AMERICA'S CHANGING PROFILE

AF781026

HEARINGS

BEFORE THE

SUBCOMMITTEE ON CENSUS AND POPULATION

OF THE

COMMITTEE ON POST OFFICE AND CIVIL SERVICE HOUSE OF REPRESENTATIVES

ONE HUNDRED SECOND CONGRESS

SECOND SESSION

MAY 26, 27; JUNE 23, 24; JULY 28, 29; SEPTEMBER 22, 1992

Serial No. 102–64

Printed for the use of the Committee on Post Office and Civil Service

U.S. GOVERNMENT PRINTING OFFICE

61–412 ⇆ WASHINGTON : 1994

For sale by the U.S. Government Printing Office
Superintendent of Documents, Congressional Sales Office, Washington, DC 20402
ISBN 0-16-043596-X

COMMITTEE ON POST OFFICE AND CIVIL SERVICE

WILLIAM L. CLAY, Missouri, *Chairman*

PATRICIA SCHROEDER, Colorado
GUS YATRON, Pennsylvania
MARY ROSE OAKAR, Ohio
GERRY SIKORSKI, Minnesota
FRANK McCLOSKEY, Indiana
GARY L. ACKERMAN, New York
MERVYN M. DYMALLY, California
THOMAS C. SAWYER, Ohio
PAUL E. KANJORSKI, Pennsylvania
CHARLES A. HAYES, Illinois
MICHAEL R. McNULTY, New York
JAMES P. MORAN, Jr., Virginia
ELEANOR HOLMES NORTON, District of Columbia
BARBARA-ROSE COLLINS, Michigan

BENJAMIN A. GILMAN, New York
FRANK HORTON, New York
JOHN T. MYERS, Indiana
DON YOUNG, Alaska
DAN BURTON, Indiana
CONSTANCE A. MORELLA, Maryland
THOMAS J. RIDGE, Pennsylvania
ROD CHANDLER, Washington

Gail E. Weiss, *Staff Director*
Robert E. Lockhart, *General Counsel*
Doris Moore-Glenn, *Deputy Staff Director*
Joseph A. Fisher, *Minority Staff Director*

SUBCOMMITTEE ON CENSUS AND POPULATION

THOMAS C. SAWYER, Ohio, *Chairman*

MERVYN M. DYMALLY, California
MICHAEL R. McNULTY, New York

THOMAS J. RIDGE, Pennsylvania
ROD CHANDLER, Washington

TerriAnn Lowenthal, *Subcommittee Staff Director*

CONTENTS

MAY 26, 1992

MAY 27, 1992

JUNE 23, 1992

AMERICA'S CHANGING PROFILE: "WHO WE ARE: SIGNIFICANT U.S. POPULATION TRENDS"

TUESDAY, MAY 26, 1992

HOUSE OF REPRESENTATIVES,
SUBCOMMITTEE ON CENSUS AND POPULATION,
COMMITTEE ON POST OFFICE AND CIVIL SERVICE,
Washington, DC.

The subcommittee met, pursuant to call, at 1 p.m., in room 311, Cannon House Office Building, Hon. Thomas C. Sawyer (chairman of the subcommittee) presiding.

Member present: Representative Sawyer.

Mr. SAWYER. Good afternoon. I am pleased to welcome our witnesses and our guests to this afternoon's hearing. This is the first in a series of hearings entitled "America's Changing Profile." It is designed to examine demographic trends and their policy implications over the near and far terms.

Over the last several years, the subcommittee has been overseeing, planning, and sharing in the implementation of the 1990 census. Now we are ready for the much more serious work of studying the product of that effort.

Census data provides a detailed portrait of our Nation's population. The demographic trends that the census reveals create a vision of the future. We need to know what kind of nation we are becoming, where we will be in 20, 30, 40 years from now, in order to plan the activities that we undertake today.

There are an awful lot of people who would suggest that our Nation is undergoing a more rapid and profound change than we have witnessed in perhaps a century. Population changes are a central element in that vast transition. They affect the social and economic landscape today and have enormous policy implications for us now and well into the next century.

The United States is a uniquely diverse nation. Our population is bound together by common interests that we share as Americans, but we are also marked by distinct and sometimes disparate needs. The ongoing changes in that human fabric may lead to a collision of needs between different segments of our population. It has become almost commonplace to suggest in the last few days that the recent events in Los Angeles and in urban communities across the country have brought into sharp focus the effects of demographic forces on the quality and stability of life in our communities.

Suddenly, the implications of the enormity of that change over the past few decades has become alarmingly clear very, very quickly.

We have an opportunity to bring the future into focus and to develop policies that are sensitive to the needs of today and which anticipate the conditions of tomorrow, but if there is one thing that the unrest in Los Angeles revealed, it is that events may be overtaking our capacity to react to them.

We just can't let that happen if we are going to manage our future in any meaningful way. I am not even sure that "manage" is the word that I want to use. Choose a future among the several potential futures that lie before us. But all of that doesn't have to happen. We have the ability to see over the horizon at least in some ways and to exercise the foresight that is needed to address those conflicts before they occur.

Clearly, we have got to put out whatever fires may be burning right now, but we can't let that important work distract us from the important task of practicing fire prevention. We have the ability to do both. If we don't, we will do nothing but fight fires well into the 21st century.

We can develop responsible strategies to meet the challenges of tomorrow, and if we do, we will be able to nurture the full potential of our human resources. Our Nation will be stronger if we meet the challenges of that future today. We will continue hearings on America's changing profile in June, July, and September.

I am genuinely excited by this opportunity to explore that place where information and policy come together. We will examine a broad range of demographic issues and consider how they are shaping our future today. We will look at who we are and how we live, where we are going and how we compare globally. It is an undertaking of some size.

Our goal is to try to bring into clear focus the data that will define the direction in which our Nation is moving.

Our job here isn't so much to solve problems in these hearings as it is to identify them. We will begin our hearings today by focusing on population growth and distribution in the changing racial and ethnic composition of our population. Tomorrow we will address the urban, suburban and rural distribution as well as the age structure of our population.

Our witnesses here today are among the leading experts in their fields. I look forward to our review and discussion.

Before we begin, I want to recognize the Population Resource Center for its enormous assistance and effort in helping us prepare for these hearings. In particular, I want to thank Jane DeLung and Shelley Kossack for their many hours of work and consultation with my staff in preparing for our proceedings today. I also want to thank Jennifer Williams and her colleagues at the Congressional Research Service for serving as a source of information and materials as well as ideas as we develop our review of important demographic issues.

Our first witness today is Mrs. Paula Schneider. She is the Chief of the Population Division of the U.S. Bureau of the Census. She will give us an introduction and overview of much of the data from which we will be working over these coming weeks. Welcome.

STATEMENT OF PAULA SCHNEIDER, CHIEF, POPULATION DIVISION, U.S. BUREAU OF THE CENSUS

Ms. SCHNEIDER. Thank you. I was going to introduce myself but thank you for doing it for me so I can get right into the numbers.

Mr. Chairman, I would like to thank you for this opportunity to share some of the important results from the 21st decennial census. The 1990 census is yielding a wealth of data vital to efficient and productive government, as well as the private economy and to our institutions. We are pleased that we have not only met our deadlines for publishing census data products, but are releasing many products ahead of schedule.

Today, as requested by the subcommittee, I will summarize some results of the 1990 census. I will give an overview of the national and regional population growth, metropolitan and non-metropolitan population trends, changing racial and ethnic composition, and our aging population.

I expect the other witnesses will discuss these topics in further detail.

Results in the census are being released every week. In subsequent hearings, the Census Bureau welcomes the opportunity to address other important social, demographic, and economic trends that are portrayed by the census data.

Let me start first today with population growth. In 200 years we have grown from a Nation with a resident population of 3.9 million to a population as of 1990 of 248.7 million. That is an increase of more than 60 fold in two centuries. The majority of this growth has come from natural increase, births over deaths. However, an increasing share of the U.S. population growth comes from net immigration which accounted for about 30 percent of the population growth during the 1980's.

The 9.8 percent population growth rate last decade was the second slowest rate in history. Only the Depression decade of the 1930's had a smaller percentage increase. However, the numerical gain of the 1980's of 22.2 million persons was the fourth biggest gain ever and was topped only by the three preceding decades.

The decline in the national growth rate is attributable mainly to the long-term decline in the childbearing rate. Despite the downsizing of the American family, however, births during the 1980's rose steadily, reaching 4.2 million by 1990 according to the National Center for Health Statistics. The mothers of many of these babies are from the post-World War II baby boom. Many of these women postponed marriage and motherhood to complete their education and launch their economic careers, contributing to a drop in births from the mid-1960's to the mid-1970's, and while they are now choosing to have small families, there are so many more of them to have babies that they are triggering what has been called the echo baby boom.

But the number of births may level off or decline soon as the older members of the baby boom generation pass through their childbearing years.

Let me turn now to regional population growth. One unmistakable conclusion of the 1990 census is that the dramatic growth of the past decade has been disproportionately in the West and South.

Over half of the numerical increase in the past decade came in only three States, California, Texas, and Florida. A large proportion of these gains is the result of migration, both migration from other States as well as immigration from abroad.

Jobs remain a major factor in interstate population shifts. People may talk about the warm weather and the sunny skies in the so-called Sun Belt, but it is often a job or pursuit of one that brings newcomers to the fast growing States of the South and West.

Conversely, the major industrial centers in the Midwest and the Northeast were especially hard hit during the recession of the 1980's. Four States registered population declines in the 1980's: Iowa, North Dakota, West Virginia, and Wyoming.

I will now describe demographic trends illustrated by population data for metropolitan and non-metropolitan areas. Metro areas are defined by the Office of Management and Budget with the assistance of the Census Bureau and are due to be revised later this year based on the detailed information from the 1990 census.

The Nation's metropolitan areas continued to act as population magnets during the 1980's, as 90 percent of the growth between 1980 and 1990 took place in the Nation's 284 metropolitan areas. Nearly 20 million additional persons or a total of 193 million called metropolitan areas home.

Contributing to that growth is the spreading outward of suburbia to what had previously been classified as non-metropolitan areas. Since the 1940 census, at least half of the metropolitan population growth has taken place in suburbs, those areas outside central cities but still within the metropolitan boundaries.

The suburbs have grown from about 14 percent of the national population in 1930 to 46 percent today. We have seen concentration of more of the population into large metropolitan areas, those containing at least 1 million persons. Half of our population now lives in just 39 metropolitan areas, each of which has at least 1 million persons.

Not unexpectedly, given the regional trends I mentioned earlier, the most rapidly growing major metropolitan areas are in the South and West.

Let me turn now to racial and ethnic composition. One of the biggest stories from the 1990 census has been the differential growth in the racial and ethnic groups, especially the dramatic growth of Asians and Pacific Islanders and of Hispanics. The Asian and Pacific Islander population more than doubled to 7.3 million persons which moved it to nearly 3 percent of the country's population.

This is one reason why data users will start seeing data on Asians and Pacific Islanders from the Current Population Survey and in associated reports.

The Hispanic origin population, which may be of any race, grew by 53 percent to account for a full 9 percent of the total U.S. population. Their large increase was due to a combination of high fertility and immigration.

The black or African-American population grew 13 percent nationally, faster than the 9.8 percent national average. This was caused mainly by high fertility. Blacks now make up approximately 12 percent of the population of our country.

The growth in the American Indian, Eskimo, and Aleut populations was a surprising 38 percent over the last decade. Totaling nearly 2 million persons, this racial group makes up about 1 percent of the population. The rate of increase that was evidenced in the census is larger than can be accounted for by natural increase, births and deaths.

It appears that more persons are identifying as American Indians, perhaps because of the growing pride in their heritage as well as a realization of the political importance of being counted as an American Indian.

One-fourth of us are now either African-American, American Indian, Eskimo or Aleut, Asian, Pacific Islander, or Hispanic.

It is fair to conclude that there has been more increase in ethnic diversity than at any time since the great waves of immigration at the turn of the century or during the late 19th century.

The effects are far reaching. For example, California, with the Nation's largest Asian and Pacific Islander population, has emerged as a gateway to businesses in Asia. Miami, with its large Hispanic population, has become a financial and trading center for those doing business with Latin American countries.

Finally, let me turn to the aging of our population. The reasons include both low fertility and increased life expectancy and the fact that the massive baby boom generation are now 10 years older than what they were one census ago. People generally are living longer. Seniors, those age 65 and over, now comprise 13 percent of the population and number over 31 million persons.

The aging of the baby boom generation and the general rising median age of our population means that America is no longer a youth-oriented society, but is evolving into a middle-age oriented society.

As a result, we can expect that there will be more focus on issues such as health care, care for the elderly and pensions. At sub-national levels, one should note that the age distributions differ. For example, Florida residents continue to have the highest median age, 36 years, because of the steady influx of retirees. Utah has the lowest median age, 26.2 years.

The 1990 census profiles a changed America, as our censuses have done for 200 years. The implications are large. Our population is growing, changing its regional distribution, concentrating in metropolitan areas, growing more racially and ethnically diverse and aging, all at the same time.

The implication for changing demands for planning, funding programs, and delivering goods and services are there to be understood and acted upon. The 1990 census is a valuable resource to help in this undertaking. Mr. Chairman, that concludes my comments. I will answer any questions you may have.

Mr. SAWYER. Thank you very much. We couldn't have asked for a finer overview or a clearer pathway for our subsequent witnesses to follow. I don't have questions today but I want to thank you for the care with which your testimony has been prepared.

I particularly appreciate the summary, although I have to note for the record how much more thorough your written testimony is and how useful it will be as we review these documents in the light of the subsequent testimony.

Ms. SCHNEIDER. Thank you.
[The prepared statement of Ms. Schneider follows:]

PREPARED STATEMENT OF PAULA SCHNEIDER, CHIEF, POPULATION DIVISION, BUREAU OF THE CENSUS

Introduction

Mr. Chairman, I would like to thank you for this opportunity to testify about the important and, I believe, fascinating and often surprising results of the 21st decennial census. It is with pleasure that I appear here today to begin to describe the fruits of all our labors—the data that describe who we are, how and where we live and work, and where we as a Nation, a people, and a culture appear headed in this crucial decade—the gateway to the 21st century. Only a national census can give us such a full measure of our Nation's ever changing demographic landscape, identifying and quantifying our progress, our problems, our challenges, our opportunities.

The 1990 census is yielding a wealth of data vital to efficient and productive government, as well as the private economy and our institutions. As you well know, the results help determine the allocation of some $40 billion annually in Federal grants. The data were used to reapportion 435 congressional seats and also used to redistrict congressional and sub-national and sub-county political boundaries which will be in effect in this November's elections.

Census results gauge important aspects of our population, such as educational attainment, income levels, and family structure. The results provide information for the ongoing national and local debates on issues and policy and directly influence many legislative programs. We are pleased that we have not only met our deadlines, but are releasing many data products ahead of schedule.

Federal, State, and local governments, companies, entrepreneurs, marketers of all types, planners, educators, and others turn to census data to identify and quantify population shifts and needs, to better plan for the future. In a real sense, census results help determine where new roads, hospitals, malls, and factories will be, and where existing ones will be expanded or upgraded. The end result is jobs. Academics and social scientists outside the Census Bureau use census results as the baseline for all manner of sociological and economic research.

Today, as requested by the subcommittee, I will summarize data from the early results of the decennial census. I will discuss our national and regional population growth, metropolitan and nonmetropolitan population trends, changing racial and ethnic composition, and our aging population. Results from the census are being released every week. In subsequent hearings, the Census Bureau welcomes the opportunity to address other important social, demographic, and economic trends that are portrayed by data from the 1990 census.

Let me also add that the 1990 census has captured what each census starting in 1950 has shown, the large-scale suburbanization of America. 1990 census data also indicate minority Americans joining that suburbanization in ever increasing numbers.

The 1990 Census Count

On December 26, 1990, the Secretary of Commerce delivered to the President the population of the United States as counted in the 1990 census: 249,632,692. The apportionment count delivered to the President included overseas military, overseas Federal civilian employees, and their overseas dependents, as of Census Day, April 1. The 1990 resident population as enumerated was 248,709,873 persons in the 50 States and the District of Columbia.

Population Growth

In 200 years, we have grown from a Nation with a resident population of 3.9 million to 248.7 million, an increase of more than 60 fold in two centuries. The 1990 count of 248.7 million represented a growth of 9.8 percent from the resident population count of 226.5 million in 1980. A majority of this growth came from natural increase—births minus deaths. Interestingly, births reached a 29-year high in 1990.

However, an increasing share of U.S. population growth comes from net immigration, which accounted for about 30 percent of population growth during the 1980's, up from about 23 percent in the 1970's. And, it is immigration that is contributing greatly to America's growing ethnic and racial diversity. Detailed census data on the foreign born will be released in late 1992 and 1993. Based on data from the Immigration and Naturalization Service, we expect the census to show that the majority of immigrants, perhaps 80 percent, come from Asian or Latin American countries (including Mexico).

The 9.8 percent population growth rate last decade was the second slowest in history. Only the Depression decade of the 1930's had a smaller percentage increase (7.3 percent). The numerical gain in the 1980's of 22.2 million was the fourth biggest ever, reflecting the large population base, and was topped only by the three preceding decades.

The decline in the national growth rate is attributable mainly to the long term decline in the child-bearing rate. This rate dropped from about 7 births per woman of child-bearing age in the early 1800's to about two children per woman in the 1970's and 1980's.

And, there lies an anomaly. Despite the downsizing of the American family, births during the 1980's rose steadily, reaching 4,179,000 by 1990, according to the National Center for Health Statistics. The mothers of these babies are from the post-World War II baby boom, which stretched from 1946 to 1964. Many of these women postponed marriage and motherhood to complete their higher education and launch their economic careers, causing births to drop from the mid-1960's to the mid-1970's. And, while they're now choosing to have smaller families, there are so many more of them to have babies, they are triggering the echo boom. This upswing in births has boosted sales for everything from baby food and diapers to video games, blue jeans, and bicycles, while also repopulating some of our neighborhoods with children and nearby schools with pupils.

But, the number of births may level off or decline soon as the older members of the baby boom generation pass their child-bearing years.

Regional Growth

One unmistakable conclusion of the 1990 census is that the dramatic population growth in the past decade has been disproportionately in the West and South. While the Nation grew 9.8 percent, the West saw its population increase 22 percent; the South, 13 percent; the Northeast, only 3 percent; and the Midwest region but 1 percent. But not all States in the West and the South grew rapidly, and there was one State, New Hampshire in the North, that experienced growth well above the national average.

It may be of interest to note here that one effect of our population redistribution has been the moving of the center of the population about 40 miles southwest of the 1980 location near De Soto, MO. Based on the 1990 census, the center of population is now located in a spot of heavily wooded land in Crawford County, MO. In the first census of 1790, the center of population was 23 miles east of Baltimore on Maryland's Eastern Shore. By 1900, the center of population was six miles southeast of Columbus, IN. Many Americans have taken Horace Greeley's "go west" advice partially to heart, and have headed west and south.

The first obligation of the census is to provide the population counts for the purposes of congressional reapportionment, as required every 10 years by the Constitution. As a result of the 1990 census, 19 congressional seats moved. There was a net gain of 15 seats in the West and South; and a corresponding net loss of 15 seats in the Northeast and Midwest. All eight States that will gain congressional representation are in the South and West. All but 4 of 13 States losing representation are in the Northeast and Midwest. This brings to 149 the number of congressional seats in the South, while the West has 93; the Northeast, 88; and the Midwest, 105.

The redistribution of population from East and North to West and South continues a long-term pattern. At the time of the first census in 1790, the population was nearly evenly divided between States that are now in the Northeast and South census regions. One hundred years later, the 1890 census showed the country stretched from Atlantic to Pacific, with 5 percent living in the West, 27 percent in the Northeast, and 36 percent in the Midwest. The South had 32 percent of the population.

Throughout the 20th century, the Western population has grown until today it represents over one-fifth of the Nation, while the Midwest has decreased from over one-third to one-fourth, and the Northeast from over one-fourth to one-fifth. The South has held throughout the 20th century at about one-third of the Nation's population.

In the 40 years since the 1950 census, the first after World War II, the United States grew 64 percent while the West grew 161 percent, the South by 81 percent, the Midwest by 34 percent, and the Northeast by only 29 percent.

Over half of the numerical increase in the past decade came in only three States: California, Texas, and Florida. Those three States also accounted for over 40 percent of the growth between 1970 and 1980, and one-third of the growth in the three prior decades. A large proportion of these gains are the result of migration, both migration from other States as well as immigration from abroad. Sample migration data are now being released on a State by State basis as part of our summary tape file 3, which contains social and economic characteristics of the population.

The other six States with population gains of 500,000 or more also are located in the South and West—Georgia, Arizona, Virginia, North Carolina, Washington, and Maryland. These States accounted for over one-fifth of all growth.

Numerically, California was the big gainer in population. Between 1980 and 1990, California grew by over 6 million persons. Its growth alone is about as much as the current population of Massachusetts. Its 1990 size of 29.8 million made it larger than the 21 least populous States combined. Its population is about 3 million more than that of Canada, and larger than the individual populations of more than 80 percent of the world's nations.

California accounted for 27 percent of the U.S. population growth last decade. However, since the 1990 census, California's average annual rate of growth has declined from well over 2 percent to about 2 percent.

Nevada was the fastest growing State, with a 50-percent increase in population, or 400,000 persons. According to our latest estimates, Nevada grew by an estimated 82,000, or 6.8 percent, in the 15-month period between April 1, 1990 and July 1, 1991, again the fastest rate among the States. Many newcomers to Nevada are workers or job-seekers attracted by opportunities in the State's expanding gaming and resort industries; others are retirees.

Jobs, or the lack of jobs, remain a major factor in interstate population shifts. People may talk about the warm weather and sunny skies in the so called Sun Belt. But, it's often a job or pursuit of one that brought newcomers to the fast-growing States in the South and West. Not coincidentally, the majority of the new jobs created in the 1980's sprang up in these regions.

Conversely, the major industrial centers in the Midwest and Northeast were especially hard-hit during the recession of the early 1980's, when many laidoff auto and steel workers headed to Texas and California in search of work.

States such as Illinois, Michigan, and Indiana have shown little population change from their 1980 counts. They actually experienced net out-migration, but managed to show overall births over deaths (natural modest population gains because of an excess of increase). But natural increase was not enough to counterbalance out-migration in four States, which registered overall population declines in the 1980's: the farming States of North Dakota and Iowa and the mining and agricultural States of West Virginia and Wyoming. New Hampshire was the Nation's sixth-fastest growing State last decade, up 20.5 percent. A strong economy seems to have attracted a flood of newcomers.

In addition to increasing representation in the House of Representatives, the above-average growth in numerous States in the West and South often boosts the local economies and encourages further growth. But, the increasing population also increases demand for roads, water and sewers, schools, and fire and police protection, as well as the taxes to pay for them. In States with slowgrowing or declining populations, the infrastructure that already exists must be maintained, and paid for by a stable or declining tax base.

Metropolitan and Nonmetropolitan Trends

I will now describe demographic trends illustrated by population and housing data for metropolitan and nonmetropolitan areas, counties, and cities.

The general concept of a metropolitan area is that of a large population nucleus, together with adjacent counties, having a high degree of social and economic integration. A metropolitan area usually comprises a sizable city with its suburbs, and generally has a total population of at least 100,000. Metropolitan areas are defined by the Office of Management and Budget, with assistance from the Census Bureau, and are due to be revised later this year based on detailed information from the 1990 census.

The Nation's metropolitan areas continued to act as population magnets during the 1980's, as 90 percent of population growth between 1980 and 1990 took place in the Nation's 284 metropolitan areas. That amounts to a rate of increase of 11.6 percent. Nearly 20 million additional persons, or a total of 193 million, called the metropolitan areas home. Contributing to that growth is the spreading outward of suburbia to what had previously been classified as non-metropolitan areas. New Jersey is the only State that is 100 percent metropolitan, and much of that is suburban.

Nonmetropolitan areas grew more slowly last decade, increasingly only 2.1 million, or 3.9 percent, to a total of 56 million. This reverses the 1970's trend, which saw nonmetropolitan areas grow by more than 14 percent, faster than metro areas, at 10.5 percent, and the country as a whole, 11.4 percent.

Figures on metropolitan areas point to another trend: the concentration of more of the population into areas of at least a million population. While less than 30 percent of the nation's residents lived in such metro areas in 1950, that number has grown steadily, from about 46 percent in 1980 to just over 50 percent today. In other words, half our population now lives in just 39 metropolitan areas, each of which has a population of over 1 million.

Not unexpectedly, given the regional population trends I described a few moments ago, the most rapidly growing major metropolitan areas are in the South and West. Twenty of the 39 metropolitan areas over 1 million grew even faster than the 1980–90 national metropolitan growth rate of 11.6 percent. All but 1 of those 20 (Minneapolis-St. Paul) are in the South or West. Florida dominated the list of the most rapidly growing metro areas of any population size with 9 of the top 11. The other two were Las Vegas, NV, and Austin, TX.

While the three-State consolidated metropolitan statistical area centered on New York City remains the largest (18.1 million), the consolidated metropolitan statistical area centered on Los Angeles (14.5 million) is closing on it. The latter gained 3 million persons, while the former grew by only 550,000.

Since the 1940 census, at least half the metropolitan population growth has taken place in suburbs—those areas outside central cities but within metro boundaries. The suburbs have grown from 13.8 percent of the national population in 1930 to 46.2 percent in 1990, or 115 million persons. This far exceeded the counts for those living in central cities (78 million) or nonmetro areas (56 million).

Much of the 1980's population and job growth has come in second-ring, newer suburbs, where land is still plentiful and affordable, and accessible to the entire region via the ever-extending highway network. This has given a boost to some suburban cities, or what have been called "edge cities," often several within a single metro area. Many are competing against one another, and the central city, for jobs and shoppers, as well as residents.

While families can get more house and land for less money the farther out they go, the decentralization of population and jobs makes it more difficult and expensive to provide mass transit and other municipal-type services, such as sewer and water, than in smaller, more densely populated areas.

The number of cities with 1 million or more population increased from six to eight in the 1980's. The two newcomers were in the South and West: San Diego and Dallas. The other cities over 1,000,000 are: New York, Los Angeles, Chicago, Houston, Philadelphia, and Detroit. Three of these cities, Chicago, Philadelphia, and Detroit, however, actually dropped in population. The last declined from a city of 1.5 million in 1970 to a bare million today. Thanks to immigration from abroad New York City and Houston gained slightly in the 1980's. This was New York City's first population growth since the 1970 census. Overall, 195 cities now have populations that exceed 100,000, a net gain of 24 in the decade.

The 1990 census also found 30 counties with a million or more population, five more than in 1980. Los Angeles County is by far the largest, with 8.9 million people, followed by Cook County (Chicago) with 5.1 million. The three counties with the largest numerical increases were in the West—Los Angeles, San Diego, and Maricopa (Phoenix). Also, the nine counties that more than doubled in population in the 1980's are all in the South or West.

Not all counties were population winners, however. More than 45 percent lost population during the 1980's. Of the Nation's 3,141 counties or statistically equivalent entities, 1,420 declined in population compared with only 560 in the 1970's. Sixty-three percent of Midwestern counties lost population as did 39 percent of Southern counties, 30 percent of Western counties, and 27 percent of Northeastern counties. The implications for businesses operating in these environments is shrinking markets.

Racial and Ethnic Composition

One of the big stories of the 1990 census is the differential growth in racial and ethnic groups, especially the dramatic growth in the number of Asians and Pacific Islanders and Hispanics.

Asians and Pacific Islanders were the fastest growing group during the 1980's. The Asian and Pacific Islander population more than doubled (108 percent growth), which moved it from 1.5 to 2.9 percent of the country's population. By 1990, there were 7.3 million persons identifying themselves as Asians or Pacific Islanders. This is one reason why data users will soon start seeing data for Asians and Pacific Islanders from the Current Population Survey and in associated reports.

The Hispanic-origin population, which may be of any race, grew 53 percent to 9 percent of the total U.S. population, accounting for over 22.4 million persons. Hispanics had the largest numerical growth, 7.7 million, of the tallied ethnic groups. Their large increase was due to a combination of high fertility and immigration.

The black or African-American population grew 13 percent nationally, faster than the 9.8 percent national average. This was caused mostly by higher fertility rates. Blacks now make up approximately 12 percent of the population of the United States. The count of nearly 30 million blacks represented an increase of some 3.5 million from the 1980 census. Blacks are America's largest minority group.

The growth in the American Indian, Eskimo, and Aleut population was a surprising 37.9 percent. Totalling nearly 2 million persons, this racial group makes up 0.8 percent of the population. This rate of increase is larger than can be accounted for by natural increase. So it appears that more persons are self-identifying as American Indians, perhaps because of a growing pride in their heritage as well as realization of the political importance of being counted accurately.

The white population, including Hispanics who classify themselves as white, grew by only 6 percent nationally. Still, this amounted to some 11.3 million persons, the largest numeric increase of the four tallied racial groups. The non-Hispanic white population increased by 4.4 percent, or 7.9 million.

The count of persons classifying themselves as "other race" increased from 6.8 million to 9.8 million. Analysis of the questionnaire entries for this category indicate that over 95 percent of the persons are of Spanish origin. The remainder are write-ins using terms such as biracial or Cape Verdean.

The racial breakdown of the resident population of the United States as of April 1, 1990, then, is 80.3 percent white; 12.1 percent black; 2.9 percent Asian or Pacific Islander, 0.8 percent American Indian, Eskimo, or Aleut, and 3.9 percent other races. Hispanics, who may be of any race, are 9 percent of the total population. One-fourth of us are now either Afro-American, American Indian, Asian, Pacific Islander, Eskimo, Aleut, or Hispanic. A 1989 study by the Population Reference Bureau projects that these groups could represent one-third of the U.S. population by 2030.

But in numerous cities and counties, minorities already are a majority, including Chicago and New York City. Blacks are a majority in Atlanta, Detroit, and Washington, DC. Prince George's County, MD, is a majority black suburban county, which has experienced a significant influx in recent decades of middle-class blacks. Hispanics are the majority in such cities as Miami, El Paso, and San Antonio. Over half the residents in Honolulu and the Los Angeles suburb of Monterey Park are Asians or Pacific Islanders.

The growth in minority population is increasing throughout the United States as indicated by large growth rates in virtually every State and metropolitan area. But, distribution of specific racial and ethnic groups is not uniform. While blacks are more widely distributed than other racial/ethnic groups, 35 percent of blacks live in only five States: New York (9.5 percent), California (7.4 percent), Texas (6.7 percent), Florida (5.9 percent), and Georgia (5.8 percent). The distribution of other racial and ethnic groups is even more concentrated. Thus:

- Half of Asians and Pacific Islanders live in two States and two-thirds in the top five: California (39.1 percent), New York (9.5 percent), Hawaii (9.4 percent), Texas (4.4 percent), and Illinois (3.9 percent).
- Hispanics are even more concentrated than Asians and Pacific Islanders—half in two States and three-fourths in the top 5: California (34.4 percent), Texas (19.4 percent), New York (9.9 percent), Florida (7.0 percent), and Illinois (4.0).
- Nearly one-half of American Indians, Eskimos, and Aleuts live in five States, with Oklahoma having the largest number and Alaska having the highest proportion in its State population.

It is fair to conclude that there has been more increase in ethnic diversity than at any time since the great waves of immigration at the turn of the century or during the late 19th century. The effects are far-reaching. For example, California, with the Nation's largest Asian population, has emerged as a gateway to businesses in Asia. And Miami, with its large Hispanic population, has become a financial and trading center for those doing business with Central and South American countries.

Aging in America

The country's population is aging. The reasons include low fertility and increased life expectancy and the fact that the massive baby boom generation, those born between 1946 and 1964, are 10 years older now than at the last census. By 1990, they ranged in age from 26 to 44.

Numbering 77 million, baby boomers represent 31 percent of the U.S. population. As the largest age cohort, they will drive U.S. age statistics upward for the rest of our lifetimes. The median age, which was 30 in 1980, now stands at 33. Median age is projected to reach 36.5 years by 2005, and 37.0 years by 2020. Interestingly, in 1820, the median age was only 17.

People generally are living longer. While the total population this past decade was growing about 1 percent per year, the group age 65 and older grew about 2.1 percent per year. These seniors now comprise close to 13 percent of the population and number over 31 million. The oldest old, aged 85 and older, grew about 3.3 percent per year. This dramatic increase in the senior population will stimulate demand for social services, social security benefits, and health-care, as well as travel, retirement homes, and condominium construction and sales.

The largest 5-year age group at census time consisted of baby boomers aged 30–34. They accounted for 21.9 million persons, and were followed closely in number by the 25–29 year olds, the youngest baby boomers, who numbered 21.3 million. These groups are in their child-bearing years, and in fact the baby boom women are having children—though not as many per woman as their mothers had. The recent boomlet, however, is substantial in number because of the sheer size of the parent population.

In the years between the baby boom and its "boomlet," or "baby boom echo," 1965–76, a comparatively small group of 41 million people were born. In the future, we may see some hiring shortages at entry level because of their comparatively limited number. That could bid up demand for both their services and their salaries.

At subnational levels, 1990 census population age distributions differ. For example, Florida residents continue to have the highest median age, 36 years, because of the steady influx of retirees. Other States with higher-than-average median ages include: Pennsylvania, West Virginia, Oregon, and Connecticut. In some cases, median age is driven up by the exodus of younger people to other States.

On the other end, there are 10 States with median ages lower than the national average. Lower-than-average median ages for these States are in part the result of higher birth rates and an influx of young people, often families with children, pursuing opportunities. Utah has the lowest median age by far, 26.2 years. All 10 States are located in the South and West. Similar patterns are apparent for cities as well. Examples are the residents of St. Petersburg, FL, who have a median age of 38.6 years, whereas the median age in Santa Ana, CA, is only 26.

The aging of the baby boom and the general rising median age of the population means America is no longer a youth-oriented society, but is evolving into a middle-age-oriented society. As a result, we can expect that there will be more focus on issues such as health care, care for the elderly, and pensions, etc.

Earlier I discussed our changing population mix and the fast-paced growth of minority populations. These trends are interrelated with the age of our population. We know that most immigrants are young, and minorities generally have a higher birth rate than nonminority whites because they are younger and have higher fertility rates. As a result, minorities are a progressively large share of the population at younger ages. Thus, percent of the population is white, but under age 10, at age 80 or over, 90 75 percent is white.

Hispanics comprise 3 percent of our population 80 or older, but nearly 13 percent under age 10. (Remember that the overall Hispanic share of the population is 9 percent). This trend of increasing proportions of blacks, Hispanics, and Asians and Pacific Islanders in younger age groups most likely will continue and move upward as each age cohort gets older.

Because of its size, the baby boom group will continue to drive markets, housing, and social service needs. How baby boomers and the older population have changed location, type of housing, marital, and parental status in the past 10 years will be among the more interesting topics for analysis from the 1990 census.

Conclusion

The 1990 census profiles a changed America, as our censuses have done for 200 years. The implications are large. Our population is growing, changing its regional distribution, concentrating in metropolitan areas, growing more racially and ethnically diverse, and aging. The implications for changing demands for planning, funding programs, and delivering goods and services are there to be understood and acted on. The 1990 census is a resource to help in this undertaking.

Mr. Chairman, that concludes my testimony. I will answer any questions you may have.

Mr. SAWYER. Thank you.

Our first panel this afternoon, on population growth and regional distribution, will be composed of Dr. Martha Farnsworth Riche, Director of Policy Studies at the Population Reference Bureau. She is a founding editor of American Demographics Magazine, and her recent works have focused on increases in formerly small segments of the population and in declines of historically dominant segments.

The second member of this panel is Dr. Peter A. Morrison. He is the senior staff demographer at the RAND Corp. He has served as an advisor to the National Academy of Science, Congressional Research Service, the Committee for Economic Development and the U.S. Census Bureau.

If you would join us, let me say welcome, we are grateful to have you with us today, and I would invite you to take as much time as it takes to present your testimony. I read through it and found it fascinating and would urge you to summarize or expand as you find useful.

STATEMENT OF MARTHA FARNSWORTH RICHE, DIRECTOR OF POLICY STUDIES, POPULATION REFERENCE BUREAU AND PETER A. MORRISON, SENIOR STAFF DEMOGRAPHER, THE RAND CORP.

Ms. RICHE. Thank you very much, Mr. Chairman. We are glad to be here. As we just heard, the 1990 census measured an increase in the population of 9.8 percent, and that was the second lowest decennial growth rate in census history. I think that to see that change in perspective, it is good to remember that the first seven censuses each found that the population had grown by at least one person for every three people over the decade.

The next five censuses each found at least 1 person for every 5 Americans, and with the exception of that Depression decade of the 1930's, each census since 1920 has found at least 1 person for every 10. This is the first time we have dipped below the 10 percent growth mark.

As populations become larger, growth rates fall and the absolute increase becomes far more significant, and as we have just heard, the 1990 census found an increase of 22.2 million people. Well, that is more than any census up through the middle of this century but it is 1 million fewer than the 1980 census found. It is almost 2 million fewer than the 1970 census found and it is almost 6 million fewer than the 1960 census found.

Growth has been a hallmark of this Nation. Growth and population has been associated with growth in the economy and I think for many people, a slowdown in population growth is implying a slowdown of economic growth. We don't know yet if this is so and I think the economists are going to argue about it until we do know but as demographers, our job is to assess whether indeed we are seeing a slowdown and what it might mean.

The current official projections are the first to estimate an eventual decline in the size of our population. According to the middle of some 30 scenarios the Census Bureau produced a few years ago, the population will peak at just under 302 million people in 2038, and then start to decline. These projections were made in 1987 and it is already clear that our population is growing more rapidly than they estimated.

The first thing that happened since those projections appeared was that the immigration law was revised to allow more immigration. So even the highest immigration assumption of those projections is now too low. But the demographic turnaround that could get our population growing more rapidly again is really a turnaround in fertility.

As we just heard, in 1990, Americans had over 4 million babies and that was more than in any year since 1961. Now, that wasn't unexpected because due to our baby boom, so many women are of childbearing age. However, according to earlier projections, births from the baby boom should have peaked a couple of years earlier in 1988.

So some demographers are saying that births have just been postponed longer than expected and population growth really isn't going to change. Others are saying that women are having more children and that this is a new long-term trend.

In my judgment, the former view is more likely because more women are having or raising children on their own. That is another thing the 1990 census found. Almost all of this recent increase in fertility has occurred to women who are not currently married. Moreover, divorce rates are still high, especially for new marriages, and as a result, surveys tell us, women are making decisions about childbearing conscious that they might have to raise the child on their own.

So if we think of fertility and birth rates in terms of decisions made this way and then put them in the context of the current labor force participation rates for mothers of small children, another important finding of the census, it is telling, I think, that the current rates are so high, and I think they suggest a demographic universal and that is that American women are going to have an average of close to two children no matter how arduous raising them might be, but probably not more.

Now, there is one more part of those assumptions that underlie population projections and that is mortality. This is the least controversial, but demographers are currently disputing whether there are natural limits to the life-span. Certainly if the present trend toward healthier life-styles continues, the latter may be correct, and that is because the people who have made significant changes in health habits are middle-aged now and we don't know the impact on life expectancy if healthier habits persist into older age.

So in sum, based on current trends, the most likely of the current official projections is the one that is known as the "highest," because it will produce the highest population levels, and according to that projection, in 2080, the population will total 501 million people.

And probably the lowest likely level of population, again based on current trends, is the projection that assumes high immigration, and in 2080, population according to that projection would be nearly 333 million people.

So to put those two numbers—333 million versus 501 million—into perspective, let us remember that the 1990 census found nearly 249 million people. So if the lower of these two projections actually occurs, over the next nine decades we will add one American for every three that we have now. If the higher projection occurs, we will add more than one for every two people that we have now.

Based on current trends, even that high projection seems low. And at PRB we are currently using somewhat higher assumptions. But in any case, it is important to note that we are still looking at a slower growing population than we have ever had before.

Now, for policy purposes, it is important to assess what these trends tell us about the composition of the population, and that is because in a slow growth situation, different growth trends within different segments of the population transform its nature, and I think the most important thing these trends tell us is that the aging of the population is producing a profound change in our age structure.

Traditionally a population has been distributed by age in the form of a pyramid with a relatively small group of older people, a middling amount of middle-aged people and the bulk of the population being young adults, children, teenagers. And as recently as 1970 that was a pretty good representation of our population.

But demographic trends have transformed that historic pattern. The American age structure no longer resembles a pyramid, but rather a pillar, and what I mean is that there are more older people relative to young people than we have ever had before and there are more middle-aged people relative to young people than we have had before.

Now, during this decade and the next decade, this pillar is going to have a pronounced bulge in the middle because the baby boom will be swelling the middle-aged in our population, and what that means is that during this decade and the next, a record high share of the population will be in the working ages.

This factor alone should play a significant role in setting the issue agenda for Congress and for the Nation.

A second important change that Ms. Schneider has already related to us is the change in our racial and ethnic structure. The 1990 census found that non-Hispanic whites accounted for only three out of every four Americans and all projections say this share will continue to decrease.

As we just heard, thanks to immigration and fertility differences, minority populations are younger than the majority, and what that means is that the population looks very different for different age groups.

According to our projections at PRB, the 2000 census will find that nearly 71 percent of Americans will be white; however, fewer than two in three children will be non-Hispanic white while nearly 80 percent of Americans aged 45 and older will be.

Well, this shift is already having an effect on the political landscape in certain communities. For example, we have recently seen communities where older, mostly white voters defeated school bond issues where children are mostly minority children. And I think we will see more of that sort of conflict as the decade progresses.

Another demographic aspect of a slow-growing population arises from population shifts that are produced by migration. As we just heard, the South and the West together accounted for 89 percent of our population growth in the 1980's. Well, the flow of Americans from the Northeast and the Midwest toward the West and the

South has produced different age patterns in different parts of the country.

States that gained significantly from migration have younger populations on average while States with significant out-migration have older populations. We are now reaching a point where Pennsylvania, for example, is distinctly older than Texas, and unless migration flows change direction, these differences will become more pronounced because the younger populations are, of course, the ones that have more children.

Well, that is just one example of how diverging trends within a slow-growing population produce population diversity across the country. An even more telling example I think is the growing difference between the racial and ethnic composition of States and amongst communities. I think for demographers the one great surprise of the census was the great growth of minority populations but it is instructive to look at the minority population distribution across the country State by State, and when you do that you see that only one State resembles the national profile and that State is New Jersey, as we just heard. That is the one State that is all metropolitan.

So I think that for Congress, the most important meaning of the census and the trends that it depicts may be a new political geography, one that extends beyond the current redrawing of congressional boundaries that we are seeing, and that is because in a slow-growth population, differential growth amongst demographic groups shatters different patterns of domination.

As I have indicated, both older and middle-aged people are becoming more numerous relative to the young, and racial and ethnic groups are becoming more numerous relative to the majority.

The same thing is occurring for other demographic characteristics such as family and household types. Since these trends are occurring unevenly across the country, they are making communities far more diverse in terms of their nature and in terms of the issues that are important to them. I think Americans will be looking to Congress more and more to keep diversity from turning into divisiveness and to find the common denominators that facilitate consensus.

I would like to turn the microphone over to my colleague, Peter Morrison.

[The prepared statement of Ms. Riche follows:]

Prepared Statement of Martha Farnsworth Riche, Director of Policy Studies, Population Reference Bureau

The 1990 census measured an increase in the population of the United States of 9.8 percent since the 1980 census—an increase of less than 1 percent a year over the decade. This was the second lowest decennial growth rate in census history, exceeded only by the 7.3 percent increase experienced during the 1930's.

To see this change in perspective, recall that the first seven U.S. censuses each found that the population had grown by at least one person for every three over the decade. The next five censuses each found at least one person for every five. With the exception of the Depression decade, each census since 1920 has found at least one person for every ten people over the decade.

Of course, as populations become larger, percentage growth rates fall and the increase in the absolute numbers of people becomes far more significant. The 9.8 percent growth measured by the 1990 census amounted to an increase of 22.2 million people. This increase is larger than that recorded by any census through the middle of this century, but it is 1 million fewer than the 1980 census found, almost 2 million fewer than the 1970 census found, and almost 6 million fewer than the 1960 census found-our highest ever population growth.

Growth has been a hallmark of this nation—growth in population, associated with growth in the economy. Consequently, for many people a slowdown in population growth implies a slowdown in economic growth. We don't know yet if this is necessarily so, and the economists will argue about it until we do know. As demographers, our job is to assess whether this is indeed a slowdown, or just a pause.

The current official projections, prepared by the U.S. Bureau of the Census in 1987, are the first to estimate an eventual decline in the size of the population (U.S. Bureau of the Census 1989). According to the middle, "most likely," projection series (of thirty series), the U.S. population will peak at just under 302 million in 2038, and then decline. In this series, the rate of population growth between 1987 and 1995 will be smaller than for any previous period except the Depression—0.81 percent a year, compared to 0.70 percent a year during the 1930's. After 1995, the growth rate will decline below even the Depression rate, turning negative toward the middle of the next century.

Like all projections, these series are based on a range of assumptions, and the different series allow users to select assumptions they believe most likely to occur. It is already clear that our population is growing more rapidly than the official, "most likely" scenario. All the assumptions that underlie that projection series were too conservative relative to what has happened since, and most demographers have now abandoned them.

From the beginning, most demographers faulted the current projections for underestimating net immigration. The middle series assumed a continuation of recent annual totals of 600,000, dropping to 500,000 a year by 1998. As a Government agency, the Census Bureau probably felt constrained to assume that the Immigration Reform and Control Act of 1986 would reduce illegal immigration-from an estimated 200,000 a year to 100,000 a year. Demographers who considered this outcome unlikely could select a series that assumed "high" immigration—800,000 a year. Changing to this assumption eliminates the estimate of an eventual population decline—at least by 2080, the last year projected.

Since the official projections appeared, the immigration law has been revised. The provisions of the Immigration Act of 1990 took effect in November 1991, and the Immigration and Naturalization Service has projected an immediate jump in immigration, to 741,900. The service projects fewer immigrants in subsequent years, but in almost every year of the decade it still expects at least 700,000 per year (Hoefer 1991). This figure does not include refugees, who have amounted to around 100,000 a year in recent years.

Given what seems to be a renewed inflow of illegal immigrants, even the high immigration assumption of the official projections is now too low, unless emigration increases significantly. Until the Census Bureau issues a new set of projections, most demographers will use the high series or make their own projections. Based on current expectations, the Population Reference Bureau is assuming net immigration of 900,000 a year.

However, the demographic turnaround that may seriously distort the current projections—in the long, not the short term—is a turnaround in fertility. Dramatic and abrupt changes in fertility made earlier projections ludicrous—for example, according to projections made during the midst of the baby boom, the U.S. population would have reached its present size during the latter part of the 1970's (U.S. Bureau of the Census 1957). In the few years since the current projections were made, fertility has increased significantly and demographers disagree as to whether this increase represents a short-lived phenomenon or a new long-term trend.

Americans had over 4 million babies in 1990, more than in any year since 1961 (National Center for Health Statistics 1991a). This is not unexpected since, thanks to the baby boom, so many women are of childbearing age. However, according to the official projections, births from the baby boom should have peaked in 1988 (U.S. Bureau of the Census 1984). Some demographers say that births were just postponed longer than expected (a change in timing), others say that women are having more children (a change in volume).

Certainly starting in mid-1987, the fertility rate-began to move upward. Provisional data indicate that in 1990, it exceeded the level projected under the high fertility assumption, and fell only slightly in 1991. Will the rate continue to rise? Will it stabilize? Or will it fall again?

The answer lies on the interface between social and economic behavior—perhaps that is why there are so many persuasively argued yet widely differing scenarios. Some social scientists hold that births have been constrained for the baby boom because there were so many of them—they crowded first the labor market, then the housing market (Easterlin, Preston, among others). This is the view expressed most often in the popular press, and it is generally accompanied by the prediction that the baby bust will have higher fertility than the baby boom because its small size will grant it superior economic opportunities.

Others point to the relative stability in birth expectations-surveys still report that Americans want, on average, two children—and assert that the turnaround in the fertility rate simply represents the end of the transition to delayed childbearing—a delay that began with the widespread dissemination of the birth control pill. These demographers (for example, Bumpass 1990) expect that fertility will not continue to rise, or even stabilize at this new higher rate. Instead, they think the rate will resume its long-term downward trend.

The latter view seems far more likely because the proponents of the former fail to take account of a significant trend: more women are having and/or raising children on their own. Almost all of the recent increase in fertility has occurred to women who were not currently married (U.S. National Center for Health Statistics 1991b). Moreover, although the divorce rate seems to have stabilized overall, it is actually higher for new marriages—Bumpass estimates that 6 in 10 new marriages will fail, based on current age-specific rates. As a result, women are making decisions about their childbearing conscious that they may have to raise the child/children on their own (*Self* 1990 is one of many surveys).

If we think of current fertility and birth rates in terms of decisions made by women, rather than by couples, and view them in the context. of current labor force participation rates for mothers of small children, it is telling that the rates are so high. They suggest a demographic universal: that American women will have an average of close to two children, no matter how arduous raising them may be.

The 1990's will be dedicated in a major way to children and family because family life will be at its peak for the most influential generation in the population—influential by virtue of its size, and now aging into positions of influence. This shift can't help but influence decisions to have children at the margin—other things being equal, we will probably see a somewhat higher fertility rate. How high cannot be predicted, but probably not very much higher than the 2.2 in the high fertility projection series, since the opportunity costs of having children are more likely to increase than to decrease. In the longer term, fertility will probably decrease again. Whether it goes below replacement rate depends on too many factors—many of them having to do with how people perceive population growth as affecting the physical environment—to estimate with any degree of certainty. In any case, fertility is not likely to grow enough to produce a turnaround in overall population growth.

Mortality is the least controversial of the projection assumptions, although some demographers are currently disputing whether or not there are natural limits to the life span. Those who assert that there are (see Olshansky et al. for a persuasive account) would opt for the official projections' middle assumption of mortality; those who do not (see for example Preston for an equally persuasive account) choose the lower one. If the present trend toward healthier lifestyles continues, the latter may be correct. The people who have made significant changes in such health habits as avoiding smoking, using seatbelts, and exercising, are people in middle age. We do not yet know the impact on life expectancy if healthier habits persist into old age.

In sum, based on current trends the safest set to use of the current official series of projections is the one known as the "highest" because it will produce the highest population levels—low mortality, high immigration, and high fertility assumptions. In 2080, the population will total 501 million if these assumptions are met. Probably the lowest likely level of population, again based on current trends, is the one produced by assuming middle mortality, high immigration, and middle fertility: the "high immigration" set. In 2080, the population will total nearly 333 million if these assumptions are met.

To see these figures in perspective, remember that the 1990 census found nearly 249 million people. If the lower of these projections actually occurs, over the next nine decades we will add one American for every three we have now. If the higher but still slow growth projection occurs, we will more than double our present population. Based on current trends, even the higher projection seems low, and at the Population Reference Bureau we are currently using more generous assumptions for all three components of change. In any case, we are still looking at a slower growing population than we have had before.

For policy purposes it is just as important, if not more so, to assess what these trends tell us about the composition of our population. In a slow-growth situation, different trends within different segments of the population will transform its nature. The most important thing they tell us may be that the population is aging, and that the age structure of our population is undergoing a profound change.

Traditionally, a population has been distributed by age in the form of a pyramid—with a relatively small group of older people at the top, a middling amount of middle-aged people in the middle, and the bulk of the population young adults, teenagers, and children. As recently as 1970, this was a good representation of our population. But a number of trends have transformed that historic pattern.

• We had a baby boom between 1946 and 1964—births were bunched after World War II, and then unusually good economic conditions contributed to earlier and more widespread marriage and childbearing.

• Starting in 1965, women began to postpone having children and births dropped dramatically, so the generation that followed the baby boom is significantly smaller.

• Now the baby boom is having its children, but because they are doing it later, at best they will replace themselves.

• And more people are living to a ripe old age.

When we put these trends together, the American age structure no longer resembles a pyramid but rather a pillar: there are more older people, and more middle-aged people relative to young people than ever before.

Under all the projection scenarios currently deemed likely, the population will continue to age. It will continue to age because, even at a fertility rate of 2.2—the high fertility assumption—women will have fewer children in the future than women have borne, on average, in the past. Even with high immigration, higher life expectancy will offset the influx of younger people into the population. So the replacement of the traditional pyramid by the pillar is a good long-term image for the age structure of the population.

During this decade and the next, this pillar will have a pronounced bulge in the middle, as the baby boom swells the middle-aged population. This means that during this decade and the next, a record high share of the population will be in the working ages.

A second important change in the composition of the population is the change in its racial and ethnic structure, particularly at younger ages. The 1990 census found that whites accounted for 8 in 10 Americans, down from 9 in 10 as recently as 1960. Subtracting white Hispanics, in 1990 non-Hispanic whites accounted for only three out of four Americans.

Due to trends in immigration and in differential fertility, racial and ethnic minorities will continue to grow faster than the white population. By 2000, non-Hispanic whites will represent under 71 percent of the population, blacks nearly 13 percent, Hispanics over 11 percent, and Asians more than 4 percent, we project. The proportions will change even more for younger ages.

Thanks to both immigration and fertility differences, minority populations are younger than the white population. According to preliminary census tabulations, in 1990 non-Hispanic whites were far older than minority groups: their median age was 34.4 years. Hispanics were youngest, with a median age of 25.5 years. Native Americans and Alaskans were second youngest, at 26.3 years, while blacks had a median age of 28.1 years and Asian and Pacific Islanders had a median age of 29.8 years.

As a result, different age groups are becoming multicultural at different rates. According to PRB projections, although the 2000 census will find that nearly 71 percent of Americans will be white, fewer than two in three children will be—63 percent of children under age 8, 65 percent of children aged 8 to 13, and 66 percent of children aged 14 to 17. In contrast, nearly 80 percent of Americans aged 45 and older will be white.

Another demographic aspect of a slow-growing population arises from the differential effects of migration. The South and the West together accounted for 89 percent of population growth in the 1980's, down just slightly from 90 percent during the 1970's. The West grew at a slightly slower pace in the 1980's (22.3 percent) than in the 1970's (23.9 percent), but in the 1980's it outpaced growth in the other regions to an even greater degree. Growth in the South slowed sharply during the 1980's, but it was still well above the national average. In contrast, the Northeast grew at little more than a third of the national rate, and the Midwest grew only a seventh as much.

One result is that the West is no longer the smallest of nation's four census regions—the Northeast now holds that distinction. Another result is that the distribution of population among the regions has become more equal. The Northeast and West each now account for one-fifth of Americans, the Midwest for one-fourth, and the South for one-third.

However, this relatively even distribution is unlikely to continue, because the flow of Americans from the Northeast and Midwest toward the West and the South has contributed to a younger age structure in most of the receiving States. Since interstate migrants tend to be young adults, seeking new opportunities, States that suffer a net loss of migrants lose those migrants' eventual children as well.

Already the median age varies among States. According to the 1990 census, New Hampshire is the only Northeastern State with a population that is younger—barely—than the Nation as a whole. The median age for the United States was 32.9 years; for New Hampshire it was 32.8 years. Not coincidentally, New Hampshire was the only Northeastern State with a large net gain from migration during the 1980's. In contrast, most Western States were younger than the Nation as a whole.

Most States that gained significantly from migration—notably California, Arizona, and Texas—have younger populations, on average, while States with significant net outmigration—such as Iowa or West Virginia—have older populations. The difference between States as depicted in the median age is widening, making Pennsylvania, for example, distinctly older than Texas. Unless migration flows change direction, and we see no reason to expect they will, States will have increasingly different age structures.

This is one example of how diverging trends within a slow-growth population produce population diversity across the country, State to State, community to community. An even more telling example is the growing difference between the racial and ethnic composition of States.

For demographers, the great growth in minority populations was the one surprise of the 1990 census. Yet only one State has a population that looks, racially and ethnically, like the nation as a whole: New Jersey, the only State that is completely metropolitan in statistical terms. Illinois is the only other State that comes close to resembling the national distribution, but Illinois has significantly more African-Americans, and significantly fewer whites, than the Nation as a whole.

For Congress, then, the most important meaning of the census and the trends it depicts may be a new political geography that extends well beyond the changes reflected in the redrawn boundaries of congressional districts. In a slow-growth population, differential growth among traditional demographic groups shatters traditional patterns of domination. As I've indicated, older and middle-aged people are becoming more numerous relative to the young, and racial and ethnic minorities are becoming more numerous relative to the majority. The same thing is occurring for other demographic characteristics. For example, during the 1980's the traditional family of married couple with children became less numerous than married couples without children. And during the 1990's, we project that single-person households will also become more numerous than the traditional family.

Relationships among all these different trends mean that they are occurring unevenly across the country. The new congressional boundaries are being determined in large part by a single demographic characteristic—race and ethnicity, and that means that representatives will have to find new ways of forging consensus. As you do this, many of you will discover that your districts have become more different in terms of other demographic characteristics too. During the 1990's, Congress may also be the place for finding consensus across different age groups, and different family and household types.

REFERENCES

Bumpass, Larry

1990 "What's Happening to the Family? Interactions Between Demographic and Institutional Change." *Demography* 27(4): 483–98.

Easterlin, Richard A.

1980 *Birth and Fortune: The Impact of Numbers on Personal Welfare.* Basic Books.

Hoefer, Michael D.

1991 "Immigration Limits and Projected Immigration for Fiscal Years 1990–97," Statistics Division, U.S. Immigration and Naturalization Service (unpublished table).

Olshansky, S. Jay, Bruce A. Carnes, and Christine Cassel

1990 "In Search of Methuselah: Estimating the Upper Limits to Human Longevity." *Science* 250: 634–40.

Preston, Samuel H.

1991 "Demographic Change in the United States, 1970–2050." Presented at the conference on "Demography and Retirement: the 21st Century," University of Pennsylvania, May 9–10.

Self

1990 "The New Diversity: Self Magazine Reports on American Women." New York.

U.S. Bureau of the Census

1957 *Illustrative Projections of the Population of the United States, by Age and Sex, 1960 to 1980.* Current Population Reports, Series P–25, No. 187, Washington, DC.

1984 *Projections of the Population of the United States, by Age, Sex, and Race: 1988 to 2080.* Current Population Reports, Series P–25, No. 952, Washington, DC.

1989 *Projections of the Population of the United States, by Age, Sex, and Race: 1988 to 2080.* Current Population Reports, Series P–25, No. 1018, Washington, DC.

U.S. National Center for Health Statistics

1991a *Monthly Vital Statistics Report,* Vol. 39, No. 12. Public Health Service, Washington, DC.

1991b *Advance Report of Final Natality Statistics, 1989,* Vol. 40, No. 8, Supplement. Public Health Service, Washington, DC.

Mr. SAWYER. Thank you very much.

Dr. Morrison.

Mr. MORRISON. My name is Peter Morrison and I should make one minor correction. I am the former director of RAND Corporation's population research center, and my views here are my own, not those of RAND.

I thank you for inviting me to testify at your hearings today, Mr. Chairman. My testimony focuses on segments of the population that have become more conspicuous because of their geographic distribution.

First, ethnic and racial subgroups; second, the Nation's children; and third, the elderly.

My first point is that the population's ethnic and racial diversity, fueled by immigration, has become much more apparent now that we have taken the 1990 census. Our political institutions and our schools need to accommodate to the culturally more diverse future that lies ahead.

Second, many children across the Nation are submerged in poverty, and their poverty has become concentrated in families that are headed by women. And third, the aging of the population, which we have heard about already, is not going to crest nationwide for another two decades, but is already beginning to materialize in certain communities.

Now, none of these developments comes as a surprise because well before the 1990 census each of these was apparent on a national basis. But national demographic trends don't materialize evenly across the Nation, as you know. Developments that are now full-blown and clearly visible in some places may be only in their beginning stages in others, and it takes the decennial census to reveal the rich detailed diversity of these developments at the local level.

Let me turn to the first of these developments, our greater ethnic diversity across the Nation. Metropolitan areas today manifest a more complex racial and ethnic pattern than they did in 1980. I think the traditional notion of a melting pot no longer holds. Its ingredients have separated into a complex racial and ethnic mosaic in which groups of people cling to their separate identities.

Now, this is a mosaic that varies from city to city. If you look at it in St. Paul, it contains Hmong from Southeast Asia. If you look in Providence, it contains Cambodians; in Des Moines, Tai Dam and Vietnamese and here in nearby Arlington, VA, Salvadorans and other Central Americans.

In California, the State from which I come, the term "minority" is coming to sound obsolete. One of every four California cities above 50,000 in population has no racial or ethnic majority of any kind. Neither Anglos nor Hispanics nor blacks nor Asians constitute a majority of the population, and I have listed in table 1 of my prepared testimony a number of examples of such cities.

Cultural pluralism is highly visible in California, but it is visibly emerging across the Nation and, as in California, it is pulling communities in separate directions toward two different visions. One, the traditional conception of melting pot assimilation, the other a more complex racial and ethnic assertiveness that has come to be thought of as a mosaic, with an array of groups demanding equity.

The distribution of particular groups by region places extraordinary pressures on their education systems. In Florida and across the Southwest, schools must educate a diverse student population, many of whom lack basic English language skills. More generally, many people speak a language other than English and they cannot speak English very well.

In New Mexico and Florida, one-tenth of all persons 5 and older report that they do not speak English very well on the 1990 census. In California, 16 percent report that they do not speak English very well, and in south central Los Angeles, that figure is 29 percent.

Let me turn now to the second development I mentioned, that many children are submerged in poverty. The United States has been characterized as a rich nation with poor children. Demographers have chronicled the deterioration of urban childhood on a national scale for years. Now the 1990 census can reveal the specifics about poverty-stricken children: who they are, why they are poor, and where. In the city of Erie, PA, 15 percent of all adults live below poverty; but for children under 5 years old, the figure is 36 percent.

In Los Angeles County, where I reside, 22 percent of these young children under 5 are poverty stricken. And in south central Los Angeles, 44 percent of all children under 18 live in poverty. Congressman Sawyer, in your area, Summit County, OH, the corresponding data I had hoped to have are due to be released the end of this week, and we will soon know what the figures are in Ohio.

Mr. Sawyer. I assume it was only coincidental that you picked out Summit County or Erie, PA.

Mr. Morrison. Right. What these comparisons suggest is that child poverty typically exceeds adult poverty, and that I think is a reality warranting the Nation's attention.

The future, it is said, creeps in on tiny feet. Our future, regrettably, seems to be creeping in on impoverished tiny feet. High rates of poverty among contemporary children raise fundamental long-term issues about our economic competitiveness. Poverty curtails education and eventually erodes future workforce productivity.

A rich nation that tolerates poor children in its midst wastes the means to enrich itself further.

The third important development I want to underscore in my testimony has to do with our aging population and the future concerns it will pose. Today, as you have heard persons who are 65 and older are about 13 percent of the Nation's population. By the year 2020, that figure is projected to rise to about 20 percent, and the number of elderly people will have nearly doubled.

The aging of population, as I said, will not crest on a national basis for another two decades, but it has begun to materialize in certain communities already. The future challenges that have only been speculated about in recent years are now turning into real challenges in some of these communities, as we see generations who settled in communities long ago beginning to age-in-place.

By that I mean that the suburbs that housed newly-settled young families in the 1950's are now communities in which many of the same family members have grown old. As they age-in-place, the elderly will express needs in local places, intensifying the local focus on how those needs can best be met.

Now, those needs are set within living environments where other factors may exaggerate the needs or reduce them. Household living arrangements are a key feature here, and the 1990 census data that will allow us to fathom those living arrangements amongst the elderly are just being released.

We need to understand how those living arrangements evolve as people age-in-place, why they do, and what the consequences are.

In closing, let me point out that the 1990 census, like its predecessors, was a massive undertaking that provides a highly detailed statistical snapshot of the U.S. population.

One outstanding feature of the census this time, I think, is the ease with which anyone can access its products. The Census Bureau is delivering the results in forms that are more readily available to the general public than ever before, and the Bureau has in my opinion defined a new standard for user friendliness democratizing data use.

Vast amounts of information are at the fingertips of any civic-minded person with access to a personal computer.

Thank you.

[The prepared statement of Mr. Morrison follows:]

PREPARED STATEMENT OF PETER A. MORRISON, SENIOR STAFF DEMOGRAPHER, THE RAND CORP.

Thank you for inviting me to testify at today's hearings on "America's Changing Profile." My testimony focuses on subgroups within the population that have become more conspicuous and urgent: ethnic and racial subgroups; the nation's children; and the elderly.

The 1990 census, like its predecessors, was a massive undertaking that provides a highly detailed statistical snapshot of the U.S. population. One outstanding feature of this census is the ease with which anyone can access its products. The Census Bureau is delivering the results in forms that are more readily available to the general public than ever before. The Bureau has defined a new standard for "user friendliness" that is democratizing data use. Vast amounts of information are at the fingertips of any civic-minded person with access to a personal computer.

My testimony highlights what these data reveal about us as a democracy and what they suggest about the future. Three broad developments are worthy of public attention, both nationally and at local community levels:

• 1. The population's ethnic and racial diversity, fueled by immigration, has now become more apparent. Our political institutions and our schools will need to accommodate to the culturally more diverse future ahead.

• 2. The United States remains a rich nation with poor children. Many children across the nation are submerged in poverty, and their poverty has become concentrated in families headed by women.

• 3. The aging of the population, which will come to a crest nationwide two decades from now, is already materializing in certain communities.

None of these developments come as a surprise. Well before the 1990 census, each was apparent on a national basis. National demographic trends, though, materialize unevenly across the nation. Developments that are now full-blown and clearly visible in some places may be only in their beginning stages in others, and it takes the decennial census to reveal the richly detailed diversity of these developments at local scales.

1. Greater Ethnic Diversity in Communities Across the Nation

Metropolitan areas today manifest more complex racial and ethnic patterns than they did in 1980. The traditional notion of the "melting pot" no longer holds; its ingredients have separated into a complex racial and ethnic mosaic in which groups of people cling to their separate identities. The mosaic comprises not just Whites, Blacks, and Hispanics but a multitude of other nationalities and ethnic subgroups. Indeed, people responding to the 1990 census question asking how they identified their race reported upwards of 250,000 unique entries other than the 16 conventional categories of "white," "black," "Chinese," and the like.

It is a mosaic that varies from city to city. In St. Paul and Missoula, it contains Hmongs from Southeast Asia; in Atlanta and Providence, Cambodians; in Des Moines and Sioux City, Tai Dam and Vietnamese; in Arlington, Virginia, Salvadorans and other Central Americans; in Hartford, Jamaicans, Puerto Ricans, and assorted Asian populations. California's cities contain a dazzling array of nationalities and ethnic groups including Filipinos, Koreans, Vietnamese, Hmong, Armenians, and Japanese, along with Latinos and Blacks. Noncitizens add further complexity to the patterns in some areas.

The term "minority" is becoming increasingly obsolete. In a handful of the nation's metropolitan areas, the majority of residents now are members of one or another politically salient minority group. In California, one of every four cities above 50,000 in population have no racial or ethnic majority of any kind: Neither Anglos nor Hispanics nor Blacks nor Asians constitute a majority of the population (Table 1 lists several examples).

Table 1—Illustrative California Cities Without an Ethnic/Racial Majority by 1990

City	Total Population (000)	Percent White [1]	Percent Hispanic	Percent Asian/PI [1]	Percent Black
Los Angeles	3,485	37.3	39.9	9.2	13.0
San Jose	782	49.6	26.6	18.7	4.4
San Francisco	724	46.6	13.9	28.4	10.5
Oakland	372	28.3	13.9	14.2	42.8
Stockton	211	43.6	25.0	21.4	9.1
Vallejo	109	46.2	10.8	21.6	20.7
Daly City	92	27.4	22.4	42.3	7.5
Carson	84	22.1	27.9	23.7	25.6
Alhambra	82	24.3	36.1	37.4	1.8
National City	54	26.0	49.6	15.9	7.9

SOURCE: Calculated from Census of Population and Housing, 1990: Public Law 94–171 data (California)
[1] Non-Hispanic only.

Cultural pluralism is highly visible in California, but it is visibly emerging across the nation. As in California, this development will gradually transform the composition of voting electorates and, more generally, focus attention on the political means by which pluralism is to be accommodated at local scales. That issue is now at the heart of local decennial redistricting, pulling communities in separate directions toward two different visions: one, the traditional conception (however exaggerated) of "melting pot" assimilation; the other, a more complex racial and ethnic assertiveness that has come to be thought of as a "mosaic," with an array of groups demanding equity.

The distribution of particular ethnic groups by region places extraordinary pressures on their educational systems. In Florida and across the Southwest, schools must educate a diverse student population, many of whom lack basic English language skills. (The *Los Angeles Times* reports that more than 100 languages are spoken in California schools.) In ethnically diverse states, demographic change is transforming the mission of postsecondary education. In California, where many of the nation's immigrants and refugees have been settling, 54 percent of all young people enrolled in public schools statewide are members of one or another minority group. Forecasts anticipate that 65 percent of all public school enrollments will be minority by the turn of the century.

More generally, many people speak a language other than English and cannot speak English very well. In Florida and New Mexico, for example, one-tenth of persons 5 and older report they do not speak English "very well". In California, the figure is 16 percent; and in the South Central part of Los Angeles County, it is 29 percent.

Adding further complexity here is the fact that undocumented immigrants often form families and bear children who, as U.S. citizens by birth, are members of "binational" families. Concentrations of such "binational" families in certain jurisdictions complicates the issue of access to social services and how "resident" is to be defined.

2. Many Children Are Submerged in Poverty

The United States has been characterized as a rich nation with poor children. Demographers have chronicled the deterioration of urban childhood on a national scale for years. Now, the 1990 census can reveal the specifics about poverty-stricken children—who they are, why they are poor, and where:

• In Summit County, Ohio (where Congressman Sawyer resides), 10.2 percent of all adults live below poverty; but for the children under 5 years old, that figure is 21.2 percent;

• In the City of Erie, Pennsylvania (where Congressman Ridge resides), 15.4 percent of adults live in poverty; but 35.6 percent of the young children there are poverty-stricken;

• In Los Angeles County (where I reside), 22.0 percent of these young children under 5 are poverty-stricken; and in South Central Los Angeles, 44.1 percent of all children under 18 live in poverty.

As these comparisons suggest, child poverty typically exceeds adult poverty—a reality that warrants this nation's attention.

Demographic shifts are influential in shaping the characteristics of those classified as poor. Two distinct demographic factors have reshaped the face of poverty: marital disruption and single childbearing. The increase in the proportion of families headed by a lone parent and of children living in such families has elevated the overall poverty rate, especially among children. The 1990 census records wide disparities from place to place:

• In Los Angeles County as a whole, married-couple families outnumber, by a ratio of 5 to 2, families headed by just one parent.

• In the South Central part of Los Angeles County, by contrast, there are slightly more one-parent families than married-couple families.

Children's poverty has come to be concentrated in families headed by women. By 1989, well over half (57 percent) of all poor children lived in fatherless families, compared with less than a quarter (24 percent) of their 1959 counterparts. The demographic etiology of poverty has produced marked racial and ethnic differences in child poverty rates. In 1989, 44 percent of Black children and 36 percent of Hispanic children were poor, compared with only 14 percent of White children.

The future, it is said, creeps in on tiny feet. Our future regrettably is creeping in on impoverished tiny feet. High rates of poverty among contemporary children raise long-term concerns about access to postsecondary education. Among Blacks and Hispanics, the proportion of 18-to-24-year-old high school graduates who enrolled in college scarcely changed during the 1980's. That proportion stood at only 31 percent for Blacks and 29 percent for Hispanics in 1989, whereas the proportion had reached 39 percent among Whites (fig. 1).

Figure 1—Percentage of High School Graduates Enrolled in College, October 1979 and 1989

	1979	1989
All races	31.2	38.1
White	31.2	38.8
Black	29.5	30.8
Hispanic origin	30.2	28.7

Source: Bureau of the Census, Current Population Reports, Series P–20, No. 443, updated.

Poverty curtails education. Eventually, it erodes future workforce productivity. A rich nation that tolerates poor children in its midst wastes the means to enrich itself further.

For many cities, the quality of their workforce and their competitiveness in the world economy will depend heavily on the future productivity of the current student population. Mounting concerns with economic competitiveness already have intensified the private-sector focus on the link between childhood poverty and future workforce quality.

Of more immediate concern are the fiscal consequences of neglecting childhood poverty. The preventable needs of children now make substantial claims on public sector resources, ranging from intensive pediatric hospital care to antidelinquency and drug-abuse programs.

3. Local Concerns Posed by an Aging Population Will Intensify

The third development has to do with our aging population and the future concerns it will pose. Today, persons who are 65 or older constitute less than 13 percent of the nation's population, but by the year 2025 that figure is projected to rise to about 20 percent, and the number of elderly people will have nearly doubled.

Although the aging of population will not crest for another two decades, its effects have begun to materialize in certain communities. The future challenges that have only been speculated about in recent years are now turning into real challenges, as generations who settled in communities long ago have begun to age in place.

A critical aspect of this population aging is the pattern of its local diffusion, in terms of timing and intensity. In future decades, the elderly population will increase in most communities (at least relative to the rest of the population). That increase will be highly variable at local levels, with widely different consequences from place to place.

Inevitably, our national concern with aging will take on a more local focus, especially on the circumstances that surround elderly people who strive to live independently. The opportunities to maintain independence in old age matter not only to the elderly and their families but also, increasingly, to the communities where they reside. Policies whose scope is national will have to address those consequences as they unfold locally. Suburbs that housed newly settled young families in the 1950's are now communities in which many of the same family members have grown old. Neighborhoods across the nation retain some of their original "single-generation" look, which portends distinctive patterns of "aging in place" in the years ahead. Journalists already are discovering the emerging manifestations of this development in what are called "naturally occurring retirement communities"—existing neighborhoods where many older adults stayed on after young people left.

As local aging in place becomes more widespread, significant numbers of older inhabitants will strive to live independently as long as they can. As they age in place, the elderly will express needs in local places, intensifying the local community's focus on how their needs can best be met. Those needs are set within a living environment where other features may either exaggerate those needs or reduce them. Household living arrangements are a key feature, and the 1990 census data for fathoming living arrangements among the elderly is just now being released. We need to understand how those living arrangements evolve as people age in place, why they do, and what the consequences are.

* * * * *

Demographic changes tend to go unrecognized until they confront society with new needs on a massive scale and create constituencies for new legislation. The three issues I have highlighted are long-term and enduring in their importance. They are emerging gradually but unevenly across the nation. The 1990 census will help to strengthen local public awareness of these issues and what policies may be needed to address their manifestations.

Mr. SAWYER. Thank you. Thank you both very much. Let me begin with a question that may sound simple. I don't mean it to be. You have both described the increase in the diversity of the country. In terms of the most intensive consequences of demographic change, we are seeing that change concentrated on either coast or several of our coasts. To put it simply, is California the future and New Jersey the present?

Mr. MORRISON. I would be willing to say California is one aspect of the future, certainly in terms of the racial and ethnic diversity we see. And I think the challenges we see in California today politically are to figure out how we can put people together so that they can vote together and have common political agendas together, foreshadowing what is going to occur elsewhere in the Nation on a much more widespread basis.

I can also tell you that in California, the action seems to be moving inland. Coastal California, as you know, is densely settled. I think the projections show that much of the future growth in California, both economic and demographic, will be centered on what we call the Central Valley (San Joaquin Valley) running roughly from Bakersfield on up to Sacramento. That is an interesting region in the sense that it is probably ethnically more diverse than any other part of California.

So in a sense, that is where we will see the future unfold. And, of course, you sometimes hear of earthquakes in California. But those of us from California know that when the big one hits, everything east of the San Andreas Fault is going to slide into the Atlantic Ocean.

Ms. RICHE. I think it is important to remember when we look at what is changing, we also look at what isn't changing and I thought the most graphic example of what the census found is a series of maps, color-coded maps showing different counties across the country by their racial and ethnic makeup. It was very striking to see the Southeast with large proportions of African-Americans. It is very striking to see the Southwest with large portions of Hispanic, Latino Americans, but it was also just as striking to look at that large central part with very small proportions of minority populations and to wonder how people in each of these different regions understand and think about the interests of other people in other regions where they are looking very different and I think that is a challenge for all of us.

Mr. SAWYER. Clearly there are some parts of the country that are not changing at all.

Ms. RICHE. Right.

Mr. SAWYER. And they may be the exceptions and the focus of problems we don't even anticipate today. I look at Montana, which overnight this year will go from being represented by two Members of Congress to one and will shift from having two of the smallest congressional districts in the Nation to the single largest district in the Nation.

What a profound change in the relationship to their Nation's governance. It changes the relationship of 800,000 people to Washington, DC.

One of the elements that you mention in your written testimony is the record high share of population in the working ages in this decade and the next. It is a classic window of opportunity whose time will pass and will shift almost immediately from a great opportunity into an enormous burden to be borne by a following population.

Could you expand on how the differences in the concentration of those working age populations from one part of the country to another will affect the kind of policymaking we ought to be doing over the next 20 years?

Ms. RICHE. Certainly, I think all of us are focused on the retirement issue that we are going to face about 20 years from now. And I think a problem for all of us is to educate the broader policymaking public as to how this is a big window of opportunity but it is a time-limited window of opportunity and we have to really be thinking now as to what we are going to do if we want to be situated better 20 years down the road.

One of the things we are also seeing is—not only are we seeing a record share of population in the working ages, we are seeing a record high share of the working-age population working or wanting to work, and that is why we are all very interested in educational efforts for people who are currently in the workforce.

A lot of people are focused on the small numbers, relatively small numbers of people who are going to be coming into the workforce over the next decade or so and they are missing the point that most of our workers who are going to help us into the 21st century are already here and efforts have to be made to help them become as productive as possible if we want to take maximum advantage of our window of opportunity.

Mr. SAWYER. Let me complicate this a little bit. For much of the last 60 years we looked at our population, and the locus of its poverty, and found that older Americans constituted an impoverished body of population. We have worked very hard over the last 60 years to overcome that.

Today we find ourselves with perhaps an even more intense concentration of poverty among our Nation's children, with a very large population in between that is finding itself in a position of having to mediate between the demands of those two ages.

In a Nation that is going to be as different from one community to another as this one is likely to be, what are the kinds of measures that we ought to look for? How should we refocus the way we are identifying the needs of a Nation in demographic terms?

Mr. MORRISON. I think you have put your finger on a very important long-term issue: the fact that we have managed to lower poverty among the elderly but seen it increase among children, and I would underscore the point that voters need to recognize that we all have a stake in what happens to these children, because it is they who will be paying taxes into the social security system when we are the beneficiaries of social security later on. In fact, there is an increasing disparity between the minority make-up among the child population and the make-up of the older population who are nearing retirement age.

The fact is that there may be differences along racial or ethnic lines but there certainly is common cause in terms of getting these kids educated, who ever's kids these are and wherever they are, to turn them into productive adults for purely economic reasons if nothing else. Because without that kind of impetus, we will not be competitive in the 21st century.

Ms. RICHE. I think another point to go along with that is in the past we have traditionally relied on parents to make the investment in children, in their upbringing and their education and their socialization, but what is happening now with this changing age distribution that I described is that at any given time, most adults, most voters, most taxpayers are not in the process of raising children.

Family life, child rearing, is taking up a smaller share of adult life. So if we continue to assume that, well, parents will take care of their children, it means that a smaller share of society at any one time is engaged in raising the next generation, so there has to be some sort of rethinking or spreading out of responsibility so that all of us at all stages of life see our Nation's children as our children too.

Mr. SAWYER. You touched on something in your testimony that goes right at that point. There are some who suggest that a large portion of the productivity increase that the United States has experienced over the past 15 to 20 years is largely attributable to the growth in the percentage of working age women who are a part of that workforce. That will top out at some point.

The consequences of that for the potential for growth goes at a phrase that you used, Dr. Riche, in characterizing the safest projection as the highest projection in 2080. I assume that you mean the safest in that it will pose the greatest number of problems. So it is the most careful projection that you can make.

Yet it seems to me that if it is the case that our current patterns of productivity growth are grounded in a larger number of people actually being a part of our workforce, that may be the most dangerous projection. And if we are thinking in terms of what we are able to produce with the human skills we have, that lower 333 million may be the safest projection because the dangers are greatest.

Would you comment on that?

Ms. RICHE. Well, yes, I think actually our productivity growth has been quite slow compared to what it had been in previous decades, and one of the reasons we think that is so is because we have been adding more women and more younger people to the workforce and we are actually beginning to see some productivity growth again, I think as our workforce growth has been slowing.

But we have to look at that in comparison to what is happening with our competitors around the world, and I think to me the significant thing there is that our workforce is growing more than those workforces in Japan and in Germany, in Western Europe in general.

We are not sure what is going to happen yet with the Eastern European changes and what kind of migration might occur there, but up until now we have seen a much slower workforce growth there and as a consequence we have seen much more investment in labor-saving technology.

And my personal fear has been, is that we won't have that much of an investment in labor-saving technology relative to those countries and that we might end up being somewhat like a first-and a-half world economy relative to the kind of production that is going on in Europe and Japan, and I think that is something we should be aware of.

Mr. SAWYER. One of the things that I am working on in another part of my work in this Congress is precisely the kinds of education issues that you are talking about. The more we work on them, the more I am struck by the desire from every side of the political spectrum to provide a measure of accountability for the work that we do in educating children. I recall a point earlier in my life when I was looking at the same kinds of measures of accountability, the ability to assess how well children are performing and how much they have learned. In my State, Ohio, is one of the great linguistic dividing lines in the Nation, the old Lincoln Highway across Ohio U.S. 40. Above it, one kind of English is spoken and below, there are substantial differences in the style of spoken language. One of the consequences of that was that on standardized tests, children above that line would identify the word "toboggan" as a bentwood sled, but below that line they would identify it as the knit cap that you wore in the winter when you rode on a bentwood sled.

It seems to me that that is a relatively minor differentiation when you compare it with the extraordinary differences you describe as a product of what we have learned from the 1990 census. I use that example only as one clearly definable problem as we try to measure the performance of children across this hugely diverse mosaic that you describe.

But my question is this, at what point will we begin to have to consider law, programs, standards, regulations, and measurements that are regional or local rather than national in character, in order to begin to address this monumental diversity?

Ms. RICHE. That is a huge question. I would like to make one point backing up something Dr. Morrison said. The 1990 Census is being delivered in a way that enables more people to use data than ever before. That means that we have the possibility, if we want to have more State and local decisionmaking, we have in our hands the tools that will enable us to do that in a more precise way than we have done in the past and still fit them into whatever the national goals might be.

I really want to underscore the use of the Census as a tool, and I think that is going to be changing in a major way.

Mr. MORRISON. I would just underscore that there are common demographic underpinnings here causing these problems to materialize in different ways in different places, but the underlying problems themselves are the same.

In the Los Angeles school system, it said there are 100 different languages spoken by all the students in attendance. Those languages may not be the same in other parts of the country, but they pose the same problem and the same issue and the same differences of opinion among those who would advocate English only and those who would recognize that if you don't get kids started learning in a way that they don't find frustrating because they can't understand what is going on in the classroom, you are going to lose them.

I do think this is something that should be addressed locally and people locally should make that decision, but they should do so with the knowledge that if those kids aren't turned into productive workers in the future because they couldn't start out understanding what was going on, they will be a very heavy burden on the taxpayers of the future in those localities.

Mr. SAWYER. Let me touch on a question that you haven't talked about. Of the huge forces on population change over the millennium—war clearly has been one, disease is another—the concentrations of disease, particularly in urban settings where populations are thrown together in much more intensive ways than elsewhere, and particularly the concentrations of populations that have seen a faster spread of sexually transmitted diseases—have you given much thought to the consequences of that sort of phenomena on the accuracy and usefulness of population projections into the near and longer term?

Mr. MORRISON. I am not really qualified to comment on that except to make the obvious point that some of these diseases are going to rob us of people relatively early in their productive lives. So in that sense, they represent a costly loss of human resources. I do know that there are, just to touch on more commonplace diseases, things like measles—lots of kids are coming down with measles today. I don't know why. We thought we were rid of that.

We know how to administer inoculations——

Mr. SAWYER. But you have to do that before they work.

Mr. MORRISON. That is right, but if you look at it from a purely economic standpoint, it is a very cost-effective investment to make.

We see circumstances in which there are too many kids who haven't been inoculated against early childhood diseases, and it is costing us not only in terms of the health care bill, but somebody's mother or father who didn't go to work that day.

There are many opportunities to deal with these in ways that can have an immediate impact. The problem of the sexually transmitted disease is more profound because we don't know how to cure it or how to get rid of it or how long it will be until we can.

Ms. RICHE. I think that these things still have to be seen in perspective with worldwide population growth. It is important to remember that that growth is taking place, not in our country or in countries of similar economic level of development.

About every minute I think 176 new people are added to the world and it is important to remember that only 12 of those people are in developed countries. I think that is where the kind of issues you are raising about the effect of mass diseases probably are really far more unpredictable than in our country.

Another point that I think is important to remember about the census is that all these numbers are going to be calculated in special tabulations for almost all policy-making departments, Department of Transportation, Department of Housing, and planners in the government, whether at the State or national level will be able to use these figures in a way they haven't been able to before to target programs to say we have a bunch of children out there who need to be inoculated for measles.

There is a lot of room for much more strategic planning. That is going to be different in this decade because computers give planners an opportunity to use data like these in a way they have never done before.

Mr. SAWYER. I would hope that you would be willing to respond to written questions later on. Your testimony is enormously helpful to us today.

I have one other question that I would like to pose to both of you as thoughtful users of this data. That is, the difficulty in planning for a census that functions well in this kind of environment of change is one of the real scientific challenges that lie before this government.

We are looking at a variety of means of conducting a census, the kind of information that is gathered by the census, who ought to do it, and the ways in which modern statistical technique might supplement the actual head counts that have been the traditional conduct of the census.

Would either of you care to comment about the way in which the census ought to evolve over the next decade or 20 years?

Let me say, I ask that in terms of 20 years, because I am one of those people who believes that we probably cannot get to where we need to be in the course of this decade.

We have about 18 months left in which to have in place new ideas in order to be usable by 2000 and therefore we probably ought to plan 2000 with 2010 carefully in mind.

Over the next 10 or 20 years, what kind of changes, given the rates of change in our population, do you think the Census ought to anticipate?

Ms. RICHE. We are all looking at a variety of advanced techniques, new ways to conduct the census. We shouldn't forget some of the basic things. The most basic thing about the census is it is the one thing everybody in the country does 1 day every 10 years.

The diverseness that we see portrayed in the Census makes us ask what can we find that is common for all Americans, what brings us together, and that sense of a community event is something that can be very important to all of us.

One thing that I hope you do as you are looking toward the census is asking the American people how the census could be conducted in a way that would enable them to feel that they are still a part of it.

Mr. MORRISON. The only comment I have is to point out that the Census Bureau has a pretty thorough process of strategic planning under way and has had it under way for at least several years.

I have been very impressed by what I have seen happening, because they have started from the foundations of why we take the census and asked the question, how do we want to do this and what else do we want to do and how else might we do it.

They have examined a number of different alternative ways of thinking about the census and the information needs it meets.

We have to recognize that the decennial census which is an event that happens once every decade is only one part of an important broader function that the Bureau performs, which is it keeps us posted on all sorts of developments during the interim years. That is not a function that can be ignored.

The Bureau, I think, is anticipating changes in technology that might facilitate different ways of collecting information. Of course we are all aware that we can't predict 5 or 10 years from now what is going to be on our mind that we want to know about.

In that sense, we have to keep our options open and we have to plan for a way to collect information that not only meets the basic constitutional mandates, but keeps us informed how our population is changing on dimensions that are a current public policy concern.

Mr. SAWYER. I hope it will comfort you to know that this subcommittee has been working closely with the Bureau toward those ends, in addition to commissioning a study by the National Academy of Sciences to undertake a fundamental review of planning for 2000.

I think it is clear that some of the difficulties in the conduct of the 1990 census weren't problems of execution, but rather problems of design. There are serious changes going on both in the size and the complexity of the population that make some of the previous techniques not as effective as they might have been.

But you are absolutely correct—understanding the fundamental purpose for the Census and not throwing the good out in the name of change is enormously important. Comparability of data over time is really a key ingredient in being able to see beyond that horizon.

In any event, I thank you both very much for being here and for the quality of your testimony. I look forward to seeing you again.

Our second panel today has been cut in half by an inadvertent absence, but we are pleased to welcome back Dr. William P. O'Hare, who is the director of population and policy analysis at the Urban Research Institute of the University of Louisville.

Did I get that right?

Mr. O'HARE. I haven't been there long enough to tell you whether that is right or not.

Mr. SAWYER. He is also the former director of policy studies at the Population Reference Bureau, and he is a good friend of this subcommittee.

STATEMENT OF WILLIAM P. O'HARE, DIRECTOR OF POPULATION AND POLICY ANALYSIS, URBAN RESEARCH INSTITUTE, UNIVERSITY OF LOUISVILLE

Mr. O'HARE. I would like to start by thanking the members of the House Subcommittee on Census and Population for giving me this opportunity to present my views on America's changing minority population.

Rapid growth and increasing diversity are two key trends that characterize the changes in America's minority population during the 1980's. In my oral testimony, I will briefly summarize these points. I have provided the committee with a written report which I would like to have included as part of my testimony.

America's racial and ethnic minority populations—Africa-Americans or blacks, Hispanics, Asians, and American Indians—increased from 46 million in 1980 to roughly 61 million in 1990.

The number of minorities in the United States today is nearly twice the number counted in 1970, which was 34 million. It is widely recognized that the number of minorities were significantly undercounted in the 1990 census.

Minorities are becoming a larger share of our population, a larger part of our national character, and a larger part of our future.

The 32 percent growth rate in the minority population during the 1980's contrasts sharply with the increase of only 4 percent among non-Hispanic whites. Minorities accounted for approximately two-thirds of U.S. population growth between 1980 and 1990, and they now represent nearly a quarter of our population. In a large and growing number of areas of the country, minorities are now a majority of the population.

The growth of minority groups has been accompanied by increased demographic and socioeconomic diversity. Just a few generations ago, African-Americans were the vast majority of the minority population and the vast majority of all African-Americans were poor.

African-Americans are now less than half of the minority population and the socioeconomic status of minorities, including African-Americans, is more diverse than a generation or two ago.

Much of the recent growth of America's minority population has been fueled by immigration. About half of the growth of Hispanics during the 1980's can be attributed to immigration, and nearly three-quarters of the growth among Asian-Americans during the 1980's was due to immigration. Even African-American population growth was affected by immigration.

About one-sixth of the black population growth during the 1980's was due to immigration. The presence of foreign-born members adds diversity to each minority group as well as to the society at large.

The minority groups growing most rapidly are Asians and Hispanics. The Asian-American population, including Pacific Islanders, doubled during the 1980's. The Hispanic population grew by more than 50 percent. The rapid growth of Hispanic and Asian subgroups has fueled demographic diversity within the American minority population.

There are at least three clearly identified Latino subgroups: Mexican Americans, Puerto Ricans, and Cubans. Newly arriving immigrants from Central and South America are also important segments of the Hispanic population in certain locations. While these groups share certain cultural similarities, language and religion, for example, they also exhibit many dissimilarities.

Asian-Americans may be the most diverse subgroup. Among the 7.3 million Asian-Americans, there are six groups of a half million or more, Chinese, Japanese, Filipino, Asian Indian, Vietnamese, and Koreans; a decade ago, in 1980, there were only three Asian groups of this size. These groups often have little in common other than ties to a distant continent.

While minorities still constitute a disproportionately large share of the poverty population, some segments of the minority community are thriving. For example, in 1990, the median household income of Asian-Americans was 18 percent higher than that of Anglos or non-Hispanic whites.

Furthermore, there is a growing share of blacks and Hispanics who are affluent. Among blacks, the number of households with income of $50,000 or more, in 1990 dollars, has grown by 73 percent since 1980, and the number of affluent Hispanic households has grown by 81 percent during this period.

What are the implications of these changes in America's minority population?

Let me mention a couple.

The new demographics of American minorities are forcing us to rethink what it means to be a minority in America. Neither the conception of minorities derived from European immigrants of a century ago, nor the black/civil rights model of a generation ago, adequately reflect the experiences of today's minority population.

The treatment of minorities by public policies is now being reexamined in light of changing minority demographics.

The new demographics of diversity have also altered intergroup dynamics, both majority/minority relations and relationships among different minority groups. The new diversity in America's minority population is forcing Anglos to reexamine their concept of minorities.

Also, the growing numbers of "new minorities" have provided opportunities for progressive coalitions, but they have also elevated tensions among minority groups in some cities.

The large, rapidly growing, and increasingly diverse minority population in America is forcing us to rethink what it means to be a minority in America and to contemplate how our public policies should change to accommodate the new demographics of diversity that will characterize America in the 21st century.

That concludes my remarks. I would be happy to answer questions or add some additional comments about implications.

[The prepared statement of Mr. O'Hare follows:]

PREPARED STATEMENT OF WILLIAM P. O'HARE, DIRECTOR OF POPULATION AND POLICY ANALYSIS, URBAN RESEARCH INSTITUTE, UNIVERSITY OF LOUISVILLE

Introduction

The increasing size and diversity of America's minority population were two of the most striking facts revealed by the results of the 1990 Census. This paper reviews some of the major shifts in the U.S. minority population during the 1980s and offers comments on their significance.

Following a brief background section, the paper is divided into three sections. First, a discussion of the changing size of minority groups is provided. Second, the growing socioeconomic diversity within the minority population is explored. Finally, I offer a few thoughts about some of the implications of these facts and figures.

Background

Exactly who is a minority is a matter of perception. In some respects we are all minorities. For example, there is no single ancestry group that is more than half the population. There are also some groups, such as Jews and Arabs, for which there is no Government data, and very little data of any sort.

While the Decennial Census questionnaire identifies many racial and ethnic groups, it is important to note that Census data are based on self-identification. An individual, or someone in the individual s household, reports the racial and Spanish Origin status of the individual. The census data are not based on some objective standard for assigning individuals into racial or ethnic categories.

Another drawback of data from the Decennial Census is the way that race and Spanish Origin status are measured. First respondents are asked to identify their racial group and are offered five choices; white, black, American Indian/Eskimo/Aleut, Asian or Pacific Islander, or "other race." In a different question, individuals are asked if the respondent is a person of Spanish origin and if so, what particularly national origin subgroup they belong to (i.e. Cuban, Mexican, Puerto Rican, etc). Therefore race and Spanish origin status are not mutually exclusive categories.

About half of those identifying themselves as being Hispanic (being of Spanish origin) also identify themselves as white and about half identify themselves as belonging to "other races." The inclusion of large numbers of Hispanics in the white category can often provide misleading information. For example, in cities where there are large numbers of Hispanics, the income figures for whites can be misleadingly low because many Hispanics are included in this group. The most useful categorization of race/ethnicity from census data is that which identifies non-Hispanic whites, blacks, Indians and Asians separately, but such data are not always available.

In this report, I have used non-Hispanic racial categories along with Hispanics whenever possible in order to present mutually exclusive categories. Also, I use the term "Anglo" in places to refer to non-Hispanic whites.

While basic demographic information (age, sex, race/Spanish Origin status, marital status and household relationship) are now available from the 1990 Census of Population and Housing, social and economic data are not yet available for the country as a whole. Where possible I have utilized the 1990 Census data in this analysis. Where data from the Decennial Census are not yet available, I employed data from other census datafiles such as the Census Bureau's Current Population Survey.

Section 1—America's Growing Minority Population

The bulk of the population growth in the United States during the 1980s was due to increased numbers of minorities. There were about 46 million minorities counted in the 1980 Census and 61 million counted in the 1990 Census (see table 1.1). In other words, minorities accounted for 64 percent of the 22.2 million population increase between 1980 and 1990.

Table 1.1—Growth of American Population Groups: 1980–90

[in thousands]

	1980	1990	Change 1980–90 Number	Change 1980–90 Percent of Total	Change 1980–90 Percent
Non-Hispanic:					
White	180,603	188,129	7,526	34.0	4.2
Black	26,092	29,216	3,124	14.1	12.0
Asians	3,551	6,970	3,419	15.4	96.3
Indian/Eskimo/Aleut	1,433	1,794	361	1.6	25.2
Other races	264	249	−15		
Hispanic	14,604	22,354	7,750	35.0	53.1
Total minorities	45,944	60,583	14,639	66.0	31.9
Total	226,547	248,712	22,165	100	9.8

Source: 1980 Figures from U.S. Bureau of the Census, 1980 Census of Population, ***General Social and Economic Characteristics***, PC80–1–C1, Table 75, Dec. 1983; 1990 Figures from P.L. 94–171 files on CD-ROM.

The trend in the 1980s followed rapid growth of minorities in the 1970s. In 1970, the minority population numbered about 34 million. Between 1970 and 1980, 53 percent of U.S. population growth was due to increased numbers of minorities.

It is widely known that the number of minorities is actually larger than the number reported by the Census Bureau because the Census misses minorities at a higher rate than non-Hispanic whites. The 1990 Census undercount rates for minorities, based on the Post-Enumeration Survey, are provided in table 1.2. Based on the undercount rates reported in table 1.2 and the minority populations shown in table 1.1, there were actually about 63.5 million minorities in the United States in 1990.

Table 1.2—Undercount of Various Groups in the 1990 Census Based on Postnumeration Survey

	Percent [1]
Total	2.1
Male	2.4
Female	1.7
Black	4.8

Table 1.2—Undercount of Various Groups in the 1990 Census Based on Postnumeration Survey—Continued

	Percent [1]
Male	5.4
Female	4.3
Asian/Pacific Islander	3.1
Male	3.5
Female	2.6
American Indians	5.0
Male	5.6
Female	4.4
Hispanic	5.2
Male	5.8
Female	4.7

Source: Hogan, Howard, 1991, "The 1990 Post-Enumeration Survey: Operation and Results," Table 3.1, paper delivered at the 1991 Annual Meetings of the American Statistical Association, Atlanta, GA, August 19–22, 1991.

[1] Based on smoothed estimates.

The overall growth rate for the minority population during the 1980s (31.9 percent) was much higher than that for non-Hispanic whites (4.2 percent). However, the overall growth rate for minorities masks extensive variation in population growth among the various minority groups.

The growth rates of individual minority groups as well as non-Hispanic whites are shown in table 1.1. The figures in the racial categories shown in table 1.1 include non-Hispanics only in order to derive the total number of minorities. Therefore the number of racial groups in table 1.1 are not as large as the numbers typically quoted for a racial group. While most Hispanics chose the white or "other races" designations on the Census race question, some selected other race groups. For example, there were 770,000 black-Hispanics, 304,000 Asian-Hispanics (mostly Filipinos I suspect), and 165,000 American Indian-Hispanics.

Asian-Americans, who grew by 96 percent, are the most rapidly growing minority group. The Asian-American population was also the fastest growing population during the 1970s, increasing by 128 percent.[1]

Hispanics were the second fastest growing minority population; increasing by 53 percent during the 1980s compared to 61 percent during the 1970s. American Indians grew by 25 percent during the decade, compared to 72 percent during the 1970s. The African-American population was the slowest growing minority population, growing by only 12 percent during the 1980, down from 17 percent during the 1970s.

In other words, blacks are increasing at 3 TIMES the rate of Anglos, Indians are increasing at 6 TIMES the rate of Anglos, Hispanics are increasing at 12 TIMES the rate of Anglos, and Asian-Americans are increasing at 24 TIMES the rate of Anglos.

The rate of increase is due in part to the size of the group at the initial point in time. Smaller groups tend to show higher percentage increase than larger groups. Therefore it is also important to look at absolute increase as well as percentage increase.

Table 1.1 shows the 1980s changes in terms of absolute numbers. Hispanics had the largest increase (7.8 million), followed by Asians (3.4 million), blacks (3.1 million), then American Indians (361,000).

In addition to growing larger, the U.S. minority population is becoming more diverse in terms of demographic subgroups within the minority population. A few generation ago, blacks were the vast majority of all minorities. Now, blacks are less than half of all minorities.

While blacks are typically seen as a relatively homogenous population, the minority groups that are growing most rapidly, Hispanics and Asians, are composed of many distinct subgroups.

The "new minorities," Asians and Hispanics, are growing much more rapidly than blacks or American Indians. The number of Asian-Americans (including Pacific Islanders) nearly doubled during the 1980s. The number of Hispanics increased by more than 50 percent. By contrast, the African-American population grew by only 12 percent during the decade.

[1] U.S. Bureau of the Census, 1991, "Race and Spanish Origin," *1990 Census Profile,* Number 2, June.

The Census Bureau identifies numerous subgroups among Asians and Hispanics. Results of the 1990 Census indicates there were 13.5 million Mexican-Americans, 2.7 Puerto Ricans (living on the mainland), and 1 million Cubans (see table 1.3). Newly arrived immigrants from Central and South America are also important segments of the Latino population. The 1991 Current Population Survey indicates that there were nearly three million people who identified themselves as being Hispanics of Central or South America origin.[2]

Table 1.3—Detailed Changes in the Hispanic Population: 1980–90

[in thousands]

Hispanic Subgroup	1980	1990	Change 1980–90 Number	Change 1980–90 Percent
Mexican	8,740	13,496	4,755	54.4
Puerto Rican	2,014	2,728	714	35.4
Cuban	803	1,044	241	30.0
Other Hispanic	3,051	5,086	2,035	66.7
Total	14,609	22,354	7,745	53.0

Source: U.S. Bureau of the Census, Press Release CB91–216, released June 12, 1991.

While these Hispanic groups share certain cultural similarities (language and religion, for example) they also exhibit many dissimilarities. For example, they typically live in different parts of the country. Nearly two-thirds (63 percent) of the Mexican-Americans are located in the Southwest (including Texas where there were 3.9 million Mexican-Americans in 1990), 68 percent of the Puerto Ricans are in the Northeast, and 70 percent of Cubans are in the South, primarily in Florida.

Asian Americans may be the most diverse minority group. Among the 7.3 million Asian-Americans, there are six-groups of a half million or more (Chinese, Japanese, Filipino, Asians Indians, Vietnamese, and Koreans)—84% of all Asian-Americans are in one of these top six groups (see table 1.4). In 1980 there were only three Asian groups of this size.

Table 1.4—Detailed Changes in the Asian and Pacific Islander Population Between 1980 and 1990

[in thousands]

Asian/Pacific Islander Subgroup	1980	1990	Change 1980–90 Number	Change 1980–90 Percent
Chinese	806	1,645	839	104.1
Filipino	775	1,407	632	81.6
Japanese	701	'848	147	20.9
Asian Indian	362	815	454	125.6
Korean	355	799	444	125.3
Vietnamese	262	615	353	134.8
Hawaiian	167	211	44	26.5
Cambodians	16	147	131	818.8
Laotian	48	149	101	210.4
Thai	45	91	46	102.2
Hmong	5	90	85	1700.0
Pakistani	16	81	65	406.3
Samoan	42	63	21	50.1
Guamanian	32	49	17	53.4
Indonesian	10	29	19	190.0

Source: U.S. Bureau of the Census, Press Release CB91–215, Issued June 12, 1991.

*This is number based only on nine specific Asian categories used in 100% questionnaire in 1980. When sample data are used the 1980 count of Asians and Pacific Islanders was 3,726,000. Growth over decade was 95.2%.

[2] U.S. Bureau of the Census, 1991, "The Hispanic Population of the United States: 1991," *Current Population Reports,* Series P–20, No. 455, Oct.

Table 1.4 shows changes in the size of these subgroups during the 1980s. While four of the largest subgroups doubled in size during the 1980s (Chinese, Asian Indians, Koreans, and Vietnamese) other subgroups (for example, Japanese and Hawaiians) grew relatively slowly.

These groups often have little in common other than ties to the same continent. In their homelands, they may have actually been adversaries.

Understanding America's minority population is further complicated by the fact that much of the population growth among minorities during the 1980s was due to immigration. Immigration accounted for about half of all Hispanic population growth, and nearly three quarters of all Asian-American population growth.

Immigration also contributed to black population growth during the 1980s. About one-sixth of black population growth during the 1980s was due to immigration from Africa and the Caribbean.[3]

The presence of foreign-born members adds diversity to each minority group as well as to the society at large. The presence of large numbers of foreign-born individuals in some minority groups complicate assessment of their socioeconomic status.

Section 2—Changing Socioeconomic Status Among Minorities

The view that all, or nearly all, minorities are poor is no longer accurate. While only a few generations ago the common image of America's minority population was one comprised primarily of poor blacks, particularly one with close ties to the rural South, this image is now outdated.

Minorities are still over-represented among the poor, but recent changes have resulted in a minority population that is more economically diverse. To some extent, the minority population is becoming economically polarized. The immigration of highly educated minorities, particularly from Asia, along with economic advancement among segments of the black and Hispanic populations, has lead to a significant increase in the number of middle and upper income minorities. Yet large segments of the minority population remain impoverished and powerless.

While minorities still lag well behind Anglos on most measures of socioeconomic status, some segments of the minority community are thriving. For example, the 1990 median household income[4] of Asians and Pacific Islanders ($38,450) was significantly higher than that of non-Hispanic whites ($32,500).

Table 2.1 provides information on median household income for groups in 1979 and 1990. The 1979 data are from the 1980 Census while the 1990 data were gleaned from the March 1991 Current Population Survey. The median income of groups is compared to that of non-Hispanic whites to gain a better of understanding of their socioeconomic position at each point in time.

Table 2.1—Median Household Income for Various Groups: 1979 and 1990

[in 1990 dollars]

	1979		1990	
	Median	As a percent of non-Hispanic whites	Median	As a percent of non-Hispanic whites
White	$31,829	99.3	$31,231	96.1
Non-Hispanic Whites	32,065	100	** 32,500	100
Black	19,700	61.4	18,676	57.5
Indian/Eskimo/Aleut	22,064	68.8	N/A	N/A
All Hispanic	24,307	75.8	22,330	68.7
Mexican	24,885	77.6	22,439	69.0
Puerto Rican	22,997	71.7	16,169	49.8
Cuban	35,082	109.4	25,900	79.7
Central/South American			23,568	72.5
Other Hispanics*	31,989	99.8	25,635	78.9
All Asian and Pacific Islanders	35,944	112.1	38,450	118.3

[3] U.S. Bureau of the Census, 1990, "U.S. Population Estimates by Age, Sex, Race and Hispanic Origin: 1989," *Current Population Reports,* Series P–25, No. 1018, GPO, Washington, DC.

[4] U.S. Bureau of the Census, 1991, "Money Income of Households, Families, and Persons in the United States: 1990," *Current Population Reports,* Series P–60, No 174, Table a, August.

Table 2.1—Median Household Income for Various Groups: 1979 and 1990—Continued

[in 1990 dollars]

	1979		1990	
	Median	As a percent of non-Hispanic whites	Median	As a percent of non-Hispanic whites
Japanese	40,537	126.4	N/A	N/A
Chinese	35,215	109.8	N/A	N/A
Filipino	39,473	123.1	N/A	N/A
Korean	32,666	101.9	N/A	N/A
Asian Indian	37,082	115.6	N/A	N/A
Vietnamese	22,592	70.5	N/A	N/A
Hawaiian	29,872	93.2	N/A	N/A
Guamanian	30,414	94.9	N/A	N/A
Samoan	24,930	77.7	N/A	N/A
Other Asians	22,891	71.4	N/A	N/A

Source: 1980 Census of Population, ***General Social and Economic Characteristics,*** PC80–1–C1; U.S. Bureau of the Census, ***Current Population Reports,*** Series P–60, No. 174, Table A; U.S. Bureau of the Census, 1991, "The Hispanic Population in he United States: March 1991, ***Current Population Reports,*** Series P–20, No. 455.

* Includes central and South American in 1980.

** My calculation from the March 1991 CPS Tape.

ANote: The 1979 data are from the 1980 Decennial Census and the 1990 data are from the March 1991 Current Population Survey. Since these two data sources use slightly different methods to collect data on income, caution should be used in making direct comparisons of changes over time.

While some patterns are apparent, there is also a great deal of diversity among and within groups. Asians median household income was 12 percent higher than that of Anglos in 1979 and by 1990 their median household-income was 18 percent higher than that of Anglos. However, data from 1980 indicate that not all Asian subgroups are thriving. Several subgroups (namely Vietnamese, and Samoans) have average incomes well below Anglos. The same is true for the Hispanic subgroups.

Mexican-Americans and Puerto Ricans have average incomes well below Anglos, but the median 1990 household income of Cubans was 9 percent above that of Anglos.

Furthermore, among blacks and Hispanics there is a growing share of the population that is affluent. Among blacks, the number of households with incomes of $50,000 or more (in 1990 dollars) has grown by 73 percent since 1980, and the number of affluent Hispanic households has grown by 81 percent during the same period (see table 2.2). By 1990, nearly one out of every seven black households was affluent, and one out of every eight Hispanic households was affluent.

Table 2.2—Number and Percentage of Affluent Black and Hispanic Households: 1967–1990

[in thousands]

	Blacks			Hispanics		
	Households	Percent affluent	Affluent households	Households	Percent affluent	Affluent households
1990	10,671	11.9	1,270	6,220	13.4	833
1989	10,486	12.9	1,353	5,933	15.5	920
1988	10,561	12.5	1,320	5,910	13.9	821
1987	10,192	11.2	1,142	5,642	14.2	801
1986	9,922	10.9	1,081	5,418	14.1	764
1985	9,797	10.3	1,009	5,213	12.3	641
1984	9,480	10.0	948	4,883	12.4	605
1983	9,243	8.5	786	4,666	10.8	504
1982	9,916	7.2	642	4,085	10.6	433
1981	8,961	8.1	726	3,980	11.8	470
1980	8,847	8.3	734	3,906	11.4	445
1979	8,586	9.8	841	3,684	13.2	486
1978	8,066	11.0	887	3,291	12.4	408

Table 2.2—Number and Percentage of Affluent Black and Hispanic Households: 1967–1990—Continued

[in thousands]

	Blacks			Hispanics		
	Households	Percent affluent	Affluent households	Households	Percent affluent	Affluent households
1977	7,977	9.0	718	3,304	10.9	360
1976	7,776	8.6	669	3,081	10.2	314
1975	7,489	7.8	584	2,948	8.9	262
1974	7,263	8.9	646	2,897	10.8	313
1973	7,040	8.6	605	2,722	12.6	343
1972	6,809	9.0	613	2,655	10.2	271
1971	6,578	7.7	507	N/A	N/A	N/A
1970	6,180	8.5	525	N/A	NJA	N/A
1969	6,053	7.0	424	N/A	N/A	N/A
1968	5,870	6.8	399	N/A	N/A	N/A
1967	5,728	5.9	338	N/A	N/A	N/A

Source: U.S. Census Bureau, ***Current Population Reports,*** Series P–60, No. 174, Table B–2.

The result of rapid growth among high-earning Asians and growth of affluent groups among blacks and Hispanics has produced a segment of the minority population that is economically well off, while another large segment is stuck in poverty.

The poverty rates for all minorities are significantly above those of Anglos. Even Asian-Americans whose average income is higher than that of Anglos have a poverty rate that is nearly 50 percent above the Anglo rate (see table 2.3).

Table 2.3—Poverty Rates of Persons in Various Groups: 1979 and 1990

	1979		1990	
	Poverty rate	As a percent of non-Hispanic whites	Poverty rate	As a percent of non-Hispanic whites
White	9.4	106	10.7	122
Non-Hispanic White	8.9	100	8.8	100
Black	28.7	323	31.9	363
Indian/Eskimo/Aleut	27.5	308	N/A	N/A
All Hispanic	23.5	264	28.1	319
Mexican	23.3	262	28.1	319
Puerto Rican	36.3	408	40.6	461
Cuban	13.2	148	16.9	192
Central/South American	20.3	228	25.4	289
Other Hispanics*	17.2	193	21.5	244
All Asian and Pacific Islanders	13.1	147	12.2	139
Japanese	6.6	74	N/A	N/A
Chinese	13.5	152	N/A	N/A
Filipino	7.1	80	N/A	N/A
Korean	11.7	131	N/A	N/A
Asian Indian	9.9	111	N/A	N/A
Vietnamese	35.5	399	N/A	N/A
Hawaiian	15.8	178	N/A	N/A
Guamanian	13.9	156	N/A	N/A
Samoan	29.5	331	N/A	N/A
Other Asians	35.5	399	N/A	N/A

Source: 1980 Census of Population, ***General Social and Economic Characteristics,*** PC80–1–C1; U.S. Bureau of the Census, ***Current Population Reports,*** Series P-60, No. 175, Table A; U.S. Bureau of the Census, 1991, "The Hispanic Population in the United States: March 1991", ***Current Population Reports,*** Series p-20, No. 455; 1980 Poverty rates for these two groups are taken from Bean, Frank and Marta Tienda, 1987, ***The Hispanic Population of the United States,*** Russell Gage Foundation, New York, Table 10.7.

Note: The 1979 data are from the 1980 Decennial Census and the 1990 data are from the March 1991 Current Population Survey. Since these two data sources use slightly different methods to collect data on income, caution should be used in making direct comparisons of changes over time.

While the poverty rate for Anglos remained virtually stagnant at just below nine percent between 1980 and 1990, the poverty rates for blacks and Hispanics increased during the 1980s.

Another barometer of economic well-being is the rate of business-ownership within a group. Data from a Census Bureau survey taken in 1987 provide evidence on the extent to which different minority groups are likely to own a business.

Table 2.4 shows that Asian-Americans have much higher rates of business-ownership than other minority groups, except Cubans. The rate of Asian business ownership is nearly as high as that of Anglos. Business ownership among blacks and American Indians trails far behind that of Asians. While the business-ownership rate for Asian-Americans was 57 businesses per 1,000 people, the rate for blacks was 14.6 and the rate for American Indians was slightly lower at 13.9. Overall the rate for Hispanics was 20.9; somewhat higher than blacks or American Indians, but well below the rate for Asians.

Table 2.4—Rate of Business Ownership Among Minorities

[Number of firms per 1,000 population]

	1982	1987
Major Groups:		
Non-Hispanic whites	61.9	67.1
Black	11.3	14.6
Hispanic	14.3	20.9
Asian*	46.3	57.0
American Indian **	8.8	13.9
Subgroups:		
Mexican	13.7	18.8
Puerto Rican	6.3	10.9
Cuban	41.4	62.9
Other Hispanic	14.2	22.9
Aleut	58.5	54.0
Eskimo	36.8	44.4
American Indian	7.4	10.3
Asian Indian	65.7	75.7
Chinese	49.1	63.4
Japanese	59.3	66.1
Korean	68.0	102.4
Vietnamese	14.6	49.3
Filipino	25.5	32.8
Hawaiian	16.6	21.5

Source: O'Hare, William, 1992, "Reaching for the Dream," ***American Demographics,*** Vol 14, No. 1, Jan.
* Includes Pacific Islanders.
** Includes Eskimos and Aleuts.

Within the Hispanic community, Cubans have the highest rate of business ownership by far (62.9 businesses per 1000 people). The rate for Mexican-Americans was 18.8, and the rate for Puerto Ricans (10.9) trails even blacks and American Indians.

Among Asians, Koreans stand out as a group with an extraordinarily high rate of business-ownership. More than 1 out of 10 Koreans was a business owner in 1987. Asian Indians, also have a high rate of business ownership (75.7 per 1000 people). On the other hand, Filipinos and Hawaiians, have very low rates of business ownership relative to other Asian groups.

The social status of a group has important implications for the spatial distribution of that group. The most commonly used indicator of residential segregation is the Index of Dissimilarity which reflects how evenly minorities are spread across the neighborhoods of a city or metropolitan area. The higher the index, the more segregated a group is.

Average segregation scores for minority groups are presented in Table 2.5. The average score for blacks was .686, compared to .507 for Hispanics, .416 for Asians, and .353 for American Indians.

Table 2.5—Residential Segregation and Suburbanization in Metropolitan Areas: 1990

	Weighted Mean Index* of Dissimilarity	Percent of Metro Area Residents Living in Suburbs
Blacks	.686	3.2
Hispanics	.507	43
Asians	.416	51
Indians	.353	N/A

Source: Harrison, Roderick, J., and Daniel H. Weinberg, ***1992, Racial and Ethnic Residential Segregation in 1990,*** Paper delivered at the Population Association of American Meeting, Denver CO. May 1992; William H. Frey, 1992, ***Minority Suburbanization and Continued "White Flight" in U.S. Metropolitan Areas: Assessing Findings from the 1990 Census,*** Paper delivered it the Population Association of American Meeting, Denver Co. May 1992.

* This reflects dissimilarity between each minority and non-Hispanic whites. The higher the value of the index the more segregated a group is.

Note: Only areas with 2 percent or more racial or ethnic population were included (1 percent for American Indians, Eskimos, and Aleuts).

Clearly, blacks are more segregated than Asians, Hispanics, and American Indians. Blacks are almost twice as segregated as Indians. Although it should be noted that these figures are only from metropolitan areas, and does not reflect that segregation of Indians on reservations which are located mostly outside metro areas.

Past research has indicated that the residential segregation of blacks is not due to income differences between whites and blacks. Poor blacks seldom live in the same neighborhood as poor whites, for example.

Table 2.5 also provides data on suburbanization of minorities. The groups follow the familiar pattern of Asians having the highest level of suburbanization, and blacks the lowest. Hispanics are in between Asians and blacks. Asians are the most suburbanized group, followed by Hispanics and finally blacks. Similar data for Indians were not available.

The results of this analysis suggest that there is a clear ranking of minority groups on most measures of status. Asians are on top, followed by Hispanics, with blacks and American Indians at the bottom. It should also be noted that with the Asian and Hispanics groups, there is significant variation among subgroups, and that a segment of the black population has become more affluent.

Section 3—Summary and Implications

America's minority population is growing much more rapidly than the nonminority population, and therefore becoming a larger share of our total population. As minorities increase their share of our total population, they will increasingly shape our national character.

In addition to rapid growth, minorities are adding diversity to our population. Blacks who made up the overwhelming majority of all minorities just a few generations ago, are now less than half of all minorities. New minority groups are growing rapidly, and the uniformly low economic status that once characterized minorities is no longer evident. The recent changes in America's minorities mean that the image that characterized the U.S. minority population a few generations ago, is now outdated.

Historically, the conception of minorities in America has developed along two different lines. One image is based on the European immigrants of the 19th and early twentieth century. Most of these groups were eventually absorbed into broader society leading to a vision of a "melting pot" in which ethnic minorities were brought into the mainstream of society a generation or two after arrival.

The second conception, of minorities that has dominated our thinking stems from the civil rights movement of the 1950s and 1960s. in this image, minorities (primarily blacks) are seen as a long-oppressed racial group for whom the "melting pot" has not been accessible.

Both of these conceptions tend to become muddled in discussions of minorities today. Neither model fits all of today's minority groups very well. Immigration is an important factor in understanding the status of some minority groups, namely Hispanics and Asians, but it is irrelevant for others (blacks and American Indians). Even among groups that have high numbers of immigrants, such as Hispanics, immigration alone is not an adequate explanation for their low socioeconomic status. Native-born Hispanics still have lower socioeconomic status than Anglos.

While many of the "new immigrant" groups seem to be following the path of European ethnics a century ago, the fact that blacks and American Indians remain stuck at the bottom of the socioeconomic ladder, challenges our image of America as a "melting pot. " On the other hand, upward, mobility of some minority groupsl primarily Asians and Cubans, suggests that minority status itself is not a barrier to success. This challenges the "civil rights" model of minorities.

Today's minority population is diverse and multi-faceted. We need to reconceptualise what it means to be a minority in America in light of a rapidly growing complex minority population.

The recent demographic changes in the American minority population have produced changes in intergroup relations. First, it is changing the way the majority population views minorities. The increased diversity of America's minority population is calling into question policies that lump all minorities into a single group. When blacks dominated our vision of minorities, public policies which offered assistance to minority groups seemed appropriate. Such policies may seem unnecessary or unwise given today's more diverse minority population.

Furthermore, the fact that some segments of the minority population have achieved middle-class economic status, and in some cases affluence, has lead to questioning the need for continued government programs to assist minorities. I think this changing view of minorities is reflected in recent Supreme Court decisions regarding civil rights.

Second, the rapid increase of "new minorities" has elevated tensions among minority groups in some cities such as Los Angeles, Miami, New York and Washington. In locations where blacks have seen "new" groups surpass them in number and economic status, tensions between minority groups have been magnified. In addition, the white power structure sometimes uses intergroup tensions among minorities to forward its own agenda.

What does all of this mean for public policy? As we move toward the 21st century, governments at all levels will be grappling with the realities of America's new minorities. The new complexity and diversity that characterizes today's minority population will need to be recognized as we move toward re-consideration of existing public policies. On the one hand, minority status no longer automatically signifies oppressed impoverished groups, but on the other hand segments of the minority community still suffer from discrimination and encounter barriers to upward mobility. New public policies will have to be sensitive to these contrasting aspects of the U.S. minority population.

Mr. SAWYER. Thank you very much.

Clarence Wood, who was our other witness today, is the Director of the Human Relations Foundation in Chicago. He is unable to be with us at the last minute due to an emergency meeting that was called by Mayor Daley.

[The prepared statement of Mr. Wood follows:]

PREPARED STATEMENT OF CLARENCE N. WOOD, PRESIDENT, HUMAN RELATIONS FOUNDATION OF CHICAGO [1]

A key finding in The Chicago Community Trust Human Relations Task Force's 1989 report on ethnic and racial tensions in Chicago was that:

> Poverty and race often overlap. But, they are not interchangeable, for if black or brown skin caused poverty, there would be no poor whites and no affluent minorities.[2]

This finding is a key factor in addressing racial and ethnic tensions because attempts to redress the abuses of racial discrimination are usually presented in the form of economic programs. Conversely, economic needs of citizens, whatever their skin color, are often dismissed as the results of discrimination.

> * court decisions, and thousands of brave words about Negro rights had barely touched the life of Chicago's Negroes.[3]

---

[1] I wish to thank Dr. Bruce Hatton Boyer for his help in preparing this paper.

[2] Chicago Community Trust Human Relations Task Force, "A Report On Race, Ethnic and Religious Tensions in Chicago," (1989), p. 18.

* NOTE: A page of testimony was missing from the original submission.

[3] Allan H. Spear, *Black Chicago: The Making of a Negro Ghetto, 1890–1920,* (Chicago: University of Chicago Press, 1967), p. 224.

This lack of effect from civil rights laws had a perverse positive consequence; the black ghetto in Chicago was still a functioning community as late as 1966. Blacks still provided most of the community services, they still owned the small shops and businesses, and black professionals still provided help to black citizens. There was a vertical integration that provided social cohesion:

> In short, unlike the present period, inner-city communities prior to 1960 exhibited the features of social organization-including a sense of community, positive neighborhood identification, and explicit norms and sanctions against aberrant behavior.[4]

This vertical integration and subsequent self-sufficiency existed in other minority communities as well. Andrew Greeley showed clearly how Catholic and non-Catholic vertical stratification co-existed in "Westwood" without disrupting the overall well-being of the community at large.[5] His work and that of his colleagues showed how white ethnic communities had prospered prior to the 1960's:

> Because the ethnic subcommunity is, at least if it's big enough, a comprehensive substructure, it is possible for an upwardly mobile professional and businessman to build his entire career almost entirely within its confines. Not only a practitioner, but even a surgeon, can have patients almost all of his own ethnic background; a Catholic academician can achieve a position within the system of Catholic colleges (which are, for the most part, Irish Catholic colleges) that he would not enjoy in the larger academic system; a political leader can gain far more power as the head of an ethnic faction within the party than he would if he tried to operate without such a proven base; . . . even a racketeer, though he may be viewed with contempt by the larger society, may be respected for his success and affluence within his own substructure.[6]

Such is no longer the case, particularly in older northern cities such as Chicago. Patterns of successful intra-urban community life that developed in the 1920's and 1930's were rent apart in the late 1960's and 1970's by a variety of forces. Factory closings and relocations removed many city jobs, for one thing, while the well-documented shift from blue-collar to white-collar jobs upset once stable employment opportunities. Gentrification and an attractive suburban diaspora lured many city dwellers away from traditional neighborhoods. While both white ethnics and blacks were affected by these shifts, Blacks were hit harder because the exodus of some middle-class blacks to suburbs and previously all-white neighborhoods left black communities more bereft of effective local leadership.[7]

The result of these demographic shifts is clear today. There remains in most major American cities, Chicago among them, an urban underclass that is largely minority, that suffers disproportionately from unemployment and other economic measures, that has a fragmented community and family structure, and that is by far the most devastated by such modem urban scourges as gangs, crime and drugs.

The principal difficulty in addressing the problems of this underclass has been, in my view, an often-unconscious assumption that because many of its members are minorities, poverty itself exists mostly as a minority problem. It does not. People are poor because they are uneducated or untrained, because they lack work skills or opportunities, because they do not know how to hold down a job successfully, or some combination of these factors. The reasons why the poor lack remedies to poverty are highly linked with racism, but the poverty itself is an economic problem. It is this confusion of race with poverty that has all too often obscured the real needs of minority communities.

The simple proof of this assertion is the fact that not all of the persons living in poverty in this country are from minority classes—a 1983 congressional study, for example, determined that two-thirds, or 23,000,000, of the people living in poverty in the United States in 1982, were indeed white.[8] Clearly, whites lack job opportunities

---

[4] William Julius Wilson, *The Truly Disadvantaged: The Inner City, the Underclass, and Public Policy* (Chicago: University of Chicago Press, 1987), p. 3.

[5] Andrew M. Greeley, *Why Can't They Be Like Us* (New York: E.P. Dutton, 1975), pp.103–19.

[6] *Ibid.*, pp. 50–1.

[7] The exodus of middle-class blacks is the principal reason that the black community today is so helpless, argues William Julius Wilson in many of his works, especially *The Truly Disadvantaged.* Recently scholars have disputed Wilson's reliance on this premise. But the fact remains that this notion remains an important explanation, if not the primary one, for intra-urban decay in black neighborhoods.

[8] Ways and Means Committee, U.S. House of Representatives, October 17, 1983, in Thomas J. Hynes, Jr. and William F. Campbell, eds., *An End to Poverty* (Chicago: National Textbook Company, 1984), p. 4.

and training as well as minorities and, just as clearly, poverty is not *ipso facto* a minority problem. This idea cannot be too strongly emphasized.

In addition, Great Society programs such as Aid To Families With Dependent Children (AFDC) were not designed to benefit minorities exclusively; they were designed to benefit the poor, many of whom happen to be black or Hispanic. The problem of affordable housing, for example, is not a minority problem alone. It does, however, as I noted above, affect minorities more acutely. For example, Chicago and the Nation face a housing crisis that crosses racial and ethnic lines. The well-documented mediocrity of the public school systems in Chicago and other major urban centers, to cite another instance, has caused both minorities and whites to suffer from poor educational opportunities.

However, minorities appear to suffer disproportionately from poverty because they usually live in major cities where their poverty is highly visible and more intractable. This situation is in direct contrast to that for poor whites, who tend to live in rural settings where subsistence existence is more manageable, and where the hazards associated with overcrowding are minimized. To cite two quick examples, black households live in substandard or overcrowded housing, or pay over 30% of their income for housing, in numbers nearly three times their population rate.[9] 44% of all murder victims nationally were black even though blacks constitute only 12% of the overall population; homicide was in 1987 the leading cause of death for all blacks between the ages of 15 and 34.[10] The statistics show similar trends among Hispanics.

The question therefore is, why do minorities suffer so horribly from poverty? The answer lies, paradoxically enough, in the very successes that they achieved with the 1960's civil rights laws. It was the enfranchisement of minorities under the Voting Rights Act of 1965, the dropping of formal racial barriers under the Civil Rights Act of 1964, and the entry of some minorities into mainstream economic life at least in part as a result of affirmative action, that split minority communities apart. Upper-middle class blacks moved on and prospered, and thus "decapitated" the vertical integration that Spear observed in 1966 Chicago.

That white ethnic neighborhoods did not suffer from the same phenomenon is instructive. Because businesses and real estate in these neighborhoods were locally owned, many ethnics who could afford to move to suburbs, stayed in traditional neighborhoods by choice. White ethnic communities, e.g. Italians in Elmwood Park, Lithuanians in Marquette Park and Ukrainians in Wicker Park, continue to exhibit this vertical integration.

Clearly, something is still holding minorities back when it comes to economic prosperity and community development. While the debate to define this "something" has caused much acrimony among social critics, one fact does stand clear: that "something" is real, it is operating even as these words are penned, it is unaffected by legal remedies, and it is still keeping minorities in this country from realizing the "American dream."

Not surprisingly, this debate often follows pre-conceived political ideologies. The two principal sides of the argument can be essentially represented by the works of Daniel Patrick Moynihan on the one side, and sociologist Charles Murray on the other, particularly as they swirl around two key phenomena that today continue to plague urban minorities.

The first of those problems is the breakdown in family. As early as 1963 Moynihan, then serving as Assistant Secretary of Labor in the Kennedy Administration, saw that the disintegration of family had a great effect on job stability. He later converted this observation into the cornerstone belief of the Great Society, namely, that eliminating legal segregation would be meaningless without a corresponding effort to raise the economic and social status of once-oppressed minorities.[11] He saw that minorities were being held back by powers that extended far beyond legal sanctions. This position, in turn, led to his famous—and for a long time, infamous comment during the Nixon administration that "the time may have come when the issue of race could benefit from a period of benign neglect." [12] He meant by this

---

[9] Philip Clay, "House Opportunity: A Dream Deferred," in Janet Dewart, ed., *The State of Black Africa 1990* (New York: National Urban League, 1990), p. 75.

[10] Carl C. Bell, M.D. and Esther J. Jenkins, Ph.D., "Preventing Black Homicide" in Dewart, p. 143.

[11] See Daniel Patrick Moynihan, *The Negro Family: The Case for National Action* (Washington, D.C.: Office of Policy Planning and Research, U.S. Department of Labor, 1965).

[12] Daniel Patrick Moynihan, *The Politics of a Guaranteed Income: The Nixon Administration and the Family Assistance Plan.* (New York: Random House, 1963), p. 41.

that the removal of legal barriers was not sufficient to remedy the economic and social inequalities in American society. He believed that minorities needed time to build up systems of self-reliance and self-help, and to develop an effective work ethic that inhabited entire communities, entities that could not be purchased with government funds or waved into existence by government fiat.

Moynihan's work was, as William Julius Wilson has pointed out, so controversial in its analysis of the blight of urban minorities that it scared a generation of liberal scholars away from examining the plight of minorities.[13] The vitriol which was leveled at Moynihan served as a warning; better to do something, anything, so critics implied, than to be accused of ignoring the issue of race. As a result, researchers turned their attention away from the important issues of race, family and social structure just as they were becoming crucial factors within the inner city, and looked instead to economic issues alone as the cause of inter city problems.

As a result of this neglect, the social evils that Moynihan so presciently identified were not addressed. Accordingly, his expected readjustment never occurred, and today's cities are immersed in a crisis of family. Never before have so many households with children been headed by single parents, a fact that applies to whites as well as blacks.

But, it must be remembered, the breakdown of the family within the inner ciry differs only in degree, not in kind, from those occurring in the rest of society. Whites, blacks and most other minorities have all suffered from the upheavals of the last two decades. In 1965, for example, 10.5% of families in this country were headed by a single female; by 1983, that figure had grown to 15.4%, a 47% increase. Again, this burden was shared disproportionately by minorities, but it was not exclusively a minority problem. In 1965, 28.3% of black families were headed by a single female as opposed to only 9% of white families; by 1983, those figures had leaped to 41.9% and 12.2% respectively. Nor were other minorities spared: in the ten years between 1973 (the first year for which such statistics are available) and 1983, the number of Hispanic families headed by a single female rose from 16.7% to 22.8%.[14]

The principal complication of the single-parent family is worth repeating: it is far more likely to be poor. Statistics show that the number of single-parent families that were poor in 1979 was 52.1%. Among blacks, that figure rose to 75.2%.[15] Second, there is less familial cohesion and hence less transmission of those social values required to advance economically. Michael Harrington has suggested, for example, one compelling explanation for the growth in teen-age pregnancies among the poor:

> In many of the subcultures of poverty—the Appalachian white, as well as the Hispanic and black—it is "macho" for a young man to get his girlfriend pregnant. And young girls, I suspect, living in a harsh and sometimes loveless world, subjected, as Silberman says, to all the romantic values of the mass media but without the means of acting upon them possessed by the middle class, willingly court pregnancy as a way of finding love. In the process, they can sentence themselves to a life of poverty.[16]

The absence of love and positive nurturance are critical factors not only in the perpetuation of poverty but, as I will discuss later, in the establishment and maintenance of racism.

Unemployment remains another major problem. Between 1972 and 1989, unemployment for blacks increased 8.65% while the same rate for whites decreased 11.76%; the absolute rate of unemployment for blacks was over two and half times greater than that for whites as late as 1989.[17] Explanations for this disparity are many, and they vary from region to region but they may be summed up as follows: blacks and other minorities are less likely than whites to achieve the levels of schooling and training needed to compete effectively in an increasingly post-technological society. This phenomenon is most pronounced in the major Rust Belt cities such as Chicago, Detroit and Cleveland, where the increase in service-industry jobs is mirrored by a corresponding decline of unskilled and semi-skilled jobs in manufacturing, but it is universal around the country. As one analyst writes:

---

[13] Wilson, p. 4.

[14] Wilson, p. 65.

[15] Mary Jo Bane, "Household Composition and Poverty," in Sheldon H. Danziger and Daniel H. Weinberg, eds., *Fighting Poverty* (Cambridge: Harvard University Press, 1986), p. 218.

[16] Michael Harrington, *The New American Poverty* (New York: Holt, Rinehart and Winston, 1984), p. 196.

[17] David H. Swinton, "Economic Status of Black Americans During the 1980's," in Dewart, p. 47.

The fact that black/white youth unemployment differentials seem to persist for all geographic locations, for all family types, and for all income groups clearly suggests that the cause is something more fundamental than the growth of welfare programs.[18]

It is this "growth of welfare programs" that is most often cited by conservatives as the sure sign that anti-poverty programs do not work. Welfare programs, so goes the reasoning, support the poor in their poverty, and offer no way out. The leading exponent of this charge, Charles Murray, has gone so far as to blame the rise of the underclass directly on the antipoverty programs themselves:

The first effect of the new rules was to make it profitable for the poor to behave in the short term in ways that were destructive in the long term. Their second effect was to mask these long-term losses-to subsidize irretrievable mistakes. We tried to provide for the poor and produced more poor instead. We tried to remove the barriers to escape poverty, and inadvertently built a trap.[19]

Murray goes on to cite how he believes that welfare payments have income incentives for the poor to stop working; how programs such as AFDC have directly caused family breakdown instead of alleviating its aftermath; and how the ghettoization of urban minorities has destroyed the status rewards associated with self-improvement.

Murray's thesis contains important truths and several flaws.[20] One fact that Murray conveniently overlooks is that many programs were never adequately funded, i.e. up to the levels at which they were designed to operate. The Office of Economic Opportunity (OEO), for example, received a maximum of $6 billion in 1968 when estimates for fully funding its programs ran as high as $40 billion.[21] And expenditures under AFDC, even at its most generous levels, never exceeded one percent of the Federal budget.[22] What is more, a 1983 Congressional study showed that half of the fifty states paid AFDC benefits that were below 50% of the poverty threshold for a three- or four-person family, and that in over 80% of the states, the AFDC payment was at least one-third below the established poverty benchmark.[23] Is it any wonder that these programs have not fulfilled the expectations that gave them birth?

But in Murray's defense, many government programs were hastily designed or poorly executed.[24] In addition, attempts to apply Federal standards to hundreds of different communities are inherently flawed. Rather, as economic conditions vary considerably between, say, a Chicago and a Miami, so should the solutions. The line between government assistance that helps pull people out of poverty, and assistance that breeds dependence and so keeps people mired in poverty, is difficult to ascertain. And finally, Murray's depiction of "bureaucratic tangles" involved in administering War on Poverty programs, and his implicit assertion that the programs served the middle-class government functionaries more adequately than they did the urban poor, is certainly a valid interpretation.

Murray's argument falters most conspicuously because he confuses "poverty" programs with "social" programs. Here, dollar figures do become alarming, for one of the fastest rising segments of the Federal budget in the past twenty years has been that for "social" programs. But despite popular notions, the greatest share of these programs is devoted not to "poverty" or "welfare" but to Social Security and Medicare, both staunchly middle class programs. For example, between 1970 and 1980, Social Security Old Age and Survivors outlays nearly doubled, from $60.7 to $104.7 billion, while AFDC payments went from $10.3 to only $12.5 billion. In the same time period, General Assistance payments rose from $1.3 to $1.4 billion, a modest 8% rise during a period of wildcat inflation.[25]

---

[18] David T. Ellwood and Lawrence N. Summers, "Poverty In America" in Danziger and Weinberg, p. 101.

[19] Charles Murray, *Losing Ground: American Social Policy, 1950–1980* (New York: Basic Books, 1984), p. 9.

[20] See Robert Greenstein, "Losing Faith in Losing Ground," *The New Republic* (March 25, 1985), pp. 12–17.

[21] Harrington, p. 21.

[22] Haley Brooks, "Seeking Equity and Efficiency: Public and Private Roles," in Brooks, Liebman and Schelting, eds., *Public Private Partnership* (Boston: American Academy of Arts & Sciences; Ballenger Publishing Company, 1984), p. 4.

[23] Ways and Means Committee, U.S. House of Representatives, October 17, 1983, p. 106.

[24] John C. Donovan's *The Politics of Poverty* (New York: Pegasus Books, 1967) preserves the flavor of optimism from those times while rationally discussing the practical difficulties that doomed many OEO programs from the outset.

[25] Ellwood and Summers, p. 85.

Yet the notion that "welfare" programs are the cause of poverty has immense popularity. Its simplicity was especially alluring as the 1980s opened after a decade of economic stagnation. Indeed, Ronald Reagan won two stunning Presidential victories on the premise that the government, by withdrawing support for social programs and by cutting taxes, could let the economy expand and cure poverty all by itself. This is the much touted "trickle-down" effect. Another way of expressing it is the apt metaphor that a rising tide lifts all boats." Such a theory holds true, of course, only if the hulls of all the boats are sound.

The sad fact, as we have seen, is that all boats were not lifted during the past two decades. The underfunding and mismanagement of anti-poverty programs in the 1970s, and the active diminution of such programs during the 1980s, have had their depressing effects on poverty rates among minorities. The programs did help some whites some of the time and some minority individuals were helped, but the main trend is clear: poverty among minorities continues to rise even today, in the absence of sufficient constructive help, and at a rate that is faster than that for whites.

Statistics show, for example, that white poverty rates have more or less followed the leading economic indicators over the past two decades; they fell in periods of prosperity and rose during recessions. The official poverty rate in 1964, before the War on Poverty programs were put in place, was 19%; nearly twenty years later, in 1983, the official poverty rate had dropped to 15.2%. Among blacks, however, the 1964 and 1983 rates were, respectively, 49.6% and 35.7%, making the poverty rate among blacks in 1983 twenty percentage points higher than the rates for all persons in 1964.[26] Particularly alarming has been the concurrent trend of skyrocketing poverty among selected groups within these wider groups, most notably among black males and black females with children.

The conservative explanation for this phenomenon is simple: since those who wanted to rise out of poverty had the means to do so during the recent economic expansion, those who did not rise must enjoy remaining poor. Murray's thesis that the poor are free to change their lot if they only so desired is typical:

> People—all people, black or white, rich or poor—may be unequally responsible for what has happened to them in the past, but all are equally responsible for what they do next. . . . A person can fall repeatedly and always be qualified for another chance—to try again, to try something easier, to try something different. The options are always open. Opportunity is endless. There is no punishment for failure, only a total absence of rewards.[27]

In an ideal world, Murray's sentiment would perhaps pertain. But to say "opportunity is endless" is to be blind to the actual workings of our American society. Surely the countless successful discrimination suits and prosecutions over the past two decades suggest that opportunity is more endless for some portions of our society than for others. The fact that women and minorities are still significantly underrepresented in top management of our society's institutions even after twenty years of anti-discrimination efforts suggests the same thing. And to state, as Murray does, that "there is no punishment for failure" ignores the fact that the millions of poor minorities huddled in public housing with little food, scant clothing and no hope of escape are indeed being punished for their inability—self-inflicted or otherwise—to move out of poverty. At the very least, given the economic disruptions of the past two decades, minorities would not have suffered all out of proportions to their numbers—as they have done—if Murray's simple world were the real one.

Murray's argument conveniently ignores the psychological and social forces at work in our society today. The long-term effects of poverty on nutrition, on education, on health, not to mention on self-esteem and emotional development, are too well-known for Murray's grade school Social Darwinism to be a useful construct. It is too simplistic and too uncognizant of simple realities to be true.

Yet, as we noted earlier, "something" is causing all of this poverty among minorities. Since it is not welfare, or social programs, or legal barriers, it must be some phenomenon from the realm of psychology and social structure. To find the reason for these disproportionate poverty rates between whites and minorities, I believe we must look beyond the realm of economics.

II. Racism

If the old racism was the systematic, conscious exclusion of blacks from white life through law and flat, the New Racism is more subtle. It consists of behavior on the part of both whites and minorities that continues to erect racial barriers at all

---

[26] Sheldon H. Danziger, Robert H. Haveman, Robert D. Plotnick, "Antipoverty Policy: Effects On the Poor and the Nonpoor," in Danziger and Weinberg, pp. 55–6.

[27] Murray, p. 234.

levels of society. These barriers are often subtle or even unconscious; for whites, they can take the form of silent acquiescence to exclusionary customs in churches or clubs, while for blacks, they can be social envy subtimated as racial pride. Whatever their form, they undeniably exist because there is no other plausible way to explain why the gap between white affluence and minority poverty is widening.

The New Racism is a social game played on an unequal playing field. One team has the newest uniforms, the finest equipment, the best training facilities, the best farm system, the most experienced coaches and the best-prepared reserve bench. The other team has none of these. Not surprisingly, the first team wins most of the games and then says, in effect, "See, we've let you play in our league and you still can't make the grade! Why don't you go back down to the minor leagues where you belong?"

This new racism is the result of many factors. As we have seen, it gains force from new economic realities but its true etiology is social and psychological. New economic realities have not created the New Racism, they have merely allowed it to surface and flourish.

Since 1970, and during the past decade in particular, gaps in income between rich and poor and between whites and non-whites have been growing. Kevin Phillips has traced in detail how the Reagan administration tax policies deliberately shifted income away from the lower and middle classes toward the very richest 5% of our society.[28] The resultant "falling expectations," as Barbara Erhenreich has dubbed them,[29] have rekindled old hatreds and manifested themselves in a new set of truisms. Murray describes it as follows:

> It is the inarticulate constellation of worries and suspicions that helped account for Ronald Reagan's victory in 1980. . . . [It] is characterized by hostility toward welfare (it makes people lazy), toward lenient judges (they encourage crime), and toward socially conscious schools (too busy busing kids to teach them how to read). The popular wisdom disapproves of favoritism for blacks and of too many written-in rights for minorities of all sorts. It says that the government is meddling far too much in things that are none of its business.
>
> The hostility one hears in the vox populi may account for the reluctance of many intellectuals to consider whether this view might not be right. To listen carefully to the popular wisdom is also to hear a good deal of mean-spirited (often racist) invective. Acknowledging the merits of its insights is seen as approving of the invective as well.[30]

Murray then attempts to discuss these perceptions "stripped of the prejudices and bombast" but finds the going slippery as the facts simply do not support the perceptions.

To take just one example, Murray contends that "lenient judges" are seen as encouraging crime by refusing to incarcerate malefactors. The fact is that incarceration rates have soared in the past decade. During the first six months of 1987 alone, the United States prison population grew at a rate of five percent, or 1000 new prison beds every week.[31] Indeed, these rates out-stripped the crime rate, which according to the F.B.I. grew only 1.4% during that entire year.[32] And incarcerations in state prisons rose at a faster rate than those for federal prisons, a significant trend because crimes of violence and property-the heart of the "crime problem" are adjudicated at the State level.

It is difficult, therefore, to make a factual case that "lenient judges" are "encouraging crime." Yet politicians make this charge every day. And though the charge is overtly non-racial, the fact that minorities get caught committing proportionately more crimes is well-known enough to scare many whites.[33] This type of appeal is

---

[28] Kevin Phillips, *The Politics of Rich and Poor* (New York: Random House, 1990), pp. 52–73.

[29] Barbara Ehrenreich, *Fear of Falling: The Inner Life of the Middle Class* (New York: Pantheon Books, 1989).

[30] Murray, p. 146.

[31] Incarceration rates among certain sub-groups show some highly significant trends. The number of female inmates rose 111% in just seven years between 1980 and 1987, a figure not coincidentally related, I believe, to the number of single-parent families and its accompanying increase in the poverty rate among women. Source: *World Almanac* 1989, p. 821.

[32] *Ibid.*, p. 818.

[33] I say "get caught commiting . . ." rather than "commit" because some critics believe that black criminals are more tenaciously pursued by police, more vigorously prosecuted by district attorneys, and more likely to suffer from inadequate legal counsel than whites, thus raising the possibility that white criminals more often escape conviction. It is difficult to find hard data to support this conclusion, so I will only raise the question for the reader to consider.

the heart and soul of the New Racism; it attacks minorities not with overt invectives but relies instead on insinuation and guilt by association to maintain racial barriers.

Murray accuses intellectuals of not listening to these ideas because of the attached racial invective, but I submit that intellectuals cannot take the ideas seriously because these fears are essentially psychological rationalizations formed in direct reaction to fundamental economic changes in this country.

The fears stem from America's receding from world-wide economic power. This retreat is real, and its effects are slowly working their way into the American economy through lay-offs, corporate reorganizations and direct foreign ownership of many American companies.[34] This economic retrenchment has led in turn to a psychological retreat of the forces that bring sense, order, unity and dignity to everyday life. As Harrington writes, Kevin Phillips' analysis on this point is forthright and notes that by 1988, 2% of America's manufacturing assets were foreign-owned, a figure almost 50% higher than the previous record levels of the pre World War I era.

> In the seventies and eighties we had both inflation and recession, which subverted the liberal wisdom; the highest unemployment rate since the Great Depression; and a consequent loss of political and social nerve. Crises, particularly at first, do not make people radical or compassionate. They are frightening, and most people concentrate on saving themselves. Thoughts of "brothers" and "sisters" who are moral kin but not one's blood relatives, are a luxury many cannot afford . . . It is somewhat more problematic to summon the average American to such a struggle in the midst of declining real wages and chronic unemployment.[35]

It is this fracturing of the social fabric that has given vent to the New Racism. It is not difficult to imagine, as many whites did during the optimistic 1960s, that liberating oppressed minorities in this country is a noble and deserving act; the white Freedom Riders of that time, the white students who went into the Deep South under the banner of SNCC, the widespread denunciation by whites all across the country of Jim Crow segregation, were all made possible by a rising economy. Blacks were not a threat to most whites in 1965.

Today, they appear to be—A shrinking industrial base combined with demographic changes caused by the "baby boom" have seemingly turned the unlimited opportunity ethic of the 1960s into a zero-sum game. Again, this phenomenon is more a perception than a fact. Not all industries have suffered and large numbers of new jobs have been created during the past 10 years. The possibility that the United States can create enough new jobs in this post-industrial era to once again produce a generally widespread affluence certainly exists. But for now, the idea of a "fortress America" that can stride the world with unlimited economic and military power is not readily accepted by any except the most ardent jingoists.

Racism is therefore a perceptual state. And since it lies in the eyes of the beholder, its etiology and its cure lie in the realm of psychology. One classic study of racism and mental health states the premise well:

> Mental health encompasses the issue of the availability of the "good life" within a given social, political, and economic context. The absence of opportunities to meet basic and culturally determined needs constitutes the gap between individual aspiration and the availability of satisfaction. This gap is the source of a great deal of mental anguish and sometimes precipitates or complicates mental illness.[36]

Dr. Thomas Pettigrew has made the critical distinction between individual racism and institutional racism.[37] The former, he found, is maintained by an individual sense of inadequacy, particularly in the case of whites with the authoritarian upbringings that are especially common in lower middle- and lower class households. In such individuals, the psychological mechanisms are well understood if not immediately obvious: anger toward harsh parents that was unexpressable in childhood becomes, in adult life, projected onto outsiders. Numerous studies show that such individuals lack the ability for introspection, indeed, that such an ability is walled off

---

[34] See *Politics of Rich and Poor,* pp. 139; 125.

[35] Harrington, p. 3.

[36] Claudewell S. Thomas and James P. Comer, "Racism and Mental Health Services," in Charles V. Willie, Bernard M. Kramer and Bertram S. Brown, eds, *Racism and Mental Health* (Pittsburgh: University of Pittsburgh Press, 1973), p. 166.

[37] Thomas F. Pettigrew, "Racism and the Mental Health of White Americans," in Willie, Kramer, Brown, pp. 269–298.

by defense mechanisms.[38] This denial leads to an apparent mastery of the environment that is only temporarily satisfying.

One thinks here of Murray's grumbling whites. We cannot strip away their bigotries because their bigotries are essential to their own sense of self-esteem. Such debasement of minorities and the subsequent feeling of superiority, belies their actual life situations. In other words, a white who feels like a failure can blame one of two people: him or herself or "that pushy nigger down the street." The latter course is not only easier, it brings better temporary relief:

> It can be argued that the bigot's environmental mastery is enhanced by prejudice when it bolsters his sense of worth and effectively organizes his world. But here again, it is not difficult to think of situations where these personality functions of prejudice would fail the bigot. . . . Prejudice becomes for such individuals "a crutch" upon which to limp through life. Lacking insight into their inner feelings, they project their own unacceptable impulses on the minorities whom they regard as beneath them.[39]

This pattern of racism is familiar. It is classic bigotry, the basis of most anti-Semitism and skinhead movements. This behavior is disturbing to sensitive people but it is usually excused as aberrant. And it may well be aberrant, since few statistics exist to track its extent with any reliability.

But similar strains of racism can be found throughout our society, even among the best educated and most affluent segments. In these places it is less raw, perhaps, but it is present nonetheless. Harvard psychiatrist Robert Coles' classic multivolume study, Children of Crisis, shows how racism develops even among America's most privileged classes. One articulate child from upper-middle class Boston, for example, presented the following as accepted truth:

> I don't think some of our teachers really like this town; they try to preach to us how we did a lot of harm to the Indians and to the black people. My father says it'll always be like that; there are people who are prejudiced against anyone who has tried to work hard and make some money, and prejudiced in favor of the people who don't care if they work or not, so long as they collect welfare.[40]

Here is Murray's vox populi again, supposedly "stripped of prejudices and bombast," and it is no less racist. Even among less dogmatic rich whites, Coles records how efforts to bridge the gaps between whites and minorities often disintegrate into racist stereotypes:

> One day Daddy will like the black people, and tell us how he'd like to help them, and sometimes he does. But another day will come when he's changed his mind. Then he's all against them. He says it'll soon be so bad in the city, because of the black people, that we'll have to go live in our country home, or in one of the tall apartment houses that Daddy's company owns; they have police guarding them all the time, and they have to, because if they didn't, everyone would be robbed.[41]

Thus racism begins early in life. It is a social disorder with psychological roots; wherever there are parents who destroy their children's self-esteem, there will be prejudice.

The New Racism is insidious because it manifests itself in the corners of society, away from the glare of affirmative action. It is more often than not racism by omission, not commission. Because it is more difficult to isolate and identify, it is therefore more dangerous. It is an institutional racism.

Many whites assume that institutional racism was banished with the civil rights laws of the 1960's. Nothing could be further from the truth. Formal, verbal and written forms of this racism have been largely eliminated but its unconscious forms are still flourishing. Its intensity seems to grow in inverse proportion to economic prosperity.

Pettigrew defines institutional racism as "that complex of institutional arrangements that restrict the life choices of black Americans in comparison to those of White Americans." [42] His language is particularly useful because he talks of "life

---

[38] Pettigrew's citations are complete and so have not been reproduced here.

[39] Pettigrew, p. 285–8.

[40] Robert Coles, M.D., *Children of Crisis,* Vol. 5 Privileged Ones (Boston: Little, Brown and Company, 1977), p. 259.

[41] *Ibid.,* p. 296.

[42] Pettigrew, p. 274. It is important to note, as Pettigrew does, that the concept "black Americans" can also be used to describe any ethnic or religious minorities undergoing attack.

choices." To exclude a qualified minority from law school is illegal; to exclude a qualified minority law school graduate from working at a particular law firm is also illegal though more difficult to establish as an act of discrimination; to exclude a qualified minority law school graduate with a good work record from partnership in a law firm is illegal, though extremely difficult to prove as an act of discrimination; to exclude a qualified minority law school graduate law firm partner from a lunch at which business matters are discussed is, for all intents and purposes, an invisible, unprovable act of discrimination but it does limit the "life choices" of that individual.

These distinctions are important because while researchers have found hard cases of individual prejudice to be few in number, they have found that instances of institutional or situational prejudice to be widespread. Pettigrew estimates that at any given moment, 60% of white Americans will act in a racist manner toward a given issue.[43] He notes carefully that:

> for many whites, anti-black views and behavior are not nearly so expressive as they are socially adaptive in a racist society. In sharp contrast to the deeply-rooted bigotry of authoritarianism, the bigotry of "conformity" requires prejudice as a social entrance ticket.[44]

It is not difficult to spot such behavior in everyday life. The father of the child cited above, who alternates between supporting and hating blacks, is one example. Another, more prototypical example might be a white who feels uncomfortable with an unspoken color or religious restriction at a country club or, on a different socioeconomic level, at a Moose or Elks lodge. How can such doubts be expressed? One can seek out members who share his views and hope their numbers are sufficient to support a change. This is the idealistic view, and it does happen from time to time. More likely, however, one will tolerate, even rationalize, the restrictions on the grounds that "they don't want to be members here anyway, they wouldn't be comfortable here," or "it's not really hurting anybody and besides, I associate with plenty of blacks (or Jews or Poles) in other places I frequent." Occasionally, given an external prod, one will resign from the club. But, and this is the important point, the club and the institutional racist arrangement more often than not remain intact. The courts have held that such private clubs can discriminate if they so choose, so the exclusionary practices are legal. But they are not moral, they are not useful, and they are indeed socially disruptive because they perpetuate racism.

Such a dynamic is even more complicated in the case of housing. Financial means is, according to the law, the sole criterion for refusing to sell a house. But, as dozens of studies in Chicago alone have demonstrated, steering goes on daily as blacks are kept out of white neighborhoods, Jews are often told to consider certain North Shore suburbs other other ones, and so forth. Even if individual homeowners express no particular prejudice, the institutional racism of the real estate industry, the banking industry and the neighborhood organization will operate quietly but firmly to maintain the status quo.

This phenomenon is not fomented by bigots nor perpetuated by them. It is the result of Pettigrew's 60% accepting situational ethics.

In the 100-plus focus groups conducted in Chicago during the summer of 1989 by The Chicago Community Trust Human Relations Task Force, such situational attitudes were found throughout the city:

> Maybe you don't feel like that, but in my community I know we have blacks (inaudible) we've got blacks on the corner. Nobody bothers them. We all ignore them. We don't have anything to do with them.
>
> I think people panic when they see a black. I'm in business here and I see that what they see a black person come into a store, they panic immediately thinking this black person is going to rob me. While I'm watching the black person, some Polish immigrant is robbing me.
>
> They don't really communicate between each other. They stay with their own race. They stay with their own race, [we stay] with our own race. We don't like to be with their kind, and they don't like to be with us.[45]

Protestations of self-innocence when it comes to racism were common in these interviews; successfully-integrated neighborhoods appeared to be the perceptual norm. Disharmony was always caused by "outside" forces—the police, the media, politicians, real estate operators, big corporations, etc. Time after time, the source of racial tensions was projected out from the individual, out from the neighborhood

---

[43] Pettigrew, p. 289–90.

[44] *Ibid,* p. 288.

[45] See, for example, the Chicago Urban League's report, "Where Blacks Live: Race and Residence in Chicago in the 1970's" (Unpublished MSS, 1978), *passim.*

and onto society-at-large, where it could rest without immediate psychological threat.

The end effect of this institutional process is harmful to minorities and whites alike. For minorities, it means harder work than their white counterparts to achieve social status. Open housing notwithstanding, homes in nice neighborhoods are more difficult to buy. Civil rights legislation notwithstanding, club memberships must be extracted from reluctant whites with greater personal effort. Affirmative action notwithstanding, minorities in law firms and corporate headquarters and university departments must be more careful—often to the point of self-consciousnes—about their work habits, their speech, and even their dress. Overall, institutional racism moves the carrot farther out for minorities than for whites; despite the common complaint that blacks and other minorities "have it all made" [46] in companies because of their skin color, the psychological price they pay is often far higher than for their white brethren.

For whites, the burden is different but equally onerous. We have asked some of our citizens to bear a disproportionate load of our efforts to cure the social and economic problem of segregation. It should not surprise us, therefore, that middle-class whites grumble when their children are subjected to busing by judges who send their own children to all-white private schools. It should be easier for us to be attuned when whites feel threatened by minorities that have leap-frogged over the very seniority systems that whites were forced to endure. If we attend to the plight of whites who have been hard hit by recent economic disruptions, we will better understand why they can so easily blend racism into economic issues.

And for both of these groups, the psychological costs are real costs. Ulcers and chronic fatigue are real disturbances, as are substance abuse, divorces and other forms of personal breakdown. Our hospitals and divorce courts are filled with the casualties of our modern lifestyles exacerbated by these social and economic upheavals. And while minorities may suffer from these ailments in higher numbers, both minorities and whites suffer from them to unacceptable degrees.

We need as a society, therefore, to attack the mental disease of institutional racism if we are ever to attack the problem of poverty effectively. This attack involves a long-term commitment by the leaders of all segments of our society to practice what they preach. Chief executive officers of companies should be the first to hire minority aides instead of forcing other departments to meet quotas that they themselves ignore. Production foremen should leave their offices and help acclimate minority workers to factory life in person. Churches should work to place black clergy in white parishes, educators should strive to see that predominantly white schools have significant numbers of minority teachers, and cultural organizations should ask themselves if the programs they produce are conducive to effective minority representation.[47]

All of our leaders must take the initiative to help accomplish these ends.

Such leadership will help us immensely. I believe that people will follow positive examples, especially when they eliminate the bad examples so common today. The idea of a shared burden is not anathema to most American-the Depression and the Second World War proved as much-providing that the burden is perceived as affecting all people. It is that sharing which is missing today and which contributes so mightily to social discord. With luck, positive leadership will force institutional racism into remission until we can bring about a true cure, a matter I will touch upon later in this paper.[48]

In sum, institutional racism is a mental condition overlaid onto certain economic and social realities in this country. The two operate synergistically to create an approach to the political process that is particularly harmful in the present state of our society. It is this approach that I call Balkanization.

III. Balkanization

In 1972, Michael Novak, now of the American Enterprise Institute, published one of the seminal books in the white ethnic movement, The Rise of the Unmeltable

[46] These and other comments are taken from the unpublished transcript summaries of focus groups conducted by the Human Relations Task Force under the direction of Michael Glass. The summaries were prepared by Dr. Bruce Hatton Boyer.

[47] The controversy in 1990 between Actor's Equity Association and a New York producer over the hiring of a white actor to play a Eurasian role is instructive. The issue was raised because pad for minority actors in New York are rare; if theaters in New York produced plays that provided opportunities "roughly equivalent" for minority and white actors, there would have been no impulse to clamor for special privilege in the first place.

[48] See p. 40.

Ethnics.[49] In it, he called for a renewed interest in ethnic origin as a fountainhead for community identity:

Delight comes from sharing a communal sense of reality, from being faithful to a set of communal stories, from rejoicing in command and personal symbols. any rootless Americans could use more delight. And indeed, our conception of what America is, and what political activity ought to be, might well be revolutionized if we take seriously our cultural pluralism; it operates within us even when we perceive a headache or an uneasy stomach. A strong politics might be based upon that proposition. A proportion of our widespread anomie might be healed by strengthening the organs and institutions of such differences.[50]

Nearly thirty years later, however, the same Michael Novak lamented the growth of ethnic fractionalism, seeing everywhere signs of political gridlock that seriously threaten the vitality of this country:

Suddenly, ethnicity has turned virulent. Last July the New York State Commissioner of Education issued a report calling "European culture and its derivatives" oppressive. The report debunked "the European-American monocultural perspective." In short, it suggested that the American way of pluralism was a bad thing and that "the American Idea" was a fraud. . . .

[This report] portends ethnic splintering and institutional disarray. What this can lead to is painfully evident outside the shops of Korean merchants in New York City by certain extremists, and in many other ill omens.[51]

The ethnic strife in New York to which Novak refers is certainly echoed in Chicago. Indeed, the Human Relations Task Force focus groups uncovered similar ethnic fractionalism in every corner of the city:

I don't think anyone has said anything about the Arab stores. We are really abused by them. I don't shop in them and I certainly wish we could form something to get the children to stay out of them. They have guns and they walk around in the stores where everybody could shop. I don't think that's (inaudible.) We spend our money there. They should be glad that we're shopping there. Instead they abuse us, plus they give nothing to the community. They take everything out and give us nothing.

You take like the Arab businesses in black neighborhoods. [We're] having at the very least two Arab businessmen killed every year. There's no investigation done. Nobody takes an action. There's nothing in the media about it. It's like a fly that just dropped dead and nobody cares about it. We're not accepted by the whites. We're not accepted by the blacks.

Wherever blacks or Hispanics move in, the neighborhood does deteriorate. They don't come and live as you live and keep the homes clean as you do, or abide by the rules. Maybe it's their upbringing, maybe it's the area they come from. I don't think they know how to cope with an established community. They come in and bring in, not their best, but sometimes they're worst.

If they prefer their own nationality, you cannot force them to get [used to] other nationalities. At least the Latinos and the Orientals are quiet people. Especially the Orientals. They are very quiet people. They're not like the colored people. They are very quiet and they mind their own business. They are working people.[52]

There has also been a shift in the nature of pluralism, as traditional community divisions have been overlaid with a network of gigantic institutions-schools, corporations, hospitals-whose duty is self-preservation first and service for constituents second. Blacks and whites can both agree, for example, that good education is vital for the urban underclass, but both groups find increasing frustration dealing with a giant bureaucracy like the Chicago Board of Education. The fact that the Chicago public educational establishment has a black superintendent, a black Board President, many black executives and even a black president of its teachers' union increases the irony of poor education for blacks in Chicago. Poles and blacks, Lithuanians and Hispanics alike find their agendas thwarted by such an institution and in the end, no one wins.[53]

The result is a fractured sense of responsibility. Causes become more important than end results, and the battle for a "piece of the action" often becomes more significant, more unifying than the piece of the action itself. There is a fine line be-

---

[49] Michael Novak, *The Rise of the Unmeltable Ethnics* (New York: Macmillan Publishing Company, 1972).
[50] *Ibid.*, p. 54.
[51] Michael Novak, "A Call for Disunity", *Forbes Magazine* (Vol 146, No. 1, July 9, 1990), p. 65.
[52] Human Relations Task Force focus groups.
[53] Peter Drucker, *The New Realities* (New York: Harper & Row, 1989), p. 93.

tween ethnic or racial pride and ethnic or racial superiority, a line which many groups have crossed in their attempts to secure economic and social gains in an era of diminishing resources. This phenomenon is the essence of Balkanization. Kevin P. Phillips first used this term to describe the fractionalization of American political life back in 1978. He elaborated on it in his study, Post-Conservative America.[54] It is a useful simile. Like the system of political alliances that triggered World War I from which it gets its name, Balkanization is an unstable state of social affairs. The tensions it engenders are destructive because they prohibit action by any one group that might be perceived as detrimental to another group. It lacks the spirit of comity upon which the entire American notion of community has traditionally been based.

Balkanization occurs when group loyalty supersedes community need. Often its origins are benign. Certainly the "white ethnic" movement of the 1970's that Novak and Greeley so vigorously championed had a positive goal in the beginning. As with the black civil rights movement of the early 1960's, it was an attempt to force recognition that many white immigrants, principally those from eastern and southern Europe, had been discriminated against.[55]

With the economic dislocations of the 1970's, however, that recognition took on a sinister aspect. Anti-discrimination programs that appeared to favor blacks over whites began to be seen as threats to white economic survival, as Glazer suggested in 1975:

> There is indeed a special edge, a special tension, in the relationships between white ethnics and blacks, and rising minorities. Undoubtedly this arises in large part, out of general racist sentiments. In more substantial part it arises out of the conflict over jobs. The later white ethnic groups are strongly represented in the trade unions and the areas of construction, transportation and manufacturing in which trade unions are powerful. Their progress has been based in large measure on union strength. They are committed to the rules and principles that union strength has established, for example, the overriding role of seniority in determining opportunities for advancements and protection from layoffs and dismissals. They see these principles now challenged and restricted by affirmative action and quotas for blacks and other groups.[56]

That the tensions exist between all racial groups, and increasingly between a whole array of groups created to protect religion, gender or sexual orientation, only exacerbates the difficulties encountered in attempting to govern. Indeed, Balkanization in an era of declining comity does not eliminate racism, it brings it to center stage:

> For public authorities to allocate jobs, school positions or apartments to blacks or Jamaicans rather than whites or Dutchmen is to put renewed emphasis on group consciousness, organization and politicking. No system can allocate benefits by race and ethnic group without making racial and ethnic group competition an overt component of politics.[57]

Today, minorities and ethnics are squared off against each other, and Chicago, in common with other major cities of the Northeast, is a checkerboard of enclaves. The fortress mentality destroys cross-group communication; the report of the Human Relations Task Force found this social isolation endemic in Chicago:

> The Task Force found a shocking lack of contact between the diverse populations in Chicago. As the focus group discussions reveal, this isolation has bred myths and "beliefs" that are conspiratorial, destructive, polarizing and simply untrue.[58]

One would expect racial incidents to flourish in such an atmosphere, and indeed they have. Crimes of bias were up 25% in Boston during 1989, for example, and 12% in New York City, while the Anti-Defamation league of B'nai B'rith reported a 12% increase in anti-Semitic incidents during the same time period.[59] Closer to home, the Chicago Commission on Human Relations received 15% more reports of hate crimes in 1990 than in the previous year. More ominously, the Commission also reported that 1990 had the highest percent of violent hate crimes reported in the past five years.

Balkanization feeds upon the New Racism, and vice versa. Balkanization is the political and social manifestation of the psychological state of the New Racism. We

---

[54] New York: Vintage Books, 1983.
[55] See Nathan Glazer, Affirmative Discrimination (New York: Basic Books, 1975), pp. 168–95.
[56] *Ibid.*, pp. 186–7.
[57] Phillips, p. 78.
[58] Human Relations Task Force Report, p. 19.
[59] *New York Times*, May 29, 1990.

must therefore strive to eliminate the New Racism if we are ever to begin tackling the problems of political infighting that in turn have helped perpetuate the urban poverty that so plagues our cities today.

IV. Solutions

Solutions to this sorry state are not easy to come by, and they are certainly not fastacting. As racism has built up over generations, it will take generations to be dlsmantled. But there are steps we can take today to establish an environment in which racism will wither from social malnutrition.

First and foremost, we must clearly define the problems we are dealing with. Poverty is an economic problem; racism is a mental health problem. No amount of social work, counseling, good will or community renewal will solve poverty in our cities today; only money can, and the best source of that money is jobs for the unemployed. AFDC, welfare, unemployment insurance, the entire raft of transfer payments are stop-gap measures and must be regarded as such by all members of society.

Liberals have fought to protect welfare under the fallacious notion that measures to eliminate such programs were racially motivated. Even where such racism does exist in the minds of critics, the fact that well over half of the recipients of welfare are, as we have seen, white makes such racism largely irrelevant. Minorities have fought to protect welfare out of necessary self-interest. Conservatives such as Murray have sought to eliminate welfare because they believe such payments are fruitless and even destructive.

Our solution is to view social welfare programs as temporary expedients along the road to full economic enfranchisement. Welfare, in all of its forms, can only be eliminated when businesses and local governments successfully create jobs.

Conversely, no amount of welfare, cash transfers, high-paying jobs or upward financial mobility can eliminate racism in our society. We have made a good start in this country over the past three decades by making public racism a social disgrace. But we cannot eliminate private racism until we attack its root causes: low self-esteem among both whites and minorities.

Accordingly, we must address our child-rearing practices in this country. Psychologists have long understood that authoritarian upbringings, rigid social expectations, and a lack of parental nurturance are the cause of the mental disturbances that give rise to racism:

> Contempt is the weapon of the weak and a defense against one's own despised and unwanted feelings. And the fountainhead of all contempt, all discrimination, is the more or less conscious, uncontrolled, and secret exercise of power over the child by the adult . . . Let us hope that the degree to which this discrimination is persistently transmitted from one generation to the next might be reduced by education and increasing awareness.[60]

Professionals in the mental health field must commit themselves to seeing racism as being, in large part, a psychological problem:

> If racism is our endemic mental illness, then it follows that a major task for mental health is to discern its causes and direct its cure. Certainly a scientific challenge for psychology, psychiatry, sociology and anthropology is to discover the causes, consequences and means of control of maladaptive behavior.[61] [Emphasis added.]

I have emphasized the concept "means of control" because laws and social sanctions alone cannot end the spread of racism. We must as a society develop mechanisms that can assist people in understanding the psychological distortions that give rise to racism. Social workers and psychologists are trained in this work, of course, but we must not neglect the other significant resources that are available in each and every local community: teachers, school guidance counselors, physicians, clergypeople and other persons in the mendicant professions. Drop-in centers, in-service programs, community houses and church parishes all offer venues for the transmission of positive messages concerning race and mental health.

Second, we must recognize the crucial role that schools can play. School integration has acquired a bad name over the past two decades because it has emphasized busing as a means of compensating for unequal economic status. Busing is expensive and disruptive, say its critics. But this disruption has a positive value as well: it disrupts patterns of familial and neighborhood racist thinking. Removing a white child from a white neighborhood for several hours a day—provided that it is done

[60] Alice Miller, *Prisoners of Childhood* (New York: Basic Books, 1981), p. 69.

[61] Bernard M. Kramer "Racism and Mental Health as a Field of Thought and Action", in Willie, Kramer, Brown, eds., pp. 15–16.

without rancor—is a benefit to that white child for it disrupts his or her narrow social perspective. Similarly, such transfers allow minority children to see that affluent whites, for example, are no less immune to social stresses and periods of unhappiness than they themselves are. In short, it teaches humanity and humility, essential antidotes to the poison of racism.

Critics of school integration contend that shifting students around causes education to "take the back seat." They cite declining test scores as "proof" that schools have declined since integration was mandated thirty years ago.

This charge has little merit. First, the validity of test scores as a measure of school "quality" has long been challenged.[62] Second, there are many school districts where integration has had no significant negative effect on the academic achievement of white children,[63] and conversely, many districts where no busing has occurred that have experienced an overall decline in test scores. Second, the tablulations over the lack of fundamental skills in many young people applies to whites as well as to minorities; if schools have failed, they have failed all students, albeit in different proportions. Finally and most fundamentally, what is education if it is not a process of socialization? The ability to get along with one's neighbor or co-worker, to understand his or her beliefs and goals, is no less useful a skill than the ability to add and subtract. Indeed, one can well argue that the ability to add and subtract is less important to a successful and healthy life than the ability to form fulfilling relationships.

Schools represent our best, though by no means our only, vehicle for the transmitting positive values concerning race. They must be supported in these efforts if we are to live harmoniously with each other. In this process, minorities bear a special burden. The social isolation of the urban ghetto is frightful, and it can breed incredible amounts of hatred and envy. Worse, minority children growing up amid urban poverty usually lack positive role models on which to base their own actions. Wilson's point in this regard is worth mentioning:

> In a neighborhood with a paucity of regularly employed families and with the overwhelming majority of families having spells of long-term joblessness, people experience a social isolation that excludes them from the job network system that permeates other neighborhoods, and that is so important in learning about or being recommended for jobs that become available in various parts of the city. And as the prospects for employment diminish, other alternatives such as welfare and the underground economy are not only increasingly relied upon, they come to be seen as a way of life.[64]

Minorities must fight this isolation tooth and nail; they must be willing to risk ventures into the larger community, and they must be willing to have their children exposed to alternative lifestyles. To practice, as many minorities do, a "voluntary apartheid" inside the seeming comfort of their urban fortresses is a false step toward the solution of our racial problems. In this, blacks face the heaviest burden because they are disproportionately trapped in these fortresses. The black scholar Shelby Steele has offered the highly controversial idea that some part of this mentality is self-inflicted:

> We hold a victim-focused identity that tells us there is less opportunity than there actually is. And, in fact, our victimization itself has been our primary source of power in society-the basis of our demands for redress.
>
> The paradoxical result of relying on this source of power is that it rewards us for continuing to see ourselves as victims of a racist society, and implies that opportunity itself is something to be given instead of taken.[65]

Make no mistake, this victimization complex comes from exactly the same cause as the Ku Kux Klan: low self-esteem. In Chicago, it led to the Steve Cokely incident of 1989, where a black aide to then-Mayor Eugene Sawyer made accusations of genocide against Jews. Such wild charges are at least equally destructive to black opportunity as are its white counterparts, and it must be denounced by community leaders whenever it occurs.

---

[62] The most cogent summary of the unreliability of such tests is Stephen Jay Gould's *The Mismeasure Of Man* (New York: W.W. Norton, 1981).

[63] 2. The Chicago suburb of Evanston is a case in point. Evanston's elementary schools are fully integrated, i.e. no one racial group constitutes less than 40% or more than 60% of each school body. And while blacks fare less well than whites as a whole, the majority black schools such as Washington School show test scores and academic achievement that equal or surpass majority white schools such as Willard School.

[64] Wilson. p.57

[65] Shelby Steele, "Pride and Possibility," Chicago *Sun-Times*, June 10, 1990.

Next, we must define our goals, and I submit that our goal is a simple one: true and complete integration.

When The Chicago Community Trust's Human Relations Task Force issued its report in 1989, several journalists complained that it offered no new vision. In calling for integration, the criticism went, the Task Force was turning to an outmoded and disproven notion. I must reject that charge categorically.

Racism exists wherever people regard peoples of different skin color, religion or national origin as suspect because they do not have the vision or the opportunity to know these people as individuals. Integration does not mean that our goal is to have whites and minorities love one another as brothers and sisters. That notion is patently unrealistic. Even the best adjusted people dislike other people of their own race or religion. But—and this is the crucial difference—people usually learn to control these personal dislikes within their communities. They have been taught the positive social value of community harmony.

Our goal should be no less for interactions between communities. Only when blacks can live in Kenilworth and socialize easily with their neighbors, and when whites are not terrified to even set foot on the "South Side," will racism be eliminated in our society. I frankly do not expect to see this in my lifetime, but I argue that we must begin work now to achieve that goal within the lifetime of our children.

The process will not be an easy one. Four centuries of exploitation and social humiliation have made different groups suspicious of one another. Years of Polish jokes and anti-Semitic literature and burning crosses have taken a tragic toll. In particular, minorities on the receiving end of such stigmatization look suspiciously at extended white hands for good reason; they have reached out in the past only to be slapped down.

A special danger exists, therefore, when well-intentioned whites attempt to bridge racial gaps. There are different expectations, different styles of behavior, different speech patterns, different hopes among minority communities, and the white who ventures into these groups often offends without so intending.

Therefore, we must facilitate the intermingling of the races. Chicago addressed this problem one hundred years ago through the agency of the settlement house. Jane Addains, Mary McDowell and Graham Taylor led this city and this nation into the future, and we must go back to the lessons they taught. First, social workers must live in the areas in which they work, and they must become "of" that community. They must understand the particular institutions—often invisible to the visitor—that hold that small, manageable urban unit together. Underwriting this type of social work is, I submit, the highest priority of private philanthropy.

Second, ethnic and racial identities must be made secondary to an over-arching sense of the broad American community. In the 1970's, it became fashionable among revisionist historians to debunk the "Americanization" efforts of Addams and other Progressives. The forced renunciation of Old World customs that Addams demanded, so goes the theory, stripped immigrants of social skills and connections vital to survival in their adopted country.

Yet in recent years, even this revisionist thinking is being discarded. Looking behind the words of the Progressives, we see a pragmatic spirit among immigrants that mixed Americanism with native interests freely. Addams never succeeded in eradicating nativist ways, even had that been her intent; instead, she succeeded in giving immigrants the hyphenated identities, e.g. Norwegian-American, that served them well up until the Balkanization process began in earnest in the 1980's. One recent study of Polish and Italian immigrants in Chicago, for example, found that these two communities picked and chose the institutions they found useful from the smorgasbord that reformers presented to them:

> The biases of social reformers notwithstanding, Italians and Poles appeared remarkably free to adopt those values and institutions that best fit their goals and expectations . . . Italians hoping to return to the paese forged temporary yet meaningful worlds. Neither participation in American institutions nor minimal support for the ethnic parish indicated the jettisoning of old world values. Poles, too, developed complete, stable, and satisfying communities around institutions, ethnic by definition, that inculcated respect for American values and traditions. Both processes were at work in the 1910's, confounding social reformers and disproving the validity of Anglo conformity as a model of assimilation.[66]

[66] Catherine Sardo Weidner, "Building a Better Life," *Chicago History* (Vol. XVIII, No. 4, Winter, 1989–90), p. 25.

We have much to learn from the work of Hull House and Chicago Commons. As social work must look into the neighborhood, so must it also look out toward the broader community. We must continue to remind our children; for example, that all of us, as Americans, have common needs. We need to understand, when we go before our local school councils, or visit our aldermen, or write to our Congresspersons, that the desires of other people for housing or education or simple pleasures that differ from ours, are not threats.

We must create common grounds upon which diverse people can meet. These grounds should be physical and they should be specific. It is not enough to say "the workplace is a meeting place." We should help companies institute simple programs; lunchroom programs on different cultures, panel discussions, even movies about social problems can stimulate thought and help break down barriers. Similarly, community houses should establish pro-active racial programs. Athletic counselors, for example, should work hard to integrate after-school basketball games and to set up leagues where youths of different colors can harmoniously meet.

These grounds should also be psychological. Companies and schools should work to devise ways to subtly break-down the voluntary segregation that inhabits cafeterias, gyms, even company snack bars. When ad hoc committees are set up within groups to study problems, leaders should take care to integrate them.

None of these measures are complicated or costly. They do not require massive bureaucracies or complex guidelines to operate. But well-intentioned people do need help to set such programs up, and this is where social workers, neighborhood workers and community leaders can provide invaluable services at a low cost.

We must return to some elementary truths: the premises of this country as stated in the Declaration of Independence, the Constitution and the Bill of Rights. Jefferson's words that "all men are created equal" and the provisions of the Fourteenth Amendment that no state shall "deny to any person within its jurisdiction the equal protection of its laws" are phrases that form the heart of our body politic. They have been repeated so often, and by people of all political stripes and purposes, to the point that they have nearly lost their meaning. But they remain valid; there is no innate difference between a black man and a white man, or a yellow man and a red man. Each is a human being worthy of dignity and respect.

Liberals, confronted with the massive inequalities of our social structure, have in recent years winced at these words, which they regard as false promises. Among the intelligentsia that forms the core of the liberal establishment, cynicism is endemic. Because we as a nation cannot afford an alienated intelligentsia any more than we can afford an underclass, we must redefine patriotic sentiments that have become almost the exclusive property of the conservative and far right wings of our society, the very groups where racism has its most overt hold.

Our political debate has been so diluted that amendments banning flag-burning have become the litmus test for "patriotism." Our leaders must condemn politicians who exploit such cheap tricks, and our election-monitoring systems must bring liberals and conservatives, Democrats and Republicans, together to fight such mud-slinging.

We must also return to the notion of the "melting pot" long enough to recognize the lessons that the Irish and the Polish and the Slovaks taught us a century ago: that we all must adjust, we must give a little in order to receive something else back, that we must not let notions of "purity" disrupt our efforts to live peacefully with each other.

This failure of the progressive elements in our society to seize the high ground, to declare emphatically that equality of access to the American dream is not the white man's gift to give, but the birthright of all Americans, has been a major element in the continuation of racism. These people, whatever their skin color, must declare that those who agitate for social progress are not the enemies of democracy but its true defenders.

We must adopt a strategic plan that aims to eradicate racism by the year 2010. The Human Relations Foundation of Chicago has been created to perform just such a task. This strategic plan must include specific timetables for programs and methods for measuring progress. It must demonstrate convincingly that racism is an economic and social drain on our society, and that its eradication will free resources to be used toward more constructive social ends. It also must provide each sector of our society with action plans that can be implemented with minimal outside assistance. It must not underestimate the scope of the work to be done. We have, in the past two decades, tinkered with our system and achieved only a tinkerer's product. We must go down to the roots of every institution, examine it for flaws, and prescribe the appropriate remedies.

61-412 O - 94 - 3

This is a tall order, but we must attempt it, for as the eminent historian John Hope Franklin has pointed out:

> There was [among the Founding Fathers] too little self-criticism, too much inclination to accept things as they were and to postpone dealing with the hard problems. It was this postponement that put Lincoln's generation in a bind and that led to the tragic events of the 1860s. If there is one lesson we should learn from this, it is to face up to our staggering problems now and not put them off for some unknowing, innocent generation to which it will cost infinitely more to solve problems we leave than it would cost to face up to them and solve them now.[67]

Only when we face up to the racism that still permeates our society can we hope to make true progress toward 1) eradicating the scourge of poverty, and 2) repairing the damage to the body politic that still infects so many parts of our nation.

Postscipt

Since these words were first written, dramatic events have only confirmed the premises which underlie them in regards to Balkanization, racism and poverty. The disintegration of the Soviet Union, the civil war in Yugoslavia, and the recent riots in Los Angles, hold grim lessons for those wise enough to examine them.

Many Americans have smugly drawn the conclusion that the agonies in these countries of the former Soviet bloc have been caused by Communism. The rhetoric of the Cold War has obscured the real issues. While Communism undoubtedly exacerbated the economic woes of those countries, the agonies have not been caused by ideology but instead by a volatile mixture of economic depression and unresolved racial animosities.

The collapse of Communism has deprived the Soviet Union and Yugoslavia of their ideological centers. Those centers, immoral or repugnant as we may have found them, held those countries together for decades. They were autocratic, often charismatic and usually ruthless but they were centers. With those centers gone, the glue that held the uneasy pieces together has disappeared.

That the same thing could happen in the United States in the next few years is a very real—and very frightening—possibility. We Americans have always felt ourselves immune to the social forces that wrack other countries, but the Los Angles riots tell us—drmatically and urgently—that this immunity is a fantasy.

Today, cries of anguish and hatred are rising in this country. An ex-Klansman and follower of Adolf Hitler was considered gubernatorial material in Louisiana. A nomination to the Supreme Court becomes the excuse for a loathsome display of pressure-group politics. A trial verdict set off riots fueled by years of rage and neglect.

The fractionalizing of what was once a healthy if imperfect alliance of peoples into highly organized groups speaks loudly of national disunity. If people continue to define themselves as blacks first, or women, or gays, rather than as Americans who happen to have any of those characteristics, we face the total disintegration of our national center.

I believe that most Americans want some form of national consensus. In periods of greatness in our history, we enjoyed such a consensus, and the recent successes of flag-waving political campaigns suggests how deeply its lack is felt. Certainly the xenophobic outburst which surrounded the Persian Gulf War represented a deep-seated yearning for America to be whole again.

There is, therefore, an urgency to the issue of race that has not been equaled since the decade prior to the Civil War. We failed to solve the issue of race after that conflict, and we failed to solve it with the Civil Rights movement of the 1960's. We have continually abandoned the agenda of race for one oriented around economics and as a result, we live in a society which is more racist, more disunited and more volatile than ever before. Can there be any doubt, following the tragic events in Los Angles, that the unfinished agenda of the 1960's continues to haunt us?

So let us listen to the lessons the Los Angles riots teach us. They teach us that racism remains the central problem in this country. They teach us that our inner city enclave—black, yellow, brown and white—have been waiting for 20 years to hear that American society is committed to eradicating racism, to healing economic deprivation, and to relieving the hopelessness which so pervades our inner cities. They teach us that the poverty in our cities cannot be eliminated without first eliminating the racism that fostered it. They teach us that racism distorts our ev-

---

[67] John Hope Franklin, "Who Divided This House?," Address to the Chicago Historical Society, July 4, 1990.

eryday life to the point that we are no longer able to marshall the forces of progress to make our cities safe, happy and prosperous.

The current disgust with our governments in Washington and the fifty state capitals is, I believe, an opportunity we cannot afford to squander. People are asking our leaders to lead before it is too late. If they do not and if our businesses and our churches and our schools, all the institutions whose primary function is to give coherence to our national consciousness, fail us as well—then surely we will face a crisis of unconscionable gravity.

Mr. SAWYER. Let me ask you a question that will let you range as widely as you care to. Many, if not most of the minorities that you describe in all of their diversity, in many different settings across the United States live in urban settings.

The experiences that those diverse minorities have found once they have gotten to those urban settings is a phenomenon that may have been precursored by a different pathway to those urban settings.

Could you comment on how those journeys into the cities may have affected the social and economic structures of minorities as they confront the future?

Mr. O'HARE. Sure. Let me preface my comments by noting that a lot of our attention is focused on urban areas now, but we shouldn't overlook the fact that there are large numbers of blacks in the rural south and American Indians in the rural parts of this country that may be as bad off as some of our city dwellers.

Mr. SAWYER. That should not go without saying.

Mr. O'HARE. To respond more directly to the question, I think there are two aspects that need to be considered. One is the circumstances and experiences of groups before they get to the city, whether they are coming from sharecroppers in the rural South or are university graduates from Japan or Korea or Singapore and the kinds of experiences those people may have had in their socialization process, the kind of training and human resources they bring with them to the city.

Second is the reception they get once they arrive in the city. Research just revealed in the last couple of weeks by the Census Bureau and other researchers talked about persistent residential segregation where blacks are still highly residentially segregated, Hispanics in between, and Asians at a much lower level. That probably reflects to some extent the experiences of those groups when they arrive in a city or wherever they tend to settle once they come into the country and those kinds of reactions, experiences, totality of circumstances, to use language from the Voting Rights Act, have an impact on how those different subgroups end up living, and, of course, family life is a key part of that living.

I think it is well noted that among blacks in particular, there is a high level of female-headed families. There is no doubt about those statistics. What is in doubt is the reason for that.

As you probably know, many researchers, including William Julius Wilson, for example, talk about the lack of jobs for black men as one of the factors that has to be considered in the high rate of female headship among blacks.

So there is a complex conundrum—if that is not a repetitive redundancy—a complex set of factors that have to be examined and the diversity among the group experiences have to be examined group by group.

Mr. SAWYER. I am from the Midwest. The problems of the cities in the Midwest may superficially be the same as those on either coast, but as you begin to look at them in their detail, they seem to be quite different, particularly when it comes to the decline of traditional industrial base and the avenue that it provides for minority mobility.

The previous witnesses talked in terms of education as not only being important in its traditional role, but in terms of actually replacing some of that role of the industrial ladder.

Could you talk about the ways in which those patterns play themselves out—not in common, but differently, in different parts of the country and different kinds of urban settings? Then could you comment on the way in which the experiences that we have had here compare with other industrialized nations of the world?

Mr. O'HARE. That is a large question. Let me offer a few thoughts in response.

One of the differences that strikes me repeatedly when I think about these things on a national scale is the difference between a place like Detroit or Akron or Cleveland, the old industrial cities where the relatively high-paid union, blue-collar jobs were a stepping stone for lots of groups, but most recently blacks, African-Americans, and those industries are going through enormous changes in the last few decades and those rungs on the ladder have been removed in many places.

I think that is part of the explanation, if you will, for what has been commonly referred to as the urban underclass; that those jobs have dried up and there is no place for those young workers to go in terms of jobs.

That contrasts strikingly like Miami, Los Angeles, San Diego, the coastal cities, Washington, where there is a thriving economy, they have ahead of the curve in adapting to the service sector as opposed to the manufacturing sector and there is need for a lot of labor.

One of the contrasts that comes to mind as I think about that is the difference between typically poorly educated blacks who come up from the South to take the industrial jobs in Northern cities versus often college-educated or highly educated person from Asia who comes to California in particular to move into relatively good jobs in the computer field and elsewhere.

There is the difference in the education those people bring to the city as well as the different kind of economic culture, status, of the cities themselves that they come to. That is one difference that seems to be obvious as you look around the country and think about the different experiences of different minority groups.

There was another part to the question. I forgot what it was.

Mr. SAWYER. The way in which those kinds of complicated patterns compare with other industrialized urban settings in industrialized nations around the world.

Mr. O'HARE. I am not sure I am able to answer that. That is not my area.

Mr. SAWYER. It is a question that I think will become increasingly interesting as we watch the diversity of Europe play itself out in traditionally industrialized settings with a far more diverse population than they have had in any single setting before.

Mr. O'HARE. Speaking of Europe, there is survey evidence that is as discouraging as survey evidence is here about racial attitudes, that they are probably worse in Europe in terms of the European Anglo's view of non-Europeans, and I suspect that doesn't bode well for the minorities in Europe.

Mr. SAWYER. We have had a good deal of written testimony comments about the enormous diversity, for example, within the Asian communities that doesn't get well reflected in the data that we collect.

My suspicion is if there is a substantial differential in success, however we define that term, among minority communities as they differentiate themselves, measuring statistics nationally may have consequences that we don't anticipate. It takes me to a series of questions that were raised during the conduct of the 1990 census about the way in which self identification plays itself out as a matter of defining who people are, their ability or willingness to respond to a census, their confidence in it, and the validity of the data that we draw from it. The questions concern the failure to deal with the enormous diversity in the Asian Pacific Islander communities, or even in the difficulty that mixed race families of every kind have in identifying themselves and their children adequately given the 1990 instrument.

Can you talk about the kind of work that you do in defining, describing, and anticipating the directions of minority populations, and the kind of changes that might be important to anticipate in the gathering of data at the end of each decade and through each decade in terms of those kinds of problems?

Mr. O'HARE. That is an excellent point and one I have thought about without, unfortunately, very clear answers. It gets back to statistical policy that the Census Bureau and Federal Government need to think about.

There are two parts of it that seem to be particularly problematic in my experience. One is the use of a Hispanic origin question in addition to the race question so that people get classified both as Spanish and non-Spanish origin and one of the racial groups. That is confusing to a lot of people and provides some information that may be misleading in some cases.

Early in the mid-1980's, I was looking at income of blacks and whites in Miami and they weren't that different until I stopped to realize that whites included a lot of Hispanics in Miami, which brought their income down.

Unless one is cognizant of that, it can provide misleading information.

The other part, the point you alluded to, was the growing minority population and significant segments of them marrying people from other racial groups, we have a lot of children who don't fit neatly into categories and it strikes me that we should, as we go through this planning for the next census and the one in 2010, think about how we could revamp our racial classifications to better reflect the kind of diversity that we have in this country.

The Brazilian Census has such classifications. One, it is a very diverse society there, a classification system that is more sensitive to differences than the kind of categorization we have.

Mr. SAWYER. If you could put your hands around a category of information that is not available in the body of data that comes from 1990, that you think would be useful as we try to deal with the kinds of problems we have heard described here today, what would you ask for?

Mr. O'HARE. Time. How people spend their time. I think more and more people are—some people—are money rich and time poor, and I feel like I am one of them, but it is not an easy thing to measure, but I think in the statistical system it is something we don't do a very good job of collecting information on, but it is something that is vital to people in terms of understanding how people live their daily lives.

Mr. SAWYER. That is a fascinating answer. Are you thinking in terms of kinds of activities, work or——

Mr. O'HARE. The only example that shows up in the census, the 1990 census asks people how long it takes to get to work or what time they leave for work. That is one aspect. Whether you take a 15-minute commute or 2 hours is a big difference in people's lives. We haven't had data like that in the past.

Another is how much time do people spend with their child. If you want to try to quantify quality time, that would be interesting. That is a real challenge.

How long do spouses spend with each other, how often do they visit their parents, how much time do they spend with their parents. It is a complex sets of categories, but even a start would provide us with a framework for thinking about the future.

I suspect as we move into the 21st century, measuring how people spend their time is something we will be thinking about more and more.

Mr. SAWYER. One of the things that I have come to use almost as a benchmark in many of the ways that I think about where we are going is the comparison between a relatively little studied period a century ago, when much of the world underwent a profound set of changes unlike perhaps anything that we have since, until now, when the mechanization of production and agriculture not only moved people across a continent and around the world, but made that movement possible. It freed people from hand labor on the farms and freed them for the kind of intensive machinated work that created a modern city.

We heard our previous witnesses talk not only about the growth of metropolitan areas, but their spread at the same time. I began to think about Akron, OH. It is a place that has been defined by an industry that has been global in its reach and transnational in its organization, the tire and rubber business, for longer than those words existed by necessity. When I was growing up it was not uncommon to be a part of a family or to know a family who had spent a substantial portion of their productive lifetimes in very remote parts of the world. Today, increasingly, a city like that can be a command and control center for an industry in which they have no active manufacturing.

That spread of what we define as work I suspect is in the process of changing productive opportunities within this country and around the world in ways that we haven't even begun to understand. We are only really beginning to fathom what happened a century ago when those kinds of changes produced tidal demographic movement.

I suspect that we are in the process of seeing those kinds of forces bringing about change in ways that we don't even see yet. If nothing else, over the last 3 years we saw events in places as remote from one another as Lisbon and Manila and Beijing and the capitals of central and eastern Europe.

We not only saw events happen one after another, it was almost as if the same event was happening over and over and over again in a way that took place over decades 200 years ago, the great revolution, of which this country's revolution was a part.

Try and understand that the pace of that change is as much of a challenge as we face in this Nation today.

So in conclusion I would like to say thank you to our witnesses today. I look forward to the continuing testimony that we will hear in days and weeks ahead.

There is no further business before us and we stand adjourned.

[Whereupon, at 2:35 p.m., the subcommittee was adjourned, subject to the call of the Chair.]

AMERICA'S CHANGING PROFILE: "WHO WE ARE: SIGNIFICANT U.S. POPULATION TRENDS"

WEDNESDAY, MAY 27, 1992

House of Representatives,
Subcommittee on Census and Population,
Committee on Post Office and Civil Service,
Washington, DC.

The subcommittee met, pursuant call, at 1:03 p.m., in room 311, Cannon House Office Building, Hon. Thomas C. Sawyer (chairman of the subcommittee) presiding.

Members present: Representatives Sawyer and Ridge.

Mr. Sawyer. Good afternoon.

Today we are going to continue our first set of hearings on significant population trends that are redefining who we are as a Nation. Yesterday we looked at population growth and its regional distribution, as well as the changing racial and ethnic composition of that population.

We looked at several things specifically. The first thing we looked at was the findings out of the 1990 census, that we have been experiencing a surprisingly rapid growth in minority populations. Virtually a quarter of our population is now nonwhite. We also found that the growing racial and ethnic diversity was not evenly spread across our country.

Second, there was consensus that the term "minority" may not even function well any more—in fact, perhaps even becoming obsolete—as a growing number of cities no longer have a racial or ethnic majority of any singular description.

Finally, we heard that children are more likely to be poor and that a disproportionate number of poor children are minorities. Even as child poverty continues to haunt the Nation, we're facing a future in which an unprecedented 20 percent of our population will be 65 or older. As the "baby boom" ages, we will be faced with the challenge of balancing the needs of a large older population and a younger minority population. The difficulty of that task remains to be defined, I suspect, at this point.

Finally, the profound demographic changes that we're witnessing are affecting different communities in different ways at different times. Assessing that effect is an important challenge not only in terms of understanding how we're changing, but in crafting policy to meet that diversity.

This afternoon we will conclude our hearings on who we are by looking at rural, suburban and urban settlement patterns; we'll focus more attention on the age structure and the implications of an aging America. Clearly, demographic forces will present challenges of significant magnitude as we move into the next century. I hope that our look into the future will lay the groundwork for policies and programs that are filled with foresight and genuinely sensitive to the needs of diverse communities.

Before we begin, without objection, I am going to submit for the record the testimony of Mr. Clarence Wood, who had planned to be with us yesterday but was unable to attend the hearing. I am grateful for his contribution to our work.

[The prepared statement of Mr. Wood appears on page 43.]

Mr. SAWYER. Our first witness today is John D. Kasarda. Dr. Kasarda is Kenan professor of business administration and director of the Kenan Institute of Private Enterprise at the University of North Carolina at Chapel Hill.

Also planning to be with us was Dr. Leo Estrada from the Graduate School of Architecture and Urban Planning at UCLA. He has been unable to join us today.

Dr. Kasarda, thank you for being with us. We look forward to your testimony.

STATEMENT OF JOHN D. KASARDA, DIRECTOR, THE KENAN INSTITUTE OF PRIVATE ENTERPRISE, THE UNIVERSITY OF NORTH CAROLINA AT CHAPEL HILL

Mr. KASARDA. Thank you, Chairman Sawyer.

As you requested in your letter, and that of your staff in telephone conversations, I took a particular approach in preparing this testimony. That is, not only to lay out what significant demographic and economic trends were affecting our cities, but also looking at the implications for programs and public policies and to share with you and your staff some views that I have developed over the past 20 years in studying urban problems, particularly issues of the transformation of cities from centers of goods processing to centers of information processing, and what that means for economic survival of those that don't have the education and skill levels to be able to take advantage of the new growth industries that are developing so rapidly in our inner cities.

Let me begin by pointing out that the recent targeted attacks of rioters in Los Angeles on Korean businesses first and foremost indicate that racial conflict in urban America is no longer a black and white issue. Rather, it has become a street-level collision of hopes and opportunities in the face of dramatically changing inner-city demographic and economic contexts. I would like to review for you briefly the basics of these contextual changes in the cities, demographically and then in terms of economic base changes.

For one, the Nation's poverty population, which was once predominantly rural, has increasingly urbanized. In 1959, only 27 percent of our poor resided in metropolitan central cities. By 1985, our central cities housed 43 percent of the U.S. poverty population. During the same period, the proportion of poor blacks living in the central cities rose from 38 percent to 61 percent. So that by 1985, the central cities housed over half of the Nation's population living in census tracts with high concentrations of poverty. This is up from just one-third in 1972.

We are still awaiting the 1990 census tract data, which already has begun to trickle out, but it will be complete by the end of this calendar year. We need this data to document the most recent trends. But we do know, looking at patterns from 1970 and 1980, and preliminary analyses based on the Current Population Survey, that populations residing in extreme poverty areas and underclass areas rose dramatically between 1970 and 1980, and indications based on the Current Population Survey and other surveys indicate that these upward trends have continued during the most recent decade.

Poverty and underclass areas have expanded in our major cities despite targeted infusions of public assistance, affirmative action programs, and civil rights legislation— programs that are traditionally supported by liberals—and they have persisted in the face of national and urban economic recovery, solutions espoused by many conservatives. One reason why neither set of prescriptions worked, I propose, is that both the liberal and conservative prescriptions were overwhelmed by fundamental changes in the structure of inner-city economies, particular affecting the employment prospects of disadvantaged black residents.

We have to recognize that the American city today is a much different place than it was in the 1960's, when our fundamental assumptions about poverty were formed. Advances in transportation, communication, and industrial technologies have interacted with the changing structure of the national and global economy, transforming our major cities from centers of material goods production, the processing and handling of goods, to centers of information exchange, finance, and administration.

Now, in this process of transformation, many of the blue-collar industries that once constituted the economic backbone of our cities and provided entry-level employment for their lesser skilled residents have vanished. These blue-collar industries were replaced in part by knowledge-intensive white collar service industries with educational requirements that preclude most poorly-educated minorities from obtaining employment.

By 1989, New York City and Boston, for example, each had more employees in white collar service functions—these are service industries where executives, managers, professionals and clerical workers dominate—than their entire manufacturing, construction, retail and wholesale industries combined. This is a dramatic change since the 1950's, when employment in these traditional urban industries that handled goods, received raw materials, manufactured products, distributed them and sold them, really dominated information processing industries by a three-to-one margin. So information processing industries now exceed goods processing industries in many of these cities when, in fact, in the past the goods processing outnumbered the information processing jobs by a three-to-one margin. You're going to see how this has substantial implications for the educational skills, numeracy, literacy and other factors that are so important to gaining and holding employment in the new information economy.

Hit hardest, of course, as I point out in the data attached to this testimony, was manufacturing. Between 1967 and 1987, Detroit lost 51 percent of its manufacturing jobs; New York City, 58 percent;

Chicago, 60 percent; and Philadelphia, 64 percent. Even Sun Belt cities such as Atlanta and Los Angeles experienced manufacturing job losses during this period.

Blue-collar employment decline in the cities was exacerbated by the urban exodus of middle income residents and the neighborhood business establishments that once served them. This exodus further drained low-skill service jobs such as domestic workers, gas station attendants, and local delivery personnel.

During the 1980's, a number of large cities came back and experienced substantial and overall employment gains, led largely by growth of their white-collar service industries. Yet manufacturing continued to decline in these cities. New York City, for instance, gained over 300,000 jobs between 1980 and 1990—this was a 10 percent increase in its overall job base after contracting for more than 25 years. It began to grow again. But it lost 160,000 jobs in its manufacturing firms, a 32 percent drop. Just at the time it was adding 300,000 jobs, led by its information processing industries, manufacturing continued to contract, a drop of just about a third during this expansion period.

While millions of blue-collar jobs were disappearing from our cities—the very jobs that in the past attracted and socially upgraded waves of disadvantaged migrants—minority residents who lack the education for employment in these new information processing industries have increased. By 1990, racial-ethnic minorities composed the demographic majority in many of our largest cities: 57 percent in New York, 62 percent in Chicago, 63 percent in Los Angeles, 70 percent in Atlanta, 79 percent in Detroit, and 88 percent in Miami. In this case, the racial-ethnic minority has clearly become the demographic majority for these cities.

Now, the fact of the matter is that many of those that moved to the cities were those that lacked the education and skills and background, and the first generation offspring of those who had moved in previous generations lacked the education skills and background, to take advantage of the new growth industries that I just described in the information processing sector. So really what we have operating in many of our cities is a residential-employment mismatch, or as I describe in the paper, demographic-economic collision course. The demographies and the economies of our cities are on a collision course, with poorly educated blacks impacted the most.

Now, while overall educational attainment for black city residents did improve during the 1970's and 1980's, as measured by years of school completed—and I have to point out here as a caveat that there's a difference between years of school completed and education—this assumes that the quality of the education remained the same or improved during this period, an assumption that is open to some question. But while the actual years of school completed by inner-city black residents during the 1970's and 1980's did improve, the gains that occurred were not nearly sufficient to keep pace with even faster rises in the education required to work in the new information processing industries beginning to dominate our urban employment bases.

You also had at the same time general improvements in city residents' education levels, regardless of race, which also meant that the least educated jobless blacks fell further and further behind in the hiring queue. As a result, unemployment among poorly educated urban blacks skyrocketed. By the late 1980's, jobless rates of central city black males who had not completed high school were 44 percent in the Northeast, 58 percent in the Midwest, 49 percent in the South, and 66 percent in the West. These are out of school black males aged 16 to 64, who had less than a high school degree.

Now, in these circumstances—I think it's very interesting, in looking at Los Angeles as a case in point—one has to wonder how it is that lesser educated Asian immigrant groups have prospered in the same inner-city areas where so many blacks seem to have slipped entirely off the socioeconomic ladder.

What are the factors? What explains the ability of these groups to succeed, many of whom move into these areas with limited education—areas that have been designated distressed with many environmental factors pointing against economic success in these areas? What can we learn? What lessons can be learned that might be translated to other groups to help them get back on that socioeconomic ladder and begin their climb upward?

Mr. SAWYER. Tell us.

Mr. KASARDA. OK.

One key factor differentiating Asian and black inner-city economic success lies in self-employment, fostered by ethnic solidarity and strong kinship networks among Asians. With little or no help from government, Asian immigrants utilize ethnic-based methods to raise money and establish their own internal markets, from video stores to green groceries, from laundries to restaurants. This allows them to circumvent discrimination and generate employment within their enclaves, insulated from the swings of the national economy—because these are internal markets—as well as from the urban industrial transformations that I just described, those white collar jobs in the downtowns replacing goods processing jobs and blue collar manufacturing jobs.

Ethnic businesses are typically family-owned and operated, usually drawing upon unpaid family and extended family labor, especially during start-up periods when money is scarce. They simply don't draw wages. Extended kinship networks also enable immigrant households to share rents or mortgages, provide free child care—and this is a child being taken care of by a relative, a loved one—and assure economic security against loss of employment by other household members.

I didn't present data here, but it's amazing when we look at the census data and examine the household structures of many of these inner-city Asian immigrants to see what large percentages are other relatives, that is, nonnuclear family relatives, in these households. I don't have time to present that data now. Suffice it to say that these households have many people in them that are related but not part of the nuclear family.

To develop, Asian enterprises depend on common ethnic contacts to obtain credit, advice and patronage. These ethnic enterprises are characterized by thriftiness and long hours of hard work, with continuous reinvestment of profits. Sociological studies show that education, individual responsibility, and achievement are valued highly and instilled in their young.

They also display strong hiring preferences for "their own," many of whom would face discrimination in outside firms, and they do business with "their own." For example, in San Francisco's Chinese community, a dollar is found to turn over five or six times before it leaves the community. In many black inner-city communities, dollars leave before they turn over even once.

Indeed, a survey by Black Enterprise magazine reported that 70 percent of self-employed blacks consider lack of community support as their most formidable problem. This absence of economic solidarity among inner-city blacks has led black TV journalist Tony Brown to comment: "The Chinese help the Chinese, the Koreans help the Koreans, the Cubans help the Cubans, but blacks help everyone else. We have conducted the most successful business boycott in history—against ourselves."

Moreover, self-employment among blacks is the lowest of any minority group. In Washington, DC, only 3 percent of blacks are self-employed, compared to nearly 20 percent of Asians and 16 percent of non-Hispanic whites. In St. Louis, Asian self-employment is 25 percent and black self-employment only 2 percent. All evidence that we have to date points to entrepreneurship and small business, not government and big business, as being the key to job creation in the inner cities.

Now, when it comes to family cohesiveness and kinship networks, so critical to Asian small business success and their social mobility, the black underclass is at a distinct disadvantage. Two-thirds of black families living in our urban ghettos are mother-only households. The link between female headship of families and welfare dependency in the urban underclass has been well-documented, as has the link to school dropout: living in a mother-only household increases the risk of dropping out of school by 70 percent.

It doesn't require a deep, sociological imagination to sense the attitudinal and behavioral consequences of growing up in an impoverished single-family household, where there is no activity associated with the world of work, and a household which, in turn, is imbedded in a commercially abandoned neighborhood where pimps, drug pushers and unemployed street people replace working fathers as the predominant role models.

Well-meaning people have called for massive government intervention, a "Marshal" Plan for cities, to weed out crime, rebuild and improve the commercial infrastructure, create jobs and upgrade skills in the inner city to match the new white collar employment requirements of our information economy. Though such policies will help, I doubt that they can have a significant impact in reducing inner-city joblessness and revitalizing the ghettos. Based on past experience, there is little concrete evidence that intervention from the outside, whether it's private or public, can generate these desired results. And, despite current responses to the Los Angeles riots, there is little evidence that most Americans possess the political will for large-scale, sustained intervention.

Most important, perhaps, government has an extremely limited capacity to affect the real root of the urban underclass dilemma—that is, the attitudes of those outside, as well as those within the ghetto.

Government cannot legislate away discriminatory stereotyping and other racist views held by many outsiders. Positive attitudinal changes will likely occur only as outsiders come to believe through the actions of the ghetto poor that, despite their social and economic disadvantages, they subscribe to traditional values of strong families, hard work, responsibility, normative order, and that they eschew self-destructive behaviors.

Government cannot weave such values back into ghetto communities, nor dictate the behavior of their residents. Almost by definition, the moral authority for these tasks must come from within the community, from charismatic leadership and from voluntary and religious organizations emphasizing family cohesiveness, educational achievement, economic self-support, and antidrug, anticrime programs. In the absence of such cultural regeneration, frankly, I don't see another promising alternative for black inner-city social mobility or ghetto revitalization.

Thank you, Mr. Chairman.

[The prepared statement of Mr. Kasarda follows:]

PREPARED STATEMENT OF JOHN D. KASARDA, DIRECTOR, KENAN INSTITUTE OF PRIVATE ENTERPRISE, THE UNIVERSITY AT NORTH CAROLINA AT CHAPEL HILL

The recent targeted attacks of rioters in Los Angeles on Korean businesses reveals that racial conflict in urban America is no longer a black and white issue. Rather, it is a street-level collision of hopes and opportunities in the face of dramatically changing inner-city demographic and economic contexts. Let's briefly look at these changing contexts.

For one, the nation's poverty population, once predominantly rural, has increasingly urbanized. In 1959, only 27 percent of our poor resided in metropolitan central cities. By 1985, central cities housed 43 percent of the U.S. poverty population. During the same period, the proportion of poor blacks living in the central cities rose from 38 percent to 61 percent. (Bureau of the Census, 1982, 1987). By 1985, the central cities housed over half of the nation's population living in census tracts with high concentrations of poverty, up from just one-third in 1972 (Reischaur, 1987).

Although we still await 1990 census-tract data to document the most recent trends, we do know that urban populations residing in extreme poverty areas and underclass areas rose dramatically between 1970 and 1980 (Jargowsky and Bane, 1991; Mincy, Sawhill, and Wolf, 1990). I have no doubt that such upward trends continued during the most recent decade.

Poverty and underclass areas expanded in our major cities despite targeted infusions of public assistance, affirmative action programs, and civil rights legislation (programs traditionally supported by liberals) and have persisted in the face of national and urban economic recovery, solutions espoused by many conservatives. One reason why neither set of prescriptions worked, I propose, is that both were overwhelmed by fundamental changes in the structure of inner-city economies, particularly affecting the employment prospects of disadvantaged black residents.

The American city is a different place today than it was in the 1960s when our assumptions about poverty were formed. Advances in transportation, communication, and industrial technologies, interacting with the changing structure of the national and international economy, have transformed our major cities from centers of material goods production to centers of information exchange, finance, and administration.

In this process, many blue-collar industries that once constituted the economic backbone of cities, and provided entry-level employment for their lesser-skilled residents, vanished. These blue-collar industries have been replaced, at least in part, by knowledge-intensive white-collar service industries with educational requirements that preclude most poorly-educated minorities from obtaining employment.

For example, as Exhibit 1 reveals, by 1989, New York City and Boston each had more employees in white-collar service industries—where executives, managers, professionals, and clerical workers dominate—than in their manufacturing, construction, retail, and wholesale industries combined. This is a dramatic metamorphosis since the 1950s, when employment in these traditional urban industries outnumbered information-processing employment by a three-to-one margin.

Exhibit 1—Central City Employment (in Thousands) by Sector: 1953, 1970 and 1989

Central City/Sector	1953		1970		1989	
	Number	Percent	Number	Percent	Number	Percent
New York City:						
Total Employment [1]	2,977	100.0	3,350	100.0	3,143	100.0
Manufacturing	1,070	35.9	864	25.8	391	12.4
Retail/Wholesale	805	27.1	779	23.3	620	19.7
White Collar Services [2]	646	21.7	1,172	35.0	1,608	51.2
Blue Collar Services [3]	344	11.6	424	12.6	377	12.0
Other	111	3.7	112	3.3	147	4.7
Philadelphia:						
Total Employment [1]	788	100.0	772	100.0	610	100.0
Manufacturing	359	45.5	257	33.3	89	14.6
Retail/Wholesale	206	26.1	180	23.3	136	22.3
White Collar Services [2]	98	12.5	220	28.5	296	48.5
Blue Collar Services [3]	85	10.8	81	10.5	63	10.3
Other	40	5.1	35	4.5	26	4.3
Boston:						
Total Employment [1]	402	100.0	465	100.0	518	100.0
Manufacturing	114	28.4	84	18.1	40	7.6
Retail/Wholesale	132	32.8	111	23.9	86	16.5
White Collar Services [2]	87	21.7	194	41.6	311	60.0
Blue Collar Services [3]	51	12.6	55	11.7	63	12.2
Other	18	4.4	21	4.6	19	3.6
Baltimore:						
Total Employment [1]	342	100.0	367	100.0	310	100.0
Manufacturing	130	38.1	105	28.6	43	14.0
Retail/Wholesale	89	26.1	94	25.5	62	20.1
White Collar Services [2]	44	12.8	108	29.5	148	47.8
Blue Collar Services [3]	51	14.9	44	12.1	40	13.0
Other	28	8.1	16	4.2	16	5.1
St. Louis:						
Total Employment [1]	431	100.0	376	100.0	290	100.0
Manufacturing	194	44.9	133	35.3	89	30.5
Retail/Wholesale	103	23.9	89	23.6	59	20.1
White Collar Services [2]	50	11.5	96	25.5	96	32.9
Blue Collar Services [3]	46	10.6	44	11.8	39	13.3
Other	39	9.1	14	3.8	9	3.2

Sources: Bureau of the Census, ***County Business Patterns,*** 1953, 1970, 1989; Bureau of Labor Statistics, ***The National Industry-Occupation Employment Matrix. 1970, 1978 and Projected 1990,*** 1981.

[1] Total classified employment and industry subcategories excluding government employees and sole proprietors.

[2] Services (excluding government, retail, and wholesale) in which more than one half of the employees hold executive, managerial, professional, or clerical positions.

[3] Services (excluding government, retail, and wholesale) in which fewer than one half of the employees hold executive, managerial, professional, or clerical positions.

Hit hardest was the manufacturing sector. Exhibit 2 shows that between 1967 and 1987, Detroit lost 51 percent of its manufacturing jobs; New York City, 58 percent; Chicago, 60 percent; and Philadelphia, 64 percent. Even Sun Belt cities such as Atlanta and LA experienced manufacturing job losses during this period.

Exhibit 2—Change in Employment (in 1000s) by Industry for Selected Central Cities: 1967–1987

Central City/Industry	1967–77	1977–87	Percent Change 1967–87
New York:			
Manufacturing	−285.6	−234.7	−58.1
Trade	−140.6	34.5	−15.2
Service	16.1	286.2	83.8
Combined *	−410.1	86.0	−16.6
Philadelphia:			
Manufacturing	−106.4	−61.6	−63.7

Exhibit 2—Change in Employment (in 1000s) by Industry for Selected Central Cities: 1967–1987—Continued

Central City/Industry	1967–77	1977–87	Percent Change 1967–87
Trade	−33.7	1.6	−19.9
Service	7.2	48.7	97.8
Combined	−132.8	−11.3	−29.9
Chicago:			
Manufacturing	−180.9	−145.4	−59.7
Trade	−79.1	−45.0	−35.6
Service	19.9	83.6	74.9
Combined	−240.1	−106.8	−33.6
Detroit:			
Manufacturing	−56.4	−51.1	−51.3
Trade	−46.9	−17.0	−53.2
Service	−10.1	10.7	1.1
Combined	−113.4	−57.4	−44.6

Sources: Bureau of the Census, Economic Censuses, 1967, 1977 and 1987.
* Combined employment is the sum of manufacturing, retail trade, wholesale trade and service employment.

Blue-collar employment decline was exacerbated by the urban exodus of middle-income residents and the neighborhood business establishments that once served them. This exodus further drained low-skill service jobs such as domestic workers, gas station attendants, and local delivery personnel.

During the 1980s, a number of large cities experienced considerable job growth led by employment gains in white-collar services. Yet, manufacturing employment in these cities continued to decline. New York City, for instance, gained 301,000 jobs from 1980 to 1990—a nearly 10 percent overall increase—but lost 160,000 jobs in its manufacturing firms—a 32 percent drop (Bureau of Labor Statistics, 1981, 1991).

While millions of blue-collar jobs were disappearing from our cities—the very jobs that in the past attracted and socially upgraded waves of disadvantaged migrants—minority residents who lack the education for employment in the new information-processing industries have increased. By 1990, racial-ethnic minorities composed the demographic majority in most of our largest cities—57 percent in New York; 62 percent in Chicago; 63 percent in Los Angeles; 70 percent in Atlanta; 79 percent in Detroit; and 88 percent in Miami. (See Exhibit 3.)

Exhibit 3—Population by Race & Ethnicity: 1970, 1980, 1990

Central City/Year	Total Population	Percentage				
		Non-Hispanic White	Non-Hispanic Black	Hispanic	Asian/Other	Total
New York:						
1990	7,322,564	43	25	24	7	57
1980	7,071,639	52	24	20	4	48
1970	7,894,851	64	19	15	1	36
Philadelphia:						
1990	1,585,577	52	39	6	3	48
1980	1,688,210	57	38	4	2	43
1970	1,948,609	64	33	2	1	36
Chicago:						
1990	2,783,726	38	39	20	4	62
1980	3,005,072	43	40	14	3	57
1970	3,362,825	59	32	7	1	41
Detroit:						
1990	1,027,974	21	75	3	1	79
1980	1,203,339	33	63	2	1	67
1970	1,511,336	54	43	2	1	46
Atlanta:						
1990	394,017	30	67	2	1	70

Exhibit 3—Population by Race & Ethnicity: 1970, 1980, 1990—Continued

Central City/Year	Total Population	Percentage					
		Non-Hispanic White	Non-Hispanic Black	Hispanic	Asian/Other	Total
1980	425,022	32	66	1	1	68
1970	497,024	48	50	1	0	52
Miami:						
1990	358,548	12	25	62	1	88
1980	346,865	19	24	56	1	81
1970	335,075	34	22	45	0	66
Los Angeles:						
1990	3,485,398	37	13	40	10	63
1980	2,966,850	48	17	28	8	52
1970	2,816,111	63	17	15	4	37
San Francisco:						
1990	723,959	47	11	14	29	53
1980	678,974	52	12	12	23	48
1970	715,674	63	13	10	14	37

Source: Bureau of the Census, ***1990 Census of Population,*** PL 94–171 CD-ROM; ***1980 Census of Population,*** STF1C machine-readable file; and ***1970 Census of Population,*** 1st Count machine-readable file.

These conflicting residential and employment base changes placed the demographies and economies of our central cities on a collision course, with poorly educated blacks impacted the most. While overall educational attainment for black city residents improved during the 1970s and 1980s, these gains were not nearly sufficient to keep pace with even faster rises in the education required to work in the new informational economy.

General improvements in city residents' education levels also meant that the least educated jobless blacks fell further behind in the hiring queue. As a result, unemployment among poorly educated urban blacks skyrocketed. By the late 1980s, jobless rates of central city black males who had not completed high school were 44 percent in the Northeast; 58 percent in the Midwest; 49 percent in the South; and 66 percent in the West. (See Exhibit 4.)

Exhibit 4—Percent Not at Work of Out-of-School Central City Black Male Residents Aged 16–64 Who Have Not Completed High School: 1968–70 to 1986–88

Region	Pooled Years			
	1986–88	1980–82	1976–78	1968–70
Northeast	44.3	45.4	43.9	18.8
Midwest	58.0	51.5	42.4	23.5
South	49.0	36.2	30.1	16.9
West	66.2	50.9	46.1	26.3

Source: Bureau of the Census, Current Population Survey, March (Annual Demographic) machine-readable files, 1968 to 1988.

In these circumstances, how is it that lesser-educated Asian immigrant groups have prospered in the same inner-city areas where so many blacks have slipped entirely off the socioeconomic ladder?

A key factor differentiating Asian and black inner-city economic success lies in self-employment fostered by ethnic solidarity and strong kinship networks among Asians.

With little or no help from government, Asian immigrants utilize ethnic-based methods to raise money and establish their own internal markets, from video stores to green groceries; from laundries to restaurants. This allows them to circumvent discrimination and generate employment within their enclaves, insulated from the swings of the national economy as well as from the urban industrial transformation.

Ethnic businesses are typically family-owned and operated, usually drawing upon unpaid family and extended family labor especially during start-up periods when money is scarce. Extended kinship networks also enable immigrant households to share rents or mortgages, provide free child care, and assure economic security against loss of employment by other household members.

To develop, Asian enterprises depend on common ethnic contacts to obtain credit, advice and patronage. These ethnic enterprises are characterized by thriftiness and long hours of hard work with continuous reinvestment of profits. Education, individual responsibility, and achievement are valued highly and instilled in their young.

They also display strong hiring preferences for "their own," many of whom would face employment discrimination in outside firms, and they do business with "their own." In San Francisco's Chinese community a dollar was found to turn over five or six times before it leaves the community. In many black inner-city communities, dollars leave before they turn over even once (Kotkin, 1986).

Indeed, a survey by Black Enterprise magazine reported that 70 percent of self-employed blacks consider lack of community support as their most formidable problem. This absence of economic solidarity among blacks has led black TV journalist Tony Brown to comment: "The Chinese help the Chinese, the Koreans help the Koreans, the Cubans help the Cubans, but blacks help everyone else. We have conducted the most successful business boycott in history—against ourselves" (Kotkin, 1986).

Moreover, self-employment among blacks is the lowest of any minority group. In Washington, D.C., a predominantly black city, only 3 percent of blacks are self-employed compared to nearly 20 percent of Asians and 16 percent of non-Hispanic whites. In St. Louis, Asian self-employment is 25 percent and black self-employment only 2 percent (Kasarda, 1989). All evidence points to entrepreneurship and small business, not government or big business, as being the key to job creation in the inner cities (Sexton and Kasarda, 1992).

When it comes to family cohesiveness and kinship networks so critical to Asian small business success and their social mobility, the black underclass is at a distinct disadvantage. Two-thirds of black families living in our urban ghettos are mother-only households (Wilson, 1987). The link between female headship of families and welfare dependency of the underclass has been well established, as has the link to school dropout: living in a mother-only household increases the risk of dropping out of school by 70 percent (McLanahan, 1985).

It doesn't require a deep sociological imagination to sense the attitudinal and behavioral consequences of growing up in an impoverished single-parent household, where there is no activity associated with work which, in turn, is imbedded in a commercially abandoned neighborhood where pimps, drug-pushers and unemployed street people replace working fathers as the predominant role models.

Well-meaning people have called for massive government intervention to weed out crime, rebuild and improve the commercial infrastructure, create jobs and upgrade skills in the inner city to match the new white collar employment requirements of our information economy.

Though such policies will help, I doubt that they can have a significant impact in reducing inner-city joblessness and revitalizing the ghettos. Based on past experience, there is little concrete evidence that intervention from outside, private or public, can generate these desired results. And, despite current responses to the Los Angeles riots, there is little evidence that most Americans possess the political will for large-scale, sustained intervention.

Most important, perhaps, government has an extremely limited capacity to affect the real root of the urban underclass dilemma—attitudes of those outside as well as within the ghettos.

Government cannot legislate away discriminatory stereotyping and other racist views held by many outsiders. Positive attitudinal changes will likely occur only as outsiders come to believe through actions of the ghetto poor that, despite their social and economic disadvantages, they subscribe to traditional values of strong families, hard work, responsibility, normative order, and that they eschew self-destructive behaviors.

Government cannot weave such values back into ghetto communities nor dictate behavior of their residents. Almost by definition, the moral authority for these tasks must come from within the community, from charismatic leadership and voluntary and religious organizations emphasizing family cohesiveness, educational achievement, economic self-support, and anti-drug, anti-crime programs. In the absence of such cultural regeneration, frankly I don't see another promising alternative for black inner-city social mobility or ghetto revitalization.

REFERENCES

Bureau of the Census, 1987, "Poverty in the United States: 1985," *Current Population Reports,* Series P-60.

Bureau of the Census, 1982, "Characteristics of the Population Below the Poverty Line: 1980," *Current Population Reports,* Series P-60.

Bureau of Labor Statistics, *Employment and Earnings,* Vol. 28 (March), 1981 and Vol. 38 (March), 1991.

Jargowsky, Paul A. and Mary Jo Bane, 1991, "Neighborhood Poverty: Basic Questions," in Jencks and Peterson, eds., *The Urban Underclass.* Washington, DC: Brookings Institution.

Kasarda, John D., 1989, "Urban Industrial Transition and the Underclass," *The Annals of the American Academy of Political and Social Science,* January, 501:26-47.

Kotkin, Joel, 1986, "The Reluctant Entrepreneurs," *Inc.,* September, 8(9):81-86.

McLanahan, Sara, 1985, "Family Structure and the Reproduction of Poverty," *American Journal of Sociology,* 90:873-901.

Mincy, Ronald, Isabel Sawhill and Douglas Wolf, 1990, "The Underclass: Definition and Measurement," *Science* 248:450-53.

Reischauer, Robert D., 1987, *The Geographic Concentration of Poverty: What Do We Know?* Washington, DC: The Brookings Institution.

Sexton, Donald L. and John D. Kasarda, 1992, *The State of the Art of Entrepreneurship,* Boston: PWS-Kent Publishing Company.

Wilson, William Julius, 1987, *The Truly Disadvantaged: The Inner City, the Underclass, and Public Policy.* Chicago: University of Chicago Press.

Mr. SAWYER. Thank you very much, Dr. Kasarda.

Let me tell you that I particularly appreciate, given the range of your observations, your comments toward the end of your testimony, that attitudinal changes may be more dependent on the changes among those with presumptions about the ghetto poor than necessarily in the behaviors of those populations themselves.

Mr. KASARDA. That's correct. I think it's very important that the attitudes of those outside the ghetto change, but they are only going to change as they come to believe that those inside possess prescribed values, that is, the values that should be, because we know that those outside the ghettos often don't practice those very same prescribed values.

Mr. SAWYER. One of the compelling phenomena that we've seen in the course of the 1990 measurement of the United States has been not only this urbanization of the American population, to a degree that we've never seen before, but at the same time we've seen an exurbanization taking place. It is leaving at the center of that classic doughnut those who are most in need with the least opportunity to respond to that, and in the broader circle beyond that, without any of the capacity for mobility or transportation to the best transitional jobs that those populations might access themselves to.

Mr. KASARDA. You're absolutely correct. If I may elaborate on that for a moment.

Mr. SAWYER. Sure.

Mr. KASARDA Because that has been the central focus of my research, which has been not only the skills mismatches in the city—that is, the resident education and skill levels being inappropriate for the new types of jobs that are growing in the cities—but the fact of the matter that many suburban and exurban businesses are facing blue-collar and lesser skilled labor shortages at the same time as we have such high unemployment rates in the central city.

So many of the lesser educated residents are doubly impacted by skills mismatches and spatial mismatches.

For example, between 1975 and 1985, my research showed that there were more nonadministrative jobs created in the fast food and drink industry in this country than exist in the entire automobile, textile, and steel industries combined. In other words, we could have wiped out those three industries entirely and there are more jobs generated, mostly in fast food——

Mr. SAWYER. Please, don't even suggest that.

Mr. KASARDA. But most of these jobs, virtually all of these jobs, grew in the suburbs, exurbs, and small cities and towns, far removed from the spatial concentrations of jobless people. So we find in our cities a labor shortage, where many of the corporate offices are even beginning to say we might relocate out of the city because we can't find lower skilled white-collar workers, secondary office functions, clerical office functions performed, let alone the higher skilled white-collar information processing jobs. At the same time we're seeing unemployment rates in these inner-city areas of 30, 40, and 50 percent among those that have less than a high school degree.

This is compounded by the fact that one finds that, as jobs have moved out from the city to the suburbs and exurbs, they have not moved in high concentrations. Yes, we have industrial parks; yes, we have office parks and suburban shopping malls. But as they have moved out, they have scattered along beltways, expressways, interstate highways, which makes public transportation access very, very difficult.

Mr. SAWYER. Exactly. Our public transportation system is structured on an hub-and-spoke——

Mr. KASARDA. A radial system.

Mr. SAWYER. You're exactly right.

What we may need is a network, a web of transportation.

Mr. KASARDA. Yes. Unfortunately, given the 7-minute limit you put on me today, I could not get into the transportation aspects. But I have looked at a number of these.

Let me point out that one of the key findings was that inner-city blacks, regardless of the urban area—I looked at the Northeast, in the South, in the Midwest and the West—have much longer commute times to their jobs than do whites. In Chicago, for example, we're just getting the 1990 commuting times now. But in 1980, inner-city blacks that commute to suburban jobs, who use public transportation, had an average journey to work, one way, of over 1 hour. But more importantly, as you say, the jobs have dispersed, which requires automobiles or private transit for the most part.

Here the data are even more discouraging. Most inner-city households lack private automobile access, well over 50 percent in most of our inner-city areas. The private vehicle is increasingly necessary to obtain and hold employment in our deconcentrating economy, which is a dispersing economy.

Public transportation is not efficient as our economy disperses. You can have it, but it won't be efficient. This is why we have looked at such factors as van pooling, public/private efforts to get together and van pool people from the inner city to their outlying areas, but also maybe change their strategy a little bit. Most of our policies to date have been jobs-to-people policies. Even our current enterprise zone legislation is jobs to people. Very little is focused on the people to jobs strategies, the ways in which we could make jobs more accessible and allow people to get to their jobs. Mobility, social mobility and spatial mobility go hand in hand in American society.

Mr. SAWYER. Let me ask you this question, then.

Is the migration of the middle class and the jobs that move with them not only a symptom but perhaps a significant cause of the economic status of those who are left behind in the inner city?

Mr. KASARDA. Oh, it's a little bit of both, but I would say it's primarily a cause. Because what has happened in our very depressed inner-city areas is that the middle income and working class minorities, blacks in particular, also have moved out. This has left behind those people with the least resources, those who did not have the resources to be able to follow the deconcentrating job base.

This is why during the 1980's we found concentrations of extreme poverty and underclass areas growing so dramatically. I think it went from 750,000 people in 1970 to 2.5 million in 1980.

Mr. SAWYER. One of the other findings from 1990 was the intensity of residential segregation, particularly among black communities. It was far less pronounced among Asian communities who had greater mobility in terms of their ability to follow jobs and to pursue opportunity.

Could you comment on that?

Mr. KASARDA. Yes, I can. There are two phenomena that came from work in looking at the Current Population Survey. I traced immigrant groups to this country and where they were residing. It's interesting that, by 1985, Asians began to settle more in the suburbs than in the central city, reversing a traditional pattern in which the migrant flows located initially close to the inner-city core and then, as they climbed the socioeconomic ladder over time, moved out to the suburbs.

Mr. SAWYER. Not only that, but that's where the jobs were.

Mr. KASARDA. Yes. So they are moving where the jobs are.

Second, there is class segregation that interacts with racial segregation, and this is what has really left a large segment of our population isolated, spatially and culturally, in our inner cities.

Mr. SAWYER. Let me ask you a broader question. Is there a workable structure by which inner cities can share in the comparative wealth of their broader metropolitan areas, in order to assure the shared survival of economic communities that are larger than smaller governmental jurisdictions?

Mr. KASARDA. There's a way, but is there a will? OK? The political realities are that such forms of consolidation, annexation, general service areas, have met stern resistance. People have moved, what sociologists refer to as new class theory, to avoid these problems and the cost of paying for the problems.

Now, when the rapid growth areas of the 1980–90 period were studied in terms of population growth and retail activity, it seemed that there was one consistent finding that came out time and time again. Some people refer to these as "edge" cities, "peripheral" cities, what have you. It was that the areas of greatest growth in the larger metropolitan areas were within the commuting shed of that metropolitan area, but as spatially removed from the concentrations of poverty as they could be. So you do have avoidance going on.

All you have to do is plot out where the rapid growth is and it's the exurbs. It's these areas that you referred to initially. It's not the inner, older suburbs. It's not even the second-ring suburbs. It's those out 30, 40, or 45 miles. So there does appear to be a pattern of avoidance.

Under those circumstances, I cannot be optimistic that the types of political decisions will be made that enable those outlying communities to provide the inner cities with the mechanism to obtain some of these resources. I don't think the will exists for those that have moved out to share those resources with the central cities. That's my own opinion.

Mr. SAWYER. During these first 2 days of hearings, we have come to find that there are enormous and intensifying differences among communities throughout this country. We heard yesterday that California characterizes one potential future that much of the rest of the country might look forward to; that New Jersey, more broadly than most places, represents the current distribution of opportunity, living patterns, ages and so forth in the country.

You speak in terms of the policies that we must anticipate in order to deal with one of those futures—largely, the California model. To what degree do we have to anticipate a range of policies to deal with a range of futures?

Mr. KASARDA. This gets to the root of can we have a national urban policy, or do we have many, many diverse urban areas, each with its unique demography, economy and set of structural constraints, each demanding a unique solution. I think this goes to the root of our urban policy formation. There are those that argue, taking that California perspective on what have you, that we cannot have a national urban policy. We need a series of local, targeted policies, predicated on the context of those areas. I have to say that I go 60–40 in that favor because there are some common characteristics, some structural changes that are taking place, and there are some tradeoffs.

If we have a jobs-to-people strategy, if we are going to target and direct our industry, through tax credits and other forms of subsidies, into areas of higher cost or lower productivity, what is the impact of that on our overall national economic competitiveness? You're going to have those from the conservative side continuously raise that issue, whereas others will come in and say "Look, the survival of our cities is the very basis of our international competitiveness."

One thing I learned a long time ago is there is no objective, clear, correct public policy. Public policy, stripped to its basics, is a choice among value alternatives. What one considers a correct policy, another person considers is a wrong-headed policy, predicated on values, beliefs, and principles.

Mr. SAWYER. That leads me to my last question for you.

So much of what we're trying to do in seeing over the horizon, trying to anticipate a series of futures from which we can choose, is based on the data that we're able to measure today, to know where we've been, where we are, and in some way to get a sense of where we're going.

Are there phenomena in our society that lend themselves to the kinds of measurements that take place on a decennial basis, or on an intercensal basis, that we ought to be measuring as a matter of national statistical policy that we're not measuring today, that would give us a clear view over that horizon?

Mr. KASARDA. Yes, Mr. Chairman. I believe that we really do need better intercensal estimates. It has been very frustrating for me to wait now almost mid-way through 1992 to see what's happened since 1980 in our inner cities, because our primary device that we use to track current trends the Current Population Survey simply is not a large enough sample size to get at some critical issues.

Mr. SAWYER. Is there specific data that you would transfer——

Mr. KASARDA. I would like to see a quinquennial census that was based on a significant sample, that is, a 5-year census.

Mr. SAWYER. Done through sampling rather than through——

Mr. KASARDA. Done through sampling, yes. Effective, large-scale samples can give the same payoff as a complete census.

Mr. SAWYER. Thank you very much. We appreciate your being here today. You have certainly crammed an awful lot of information into your 7 minutes, and what you've done with your answers. I hope that you will lend yourself to answering written inquiries at a later date.

Mr. KASARDA. I will be happy to.

Mr. SAWYER. Thank you very much for your presence here today. Our fourth panel is made up of Dr. Carol J. DeVita, who is senior research demographer and director of publications, Population Reference Bureau. She directed the PRB's publication series "America in the 21st Century". Also we have Dr. Robert H. Binstock, who is the Henry R. Luce professor of aging, health and society at Case Western Reserve University. Welcome to both of you.

Dr. DeVita.

STATEMENTS OF CAROL J. DeVITA, PH.D., SENIOR RESEARCH DEMOGRAPHER, POPULATION REFERENCE BUREAU; AND ROBERT H. BINSTOCK, HENRY R. LUCE PROFESSOR OF AGING, HEALTH, AND SOCIETY, SCHOOL OF MEDICINE, CASE WESTERN RESERVE UNIVERSITY

Ms. DEVITA. Thank you very much, Mr. Chairman. It's a pleasure to be here.

By now, almost everyone has heard about "The Aging of America," but what exactly does this mean demographically, and what does it imply about our future? We know, for example, that life expectancy has been rising, which means that people are living longer. But are older people living healthier and more active lives, or are they living with chronic and disabling conditions? We know that because women tend to outlive men, there are far more women than men in the older population, especially when it comes to extreme old age. How do widowhood and living arrangements affect the chances that an older woman will become impoverished and in need of health or housing assistance? Finally, we know that the basic age structure of our population is changing. Persistently low birth rates mean that the size of the younger age groups is declining relative to the older age groups. How will society adjust to these changes and how will we provide for the needs of both the young and the old?

These are important public policy questions that are shaped by demographic forces. What's unique about the aging of America is that it is unprecedented. At no time in our Nation's history, or in the history of any other nation, has there been such a rapid change in the size and growth of the older population. As policymakers, you are really charting new and unknown territories.

There are three important demographic changes related to the aging of America that I want to share with you today. First, the growth of the older population, both in terms of numbers and percentages; second, the distribution of the older population, how this change will affect different States and regions of the country; and third, the diversity that exists within the older population. It is not a monolithic group.

Finally, I would like to close my remarks today with some thoughts about the future—about the aging of the baby boom generation—and the need to prepare now for their years as senior citizens.

The 1990 census found that 31.2 million Americans were age 65 and older. This is a 22 percent increase over 1980. In other words, more than a half million Americans reached senior citizen status each year during the 1980's. Nearly 13 percent of the U.S. population is now age 65 or older, up from just 11 percent in 1980.

This is just the tip of the iceberg, however. Demographic projections show that the size of the older population could double over the next 40 years, increasing to roughly 65 million older people. One in five Americans, or 20 percent of the population, could be in the older age groups by the year 2030. Just to give you a point of comparison, currently in the State of Florida the older population represents 18 percent of that State's population.

What is more, the oldest of the old, those age 85 and older, make up the fastest-growing segment of the population. In the next 20 years, their numbers will double, growing from 3 million today to over 6 million in the next 20 years. By 2030, there are expected to be about 8.6 million people age 85 and older. This group of elderly, the oldest old, has the greatest need for services and places considerable demand on the service delivery system.

Let me now proceed to point two: the distribution of this population. While all States will feel the effect of the aging of the population, the impact of this demographic change will be more immediate and more evident in particular States. According to the 1990 census, the greatest number of elderly are found in California, Florida, and New York. Each of these States has more than 2 million people who are age 65 and older. This really shouldn't be surprising, since these States are among the most populous overall. Six other States, however—Pennsylvania, Texas, Illinois, Ohio, Michigan, and New Jersey—have over 1 million older people in their populations.

I have included three tables with my testimony, and I would like to ask that those be submitted as part of the record. They lay out this information in more detail for all 50 States, as well as the District of Columbia.

Mr. SAWYER. The entire testimony of all witnesses will be included as part of the record.

Ms. DEVITA. Thank you.

What we see is that during the past decade, the most rapid growth of the older population has occurred in the West and the South. In particular, the increases in Nevada, Alaska, Hawaii, Arizona, and Florida have been two to four times greater than the U.S. average, which as I said earlier was 22 percent.

While this trend reinforces the popular image that most older people move to the Sun Belt States upon retirement, the demographic reality is that only about 5 percent of the older population change their residence in any given year. Even then, most moves are local because most older people age in place; that is, they remain in the community in which they spent most of their adult years.

This has important implications, of course, for service delivery programs. Reaching this population has become more difficult logistically for service providers because the majority of older people are scattered in suburbs rather than in inner-city neighborhoods, and roughly one in four are located in rural areas.

While rapid rates of growth are occurring in the South and the West, if we look at the share of elderly in each State's population, we find that the highest percentages are found in the Northeast and the Midwest. Florida does rank as No. 1 in this category, but Pennsylvania, Iowa, and Rhode Island follow right behind. In fact, of the top 10 States with the greatest share of elderly, 7 are in the Northeast or Midwest. Again, these figures are found in the tables that I have provided.

It is also important to look at the percentage of the population age 65 and older that is age 85 and older, because this is the most vulnerable group of elderly who are likely to have the greatest service needs. For the United States as a whole, the 1990 census found that this figure was just under 10 percent, but for many Northeastern and Midwestern States, the proportion is much higher. In Iowa, for example, about one in eight senior citizens in that State are age 85 or older. Census Bureau projections forecast that in the next 20 years one in five older Iowans are going to be age 85-plus.

Finally, as policymakers, you must remember that the older population is very diverse. While all of these individuals have passed a milestone birthday marker, they do not all share the same needs. Demographic factors are important indicators of which elderly are most at risk of needing assistance.

For example, poverty rates within the older population increase dramatically with age. In 1990, about 1 in 10 persons age 65 to 74, the younger end of the spectrum, was living in poverty, but 1 in 6 of those who were age 75 and older was poor.

Similarly, the rates of poverty for minority elderly are two to three times higher than for the white population. Ten percent of white elderly lived in poverty in 1990, compared with 23 percent of Hispanic elderly and 34 percent of black elderly. Racial and ethnic minorities, as you heard yesterday, are fast becoming a larger share of the U.S. population and are expected to account for approximately one-third of the total population by the year 2030. This trend could raise poverty rates among the older population if current patterns persist.

And because women tend to outlive men, marital status and living arrangements also play an important mediating role in determining poverty rates. Older widows and unmarried women who live alone are five times more likely than their married peers to live in poverty. One in four older women who lives alone lives in poverty.

In closing, let me turn to the future. The 1990's provide us with a window of opportunity. The problems of the elderly, although not an immediate crisis, have long-range and important implications for our society. The growth of the older population will slow during the 1990's as the somewhat smaller Depression-era generation—those individuals who were born during the 1930's—begins to move into their older years. However, when the baby boom generation begins to reach retirement age around the year 2010, they will set off a senior boom. Because of its size, the baby boom generation has always put a tremendous strain on society's resources. This will be no less true in the 21st century.

For the next 20 years, the baby boom generation will be laying the foundation not only for its own retirement and older years but also for the Nation's future. Baby boomers are now entering their most productive work years and will dominate the workforce for the next three decades. They will see their children grow and their parents age. And, both directly and indirectly, they will set the agenda for the Nation's public policy choices in education, work-family policies, retirement programs and health care.

Anticipating the future will be a key component of policymaking in the 1990's, and the aging of America, I think, will be a key factor in that process. While some policymakers will be tempted to defer action on this seemingly far off problem, let me urge you to begin laying the groundwork now for this demographic inevitability.

[The prepared statement of Ms. DeVita follows:]

PREPARED STATEMENT OF CAROL J. DEVITA, SENIOR RESEARCH DEMOGRAPHER, POPULATION REFERENCE BUREAU

By now, most everyone has heard of "The Aging of America." But what exactly does this phrase mean demographically, and what does it imply about our future? We know, for example, that life expectancy has increased, which means that people are living longer. But are older people living healthier and more active lives, or are they living longer with chronic and disabling conditions? We know that because women tend to outlive men, there are far more women than men in the older population, especially at extreme old age. How do widowhood and living arrangements affect the chances that a older woman will become impoverished or in need of housing or health care assistance? Finally, we know that the basic age structure of our population is changing. Persistently low birth rates mean that the size of the younger age groups in the population is declining relative to the older age groups. How will society adjust to this change and how will it provide for the needs of both the young and the old?

These are important public policy questions that are shaped by demographic forces. What is unique about the aging of America is that it is unprecedented. At no time in our nation's history (or in the history of any other nation) has there been such rapid change in the size and growth of the older population. As policymakers, you are charting new territories.

There are three important demographic changes related to the aging of America that I want to share with you today:

- first the growth of the older population both in terms of numbers and percentages;
- second, the distribution of the older population—how this change will affect different states and regions of the country; and
- third, the diversity that exists within the older population. It is not a monolithic group.

Finally, I'd like to close my remarks with some thoughts about the future—about the aging of the baby-boom generation—and the need to prepare now for their years as senior citizens.

The Growth of the Older Population

The 1990 Census found that 31.2 million Americans were age 65 or older. This is a 22 percent increase over 1980. In other word, more than a half million Americans reached senior citizen status each year during the 1980s. Nearly 13 percent of the U.S. population is now age 65 or older, up from just 11 percent in 1980.

This is just the tip of the iceberg, however. Demographic projections show that the size of the older population could double over the next 40 years, increasing to roughly 65 million people. One in five Americans—or 20 percent of the population—could be in the older age groups by 2030. Just as a point of comparison, currently in the state of Florida, the older population represents 18 percent of that state's population.

What is more, the oldest of the old, those age 85 and older, make up the fastest growing segment of the population. In the next 20 years, their numbers will double, growing from 3 million today to 6.1 million. By 2030, there will be more than 8.6 million. This group of elderly—the oldest old—has the greatest need for services and places considerable demand on service delivery systems.

Distribution

While all states will feel the effect of the aging of the population, the impact of this demographic change will be more immediate and more evident in particular states.

According to the 1990 Census, the greatest number of elderly are found in California, Florida, and New York. Each of these states has more than 2 million persons age 65 and older. This is not surprising, as these states are among the most populous overall. Six other states (Pennsylvania, Texas, Illinois, Ohio, Michigan, and New Jersey) have over 1 million older persons. Table 1 provides detailed data for all 50 states and the District of Columbia.

Table 1—State Rankings of Population Age 65 and Older: 1990

Number of Persons 65 and Older			Persons 65 and Older as Percent of State Population		
Rank	State	Number	Rank	State	Percent
U.S.		31,241,831	U.S.		12.6
1	California	3,135,552	1	Florida	18.3
2	Florida	2,369,431	2	Pennsylvania	15.4
3	New York	2,363,722	3	Iowa	15.3
4	Pennsylvania	1,829,106	4	Rhode Island	15.0
5	Texas	1,716,576	5	West Virginia	15.0
6	Illinois	1,436,545	6	Arkansas	14.9
7	Ohio	1,406,961	7	South Dakota	14.7
8	Michigan	1,108,461	8	North Dakota	14.3
9	New Jersey	1,032,025	9	Nebraska	14.1
10	Massachusetts	819,284	10	Missouri	14.0
11	North Carolina	804,341	11	Kansas	13.8
12	Missouri	717,681	12	Oregon	13.8
13	Indiana	696,196	13	Massachusetts	13.6
14	Virginia	664,470	14	Connecticut	13.6
15	Georgia	654,270	15	Oklahoma	13.5
16	Wisconsin	651,221	16	New Jersey	13.4
17	Tennessee	618,818	17	Montana	13.3
18	Washington	575,288	18	Wisconsin	13.3
19	Minnesota	546,934	19	Maine	13.3
20	Alabama	522,989	20	New York	13.1
21	Maryland	517,482	21	Arizona	13.1
22	Arizona	478,774	22	Ohio	13.0
23	Louisiana	468,991	23	Alabama	12.9
24	Kentucky	466,845	24	District of Columbia	12.8
25	Connecticut	445,907	25	Tennessee	12.7
26	Iowa	426,106	26	Kentucky	12.7
27	Oklahoma	424,213	27	Illinois	12.6
28	South Carolina	396,935	28	Indiana	12.6
29	Oregon	391,324	29	Minnesota	12.5
30	Arkansas	350,058	30	Mississippi	12.5
31	Kansas	342,571	31	North Carolina	12.1
32	Colorado	329,443	32	Delaware	12.1
33	Mississippi	321,284	33	Idaho	12.0
34	West Virginia	268,897	34	Michigan	11.9
35	Nebraska	223,068	35	Washington	11.8
36	Maine	163,373	36	Vermont	11.8
37	New Mexico	163,062	37	South Carolina	11.4
38	Rhode Island	150,547	38	Hawaii	11.3
39	Utah	149,958	39	New Hampshire	11.3
40	Nevada	127,631	40	Louisiana	11.1
41	New Hampshire	125,029	41	Maryland	10.8
42	Hawaii	125,005	42	New Mexico	10.8
43	Idaho	121,265	43	Virginia	10.7
44	Montana	106,497	44	Nevada	10.6
45	South Dakota	102,331	45	California	10.5
46	North Dakota	91,055	46	Wyoming	10.4
47	Delaware	80,735	47	Texas	10.1
48	District of Columbia	77,847	48	Georgia	10.1
49	Vermont	66,163	49	Colorado	10.0
50	Wyoming	47,195	50	Utah	8.7
51	Alaska	22,396	51	Alaska	4.1

Prepared by Population Reference Bureau from 1990 Census of Population, STF1A data.

What we see is that during the past decade, the most rapid growth of the older population has occurred in the West and the South (see table 2). In particular, the increases in Nevada, Alaska, Hawaii, Arizona, and Florida have been two to four times greater than the U.S. average.

Table 2—Growth of the Older Population: 1980–1990

Age 65 and Older			Age 85 and Older		
Rank	State	Percent Change	Rank	State	Percent Change
U.S.		22.3	U.S.		37.5
1	Nevada	94.1	1	Nevada	105.0
2	Alaska	93.7	2	Alaska	102.1
3	Hawaii	64.2	3	Arizona	89.7
4	Arizona	55.8	4	Hawaii	87.0
5	New Mexico	40.7	5	Florida	79.1
6	Florida	40.4	6	New Mexico	62.0
7	South Carolina	38.1	7	North Carolina	54.8
8	Utah	37.3	8	Utah	53.8
9	Delaware	36.4	9	South Carolina	53.7
10	North Carolina	33.3	10	Texas	48.7
11	Washington	33.3	11	Virginia	45.2
12	Colorado	33.2	12	Georgia	45.2
13	Virginia	31.5	13	Louisiana	42.9
14	Maryland	30.8	14	Alabama	42.6
15	California	29.9	15	Maryland	42.3
16	Idaho	29.4	16	Tennessee	41.9
17	Oregon	29.0	17	North Dakota	38.1
18	Wyoming	27.0	18	New Hampshire	37.7
19	Georgia	26.6	19	Mississippi	37.5
20	Montana	25.9	20	California	37.2
21	Texas	25.2	21	Oregon	36.5
22	Connecticut	22.2	22	Washington	35.7
23	Michigan	21.5	23	Delaware	35.5
24	New Hampshire	21.4	24	Colorado	35.3
25	Ohio	20.3	25	Oklahoma	34.9
26	New Jersey	20.0	26	Idaho	34.5
27	Tennessee	19.6	27	Rhode Island	33.7
28	Pennsylvania	19.5	28	Kansas	33.6
29	Indiana	18.9	29	Wisconsin	33.5
30	Alabama	18.9	30	Missouri	33.0
31	Rhode Island	18.6	31	Kentucky	32.3
32	Louisiana	16.0	32	New Jersey	32.3
33	Maine	15.9	33	Pennsylvania	32.2
34	Wisconsin	15.4	34	Indiana	31.9
35	Minnesota	14.0	35	Connecticut	31.5
36	Kentucky	13.9	36	West Virginia	31.1
37	Illinois	13.8	37	Wyoming	31.0
38	Vermont	13.7	38	Michigan	30.9
39	North Dakota	13.2	39	Minnesota	30.4
40	West Virginia	13.0	40	Maine	29.3
41	Oklahoma	12.8	41	Illinois	28.7
42	Massachusetts	12.8	42	New York	28.6
43	South Dakota	12.4	43	South Dakota	28.0
44	Arkansas	12.0	44	Ohio	27.3
45	Kansas	11.9	45	Kansas	26.3
46	Mississippi	11.0	46	Vermont	25.2
47	Missouri	10.7	47	Massachusetts	24.8
48	Iowa	9.9	48	Nebraska	23.0
49	New York	9.4	49	Iowa	23.0
50	Nebraska	8.5	50	District of Columbia	22.9
51	District of Columbia	4.8	51	Montana	20.8

Prepared by Population Reference Bureau from 1990 Census of Population, STF1A data.

While this trend reinforces the popular image that most older people move to the Sunbelt states upon retirement, the demographic reality is that only about 5 percent of the older population change their residence in any given year. Even then, most moves are local because most older people age-in-place, that is, they remain in the community in which they spent most of their adult life. This has important implications for service delivery programs. Reaching this population becomes logistically more difficult for service providers because the majority of older people are scattered in suburbs, rather than in inner-city neighborhoods, and roughly one in four are located in rural areas.

While rapid rates of growth are occurring in the South and West, if we look at the share of elderly in each state's population, we find that the highest percentages are found in the Northeast and Midwest. Florida does rank as number 1 in this category, but Pennsylvania, Iowa, and Rhode Island follow right behind. In fact, of the top 10 states with the greatest share of elderly, seven are in the Northeast or Midwest. Again, these figures can be found in table 1.

It is also important to look at what percentage of the age 65 and older population is age 85 and older, because this is the most vulnerable group of elderly who are likely to have the greatest service needs. For the U.S. as a whole, the 1990 Census found that this figure is just under 10 percent. But for many Northeastern and Midwestern states, the proportion is much higher (see table 3). In Iowa, for example, about one in eight senior citizens in that state was age 85 or older. Census Bureau projections forecast that in the next 20 years, one in five older Iowans will be age 85-plus.

Table 3—State Ranking of Population Age 85 and Older: 1990

Number of Persons 85 and Older			Persons 85 and older as Percent of State Population 65 and older		
Rank	State	Number	Rank	State	Number
U.S.		3,080,165	U.S.		9.9
1	California	299,107	1	Nebraska	13.1
2	New York	248,173	2	South Dakota	13.0
3	Florida	210,110	3	Iowa	13.0
4	Pennsylvania	171,836	4	Minnesota	12.6
5	Texas	166,605	5	North Dakota	12.3
6	Illinois	147,549	6	Kansas	12.3
7	Ohio	138,030	7	Wisconsin	11.4
8	Michigan	106,907	8	Vermont	11.4
9	New Jersey	95,547	9	Missouri	11.3
10	Massachusetts	92,209	10	Massachusetts	11.3
11	Missouri	81,217	11	Maine	11.2
12	Wisconsin	74,293	12	Oklahoma	10.8
13	Indiana	71,751	13	Rhode Island	10.6
14	North Carolina	69,969	14	New Hampshire	10.6
15	Minnesota	68,835	15	Connecticut	10.5
16	Virginia	59,709	16	New York	10.5
17	Tennessee	58,794	17	Indiana	10.3
18	Georgia	57,244	18	Illinois	10.3
19	Washington	56,301	19	District of Columbia	10.1
20	Iowa	55,255	20	Mississippi	10.1
21	Alabama	48,507	21	Arkansas	10.1
22	Connecticut	46,993	22	Montana	10.0
23	Maryland	46,496	23	Colorado	10.0
24	Kentucky	46,367	24	Kentucky	9.9
25	Oklahoma	45,848	25	Oregon	9.9
26	Louisiana	43,633	26	Ohio	9.8
27	Kansas	42,241	27	Washington	9.8
28	Oregon	38,815	28	Texas	9.7
29	Arizona	37,717	29	Michigan	9.6
30	Kansas	35,216	30	Wyoming	9.6
31	Colorado	32,953	31	California	9.5
32	Mississippi	32,335	32	Tennessee	9.5
33	South Carolina	30,749	33	West Virginia	9.5
34	Nebraska	29,202	34	Idaho	9.4
35	West Virginia	25,451	35	Pennsylvania	9.4
36	Maine	18,226	36	Louisiana	9.3
37	Rhode Island	16,016	37	Alabama	9.3
38	New Mexico	14,232	38	New Jersey	9.3
39	Utah	13,611	39	Utah	9.1
40	South Dakota	13,343	40	Virginia	9.0
41	New Hampshire	13,286	41	Maryland	9.0
42	Idaho	11,398	42	Florida	8.9
43	North Dakota	11,240	43	Delaware	8.8
44	Montana	10,676	44	Georgia	8.7
45	Hawaii	10,397	45	New Mexico	8.7
46	District of Columbia	7,847	46	North Carolina	8.7
47	Vermont	7,523	47	Hawaii	8.3
48	Nevada	7,463	48	Arizona	7.9
49	Delaware	7,142	49	South Carolina	7.7
50	Wyoming	4,550	50	Nevada	5.8
51	Alaska	1,251	51	Alaska	5.6

Prepared by Population Reference Bureau from 1990 Census of Population, STF1A data.

Diversity

As policymakers, you must remember that the older population is a very diverse group. While all of these individuals have passed a milestone birthday marker, they do not all share the same set of needs. Demographic factors are important indicators of which elderly are most at risk of needing assistance. For example:

• Poverty rates within the older population increase dramatically with age. In 1990, about one in 10 persons age 65 to 74 was living in poverty, but one in six of those age 75 and older was poor.

• Similarly, the rates of poverty for minority elderly are two to three times higher than for the white population. Ten percent of white elderly lived in poverty in 1990, compared with 23 percent of Hispanic elderly and 34 percent of black elderly. Racial and ethnic minorities are fast becoming a larger share of the U.S. population and are expected to account for one-third of the population by 2030. This trend could raise poverty rates among the older population if current patterns persist.

• And because women tend to outlive men, marital status and living arrangements play an important mediating role in determining poverty status. Older widows and unmarried women who live alone are five times more likely than their married peers to live in poverty. One in four older women who lives alone lives in poverty.

The Future

The 1990s provide us with a window of opportunity, however. The problems of the elderly, although not a immediate crisis, have important long-range implications for society. The growth of the older population will slow during the 1990s as the somewhat smaller Depression-era generation (individuals born during the 1930s) begins to move into their older years. However, when the baby-boom generation (born 1946–1964) begins to reach retirement age around the year 2010, they will set off a "senior boom." Because of its size, the baby-boom generation has always put a tremendous strain on society's resources. This will be no less true in the 21st century.

For the next 20 years, the baby-boom generation will be laying the foundation not only for its own retirement and older years, but also for the nation's future. Baby boomers are now entering their most productive work years and will dominate the work force for the next three decades. They will see their children grow and their parents age. And, both directly and indirectly, they will set the agenda for the nation's public policy choices in education, work-family policies, retirement programs, and health care.

Anticipating the future will be a key component of policymaking in the 1990s, and the aging of America will be a key factor in that process. While some policymakers will be tempted to defer action on this seemingly far-off problem, let me urge you to begin laying the groundwork for this demographic inevitability.

Mr. Sawyer. Thank you very much, Dr. DeVita.

Dr. Binstock.

Mr. Binstock. Thank you, Mr. Chairman. I am honored to have this opportunity to present my views to you on the implications of population aging as outlined, demographically, by Dr. DeVita.

The topic encompasses, of course, an extraordinary range of phenomena, ranging from the individual life course and family through community arrangements—even, as implied by our two proceeding witnesses, the issue of the aging of people in the suburbs, a place where life is integrated by the use of the automobile, and how, as we're well aware in the last few weeks, concerns about the older driver, which have received so much attention, and may have many implications for how life will be viable to some suburban older persons. It is the broad policy consequences which, in accordance with your invitation, I will address, and even there somewhat selectively in the few minutes available to me.

I will briefly summarize my written statement and, of course, would be happy to answer any questions.

Mr. Sawyer. Let me urge you, as I probably should have the other witnesses at the beginning of today's testimony, to be as flexible as you need to be. You can summarize what you have here and expand where it's appropriate. We are constrained by the clock and the need to go to the floor and vote and return, but we want to be as flexible as we can be.

Mr. BINSTOCK. Thank you, Mr. Chairman. I have a 3 o'clock plane, too, so I have an incentive to be somewhat——

Mr. SAWYER. That sounds much more compelling than the schedule of floor votes.

Mr. BINSTOCK. A common contemporary approach for dealing with the policy implications of population aging is to engage in "apocalyptic demography"—that is, mapping the future by projecting the figures of the old-old and the oldest-old that Dr. DeVita just described, and then plugging them into our existing arrangements, the public sector, institutionally, and so forth.

Now, of course, that's a poor mode of prediction because it assumes that all those arrangements will stay the same, and we know they change every year, if not every month. But nonetheless, this is commonly used to portray foreboding caricatures of an aging society, such as one proclaimed by a noted biomedical ethicist, who has described the elderly of America as "a medical, social and economic avalanche that could ultimately—and perhaps already has done—great harm."

The principal anxiety frequently expressed through such projections is that demographic changes will make it impossible for us to sustain old-age benefits much into the next century, and moreover, that the increased numbers and proportions of older voters will virtually control our political system and thereby further their self-interests at the expense of other pressing national concerns.

In the few minutes I have available with you today, I would like to challenge the apostles of apocalyptic demography by making just basically three points.

First, there is little reason to be concerned that population aging, in itself, will have adverse economic consequences for our society. Whether we can fiscally support an appropriate array of programs on aging will depend upon the continuing productive capacity of our economy, and our continuing political resolve to transfer resources to older persons who need them.

Second, I think we must begin now to nurture that political resolve by reforming our policies on aging so that older persons share in the benefits and burdens of policies in a fashion that reflects their diversity, particularly their economic diversity.

And third, despite the conventional wisdom, older voters will not be a monolithic political obstacle to such reforms.

On the first point, economic support of an aging society, concern is expressed that increasing dependency ratios—a growth in the proportion of the retired dependent population relative to workers—will make it difficult to sustain old age benefits starting in the year 2010 when the baby boom generation cohorts begin to retire. Of course, right now we're accumulating large surpluses in the OASI Trust Fund, as I have shown in table 1, but I don't think we can count on those surpluses. As Senator Moynihan's proposed amendment illustrated in 1989, there is already a big treasure trove there ready to be raided for one purpose or another to meet a fiscal exigency.

Mr. SAWYER. Dr. Binstock, I learned when I was a mayor never to call anything a surplus.

Mr. BINSTOCK. Right.

Mr. SAWYER. I always called it a "planned fund balance." I think that probably fits this better than most of the things I called a planned fund balance as a mayor.

Mr. BINSTOCK. Indeed.

Mr. SAWYER. In truth, those dollars are spent well into a future that we can foresee; would you agree?

Mr. BINSTOCK. I agree very much, sir.

Mr. SAWYER. Go right ahead.

Mr. BINSTOCK. For a variety of reasons that I have outlined in my written statement, nonetheless, the picture is not dim in economic terms. There will be a slight decline in the proportion of workers starting in 2010, but demographic changes may contribute strongly to American economic growth in the next century. So, in the last analysis, future benefits to the aging will depend not upon the proportion of retirees to workers—in fact, we can't even assume we will be relying completely on the payroll worker-by-worker tax to finance such benefits—but on whether the American economy generates sufficient resources to be transferred and whether the will to transfer them to older persons will be present.

Now, this brings me to my second point, which is a concern that that the will to transfer resources may not be there. Even now, the political climate toward older persons is becoming increasingly hostile. From the New Deal until about the late 1970's, we had a number of compassionate stereotypes of older persons in this country, somewhat inaccurate as all stereotypes, but they were that all older persons are poor, frail, needy, and deserving. There was nothing that we couldn't do for them, which we shouldn't.

But since the late 70's, when journalists and academicians began to discover that more than a quarter of the Federal budget was spent on benefits to the elderly, those stereotypes have begun to reverse. Now in the media we have seen increasingly, over the last dozen years, portrayals of the elderly as affluent, prosperous, selfish, and in the words of one of the more appealing journalistic epithets, "greedy geezers." Fortune magazine earlier this year declaimed that "The tyranny of America's old is one of the most crucial issues facing U.S. society."

As I'm sure you're aware, Mr. Chairman, in this context demographers and others have blamed older persons for the plight of poor children, the weakened state of the economy, spiraling health care costs, and a variety of other issues for which older persons have become scapegoats and which have been thematically unified as issues of so-called "intergenerational equity."

The appeal of this construct of intergenerational equity can be understood, particularly as viewed by advocates for the children, the homeless, and all sorts of other worthy causes. The proportion of gross Federal outlays devoted to domestic discretionary spending is 14 percent. Of the mandatory categories, 60 percent is devoted to programs or benefits on aging. So, from this perspective, it is easy to understand why proponents of various social causes view the old age lobby as a prime competitor for a limited budgetary pie and perhaps not worthy, at least under present policies, of continuing support.

I think we're going to have an early test of what is politically feasible in this sort of a climate in the next few years. For example, the 1991 report of the Social Security Trustees estimated that Medicare's Part A Hospital Insurance would run out of adequate pay-as-you-go financing as early as 1995 and exhaust its reserves by 2005. This year the report moved the year for exhaustion up to 2002. I suspect next year we'll see it move up even closer.

Now, in this example, there are many ways to cope with this immediate problem, including various kinds of increases in the FICA tax, raising the age of eligibility for Medicare, cutting back on Medicare coverage and so on. I don't care for those, for a variety of reasons, and I would like instead to propose a policy approach that builds on the reality of diversity in the elderly population, a diversity that's likely to be present among older cohorts well into the next century——

Mr. SAWYER. Dr. Binstock, I'm going to give you a choice. I have to go register a vote on the floor and I'm running out of time in which to do that. What I would like to do, if it's possible with your airline schedule, is to suspend while I go and cast that vote, and return so that you can conclude with those policy recommendations.

Mr. BINSTOCK. No problem, Mr. Chairman, as long as you vote on the right side, whatever it is. [Laughter.]

Mr. SAWYER. Thank you.

[Whereupon, the subcommittee was in a short recess.]

Mr. SAWYER. Dr. Binstock, it is a quick drive from here to National Airport, so I will let you be the judge of when you have to leave.

Mr. BINSTOCK. All right. I will summarize my summary.

Mr. SAWYER. All right.

Mr. BINSTOCK. What I was suggesting is that I think what we need to do at this point is take an approach that builds particularly on the economic diversity of older persons. For example, in the case of the Medicare Part A shortfall, it would be easy enough to have the deductibles and copayments calibrated to be on a sliding scale in relation to economic status, and even in Part B, one could have an economically sensitive type premium going in.

Now, as radical a change as that may seem to some, actually it's just an incremental extension of precedents that were done and established throughout the 1980's. As you know, we began taxing Social Security at the higher income levels, we amended the Tax Code in the 1986 Reform Act to eliminate the extra exemption on the Federal income tax form for being 65 and older, and replaced it with a sliding scale credit for the lowest income elderly. The Older Americans Act has been targeting programs more and more to low income and minority older persons. And even that part of the Medicare Catastrophic Coverage Act that wasn't repealed provides Medicaid buying in to Medicare for low-income older persons who are Medicaid eligible. So this would hardly be a radical approach.

I think that this sort of an approach to policy is very much needed to nurture the political will to sustain old age transfers in the future, and I don't think it's too early to begin doing this more and more, even though some persons refer to this pejoratively as "means testing."

Now, there are those, of course—and this is my last point—who say "well, older persons will never put up with this because of their political power." I think it's important to distinguish between the old age organizations and their presence here in Washington, and how older citizens actually think and vote. Older persons do vote at much higher rates than most other Americans, and there will be more older persons. But as my table 3 indicates, with the results of election exit polls, one can see that older persons distribute their votes among candidates in just about the same proportion as any other age group. That makes sense. There is no reason to think that when people become 65 or 70 or 75 they all of a sudden become homogenized in every aspect of their political outlook. In fact, repeated opinion polls on issues, even on Social Security and Medicare, show that older persons' attitudes distribute exactly the same as those of middle-aged and younger persons.

Finally on this point, I would think that the enactment and repeal of the Medicare Catastrophic Coverage Act certainly illustrated that AARP did not speak for a monolithic block of older persons out in the country. So, in short, Mr. Chairman, I don't think there are any reasons to believe that today's older voters, or increased numbers and proportions of older voters in the future, will be an obstacle to policy reforms that will be necessary and sensible. In fact, if our political leaders have the vision and courage to propose sensible policy changes and initiatives, I'm sure that most older voters, like middle-age and younger voters, will respond very positively to them. So I don't see any horrible implications of population aging but a number of challenges that we must deal with imaginatively.

Thank you.

[The prepared statement of Mr. Binstock follows:]

PREPARED STATEMENT OF ROBERT H. BINSTOCK, HENRY R. LUCE PROFESSOR OF AGING, HEALTH, AND SOCIETY, CASE WESTERN RESERVE UNIVERSITY

Mr. Chairman and members of the subcommittee: My name is Robert H. Binstock. I am currently the Henry R. Luce Professor of Aging, Health, and Society at Case Western Reserve University, in Cleveland, Ohio.

For more than a quarter of a century my work has focused on issues of population aging and public policy, dating from my service as Director of a White House Task Force on Older Americans for President Lyndon B. Johnson in the mid-1960s. I am honored to have this opportunity to share my perspectives with you today on the implications of the demographic trends that Dr. DeVita has just outlined for you.

This broad topic encompasses a wide range of potential subjects, of course, ranging from likely impacts on the individual life course and family life, through changes in the work place and a variety of community institutions, to consequences for the public sector. In accordance with your invitation to me, however, I will focus my remarks on some of the major public policy implications; and even so, I will be necessarily selective.

A common contemporary approach for considering the policy implications of population aging for American society is to engage in "apocalyptic demography," [1]—that is—mapping the future by simply taking demographic projections of the growing numbers and proportions of older persons, and the swelling ranks of the old-old and oldest-old, and plugging them into a scenario in which it is assumed that the present array of public policies and societal institutions and arrangements will remain unchanged.

---

[1] The term "apocalyptic demography was initially used by A. Robertson to describe a political effect of a strategy engaged in by advocates for Alzheimer's disease research and services; the term is used in a broader sense here. See A. Robertson, "The Politics of Alzheimer's Disease: A Case Study in Apocalyptic Demography," in M. Minkler and C.L. Estes, eds., *Critical Perspectives on Aging: The Political and Moral Economy of Growing Old* (Amityville, NY: Baywood Publishing Company, Inc., 1991) 135–150.

This sort of extrapolation, of course, is a poor mode of prediction because our public policies, institutions, and arrangements are changing all the time.

Nonetheless, this approach is often used to sketch foreboding caricatures of an aging society, such as that proclaimed by a noted biomedical ethicist, Daniel Callahan, who has described our elderly population "a new social threat" and a "demographic, economic, and medical avalanche. that could ultimately [and perhaps already has done] great harm." [2]

The principal anxiety, frequently expressed, is that absolute and proportional increases in the older population will make it impossible, economically, for our nation to sustain public old-age benefits, such as Old Age Insurance (OAI) and Medicare, through the first half of the twenty-first century. At the same time, the apostles of apocalyptic demography warn that older voters, because of their increased numbers and proportions, will virtually control our political system, and thereby further their self-interests at the expense of other pressing national concerns.

In the few minutes I have available with you today, I would like to challenge these conventional assumptions regarding the policy implications of population aging by making three points.

First, there is little reason to be concerned that population aging, in itself, will have adverse economic consequences for our society. Whether we can fiscally support an appropriate array of programs on aging will depend upon the continuing productive capacity of our economy and our continuing political resolve to transfer resources to older persons who need them.

Second, in my view, we must begin now to nurture that political resolve by reforming our policies on aging so that older persons share in the benefits and burdens of policies in a fashion that reflects their diversity, particularly their economic diversity.

And, third, despite the conventional wisdom in the media and within the "Beltway," older voters will not be a monolithic political obstacle to such reforms.

First, let us examine the concern that "increasing dependency ratios"—a growth in the size of the retired "dependent" population—will make it difficult to sustain old age benefits in the next century. If one looks at dependency ratios in isolation—using "working age" (ages 20–64) as a proxy for labor force participation—and assumes that the bulk of old-age benefits need to be financed through FICA payroll taxes on workers (as they are now), there is some cause for concern. In the immediate future, while the Baby Boom cohort is still of working age, the dependency ratio will be relatively stable. Starting in 2010, as the Baby Boomers begin to retire, the proportion of our population that is of working age is projected to begin gradually declining from about 60% until it reaches 54% in 2035, and then remains stable after that.[3]

The 1983 amendments to Social Security are generating surpluses in the OASI trust fund (see Table 1), designed to meet the benefits that will be due to Baby Boom retirees. Indeed, the current surpluses are so large that they have generated considerable controversy concerning their near-term impact on the economy, and their inclusion as revenues in annual reports and projections regarding the size of the federal deficit.[4]

Table 1—Surpluses and Deficits (−) in the Social Security Trust Funds, Fiscal Years 1971–1991

[in billions of dollars]

Year	Surplus or Deficit (−)	Year	Surplus or Deficit (−)
1971	3.0	1981	−5.0
1972	3.1	1982	−7.9
1973	0.5	1983	0.2
1974	1.8	1984	0.3
1975	2.0	1985	9.4
1976	−3.2	1986	16.7

[2] D. Callahan, *Setting Limits: Medical Goals in an Aging Society* (New York: Simon and Schuster, 1987) 20.

[3] See J.L. Palmer and S.G. Gould, "The Economic Consequences of an Aging Society," *Daedalus,* Vol. 115, No. 1 (1986) 295–323.

[4] See H.J. Aaron, ed., *Social Security and the Budget: Proceedings of the First Conference of the National Academy of Social Insurance* (Lanham, MD: University Press of America, 1990).

Table 1—Surpluses and Deficits (−) in the Social Security Trust Funds, Fiscal Years 1971–1991—Continued

[in billions of dollars]

Year	Surplus or Deficit (−)	Year	Surplus or Deficit (−)
1977	−3.9	1987	19.6
1978	−4.3	1988	38.8
1979	−2.0	1989	52.4
1980	−1.1	1990	58.2
		1991	53.5

Source: Congressional Budget Office, U.S. Congress, ***The Economic and Budget Outlook: Fiscal Years 1993–1997*** (Washington, DC: U.S. Government Printing Office, 1992), p. 114.

Yet, Senator Daniel P. Moynihan's 1989 proposal to eliminate these reserves, and return OASI to the status of a pay-as-you-go system, illustrates that one can hardly assume that these surpluses will continue to accrue and remain intact. It is far more likely than not that the surplus in the OASI trust fund will be used for some other purpose, before it is time to draw it down for paying benefits to Baby Boom retirees.

Nonetheless, the outlook is not foreboding. Likely declines in child dependency will probably offset increases in elderly dependency.[5] Moreover, a focus on the ratio of retirees to workers does not adequately capture the range of macroeconomic elements that determine whether a society is economically capable of supporting dependents within it, or the many different sources—including general revenues—through which government could fund such support. The productive capacity of an economy is a function of a variety of factors—at least including capital, natural resources, balance of trade, and technological innovation—as well as number of workers. Hence, issues involving productive capacity and number of workers are appropriately expressed in terms of "productivity per worker." [6]

Understood in these broader terms, and freed from the assumption that benefits provided under the Social Security program must be financed wholly through a payroll tax levied on a worker-by-worker basis, the economic consequences of population aging do not appear so dim. For a variety of reasons, demographic changes may contribute strongly to U.S. economic growth in the next century.[7] In the last analysis, future benefits to the aging will not depend upon the proportion of retirees to workers, but on whether the American economy generates sufficient resources to be transferred, and whether the political will to transfer them to older persons will be present.

Even now, however, the political climate is becoming increasingly hostile to older persons, in general. From the New Deal to the late 1970s, older Americans tended to be stereotyped in compassionate terms—as poor, frail, dependent, and deserving. But since then, as journalists and academicians began to discover that expenditures on old-age benefits accounted for more than a quarter of the annual federal budget, a new set of stereotypes has emerged in the media, portraying older persons as affluent, hedonistic, selfish, and politically powerful—or as one of the common epithets expresses it, "greedy geezers." As Fortune magazine declaimed earlier this year, "The Tyranny of America's Old" is "one of the most crucial issues facing U.S. society." [8]

In this context older persons have been blamed for the plight of poor children, the weakened state of our economy, spiralling health care costs, and a variety of other societal problems which have been thematically unified as issues of so-called "intergenerational equity." The extent to which these stereotypes have taken hold was

---

[5] See J.H. Schulz, A. Borowski, and W.H. Crown, *Economics of Population Aging: The "Graying" of Australia, Japan and the United States* (New York: Auburn House, 1991).

[6] See Committee on an Aging Society, Institute of Medicine and National Research Council, *America's Aging: Productive Roles in an Older Society* Washington, DC: National Academy Press, 1986); and J. Habib, "The Economy and the Aged," in R.H. Binstock and L.K. George, eds., Handbook of Aging and the Social Sciences, Third Edition (San Diego: Academic Press, 1990) 328–345.

[7] See Palmer and Gould, op. cit.

[8] L. Smith, "The Tyranny of America's Old," *Fortune,* Vol. 125, No. 1 (1992) 68–72.

reflected in a comment that Representative Dan Rostenkowski made to the press at the end of the 1989 session of Congress:

> One of the most unhappy results of our ongoing budget gridlock has been an uneven contest between the very young and the very old. The young have lost nearly every time That's partly because the old, however frail they may be, are sophisticated enough to use the political process to press their demands. . . . The sad story of the 1980s [was that] the old have got gotten more while the young have gotten less.[9]

Although Congressman Rostenkowski may have believed his characterization of Congressional activity in the 1980s, the facts do not bear him out. There were no legislative choices or contests during the decade between the very young and-the very old, and—due to the repeal of the Catastrophic Act—the old did not get more. But his willingness to characterize Congressional activity in the 1980s in terms of intergenerational conflict reflects the trend through which this framework has become a conventional perspective for describing tradeoffs in health and social welfare polices.

The appeal that the construct of intergenerational equity has for advocates for children, the homeless, education, rebuilding the nation's infrastructure, combatting drug abuse, and a variety of other domestic concerns can be appreciated by examining Table 2, which shows the distribution of federal outlays for fiscal year 1992. The proportion of gross federal outlays devoted to domestic discretionary spending is only 14.1%.[10] Nearly half of the budget goes for mandatory programs, and expenditures through Social Security's OAI (excluding survivors and disability insurance) and Medicare, alone, constitute 46% of the category.[11] If one adds in the portions of Medicaid, SSI, food stamps, and social service programs that provide benefits to older persons, over half of mandatory spending is on elderly people. And other mandatory programs that include older people—such as retirement and disability for federal civilian and military employees (excluding veterans benefits)—bring the proportion of mandatory spending that is on benefits for the aging to about 60%. This perspective makes it easy to understand why proponents of various social causes view the old-age lobby as a prime competitor for a limited budgetary pie.

Table 2—Federal Outlays, by Category, Fiscal Year 1992

Spending Category	In Billions of Dollars	As a Percentage of Gross Domestic Product
Defense Discretionary	313	5.4
International Discretionary	20	0.3
Domestic Discretionary	214	3.7
Mandatory Spending	708	12.1
Deposit Insurance	67	1.1
Net Interest	201	3.4
Gross Total	1,523	26.0
Offsetting Receipts	−64	−1.1
Desert Storm Contributions	−5	−0.1
Net Total	1,454	24.8

Source: Congressional Budget Office, U.S. Congress, ***The Economic and Budget Outlook: Fiscal Years 1993–1997*** (Washington, DC: U.S. Government Printing Office, 1992), p. 50.

[9] M. Tolchin, "Lawmakers Tell the Elderly: 'Next Year' on Health Care," *New York Times*, November 23 (1989):10Y.

[10] Some policy analysts would argue that Social Security and Medicare expenditures should not be included in calculating the percentage of the federal budget that is available for domestic or any other category of discretionary programs. Their reasoning is based on the fact that the revenues funding Social Security and much of Medicare are dedicated to the purpose of paying benefits under those programs, and therefore should not be included in the total pool of funds available for allocation between mandatory and discretionary spending purposes. From this perspective one would deduct from mandatory outlays all expenditures on OASDI and on Part A of Medicare, thereby reducing substantially the total pool available for spending choices, and also increasing substantially the percentage of outlays on domestic discretionary programs.

[11] U.S. Congress, Congressional Budget Office, *The Economic and Budget Outlook: Fiscal Years 1993–1997* (Washington, DC: U.S. Government Printing Office, 1992) 56.

An early test of what is politically feasible in this climate will face us in the next few years. The 1991 report of the Social Security Trustees estimated that, unless payroll tax rates for financing Medicare's Part A Health Insurance (HI) are increased, or other reforms in Medicare financing are enacted, HI costs will exceed tax revenues by 1995, and by 2005 the HI trust fund reserves will be exhausted and annual costs will exceed revenues by $66 billion. The Trustees 1992 report moved the date for exhaustion of the trust fund up to 2002, and next year's report will probably move the date closer because of the continuing high rate of inflation in health care costs during a period in which the yield from the FICA payroll tax is limited by relatively high unemployment.

There are many possible ways to cope with this immediate problem. The wage and salary ceiling for the Medicare portion of the FICA payroll tax, for example, could be lifted substantially to include persons with very high incomes, following the precedent set when the Omnibus Reconciliation Act of 1990 raised that ceiling from $53,400 to $125,000 in earnings for the year 1991. Or, as some have suggested, we could raise the age of eligibility for Medicare to 67, 70, or 75, thereby reducing outlays; but such a measure would ignore the tremendous diversity within the younger elderly population—both with respect to economic status and access to health insurance.

I would like, instead, to propose a policy approach that builds upon the reality of diversity in the contemporary elderly population, a diversity that is likely to be present among cohorts of older people well into the next century. When most of our major policies on aging were enacted, the vast majority of older Americans were in poverty. But today, some older persons are very well off, a great many are economically comfortable, and about one-third are extraordinarily poor or close to it, especially among the minority elderly, older women who live alone, and the very oldest elderly persons—aged in their late 80s and beyond. A policy strategy that builds on these facts should be employed generally in reforming programs on aging, because it is a practical, just, fiscally responsible, and politically feasible approach to financing old-age programs in the future, reflecting the fact that old age is no longer an accurate categorical marker for a need for governmental subsidization.

In the immediate case of financing Medicare, we ought to redistribute burdens and benefits among persons eligible for Medicare in accordance with their economic status. Higher rates of out-of-pocket deductibles and co-payments could be established for wealthier Medicare patients on a sliding-scale basis. And Medicare's Part B premiums for supplementary Medical Insurance, which are now set at a flat rate, could be increased progressively for higher income program participants.

Such measures to redistribute financial burdens and benefits among elderly program participants would simply be increments extending a 10-year trend through which Congress has reformed policies on aging to reflect the diverse economic situations of older persons. The Social Security Reform Act of 1983 began this trend by taxing one-half of the Social Security benefits of individuals with incomes exceeding $25,000 and of married couples with over $30,000. The Tax Reform Act of 1986, even as it eliminated the extra personal exemption that had been available to all persons 65 years and older when filing their federal income tax returns, provided new tax credits to very-low-income older persons on a sliding scale. The Older Americans Act programs of supportive and social services, for which all persons aged 60 and older are eligible, have been gradually targeted by Congress to low-income older persons (see Binstock 1991). And the Medicare Catastrophic Coverage Act of 1988 continued this legislative approach in two respects, through its progressive taxation provisions and its requirement that Medicaid pay for the Part B premiums and cost-sharing expenses for Medicare enrollees who have incomes below the poverty line. (Although the former provision was repealed in 1989, the latter remains in effect.)

Despite this record of legislation during the past decade, the conventional wisdom inside the "Beltway" remains that older persons will use their political clout to resist successfully any attempts to reform old-age benefit programs in a fashion that introduces the principle of income and asset sensitivity for recipients—or, as it is pejoratively labeled, "means-testing." And this brings me to my last point—the importance of distinguishing between the attitudes and behavior of older voters, on the one hand, and the presence and representations of many of the old-age organizations in Washington, on the other hand.

Older persons do vote at much higher rates than most other Americans, comprising from 17 to 21% of those who vote in national elections. The overall voting participation rate in the 1988 presidential election was 65.9%; the youngest age group—aged 18–29—had the lowest rate of participation, just 44.8%; with each successive older age group the rate increased until it peaked in the age ranges of 60–69 years (79.5% voting) and 70–79 years (81.7% voting).[12]

But older persons do not vote as a monolithic bloc, any more than middle-aged persons or younger persons do. Consequently, the aged are not a single-issue or several-issue voting constituency.

Table 3, showing the results of election exit polls in the last three presidential elections, should make clear that the votes of older persons distribute among candidates in about the same proportions as do the votes of other age groupings of citizens. Although men and women can be seen to have distributed their votes rather differently, there are no consistent patterns in how persons in the age categories of 30–44, 45–59, and 60 years of age and older cast their ballots in these elections. Particularly notable is the 1984 election, when President Ronald Reagan was sharply criticized by Democrats for wanting to "destroy Social Security." Not only did older persons give him 62% of their votes, but the percentages in all age groups of men were virtually identical.

Table 3—Nationwide Vote Distribution, by Age Groups and Gender, in Elections for U.S. President, 1980, 1984, 1988

	The 1980 Vote			The 1984 Vote		The 1988 Vote	
	Reagan	Carter	Anderson	Reagan	Mondale	Bush	Dukakis
Percent of All Voters:							
All ages	51	41	7	59	41	53	45
18–29 years old	43	44	11	58	41	52	47
30–44 years old	54	36	8	58	42	54	45
44–59 years old	55	39	5	60	39	57	42
60 years & older	54	41	4	63	36	50	49
Percent of Men:							
All ages	55	36	7	62	37	57	41
18–29 years old	47	39	11	61	37	55	43
30–44 years old	59	31	4	62	37	58	40
44–59 years old	60	34	5	63	36	62	36
60 years & older	56	40	3	62	37	53	46
Percent of Women:							
All ages	47	45	7	56	44	50	49
18–29 years old	39	49	10	55	45	49	50
30–44 years old	50	41	8	54	46	50	49
44–59 years old	50	44	5	58	41	52	48
60 years & older	52	43	4	64	35	48	52

Sources: 1980, 1984, and 1988 nationwide exit polls conducted by the ***New York Times***/CBS News Poll, published in the ***New York Times***, Nov. 9, 1980, Nov. 8, 1984, and Nov. 10, 1988.

These data should not be surprising. There is no sound reason to expect that an age cohort—constituted of all races, religions, ethnic groups, economic and social status, political attitudes, and every other characteristic in American society—would suddenly become homogenized in its political behavior when it reaches the "old age" category. Numerous contemporary polls of political attitudes show that older people are nearly indistinguishable from younger adults—both the middle-aged and younger categories—on most issues, including aging policy issues.[13] "The elderly" is an artificial category created by policy analysts, the media, and observers who are preoccupied with interest group politics. As the enactment and repeal of the Medicare Catastrophic Coverage Act in 1988 and 1989 illustrated, neither the American Association of Retired Persons nor any other old-age interest group is capable of representing older persons as an overall constituency.

In short, there are no reasons to believe that today's older voters, or increased numbers and proportions of older voters in the future, will be an obstacle to policy reforms. If our political leaders have the vision and courage to propose sensible policy changes and initiatives, whether for programs focused on the aging popula-

---

[12] National Opinion Research Center, University of Chicago, 1986–1991. Data provided by the Roper Center, University of Connecticut, Storrs, Connecticut.

[13] See C.L. Day, *What Older Americans Think: Interest Groups and Aging Policy* (Princeton, NJ: Princeton University Press, 1990).

tion or other sectors of American society, most older voters will respond positively, just like middle-aged and younger voters.

Mr. SAWYER. Thank you very much, Dr. Binstock. I appreciate your patience. I have to tell you that your example of the catastrophic medical insurance legislation probably can be used to illustrate the phenomena that both support your contentions and refute them, at least in terms of the short-term response to specific policy proposals.

Mr. BINSTOCK. May I interpret a little on that point?

Mr. SAWYER. You may. But I am willing to concede that that can be used in both directions. I'm really interested in why you think, particularly as we see a growing population of young minority children who are clearly increasingly dependent, that that population is more likely to need less rather than more assistance, and that there would not be a competition among age groups for limited resources.

Mr. BINSTOCK. I haven't suggested that that population would need less. Indeed, I think if we have effective programs, it would be wise to invest much, much more. The whole thrust of my testimony is to suggest that we should stop having programs for the aging on the basis of age categorical criteria and continue moving in the direction of sliding scale economic sensitivity to those older persons who are in need of help through governmental——

Mr. SAWYER. Need-sensitive criteria.

Mr. BINSTOCK. Right.

Mr. SAWYER All across the age spectrum.

Mr. BINSTOCK. Right. I think that to provide the same benefits, at least nominally, to Bob Hope and our proverbial "bag lady" doesn't make a great deal of sense.

Mr. SAWYER. Let me ask you one final question before I let you go.

Are there measurements that you would find useful in advancing the views that you've drawn that we're not undertaking today? Are there changes we need to make in the near term in our statistical systems?

Mr. BINSTOCK. Aside from supporting the general suggestion that was made earlier, perhaps, about some sampling every 5 years, I actually think that we are beginning to have in place now the kinds of studies that we need. There has been the authorization and funding of a very large retirement history study through the National Institute on Aging which is looking at the dynamics of economic change among older persons on a longitudinal basis.

I do think that there are areas of greater sophistication in terms of focusing in on diversity, ethnically as well as longitudinally, that are important. Let me give you two illustrations from Florida on a point which Dr. DeVita highlighted.

She talked about aging in place, where people stay in the same place, the neighborhood changes and so on. One thing we must be very sensitive to is migration and then aging in place. Let me give you the proverbial widow of a New York policeman who retired to Florida in a trailer 20 years ago, a brand new, spanking new, beautiful trailer. The husband died 10 years ago and now the wife is living in a 20-year old trailer with no assets to change her situation and all that one can imagine with that. So that sort of migration and the consequences long term are important.

The other key thing again is to focus, as you pointed out in your opening statement, on the meanings within minority, even as applied to the elderly population. For example, several years ago a successful suit was brought in the Federal district court for Florida challenging the State of Florida's intrastate funding formula under the Older Americans Act. It was brought by a group in the Miami area, Dade County. They were successful. The State had to reformulate its formula to redistribute money among the various areas within the State.

One of the ironic consequences of this was that a great deal of money went from areas where there were poor dirt farmer, black minority elderly in the northern part of the State, to an area with a higher concentration of minority elderly in the Miami area, but not nearly as poor and without resources. So I think increasing some studies that focus on these issues and bring in the longitudinal aspects of what happens would be very valuable.

Mr. SAWYER. Thank you very much for your testimony today. You are really pressing your schedule very close.

Mr. BINSTOCK. No problem. It's been a pleasure.

Mr. SAWYER. If you would be willing to respond to written questions, it would help our record as we attempt to build that over the next several months.

Mr. BINSTOCK. I would be happy to, and also I'm sure Dr. DeVita, who I'm proud to say is a former student of mine, can answer any questions better than I can. Thank you.

Mr. SAWYER. Thank you.

Dr. DeVita, thank you very much for your patience today. You referred to the change in the characteristics of the female workforce in particular. Do you anticipate sources of income for seniors changing particularly with the increased participation of women in the workforce? Will this affect the projections of soundness of the Social Security system? Are there changes in policy that we ought to anticipate as a result of the substantially greater participation of working women and the increase in their potential income streams on retirement?

Ms. DEVITA. Well, certainly the entry of women into the labor force has been one of the major demographic changes of the last 20 or 30 years that we've seen. I think what we have to take a closer look at is both the pattern of those work histories and the kinds of jobs that women have been occupying as they've moved into the labor force.

I believe there is some research underway now, by Dr. Iams at the Social Security Administration, who is looking at the impact of this on future benefits, on the eligibility of future benefits. I have not seen the research directly. My impression, from what I have heard through colleagues discussing this work, is that many women will be able to receive Social Security benefits in their own right, based on their work histories, but many may find themselves still better off in terms of receiving a spousal benefit. I think those are the kinds of research questions that need to be looked at more carefully when you look at policies and streams of income for future elderly, particularly the baby boom generation.

I think Dr. Binstock did point out quite well that we can't assume that the policies or the assumptions that are in place today are going to carry forward into the future.

Mr. SAWYER. One set of assumptions that we've been working under for the last 25 years is that older Americans are simply older. You have pointed out the differences between the younger elderly and the older senior citizens, the difference in levels of need, the way in which they live and so forth.

Can you expand on how we might adjust both the way in which we measure needs and derive policy from that diversity within the senior population?

Ms. DEVITA. Well, I think the first factor to remember is that the elderly are a diverse group, and that any time you see a study which talks about the population 65 and older or 75 and older or whatever age group, to ask what diversity is found within that larger grouping. You don't have to scratch too far below the surface before you find some very sharp distinctions.

One issue for example is that life expectancy for women is much higher than for men; rhetorically people have asked will this become a women's issue? Will the issue of aging become a women's issue? I think there needs to be more information on the aging process, ways that could increase men's life expectancy. This could be done, in part by studies that focus on women and compare them to men. A lot of the research and statistics that have been accumulated, the larger studies, have been based on samples of men and less has been done specifically on women. I think we need research agendas that better explore differences by gender as well as by race and some of the other measures that we've talked about today.

Mr. SAWYER. I want to mention that we've been joined by my friend and colleague from Pennsylvania, Tom Ridge, who has been involved in a markup in another committee.

All of us are a part of that window of opportunity that you described. We are part of a generation that is very large, reaching both its prime productive years and it's prime earning years, and that represents a window of opportunity that will close all too soon.

How can we take advantage of that window in the course of this next decade? What are the pivotal policy decisions that you see that respond to that imperative?

Ms. DEVITA. I think first there's a need to educate the public, policymakers, the business community, about these demographic changes that are taking place, so that they're not working simply on stereotypes but on a more factual basis of what to anticipate in the future. So I would begin in that regard, by disseminating the information that we already know about these changes and formulating research agendas on the populations that will be coming up through the ranks.

In terms of policymaking, as I said in my statement, we need to look toward the future and not simply look in terms of an immediate 1- or 2-year time horizon. The time to set the ground work for the baby booms' retirement is now. Baby boomers will need to be aware of various options and problems that they will need to personally prepare for. But also I think there is a role for public policy that cannot be shunted aside. There has to be a marriage between personal responsibility and public sector responsibility. That message has to be better understood by the voting electorate and by our elected officials.

Mr. SAWYER. Let me turn to Mr. Ridge.

Mr. RIDGE. Thank you, Mr. Chairman.

First of all, I apologize to you and our distinguished panelist for being delayed. I would ask unanimous consent that what had hoped to be my opening statement be included in that part of the record that suggested I wanted to be here but couldn't.

Mr. SAWYER. Without objection.

[The prepared statement of Hon. Thomas J. Ridge follows:]

PREPARED STATEMENT OF HON. THOMAS J. RIDGE, A REPRESENTATIVE IN CONGRESS FROM THE STATE OF PENNSYLVANIA

Mr. Chairman, I would like to commend you for scheduling this series of hearings. As the subcommittee that has jurisdiction over the Bureau of Census, it would be pointless for us to have invested all the time that we have over the past four years in overseeing the 1990 Decennial Census, if once the data is released we do not conduct hearings such as these to evaluate what that data tells us about the characteristics of the American people.

Examining America's changing profile has never been as important as it is today. All you have to do is read a current newspaper or magazine to know that we, as policymakers, need a better understanding of the identity of the American people. The media has been saturated with stories on both the decline of the American cities and the decline of family values.

Once the Los Angeles riots themselves subsided, the question all public officials were faced with was what the riots were telling us about the ineffectiveness of our existing social programs. Today we will hear from witnesses about urban change and ghetto revitalization. It is my hope that the distinguished witness will be able to give us some insight into why programs will or will not work, given the current structure of our cities.

Lawmakers cannot live in a vacuum when developing programs and it would be foolish for us to implement policies without knowing who it is that would be effected by those policies. Before we create what possibly could be bad solutions to the problems facing this country, we need to have a better understanding of the people that reside in this country and what their specific needs are. If we do not, then it would be like a coach developing a game plan without first knowing who the players are and what talent they posses.

I welcome our distinguished witnesses and look forward to hearing their testimony.

Mr. RIDGE. I want to follow up with a couple of questions. First of all, I applaud you for the observation you just made, that part of the need for us in the future is to elicit some kind of marriage between the public and private, the individual and the Government, in terms of developing public policy, personal responsibility and public responsibility, I think are the terms you used. I think that is one of the challenges for both parties and the leadership at all levels in the future as we take a look at some of these very interesting and, at times, disturbing trends that will call upon us to marshal our limited resources that we have, confronting some problems that look pretty enormous, and that require some pretty clear-headed thinking. But it has to be done in conjunction with private individuals accepting some responsibility in the effort as well. So I applaud you on that and thank you for that observation.

With regard to the senior citizen population and the demographic information that you had an opportunity to review, are there any economic trends that alarm you, or any economic information that alarms you, with regard to the income security of senior citizens? You also had said earlier we have to be aware of stereotypes as we develop public policy. There is a stereotype that older Americans, senior citizens, all of whom or most of whom live on fixed incomes, have had a diminution in the purchasing power of their aggregate income over the past decade. What are the signs that you see, vis-a-vis senior citizens?

Ms. DeVita. I think one of the important factors to keep in mind is that the Social Security benefit has been indexed for inflation which makes that particular source of income resistant to inflation. Private pensions often do not have any inflation factor and, over time, they will be eroded by inflation. The particular mix of income that any individual has between private pensions, Social Security, personal savings, will be affected by inflation over years.

One way that we have kept many elderly out of poverty has been the indexing of the Social Security benefit, so that has been a positive sign, if you will, toward senior citizen income.

You asked if there were some negative signs, and I think one that I would point out, in terms of thinking toward the future, is the current economic stagnation and recessionary situation that we're in, the loss of well-paying jobs that was discussed earlier this afternoon. If we expect people to save for their income in their older years in order to have enough, in order to join pension plans, I think we have to take a very careful look at today's economy that will enable people to work toward those plans and those situations.

I think the disturbing trend, from my perspective, is the stagnation in our current economy and the need to have public polices that can help improve that situation so that we can build for the future and invest in our future.

Mr. Ridge. With regard to senior citizens' incomes, how are they beginning the decade of the 1990's, vis-a-vis the same demographic group being in the 1980's, as they relate to the rest of the people in this country?

I will frankly tell you a concern that I have and, as a policymaker, we're going to have to start addressing it. There is some indication that there's a group of senior citizens who have done quite well because of their own personal savings, the indexing of Social Security, and good pension plans. They have done extremely well. There is another group of senior citizens that are very comfortable, and, undoubtedly, there's a group of senior citizens who, but for the indexing on Social Security, would have little or no income whatsoever—and those we have to be terribly concerned about.

I happened to check into a hotel a couple of weeks ago and I saw what looked to me to be a very young man—and now that I'm 47, when you see somebody that's 55, they really look young, much younger than I thought a long time ago—pull out his AARP card and get a discount. Now, I understand that, and that's good marketing, good merchandising, and that made a lot of sense to me. But out in the car I saw a younger couple in a less fancy automobile, with two or three kids, and they were coming in and they weren't going to get the discount. So as we go about, as policymakers, trying to figure out what we ought to do to aid those who really need the assistance—and that's really a rough analogy—I'm just concerned that we target our efforts to those really in need.

That's why I asked the question, vis-a-vis other groups, younger people, ages 25 to 35. What is the relative increase or decrease in their aggregate income as opposed to senior citizens, as a demographic group? Do you have that available?

Ms. DeVita. I don't have it on aggregate income. We certainly know, in terms of poverty, that the trend in poverty over the years has gone down for elderly, and that currently almost one in five, I believe it is, children are living in households that are below the poverty level. I think that's an important statistic to keep in mind. Remember, those children are our future and we can't ignore the investment in them.

Mr. Ridge. I can't help but recall, Mr. Chairman, I had a town meeting after we voted on the catastrophic health care bill, and some woman came up to me, very irate, and said why did you do that? I explained to her that it was her demographic group that was going to be the sole beneficiary and I thought the benefits were pretty good. She said, well, you have increased my payments on this and I consider that to be a tax. I said well, I either had to do that or I had to tax your children and your grandchildren, and she said to me tax my children and my grandchildren.

Now, Heaven forbid that—Hopefully, there are very few people out there who are of the same mind, but I do think it's very important that we use these very salient demographic trends, particularly with regard to income security and income opportunity, to help us channel policy in the future.

What about the trends with regard to the location of seniors? I mean, I think Pennsylvania now has the second highest senior population, Florida the first. That obviously has some strategic and political implications as well. What could you tell me about the trends that you see there and what it means in terms of public policy?

Ms. DeVita. Certainly the concentration of elderly tends to be more in the Northeast and Midwest States. We also see a flow of the U.S. population going toward the Sun Belt States.

Since we know that elderly age in place and are going to most likely stay where they spent most of their adult years, are the younger people moving out of the area? If so, that will raise a public policy concern in terms of affording services for the older population left behind. It is particularly critical, I think, in rural communities. The need for services is a difficult one both to finance and to provide. It's going to be a public policy question and an implementation question that will need to be looked at very carefully.

Mr. Ridge. Pennsylvania has the largest rural population some say east of the Mississippi, some say in the entire country. But tell me about the concentration of seniors in rural America today. Is it increasing or decreasing?

Ms. DeVita. I believe it's increasing. It's about one in four. The 1990 census itself hasn't given this type of urban/rural breakout, yet. But based on—I believe it was a 1989 report that came out on rural communities, it looked as if about one in four older persons was living in rural areas. That is an increase from, say, 1980. So it is increasing, caused in part because of the outmigration of the younger workers. Obviously, if jobs and opportunities move into smaller towns and rural areas, it may pull some of the younger working age, middle age population back to those areas.

Mr. RIDGE. I don't know if this question was asked before, but a slightly different direction. Have you seen anything in the review of the data before you that gives us an idea of whether people, the younger generation like Chairman Sawyer and myself, or maybe even younger than that, will be inclined to work as long as our parents and grandparents or less?

Ms. DEVITA. The Social Security Administration has raised the age of retirement for baby boomers and those who come behind so that you won't be receiving full benefits until age 67 rather than 65. There has been a downward trend in the labor force participation rates of older men over the past 20 years, but I think it has plateaued a bit. I don't think that the current trend is to retire at relatively younger ages.

But then again we have an economy that is not as strong as it use to be. Some people are thinking, well, maybe I ought to hold on to this job for just a little while longer in order to make sure that I have enough income for my older years. The retirement trend is tied in part to the course of the economy. But at least based on the Social Security Administration policy, it is not only that you're going to work as long as your parents but maybe a little longer.

Mr. RIDGE. As I recall, I think I voted for that.

I thank you very much for your very stimulating and very interesting and provocative testimony. Thank you, Mr. Chairman.

Mr. SAWYER. Let me return to a question that Mr. Ridge's inquiry suggested. He was talking about sliding scales of eligibility. Dr. Binstock made reference to the importance of developing revenue streams that are more sensitive to the Nation's broader measures of productivity rather than the specific number of workers who may be in the workforce at any given time, as the FICA tax does.

Do you have any sense of what kinds of measurements of productivity might better track the development of that kind of revenue stream?

Ms. DEVITA. I think I would have to defer to Dr. Binstock and let him explain what he had in mind in that case.

Mr. SAWYER. He told us you were his student and that you could answer any questions——

[Laughter.]

Ms. DEVITA. It is true that I was his student, but I defer to the professor.

Mr. SAWYER. I can appreciate that.

Let me then broaden the question to the same question I have asked others. Are there measurements that would better serve the needs of the changing population that could refine our vision of the future, that we ought to be taking either as a matter of decennial census or intercensal measurements?

Ms. DEVITA. I think the intercensal suggestion is one that is well thought of. It is a long time between censuses, and what is really needed, I think, for many programs, not just those for the elderly and the aging, are to get data that is more specific to local communities——

Mr. SAWYER. Let me interrupt. I've gotten the same answer. What I'm asking you is not whether intercensal data makes more sense. I think we all agree that, particularly as we can use sampling to expand and make more timely our receipt of information, it's good, particularly at a time when change is so rapid. But are there specific measures that are not part of the current intercensal effort that you think we ought to focus on, that are particularly important at a time of change, at a pace that we're undergoing right now?

Ms. DeVita. Perhaps one measure that is not very detailed in our current census is a measure of disability or health. Now, there are other surveys that give you those measures, but at least for the older population, many service needs will be tied to their level of health or their level of disability. This will also apply to younger populations as well. With the Americans with Disabilities Act, I think it's important that we get better measures, particularly at a local level, so that people can better understand and plan for the needs that are out there.

Mr. Sawyer. Thank you.

Thank you very much for your testimony today. If there is no further business to come before us, we stand adjourned.

[Whereupon, at 2:47 p.m., the subcommittee adjourned.]

AMERICA'S CHANGING PROFILE: "HOW WE LIVE: HOUSEHOLD, FAMILY, AND INCOME PATTERNS"

TUESDAY, JUNE 23, 1992

HOUSE OF REPRESENTATIVES,
SUBCOMMITTEE ON CENSUS AND POPULATION,
COMMITTEE ON POST OFFICE AND CIVIL SERVICE,
Washington, DC.

The subcommittee met, pursuant to call, at 1 p.m., in room 311, Cannon House Office Building, Hon. Thomas C. Sawyer (chairman of the subcommittee) presiding.

Member present: Representative Sawyer.

Mr. SAWYER. Good afternoon. I want to welcome our witnesses this afternoon.

This is the second set in a series of hearings we are conducting this year. It is entitled "America's Changing Profile." Its purpose is to examine demographic trends and the policy implications contained within them.

The 1990 census continues to reveal striking information that is central to our ability to understand who we are as a nation and where we are going, and to take the steps today to address the needs of a nation as we move forward into the future.

Last month we looked at several significant population trends. We discussed dramatic changes in the demographic forces that are redefining who we are.

Three primary trends emerged from that hearing. First, the nation is aging. It is aging in several ways, but among the numbers that are particularly telling is the fact that by the first third of the next century, fully one in five Americans will be over 65. That is more than double the current senior population.

Second, a quarter of us today are people of color. This represents a surprisingly rapid rate of growth among minority populations. The term "minority" as we use it today may not have the kinds of meaning that it has had in the past. It may become obsolete.

We learned the growing racial and ethnic diversity of our country is not evenly spread across the country. It is not evenly spread among age groups. Far more children than older Americans will be people of color.

If we just divide our population into two halves, those over 45 and those under 45, by the beginning of the next century one in five of those over 45 will be people of color. One in three of those under 45 will be people of color. That kind of divergence of interests and needs represents a marked policy challenge.

Third, we learned that an awful lot of American children are poor. Children are more likely to live in poverty than adults, and a disproportionate share of those children are minorities.

Over the next 30 years, the interests of the oldest and the youngest among us increasingly will dominate policy debate. Our greatest challenge will be to find commonality across a chasm of years that threatens to divide us.

The growing needs of older Americans will be greater if for no other reasons than by virtue of their sheer numbers alone. At the same time, the changing structure of American families, unattended, will continue to make children even more vulnerable.

Right now a quarter of all families at any one time are headed by only one parent. That is the more than twice as many as 20 years ago. But more telling than that, more than half, about 57 percent, of all young children in single-parent families live in poverty. That is a number that ought to be chilling to virtually every American.

Last month we examined the growing elderly population in some detail. Today, we are going to focus on the changing characteristics of our children and the families they live in. Tomorrow, we will look at income patterns.

We are going to try and look at all of this together over the course of this series of hearings. I think it is important to resist the temptation to look at each of these kinds of issues in a vacuum. They are very closely connected to one another. The numbers challenge us to balance divergent interests with solutions that bridge our differences and meet our disparate needs.

The census provides the means of understanding the movement of people and to understand the change as it occurs.

Our witnesses today represent some leading authorities in their field. I look forward to our review and discussion. I want to thank the Population Resource Center and the Congressional Research Service for their continuing assistance in preparing for these hearings.

Let me at this point, without objection, insert into the record a statement by our colleague, Congresswoman Patricia Schroeder, who chairs the Select Committee on Children, Youth and Families, and thank her for her contribution to these proceedings today.

[The prepared statement of Hon. Patricia Schroeder follows:]

Prepared Statement of Hon. Patricia Schroeder, a Representative in Congress From the State of Colorado

Mr. Chairman, I commend you for holding this series of hearings on "America's Changing Profile." The recent riots in Los Angeles and other cities around the country point out the need to understand how the makeup of American citizenry is evolving and to reevaluate policies and programs in light of these changes.

As Chairwoman of the Select Committee on Children, Youth, and Families, I am particularly concerned about the changing nature of America's families and the need to develop long-term federal policies to meet their needs. Toward that end, the Select Committee held a hearing this past February on "America's Families: Conditions, Trends, Hopes and Fears." Census Bureau and Bureau of Labor Statistics experts told the Committee about major changes in family structure and family labor force participation rates that have occurred over the past 20 years. Other witnesses described additional demographic shifts and concerns based on surveys of family well-being and other measures.

What the Select Committee found—and I'm sure these hearings will confirm those findings—is that American families come in all shapes and sizes. It's time we stopped bickering over what an "Ozzie and Harriet" family is and how many of them there are, and instead focus on the fact that the diversity of families means that if we want America to have "family-friendly policies," we must recognize that we need many options for many types of families.

One of the overriding concerns of American families—whether they be one- or two-parent households—is their economic vulnerability. Survey findings presented at the Select Committee hearing documented parental concerns about their family's economic well-being and their children:

• A survey commissioned by the National Commission on Children (NCC survey) found that 55 percent of parents worry that their income won't meet their family's expenses.

• The NCC survey found that parents at every income level worry about their children's physical safety. Nearly one-half of those parents surveyed said that there was no safe place in their neighborhood for children and teens to gather.

• Dr. Vince Breglio, a Republican pollster, testified that his surveys indicate that "when shown a list of items for which families must budget . . . half of the worries focus(ed) on items related to health care cost."

• A survey commissioned by KIDS COUNT revealed "a deep concern over the diminished ability of many American families to meet the core needs of their children."

The immediate economic concerns of families are real and have been exacerbated by a prolonged recession.

They have been further exacerbated by a decline in real wages for many workers, particularly young workers.

They have been fueled by the skyrocketing cost of housing and health care.

Conservatives who have testified before the Select Committee have called for policies and programs to help bolster two-parent families so that one parent can remain at home with the children—policies such as increasing the federal dependent exemption and the recently-expanded Earned Income Credit. And they are right—for some families. If families were more economically stable, they might need to have only one worker in the labor force. But increasing the exemption or the Earned Income Credit alone cannot provide that stability for all families.

Others who have testified before the Select Committee have called for policies and programs to help bolster one-parent families and two-parent families where both parents are in the paid labor force—policies such as child care subsidies, Family and Medical Leave, and the Dependent Care Credit. And they are right—for other families. Some families cannot have one parent remain at home, either because there is only one parent or because the high cost of living and low wages necessitate two workers just to keep a family afloat financially.

America will not return to the more homogeneous 1950s-era families just as America will not return to the horse- and buggy-era days. We can't "wish away" single parents or two-earner families and it's time that we stopped blaming mothers for working—or in the case of welfare recipients, for not working—when in fact all they are doing is trying to hold their families together in the best way they can.

It's important that we understand the problems that single parents face in their parenting role as well as the impact of single-parenthood on children and society.

We need to develop federal family policies that help both the single parent and the child who is from a single-parent home.

We need to develop policies that encourage fathers to take a more active role in parenting, whether they live with their children or not.

We need to develop stronger carrot and stick approaches to ensuring that parents provide economic support for their children, whether they live with them or not.

Mr. Chairman, I am gratified that you have undertaken this series of hearings to focus attention on what the America of the 1990s and 21st century really looks like. I only hope that our colleagues are listening so that as we continue to debate policies and programs affecting families, we can at least agree on who it is we are trying to help.

I would like to submit the attached information for the record summary.

U.S. House of Representatives,
Select Committee on Children, Youth, and Families,
Washington, DC, February 19, 1992.

AMERICA'S FAMILIES: CONDITIONS, TRENDS, HOPES AND FEARS—A FACT SHEET

FAMILY SIZE CONTINUES TO SHRINK, MORE COUPLES POSTPONE STARTING FAMILIES

Families are postponing having children. and are having fewer of them. In 1973. 6 out of 10 families had at least one child under age 18 and the average number of children per family was 2.2. In 1990, only about half of all families had a child under 18, and the average number of children was 1.8. (U.S. Bureau of the Census [Census], 1992)

Of all families with children, the proportion with one parent increased from 13% in 1970 to 28% in 1990. (Census, 1990)

The proportion of households without children headed by 25 to 44 year-olds nearly doubled from 20% in 1960 to 37% in 1988. Households without children have a median income per person that is 67% higher than households with two children. (Fuchs & Reklis, 1992)

FAMILY INCOMES STAGNATE DESPITE MOTHERS IN THE LABOR FORCE

Of all families with children, the percentage with two parents or the only parent in the labor force rose from 56% in 1980 to 66% in 1991. (Bureau of Labor Statistics [BLS] 1992)

Between 1979 and 1989, two-parent families with children in the middle fifth of the income spectrum ($35,000–$47,000 in 1989) experienced a 4% increase in income. Wives' $3,300 increase in average earnings accounted for this increase, but four-fifths of this gain came from increased hours rather than from increased hourly pay. (Joint Economic Committee, 1992)

Real median income of young families with children declined from $23,705 (in 1990 dollars) in 1970 to $16,219 in 1990, a 32% decrease. (Census, 1992)

Middle-income, dual-earner families with a wife employed outside the home lose up to 56% of the additional income to work-related expenses. (Hanson and Ooms. 1991)

MILLIONS OF FAMILIES TEETER ON EDGE OF POVERTY/MANY FALL IN

From 1980 to 1990, the number of families with children living in poverty increased by 854,000 to a rate of 16.4%. (Census, 1991)

From July 1989 through November 1991, 900,000 families were added to the Aid to Families with Dependent Children [AFDC] program, reaching a new caseload record of 4.6 million families. Two thousand children a day go on AFDC; one in seven American children receives AFDC. (American Public Welfare Association, 1992)

In November 1991, 24.6 million Americans received food stamps, a 15% increase over November 1990. One in ten Americans receives food stamps. (U.S. Department of Agriculture [USDA], 1992)

Forty-three percent of the increase in poverty between 1979 and 1989 was due to the reduced effectiveness of AFDC, Food Stamps, Unemployment Insurance, and other government benefit programs. (Committee on Way and Means [Ways and Means], U.S. House of Representatives, 1991)

CHILDREN'S WELL-BEING PLUMMETS

Children are the poorest Americans. While the poverty rate for all Americans was 13.5% in 1990, 20.6% of children lived in poverty, up from 18.3% in 1980. Among children under age 6, 23% lived in poverty in 1990, up from 20.3% in 1980. (Census, 1991)

The teenage suicide rate tripled from 3.6/100,000 in 1960 to 11.3/100,000 in 1980 and 1988 alone, the teen suicide rate increased more than 30%. (Fuchs and Reklis, 1992)

U.S. school children ranked 14th in math and 13th in science abilities in a 15-country international comparison of 13-year-olds. Standardized test scores fell between 1988 and 1991, with results on the verbal portion reaching an all-time low. (Educational Testing Service, 1992; Fuchs and Reklis, 1992)

FINANCIAL PRESSURES ON FAMILIES MOUNT

It will cost a middle-income family ($26,000–$42,000 in 1987 pre-tax income) an estimated $210,070 to raise a child born in 1990 to age 17. (USDA, 1991)

Of the 36 million Americans without health insurance, children constitute 28%. Two-thirds of uninsured children live in families where at least one person was employed throughout 1990. (Employee Benefit Research Institute, 1992)

Average annual health payments by families amounted to 11.7% of average family income in 1991, up from 9% of average family income in 1980. Based on current projections, average health payments will consume 16.4% of average family income by the year 2000. (Families USA Foundation, 1991)

The cost of a college education continues to outpace inflation. In 1989/90, the average cost of a four-year postsecondary education ranged from $4,979 at a public institution to $12,348 at a private one. The comparable figures for 1976–77 were $1,935 and $3,977. (U.S. Department of Education, 1991)

Families spend an estimated $15.5 billion annually on child care. (Census, 1990)

FAMILY DEBT RISES: PERSONAL SAVINGS DECLINE

Outstanding household debt rose approximately $2 trillion (to a total of about $3 trillion) during the 1980s. (Economic Policy Institute, 1990)

The personal savings rate fell from 7.9% of disposable personal income in 1980 to 5.3% in 1991. (U.S. Department of Commerce, 1992)

INCREASING UNEMPLOYMENT THREATENS FAMILIES' ECONOMIC SECURITY

The unemployment rate rose from 5.2% in June 1990 to 7.1% in January 1992. But in 1991, just 42% of the unemployed received unemployment compensation, compared with 75% in 1975. (Ways and Means, 1992)

During the fourth quarter of 1989, 5.6% of families with children had an unemployed parent. That figure rose to 7.4% during the fourth quarter of 1991. (BLS, 1992)

The number of workers employed part time involuntarily rose from 4.4% in 1980 to 5.2% in 1991. (BLS, 1992)

PROVIDING A HOME REMAINS DIFFICULT FOR FAMILIES

Homeownership rates among young households fell sharply during the 1980s. For households aged 25–29, homeownership fell from 43% in 1980 to 36% in 1990, while for households aged 30–34, the rate dropped from 61% to 52%. (Joint Center for Housing Studies [JCHS], 1991)

Of married-couple families with children, 91% of renters and 32% of homeowners cannot afford a median-priced home in their region. (Census, 1991)

U.S. HOUSE OF REPRESENTATIVES,
SELECT COMMITTEE ON CHILDREN, YOUTH, AND FAMILIES,
Washington, DC, February 19, 1992.

HEARING SUMMARY—"AMERICA'S FAMILIES: CONDITIONS, TRENDS, HOPES AND FEARS"

On February 19, 1992, the Select Committee on Children, Youth, and Families held a hearing entitled "America's Families: Conditions, Trends, Hopes and Fears" that examined the changing demographic, economic, and social conditions of families, and children and families' concerns regarding their present well-being and prospects for the future. Statisticians and economists highlighted trends in family composition, income status, labor force participation, and economic security. Pollsters discussed families' economic, educational, employment, and health worries.

The Honorable John D. Rockefeller IV, Member, United States Senate; Chairman, National Commission on Children, Washington, DC, summarized two National Commission on Children surveys on family well-being. According to the surveys, the public believes that it is harder to be a parent today than it used to be, that parents do not spend enough time with their children, and that children are worse off today than were their parents as children. Most parents (55%) worry at least some of the time that their income will not meet their family expenses, and that they give up time with their children to make ends meet. Almost 60% of parents said they wanted to spend more time with their children. Despite economic pressures, parents and children report close relationships and family ties.

Jason Zimbler, Actor, Nickelodeon show "Clarissa Explains It All," New York, NY, reported findings of a Nickelodeon/Yankelovich Youth Monitor national poll of 1200 children ages 6–17. Despite changes in family arrangements, children report that they spend significant time with their families: 78% of children eat dinner with their parents; 90% usually spend some time with a parent each evening. Between 60% and 90% of children recognize that their parents want them to do well in school, to get their homework done, and to get into college. The chief worry of young people is the need to make money (51%), followed by AIDS (48%), getting into college (46%), and drugs (45%). Young people are concerned with important national issues, including homelessness and teacher compensation. Most children report that they like school (84%) and that they do well in class (78% average A's or B's). After-school activities include doing chores (91%), watching television (79%), eating snacks (77%) and doing homework (71%).

Celinda Lake, Vice President, Green/Lake, Washington, DC, analyzed recent polling data on family well-being. Polls show that Americans believe they live in tough times which will not soon improve. Nearly half (49%) of Americans believe that the family is worse off than 10 years ago; only 39% believe it is better off; and 70% believe that children's well-being has decreased in the last 5 years. Most Americans (88%) believe that they are middle-class, although they believe that the middle class is disappearing. A majority of Americans (57%) believe that it is now impossible to support a family on one income. Families worry about how they will make ends meet, whether someone will lose a job, and their children's futures. Americans want to make families and children a national priority, expect government to act, and are willing to hold politicians accountable.

Vincent J. Breglio, Ph.D., President, RSM, Inc., Lanham, MD, evaluated polling results on economic and family issues. Although Americans believe the national economy is extremely troubled, the number who believe their family's financial situation is in poor shape has not increased during the recession. Yet more families today report that they have cut back on savings, investments, and spending than in March 1991. Major concerns over family budgets focus on health care and education. Although 73% of families express satisfaction with their own health care, 62% are not satisfied with the cost. After health care, housing, and retirement costs, the chief cost families worry most about is college education (12%).

Donald Hernandez, Ph.D., Chief, Marriage and Families Statistics Branch, Populations Division, Bureau of the Census, U.S. Department of Commerce, Washington, DC, reported trends in family income and economic status, maternal labor force participation, and homeownership. According to Hernandez, a major change in family living situations involved the dramatic increase in dual-earner, two-parent families. Labor force participation of wives with children under age 6 doubled between 1970 and 1990, from 30% to 59%.

By 1991, 63% of all two-parent families had both a mother and father in the labor force. While real median family income for married-couple families more than doubled between 1947 and 1973, it increased only 11% between 1873 and 1990. Single-parent families fared even worse by 1990, with real median incomes only 5% higher than in 1973. Hernandez documented that family householders who are young or who have low levels of education also have comparatively low family incomes. Such families experience difficulity purchasing necessities, goods, or services, especially a home. In 1968, an estimated 60% to 82% of married couple renters with incomes of $35,000 to $60,000 could not afford to buy a median priced house. The proportion of two-parent families that owned their own home decreased from 77% in 1980 to about 73% in 1990.

Thomas J. Plewes, Associate Commissioner for Employment and Unemployment Statistics, Bureau of Labor Statistics, U.S. Department of Labor, Washington, DC, described trends in family composition and parental labor force activity. From 1980 to 1991, the percent of families with children containing one parent increased from 20% to 26%. In 1991, maternal labor force participation reached 67%, and two-parent, two-worker families grew from 42% to 48% of all families with children between 1980 and 1991. The current economic recession has hurt families: 7.4% of families with children contained an unemployed parent at the close of 1991, up from 5.6% two years earlier.

Gary L. Bauer, President, Family Research Council, Washington, DC, testified that the family unit is weaker today than a generation ago. Decreased family time and busier household schedules have left children with greater responsibility to make moral choices and decreased well-being (measured by suicide and homicide rates, SAT scores, and sexual involvement). According to Bauer, breakdowns in cultural value consensus and criminal justice effectiveness have left parents feeling isolated, without adequate support, and skeptical of social institutions that formerly reinforced family values. Bauer called for an increase in the per-child tax benefits available to wage-earning families and recommended no dramatic increase in children's program spending.

David Blankenhorn, President, Institute for American Values, New York, NY, criticized the practice of "trickle-down" polling, through which a poll is prepared to reveal a predetermined opinion. Blankenhorn accused recent polls on family and child well-being of this practice. He said these polls incorrectly link declining child well-being to declining economic conditions; more accurate "bottom-up" polls have linked child well-being to declining cultural values. Blankenhorn claimed that the result of "trickledown" polling is a widening of the gap between what Americans believe and what policymakers are told that Americans believe. He called for greater attention to cultural priorities, including parental time with children, divorce, unwed parenthood, the role of fathers, and safe places for children to play.

Robert Rector, Policy Analyst, Family and Welfare Issues, The Heritage Foundation, Washington, DC, argued that families' economic troubles are due to overtaxation, a slowdown in the growth of parents' real wages and salaries, and increases in single parenthood. Increases in taxes as a share of family income now consume over one-third of a two-parent family's income, and many families have been forced to place both parents in the work force to achieve even modest income growth. Rector claimed that a sound national family policy should include tax cuts for families, tax cuts on savings and investments, and welfare system incentives to promote responsible behavior. In order to contain the Federal deficit, he recommended matching family tax relief dollars with domestic spending reductions.

Judith Weitz, KIDS COUNT Coordinator, The Center for the Study of Social Policy, Washington, DC, reported the results of the KIDS COUNT national survey of registered voters concerning the recession's impact on children and families. Two-thirds of voters believe children are worse off than a generation ago. Voters polled demonstrated a deep concern over families' diminished ability to meet children's needs: asked to identify the chief impact of the recession on children, voters named a lack of adequate food, housing, and clothing (25%), a deterioration of public school education (22%), inadequate health insurance (18%), and inability to afford child care (14%). Voters identified several policies as the most beneficial to children—guaranteed health insurance for all children (26%), more family-oriented business practices (family medical leave, etc.) (20%), a refundable tax credit for families with children (18%), increased education funding (16%), and publicly-supported child care (12%).

Greg J. Duncan, Ph.D., Program Director, Survey Research Center, University of Michigan, Ann Arbor, testified that the middle class shrunk during the 1980s. Based on a University of Michigan longitudinal study of families, Duncan reported that the proportion of families with children in the middle class fell 11% between 1978 and 1990. Increased inequality of earned income led to three trends—upward mobility into upper-income status, downward mobility into lower-income status, and a lack of upward mobility on the part of low-income families. These trends reflected income, education, and job skills gaps, and added two million families with children to the ranks of low-income families in the 1980s. Duncan made several policy recommendations, including job training programs for unemployed parents, improved technical job training for high school students, and a refundable child income tax credit.

Mr. SAWYER. Our first panel today will be composed of two witnesses, Dr. Frances K. Goldscheider, professor of sociology, and director, population studies and training center, Brown University; and Katharine B. Hazzard, director of work/family programs, John Hancock Mutual Life Insurance Co.

Will you join us at the table, please? Welcome to you both. Thank you for being here.

STATEMENTS OF FRANCES K. GOLDSCHEIDER, PROFESSOR OF SOCIOLOGY, AND DIRECTOR, POPULATION STUDIES AND TRAINING CENTER, BROWN UNIVERSITY; AND KATHARINE B. HAZZARD, DIRECTOR OF WORK/FAMILY PROGRAMS, JOHN HANCOCK MUTUAL LIFE INSURANCE

Ms. GOLDSCHEIDER. I would like to start by raising the question of not only what is going on and who is doing it, but who is not there.

Often when we study something we miss what is not there. I learned this when I started studying living arrangements and realized everybody who was studying the family was missing the people who were not living in families.

People are used to hearing discussions of what is happening to the American family, and I am going to talk about men, the ones who are not there. We have been living through a period of very rapid family change. We are familiar with many of the changes. Some of them have been summarized before and some will be later today.

What there is less agreement about is, what does it all mean? Two issues are clear.

First, marriage between men and women has become confusing, with rules of men's and women's behavior that are changing rapidly, leaving marriages between them unstable.

Second, the alternatives to marriage have never looked better. Unmarried adults have options for independence and privacy that are unique. Prior to World War II, relatively few of the unmarried lived independently. And it is this that is the most revolutionary.

The gender role revolution is less revolutionary than many like to think. And the story is more complicated than is usually told. It is important to ignore the 1950's, and instead go back to the early 19th century, when families were relatively large, adult lives were relatively short, and the work of supporting everyone belonged to everyone and was unending.

Then men's and women's lives were not the same, but they were both responsible for producing the food, clothing, furniture, and even capital equipment on which their survival depended. They were a joint production team. They worked together to make this homes, knowledgeable and aware of what the other was doing and how good he or she was at it. Not just women looked for a provider, but men did, as well, assessing their potential wives with an eye as much to their productive capacities as to their personalities.

Further, both parents were responsible for the care, training, social, and moral development of their children, supervising them all day long. Women may have been the primary caretakers of infants, but by the time toddling children were aware of their surroundings, their fathers were as much a force in their parental relationships as their mothers, and, given their greater authority, probably even more. "Lessons" on child development were aimed at fathers, not mothers, and by ministers in sermons, rather than professionals.

That is the true "traditional family," and any time anyone uses this term to apply to anything else, pay no attention to them. Anthropologists link this term to the establishment of settled agriculture, a family which all aspired to attain. Without a family, a man had almost no stature in the community, and a woman had very little as well. The home was the center of their economic lives, but as today, it was also the center of their emotional lives. Men and women may not have chosen each other, but as with parents and children, who also don't choose each other, most learned to love each other as they learned to respect and depend upon each other in the course of living together.

This traditional family of the early 19th century is a far cry from the "traditional" family of the 1950's, which is our more common referrent, the Cleavers and all of that. The 1950's family is the family of separate spheres, by which time not only were men out in the world while women were confined to the home, but also greater ideological and psychological embroideries were constructed to echo this great split. Men were supposed to be "active" while women were "passive," even in childraising and home making, and men tough and cold while women were warm and caring.

Those of us who lived through the 1950's can remember this somewhat painfully. Many tried to convince themselves that this was the way they should be.

It was the result of a century of increasing alienation of men from their homes and families, as their non-home work hours increased; an alienation so profound that today, the only component of the father role anyone can agree on is financial.

Individual fathers who want to be good parents find themselves without guidance in choosing among being a distant, benign judge, an involved coach and mentor, or a warm and caring friend, or trying, impossibly, to be all three.

One consequence is that society polarized men and women, and focused on ways that they are different rather than placing these differences in the context of what it means to be a caring and productive adult.

This has led to the promulgation of a series of destructive myths. One, that masculine and feminine are somehow opposite ends of a single dimension. Everybody thinks that way. I have asked so many and all agree: It turns out that they are nearly unrelated—the men and women with the healthiest personalities are those that can both initiate and care when the need arises; that men and women who have blocked one or the other realm often have serious difficulties; and those who can do neither, the failed nerds of this world, are in the worst shape.

Two, another myth is that in marriage, opposites attract. There is simply no evidence for this, and every evidence that shared interests, backgrounds, activities, and daily schedules, are the major sources of marital happiness, but young courting people feel that opposites are mysterious and romantic, and then expect to build enduring marriages with the opposites they become romantically involved with.

Three, and the final myth we owe to the creation of separate spheres is that marriage is for women, that men don't like to be or need to be married. In a cartoon in Psychology Today, which I remember because they ran it over an article of mine, Woody Allen, sitting in a bar with Sigmund Freud, asks, "Is it true that married men live longer?" And Freud replies, "No, it just feels longer."

My research has seen it differently. This, despite the great wave of research showing that it is much better to be married than to be unmarried in terms of physical health, mental health, mortality, and general happiness, and that these differences are much greater for men than for women.

So we say marriage and family are for women but men benefit the most from it. Data are beginning to emerge that portray men as victims of the gender revolution in unexpected ways.

We have watched women changing for several decades. Now the critical question is, will men? Will they learn that being estranged from the children they fathered and then left is painful, and leads to a lonely old age? Will they learn that being married benefits them, and begin to communicate with, negotiate with, and respect the women who might become, or stay, their wives, and the co-parents of their children?

I am really concerned. And the men's remarriage rates after divorce or widowhood are falling. There was an article that said widowed women did not want to remarry. The proportion of first married men who say they can count on their children in a pinch is 90 percent; of remarried men is less than half.

In many ways, the contemporary gender revolution is a cry to return to productive roles for women and family roles for men. But most of the emphasis has been on the first, as women find that paychecks are useful, while few men see value in reclaiming a major role in their homes and their family's lives. I am concerned that we may have lost the way back, since it requires that we go forward.

Mr. SAWYER. Thank you.

[The prepared statement of Ms. Goldscheider follows:]

PREPARED STATEMENT OF FRANCES K. GOLDSCHEIDER, PROFESSOR OF SOCIOLOGY, AND DIRECTOR, POPULATION STUDIES AND TRAINING CENTER, BROWN UNIVERSITY

FAMILY CHANGE OLD AND NEW [1]

We have been living through a period of very rapid family change. We are familiar with many of the changes. What there is less agreement about is: what does it all mean? Two issues are clear: First, marriage has become confusing, with rules of men's and women's behavior that are changing rapidly, leaving marriages between them unstable. Second, the alternatives to marriage have never looked better. Unmarried adults have options for independence and privacy that are unique. Prior to World War II, relatively few of the unmarried lived independently. And it is this that is the most revolutionary.

The gender role revolution is less revolutionary than many like to think. It is important to ignore the 1950s, and instead go back to the early 19th century, when families were relatively large, adult lives were relatively short, and the work of supporting everyone belonged to everyone and was unending. Then, men's and women's lives were not the same, but they were both responsible for producing the food, clothing, furniture, and even capital equipment on which their survival depended. Men and women worked together to make their homes, knowledgeable and aware of what the other was doing and how good he or she was at it. Not just women looked for a provider, but men did, as well, assessing their potential wives with an eye as much to their productive capacities as to their personalities.

Further, both parents were responsible for the care, training, social, and moral development of their children, supervising them all day long. Women may have been the primary caretakers of infants, but by the time toddling children were aware of their surroundings, their fathers were as much a force in their parental relationships as their mothers, and, given their greater authority, probably even more. "Lessons" on child development were aimed at fathers, not mothers (and by ministers in sermons, rather than professionals).

That is the true "traditional family" which anthropologists link to the establishment of settled agriculture, a family which all aspired to attain. Without a family, a man had almost no stature in the community, and a woman had very little, as well. The home was the center of their economic lives, but as today, it was also the center of their emotional lives. Men and women may not have chosen each other, but as with parents and children, who also don't choose each other, most learned to love

---

[1] Reflections subsequent to publishing a book on families (*New Families, No Families: The Transformation of the American Home* with Linda Waite) University of California Press, 1991.

each other as they learned to respect and depend upon each other in the course of living together.

This traditional family of the early 19th century is a far cry from the "traditional" family of the 1950's which is our more common referent. The 1950's family is the family of "separate spheres," by which time not only were men "out in the world" while women were confined to the home, but also greater ideological and psychological embroideries were constructed to echo this great split. Men were supposed to be "active" while women were "passive" (even in childraising and home making) and men tough and cold while women were warm and caring (and many tried to convince themselves that this was the way they should be).

It was the result of a century of increasing alienation of men from their homes and families, as their nonhome work hours increased; an alienation so profound that today, the only component of the father role anyone can agree on is financial. Individual fathers who want to be good parents find themselves without guidance in choosing among being a distant, benign judge, an involved coach and mentor, or a warm and caring friend—or trying, impossibly, to be all three.

One consequence is that society polarized men and women, and focused on ways that they are different rather than placing these differences in the context of what it means to be a caring and productive adult. This has led to the promulgation of a series of destructive myths:

1. That masculine and feminine are somehow opposite ends of a single dimension. It turns out that they are nearly unrelated—the men and women with the healthiest personalities are those that can both initiate AND care when the need arises; that men and women who have blocked one or the other realm often have serious difficulties; and those who can do neither—the failed nerds of this world—are in the worst shape.

2. Another myth is that in marriages opposites attract. There is simply no evidence for this, and every evidence that shared interests, backgrounds, activities, and daily schedules, are the major sources of marital happiness, but young courting people feel that opposites are mysterious and romantic, and then expect to build enduring marriages with the opposites they become romantically involved with.

3. And the final myth the we owe to the creation of separate spheres is that marriage is for women; that men don't like to be or need to be married. In a cartoon in Psychology Today, Woody Allen, sitting in a bar with Sigmund Freud, asks "Is it true that married men live longer?" And Freud replies, "No, it just feels longer." This despite the great wave of research showing that it is much better to be married than to be unmarried in terms of physical health, mental health, mortality, and general happiness—and that these differences are much greater for men than for women.

Data are beginning to emerge that portray men as victims of the gender revolution in unexpected ways. We have watched women changing for several decades; now the critical question is: will men? Will they learn that being estranged from the children they fathered and then left is painful, and leads to a lonely old age? Will they learn that being married benefits them, and begin to communicate with, negotiate with, and respect the women who might become—or stay—their wives?

- Men's remarriage rates after divorce or widowhood are falling.
- The proportion of first married men who say they can count on their children in a pinch is 90%; of remarried men is less than half.

In many ways, the contemporary gender revolution is a cry to return to productive roles for women and family roles for men. But most of the emphasis has been on the first—as women find that paychecks are useful—while few men see value in reclaiming a major role in their homes and their family's lives. I am concerned that we may have lost the way back, since it requires that we go forward.

Mr. Sawyer. Ms. Hazzard?

Ms. Hazzard. Good afternoon. I am proud to be here representing John Hancock Financial Services in Boston.

We, as a corporation, I think, have really plugged into the changing demographics and what that means to America's workers. John Hancock does an employee attitude survey every 2 years.

Over the course of the 1980's, it became more and more clear to the John Hancock management that school-age care were more and more prevalent among employees and causing more stress and strain. At the same time, the report "Workforce 2000" was released in 1988, and it confirmed that which we were finding at Hancock.

We at that point launched into a study of work family issues as they pertained to John Hancock to see what the company could or could not do. We cannot please all the people all the time, though some of our employees would like us to.

We discussed the issues with leading experts in the field, visited child care centers, consulted with management at Hancock and other companies, and ultimately came up with proposals that went into effect in January 1990. Some of those proposals and initiatives that were agreed upon were also programs that had been in place prior to 1990 but were going to be expanded upon.

One thing I might point out is that one of the very first things Hancock did was come up with a corporate statement on how it feels to employees balancing their work and family lives. You will find a copy of that corporate statement in the "Life Styles/Work Styles" brochure.

To give you a feel for the workforce, women comprise 62 percent of the home-office population. Almost 20 percent of our employees have a school age child, more than 12 percent of our employees have primary elder care responsibilities.

Once again, our population reflects that of the nation. With this in mind, as I said, we came up with a number of initiatives, some of which I will describe. There are more outlined in the "Life Styles/Work Styles" brochure, but I will just name a few.

The company embarked upon creating its own on-site child care center. It opened in November 1990. It occupies two floors of a building within sight of the John Hancock Tower. We have room enough for 200 children aged 8 weeks through kindergarten.

As a parent, I can appreciate the fact that you can leave off an 8-week-old baby and not have to worry about care for that child again until school age care in first grade. It boggles the minds of those of us who have juggled through kindergarten double sessions.

The center is fabulous. We have a playground on one side for infants and toddlers, and one on the other side for pre-school and kindergarteners. The centers are based on the theme of Boston and a certain class is situated on streets, so a child might reside on Mt. Vernon Street to make it as homey as possible and give them a sense of community.

There is an inside playroom, although I think this is called professionally a youth coordination room. We call that the Boston Common. There is a messy room. I choose to call that the Boston Harbor. There is a drain in the middle of that floor so kids can be hosed down if necessary! There is a dry enrichment room, which is the computer room and a little bit of a library room. We are also very proud to have an area that is separately ventilated, which is a mildly ill area with a full-time registered nurse who is there. We also have an indoor garden with a running brook. For a lot of those children who have had never seen a running brook, it doesn't matter that it is man-made.

Needless to say, security is very important in a downtown location. The joke was that our security director, a ex-Marine, was going to bar code all the children and that was the only way they would get in and out! We came up with an screen identification system where the employee's face pops up on the screen so there is no chance of anyone getting in without proper identification.

Another program of which I am very proud is "Kids To Go." It was started on Martin Luther King's birthday, 1990, for children age 7 to 14. John Hancock employees expressed a concern about school holidays when school is out but Hancock is at work. Employees may bring their children in as early as 7:30 in the morning to a central location at Hancock. We do it in conjunction with Ellis Memorial and Eldredge House, Inc.; a non-profit social agency, and they loan us staff.

Essentially, the children go off and do field trips using Hancock as a home base. The cost is $20 per day per child, and it includes all costs and administration and transportation fees. The cost to us is less than $2,000 a year.

The point to that is that it doesn't necessarily have to be an expensive solution. There are ways around major bucks.

It has been extraordinarily well received by employees and children alike. In fact, my daughter has made a friend. The Kids To Go program is going on this week and they are trading households. Tomorrow night Katy comes to our place and Thursday night Laura goes to hers. I have gotten to know her father. City kids have gotten to know suburban kids, and have taught them to stay away from the third rail and why!

The third one is elder care. I understand you did elder care last time so I won't spend too much time. Needless to say elder care is doing nothing but grow. Hancock has a service where an employee can call a licensed social worker and get help with relation to a elder's health and well-being. An employee can get anything from the wording of a living will to information on health to one of my best stories, which is an employee who called and said his father had been diagnosed with a terminal disease and wanted to go back to his county in Ireland to die. The service found him a nursing home in Ireland to go to. This cost nothing to the employee. You can imagine the time that would have been spent and expense by that employee trying to make those same arrangements, and more likely than not, a good part of that time would have been spent on John Hancock time.

The fourth thing is the luncheon workshop series which we have happening almost every week during the course of the year. We offer a wide range of subjects. We get between 40 and 50 people participating in each workshop. This has been created really because in this age of dual-income families and single families, nobody has the time to go to the library, let alone read a book. This is a good way to get information to parents, caregivers or singles where they can get a bibliography if they want to pursue it afterwards. Some of the topics we've covered are childhood illnesses, Alzheimer's, introduction to adoption, sexuality in your adolescent, self-esteem in ourselves our children, and creative confrontations at home and work.

March of Dimes puts on a wonderful nine-part workshop on "Babies and You." That is is free. Supposedly I will be asked for a corporate contribution at some point. That has yet to happen.

That is what I am prepared to say now. If you have any questions, I will be happy to answer them.

[The prepared statement of Ms. Hazzard follows:]

Prepared Statement of Katharine B. Hazzard, Director of Work/Family Programs, John Hancock Mutual Life Insurance

HISTORY

John Hancock administers an employee attitude survey every two years. Over the course of the 1980's, employees expressed considerable concern over the demands that were being made on them. Child care, school-aged child care, and elder care responsibilities were becoming more and more time consuming. By 1988 with the releases of the Work Force 2000 report and the data gleaned from our employee surveys, it became clear to John Hancock that the company ought to look into Work/Family issues as they pertained to John Hancock.

We began looking at family care at John Hancock in the traditional way with a task force. We attempted to define employees' needs concerning family care issues and the appropriate employer response to those needs. Our research involved attending seminars, on-site visits to child care centers, surveying other employers, interviewing John Hancock managers, surveying John Hancock employees and consultations with the leading experts in the field. We struggled for many months with these issues recognizing that there was no one solution to meet all the needs of our employees.

At John Hancock women comprise 62 percent of the Home Office population. Almost 20 percent of our employees have at least one preschool age child and 15 percent have school age children. More than 12% of our employees have primary ElderCare responsibilities. These demographics mean aggressively creating family care policies and programs which support employee efforts to deal with a wide range of challenging family care issues—issues which can cause stress, diminish performance and even prevent an employee from coming to work. We believe that family care programs can result in savings, particularly with decreased absenteeism, lower employee turnover rates, and higher employee retention and morale.

Four of many initiatives that the company took were:

1. On-site Child Care Center—At John Hancock we estimate that the number of dual wage earners will increase from 37 percent to almost 50 percent in the 19905, and single parents will increase from 9 percent to about 14 percent. It is clear that we are going to rely on those populations to perform a growing share of the jobs at John Hancock from entry level to management.

John Hancock decided to offer on-site child care early and to do it right. The John Hancock Child Care Center, which opened almost a year and a half ago is a major investment in the future quality and diversity of our work force. It will assure that we can recruit and retain the caliber of workers who will keep John Hancock competitive in the marketplace well beyond the year 2000.

The Center is a state-of-the-art facility with a planned capacity for 200 children ranging in age from 8 weeks old through kindergarten.

The bright and airy Center occupies the first two floors of an office building, within sight of the John Hancock tower.

The Center has several unique features, such as two adjacent playgrounds rare to an urban setting. The playgrounds, designed by a landscape architect, are covered with several different surfaces including a spongy protective surface made from shredded tires. A large indoor playroom with swings is covered with a similar spongy surface and a simulated wood surface around the perimeter for riding tricycles. There is also a mildly ill area, staffed by a full-time nurse, with a separate ventilation system to minimize the spread of germs. There is a dry enrichment room with tiny computer keyboards and a wet enrichment room with sinks and a floor drain for messy activities such as finger-painting. The Center also features an indoor garden with a brook and plants sprouting from flower beds mulched with wood chips.

As well as being beautiful, the Center is designed to be a safe and secure facility. A Security Officer, trained in CPR and first aid, is at the Center during all hours of operation. In addition, a sophisticated security identification system provides positive identification of all staff members, parents, and children who enter and leave the Center.

2. Kids-to-go—Kids-to-go is a program that John Hancock developed in conjunction with Ellis Memorial, a non-profit social service agency, to provide activities for the 6 to 13-year old children of Hancock employees on certain school holidays and vacations when John Hancock is open. Parent may drop off their children as early as 7:30 a.m. and pick them up at 4:30 p.m. Staff from Ellis Memorial group the children by age and provide activities such as arts and crafts, movies or trips to museums. Kids-to-go is a wonderful program that has become such a special treat for the

children that parents often sign up even when they have other child care alternatives for the day.

3. ElderCare Connection—Through John Hancock's ElderCare Connection Program employees can call a licensed, independent social worker. The social worker is able to provide a wide range of services ranging from giving the employee resource information to making an in-depth analysis of the employee's situation and recommendations for intervention. And over time, the social worker keeps in touch with the employee to make sure that elder care responsibilities remain as manageable as possible. The program also includes a Social Services Fair that give employees an opportunity to meet with representatives from organizations who are experts in elder care services.

4. Lunchtime Workshop Series—The Work/Family Programs Unit runs an extensive lunchtime workshop series with a workshop scheduled almost every week from September through June. The workshops are well attended (40–50 employees with men and women well represented) and cover a wide variety of topics. A partial listing of the 1991–92 series is listed below:

Common Childhood illnesses
Alzheimer's Disease & Related Dementia's
Introduction to Adoption
Sexuality and Your Adolescent & what you want them to know
Self-Esteem in Ourselves and Our Children
Creative Confrontations at Home and at Work
March of Dimes nine session workshop "Babies & You"

Mr. SAWYER. Thank you both very much.

You have raised some interests and concerns, and I would like you to expand on them, either of you or both of you.

The first is a comment that I found in some reading that I had done last week. In his 1990 Presidential address to the Population Association of America, Larry Bumpass said something to this effect. I have the sense of it, not the quote exactly. He said that what is at issue right now is not the existence of the American family, but the way we respond to its changing nature and what that means. He said that understanding long-term change should direct policy toward the amelioration of negative consequences, rather than toward attempts to reverse the tide.

Now, it seems to me that what John Hancock is doing is identifying the condition of American families and how they exist and where they are working, rather than attempting to turn the tide.

A second observation goes right to the question of whether the current condition of the American family is, in fact, the character of country, the nature of the demographics. The ways in which we live and earn our livings have not changed just once in the last century, but are probably at least in their second tectonic shift. The first shift probably occurred about a century ago when we moved from hand labor on farms, when it took half of us to feed all of us and when that production unit you described was necessary for all of us.

Through this part of the century, we have seen the family centered in urban areas where people came together to work in highly concentrated settings. Today, we are seeing work itself redefined.

John Hancock is a company that relates to people across the continent. You can be a continent away and working with someone at a desk thousands of miles apart. The requirement that people live together in order to work and survive together, that fundamental glue seems to have changed in ways that are driving economic, social and familial decisions in directions that we are trying very, very hard to understand.

Having said all that, let me ask you, Dr. Goldscheider, have you taken a look at the consequences of that removal of the man that you find missing on the children and the likelihood of their behaviors half a generation away?

Ms. GOLDSCHEIDER. I think there is an enormous body of research on the consequences for children, a lot of it focusing on financial which we continue to hear about, that somehow the redistribution of resources distribution to children get short-circuited when men are no longer in their vicinity.

There is a wealth of research on psychological consequences.

The reason I cast my remarks the way I did was not to make men feel guilty. You talk about the consequences for men of beginning relationships and then walking out on them not only with wives but also with children, or maybe being thrown out. I am not trying to blame anybody. I am talking about a larger system that, by the 1950's, had in some sense was in a separate sphere or world where a zipper was created down the American family with the women and children on one side and the men on the other sort of coming together between the hours of 8 at night and 6 in the morning.

When the second stage as you described it occurred, that being men's removal productively from the household, the second being women's, that zipper became unzipped. Now we have policies designed for women and children, welfare or school policies that assume men have nothing to do with children and therefore doesn't encourage, reward, frighten, entice or whatever, men to spend more time and be more involved with their children.

So some of the terms that you had described I am not sure they will go as far as you think they are. People still go to work at John Hancock.

Ms. HAZZARD. We have some telecommunicating.

Ms. GOLDSCHEIDER. It is going to be hard to set up a world where everybody is in their family and people won't have to go to the office. Maybe we will get to that and families will be enormously strengthened.

Mr. SAWYER. Let me give you an example. I live in Akron, OH. At the beginning of this century, it was the center of the growth of the Midwest's industrial concentration in tires and rubber. Beginning in the 1920's, that production began to spread across the country. Because of the nature of the industry, it had always been an industry that was spread around the globe. Today, that company is in every country where specific automotive production takes place and production decisions can be shifted almost as quickly as the change in the value of the currencies of the nations with whom they are dealing. People who are engaged in the production of raw materials, the production of end products and the research and development that goes on in between literally are half a world apart, and yet very close together.

Ms. GOLDSCHEIDER. I am not sure that works for families. I am talking about producing family relationships and producing relationships between men and women and children. That is a hands-on job.

Mr. SAWYER. I understand that. The world appears to be driven if not totally as I described, certainly more so than a century ago, and far more than two centuries ago. I am asking about the amelioration of the negative effects.

I am looking this year at a reauthorization of a Higher Education Act that presumes support for higher education predicated on a family, mother and father, and the standard of income necessary for an 18- to 22-year-old offspring to go to college or to preparatory school. That is hardly a portrayal of the demographics of need on college campuses today. As often as not, the recipient of aid is one or both of the members of the parenting generation trying to sustain work and children at the same time, both trying to hold together that family.

It has produced economic imperatives that are vastly different. I am looking at a nation that is trying to adapt its housing needs to a very different family structure than was prominent when most of that housing infrastructure was constructed. I am looking at employers who are trying desperately to attract the most skilled and talented of a generation to come and a work at the time those economic pressures are greatest. I am looking for a way to understand the consequences of all of this. I am not sure that it is sufficient at least for the near term to help men understand how much they are losing by leaving.

Ms. GOLDSCHEIDER. I can only disagree with you, I guess.

Mr. SAWYER. I understand. How do you respond to Dr. Bumpass, who says the task is not to turn the tide?

Ms. GOLDSCHEIDER. I am not trying to turn the tide. I think perhaps the communalists on the right are trying to bring us back to the 1950's and I don't see a conceivable way to do that.

I think the direction we are moving in continue to separate men from long-term relationships. I think they are counting on a lot of continuities that are not going to be out there.

If you talk to the young unmarried men in Washington today, they assume there is plenty of time and sometimes in their late 30's or early 40's, they will be out there waiting for them. They have heard the demographics, that there are more unmarried women than men, so they feel they will fall into their laps and take care of them.

What we are seeing in terms of women's roles, which are taking them away from all kinds of family responsibilities, we worry about working woman spending less time with children and dependent elderly. I think it is about time that men should start worrying that working women are not going to be taking care of them.

Mr. SAWYER. I would not disagree with that.

Ms. Hazzard.

Ms. HAZZARD. I would just like to comment that I think a flexible workplace—I have seen men who want to have paternity leave. Now, John Hancock does not have paternity leave. However, it does not have maternity leave either. John Hancock has a leave of absence policy where the company will allow you to take up to 1 year of leave with full benefits subsidized by the company. You are guaranteed your same job up to 6 months and from 6 months to 12 months you are guaranteed a like position. Anybody is eligible to apply for that personal leave.

Now, needless to say, Many woman who give birth have a period of disability and then a leave of absence. The leave of absence is also available to the father who wants to be home. Several instances have come to my attention where the mother is home for 4 or 5 months and she has to go back to work, and then the father wants to stay home for a few months so then the child is 7 or 8 months before they have to turn it over to someone else to care for.

I would say in a limited way men are taking more and more of an interest, and when given the chance, they are willing to take responsibility as well. Of the elder caregivers discussion group, 75 percent of them are men. In the lunchtime workshop series, many men are beginning to show up as much as women did from day one. It was not true at the beginning. It is giving the men the flexibility and giving them the opportunities.

If corporate America can support that and what it means in male and female run families, over the long run we may mold ourselves to the family of the year 2000 which will not resemble "Leave it to Beaver." The figure now that is being bandied about is that percentage in the country that is that family is 7 percent. So we have 93 percent. Maybe I am an optimist.

Mr. SAWYER. I think it is probably fair to say it never was as many would have portrayed it.

Ms. GOLDSCHEIDER. It was an ideal. The question is, do we believe it as an ideal? We are not disagreeing. We are not disagreeing with Larry Bumpass. I am talking about the personal family level and the relationship between the parents.

I think that industry should take a responsibility is wonderful, and I would be delighted if government would help out, too, because the figures which we start with show that children are in trouble.

Mr. SAWYER. That is particularly true, particularly as we see one generation after another having more and more diverse needs, once cared for in a single-family unit and today clearly more dispersed across the geographic landscape.

Does John Hancock provide time for families to care for children?

Ms. HAZZARD. Yes, it can be caring for any relative. They can use 3 of their existing sick days, and that is usually 10 a year, to care for a sick child or a relative; perhaps a spouse having outpatient surgery and needing them to drive them to and from.

Mr. SAWYER. Are you keeping track of this? It may be a relatively small population, but I suspect it is as diverse as much of the surrounding population. You have a wealth of longitudinal data on a lot of families that make John Hancock their career.

Ms. HAZZARD. I would like to start my own Framingham heart study, and follow people from getting pregnant and doing the March of Dimes series. There is not that much available. We will get that. Yes, you are quite right.

Mr. SAWYER. Thank you very much.

I hope we might be able to submit some written questions to you both if you would be willing to respond for the record.

Ms. GOLDSCHEIDER. Absolutely. Thank you for the opportunity.

Mr. SAWYER. We are going to suspend for a moment. We have a vote on the floor.

[Recess.]

Mr. SAWYER. Well, I think I am back for a while. It is one of those days on the floor.

Let me introduce our second panel. The first presenter is Dr. Kristin Anderson Moore, who is the director of research at Child Trends, Inc., and a former research associate with the Urban Institute, studying the effects of the Federal jobs program on children ages three to five whose mothers receive AFDC. That is a wide range of research interests. And Clifford Johnson, director of family support at the Children's Defense Fund, who served as a research associate at George Washington Research Center for Social Policy, in addition to previously being a chief legislative aide to a U.S. Congressman. We will not hold that against you if nobody else will. He is a writer of some breadth, including coauthorship of a book, "Beyond the Safety Net."

Welcome to you both. If you would proceed as you will and please introduce your colleague.

STATEMENT OF KRISTIN A. MOORE, DIRECTOR OF RESEARCH, CHILD TRENDS, INC., AND CLIFFORD M. JOHNSON, DIRECTOR OF FAMILY SUPPORT, CHILDREN'S DEFENSE FUND

Mr. JOHNSON. Thank you. I am joined today by Dr. Paul Smith, who is our director of research at the Children's Defense Fund.

Mr. SAWYER. Very good.

Ms. MOORE. I will be talking about trends so I hope you have the testimony in hand.

Mr. SAWYER. Let me urge you not to compress your testimony if you feel it would be benefited by expansion, and feel free to focus where you wish.

Ms. MOORE. I will start with table 1, which is the first table after the brief text section. On page 1, you will see on the top row that the child population in the United States grew during the 1980's. It was 64,137,000 in 1990. This increase is due to an increase in minority populations.

The number of white children has declined and the number of Hispanic children is growing particularly rapidly. In fact, the total U.S. population is growing rather rapidly, from 181 million in 1960 to 250 million in 1990.

Other segments of the U.S. population are growing faster than the child population, which is actually declining as a proportion of the population. During the baby boom, children under age 18 accounted for 35 percent of the U.S. population. Now they account for 26 percent.

Please turn to the chart on page 3. There are just over 4 million births annually in the United States right now. As you can see, the proportion of all births that occur to unmarried mothers has been increasing steadily among whites and non-whites. More than one quarter of all births, 27 percent, are outside of marriage. With 4 million births annually, that is more than 1 million nonmarital births each year.

Please turn to the figure on page 4. In part because of this increase in nonmarital childbearing and in part because of a substantial increase in marital disruption that has occurred over the last several decades and a decline in remarriage, a substantial increase has occured in the proportion of children living with just one parent. Nineteen percent of white children, 30 percent of Hispanic children, and 55 percent of black children live in a single-parent family.

Please turn to page 8. The top set of three bars shows the much higher incidence of poverty found among black and Hispanic families with children. Compared to white families, 13 percent of white families, 37 of black families and 31 percent of Hispanic families with children are living in poverty. Much of this difference, but not all, is due to differences in family structure.

For example, looking at the second set of bars on page 8, among single-parent families headed by a woman, 38 percent of white, 56 percent of black and 58 percent of Hispanic families with children are in poverty. Many others are near the poverty line; few are affluent. Among families headed by a married couple, only a minority are in poverty: 7 percent of white, 14 percent of black, and 21 percent of Hispanic families with children.

One reason that children in single-parent families are poor is that children tend to lose access to their father's income when there is no marriage or when marriage ends. Many absent fathers do not pay child support at all, or they pay irregularly, and the amounts they pay tend to be small.

In addition, women's earnings tend to be low, making it difficult for most mothers to support a family much above the poverty line. While increases in employment among mothers have occurred during the past several decades, they have been most notable among married mothers.

Please turn to page 10. The top set of bar graphs shows that the percent of mothers in married couple families working full-time, full-year rose from 15 to 30 percent between 1971 and 1987. Among mother-only families, the proportion rose from 27 to 33 percent. Thus, the percentage of mothers in married couple families working full-time, full-year is about the same as the proportion in mother-only families.

The bottom set of bar graphs shows the percentage of mothers that did not work at all was actually somewhat higher among single mothers than married, 38 percent compared with 32 percent.

Although there is considerable and justifiable concern about changes in family structure and increases in poverty, it is important to recognize the diversity among American families. Although poverty among families with children has risen, it is not universal even among single-parent families, and not all families need help. Consequently, the task of helping families is not hopeless, or overwhelming or impossible, because most families do not need help or may need just some help.

In addition, there is good news in this set of tables. You can read the details later; let me summarize now.

First, levels of parents' education have risen. Higher parent education is generally linked with more optimum child rearing and better child outcomes, so increased education among parents can be viewed as good news.

Also, there are fewer very large families today. Given trends toward single-parent families and more working parents, the availability of time for children has become an important issue for parents. Because families have gotten smaller, parents can have more time per child. Economic resources are less often stretched across very large numbers of children.

Unfortunately, some of the trends reported do signal problems for children. Poor children and children from single-parent families do tend to be disadvantaged in a variety of ways. For example, children from low-income families are more likely to worry that they are not safe even in their own homes. In addition, poor children in two-parent families more often worry that their parents will divorce than children in higher-income two-parent families.

I want to insert a comment about the data on page 16. Dr. Goldscheider referred to the data from fathers where once married fathers, 90 percent of them, felt that they could count on their children, but among fathers who had been absent only half felt they could count on their children.

You see in the top bar on page 16, virtually all children in intact two-parent families feel that their biological mother and biological father really care, but the proportion of them that feel the biological father really cares drops to 71 percent and 55 percent in mother-only families. Among children who do not live with either parent, a much smaller percent feel their mother or father really care about them.

Parents in two-parent families tend to be more involved with their children's activities. Please turn to page 17. The bottom chart shows at least one parent attend PTA events at least some time during the school year in most family types. However, parents in intact two-parent families seem to take on the more time-consuming tasks such as coaching a team or working with a youth group. This association does not seem to be due to just the number of parents, however. Step-parent families are somewhat less likely to be involved than single-parent families.

A multitude of research studies indicate that while most children raised by single parents and in step-parent families develop well, children raised by two biological parents are at an advantage, particularly if those parents have maintained a happy marriage.

In summary, the data indicate that many families have considerable internal resources; but many also face considerable challenges. Recognizing this and focusing on the needs of contemporary children is most appropriate.

Thank you.

[The prepared statement of Ms. Moore follows:]

PREPARED STATEMENT OF KRISTIN A. MOORE, DIRECTOR OF RESEARCH, CHILD TRENDS, INC.

A picture of the nation's children must begin with a chart showing how many children there are, which was 64.1 million in 1990. In table 1, you can see that the total child population fell between 1970 and 1980, but rose between 1980 and 1990. This increase is entirely due to increased numbers of minority children, with the Hispanic population increasing particularly rapidly. However, as a proportion of the entire U.S. population, the number of children has declined. As of 1990, children under 18 accounted for 26 percent of the population, compared with more than a third in the 1960s.

Table 1—The Number of Children Under Age 18 in the United States

[in millions]

	1990	1980	1970	1960
Total number of children	64.1	63.4	69.2	63.7
White children	51.4	52.2	58.8	55.1
African American children	10.0	9.4	9.4	8.7
Hispanic children (ethnicity can be of any race)	7.2	5.5	4.0	
Total population	250	228	205	181
Percent under age 18	26	28	34	35

Although the birth rate and the fertility rate are much lower than they were several decades ago (shown in table 2), the number of births has increased to over 4 million births annually during the past several years. A substantial change has occurred in the composition of these births, such that more than a quarter of all births—more than one million annually—now occur to unmarried mothers.

Table 2—The Number and Rate of Births per Year

	1991	1990	1989	1980	1970	1960	1950
Total number of births (in millions)	4.1	4.2	4.0	3.6	3.7	4.3	3.6
Birth rate (births per 1,000 population)	16.2	16.7	16.3	15.9	18.4	23.7	24.1
Fertility rate (births per 1,000 women aged 15–44)	68.33	70.0	69.2	68.4	87.9	118.0	106.2
Percent of all births to unmarried women	na	na	27	18	11	5	4

Non-marital births account for a higher proportion of all births to African American mothers than white mothers; however, the proportion of births occurring outside of marriage has increased for all population groups (table 3). In addition, the frequency of non-marital childbearing has increased among older women as well as among teens.

Table 3—Nonmarital Births as a Percent of All Births, 1940–89

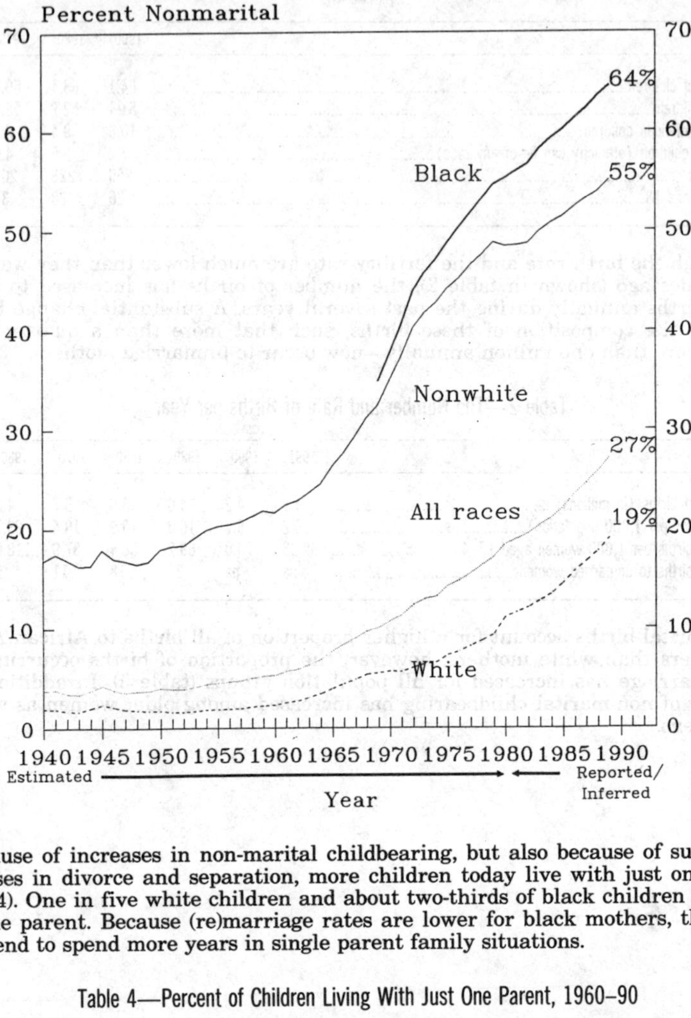

Because of increases in non-marital childbearing, but also because of substantial increases in divorce and separation, more children today live with just one parent (table 4). One in five white children and about two-thirds of black children live with a single parent. Because (re)marriage rates are lower for black mothers, their children tend to spend more years in single parent family situations.

Table 4—Percent of Children Living With Just One Parent, 1960–90

	1960	1970	1980	1990
Black	22	32	46	55
Hispanic			21	30
White	7	9	15	19

One consequence of the increase in single-parent families has been an increase in the proportion of children who live in poverty (table 5). In 1990, 23 percent of all children under age 6 were in poverty, as were 19 percent of all children ages 6–17, compared with 11 percent of adults aged 18–64 and 12 percent of the elderly. In fact, the incidence of poverty has fallen substantially among the elderly over time (table 6), while among children the poverty rate during the 1980s was higher than it was during most of the 1970s. Hence, poverty today is considerably more common among those just starting life than it is among the elderly, an historically vulnerable group.

Table 5—Poverty Rates by Age Group, 1987 [1]

	Percentage Rate
Children under 6	23
Children 6–17	19
Adults 18–64	11
Adults 65+	12

[1] Poverty rate for all—13.5%.

Table 6—Percent of Children and Elderly in Poverty, 1959–90

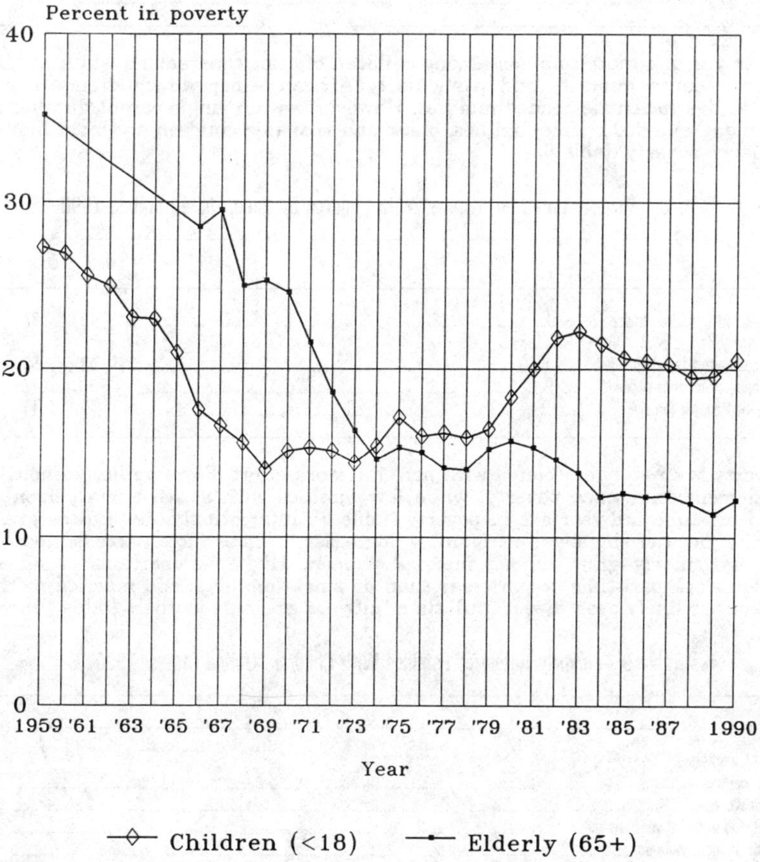

Poverty is particularly common among female-headed families (table 7). More than 37 percent of persons in female-headed families lived under the poverty line in 1990, compared with 12 percent among all persons in families.

Table 7—Poverty Rates for Families and Persons, United States, 1990

[in millions]

	Number	Percentage Rate
All families	7.1	10.7
All families with children under 18 years	5.7	16.4
All persons	33.6	13.5
Persons in families	25.2	12.0
Persons in female-headed families, no husband	12.6	37.2
Unrelated individuals	7.4	20.7
All children under 18 years	13.4	20.6
All persons 18–64 years	16.5	10.7
All persons 65 years and over	3.7	12.2

Poverty is also more common among children of color than among white children, in part because minority and particularly African American children are more likely to live in female-headed families. However, within single-parent families and also among married couple families, black and Hispanic children are more likely to experience poverty (table 8).

Table 8—Poverty Rates for Families With Children by Race, United States, 1990

	White	Black	Hispanic
All families with children under 18	13	37	31
Type of family:			
Single-parent female-headed	38	56	58
Single-parent male-headed	16	27	28
Married couple families	7	14	21

Poverty is strongly associated with parental work effort. Few families without employed members escape poverty, while few families with at least one person employed full-time full-year are in poverty (table 9). Interestingly, despite the greater economic need of single-parent families, increases in labor force participation have been particularly great among married women. Higher proportions of married mothers work part-time or part-year than do single mothers; and married mothers are about as likely even to work full-time full-year as single mothers (table 10).

Table 9—Poverty Rates for Families With Children, United States, 1990

	Percent
Number of workers:	
No workers	86
One worker	24
One full-time full-year worker	5
Two or more workers	5
Two or more full-time workers full-year worker	1
Education of householder:	
Did not complete high school	31
High school graduate, no college	11
Some college	6
College graduate	3

Table 10—Labor Force Participation of Mothers by Family Type, 1971 and 1987

	1971	1987
Worked full-time, full-year:		
Mother only	27	33
Married couple	15	30
Worked part-time or part-year:		
Mother only	31	29
Married couple	32	38
Did not work during year:		
Mother only	42	38
Married couple	53	32

Another reason that poverty is a particular risk among children in single-parent families is that only a minority of single mothers receive child support payments. In fact, only 14 percent of never-married mothers received child support from the child's father in 1989, as did 31 percent of separated mothers, 54 percent of divorced mothers, and 48 percent of (re)married mothers (table 11). Even among mothers who do receive payments, amounts averaged just about $3,000 annually.

Table 11—Percent of Custodial Mothers Receiving Child Support Payments From Absent Fathers, by Current Marital Status, 1989

	Percent
Never married	14
Separated	31
Divorced	54
Currently married	48

Although there is considerable and justifiable concern about changes in family structure and increases in poverty among American children, it is worth noting that from the point of view of children, some positive changes have also occurred. For one, there are fewer very large families (table 12). This trend tends to counterbalance the trend toward more single-parent families and more working parents, in the sense that family time and economic resources are less often stretched across very large numbers of children.

Table 12—Distribution of Families by Number of Own Children Under Age 18, 1960–90

	1960	1970	1980	1990
4 or more children	9	10	4	3
1–3 children	48	46	48	46
No children	43	44	48	51

It is also important to acknowledge the diversity among families. Although poverty among families with children has risen, most families are not poor. Even among single-parent families, poverty is not universal. Thus, the cup can be viewed either as half full or half empty. Sometimes it is necessary to note that many families are doing well, that not all families need help, because it means that there is hope and a greater probability that resources exist to assist those who really do need help.

In addition, today's parents are better-educated (table 13). Parent education is generally linked with more optimal childrearing and child outcomes, so increased education among contemporary parents can be viewed as another piece of good news.

Table 13—Percent of Elementary School Aged Children Whose Parent Had 12 or More Years of Education, 1970–90

	1970	1979	1985	1987	1988	1990
White	66	75	80	81	82	83
Black	36	51	67	70	69	74
Hispanic			41	45	46	48

Unfortunately, there is some bad news and the bad news is meaningful. Poor children and children in single-parent families are disadvantaged. Surveys of a nationally representative sample of children conducted for the National Commission on Children in 1990 indicate that poor children worry more about a variety of topics. These worries are discussed at some length in "Speaking of Kids" released by the National Commission on Children, Several results are highlighted here on table 14. Clearly, poorer children more often worry that they are not safe, even in their own homes. In addition, poor children in two-parent families more often worry that their parents will divorce than children in more financially stable two-parent families.

Table 14—Percentage of Children (Age 10–17), by Family Income, 1990, Who Worry "A Lot" That:

	<$10,000	$10,000–$20,000	$20,000–$30,000	$30,000–$30,000	>$40,000
They are not safe in their homes	16	10	7	4	4
Their parents will divorce	42	18	19	13	8

Moreover, children in single-parent families and step-families seem to have less satisfying lives. For example, children who live with both of their natural or biological parents are far less likely to report that their fathers miss events that the child considers important (table 15). In addition, children who live with both parents almost all feel that both of their parents really care about them, while only 71 percent of the children in step-families feel that their biological father really cares about them, as do just 55 percent of the children in single-parent families (table 16).

Table 15—Percentage of Children (Age 10–17) Who Report That Their Mother or Father Often Misses Events and Activities That Children Consider Important, by Family Type, 1990

	Mother	Father
Intact, both parents	5	10
Stepfamily	18	44
One parent only	13	33

Table 16—Percentage of Children (Age 10–17) Who Feel That Their Biological Mother or Father "Really Care," by Family Type, 1990

[Children with living parents only]

	Mother	Father
Intact, both parents	97	96
Stepfamily	93	71
One parent only	94	55
No parent	55	40

Finally, parents in intact families tend to be more involved in their children's lives (table 17). While a majority of parents manage to attend a PTA meeting regardless of family type, parents in two-parent families are more likely to find time for more intensive activities, such as coaching a team or working with a youth group.

Table 17—Percentage of Parents of Children (Age 6–17) Who Have Taken Part in School-Related Activities in the Past Year, by Family Type, 1990

	Intact, both parents	Stepfamily	One parent only
Attended PTA or other school meeting	71	72	66
Worked with youth group or sports team	47	28	33

The difficulties experienced by children who live in families other than those headed by both of their biological parents are reflected in their psychological well-being as well (table 18). While children in intact, two-parent families have problems, the incidence of emotional or behavioral problems is considerably higher among children living on other family types.

Table 18—Percent of Children Having Psychological Problems,[1] by Family Type, 1990

	Rate
Intact two parent	8
Mother only	19
Mother and stepfather	24
All other	22

[1] Children 3–17 with emotional or behaviorial problem lasting 3 or more months or needing treatment.

We speak often of how the experience of childhood varies for children in different economic groups and family types. It is important to acknowledge how much children's experiences vary by age as well. And it appears that parents withdraw considerably as children grow older. Perhaps it is not surprising that parents become less likely to play a game or sport with their adolescent or teenager as the child grows up; but the decline in parental involvement with school and school work seems more troubling (table 19). The academic, social, and psychological challenges faced by adolescents are substantial and require the continued involvement of parents. We are reminded of the long-term obligations of parenthood by the data on table 20.

Table 19—Parents' Involvement With Their Children's School and Activities, by Age of Child, 1990

	Rate
Play a game or a sport with child at least once a week:	
Childs's age: 6–9 years	85
Childs's age: 10–13 years	61
Childs's age: 14–17 years	34
Attended PTA or other school program in the last year:	
Childs's age: 6–9 years	78
Childs's age: 10–13 years	73
Childs's age: 14–17 years	64
Does homework or a school project with child at least once a week:	
Childs's age: 6–9 years	90
Childs's age: 10–13 years	76
Childs's age: 14–17 years	43

Table 20—Teen Birth Rate, 1970–89

	1970	1975	1980	1985	1986	1987	1988	1989
Births per 1,000 women aged 15–17	38.8	36.1	32.5	31.1	30.6	31.8	33.8	36.5
Births per 1,000 women aged 18–19	114.7	85	82.1	80.8	81	80.2	81.7	86.4

After declining during the 1970's, the teenage birth rate stabilized during the 1980's. Then, during the late 1980's, the rate of births to U.S. teens began to rise again, ensuring that you and I will be faced with the need to worry about America's children for the foreseeable future.

Mr. JOHNSON. Thank you very much. The Children's Defense Fund is particularly pleased to have this opportunity to testify today.

In any democracy the first duty of government is to ascertain accurately and report truthfully to the people what they need to know in order to make their civic choices. The leadership of the subcommittee in protecting and strengthening the quality of Federal data sources that makes such truthful reporting and informed choice possible is vitally important and deeply appreciated.

We also offer our thanks and admiration to the Census Bureau's decennial staff for their impressive and perhaps unprecedented accomplishments in making the 1990 census data available ahead of their own schedule and beyond anyone's expectations. The Bureau has been very responsive in providing a very high degree of access to a very wide audience. We much appreciate their efforts in that regard.

Let me begin by briefly discussing a few key demographic and economic trends, including the growth of child poverty, increase in single-parent families and the rising share of young Americans who are minority. Then, with the subcommittee's indulgence, I will conclude my remarks by offering CDF'S recommendations on steps that the Congress should consider to ensure that we can continue to monitor the nation's progress in these and other critical areas.

The sharp rise in the proportion of American children growing up in poverty since the late 1970's poses a greater threat to the Nation than any external enemy. More than 3 million children joined the ranks of the poor between 1979 and 1990.

Young families with children were hardest hit. The poverty rate for children living in young families nearly doubled from 24 percent in 1979 to an incredible 40 percent in 1990.

The consequences of tragically high and rising child poverty rates are all too often ignored in national policy debates, but for poor families they are inescapable. Families with incomes below the poverty threshold face impossible choices. Many poor families manage by cutting back on food, jeopardizing their health and the development of their children, or by living in substandard and sometimes dangerous housing. Some do without heat, electricity, telephone service, or plumbing for months or years. Many do without health insurance, health care, safe child care, or reliable transportation to take them to or from work.

For some children, the consequences of poverty can be deadly. Several years ago the Maine Health Bureau found that poor children were more than three times as likely as other children to die during childhood.

While the vast majority of poor children do not die from poverty, their health and development and eventual capabilities and productivity as workers, parents, and citizens often are damaged by the deprivations of growing up poor.

Poor children are more likely to be disabled or to die in infancy.

They are less likely to receive key building blocks of early development—adequate nutrition, decent medical care, a safe and secure environment, and access to early childhood development programs.

In virtually every critical area of development and healthy maturation, poverty creates major roadblocks to individual accomplishment, and economic self-sufficiency, as well as to national progress.

These recent trends present a compelling case for sweeping new Federal initiatives designed to dramatically reduce or eliminate child poverty between now and the next decennial census in the year 2000.

Because the economy has unravelled for many families with children, and particularly for young families, much of the increase in poverty during the past decade would have occurred even if today's families looked exactly like those in the generation preceding them.

But the rise in the proportion of American families headed by single women also has been a major factor fueling the growth of child poverty.

Women's wages typically are lower than those of men, and female-headed families have far fewer alternatives to cope with economic adversity than do married couple families. They do not have a second adult who can enter the job market to help support the children unless they can obtain child support from an absent father, and even the earnings of the female head of household often are limited by the burden of fulfilling parental responsibilities alone.

The growth in female-headed families with children is in part a reflection of changing values. But the economic hardships associated with falling earnings and persistent joblessness among young adults also have contributed significantly to falling marriage rates because young men with the financial ability to support a family are far more likely to be married, on average, than those without such ability.

The implications of recent growth in single-parent and dual-earner families are far-reaching. Among the most obvious are burgeoning needs for child care assistance to support the work efforts of low-income workers and for a combination of stronger minimum wage policies and wage subsidies to ensure that full-time work yields family-supporting earnings.

The growth in single-parent families also underscores the need for fundamental reforms in our current welfare and child support systems, including the adoption of more universal income supports for families with children such as a refundable children's tax credit and the creation of a child support assurance system that shields children from the most extreme economic hardships associated with the departure or absence of a parent.

Finally poverty rates among America's children and families also have been pushed higher in recent years because an increasing share of the nation's younger population are minority, compounding the problems already facing America's children and youth and increasing to an even greater extent the need for effective responses from both public and private sectors.

Let me turn to some brief suggestions regarding steps the Congress should consider in order to preserve and strengthen the quality of the essential Federal data sources on which we rely to tell these stories today.

The decennial Census of Population and Housing, because of its enormous cost and size, is taken only every 10 years. But 10 years is simply too long to go without a reasonable source of State-level data on the lives of families and Americans overall. This problem was properly and inexpensively solved in the 1970's by mandating a mid-decade expansion of the Current Population Survey, from 60,000 to 300,000 households. Of course, the corresponding survey in the mid-1980's was cancelled.

Congress should resume funding a proper and official expansion of the CPS once in the middle of each decade. This mid-decade expansion would not only provide stable and timely estimates of State figures, but would also give us the statistical power to test for new trends and patterns without waiting for each decennial census. In addition, some special augmentation of the Current Population Survey is needed to provide accurate annual national estimates for smaller portions of the population, including national estimates for ethnic subgroups and narrow age ranges.

There are several techniques that could be used to augment the Current Population Survey so that subethnic and narrow age estimates are improved.

With regard to the decennial census, we do not think that the S-Night count of the sheltered and homeless populations provides an adequate basis for national, State, or local planning.

In addition, we are aware of no nationally representative survey or census data that identifies children in migrant farm worker families or their characteristics.

Currently the Bureau needs to be funded to develop better ways of counting these desperately poor individuals and families. These developments should start now and be applied to special counts taken each year or each 2 years so that they will be mature and effective, thoroughly tested for use in the census of 2000.

I thank the Chairman for his patience and attention. We would welcome any questions that you might have.

[The prepared statement of Mr. Johnson follows:]

Prepared Statement of Clifford M. Johnson, Director, Family Support Division, Children's Defense Fund

Good afternoon. I am Clifford Johnson, director of family support for the Children's Defense Fund (CDF). I am joined here today by Paul Smith, CDF's director of research and undoubtedly one of the nation's most insatiable consumers of the federal data under the jurisdiction of the Subcommittee.

We are particularly pleased to have this opportunity to testify before the Subcommittee today, as CDF has long relied upon data from the decennial census, the Current Population Surveys, and other key data series produced by the U.S. Bureau of the Census to assess the well-being of America's children and youth. In any democracy, the first duty of government is to ascertain accurately and report truthfully to the people what they need to know in order to make their civic choices. The leadership of the Subcommittee in protecting and strengthening the quality of federal data sources that make such truthful reporting and informed choice possible is vitally important and deeply appreciated.

Let me begin by briefly discussing the implications of just a few of the key demographic and economic trends that are apparent in recent data from the decennial census and Current Population Surveys: the growth in the proportion of American children living in poverty; the increasing likelihood that families with children are headed either by single parents or by two parents who both work outside the home; and the rising share of young Americans who are minority. Then with the Subcommittee's indulgence I will conclude my remarks by offering CDF's recommendations on steps that the Congress should consider to ensure that we can continue to monitor the nation's progress in these and other critical areas during the 1990s and into the 21st century.

Growth in Child Poverty

The sharp rise in the proportion of American children growing up in poverty since the late 1970s, reflected in both the decennial census and the annual March supplements to the Current Population Surveys, poses a greater threat to the nation than any external enemy. More than 3 million children joined the ranks of the poor between 1979 and 1990, leaving a shocking one in every five children beneath the official federal poverty line. Young families with children (those headed by persons younger than 30) were hardest hit by economic, social and public policy changes during the 1980s: the poverty rate for children living in young families nearly doubled from 24 percent in 1979 to an incredible 40 percent in 1990.

The consequences of tragically high and rising child poverty rates are all too often ignored in national policy debates, but for poor families they are inescapable. Families with incomes below the poverty threshold face impossible choices. Many poor families manage by cutting back on food, jeopardizing their health and the development of their children, or by living in substandard and sometimes dangerous housing. Some do without heat, electricity, telephone service, or plumbing for months or years. Many do without health insurance, health care, safe child care, or reliable transportation to take them to or from work.

Without at least some of the basic necessities of life and lacking any cushion of savings or assets, both children and adults in poor families disproportionately suffer an erosion of their health, their hopes, their spirit, and their family togetherness. Many are just one illness, job loss, or family crisis away from homelessness or family dissolution.

Yet it is poor children, already vulnerable as they pass through their crucial developmental years, who often suffer the most. For some children, the consequences of poverty can be deadly. Several years ago the Maine Health Bureau found that poor children were more than three times as likely as other children to die during childhood.

While the vast majority of poor children do not die from poverty, their health and development and eventual capabilities and productivity as workers, parents, and citizens often are damaged by the deprivations of growing up poor:

• Poor pregnant women are more likely than other women to have received late or no prenatal care and to deliver low-birthweight babies, who are more likely to be disabled or to die in infancy.

• Poor children are less likely to receive key building blocks of early development—adequate nutrition, decent medical care, a safe and secure environment, and access to early childhood development programs to supplement learning opportunities in the home.

• Poor children are far more likely to be hungry. The Food Research and Action Center's Community Childhood Hunger Identification Project (CCHIP) projected in 1991 that 5.5 million American children younger than 12—one in every eight in this age group—do not consistently get enough to eat or experience food shortages. Children who are hungry are more likely to suffer fatigue, dizziness, irritablity, headaches, ear infections, frequent colds, unwanted weight loss, inability to concentrate, and increased school absenteeism.

• Poor children are far more likely to fall behind in school. The U.S. Department of Education found that, even for students from families with similar current incomes, those who had spent more years in poverty were significantly more likely to fall behind grade level.

• Teenage women who are poor and who have below-average basic skills, regardless of their race, are five and a half times more likely to have children than nonpoor teenage women with average or better basic skills.

In virtually every critical area of development and healthy maturation, poverty creates major roadblocks to individual accomplishment, economic self-sufficiency, and national progress. The growth of child poverty poses such fundamental dangers and immense social and economic costs for America that we can no longer risk or afford inaction. These recent trends present a compelling case for sweeping new federal initiatives designed to dramatically reduce or eliminate child poverty between now and the next decennial census in the year 2000.

Increases in Single-Parent and Dual-Earner Families

Because the economy has unravelled for many families with children, and particularly for young families, much of the increase in poverty during the past decade would have occurred even if today's families looked exactly like those in the generation preceding them. Family-supporting jobs increasingly are being replaced by jobs with wages and benefits that are inadequate to support the formation and maintenance of stable families—a shift that hurts most those young adults just entering the work force. At the same time, government assistance programs have grown less effective in lifting low-income families and children out of poverty.

But the rise in the proportion of American families headed by single women also has been a major factor fueling the growth of child poverty. Women's wages typically are lower than those of men, and female-headed families have far fewer alternatives to cope with economic adversity than do married couple families. They do not have a second adult who can enter the job market to help support the children (unless they can obtain child support from an absent father), and even the earnings of the female head of household often are limited by the burden of fulfilling parental responsibilities alone.

The growth in female-headed families with children is in part a reflection of changing values. But the economic hardships associated with falling earnings and persistent joblessness among young adults also have contributed significantly to falling marriage rates and the increasing rates of out-of-wedlock childbearing. As Benjamin Franklin wrote more than two centuries ago: "The number of marriages . . . is greater in proportion to the base and convenience of supporting a family. When families can be easily supported, more persons marry, and earlier in life."

Young men with the financial ability to support a family are far more likely to be married, on average, than those without such ability. In 1990 men in their twenties who had earnings sufficient at least to lift a family of three above the federally defined poverty line were three to four times more likely to be married than those with below-poverty earnings. As the share of young men without adequate earnings has risen since 1973, their marriage rates have fallen by 40 percent. At least one-fourth of the overall decline in marriage rates among young men, and between one-third and one-half of the decline for high school dropouts (who suffered the most severe earnings losses), can be attributed directly to the increased proportion of young men who had earnings that are inadequate to support a family.

Just as growing economic pressures have contributed to increases in the number of single-parent families, they have forced more and more married-couple families to send both parents into the paid labor force. Since the early 1970s, women in married-couple families have worked increasing numbers of hours outside the home. In the absence of these attempts to respond to a tightening economic vise, the income loss suffered by families with children during the 1980s would have been even greater.

But these changes in behavior cannot solve the economic problems of America's families with children. Whether by working more, having fewer children or postponing childbearing, parents cannot adapt fast enough or thoroughly enough to cope with rapidly deteriorating prospects for many workers in the wider economy. Nor should they have to. Their coping strategies have obvious limits and pronounced negative effects for this society's future: At some point, further efforts to increase parents' labor force participation or reduce family size become counter-productive or impossible and pose grave new threats to society's well-being.

The implications of recent growth in single-parent and dual-earner families are far-reaching. Among the most obvious are burgeoning needs for child care assistance to support the work efforts of low-income workers and for a combination of stronger minimum wage policies and wage subsidies to ensure that full-time work yields family-supporting earnings. The growth in single-parent families also underscores the need for fundamental reforms in our current welfare and child support systems, including the adoption of more universal income supports for families with children such as a refundable children's tax credit and the creation of a child support assurance system that shields children from the most extreme economic hardships associated with the departure or absence of a parent.

Changing Racial and Ethnic Composition

Poverty rates among America's children and families also have been pushed higher in recent years because an increasing share of the nation's younger population are minority. Black and Hispanic parents are far less likely to have earnings sufficient to lift their children out of poverty. As a result, black and Hispanic children are nearly three times more likely than white children to be poor.

Of course, minority children—due in large part to their far higher poverty rates—also are much more likely to encounter a host of other difficulties during their crucial developmental years. From low birthweight, inadequate nutrition and increased risk of disability or developmental delay early in life to high rates of school failure, teenage childbearing and unemployment during adolescent years, the changing racial and ethnic composition of the nation's younger population threatens to compound the problems already facing America's children and youth and increase to an even greater extent the need for effective responses from both public and private sectors.

Recommendations to Preserve and Strengthen the Quality of Data from the Decennial Census and Current Population Surveys

It would be impossible to examine the scope or implications of any of the demographic and economic trends we have been discussing today without the comprehensive data generated through the decennial census and Current Population Surveys. For this reason, I would like to turn to some suggestions regarding steps that Congress should consider in order to preserve and strengthen the quality of these essential federal data sources.

The Census Bureau completed the release of the sample data from the decennial Census of Population and Housing on June 1st of this year. Overcoming a historically low mailback rate, the requirement to attempt to count those—the homeless—whom no one has counted, and a new geographic system of unprecedented power and complexity (along with the corresponding local adjustments), the Census Bureau completed its basic work in record time and with a minimum of unavoidable error. At the end, data for states were being released at a rate of four or five per day, and on one single day data covering 30 million Americans flowed from the Bureau's computers. Within a week of the riots in Los Angeles—and without interrupting the flow of data for other states—special tabulations of all critical data for the riot-torn neighborhoods were released along with that for the rest of California. These achievements are far ahead of the Bureau's own schedule and anyone's expectation. We offer our thanks and admiration to the Bureau's decennial staff for their impressive and perhaps unprecedented accomplishments.

The Bureau also, for the first time, made decennial counts available instantly to a very wide audience. The CENDATA system made available the Bureau's press releases and data sheets within days (and in some cases, hours) of their official release to anyone with a small computer, a modem, and a few dollars. One benefit of such swift and complete release may have been unexpected: ordinary data users caught a few of the inevitable errors and inconsistencies and reported back to the Bureau, often in time for the correction of final reports. No one can weave a tapestry as large as the decennial census without error, but in an era of diminished confidence in government it is a special gift to the nation that the Bureau chose to facilitate quick, cheap, and complete public access, entirely beyond any government control. May other statistical agencies be inspired by the Census Bureau's example.

Our praise for the professional performance of the Census Bureau does not mean that we agree with all the constraints under which it was carried out. We think that the substantial consensus among statisticians that the decennial counts can be safely adjusted for systematic undercounts should be heeded; on the other hand we remain uncomfortable with the small size of the Post Enumeration Survey (150,000 households) on which an adjustment would depend. That size may be adequate to adjust, but we are not sure that it also is large enough to estimate the accuracy of the adjustments made. Congress, for example, needs not only the most accurate figures for funding distribution formulas, but also a measure of the accuracy of the figures provided, since it may easily build in safety margins in allocations where the requisite data are available. Some federal funding formulas—Chapter 1 is an example—reach to the county level, and the 150,000 households of the PES would be spread thinly over the more than 3,000 U.S. counties.

We do not think that the S-Night count of the sheltered and homeless populations provides an adequate basis for national, state or local planning. Clearly the Bureau needs to be funded to develop both a better (and permanent) facility registry of shelters and other transient residential quarters and also a redundant family of methods for counting the people living in streets, vacant lots and cars. These developments should start now, and be applied to special counts taken each year or each two years so that they will be mature and effective for the Census of 2000. Perhaps we could look back to the Census of 1940 which seemed to have better success in finding and enumerating the Depression-era railside camps of homeless persons.

In addition, we are aware of no nationally representative survey or census data that identifies children migrant farmworker families or their characteristic informal estimates of the number of such children vary widely, ranging as high as 1 million. In light of evidence that many of these children live in desperately poor and often dangerous conditions, the decennial census in the future should include efforts to collect data of this nature.

The last items produced in the decennial cycle are the Subject Reports which give greater detail on special topics (but for more limited geography) than do the main state reports. In the 1980 cycle, the Bureau apparently ran out of money, and the planned Subject Reports for the Black and Hispanic subpopulations were cancelled, while those for the American Asians and American Indians were not completed until the very late 1980s. The 1990 state volumes, as planned, will offer even less such detail than did those produced from the 1980 Census, so it is crucial that we do not suffer another wholesale cancellation of Subject Reports.

Another, more technical, matter is in danger of being overlooked: the Census Bureau may simply put itself out of the business of providing small area estimates to both Congress and our state and local governments in a year or two, because it inadvertently gives up too much of its computer processing power. Once the main processing job is complete there has been a tendency to assume that no further analyses will be required than those already planned, and thus the Bureau gives up too much of its technical muscle. This Committee may want to encourage the Bureau to believe that the decennial census is so valuable to the nation that we ought not give up our ability to put it to new or more intense use. It is important to remember that only the Bureau can process the raw data files, since privacy requires that no person or organization outside the Bureau ever be given access to individual responses.

The decennial Census of Population and Housing, because of its enormous cost and size, is taken only every 10 years, while every other census—including those of governments, agriculture, transportation, and business—are taken every five years. Ten years is simply too long to go without a reasonable source of state level data on the lives of people. The states cannot fulfill the role of the laboratories of democracy if the federal government only turns on the microscopes once a decade.

This problem was properly and inexpensively solved in the 1970s by mandating a mid-decade expansion of the Current Population Survey from 60,000 to 300,000 households, then called the Survey of Income and Education. The corresponding survey in the mid-1980s was cancelled. While it is possible to construct surrogates from multi-year or multi-panel pooling of CPS data, these substitutes have serious flaws and in many situations are virtually useless. The right answer is for Congress to resume funding a proper and official expansion of the CPS once in the middle of each decade. This mid-decade expansion would not only provide stable and timely estimates of state figures, but would also give us the statistical power to test for new trends and patterns among the conditions impacting the lives of Americans—especially where those patterns vary among the states.

A mid-decade expansion of the Current Population Survey also would allow the Bureau to check that the selection of clusters (small geographical areas) upon which the CPS is based remains representative for all individual states as well as for the nation as a whole throughout the entire decade. This will improve the quality—or at least assure us that the quality remains—of the CPS state estimates now published each year in, for example, the poverty report in the P–60 series.

Some special augmentation of the Current Population Survey is needed to provide accurate annual national estimates for smaller portions of the population. For example, national estimates for subgroups of Hispanic youth—Mexican American, Puerto Rican, Cuban-American, and other Latin American—are not usually published. For issues that impact a narrow age range (e.g., school dropouts, adolescent childbearing, family formation), the Current Population Survey as presently designed often does not generate usable estimates even for major racial and ethnic groups. We have little hope of making progress on key issues like school completion or the creation of prosperous young families if we lack powerful and timely national estimates, whose statistical stability is beyond question.

There are several techniques that could be used to augment the Current Population Survey so that sub-ethnic and narrow age estimates are improved. Some would enlarge the sample with special subpopulations (that is already done in the Survey of Income and Program participation) while others would take advantage of the fact that the CPS is taken monthly, and an annual average tape with 12 months (3 rotation groups) of data is already prepared each year by the Census for the Bureau of Labor Statistics.

Finally, we must mention that the Current Population Survey panel on the fertility of American women is now taken only every second year, rather than every year. Teenage childbearing is a problem where knowledge of trends and changes in trends are vital to our ability to make progress. In order to monitor trends, many years of data are needed. When a survey is taken only half as often, the time needed for the nation to detect and react to changes is doubled. We would never cut the power of our radars in half, just when we are alerted that enemy planes may be approaching our coasts—why would we cut the frequency of this survey in half at the beginning of a comparable crisis for the nation? It should be restored to its annual schedule.

We thank the Chairman and members of the Subcommittee again for your patience and attention to these important issues, and would welcome any questions you might have.

Mr. SAWYER. Thank you. Let me comment not only on the child poverty rates that you find at this point, but recognizing that those rates have been abiding for most of this past decade, have we developed an understanding of what prolonged consequences arise from the concentration of child poverty rates?

Mr. JOHNSON. I think we have quite good evidence at this point of the broad and pervasive impacts of poverty on children and how it affects their development in virtually every significant area of concern.

The persistence and, in fact, the substantial growth in poverty during the 1980's has gotten much debate. It is clear to us at the Children's Defense Fund, having analyzed that data carefully, that the main driving engines behind the growth in child poverty during the 1980's actually have been the disintegration of the economy for many families with children and the reduced effectiveness of Government programs in lifting families with children out of poverty.

Only about one quarter of the increase of poverty in families with children that occurred since 1979 can be attributed to the growth in single-parent families which is, of course, the popular image of why child poverty has been increasing.

We have to work harder at addressing the underlying economic problem and the reductions in public support for families with children that are driving these increases.

Mr. SAWYER. I want to get back to that in a moment. Dr. Moore, you have done substantial research on non-traditional family conditions and whether or not they specifically cause impediments in child development.

Could you expand on that?

Ms. MOORE. You mean family forms other than a two-parent family?

Mr. SAWYER. Yes.

Ms. MOORE. The literature is very clear on single-parent families. In outcome after outcome children from single-parent families do compare less favorably than children from two-parent families. The question is, "Why is that the case? "Estimates vary, but some substantial portion of that disadvantage is indeed due to the lower incomes of the single-parent families.

The question that is still being resolved is "What is the source of that remaining difference?" Some of it appears to be due to conflict. It is very clear that the children that are most advantaged are children from two-parent, low conflict families. Conflict can be very harmful to children's long-term development.

There are other questions about whether or not there are other kinds of differences between single-parent and two-parent families that have not been resolved, for example, differences in supervision, role models, neighborhood variations and other kinds of hypotheses.

Mr. SAWYER. We are in the process of watching the Census Bureau attempt to come to grips with a rapidly changing data requirement. There is potential to use a variety of alternative techniques in this decade or beyond. Are there specific vacuums in data that would assist in addressing the consequences that we are talking about today that would benefit researchers and others as we try to measure who we are and where we are going?

Ms. MOORE. There is no data set that focuses on children. Children are usually an adjunct to other data collection efforts. To the extent that there are studies that focus on children, they tend to be somewhat narrow. For example, there might be a study focused on education. There might be one focused on health. In fact, one's education can affect health, and one's health can affect schooling.

What we really need is information about the whole child, the child's family situation, the neighborhood situation, the health of the child and what happens to that child over time . We need longitudinal data focused on children. In other words, an occasional cross-sectional survey will not give us the information that we need to sort it out and answer the kinds of questions that you are asking today.

Mr. JOHNSON. That is quite a thoughtful question and we would like to come back to the subcommittee with a thoughtful set of answers. But do we have one quick response off the top of our heads.

In our written testimony we comment on the problem of teenage childbearing. Knowledge of trends related to teenage childbearing is vital to our ability to make progress in this area but the surveys that are taken in this area have been cut back so they are only being taken half as often as previously and it now takes twice as long to get any sense of certainty about the trends in teenage childbearing. Particularly with the implications for both young parents and their children and the implications for public policy in this area, that seems to be a mistake.

Mr. SAWYER. I am trying real hard not to get myself into this controversy that is ranging around the country about family structure and values, however they might be defined. But it seems to me that there are advantages and disadvantages in having both parents in a two-parent family who work. The value of incomes and what you can do with them has shifted remarkably in the last 20 years or so, despite the presence of two parents. The lowered income of a single-parent, single-earner family has advantages and disadvantages weighted against the two-income family.

Can you comment on the effect of two-worker families on the progress and development of children, particularly pre-school children?

Ms. MOORE. There is an enormous literature on the effects of maternal work on children but far less on fathers. Researchers find no universal impact of employment of the mother on the child.

I think that this literature, which hypothesizes negative effects of maternal work, needs to be compared to the literature on preschool education, where people who study programs like Head Start have hypotheses for positive effects on children. I think the real issue has to do with quality of care. If there are effects, there are subgroup effects, and the most important factor to look at is quality and continuity of care for the child.

Mr. JOHNSON. I strongly agree with that. I think the literature is clear that poor quality child care can have harmful effects on the development of children. It forces you to think about the public supports we have in place for child care, particularly for low income working families and also the ways in which the economic pressures on families with children and the low incomes of single-parent families with children may put them in situations where they are unable to purchase child care that is at all reasonable.

One of the most discouraging things in the data about family incomes over the last decade or so is, in fact, that families have had to run faster to stay in the same place. Many of those families would have lost much more income had their work effort, typically of the mother, not increased. That is quite disturbing, in part because it means our data typically understates the losses that our families are suffering. Certainly you lose something when you have to increase work effort that much, even if it is measured not in dollars and cents but in terms of time spent with children.

Ms. MOORE. I did the polling work for the National Commission on Children. That was one of the clear tensions that came back from the national sample. It was the tension between money and time. You had to work more hours to make more money and then you have less time to spend with the children. Parents feel really bad about the both the lack of money and the lack of time.

I think the experience of the Hartford Co. is very relevant here because one of the things a lot of parents don't have is the flexible opportunities to do both of those things. If they go part-time they might sacrifice benefits. Many men and woman don't have the opportunity to go part-time any way.

Mr. SAWYER. Are there specific kinds of arrangements that seem best suited to children's maturing? Are there nurturing kinds of environments that we ought to be trying to encourage? Are there specific negatives we ought to be trying to ameliorate?

Mr. JOHNSON. In part we need to insure that there are stable, long-term trusting relationships between children and caregivers. The literature is quite clear that that is one of the most important things. The rapid turnover in who is caring for an individual child can be devastating in terms of forming bonds of trust and that sort of thing.

We also know a lot about the kind of stimulation children need. They need age-appropriate activities that are challenging them, giving them opportunity to learn. They need to be in safe environments that allow them to experiment or take risks or simply to be children and have fun without risking their own health and safety. Some of that requires training. I think we have had the presumption that parents learn on their own and therefore that other caregivers can just pick up and do this.

In some ways parents do learn on their own with their own children, but they have some time span in which to learn. But an individual hired with no previous training or experience in a child care center and immediately thrown in—not with one child, but with substantial numbers of children—to a child-care program will have a hard time protecting the health and safety of those children and creating a stimulating an environment to help those children grow.

Mr. SAWYER. The Children's Defense Fund had a great deal to say with regard to the development of several proposals aimed at enactment of child care laws in the last Congress. The final enactment was substantially different from that which was anticipated in either case.

Have you prepared to track the consequences of even that relatively smaller effort with regard to quality of care and consequences?

Mr. JOHNSON. We are in the midst of tracking those outcomes from the new legislation as we speak. It is a little too early to tell. The States have just within the last year gotten their implementation efforts fully up and running with the first year of child care funding.

What is clear already, however, is that the new Federal child care funds have had a very substantial impact on the availability of child care and availability of help for low-income families. The State of Ohio is one of the more striking examples where child care funding has tripled as a result of both the new Federal dollars coming in and a decision by the State of Ohio to increase its commitment for child care funding. For families in Ohio that has had a dramatic impact in terms of availability of child care help.

We don't know what impact the new Federal child care funds will have on the quality of child care assistance. There were some provisions in the legislation passed by Congress to encourage States to bolster the quality of care. Some States are taking that challenge quite seriously.

Mr. SAWYER. Dr. Moore, could you expand on your data with regard to the growing educational level of parents and the consequences on their children.

Ms. MOORE. Yes. It is interesting to me. In two ways, certainly in studies of child development, better educated parents seem to do things for and with their children that foster their development. Some of that has to do with the greater income they bring to the task of child bearing, their neighborhoods and probably access to health care. Another has to do with stimulating activities that are available to their children.

One of the interesting unanswered question to me as someone who is involved in evaluating the new Family Support Act is that the JOBS Program has as one of its goals "human capital development." This goal, in other words, is to increase the educational level of the parents, and a substantial portion of the at-risk children in this country in AFDC families. What will be the consequences of that intervention for those children?

Mr. SAWYER. Is there anything either of you would like to add today? There are a number of written questions we would like to submit to you for response at a later time. We will be putting this record together during the course of the entire summer.

Ms. MOORE. I just want to add one thought. The final table, one of the ones I did not talk about, shows an increased rate of teenage childbearing. Also, there has been no decline in the incidence of abortion in the United States. There has been an increase in unwanted and unintended or mistimed childbearing. There has been a decline in family planning services in inflation-adjusted dollars.

I can make no statement that those two trends are causal, but those trends are going on. I observe them simultaneously and, speaking as a private individual, I think they are a source of concern.

Mr. SAWYER. Thank you. Mr. Johnson, tying back to the child care discussion we just had about implementation and the quality of care going on in States, this administration, the Department of Health and Human Services in particular, has been quite unhelpful and in many cases part of the problem in allowing States to do a reasonable job in promoting the quality of child care under the new Federal legislation.

Congress clearly intended not to mandate Federal standards in many areas, but certainly intended to give States relatively free hands to take steps they thought were prudent, and encouragement to do so.

Mr. JOHNSON. Yes, and encouragement to do so. HHS has not provided that encouragement in any significant way, but has tied States' hands in very substantial ways through their writing of the regulations governing State implementation. The State of Ohio, which has a long history—we happen to have an office in the State of Ohio so we are a little more familiar with things there——

Mr. SAWYER. It would not have anything to do with the representation of the Chair?

Mr. JOHNSON. Absolutely not. In the State of Ohio they have had a longstanding practice with State child care dollars of tying certain quality protections for children to those funding sources and providing the assistance to child care providers on the condition they made sure those protections for children were in place. They have done this with public funds—when they were paying for the care with public State dollars—in a way that they would not do if the individual parent were making their own arrangements. They were not regulating the whole industry but they said, "Well, when we pay for the care, we have an interest in making sure it is safe." That is a reasonable position for the State of Ohio.

The Department has been in the position of saying to the States that they cannot do that, that States cannot tie protections for children solely to that care which they paid for. HHS has defended this position with a very arcane set of arguments, but without elaboration I wanted to let you know that the Department is pushing on the wrong side of this and it maybe something we will have to deal with in Congress.

Mr. SAWYER. Anything you would add to that for the Education and Labor Committee I am sure it will be welcome.

Mr. JOHNSON. Thank you.

Mr. SAWYER. I thank you both for your comments. If there is no further business before us today, we stand adjourned.

[Whereupon, at 2:55 p.m., the subcommittee was adjourned, subject to the call of the Chair.]

AMERICA'S CHANGING PROFILE: "HOW WE LIVE: HOUSEHOLD, FAMILY, AND INCOME PATTERNS"

WEDNESDAY, JUNE 24, 1992

House of Representatives,
Subcommittee on Census and Population,
Committee on Post Office and Civil Service,
Washington, DC.

The subcommittee met, pursuant to call, at 1:05 p.m., in room 311, Cannon House Office Building, Hon. Thomas C. Sawyer (chairman of the subcommittee) presiding.

Member present: Representative Sawyer.

Mr. Sawyer. Welcome. I am pleased to have both of you here this afternoon, in addition to our guests.

This is our second set of hearings in the series of "America's Changing Profile." We are trying to look at a range of demographic trends and their implications for our Nation's policy making. Our focus in these hearings is on our Nation's children, the families, the households, the way in which we organize our lives as individuals. Today we will look at the effects of changing income distribution on how we live.

Yesterday we saw two essential trends. First, put at its most basic, more children are poor than has been the case in the recent past. Nearly a quarter of all children under the age of 6, by current definition, are poor, and well over half of young children in single parent families live in poverty, the single, fastest growing family characteristic in the Nation. And the rates of both of those are rising.

The implication in terms of a wide range of policy areas is very serious. You have to think in terms of educational attainment, labor force participation, income dependency.

The second trend is that the composition of families is changing rapidly. The family of yesterday isn't the family of today, and it's not likely to be the family of tomorrow. That pace of change is both being driven by factors and driving other factors that are important for policy makers to recognize, learn to measure, understand, and ultimately to be able to act on.

More parents than at any time in our history are raising children alone, and in a very large percentage of two-parent families, both parents work outside the household. Clearly, the need for support systems that also go outside that household has become acute. It's clear that employers who are sensitive to rapidly changing family situations are in the best position to be competitive, to attract and retain skilled and productive workers, and to provide families with the kind of environment that can nurture further generations of productive workers.

We hope to expand on some of that today and take a look at the way in which income distribution, at least in its largest sense, affects the kinds of consequences that we've looked at in detail over the last couple of days.

Our witnesses today are Patricia Ruggles, senior research associate at the Urban Institute, a member of the National Advisory Committee of the Institute for Research on Poverty, and author of the recently published book, "Drawing the Line; Alternative Poverty Measures and Their Implications for Public Policy."

With her is Dr. Margaret Simms, who is the director of research programs at the Joint Center for Political and Economic Studies, a former director of the Urban Institute's Minorities and Social Policy Program, has served as editor of the Review of Black Political Economy, and a consultant to a number of different organizations. We're glad to have you here this afternoon and look forward to hearing what you have to say.

Ms. Ruggles.

STATEMENTS OF PATRICIA RUGGLES, SENIOR RESEARCH ASSOCIATE, THE URBAN INSTITUTE; AND MARGARET C. SIMMS, DIRECTOR OF RESEARCH PROGRAMS, JOINT CENTER FOR POLITICAL AND ECONOMIC STUDIES

Ms. RUGGLES. Thank you, Mr. Chairman.

I am happy to be here today to discuss trends in the distribution of incomes among American families. Recent trends toward increasing inequality in the distribution of family income have important implications for the economic well-being of many families.

These changes in incomes and in opportunities affect not only the families involved, but also the public programs and policies designed to help these families. Income support programs, like social security and the various welfare programs, consume an increasing share of Federal and State budgets, but poverty, especially among children, is on the rise—as you pointed out. In difficult budgetary times, it is tempting to cut back our commitment to aid for low-income families, but if we underinvest in the education and well-being of today's poor children, we will leave them poorly prepared to become the workers and the parents of tomorrow.

There are four main issues I would like to explore in my statement today. These are: recent trends in the distribution of family incomes; the impacts of distributional trends on the well-being of American families; the major factors behind the changing trends; and the implications of these trends for public policy.

By now it is widely known that the overall distribution of income has become more unequal over the past decade or so. While the specific details of this shift depend on many factors—such as the years that are chosen for comparison, whether or not incomes are adjusted for family size, whether pre- or posttax incomes are compared, whether adjustments are made for capital gains and other sources of unearned income, and so forth—the overall story of rising inequality is so well documented as to be compelling.

I'm not going to go into the details here. In the background material for my testimony I present distributions of income under various different measures of income, and as I think that illustrates, adjusting for family size and for taxes paid does produce some changes in the magnitude of the decline of income for low-income families. But overall, the story remains pretty much the same, no matter how we calculate income.

The average incomes of families in the lowest 20 percent of the distribution fell between 1979 and 1989, those in the middle made small gains in income, and those in the top 20 percent made large average gains. In every income category, families with children fared worse than did families as a whole.

These trends are part of a longer term trend toward increasing inequality, and that trend has been in place since the mid-1970's or so. But it accelerated rapidly in the 1980's, as Table 2 illustrates. The share of all income that was received by the bottom 20 percent of American families was about 5.5 percent in 1970. It has declined to about 4.6 percent today. Two-thirds of that decline took place after 1980. For families in the middle 20 percent, shares of total income were pretty stable until 1980, but their share has also declined since then. All that money has to be going somewhere, and as table 2 shows, most of it went to families in the highest 20 percent, who increased their share from about 41 percent of all income in the 1970's to 44.3 percent in 1990. Gains for the top 5 percent of all families were particularly large between 1980 and 1990, when their share rose from 15.3 percent of all income to 17.4 percent. That's a very substantial rise in the scheme of things.

In other words, the 5 percent of families at the top of the income distribution now have almost four times more income than the whole 20 percent at the bottom, or on a per family basis, they have about 15 times as much income per family as families in the bottom part of the income distribution.

This ratio has increased substantially since 1970, when the top 5 percent had about three times as much as the bottom 20 percent, about 11 times as much per family. Almost all of this increase in the relative share of those at the top has occurred since 1980.

What do these trends mean for American families? If incomes are growing for most people, does it matter that the overall distribution is getting more unequal? And, for that matter, are incomes growing for most people?

Measuring income growth over time is fairly difficult conceptually. Comparing people who are at the same point in the over distribution of income at two different points in time is unsatisfying because they will almost always be different people with different characteristics. But if we follow specific individuals and their incomes over time, our question isn't really answered either. Most people do experience some growth in their income as they get older—at least until they reach retirement age—but much of that growth comes from their own increasing education and work experience.

Finding that the real incomes of families in the lowest 20 percent have stagnated or even fallen does tell us something useful: presumably, it will be harder for such families to make ends meet than it used to be. But, of course, most of the actual people who were in the bottom 20 percent in 1970 are not still there in 1990. As those at the bottom in 1970 have gotten older, their earnings may have increased or, if they were children, they may have become old enough to get a job. Many of the low-income elderly in 1970 will have died by 1990, and the bottom income category in 1990 will include many people who were not born in 1970.

Comparing distributions of income across time, therefore, doesn't necessarily tell us much about the income changes experienced by specific people. Over time, most low-income people do experience increases in income. Only a tiny percentage of the population remains poor for as long as 20 years at a time, for example. For the individuals involved, this is surely good news. Most of today's poor can expect to be better off in the future.

Over the past two decades, however, two disturbing trends appear to have limited the gains of poor families and worsened the degree of hardship experienced by those who are poor. First, although almost all of today's poor will eventually leave poverty, it will probably happen more slowly for today's youngsters than for yesterday's. And second, today's young families can expect smaller gains in their incomes as their earners age than the gains experienced by similar families in the 1950's and 1960's, even though today's family typically has more workers and puts in more hours of work than families did 20 or 30 years ago.

The causes of these trends are explored in more detail below, but first I think it's important to understand what they mean for American families. Overall, about 13.5 percent of Americans were officially counted as poor in 1990. Families with children were more likely to be poor in the 1980's than at any time since we started keeping track of official poverty rates in the late 1960's. In 1990, more than 20 percent of American children—one child in five—lived in a family with an income below the poverty line. In comparison, in 1970, just over 15 percent of American children were poor. Poverty rates for children peaked during the last recession at over 22 percent—the highest level since 1964—and are likely to reach similar levels when the new 1991 data become available.

What does it mean to live in a family with a below-poverty level of income? The 1990 poverty line for a family of three was $10,419, for example. That means that a family with as much as $10,420 would not be considered poor. This level of income is less than 30 percent of the median income for American families in general, and it represents a very low standard of living. For example, if such a family spent as little as $275 a month on food—which is what the thrifty food plan that is the basis for food stamps calls for families to spend as an emergency minimum—and $550 per month on total housing—that is to say, rent, utilities, everything—and both of these are extremely low estimates of family needs—they would have only $43 per month left to pay for everything else, including clothing, transportation, child care, and work or medical expenses. It's hard to see how such a family could make ends meet.

Although the poverty line is adjusted over time to take account of general changes in prices, I have argued elsewhere that these adjustments are inadequate. Housing costs in particular have risen much faster than overall prices over the last decade or so, and the poor spend a disproportionate share of their incomes on housing. Also, income levels in general have risen since the poverty line was first estimated in 1963, and as growth in income occurs, it is to be expected that the standard of living that society considers minimally acceptable will rise also.

The poverty line for a family of three has fallen as a share of median income over time, however, from almost 40 percent in 1963 to less than 30 percent today. If we instead measured poverty using a definition that was comparable to the 1963 definition in terms of the relationship to median income, the 1990 poverty cutoff for a family of three would have been about $13,800. Under cutoffs at this level—still not a luxurious standard—today's poverty rates would be much higher. About 20 percent of the population as a whole, and almost 30 percent of American children, would be counted as poor.

As poverty rates rise, the probability that a poor family will remain poor increases. When unemployment is high and many low-skilled jobs also pay very low wages, it is likely to take longer for families to work their way out of poverty. While very long spells of poverty are still quite uncommon, it is unfortunately not uncommon for today's poor children to spend much of their childhoods living in poverty. And if the distribution of earnings continues to become more unequal over time, and income growth remains poor for younger, less-skilled workers, these trends in poverty will almost certainly continue.

Why have family incomes declined so much for families at the bottom of the income distribution? Why has income growth been so slow even for families in the middle, while families at the top have seen big increases in income? Most of the answers have to do with changes in the distribution of total earnings that have taken place since the late 1970's.

The past decade has seen increases in inequality within every age group, but the incomes of younger families have been particularly hard hit. Low-income people in families with heads under age 35 saw a decline in average pretax income of almost 24 percent between 1979 and 1989. In fact, the average income for all people in families with a head under age 35 declined by about 4 percent. For all other age groups, income even for those at the bottom rose at least a small amount over this period.

These declines in average income occurred in spite of increases in hours worked. Overall, families worked about 2 percent more in 1989 than in 1979, and families in the bottom fifth worked about 5 percent more. There were small declines in men's hours of work, but these were more than offset by large increases in women's hours of work. But in spite of the fact that families were working more hours, those families at the bottom earned about 3 percent less than they did a decade ago.

As these findings imply, changes in relative wages account for most of the increase in income inequality over the past decade. Younger workers, especially those with a high school education or less, receive substantially lower wages today than similar workers did a decade or two ago.

Although the country as a whole experienced a reasonably strong recovery after the recession of the early 1980's, this recovery did not translate into wage gains for those at the bottom, or even in the middle, of the income distribution. If wages had responded to declining unemployment and rising productivity in the 1980's, in the same way that they did on average over the rest of the postwar period, incomes in the bottom fifth of the population would have been about 20 percent higher than they were in 1990. Incomes for the middle fifth would have been about 8 percent higher, while those of the top fifth would actually have been about 7 percent lower, if we had seen the same kind of response to growth that we've seen in previous decades.

Why have lower income workers stopped benefiting from the overall growth of the economy to the same extent that they did over most of the postwar period? This is a complex question and the answer undoubtedly involves many factors, including changes in family structure, changes in the industrial mix of the economy, and changes in the supply of labor. Overall, however, several studies have found that the most important factor is probably declining demand for lower skilled workers in industrialized countries, which in turn appears to be related to technological changes and increasing international competition for these jobs.

As markets become more international, jobs that were once performed by lower skilled workers in the United States are increasingly likely to go to lower paid workers overseas. If U.S. businesses are to offer their goods at prices that are competitive in world markets, they must either pay lower wages to their U.S. workers or hire cheaper labor abroad. Other technological changes—for example, increasing computer usage—have also reduced the demand for low skilled workers. As a result, wages for lower skilled workers and the supply of jobs for these workers are lower than they were a decade or so ago. This decline has had the most impact on younger workers who have entered the labor force during this period, because they haven't had a chance to build up experience and on-the-job skills that might make them more valuable, and they have faced the most direct competition for the lower skilled jobs that are available.

It should be emphasized that these changes aren't the result of any particular Government policy. Indeed, similar changes in the distribution of earnings have occurred in most industrialized countries. Policies that mandate higher wages for low skilled workers or that severely limit international competition are likely to be counterproductive, resulting in higher costs of production and lower demand for U.S. goods, and ultimately lower growth in productivity and earnings for the United States as a whole.

In summary, then, the distribution of income, and especially of earnings, has become substantially more unequal over the last decade or so, no matter how we measure it. Lower skilled workers are working more hours at lower wages, and even so, the total incomes of those near the bottom of the distribution have actually fallen. Younger families and families with young children have been particularly hard hit, with the result that as many as 30 percent of American children are currently living in families whose incomes are not adequate to provide basic necessities. This is a scandal in a country with the resources of the United States. It also bodes ill for our future, as these children grow up inadequately prepared to become the workers and parents of tomorrow.

What can public policy do to rectify or at least ameliorate these problems?

Mr. SAWYER. It is precisely at that point—I have been looking for a great place to break, and that is exactly the point. I have to go vote. We will suspend these proceedings for a few minutes, and when we come back, we can hear your recommendations.

Thank you.

[Whereupon, the subcommittee was in recess.]

Mr. SAWYER. As you were saying——

Ms. RUGGLES. Thank you, Mr. Sawyer.

What can public policy do to rectify or at least ameliorate these problems? As discussed above, large increases in minimum wages or more protectionist trade policies probably aren't the answer and are likely to hurt rather than help the U.S. economy as a whole. Similarly, policies such as mandated work programs for welfare recipients are almost entirely beside the point. The problem isn't that the poor won't work; it's that they can't earn enough to make ends meet. And while increases in the number of single parent families has added to the burdens facing today's children, there's no evidence that Government policies have caused these increases and I believe, at least, there is very little that we can do through public policy to prevent family breakups or out-of-wedlock births. Those are basically private decisions.

If no interventions along those lines are likely to do much good, what can we do? Well, taking a cue from other industrialized countries that have seen similar shifts in the distribution of earnings, but without similar increases in child poverty, we could consider more direct support for families with children who are trying to make ends meet. The costs and quality of child care in the United States, for example, pose a major problem for mothers of young children who must work to support their families. We could do more to ensure the availability and affordability of decent care for such families. Similarly, most other industrialized countries provide some form of family allowance to help support young families who are struggling to make ends meet. Even when earnings are inadequate by themselves, such allowances can help maintain the family and can substantially improve the circumstances of young children.

In the longer run, if we want to promote higher growth and greater opportunity to tomorrow's economy, we must invest more in the education and well-being of our children today. The changes in the distribution of income that have occurred recently can only be reversed if more of today's children grow up to become skilled and productive as workers and as parents in the world of tomorrow. Accomplishing that goal means giving more support to the young families of today.

[The prepared statement of Ms. Ruggles follows:]

PREPARED STATEMENT OF PATRICIA RUGGLES, SENIOR RESEARCH ASSOCIATE, THE URBAN INSTITUTE

Chairman Sawyer, I am happy to be here today to discuss trends in the distribution of incomes among American families. Recent trends toward increasing inequality in the distribution of family income have important implications for the economic well-being of many families.

These changes in incomes and in opportunities affect not only the families involved but also the public programs and policies designed to help families in need. Income support programs such as Social Security and the various welfare programs consume an increasing share of federal and state budgets, but poverty, particularly among children, continues to rise. In difficult budgetary times it is tempting to cut back our commitment to aid for low-income families, but if we under-invest in the education and well-being of today's poor children we will leave them poorly prepared to become the workers—and the parents—of tomorrow.

There are four main issues that I would like to explore in my statement today. These are:

- Recent trends in the distribution of family incomes;
- The impacts of distributional changes on the well-being of American families;
- The major factors behind the changing trends; and
- The implications of these trends for public policy.

TRENDS IN THE DISTRIBUTION OF INCOME

By now it is widely known that the overall distribution of income has become more unequal over the past decade or so. ale the specific details of this shift depend on many factors, such as the years chosen for comparison, whether or not incomes are adjusted for family size, whether pretax or post-tax incomes are compared, whether adjustments are made for capital gains and other sources of unearned income, and so forth, the overall story of rising inequality is so documented as to be compelling.

As an illustration of this point, Table 1 shows the percentage change in average incomes for families in three different parts of the income distribution between 1979 and 1989 under three different methods of measuring income. The first panel shows changes in average family income before taxes, the second shows these changes after adjustment to take account of differences in family sizes in the different income categories, and the third panel shows these changes after adjustment both for family size and for taxes paid.

Table 1—Percentage Change in Average Incomes, 1979–1989, Under Various Income Definitions

	Lowest 20 Percent	Middle 20 Percent	Top 20 Percent
Percentage change in average pre-tax cash income, 1979–89:			
All Families	−2.1	0.8	13.9
Families with Children	−17.7	−0.8	12.3
Percentage change in average pre-tax income, adjusted for family size:			
All Families	−4.3	6.7	19.6
Families with Children	−11.9	3.3	17.1
Percentage change in average post-tax income, adjusted for family size:			
All Families	−2.1	6.4	20.4
Families with Children	−6.2	2.9	17.4

Source: U.S. House of Representatives, ***Green Book: Background Material and Data on Programs Within the Jurisdiction of the Committee on Ways and Means,*** pp. 1371 and 1383, Committee on Ways and Means. Washington, D.C.: Government Printing Office, May 15, 1992.

Thus, for example, average real family cash incomes fell by about 2 percent for families in the bottom 20 percent of the income distribution between 1979 and 1989, but rose by about 14 percent for families in the top 20 percent. Adjusting for differences in family size, the gap is even bigger—a decline of more than 4 percent for the lowest group, and an increase of almost 20 percent for the highest. After taxes paid are taken into account as well, however, the decline for families at the bottom is back around 2 percent, although those at the top have still gained about 20 percent on average.

Dramatic as these changes are, the changes in average incomes among families with children have been even larger. Families with children have slightly higher incomes, on average, than do all families, but their incomes have declined more in relative terms over the past decade. In 1989, for example, the average income for all families in the bottom 20 percent of the distribution was $5,866, while the average for a family with children was $7,714. For all families in the bottom category, this average represented a decline of $128 between 1979 and 1989. For families with children, however, the 1989 average was $1,655 lower than the 1979 average for the bottom 20 percent of such families—a decline of almost 18 percent.

Again, adjusting for family size and for taxes paid produces some changes in the magnitude of the declines for low-income families, but the overall story remains the same. The average incomes of families in the lowest 20 percent fell between 1979 and 1989, those in the middle made small gains in income, and those in the top 20 percent made large average gains. In every income category, families with children fared worse than did families as a whole.

These trends are part of a longer term trend toward increasing inequality in the distribution of income, although that trend accelerated during the 1980s, as Table 2 illustrates. The share of all income that was received by the bottom 20 percent of American families was about 5.5 percent in 1970, and has declined to about 4.6 percent today. Two-thirds of that decline took place after 1980. For families in the middle 20 percent, shares of total income were fairly stable until 1980, but have declined since then. All that money has to be going somewhere, and as Table 2 shows most of it went to families in the highest 20 percent, who increased their share from about 41 percent of all income in the 1970s to 44.3 percent in 1990. Gains for the top 5 percent of all families were particularly large between 1980 and 1990, when their share rose from 15.3 percent of all income to 17.4 percent.

Table 2—Shares of Total Income Received by Families in Various Income Categories

	Lowest Fifth	Middle Fifth	Highest Fifth	Top 5 Percent
1970	5.5	17.6	40.9	15.6
1975	5.5	17.6	41.1	15.5
1980	5.2	17.5	41.5	15.3
1985	4.7	16.8	43.5	16.7
1990	4.6	16.6	44.3	17.4

Source: U.S. Bureau of the Census Current Population Reports Series P–60, No. 174, Table B–13.

In other words, the 5 percent of families at the top of the income distribution now have 3.8 times more income collectively than do the 20 percent of families at the bottom, or about 15 times as much income on a per family basis. This ratio has increased substantially since 1970, when the top 5 percent had about 2.8 times as much as the bottom 20 percent, or about 11 times as much income per family.[1] Almost all of this increase in the relative share of those at the top has occurred since 1980.

IMPACTS OF RISING INEQUALITY FOR AMERICAN FAMILIES

What do these trends mean for American families? If incomes are growing for most people, does it matter that the overall distribution is getting more unequal? And for that matter, are incomes growing for most people?

Measuring income growth over time is fairly difficult conceptually. Comparing people who are at the same point in the overall distribution of income at two different points in time is unsatisfying, because they will almost always be different people with different characteristics. But if we follow specific individuals and their incomes over time, our question isn't really answered either. Most people do. experience income growth as they get older, at least until they reach retirement age—but much of that growth comes from their own increasing education and work experience.

Finding that the real incomes of families in the lowest 20 percent have stagnated or even fallen does tell us something useful—presumably, it will be harder for such families to make ends meet than it used to be. But of course most of the actual people who were in the bottom 20 percent in 1970 are not still there in 1990. As those at the bottom in 1970 have gotten older, their earnings may have increased or, if they were children, they may have become old enough to get a job. Many of the low-income elderly in 1970 will have died by 1990, and the bottom income category in 1990 will include many people who were not born in 1970.

Comparing distributions of income across time, therefore, doesn't necessarily tell us much about the income changes experienced by specific people. Over time, most

[1] Calculated from U.S. Bureau of the Census, *Current Population Reports* Series P–60, No. 174, Table B–13.

low-income people do experience increases in income—only a tiny percentage of the population remains poor for as long as twenty years at a time, for example. For the individuals involved, this is surely good news: most of today's poor can expect to be better off in the future.

Over the past two decades, however, two disturbing trends appear to have limited the gains of poor families and worsened the degree of hardship experienced by those who are poor. First, although almost all of today's poor will eventually leave poverty, it will probably happen more slowly for today's poor youngsters than for yesterday's. And second, today's young families can expect smaller gains in their incomes as their earners age than the gains experienced by similar families in the 1950s and 1960s—even though today's family typically has more workers and puts in more hours of work than families did 20 or 30 years ago.

The causes of these trends will be explored in more detail below, but first it is important to understand their impacts. Overall, about 13.5 percent of Americans were officially counted as poor in 1990. Families with children were more likely to be poor in the 1980s than at any time since we started keeping track of official poverty rates in the late 1960s. In 1990, more than 20 percent of American children—one child in five—lived in a family with an income below the poverty line. In comparison, in 1970 just over 15 percent of American children were poor. Poverty rates for children peaked during the last recession at over 22 percent—the highest level since 1964—and are likely to reach similar levels when the new estimates for 1991 become available.

What does it mean to live in a family with a below-poverty level of income? The 1990 poverty line for a family of three was $10,419, for example—so families with as little as $10,420 in annual income could be counted as "non-poor".[2] This income level is less than 30 percent of the median income for American families in general, and it represents a very low standard of living. For example, if such a family spent as little as $275 per month on food and $550 per month on total housing costs—both low estimates of likely family needs—they would have only $43 per month left to pay for everything else—including clothing, transportation, child care, and any work or medical expenses. It is hard to see how such a family could make ends meet.

Although the poverty line is adjusted over time to take account of general changes in prices, I have argued elsewhere that these adjustments are inadequate.[3] Housing costs in particular have risen much faster than overall prices over the past decade or so, and the poor spend a disproportionate share of their incomes on housing. Also, income levels in general have risen since the poverty line was first estimated in 1963, and as growth in income occurs it is to be expected that the standard of living that society considers minimally acceptable will rise also.

The poverty line for a family of three has fallen as a share of median income over time, however, from almost 40 percent in 1963 to less than 30 percent today. If we measured poverty using a definition that was comparable to the 1963 definition in terms of its relationship to median income, the 1990 poverty cutoff for a family of three would have been about $13,800. Under cutoffs at this level-still not a luxurious standard—today's poverty rates would be even higher. About 20 percent of the population as a whole—and almost 30 percent of American children—would be counted as poor.

As poverty rates rise, the probability that a poor family will remain poor increases. When unemployment is high and many low-skilled jobs also pay very low wages, it is likely to take longer for families to work their way out of poverty. While very long spells of poverty are still quite uncommon, it is unfortunately not uncommon for today's poor children to spend much of their childhoods living in poverty. And if the distribution of earnings continues to become more unequal over time, and income growth remains poor for younger less-skilled workers, these trends in poverty will almost certainly continue.

WHAT'S BEHIND THE CHANGING TRENDS?

Why have family incomes declined so much for families at the bottom of the income distribution over the past decade or so? Why has income growth been so slow even for families in the middle, while families at the top have seen big in-

[2] Poverty thresholds vary slightly depending on the numbers of children versus adults in the family, but the highest level for a family of three would be only $10,530. The average across all family types for a three person family is the $10,419 cited above.

[3] See Patricia Ruggles, *Drawing the Line,* Urban Institute Press: Washington D.C. (1990).

creases in income? Most of the answers have to do with changes in the distribution of total earnings that have taken place since the late 1970s.

The past decade has seen increases in inequality within every age group, but the incomes of younger families have been particularly hard hit. Low-income people (the bottom 20 percent) in families with heads under age 35 saw a decline in average pre-tax income of almost 24 percent between 1979 and 1989. In fact, the average income for all people in families with a head under age 35 declined by about 4 percent. For all other age groups, income even for those at the bottom rose at least a small amount over this period.[4]

These declines in average income occurred in spite of increases in hours worked. Overall, the average family worked about 2 percent more hours in 1989 than in 1979; in the bottom filth, family members worked almost 5 percent more hours. For couples with children, small declines in the hours worked by adult males were more than offset by large increases in adult women's hours. Even though such families in the bottom 20 percent worked almost 5 percent more hours in all than had similar families a decade earlier, they earned almost 3 percent less.[5]

As these findings imply, changes in relative wages account for most of the increase in income inequality over the past decade. Younger workers, especially those with a high school education or less, receive substantially lower real wages today than did similar workers a decade or two ago.

Although the country as a whole experienced a reasonably strong recovery after the recession of the early 1980s, this recovery did not translate into wage gains for those at the bottom—or even the middle—of the earnings distribution. If wages had responded to declining unemployment and rising productivity in the 1980s in the same way that they did on average over the 1947–1979 period, incomes in the bottom fifth of the population would have been about 20 percent higher by. 1990 than they actually were. Incomes for the middle fifth would have been about 8 percent higher, while those of the top fifth would have been about 7 percent lower.[6]

Why have lower-income workers stopped benefitting from the overall growth of the economy to the same extent that they did over most of the post-war period? This is a complex question, and the answer undoubtedly involves many factors, including changes in family structure, changes in the industrial mix of the economy, and changes in the supply of labor. Overall, however, several studies have found that the most important factor is probably declining demand for lower skilled workers in industrialized countries, which in turn appears to be related to technological changes and increasing international competition for these jobs.[7]

As markets become more international in nature, jobs that were once performed by lower-skilled workers in the U.S. are increasingly likely to go to lower-paid workers overseas. If U.S. businesses are to offer their goods at prices that are competitive in world markets, they must either pay lower wages to their U.S. workers or hire cheaper labor abroad. Other technological changes—for example, increasing computer usage—have also reduced demand for low-skilled workers. As a result, wages for lower-skilled workers—and the supply of jobs for these workers—are lower than they were a decade or so. This decline has had the most impact on younger workers who have entered the labor force during this period, because they have not had a chance to build up experience and on-the-job skills that might make them more valuable, and they have faced the most direct competition for the lower-skilled jobs that are available.

It should be emphasized that these changes are not the direct result of any government policy—indeed, similar changes in the distribution of earnings have occurred in most industrialized countries. Policies that mandate higher wages for low-skilled workers or that severely limit international competition are likely to be counter-productive, resulting in higher costs of production and lower demand for U.S. goods—and ultimately lower growth in productivity and earnings for the U.S. as a whole.

---

[4] Calculated from Table 50 p. 1385, *1992 Green Book.* Adjusted for family size; quintiles based on number of persons, not families.

[5] *1992 Green Book,* pp. 1424–1432.

[6] See Patricia Ruggles and Charles F. Stone, "Income Distribution Over the Business Cycle: the 1980s Were Different," Urban Institute (1991) and Journal of Policy Analysis and Management (forthcoming) for details on these findings.

[7] For a summary and assessment of this literature, see for example John Bound and George Johnson, "Changes in the Structure of Wages in the 1980's: An Evaluation of Alternative Explanations," *American Economic Review* June 1992.

WHAT SHOULD WE DO?

In summary, then, the distribution of income and especially of earnings has become substantially more unequal over the past decade or so, no matter how we measure it. Lower-skilled workers are working more hours at lower wages, and even so the total incomes of those near the bottom of the distribution have fallen. Younger families and families with young children have been particularly hard hit, with the result that as many as 30 percent of American children are currently living in families whose incomes are not adequate to provide basic necessities. This is a scandal in a country with the resources of the United States. It also bodes ill for our future, as these children grow up inadequately prepared to become the workers and parents of tomorrow.

What can public policy do to rectify or at least ameliorate these problems? As discussed above, large increases in minimum wages or more protectionist trade policies probably aren't the answer, and are likely to hurt rather than help the U.S. economy as a whole. Similarly, policies such as mandated work programs for welfare recipients are almost entirely beside the point—the problem isn't that the poor won't work, it's that they can't earn enough to make ends meet. And while increases in the number of single-parent families have added to the burdens facing today's children, there is no evidence that government policies have caused these increases, and there is little that can be done through public policy to prevent family break-ups or out-of-wedlock births.

If none of these options is likely to do much good, what can we do? Taking a cue from other industrialized countries that have seen similar shifts in the distribution of earnings—but without similar increases in child poverty—we could consider more direct support for families with children who are trying to make ends meet. The costs and quality of child care in the United States, for example, pose a major problem for mothers of young children who must work to support their families, and we could do more to ensure the availability and affordability decent care for such families. Similarly, most other industrialized countries provide some form of family allowance to help support young families who are struggling to make ends meet. Even when earnings are inadequate by themselves, such allowances can help maintain the family and can substantially improve the circumstances of young children.

In the longer run, if we want to promote higher growth and greater opportunities in tomorrow's economy, we must invest more in the education and well-being of our children today. The changes in the distribution of income that have occurred recently can only be reversed if more of today's children grow up to become skilled and productive as workers and parents in the world of tomorrow. Accomplishing that goal means giving more support to the young families of today.

Mr. SAWYER. Thank you very much.

Dr. Simms.

Ms. SIMMS. Thank you, Mr. Chairman. I appreciate the opportunity to address the Subcommittee on Census and Population on the issue of "How we Live: Household, Family, and Income Patterns".

I have been asked to address the issue of income distribution, economic opportunity, and expectations for families and individuals, and I do so with a special focus on the black population, a group of particular interest to the Joint Center for Political and Economic Studies.

Over the past 20 to 30 years, there has been a gradual transformation in family structure, household composition, employment and income. Several features of this trend are noteworthy in terms of their implications for family income. First, there has been a rapid growth in women's labor force participation, especially among married women with children, and second, there has been a growth in the proportion of families that are headed by women.

These two factors are particularly important for understanding income distribution because they have contributed to a widening gap in that distribution. Married couple families with two earners have generally fared a lot better than families headed by women alone. Moreover, there are significant differences between the black and white populations in terms of the proportion of families in each of these categories, with black families much more likely to be headed by single women.

Currently, black family income is approximately 58 percent of white family income, a number that is little different from the 1960's. However, income for both blacks and whites has changed within the population. Income disparities have grown, as has already been noted, and the aggregate proportion of income going to households at the low end of the income distribution decreased while that for the top 20 percent increased. Within the black population, those disparities are somewhat higher than they are within the white population.

The proportion of black families with incomes over $50,000 nearly doubled over the last 20 years. A substantial proportion of those families are headed by a husband and wife who both work. As a group, these black married couple families have also made advances relative to their white counterparts.

The advances are associated with two phenomena: increased access to higher education, and equal employment opportunity policy. However, two-earner married couple families constituted only 31 percent of all black families in 1990, compared to 48 percent of white families. In contrast, female-headed families, which have the lowest median incomes, were 46 percent of black families compared to 13 percent of white families.

The close link between family structure and income level has led many to assume that the major cause of the stagnation in black family income has been the growth in female-headed families among the black population. However, work completed at the Joint Center suggests that changes in economic opportunity for different segments of the population have been at least as important as family structure in explaining the declining economic status of black families with children.

Our study used decennial census data from 1960, 1970, 1980, and CPS data from 1985 to examine the changing structure of the black family and the implication of those changes for black children. Our analysis sought to answer questions around the extent to which increased poverty was associated with changes in family structure and with economic factors unrelated to family structure. We also looked at differences in black child poverty by region, by children's age, and by characteristics of their mothers.

As might be expected, our analysis showed that family structure was an important factor in the growth of poverty among black children. If family structure had not changed after 1960, the poverty rate for black children would have been approximately 25 percent lower than it actually was over the period studied. However, our study also showed that more restricted economic opportunity for single black mothers and for young parents in general may have played an even larger role in the declining economic status of black children. If black female-headed families had been able to "hold their own" relative to other family types, the poverty rate for black children would have been about 36 percent lower over the period under examination.

The data on black child poverty in different regions of the country tend to corroborate these findings. Poverty increased in the north and midwest, areas where economic growth was slower, and the disappearance of manufacturing jobs resulted in a loss of high wage jobs. Poverty declined in most of the southern cities that we examined, with the regional differences in poverty that were common before 1970 virtually disappearing.

These differences in economic opportunity are also reflected in the distribution of families headed by single women and the extent to which black families with children are dependent on public assistance.

Another aspect of black child poverty that is disturbing is the fact that it is worsening among young children. Those under the age of three are especially vulnerable. This is associated with the fact that their parents tend to be young, and the incomes of younger parents—whether single or married—have tended to decline relative to their older counterparts, as was noted earlier.

We are faced with the prospect of a growing proportion of our Nation's youth growing up in poverty, and we need to develop new initiatives and expand successful programs in ways that can address the long-term problem of America's families, problems which cut across the entire population of our country. In fact, some of these trends are worldwide.

A recent Joint Center project indicates that the United States was not alone in experiencing slow economic growth and declining real wages over much of the 1980's. In fact, the United States had better economic experiences overall than many other industrialized nations. What distinguished the United States from its counterparts was its failure to offset adverse economic changes with supportive public policy programs.

While it is not possible to import programs that have been successful in other countries and apply them here without consideration of our unique situation, the crisis that we are facing dictates that we examine alternatives to our current set of policies. Failure to do so could endanger the Nation's future.

Thank you.

[The prepared statement of Ms. Simms follows:]

Prepared Statement of Margaret C. Simms, Director of Research Programs, Joint Center for Political and Economic Studies

Mr. Chairman and Members of the Committee:

I appreciate the opportunity to address the Subcommittee on Census and Population on the issue of "How We Live: Household, Family and Income Patterns" and I applaud the committee for taking the time to examine what we have learned and can continue to learn from the enormous undertaking that is the U.S. decennial Census.

I have been asked to address the issue of income distribution, economic opportunity, and expectations for families and individuals. I do so with a special focus on the black population, a group of particular interest to the Joint Center for Political and Economic Studies.

Since it is too early to have complete analyses of the 1990 Census, I will focus on findings from analyses of earlier decennial Censuses and Current Population Surveys. These tell us what has happened to family income in recent years and highlight the kinds of questions that will need to be addressed with income and family data from the 1990 Census. For my remarks, I have drawn on several studies completed by the Joint Center.

INCOME TRENDS AND FAMILY STRUCTURE

Over the past twenty to thirty years, there has been a gradual transformation in family structure, household composition, employment and income. Several features of this trend are noteworthy in terms of their implications for family income. First, there has been a rapid growth in women's labor force participation, especially among married women who have children. Second, there has been a growth in the proportion of families that are headed by women.

These two factors are particularly important for understanding income distribution because they have contributed to a widening gap in income distribution. Married-couple families with two earners have generally fared a lot better than families headed by women alone. Moreover, there are significant differences between the black and white populations in terms of the proportion of families in each of these categories, with black families much more likely to be headed by single women.

Overall, median family income has grown very little in real terms and the ratio of black to white family income has declined slightly. In 1970, median family income for whites was $34,481 in 1990 dollars compared to $21,151 for black families, giving a black-to-white income ratio of .61. These numbers rose slightly over the decade, with a peak black-to-white income ratio of .62. During the 1980s, median family income First declined and then rose, with the black to white income ratio fluctuating between .56 and .58.[1] (See Table 1)

Table 1—Median Family Income, by Race, Selected Years

[in 1990 CPI–U Adjusted Dollars]

Year	Black	White	Black-White Ratio
1970	$21,151	$34,481	.61
1975	21,327	34,662	.62
1980	20,103	34,743	.58
1985	20,390	35,410	.58
1990	21,423	36,915	.58

Source: U.S. Bureau of the Census, Current Population Reports, Series P–60, No. 174, ***Money Income of Households, Families, and Persons in the United States: 1990,*** U.S. Government Printing Office, Washington, D.C., 1991.

These aggregate income figures disguise shifts in family income for both blacks and whites. Within each population, income disparities grew. The proportion of aggregate income going to households at the low end of the income distribution (the bottom 40%) decreased, while that for the top 20% of households increased. As can be seen in Table 2, the disparities within the black population were somewhat higher than they were within the white population. For example, in 1990 the top 20% of black households had nearly one-half of the income within the black community while the bottom 20% had only 3.1% of the income. In contrast, the bottom 20% of the white population had 4.2% of the household income compared to 46% for the top 20%. (Table 2)

Table 2—Share of Aggregate Income Received by Each Fifth of Households, 1970 and 1990, by Race

Year	Lowest Fifth	Second Fifth	Third Fifth	Fourth Fifth	Highest Fifth
White Households:					
1970	4.2	11.1	17.5	24.3	42.9
1990	4.2	9.9	16.0	23.9	46.0
Black Households:					
1970	3.7	9.3	16.3	25.1	45.5
1990	3.1	11.1	17.5	24.3	49.0

[1] The official price deflator for income that is used by the Bureau of the Census is thought to overestimate inflation prior to 1983 and therefore to underestimate positive changes in real income. Alternative measures show a greater increase. However, since the same deflator would be used for both black and white income, the ratios remain the same regardless of which deflator is used. For further discussion of this issue, see *Money Income of Households, Families, and Persons in the United States: 1990,* P–60, No. 174.

Source: U.S. Bureau of the Census, Current Population Reports, Series P–60, No. 174, ***Money Income of Households, Families, and Persons in the United States: 1990,*** U.S. Government Printing Office, Washington, D.C., 1991.

The proportion of black families with incomes over $50,000 climbed from 6.7% in 1970 to 12.6% in 1988. A substantial proportion of those families are headed by a husband and wife who both work. As a group, these black married-couple families have also made advances relative to their white counterparts. In terms of annual income, the 1990 ratio was 85 % compared to 72% in 1967.

The advances made by these black families are associated with two phenomena—1) increased access to higher education due to Title VI of the Civil Rights Act of 1964 and grants for low- and moderate-income students and 2) equal employment opportunity policy, established under Title VII of the same Act, which opened up new occupations to blacks. The proportion of the black population with a college degree tripled between 1970 and 1990 and the proportion of black workers who were in managerial, professional and related occupations jumped from 24% to 44% in the same twenty year period.

However, two-earner married couple families constituted only 31% of all black families in 1990 compared to 48% of white families. In contrast, female-headed families, which have the lowest median incomes, are 46% of black families compared to 13% of white families. Black families headed by women are more likely to be in poverty than other types of families (48% were poor in 1990) and are more likely to have no earners in the household (28% had no earners in the household in 1990).

THE ROLE OF FAMILY STRUCTURE IN ECONOMIC STAGNATION

Explaining the lack of gains among the remainder of the black population has been somewhat more complicated. The close link between family structure and income level has led many to assume that the major cause of the stagnation in black family income has been the growth in female-headed families among the black population. However, work completed at the Joint Center suggests that changes in economic opportunity for different segments of the population have been at least as important as family structure in explaining the declining economic status of black families with children.

Our study used data from the 1960, 1970 and 1980 decennial Censuses and additional information from the 1985 Current Population Survey to examine the changing structure of the black family and implication those changes had for black children.[2] Our analysis sought to answer the following questions:

- To what extent is the increased poverty among black children associated with changes in family structure?
- To what extent is growing child poverty the result of economic factors unrelated to family structure, such as the availability of employment, prevailing wage levels, or public assistance levels?
- How do economic conditions differ for children in different regions of the country and to what extent have these differences changed over time?
- Are children in certain age groups more likely to be poor than others? How likely are poor black children to "grow out of" their poverty as they get older?
- Do all children in female-headed families face similar conditions, or is their economic well-being affected by such factors as their mothers' age and previous marital status?

As might be expected, our analysis showed that family structure was an important factor in the growth of poverty among black children. If family structure had not changed after 1960, that is if the percentage of black families headed by women had not risen, the poverty rate for black children would have been 29% in 1979 rather than 38%. In 1984, only 34% of black children would have been poor, instead of 47%.[3] However, our study also showed that more restricted economic opportunity for single black mothers, and for young parents in general, may have played an even larger role in the declining economic status of black children. If black female-headed families had been able "to hold their own" relative to other family types, that is if the gap in poverty rates had remained the same over time, the poverty rate for black children would have been 24% in 1979 and 30% in 1984. (Figure A)

---

[2] See *The Declining Economic Status of Black Children: Examining the Change, Summary of Findings* (Washington, D.C.: Joint Center for Political and Economic Studies, 1990), copy attached. This research was funded by the Carnegie Corporation of New York. The full study is scheduled for release at the end of this year.

[3] This scenario assumes that the poverty rates for each family type would have continued to change as they actually did.

Figure A—Hypothetical Poverty Rates for Black Children: 1969–1984

[Percent in Poverty]

	1969	1979	1984
Actual poverty rate	42.4	37.9	46.5
Scenario 1 *	38.2	28.8	33.6
Scenario 2 **	34.0	23.8	30.2

* The figures show what the poverty rate would have been for black children if (a) family structure had remained the same as in 1960 (that is, with no increase in the percentage of female-headed families), but (b) the poverty rates for each family type continued to change as they actually did.

** The figures show what the poverty rate would have been for black children if (a) the poverty rates for each family had remained as they were in 1960, but (b) black family structure continued to change as it actually did.

The data on black child poverty in different regions of the country tend to corroborate these findings. Poverty increased in the North and Midwest, areas where economic growth was slow and the disappearance of manufacturing jobs resulted in a loss of high wage jobs. Poverty declined in most of the Southern cities that we examined, with the regional differences in poverty that were common before 1970 virtually disappearing.

These differences in economic opportunity are also reflected in the distribution of families headed by single women and the extent to which black families with children are dependent on public assistance. Young black mothers who have never married are more heavily concentrated in the North, an area that has had lower employment growth for black males. During the 1970s, employment for black males decreased more than twice as much in Northern cities as in Southern cities, and unemployment rates for black males increased approximately 60% more in the North than in the South. Likewise, there were more employment opportunities for black female family heads in the South, as jobs which are heavily dominated by women grew more rapidly in this region.

Poor black families with children in the North were also more likely to be dependent on public assistance for at least one-half of their income than they were in the South. Even in the Northeastern and Midwestern metropolitan areas where the proportion of black children in poverty changed very little, the nature of their poverty changed. Black children were less likely to be living in working poor families and more likely to be living in dependent poor families. Poor children in the South, on the other hand, were more likely to be in working poor families.

Another aspect of black child poverty that is disturbing is the fact that it is worsening among young children. Those under the age of three are especially vulnerable. This is associated with the fact that their parents tend to be young, and the incomes of younger parents (whether single or married) have tended to decline relative to their older (over 30) counterparts. However, preliminary analysis based on CPS data suggest that these children are not going to "grow" out of poverty.

While the employability of single mothers is a major determinant of black child poverty, another important factor is the changing composition of the households which are headed by black women. In 1960, more than two of every five households (44%) headed by never-married or divorced black women had other adults in them. For divorced women that proportion has remained relatively constant (41% in 1985), but it has dropped significantly for never-married mothers. Only 15% of these households had other adults in them in 1985. That means that there are no additional adults to serve as wage earners or caretakers, reducing the possibilities for supplementing the household head's income and increasing the problems of child care.

POLICY IMPLICATIONS

The findings from the Joint Center's study reinforce those of other institutions. For example, studies by the Children's Defense Fund and Northeastern University show a decline in the real earnings for young males, which has implications for family formation and well-being.[4] Also, a recently released study by the Institute for Women's Policy Research indicates that it is the return to work rather than the

[4] Clifford M. Johnson, Andrew M. Sum, and James D. Weill, *Vanishing Dreams: The Economic Plight of America's Young Families* (Washington, D.C.: Children's Defense Fund, 1992).

willingness to work that affects the economic status of children in single parent households.[5]

If detailed analyses of the 1990 Census confirm these findings, as I suspect they will, we are faced with the prospect of a growing proportion of our nation's youth growing up in poverty. The consequences of this for both the individuals and the society are well-known.

Our recent experiences with the violence in Los Angeles and other urban areas around the country have placed urban policy on the agenda once again. We have an opportunity to develop new initiatives and expand successful programs in ways that can address the long-term problems of America's families, both urban and rural, whether black, white or members of other groups. For while the problems are most acute among minority households, these problems cut across the entire population of our country. In fact, some of these trends are worldwide.

Last fall, the Joint Center held a conference on "Poverty, Inequality and the Crisis of Social Policy." That meeting brought together scholars from eight industrialized countries to compare the experiences of families and young workers during the 1970s and 1980s in each of these countries.[6]

The findings from this project indicate that the United States was not alone in experiencing slow economic growth and declining real wages over much of the 1980s. In fact, the U.S. had better economic experiences overall than many other industrialized nations. What distinguished the United States from its counterparts was its failure to offset adverse economic changes with supportive public policies and programs. These programs fall into two basic areas—support for economically vulnerable families and employment and training programs for workers, particularly those at the early stages of their work careers.

While it is not possible to summarize all of the study findings in the time available to me, I would like to point to the following: [7]

- A major factor in the declining status of black children has been declining real earnings for young workers. These decreases are associated with education and skill levels. Therefore, programs to train and retrain workers are an essential ingredient for the long-run well-being of children and the families in which they live. Most of the European countries in our study have fairly comprehensive programs for training young workers and retraining adult workers who are displaced as a result of economic change.
- Children who live in families with low wage workers or, alternatively, no employed workers, are likely to live in dire economic conditions. A more systematic approach to provide economic support for children is needed. Many European countries have child allowances or other guaranteed support systems that reduce the likelihood that children grow up in poverty.
- In addition to increased employment opportunities, single mothers are in need of child care assistance and other programs that facilitate combining parenting and work. Those European countries with child care programs and child allowances that do not penalize women who enter paid employment tend to have higher labor force participation by single mothers.

While it is not possible to import programs that have been successful in other countries and apply them here without consideration of our unique situation, the crisis that we are facing dictates that we examine alternatives to our current set of policies. Failure to do so could endanger the nation's future.

CENSUS SOURCES

U.S. Bureau of the Census, Current Population Reports, Series P–20, No. 448. *Black Population in the United States. March 1990 and 1989.* U.S. Government Printing Office, 1991.

U.S. Bureau of the Census, Current Population Reports, Series P–60, No. 172. *Money Income of Households, Families, and Persons in the United States: 1989 and 1989.* U.S. Government Printing Office, 1991.

---

[5] Roberta Spalter-Roth, Heidi I. Hartmann, and Linda Andrews, *Combining Work and Welfare: An Alternative Anti-Poverty Strategy* (Washington,D.C.: Institute for Women's Policy Research, 1992).

[6] The countries were the United States, Canada, the United Kingdom, Germany, the Netherlands, France, Italy, and Sweden.

[7] For additional information, see Katherine McFate, *Poverty, Inequality, and the Crisis of Social Policy: Summary of Findings* (Washington: Joint Center for Political and Economic Studies, 1991) and Katherine McFate, "Innovations, New Directions, and New Convergences in Poverty Alleviation", testimony before the Select Committee on Hunger, U.S. Congress, May 21, 1992.

U.S. Bureau of the Census, Current Population Reports, Series P–60, No. 174. *Money Income of Households, Families, and Persons in the United States: 1990.* U.S. Government Printing Office, 1991.

U.S. Bureau of the Census, Current Population Reports, Series P–60, No. 167. *Trends in Income, by Selected Characteristics: 1947 to 1988.* U.S. Government Printing Office, 1990.

The Declining Economic Status of Black Children, Examining the Change

(Principal researcher: Cynthia Rexroat, Ph.D., Clemson University)

During the past three decades, the economic picture for black Americans has increasingly become a study in contrasts. On the one hand, there is a growing middle class that has made great strides toward closing the gap between blacks and whites with respect to education, employment, and, therefore, economic resources and stability. At the same time, a growing segment of the black population is increasingly mired in poverty. While legal guarantees of equal opportunity have been the catalyst for upward mobility for many poor and working class blacks, many others have not been able to reap the benefits of these changes. Indeed, the plight of many has worsened.

Among blacks in poverty, no group more fully dramatizes the depth of the problem before us than the children. They are not only the most vulnerable victims of poverty; they are also, literally, the future. If current trends hold, these children will be increasingly hard-pressed to overcome the burdens imposed by poverty. Growing numbers of them will not succeed.

FOCUS OF THIS STUDY

This study examines changes in the economic well-being of black children and their families over the period from 1960 to 1985. The findings are based on data from the decennial censuses of the U.S. population for 1960, 1970, and 1980, and mid-decade information from the Current Population Survey. In addition to providing a national overview, the study examines changes in the economic status of children by region and for 45 metropolitan areas with a black population of at least 100,000 in 1980. These cities, 11 of them in the Midwest, six in the Northeast, three in the West, and 25 in the South, were home to over half the nation's black population in 1980. The study findings will be published in full as a Joint Center monograph in 1991.

This research in some instances confirms and in others confounds conventional wisdom about black poverty. As expected, the findings show that out-of-wedlock births and female-headed families are strongly linked to growing childhood poverty. But they also indicate that the changes in family structure, alone, are not enough to account for the growing numbers of black children in poverty. In fact, declining economic opportunity has played at least as great a part in increasing the prevalence of childhood poverty as the change in family structure.

Finally, in other areas, this research brings to light unexpected information that raises new questions to be addressed in the future. For example, the growing divergence in economic standing between single-parent households headed by women who were previously married and those headed by women who were never married deserves further study and analysis.

KEY FINDINGS

This research provides new insights in three broad areas. The first is the relationship between family structure and poverty.Because increases in poverty have occurred at the same time that family structure has been changing, it is widely assumed that the latter is the cause of the former. This research tested the validity of that assumption and found that family structure is not the sole, and probably not even the most significant, factor in the growth of poverty.

Second, these findings provide a more detailed look at the contours of poverty itself. Of particular importance are findings regarding the deepening of poverty, with the slide of many black families from the working poor category to the ranks of the dependent poor. Families caught in this downward shift are not only subject to greater economic deprivation; but without employment they also have less opportunity to enter the economic mainstream.

Another significant factor that emerges is the growing disparity between children in families headed by women who have never been married and those whose mothers were formerly married These findings show a new and important divergence in poverty levels for children in those two types of female-headed households.

Finally, by combining a comprehensive national portrait with more precise information by region and metropolitan area, these findings provide, for the first time, a detailed "map" of poverty. The findings reveal important regional differences in both the character and the leading causes of black childhood poverty.

FAMILIES IN CHANGE IN A CHANGING ECONOMY

While family structure is an important factor in determining whether a black child will be poor, the decline in marriage and the increased proportion of births occurring out-of-wedlock do not account fully for the decline in children's economic well-being. Indeed, the study revealed that the economic slippage experienced by all types of black families—whether headed by married couples, never-married women, or formerly-married women-played at least a great a role a family structure change in the worsening status of black children.

• The rising proportion of births to never-married women, plus increasing rates of separation and divorce, have doubled the proportion of black families headed by women: from 25 percent of all black families in 1960 to over 50 percent in 1985.

• Most of this growth in the number of female-headed families stems from the increasing proportion of black families headed by women who have never married, as opposed to those who are separated, divorced, or widowed. The number of families in the former category rose from about 10 percent in 1960 to 33 percent in 1985.

• Changing family structure is only one of several factors that have caused the increase in poverty among black children. If family structure had remained the same as in 1960, that is, if the percentage of black female-headed families had not risen at all, the percentage of poor black children in 1984 would have been about one-sixth lower than it actually was in that year (33 rather than 47 percent of all black children). (See Figure A, scenario 1.)

• Black families of every type experienced some real decline in their economic status at some time during the period, contributing significantly to the overall deepening poverty levels for black children. If female-headed families had been able to "hold their own," that is, if their poverty rates had changed in the same way that those rates changed for married-couple families from 1960 to 1984, only 30 percent of all black children (rather than the actual 47 percent) would have been poor in 1984—even with the increased proportion of children living in female-headed families. (Figure A, scenario 2)

Figure A—Hypothetical Poverty Rates for Black Children: 1969–1984

[Percent in Poverty]

	1969	1979	1984
Actual poverty rate	42.4	37.9	46.5
Scenario 1 *	38.2	28.8	33.6
Scenario 2 **	34.0	23.8	30.2

* The figures show what the poverty rate would have been for black children if (a) family structure had remained the same as in 1960 (that is, with no increase in the percentage of female-headed families), but (b) the poverty rates for each family type continued to change as they actually did.

** The figures show what the poverty rate would have been for black children if (a) the poverty rates for each family had remained as they were in 1960, but (b) black family structure continued to change as it actually did.

It is well known that black female-headed families experience greater economic hardship than married-couple families. While this research confirms that female-headed households bear a disproportionately high share of the poverty burden, it also found a slight overall improvement in the economic status of these families. Among these families, however, the research also uncovered a growing economic disparity between families headed by never-married versus formerly-married women. In 1959,78 percent of each type was poor; by 1984, that percentage had declined to about 50 percent among the previously-married, but remained over 67 percent for the never-married.

• Because of a drop in employment and earnings for workers in their 20s, young black families were much more likely to be poor in 1984 than in 1979, regardless of their family structure. Older families, on the other hand, including those headed by never-married women, were neither more nor less likely to be poor in 1984.

THE FACE OF CHILDHOOD POVERTY

The children who fare worst are those who face multiple risks. They are born to young never-married mothers who live in economically depressed areas and are very likely to be on public assistance. The concentration of poverty is highest for the youngest black children, who are much more likely to be poor than older children.

• In 1969, the poverty rates of black children did not vary in relation to the age of the family head. By 1984, children in young families (where the head of household is under 30) were twice as likely as children in older families to be poor.

• Many poor black children are becoming even poorer. In 1969, about 3.5 times as many black children lived in working poor families as lived in families dependent on public assistance (around 40 percent compared to 11 percent). By 1984, this ratio had shrunk to 1.5 (33 percent compared to 21 percent).

• Black children in families headed by never-married women today are much more likely to be impoverished than are children in married couple families or in families headed by a formerly-married woman.

Figure B.—Regional Change in the Poverty Status of Black Children: 1979–1984 *

[In percent]

Region	1979			1984		
	Non-poor	Working Poor	Dependent Poor	Non-poor	Working Poor	Dependent Poor
Northeast	55.0	21.8	21.0	46.5	22.4	30.7
Midwest	56.7	21.3	20.2	38.6	24.1	37.1
South	50.8	36.9	10.5	46.2	40.8	12.5
West	62.5	20.6	14.7	54.3	24.9	19.0

* Poverty status is defined as falling below 125% of the poverty threshold. Children living in families with no reported income are not included here.

• The very youngest black children, those under the age of three, have become especially vulnerable economically. Not only are they the poorest black children, they are also the ones with the fastest rising poverty rates. By 1984, over half of all black children under the age of three were poor, an increase of over 10 percent just since 1979. Children younger than three in families headed by never-married women have the highest poverty rate of all: 87 percent in 1984 (up from 76 percent in 1979).

• Compared to other family heads, black mothers who have never married are more likely to be in their 20s. By 1985, nearly 60 percent of all never-married female heads were in this hard-hit age bracket, while just 25 percent of household heads in married-couple families and fewer than 15 percent of formerly-married female heads were in this age group.

• The high poverty rate among never-married mothers in their early 20s reflects their education and employment status. The percentage of these women who had completed at least one year of college declined slightly, from 21 to 18 percent, between 1980 and 1985, while employment dropped from 45 to 35 percent. These trends are probably related, in turn, to the general drop in employment and earnings among workers in their 20s and to the sizable proportion of young never-married mothers living in economically depressed areas.

• The economic status of young never-married black mothers who were between the ages of 20 and 24 in 1979 had changed little by 1984, when they were 25 to 29. Three out of four of these young women continued to live below the poverty line.

• Most importantly, young black children are not likely to "grow out of" poverty as they age, because an increasing number live in families headed by a never-married woman who is in her 20s, lives in an economically depressed area, and is herself unlikely to escape from poverty. Based on calculations from the 1980 census data, the average black child who continues to live with his or her never-married mother will spend 15 years of childhood in poverty. In other words, the life chances of the very youngest generation of black children are those most seriously jeopardized by the combined trends discussed in this study.

Figure C—Distribution of Black Children Under Age Three, By Family Type and Poverty Status: 1969, 1979, 1984 *

[in percent]

Family Type and Poverty Status	1969	1979	1984
Never-married female-headed families:			
Not in poverty	17.3	17.2	11.5
Working poor	30.1	28.5	25.3
Dependent poor	43.5	49.1	63.2
No income	9.1	5.2	
Formerly married female-headed families:			
Not in poverty	21.2	28.6	25.7
Working poor	42.3	40.0	40.4
Dependent poor	31.0	27.9	32.5
No income	5.6	3.5	1.3
Married couple families:			
Not in poverty	59.5	71.2	65.4
Working poor	38.0	25.0	31.3
Dependent poor	2.0	2.8	2.6
No income	0.5	1.0	0.7

* Includes only children related to the household head.

THE GEOGRAPHY OF POVERTY

Poverty differs substantially by region. In the North, black children were more likely to be in poverty in 1984 than in 1969. Moreover, Northern children in poverty were also more likely in 1984 to fall into the most disadvantaged subcategory: the "dependent poor" families, who derive most of their income from public assistance. Black children in the South, on the other hand, were slightly better off in 1984 than in 1969, and the families of those below the poverty line were more likely to be classed as working poor rather than dependent poor.

- In the 20 metropolitan areas outside the South, poverty increased among black children, on average, from 30 percent to 35 percent from 1969 to 1979. This trend is largely due to declines in black male employment in those areas (down from 66 percent to 55 percent, on average), and to increases in the proportion of children living with never-married mothers (up from six percent to 15 percent, on average).
- During that same period in metropolitan areas outside the South, black children—whether above or below the poverty line—became poorer. More specifically, the proportion of black children above the poverty line declined two percentage points and those in working poor families decreased three points, while the percentage dependent on public assistance grew by more than five points. In some cities, black children suffered especially sharp setbacks. In Milwaukee and Cincinnati, for example, the proportion of black children in dependent poor families increased by approximately 11 points and in Buffalo the increase was 10 points.
- Even in the Northeastern and Midwestern metropolitan areas where the proportion of black children in poverty changed very little, there was, nevertheless, substantial erosion in the relative status of black children already classified as poor during this period. For these metropolitan areas, the declining number of children in working poor families and the increasing number of those in dependent poor families balanced each other out. In Indianapolis, for instance, there was a 10.1 point decline in the proportion of black children in working poor families, and a corresponding 10.9 point increase among those classed as dependent poor.
- Between 1979 and 1984, the deepening of poverty for black children was most pronounced in the Midwest. There, 37 percent of all black children relied on public assistance in 1984, up from 20 percent in 1979. During that same period, the percentage of dependent poor black children grew from 21 to 31 percent in the Northeast, and from 10.5 to 12.5 percent in the South.
- From 1969 to 1979, the six Northeastern metropolitan areas that were studied averaged a 3.4 point increase in the proportion of black children living in dependent poor families, while the 11 Midwestern metropolitan areas averaged a 7.2 point increase.
- In the 11 Midwestern cities and the six Northeastern cities studied, the increasing percentage of children living with never-married mothers was more closely associated with declines in black male employment than with any other trend.

• Black families headed by never-married women in their 20s were much more likely than other young families to live in economically depressed regions. For example, in 1985 more than 50 percent of families headed by young never-married women lived in the Northeast and the Midwest, compared to fewer than 25 percent of the young married-couple families.

• In the South, on the other hand, the economic situation of black children improved. Between 1969 and 1979 the poverty rate for black children declined from 43 to 37 percent for the region as a whole, rising only in Atlanta, Birmingham, and Jacksonville, of the 25 Southern cities studied.

• This improvement seems to be associated with the expansion of economic opportunities in the South, enabling black family heads to improve their earnings. Thus, growth in the proportion of black children who had risen above the poverty line (9.5 percentage points) coincided with a 12 point decline in the number of children whose families were classified as working poor.

• While the proportion of black children living in female-headed families increased in the South during this period, this trend was not related to changes in black child poverty rates in three-quarters of the Southern metropolitan areas studied.

• Southern black children in rural areas were considerably more likely than urban children to be poor, both in 1979 and 1984. Nevertheless, black children in the rural South faced a lower degree of economic deprivation than those in urban areas outside the South.

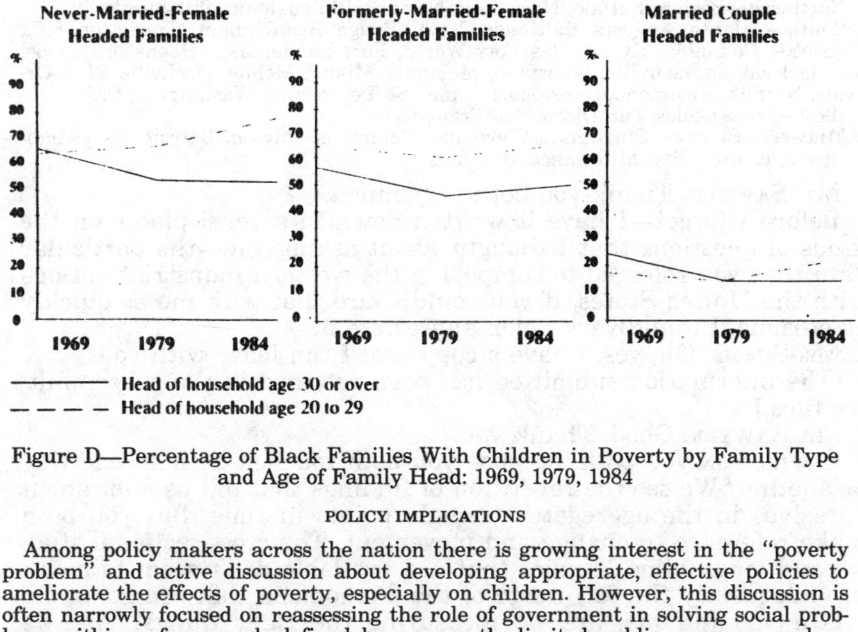

Figure D—Percentage of Black Families With Children in Poverty by Family Type and Age of Family Head: 1969, 1979, 1984

POLICY IMPLICATIONS

Among policy makers across the nation there is growing interest in the "poverty problem" and active discussion about developing appropriate, effective policies to ameliorate the effects of poverty, especially on children. However, this discussion is often narrowly focused on reassessing the role of government in solving social problems within a framework defined by apparently limited public resources and an economy that is growing slowly or not at all. Therefore, the imperative is for cost-effective measures that could open pathways to economic independence and stability.

The findings of this study indicate that the situation for black children has deteriorated, not only because of the decline in marriage, but also because of changes in the economic opportunities available to the heads of households in which these children live. The specific circumstances of black children in poverty vary by family type, region, and age of child. These variations must be accounted for, so that policy solutions can be appropriately targeted to address specific needs.

The Family Support Act (FSA), passed by Congress and signed into law in 1988, is one major program crafted in the new era of concern about the poverty problem. This act strengthens the legal child support mechanism and provides for the establishment of structured employment and training programs for individuals on public assistance. FSA has potential for addressing some of the needs of black children. However, the program's overall effectiveness will be determined by how well the act is implemented at the state level and by how much funding is available. Moreover, FSA is unlikely to have much impact on the large number of working poor families in the South. Nor will it lift children from poverty if their parents are merely shifted from the dependent poor to the working poor column.

In the long run, even a 'Family Support Act that is appropriately implemented and adequately funded cannot stand alone as the sole means for improving the well-being of children. Rather, the situation calls for comprehensive strategies and programs to improve the quality of education, provide skills training for the jobs of the future, and ensure equal access to employment opportunities.

Additional research is also needed to provide the necessary foundation for sound policy. The Joint Center for Political and Economic Studies has several current research programs underway that explore a number of particularly relevant poverty-related questions. For example:

- What are the implications of the Family Support Act for the economic status of black families?
- Does economic expansion lead to improved well-being for female-headed households in different regions?
- How effective are innovative vocational education programs at moving disadvantaged young blacks into the economic main-stream?
- How are community-based organizations trying to address the crisis now confronting black male children?

METROPOLITAN AREAS STUDIED

Northeast—Boston, Buffalo, New York, Newark, Philadelphia, Pittsburgh.

South—Atlanta, Augusta, Baltimore, Baton Rouge, Birmingham, Charleston, S.C., Charlotte, Columbia, S.C., Dallas/Fort Worth, Fort Lauderdale, Greensboro, Houston, Jackson, Jacksonville, Louisville, Memphis, Miami, Mobile, Nashville, New Orleans, Norfolk, Richmond, Shreveport, Tamp/St. Petersburg, Washington, D.C.

West—Los Angeles, San Diego, San Francisco.

Midwest—Chicago, Cincinnati, Cleveland, Columbus, Dayton, Detroit, Gary, Indianapolis, Kansas City, Milwaukee, St. Louis.

Mr. SAWYER. Thank you both very much.

Before I forget—I have it written down in several places on the kinds of questions that I thought about asking you—the particular data that you referred to comparing the western industrial nations with the United States, if you could share that with me as quickly as possible, I would very much appreciate it.

Ms. SIMMS. Oh, yes. I have a copy that I can leave with you.

[The information submitted has been retained in the subcommittee files.]

Mr. SAWYER. Good. Thank you.

Let me ask you both, because you both touched on it in one way or another. We see the repetition of findings that tell us a lot about ourselves in the aggregate at single points in time. But you both make reference to change and movement. The cross-sectional studies and longitudinal studies that are available don't seem to measure adequately the full range of the phenomena that are going on.

Can you tell me, are we measuring the right things? Are we asking ourselves enough about questions like the consequences of the number of person years in poverty, the consequences of duration or action during poverty? Do we have the tools with which to measure those kinds of things in large terms across the country, or are they still limited to being able to be studied only in small and focused research projects?

Ms. RUGGLES. Well, I think that you're absolutely right. Those are important questions that are pretty hard to study with existing data, particularly existing census data. The data that we have do tend to be cross-sectional and longitudinal rather than following people over a period of time. The relatively new survey of income and program—I guess it's not really new any more—of income and program participation does follow people over a 2½ year period. That's enough to get some idea how people move in and out of the most dire stage of poverty because people typically don't stay in, you know, really extreme poverty for long periods of time.

Mr. SAWYER. But we're seeing an enduring higher level of poverty which has been a decade or more in its length. I guess the question becomes, are we looking at new baselines?

Ms. RUGGLES. I think that's right. I think that we have seen a basic structural shift in what the distribution of income looks like in this country, and I think we essentially have a new baseline for poverty and for low income that is higher than it was a decade ago.

I think that if you want to look at the experience of particular families, you don't see very many families who spend 20 years in poverty. But we do have data from the panel study of income dynamics and we know that that might be 1 or 2 percent of those who enter poverty who spend a long time in poverty.

But what I think has happened is that opportunities are not there for the young workers of today to earn enough money, particularly single mothers, low skilled workers. The opportunities aren't there and we just see less chance for them to earn their way out of poverty.

Mr. SAWYER. You just took me right out of the order of questions I was going to ask you, but that's OK. We have seen a change in the locus of opportunity. A hundred years ago we saw poverty spread very broadly across an enormous rural landscape, and much of that abided through the first half or two-thirds or three-quarters of this century, and much of that remains. I don't mean to suggest that it's not there. But in terms of the total proportion of poverty in this country, it is less than it once was.

But we are seeing again a change in the locus of opportunity, having moved from farm to city, and people having followed it. We're seeing a spread of opportunity for work, for education, in ways that are less centrally located than perhaps even as little as 20 or 30 years ago.

Can you comment on those kinds of questions, questions like the location of transportation, of living arrangements, of educational opportunity, in terms of tangible limitations in the opportunity to get out of poverty?

Ms. SIMMS. If I could just say something about that and join——

Mr. SAWYER. Just jump in, back and forth, really.

Ms. SIMMS. In my written statement I pointed out the impact of differences in region in terms of the nature of economic opportunity, particularly for black families. While it is true that, overall, the proportion of the population that is in poverty over long periods of time is quite low, for many black families it is an extended period of time. Estimates on the number of years that black children may remain in poverty could be 16 of their 18 years for vast majorities of those who were born in single parent households.

In looking at differences, for example, between the northeast and midwest and in the south, you see that in some sense poverty is leveling compared to what it used to be, where poverty has over some periods increased in the northeast and midwest, and it's associated with changes in employment opportunities. So that in the northeast and midwest, even in those areas where the overall level of poverty has not changed, the proportion of those households who are dependent and receive most of their income from public assistance has grown. In the south, they are more likely to be working poor families; that is, they're taking advantage of the growth in jobs that has existed in the south, but they are unable to earn enough to support their families above the poverty line.

Ms. RUGGLES. Overall, I think another aspect of location that you might have been referring to is the difference between inner city poor and rural poor.

Mr. SAWYER. Yes.

Ms. RUGGLES. Overall poverty rates are very close to being the same in rural areas and in inner city areas. They run around 20 percent in both places. And both places have in common the infrastructure to help people who are in poverty tends not to be very strong in either kind of place.

Mr. SAWYER. People in rural settings were always isolated. They have been for a long time.

Ms. RUGGLES. That's right.

Mr. SAWYER. But increasingly, people in impacted urban settings are being isolated in a different way in great numbers and in great concentration. It's not normal to think of isolation in those terms. But in truth, instead of seeing huge employment opportunities, tens of thousands of people in large factories concentrated in the middle of cities, we're seeing a more diffused employment opportunity. Even when it exists, it is very difficult to access because of distance and the fact that transportation systems are established in almost hub-and-spoke patterns that don't fit the diffusion of work, schooling, employment, and other kinds of opportunity.

Ms. RUGGLES. I think that's an important set of concerns. I think perhaps an even more important set of concerns is the fact that those jobs are just disappearing. So it's not even so much that they've moved to the suburbs as it is they just don't exist any more. The kinds of jobs that lower skilled workers might have entered a decade ago and earned a reasonable amount of money just aren't there. It's more that than an inability to get to the jobs, I think, that accounts for increasing poverty rates and increasing isolation, and increasing joblessness in inner city areas.

Mr. SAWYER. You have both referred, in one way or another, to the decline in manufacturing and the increase in service as a cause of that lack of opportunity. It seems to me that we don't even define what we mean very well when we're talking about manufacturing and service.

I live in a community that used to have large numbers of manufacturing jobs, Akron, OH, a huge tire manufacturing center. There are no passenger car tires at all manufactured now in Akron, OH. But what used to be thought of as one kind of service—engineering services, legal services, accounting services and others—that used to be classified as manufacturing under the roof of a large company, have now been dispersed in a variety of different kinds of settings. These settings include the entry level opportunities from large employers that have and continue to have an interest in a broad spread of employment opportunities across the entire population, to smaller, more diffused employment opportunities which, even where the numbers remain the same, we find them dispersed across a geography that is much wider, with limited opportunity to access even the entry level opportunities that used to exist. The other side of the service is the more conventional definition that most people think of when they talk about a service-based economy, the very low wage, no ladder initial employment opportunity.

I mean, that whole division of employment opportunity, coupled with its diffusion, is a part of the chicken and egg problem that we face. That is, opportunities that are declining are the consequences of effects, that the lack of opportunities themselves exacerbate.

Ms. RUGGLES. I think that's true. I think the way to get out of that cycle is to invest more in our young entry level workers and to help them qualify better for the kinds of jobs that are likely to be available in the future. But, unfortunately, this is a time of very tight budgets at both the State, local, and Federal level, and it is very difficult to come up with the kind of money that it would take to really make a difference.

Mr. SAWYER. Dr. Simms?

Ms. SIMMS. Yes, I would agree that one of our big issues is investment, because as you indicated, there are different kinds of jobs that we define as service jobs. There are the ones that are professional and usually require, if not as college degree, some postsecondary education, and then we have low wage, low skilled service jobs. If you're the younger equivalent of someone who had a manufacturing job, you probably qualify more for the low level, low wage job than you would for the entry level or professional type service job.

The United States has really done very poorly, nationally speaking, in terms of trying to address training for young people who don't go to college. We could say well, everybody could get a college education, but that's quite expensive, particularly if you don't have adequate public scholarships or grants.

Mr. SAWYER. It is particularly difficult—I can't resist the opportunity to raise it, because I raise it every chance I get, but it is particularly difficult in a time when we're still trying to dispense that kind of assistance based on definitions that don't apply any more. The whole business of qualifying for that kind of assistance is predicated on a family in which an 18 year old winds up going off to school and is the dependent of the parents whose income is measured. In fact, a larger and larger proportion today represent a student population who are themselves parents trying to sustain a family and go to school at the same time and find that the tension between those two goals is just unsustainable.

Ms. SIMMS. And certainly there are other industrialized countries that have addressed this in a more systematic manner by developing a whole stream of training opportunities that are alternatives to college. We have kind of left a void between a high school diploma and a college degree, leaving even those students who successfully complete high school relatively unskilled for today's workforce.

Ms. RUGGLES. I think that Margaret is absolutely right. The failure to deal with the school-to-work transition or additional training for kids who don't go to college is an important problem. But I think at least as important is the fact that the proportion of kids who do go on to college is declining in this country. It has fallen substantially over the last decade or two. I think the reason for that is the cost of college has gone up so much relative to people's incomes, and we haven't expanded our student loan programs or done anything really to help students, as you say, go on to college. That, I think, is a serious problem in an economy that's going to be supplying more jobs for that kind of person and fewer for people who don't have those skills.

Mr. SAWYER. Going to college or getting some other alternative in the form of postsecondary education.

Ms. RUGGLES. That's right.

Mr. SAWYER. You know, we keep asking ourselves questions, and we poll ourselves endlessly. Do we think the current generation of children and young adults will do better than their parents? Are people working longer and harder just to maintain their current condition? We keep asking ourselves these things over and over in terms of perception.

How well are we able to measure those concerns? We had a witness yesterday who made a powerful point, talking about the myth of the paradigm of the 1950's. She suggested that the independent family unit, in a trade craft household, or in a family farm, was the real unit of productive comparison that we ought to be talking about. I suspect that's as much a myth a century and a half ago as the "Ozzie and Harriet" family of 40 years ago is.

My question is whether or not we need to measure ourselves differently, in terms of what works. What is a comparison of comfort or absence of poverty from one generation to another?

Ms. RUGGLES. I think we definitely need to reform our measures in that area. I think that our poverty line was put together in a period when there an explicit expectation that there was going to be somebody at home, and it has built into it the assumption that there are certain services being provided at home. One reason why you see parents working more hours and earning lower wages at the bottom end of the distribution right right is because an awful lot more of those parents are women and their earnings are lower than men's earnings. They don't have someone at home who is providing child care for free, or who is providing other domestic services. I think that it's not really very healthful to compare today's poverty line, you know, incomes, with those of 40 years ago, when they actually involved very, very different kinds of family structures and very different kinds of expenses that those people faced in terms of actually going out and earning a living.

So yes, I think we need to revisit the question of what is an adequate level of income and we need to explicitly take into account the fact that today's families typically have to pay for, at a minimum, child care in order to actually go out and earn a living.

Mr. SAWYER. Should I assume from what you've suggested that you don't view these differences as being lifestyle choices but, rather, imperatives that are being driven by forces outside the——

Ms. RUGGLES. Yes. I think that it's not lifestyle choices in the sense that—I mean, in a sense, I suppose you could say that becoming a single parent is a lifestyle choice, but once it has happened, you are a single parent and you still have to support the child somehow. I think it's very difficult for single mothers who have no access to child care, and I think we should take that into account in figuring out how well off they are.

Mr. SAWYER. Dr. Simms?

Ms. SIMMS. I think certainly if you look at the growth of married women in the workforce, it's an indication that what we're facing is ways in which people try to maintain or improve their standard of living. The problem is that some families have more workers to send into the workforce than others do. So that when you say lifestyle choices, a lot of these are necessities, you might say, in order to maintain quite modest standards of living in some cases and are fundamentally related more to economic opportunity than to decisions about how you live.

In fact, if one looks at the whole question of single parenting, family formation may, in fact, be related to economic opportunity when, if the father is unable to support the family, there may be little to make for a stable marital relationship. So even being a single parent isn't necessarily always a lifestyle choice. It's just something that, in fact, happened that didn't happen 40 years ago because the result might have been different.

Ms. RUGGLES. I think it's hard to say. One thing we know for sure is that men's wages have been declining relative to women's wages, particularly for low skilled workers. That has a lot of consequences in terms of who supplies labor——

Mr. SAWYER. Is that because men's wages are actually dropping or because women's have increased so substantially?

Ms. RUGGLES. Both.

Mr. SAWYER. Let me share with you something I said twice yesterday, and I apologize to everybody who has been here both days. But Larry Bumpass, in his presidential address to the Population Association of America, concluded by saying that "Understanding the long-term character of institutional change should direct social policy toward the amelioration of negative consequences rather than toward attempts to reverse the tide."

Is that essentially what you both just said?

Ms. RUGGLES. That's exactly right.

Mr. SAWYER. Let me go back to something that Dr. Simms suggested in her written testimony, and that is what you really have said today is based on past census data and Current Population Surveys.

As we watch the unfolding and the flowering of data from 1990, what should we look for? What are the critical measures that will emerge from this data based on what you've learned from the previous studies? What are the critical things we ought to look for?

Ms. SIMMS. I think we need to look for some of the issues that both Pat and I have discussed today, and that is growing poverty among certain household types or family types.

It is particularly important, I think, to look at what has happened using the 1990 census data, because when our analysis stopped in the mid-1980's, the argument could be well, we're just beginning our economic recovery from 1982 and, therefore, what you see is the low point for many families because—In fact, 1984, for example, was a year in which the poverty level did not drop, even though employment had already begun to increase. And to look then at what has happened over the full decade, when we've had economic recovery and when employment has expanded fairly rapidly—though not as rapidly as in some previous periods—would be particularly useful, because it tells us more about this difference between economic opportunity and family structure.

Ms. RUGGLES. I think another thing that the 1990 census is particularly important for is looking at what's happened to specific areas, to specific small groups of the population. We have used the Current Population Surveys, which are done annually, to look at trends in poverty over time. I think they do a pretty good job. But you need something as big as the decennial census to really look at what kinds of standards of living people have in different parts of the country and different types of cities, that kind of thing, how people's housing costs, standard of housing, compares to their income, what a given income gets you in terms of standard of living, that kind of thing can be investigated in much more detail in the decennial census than we can without that data.

Mr. SAWYER. That's not what we're looking at today, but that's what I asked you about. You have touched on something that is critical to a set of decisions that have to be made in the next 18 months, and that is, what will the instrument look like in 2000? What alternatives between now and then can we begin to explore? What better measurements and modes of measurement might, in fact, supplant the decennial document, and perhaps even improve on it, in the course of continuous measurement throughout the Nation, over time, that doesn't require the enormous refinement of small area data?

We face some very difficult choices. The difficulties that were encountered in 1990 were, as much as anything, a product of a design that may no longer be well suited to the size and complexity, the rate and depth of change, going on in the country that we're seeing right now. The need for data is enormous. The suitability of an every household mail out/mail back survey for the gathering of that data is very much open to question, and yet, clearly, we can't do without it. I believe we're in a time of extremely rapid change, a depth of change that we haven't seen for a century or so. As a consequence, we really need to know what to look for as data emerges, because we may well see the kinds of events that are happening worldwide begin to happen here. That is to say, not necessarily a quarter of a million people sitting in the middle of a town square in order to depose an entire government, but that has happened in one capital after another across the globe, not one following another, but I suspect each the same event happening over and over again in response to many of the same kinds of forces. Similarly, the conditions of poverty that you describe are not necessarily isolated to the conditions in any one country, but rather, the consequences of global phenomena that are affecting each country differently, perhaps, but nonetheless affecting each industrialized nation.

Let me ask you one last question. There are so many things I want to ask you about. I guess this is as important to me as anything because it is one of the ways in which people in this institution can have a consequence, large or small.

One of the enormous shifts that we've seen talked about is the question of whether the middle class is vanishing or whether, in fact, high income households are receiving a dramatically disproportionate share of that rising tide that may not be lifting all ships but is doing very well on the average. Some families, some populations, respond better to rapid institutional change. We talk about work opportunities, manufacturing jobs. Are we seeing an increase in institutional obsolescence?

People talk about the labor unions. We talk about the quality of public school education, and we talk about the access and opportunity to take advantage of health care in traditional hospital settings. We talk about housing stock and the size of units that are available in this country, with huge numbers of people living alone in far greater numbers than we've seen in the past, where older people are dispersed across a population and a geography living alone in ways that they had not done in the past, in addition to single people living alone.

What kinds of measures of institutions to go along with measures of population would make sense, if it makes sense at all?

Ms. RUGGLES. That's an interesting question.

Mr. SAWYER. I know what some people mean when they say that to me. It's boy, was that goofy.

[Laughter.]

It's a part of the "chicken and egg" syndrome. But it is one of those areas where government can have a consequence. You know, we talk about the inability to deal broadly with massive public policy on huge and dispersed populations, and I quite agree with that. It's very difficult to deal with. But if we watch institutions becoming more or less useful in a society, then those are the kinds of tools, in the largest sense, that government can affect. What do we need to look for?

Ms. SIMMS. Well, I could just talk a little bit about two of the institutional frameworks that you mentioned. For example, in education, when we talk about the failure of public education, we're often ambiguous about what we mean. If we use, for example, years of education completed, our data seem to indicate we've continued to make progress in that regard, that the median number of years completed has risen for disadvantaged populations. Like for blacks, the proportion who complete high school has risen and the gap between blacks and whites appears to be much smaller.

Mr. SAWYER. In fact, in those populations that over the longer period of time have been the most impoverished, the gains are the most dramatic.

Ms. SIMMS. Yes.

Mr. SAWYER. Absolutely.

Ms. SIMMS. And yet you hear at the same time employers and others saying that they can't find skilled workers, that even problems like basic functional literacy are not widespread in the population that they see for low level, entry level jobs. That suggests that perhaps, as we measure educational success, certainly on many of our national surveys, maybe we're not capturing what we really mean when we talk about an educated populace.

The same thing could be said to be true of how we measure housing and housing quality, that the standards we have used over a series of decennial censuses have sort of lost some of their meaning. For example, we talk about flush toilets as one standard that many years ago did give you a good indication of the overall quality of the dwelling unit, but that no longer has the same ability to distinguish housing quality one from another. So there are certainly some ways in which we need to either rethink or supplement some of the measures that we have used to measure progress in a number of areas, and those are two that come to my mind.

Ms. RUGGLES. I think that you said earlier that we are looking at a real structural change in our wage distribution, and I think that that's right. I think our institutions are going to have to adapt to that.

I think that if our labor force is going to match up to the kinds of jobs that are going to be available, we do have to change the way that we educate young people and we have to particularly produce more educated young people. So I think there is a need for an institutional response there.

I think that many of the kinds of measures that we have are affected by changes in our institutional structure. I think, for example, a big piece of why we can't find large parts of the low-income population when we do these surveys is because they are in prisons, or they are in places that are outside the scope of our surveys. I think on the measurement front we need to work a little harder to see if we can come up with a sample that is a little bit more meaningful and that takes into account a larger part of particularly this low-income population.

I agree with you. It's very difficult to figure out how to respond to change if you aren't doing a very good job of measuring change.

Mr. SAWYER. Yesterday one of the witnesses brought up the difficulty in measuring the homeless population, the great logistical difficulties that were encountered 2 years ago. We have to be able to define what homelessness means in a way that's useful before we can even begin to count. I mean, do we count simply those people living in shelters or on the street on any given night, or do we count people illegally doubled up in public housing, or sleeping in a loft in the garage in a relative's home, or in a car, or from one car to the next, night to night? It is a changing definition that we haven't really done very well. I'm not sure that the definitions really serve——

Ms. RUGGLES. As a matter of fact, I think that's not the only definition of that type. I think our definition of what constitutes a household or a family is undergoing a lot of change. I think that our definition of what constitutes an adequate income or a nonpoverty level of income should have undergone more change than it has. I think in terms of measurement we need to be more flexible about trying to adapt our measures to the changing reality that's out there.

Mr. SAWYER. Is there anything you would like to talk about that I haven't asked you about?

Ms. SIMMS. Well, there are some that I understand that were raised yesterday. For example, a more systematic approach to supporting children, whether it's an income guarantee or an alternative system. Because as has been indicated, economic opportunity has changed, so it is not really an individual's lack of a will to work so much as their inability to provide, even if they do work, that's at issue, and whether part of our investment really means providing some basic living standards for children to ensure they are able to benefit from other kinds of investments we wish to make in them, such as education.

Ms. RUGGLES. Institutions don't change overnight. There are a lot of people who get caught in the transition. Today's young families, families with young kids, particularly with lower skilled parents, are some of the people currently caught in that transition.

I think Margaret is absolutely right. If we want to improve the circumstances of these kids over the longer run, we have to make it possible for them to stay alive and to have an adequate diet, to have adequate health care and so on in the meantime.

Mr. SAWYER. You haven't said much today in terms of a phenomenon that we've heard others talk about, and that is the shift of poverty from 60 years ago being concentrated very heavily among the oldest among us and the movement to a much younger segment of our population. In 1940, one of every four program beneficiaries of social security was a child. Today it's one in 12. When we talk about social security, we don't even think of children—too few of us do, in any case. And yet, that is a substantial shift and there has been nothing comparable to deal with the every bit of fragile existence of young children as we have done to address the needs of the oldest among us.

I'm not sure that opening that today is necessarily going to solve the problem, but it certainly is one of the things that we all need to bear in mind. If we do not, we will see an exacerbation of a tension between generations that is just not productive or constructive.

Thank you very much for being with us today. I appreciate your time and I appreciate your patience while I had to run back and forth.

If there is nothing more to come before us, we stand adjourned.

[Whereupon, the subcommittee adjourned at 2:35 p.m.]

AMERICA'S CHANGING PROFILE: "WHERE WE'RE GOING: EDUCATION AND WORKFORCE TRENDS"

TUESDAY, JULY 28, 1992

House of Representatives,
Subcommittee on Census and Population,
Committee on Post Office and Civil Service,
Washington, DC.

The subcommittee met, pursuant to call, at 1:15 p.m., in room 311, Cannon House Office Building, Hon. Thomas C. Sawyer (chairman of the subcommittee) presiding.

Mr. Sawyer. I'm pleased to welcome our witnesses and guests to the hearing this afternoon. This is the third set of hearings in a series to look at demographic trends and their policy implications for the United States.

In our earlier hearings, we discussed demographic change that is redefining who we are and how we live. We have certainly not attempted to make those hearings exhaustive but, rather, exemplary and point out some of the ways in which the change that is affecting this Nation today has direct consequences in the way in which we manage our public lives.

Among the wealth of numbers that has emerged from the 1990 census, there are some that are just indelible in their impression. Minority populations are the fastest growing populations in the United States. Virtually a quarter of us are people of color. That surprisingly rapid increase has been fueled in part by record numbers of immigrants today. An unprecedented 20 million Americans are foreign born.

During the 1980's, almost all of our population growth took place in urban areas. For the first time we have crossed another one of those thresholds that we like to point out. A century ago, or a little more than a century ago, half of us lived in cities. Today, three-quarters of us live in what we broadly define as metropolitan areas. Metropolitan areas extending far beyond their original centers, but poverty is increasingly concentrated in the inner cities and continues to be greatest among minority populations.

The Nation is aging. In this last decade alone, the average age in the United States leaped nearly 3 years. Within 40 years, for the first time, one in five Americans will be elderly.

But increasingly it is the children who are becoming more and more poor and more culturally diverse. The poverty of childhood is concentrated in the growing number of single-parent families, a confluence of phenomena that has consequences that we simply cannot afford to ignore. This sea change will create an enormous tension in many areas of policy-making. Its effects, however, will be felt most sharply and most immediately in our schools and subsequently in the workplace.

Let me just share with you today a portrayal of a rapidly emerging future. It will be a future that will be defined in many different ways, but one way is to look at it in terms of two generations. The next generation of students will challenge educational institutions like never before: children living in poverty, children living with only one parent, children of differing backgrounds, children speaking many different languages other than English. Schools must prepare that generation to be productive in emerging American workplaces, and it won't be easy. It will stretch our resources and test our ingenuity.

At the same time, the so-called baby-boomers, the single largest population bulge in our Nation's history, are today reaching their peak productive years. In only two decades many of them will be retiring, and that represents a very narrow and predictable window of opportunity to find solutions for a whole new wide range of pressures that this shift in age structure will trigger.

The needs of older Americans in the next century will be enormous by virtue of their sheer numbers alone. We have to ask ourselves: will the generation that follows, one of much smaller numbers, be productive enough to ensure that this Nation can meet its needs? We are not responding to that inevitable movement of the population right now, but clearly we ought to be.

So we are here today with two generations, one that is younger, less white, more mobile, increasingly foreign born, and an older generation that is indigenous, more place bound, and numerically large. Two generations whose needs and expectations will be great, whose needs and expectations will often be widely, if not to say wildly, divergent, and two generations in intense competition for the same limited resources.

The challenge that we face is clear, and the burden of that challenge will fall on working Americans caught in the middle of enormous and competing needs. The force and pace of change is as intense as any that we have experienced in a century. We need to measure that change in order to understand it. We need to understand it to get a sense of where it is going to lead us, and we need to set a course to get us there before we find ourselves simply in a condition of drift in the midst of that kind of sea change.

Today we are going to examine demographic trends affecting our Nation's education system. We will also look at the pivotal transition from schools to work, and tomorrow we will be looking at the emerging American workplace itself.

Our witnesses today are each in their own right leading experts in their fields. I look forward to their testimony and want to thank again the Population Resource Center and the Congressional Research Service for their continuing assistance in preparing for these hearings.

Let me, before we begin, just suggest to this panel of witnesses and the subsequent panel that, although you have been given time limits for your testimony, I realize that those time limits constrain the amount of material that you have to present. We will be as flexible as we can be, given the constraints of the clock. I'm more interested in having you say what you came here to say and for us to have a chance to talk about it than to living up to any rigid time limitations.

With that having been said, our first panel today consists of two witnesses, Dr. Dave Sweet and Dr. Shirley McBay. Dr. Sweet is the dean of the Levin College of Urban Affairs at Cleveland State University. He is the chairman of the Ohio Board of Regents Urban University Program Advisory Committee. He has been instrumental in establishing the National Regulatory Research Institute at the Ohio State University. In a previous life, he was commissioner for the Ohio Public Utilities Commission and, for most of the last 20 years, a good friend—glad to have you here, Dave.

Our second witness is Shirley McBay, who is the president of the Quality Education for Minorities Network. She is the former dean for student affairs at MIT, director of the Quality Education for Minorities Project for 3 years, and has served as program manager and director in the Science Education Directorate of the National Science Foundation.

It is a pleasure to have you both here, and, with that, let me turn to Dr. Sweet to begin.

STATEMENTS OF DAVID C. SWEET, DEAN, LEVIN COLLEGE OF URBAN AFFAIRS, CLEVELAND STATE UNIVERSITY; AND SHIRLEY McBAY, PRESIDENT, QUALITY EDUCATION FOR MINORITIES NETWORK

Mr. Sweet. Thank you, Chairman Sawyer. It is a pleasure to be here and to share some perspectives related to the topic at hand.

You have focused in your statement about population changes affecting the social and economic landscape in our Nation, and I would particularly like to focus in on one geographic dimension of that, and that is specifically the gap that is increasing between the socio-economic conditions of our populations in our central cities and the suburbs that surround these central cities.

My remarks will focus on the emerging demographic and workforce trends which reveal a growing socio-economic gap—and you will hear that term "gap" frequently in the various indicators—between central cities and the suburbs and the challenges this poses for all educational systems, but particularly (since I speak from a vantage point of higher education) for those of us that are in urban universities and addressing the students that emerge from this particular condition.

I will begin by describing the growing gap in income, educational attainment, and the access to jobs between central cities and the suburbs. These gaps present significant challenges for universities which are also facing the needs of a changing student population and workforce as well as the need to educate a more diverse workforce and provide the community with policy-oriented research and action-oriented public service.

As a former mayor, I know you are well acquainted with the abilities of urban universities to address action-oriented research agendas and assist local administrations, and I think it is important to recognize that all of this kind of work can only be accomplished through the use of important demographic and related data such as those provided by the Census Bureau, and first let me say that my presentation today and those that both preceded mine and follow would not be possible without the tremendous undertaking of the U.S. Bureau of the Census.

I hope to demonstrate, however, that the vast amount of important data collected by the Bureau must be coupled with mechanisms to ensure that these data are used for critical public policy issues analyses and action-oriented solutions. I will conclude my comments with a specific proposal to address this particular need.

Let me begin by presenting some empirical analyses that, while focusing mostly on the trends in Ohio's metropolitan areas, are reflective of trends in other similar metropolitan areas in our country. The Nation's central cities continue to face a multitude of social and economic problems, including increased poverty and unemployment. These problems are aggravated by both industry and job relocation to the suburban fringes of our metropolitan areas.

While this is a national trend, let me draw your attention to some dramatic data which is being collected by researchers at the Levin College; this is a specific example drawn from our analysis of the ES–202 tapes which are being provided by the Ohio Bureau of Employment Services.

From the first quarter of 1989 to the first quarter of 1991, the city of Cleveland lost approximately 18,500 jobs, in that 2-year period. The suburbs of the county—our county is Cuyahoga, as you are aware—gained 7,100 jobs, and in the period of 1981 through 1991 two suburban counties in the Cleveland area, Lake and Geauga, gained approximately 500 new establishments and over 10,000 new jobs.

This relocation of jobs has had a devastating effect on our metropolitan areas, both demographically and economically, and has specifically wreaked hardship on the residents of our central city and their ability to get to these suburban-oriented jobs

During the 1980's, many central cities in the so-called Rust Belt lost population to their surrounding neighbors. Cities such as Detroit, Pittsburgh, St. Louis, and Cleveland lost more than 10 percent of their population from 1980 to 1990, and I have attached a table that illustrates that particular well-known trend.

The relocation of jobs and population from the central cities to the suburbs and outlying counties is reflected in the growing gap in the socio-economic conditions of citizens in these areas. Population and job flight to the suburbs and outlying counties contribute to the unemployment and poverty rates in the central cities.

In 1980 the unemployment rate for the central cities in Ohio was 10 percent compared to 6.6 percent for the suburbs, a gap of 3.4 percentage points. These gaps are illustrated in charts which are attached to my testimony.

While the size of the gap itself is important, our focus is on the change between 1980 and 1990. Thus, despite the fact that overall unemployment was slightly down in the metropolitan areas of our State in 1990, the difference between the central city unemployment rate and that of the suburbs—the gap, in essence—grew to 4.4 percent by 1990, up again from 3.4 in 1980.

Clearly, a lack of job opportunities affects income. In 1980, central city family income was 76 percent that of the suburban family income. The gap increased by 1990 such that the central city family income decreased to 69 percent of suburban family income by 1990.

Household income for central city residents was approximately 72 percent that of suburban households in 1980 and decreased to 67 percent in 1990. Poverty rates increased, and the gap in poverty rates between the central city and the suburbs also increased, as I have documented with the data from the census.

The growing disparities in income and poverty rates between central cities and suburbs will continue as long as job opportunities and accessibility to jobs decrease for central city residents. Central city residents continue to largely have blue-collar, service, and sales occupations, occupations which tend to require less skills and pay lower wages. Suburban residents, on the other hand, are more often found in occupations that require a college education and tend to pay higher wages.

The occupational gap between central cities and suburbs in metropolitan Ohio narrowed or stayed the same during the 1980 to 1990 decade for all but one of the major categories of occupations. Importantly, the exception to this relatively stable occupational gap was among those occupations for which a higher education is required, occupations which mostly directly affect the management of our cities and Nation. This occupation group of executives, managers, administrators, and professionals grew from 22 percent of the metropolitan Ohio's labor force in 1980 to 26 percent in 1990. Significantly, however, the gap between central cities and the suburbs again grew from 3.7 percent in 1980 to 4.4 percent in 1990.

That is, while the percent of labor force in these occupations rose 3.5 percentage points from 20 to 23 percent in central cities, it grew from 23 percent of the suburban labor force in 1980 to 27 percent in 1990, a gain of 4.1 percentage points. In other words, despite general increases in these occupations, central cities lost ground to suburbs in terms of having a highly skilled, higher-paid labor force.

The management and professional occupations are largely supplied by graduates of higher education. While primary and secondary education provide the fundamental skills and basic knowledge for all of our citizens, it is the colleges and universities that train professionals and administrators and managers who have leadership roles in business, government, and the community.

The good news is that more persons are college educated today than ever. Overall in Ohio, the percentage of population with at least 4 years of college increased from 14 percent in 1980 to 18 percent in 1990. This increase is seen in central cities and in suburbs, but the distressing news is that, again, the central cities are falling further behind the suburbs.

The spread between the percent of those with four or more years of college in central cities and those in the suburbs increased from 4 percent to 5.3 percent, again an increase in that gap as seen in the graph attached to the testimony.

It is also true that the gap has narrowed in terms of the people with some college education, and I think a lot of this can be attributed to the effective work of our community colleges in our Nation's central cities. Even if it is less than the standard 4 years required for a bachelor's degree, getting into college and picking up some technical skills, particularly in a community college, can be very useful in entering today's workforce.

In this regard, the central cities in Ohio are gaining on their surrounding suburbs. The percent of persons aged 25 or older with some college education but less than a completed degree increased in the central cities by over 13 percent while the increase in the suburbs was about 6 percent over the last decade.

This encouraging trend in the central cities illustrates a demographic change that has been occurring on our college campuses. No longer is it uncommon for individuals to begin their college careers in their mid to late 20's, 30's, or even 40's. The traditional 18-year-old who enters college right out of high school and studies full time is becoming less and less the norm. Nontraditional students, such as those aged 25 or older, who attend school intermittently and often part time, are common on today's college campuses. Blacks and Hispanics, while still underrepresented, are increasing in number across our college campuses. Female students are increasingly becoming the majority, surpassing males in enrollment numbers.

Enrollment trends at Cleveland State University are similar to the national trends. Female student enrollment increased from 47 percent in 1985 to over 50 percent in 1991. The average age of our undergraduate increased from 24 and a half in 1985 to 26, nearly 27, years in 1991. Although a majority of CSU students are white, the proportion that are black and Hispanic increased slightly each year from 1985 to 1991, and the percentage of undergraduate students attending school part time in 1991 was 33 percent.

So increasingly the nontraditional students, as we have often referred to them, are becoming the traditional students of our Nation's urban universities. Such trends require urban universities such as Cleveland State to offer more classes in evenings and on weekends to adjust to students working full time and attending school part time.

Partnerships linking universities and community colleges are important to ease the transition for many nontraditional students who begin their education at 2-year colleges. Urban universities also need to be more receptive to the needs of the underrepresented minority students. Educators must learn to teach a more diverse population of students and to change both curriculum and methods of instruction.

Changes in the economy require a much higher-skilled and educated labor force which increases the demands on urban universities to provide accessible training and educational opportunities. The well known loss of both blue-collar jobs and middle management positions in our metropolitan areas is causing many nontraditional students to return to universities for career changes, advanced degrees, or more training to keep pace with the technological changes in our society.

Urban universities are not only faced with the challenge of the changing educational needs of our economy and a more diverse and changing student body but also with the widening socio-economic gap between our central cities and suburbs. This growing gap not

61-412 O - 94 - 7

only challenges urban universities but also local governments and communities who struggle to effectively manage and provide public services to a decreasing and more impoverished population and, as you are well aware, a decreasing tax base to support these public services.

Today's urban universities are being asked by the local community to come out of the ivory tower and participate in meeting critical needs and solving critical public problems. Indeed, providing public service has become a central mission, along with the traditional teaching and research functions, of many urban universities.

The educational needs of today's and tomorrow's students together with a need to provide greater public service to the community, offers a great challenge but also an opportunity to the urban university. In many cases, we are using this field experience—internships and working in neighborhood organizations—as one of the critical elements in training our students to deal with the challenges of today's central city management.

This challenge and opportunity is to better focus research on the urban policy and problem-solving matters of our central cities and metropolitan systems. The urban university is the single most appropriate institution to perform this vital role with the available data and research and analysis capacity on hand.

The Census Bureau alone cannot provide all the research and the public service programs needed. Of the 10-year $2.5 billion budget for the 1990 census, only 5.8 percent is used for data dissemination, and a much smaller fraction is dedicated to the substantive demographic research using the data collected.

An immense amount of valuable data is distributed by the Bureau to public institutions. The Bureau estimates that the market value (as determined by the Bureau's modest cost recovery pricing schedule) of computer tapes, discs, and printed material distributed to the depository libraries, State data centers, the University Consortium for Political and Social Research, and the five Census Information Centers which serve selected minority populations amounts to approximately $1.3 million.

An additional $1.5 million is invested in the State Data Center Program, which is extremely successful in distributing data through the Census Bureau's affiliate networks.

The Bureau should be applauded for its excellent job in ensuring that census data is available to those of us who want to use it. While a significant amount of very important data is distributed, there are few Federally funded efforts to ensure that important urban policy and action-oriented issues are addressed through research and technical assistance in our communities using this most valuable data.

I would like to commend you, Chairman Sawyer, for your leadership in securing this year's reauthorization of title XI of the Higher Education Act, otherwise known as the Urban Community Service Program. This program, the first grant proposals which are now just being reviewed by the Department of Education, is the only existing Federal effort to support university-based applied research and outreach activities on urban issues by our urban universities.

I am also pleased to note that the House and Senate Banking Committees may take steps on this year's housing bill to authorize local governments and their local universities to collaborate on projects of importance to the community, drawing on funds managed by the Department of Housing and Urban Development.

It would be good to have HUD back in the business of supporting local urban research and technical assistance work by universities. I feel strongly that a program of funded demographic research and public service be established on a university level to fulfill the pressing needs of our urban areas.

At the Levin College of Urban Affairs at Cleveland State, with the use of funding from a unique State appropriation supporting public service at urban universities, Ohio's Urban University Program, we have established a large data base and analysis capacity. This capacity has enabled us to bring together vast data sets including census, county real property records, and the establishment of specific employment data, which is the ES–202 file that I mentioned earlier, so that cross-cutting action-oriented analyses are possible.

We have assembled 5,000 data bases which together include 10 billion bytes of information. Regardless of how you count it, that is a lot of data.

The potential policy and action impacts of university research based on a combination of these data is exemplified by the recent reconsideration by a Cleveland Area Council of Governments whether to approve Federal highway funds for a highway expansion into one of our suburban counties which would contribute to the continued outward flow of jobs and population from the central city of Cleveland and nearby communities to adjacent counties whose infrastructure is inadequate to support dramatic growth in housing and population.

We have underway in our community, for the first time ever, a question being raised as to whether highway funds should be used to expand suburb freeway systems to allow the more rapid transportation of people to their residences in the suburb and exurban areas which are inadequately prepared to provide the infrastructure for the new housing units that are being constructed there.

We are encouraged by this type of policy discussion, and it is made possible by the analysis and availability of data such as is provided by the U.S. Census. Such a direct impact by local research on political and policy decision-making processes is a virtual first in my years of observing local government development decision processes.

As many observers have remarked, we live in an age which generates an impressive amount of information but which is not used for improving the life in the community. Information is both a resource and a currency in our society and ideally needs to be channeled through organizations which can help ensure its use and accessibility.

Historically, we have created public schools and libraries which prepared citizens to use and access the information of the print era. What we are proposing for the next generation is the preparation of and access to electronic information. If we do not create new institutions for this purpose, then information will increasingly be the currency which separates the haves from the have-nots.

I have proposed the creation of a demonstration census data and education center which would be the focus of electronic and organizational networks, information which would be received from the Census Bureau and augmented with data and research from universities, State and local agencies, and organizations. The resulting information would then be disseminated through teaching, further research, public service, and public access.

This synergy builds on the existing teaching, research, and public service, and technical assistance programs of our universities, increases their capabilities, and provides access to the general community, thus providing a means for public policy development to be debated on common ground.

In essence, the census data and education center would become an information and activity hub that connects levels of government, academic research across disciplines, and the public. With this mechanism, not only is the public provided access to understandable information, but that information is used to train the next generation of citizens.

A widespread dissemination role must be an ongoing function of educational institutions. Citizens must be connected to the educational institutions that can tap and assemble the data that is needed to improve the quality of life in our communities.

I appreciate the opportunity of appearing before this committee and commend its work in providing the universities with the data that is so essential to the analysis and the work that we undertake.

[The prepared statement of Mr. Sweet follows:]

PREPARED STATEMENT OF DAVID C. SWEET, DEAN, LEVIN COLLEGE OF URBAN AFFAIRS, CLEVELAND STATE UNIVERSITY

Chairman Sawyer and Subcommittee members, I appreciate the opportunity to testify at the hearings on "Education and Workforce Trends." My remarks will focus on the emerging demographic and workforce trends which reveal a growing socioeconomic gap between central cities and the suburbs and the challenges this poses for higher education institutions. I will begin by describing the growing gap in income, educational attainment, and access to jobs between the central cities and the suburbs. These gaps present significant challenges for universities which are also facing the needs of a changing student population and workforce, as well as the need to educate a more diverse workforce and provide the community with policyoriented research and action-oriented public service.

All of this must and can only be accomplished through the use of important demographic and related data such as those provided by the Census Bureau. First, let me say that my presentation today, and those that both preceded and follow mine, would not be possible without the tremendous undertaking of the Census Bureau. I hope to demonstrate, however, that the vast amount of important data collected by the Bureau must be coupled with mechanisms to ensure that these data are used for critical public policy issue analyses and action-oriented solutions. I will conclude my comments with a specific proposal to address this need.

Let me begin by presenting some empirical analysis that, while focusing mostly on trends in Ohio's metropolitan areas, is reflective of trends in other similar metropolitan areas.

The nation's central cities continue to face a multitude of social and economic problems, including increased poverty and unemployment. These problems are aggravated by both industry and job relocation to the suburban fringes of our metropolitan areas. While this is a national trend, let me draw your attention to some dramatic data being collected by researchers at my College.

From the first quarter of 1989 to the first quarter of 1991, the City of Cleveland lost approximately 18,500 jobs. The suburbs of the county (Cuyahoga) gained 7,100 jobs. And in the period of 1989 through 1991, two suburban counties in the Cleveland PMSA, Lake and Geauga, gained approximately 500 establishments and over 10,000 jobs. This relocation of jobs has a devastating effect on our metropolitan areas, both demographically and economically.

During the 1980s many central cities in the so-called "rust belt" lost population to their surrounding neighbors. Cities such as Detroit, Pittsburgh, St. Louis and Cleveland lost more than 10% of their populations from 1980 to 1990 (see Table 1 and Graph 1).

"Major" Central City *	1980			1990			Percent Change 1980–90		
	PMSA	"Major City"	Percent	PMSA	"Major City"	Percent	PMSA	"Major City"	PMSA Balance
Cleveland	1,898,825	573,822	30.2	1,831,122	505,616	27.6	−3.6	−11.9	0.0
St. Louis	2,356,460	453,085	19.2	2,240,048	296,685	17.7	−4.9	−12.4	−3.2
Milwaukee	1,397,143	636,212	45.5	1,375,191	628,088	45.7	−1.6	−1.3	−1.8
Pittsburgh	2,263,894	423,938	18.7	2,030,689	369,879	18.2	−10.3	−12.8	−9.7
Buffalo	1,242,826	357,870	28.8	968,532	328,123	33.9	−22.1	−8.3	−27.6
Detroit	4,353,413	1,203,339	27.6	4,188,153	1,027,974	24.5	−3.8	−14.6	0.3
Cincinnati	1,401,491	385,457	27.5	1,452,614	364,040	25.1	3.6	−5.6	7.1
Average	2,130,579	576,246	27.0	2,012,336	517,201	25.7	−5.5	−10.2	−3.8

* Note: Some PMSAs include more than one central city. Population for "major" central cities are reported in the table.
Source: 1980 and 1990 Census of Population and Housing.

Graph 1—Population Change in the Cleveland MSA, 1980 to 1990

	1980	1990
Cleveland	573,822	505,616
Balance of MSA	1,325,003	1,325,506
Total	1,898,825	1,831,122

Source: 1980 and 1990 Census of Population.

The relocation of jobs and population from the central cities to the suburbs and outlying counties is reflected in the growing gap in the socioeconomic conditions of the citizens in these areas.

Population and job flight to the suburbs and outlying counties contribute to the unemployment and poverty rates in the central cities. In 1980, the unemployment rate for central cities in Ohio was 10% compared to 6.6% in the suburbs, a gap 3.4% percentage points (see Graph 2). While the size of the gap itself is important, our focus is on the change between 1980 and 1990. Thus, despite the fact that the overall unemployment was slightly down in the metropolitan areas of the State in 1990, the difference between the central city unemployment rate and that of the suburbs grew to 4.4% by 1990, up from 3.4% in 1980.

Graph 2—Unemployment: Central City vs. Suburbs, Ohio MSA's, 1980 and 1990

[In percent]

	1980	1990
Central City	10.0	9.2
Suburbs	6.6	4.9

Source: 1980 and 1990 Census of Population.

Clearly, a lack of job opportunities affects income. In 1980, central city family income was 76% that of suburban family income (see Graph 3). The gap increased in 1990 such that the central city family income decreased to 69% of suburban family income in 1990. Household income for central city residents was approximately 72% that of suburban households in 1980 and decreased to 67% in 1990.

Graph 3—Central City Average Income as a Percent of Suburban Average Income, MSA's in Ohio, 1980 and 1990

[In percent]

	1980	1990
Family income	76.3	69.3
Household income	71.5	66.9

Source: 1980 and 1990 Census of Population.

Poverty rates increased significantly in the 1980s and, not surprisingly, faster in the central cities than in the suburbs of Ohio's metropolitan areas. The poverty rate in central cities grew from 17.2% to 21.7%, an increase of approximately 26% (see Graph 4). The poverty rate also increased in the suburbs from 5.9% to 6.9% in the decade, an increase of 17%. The difference between central city and suburban poverty rates increased from 11.3% in 1980 to 14.8% in 1990.

Graph 4—Poverty Rate: Central City vs. Suburbs, Ohio MSA's, 1980 and 1990

[In percent]

	1980	1990
Central City	17.2	21.7
Suburbs	5.9	6.9

Source: 1980 and 1990 Census of Population.

The growing disparities in income and poverty rates between central cities and suburbs will continue as long as job opportunities and accessibility to jobs decrease for central city residents. Central city residents continue to largely have blue collar, service, and sales occupations, occupations which tend to require less skills and pay lower wages. Suburban residents, on the other hand, are more often found in occupations that require a college education and tend to pay higher wages.

The occupational gap between central cities and suburbs in metropolitan Ohio narrowed or stayed the same during the 1980–1990 decade for all but one of the major categories of occupations. Importantly, the exception to this relatively stable occupational gap was among those occupations for which higher education is required and occupations which most directly affect the management of our cities and nation.

Executives, managers, administrators, and professionals grew from about 22% of the metropolitan Ohio's labor force in 1980, to about 26% in 1990. Significantly, the gap between central cities and suburbs grew from 3.7% to 4.4% (see Graph 5). That is, while the percent of the labor force in these occupations rose 3.5 percentage points (from 20% to 23.5%) in central cities, it grew from 23.7% of the suburban labor force in 1980, to 27.8% in 1990, a gain of 4.1 percentage points. In other words, despite general increases in these occupations central cities lost ground to suburbs in terms of having a highly skilled, higher paid labor force.

Graph 5—Executives, Managers, Professionals, Ohio MSA's, 1980 and 1990

[Percent of labor force]

	1980	1990
Central City	20	23.5
Suburbs	23.7	27.8

Source: 1980 and 1990 Census of Population.

The management and professional occupations are largely supplied by graduates of higher education. While primary and secondary education provide the fundamental skills and basic knowledge for all our citizens, it is the colleges and universities that train the professionals, administrators, and managers who have leadership roles in business, government and the community.

The good news is that more persons are college educated today than ever. Overall in Ohio, the percent of the population with at least four years of college increased from 14% in 1980 to 18% in 1990. This increase is seen in central cities and in suburbs, but the distressing news is that, again, the central cities are falling further behind the suburbs. The spread between the percent of those with four or more years of college in central cities and those in suburbs increased from 4% in 1980, to 5.3% in 1990 (see Graph 6).

Graph 6—College Degree: Central City vs. Suburbs, Ohio MSA's, 1980 and 1990

[Percent of persons 25 years or older]

	1980	1990
Central City	12.3	15.3
Suburbs	16.2	20.6

Source: 1980 and 1990 Census of Population.

Yet, it is also true that the gap has narrowed in terms of people with some college education, even if it is less than the standard four years required for a bachelor's degree. In this regard, the central cities in Ohio are gaining on their surrounding suburbs. The percent of persons aged 25 or older with some college education but less than a completed degree increased in the central cities by over 13%, while the increase in the suburbs was about 6% from 1980 to 1990. This encouraging trend in the central cities illustrates a demographic change that has been occurring on our college campuses. No longer is it uncommon for individuals to begin their college careers in their mid- to late twenties, thirties or even forties.

The traditional eighteen year old who enters college right out of high school and studies full-time is becoming less and less the norm. Non-traditional students such as those aged 25 or older, who attend school intermittently and often part-time are common on today's college campuses. Blacks and Hispanics, while still underrepresented, are increasing in number across college campuses. Female students are increasingly becoming the majority, surpassing males in enrollment numbers.

The enrollment trends at Cleveland State University (CSU) are similar to the national trends. Female student enrollment increased from 47% in 1985 to 50.7% in 1991. The average age of an undergraduate at CSU increased from 24.6 in 1985 to 26.8 in 1991. Although a majority of the CSU students are white, the proportion that are black and Hispanic increased slightly each year from 1985 to 1991. The percentage of undergraduate students attending school part-time in 1991 was 33%.

Such trends require urban universities such as CSU to offer more classes in evenings and on weekends to adjust to students working full-time and attending school part-time. Partnerships linking urban universities and community colleges are important to ease the transition for many non-traditional students who begin their education at two-year colleges. Urban universities also need to be more receptive to the needs of underrepresented minority students. Educators must learn to teach a more diverse population of students and to change both curriculum and methods of instruction.

Changes in the economy require a much higher skilled and educated labor force which increases the demand on urban universities to provide accessible training and educational opportunities. The well-known loss of both blue collar jobs and middle management positions in our metropolitan areas is causing many non-traditional students to return to universities for career changes, advanced degrees or more training to keep pace with the technological changes in our society.

Urban universities are not only faced with the challenge of the changing educational needs of our economy and a more diverse and changing student body, but also with this widening socioeconomic gap between central cities and the suburbs. This growing gap not only challenges urban universities but also local a governments and communities who struggle to effectively manage and provide public services to a decreasing and more impoverished population.

Today's urban university is being asked by the local community to come out of the ivory tower and participate in meeting critical needs and solving critical public problems. Indeed, providing public service has become a central mission, along with the traditional teaching and research functions, of many urban universities.

The educational needs of today's and tomorrow's students, together with the need to provide greater public service to the community, offers great challenge, but also an opportunity, to the urban university. This challenge and opportunity is to better focus research on the urban policy and problem-solving matters of our central cities and metropolitan systems. The urban university is the single most appropriate institution to perform this vital role with the available data, research and analysis capacity on hand.

The Census Bureau alone cannot provide all of the research and public service programs needed. Of the 10 year 2.5 billion dollar budget for the 1990 Census, only 5.8% is used for data dissemination and a much smaller fraction is dedicated to substantive demographic research using the data collected. A lot of valuable data is distributed by the Bureau to public institutions. The Bureau estimates that the market value (as determined by the Bureau's modest cost recovery pricing schedule) of computer tapes, disks, and printed material distributed to depository libraries, state data centers, the Inter-university Consortium for Political and Social Research, and the five Census Information Centers, which serve selected minority populations, amounts to approximately 1.3 million dollars.

An additional 1.5 million dollars is invested in the State Data Center program, which is extremely successful in distributing data through the Census Bureau's affiliate networks. The Bureau should be applauded for its excellent job in ensuring the Census data is available to those who want to use it.

While a significant amount of very important data is distributed, there are few federally-funded efforts to ensure that important urban policy and action-oriented issues are addressed through research and technical assistance in our communities. However, I would like to commend you, Chairman Sawyer, for your leadership in securing this year's reauthorization of Title XI of the Higher Education Act, otherwise known as the Urban Community Service Program. This program, the first grant proposals which are just now being reviewed by the Department of Education, is the only existing federal effort to support university-based applied research and outreach activities on urban issues.

I am also pleased to note that the House and Senate Banking Committees may take steps in this years housing bill to authorize local governments and their local universities to collaborate on projects of importance to the community, drawing on funds managed by the Department of Housing and Urban Development (HUD). It would be good to have HUD back in the business of supporting local urban research and technical assistance work by the universities. I feel strongly that a program of funded demographic research and public service be established on a university level to fulfill the pressing needs of the our urban areas.

At the Levin College of Urban Affairs at CSU, with the use of funding from a unique state appropriation supporting public service at urban universities, Ohio's Urban University Program, we have established a large database and analysis capacity. This capacity has enabled us to bring together vast datasets including Census, county real property records, and establishment specific employment data—so that cross-cutting action-oriented analyses are possible. We have assembled 5,000 databases which together include over 10 billion bytes of information.

The potential policy and action impacts of university research based on a combination of these data is exemplified by the recent re-consideration by a Cleveland area council of governments of whether to approve federal highway funds for a highway expansion which would contribute to the continued outward flow of jobs and population from the city of Cleveland and nearby communities to adjacent counties whose infrastructure is inadequate to support dramatic growth in housing and population. Such a direct impact by local research on a political and policy decision-making process is a virtual first in my years of observing local development decision processes.

As many observers have remarked, we live in an age which generates an impressive amount of information but which is not used for improving life in the community. Information is both a resource and a currency in our society, and ideally needs to be channelled through organizations which can help ensure its use and accessibility. Historically, we created public schools and libraries which prepared citizens to use and access the information of the print era.

What we are proposing for the next generation is the preparation of and access to electronic information. If we do not create new institutions for this purpose, then information will increasingly be the currency which separates the "haves" from the "have nots".

I propose the creation of The Demonstration Census Data and Education Center which would be the focus of electronic and organizational networks. Information would be received from the Census Bureau and augmented with data and research from universities, state and local agencies and organizations. The resulting information would then be disseminated through teaching, further research, public service and public access.

This synergy builds on the existing teaching, research, public service and technical assistance programs of our universities, increases their capabilities and provides access to the general community, thus providing a means for public policy development to be debated on common ground. In essence, the Census Data and Education Center would become an information and activity hub that connects levels of government, academic research across disciplines, and the public.

With this mechanism, not only is the public provided access to understandable information, but that information is used to train the next generation of citizens. A widespread dissemination role must be an ongoing function of educational institutions. Citizens must be connected to the educational institutions that can tap and assemble the data that is needed to improve the quality of life in our communities.

Mr. SAWYER. Thank you very much for your presentation this morning.

I couldn't help but notice in this morning's Cleveland Plain Dealer as I was flying from that city's great airport to this city that there was an editorial to the effect that that newspaper supports the use of Ohio's ivory towers in solving broad-based problems. I read to you in part from their comment on the proposal of Ohio State University President E. Gordon Gee to undertake such a broad-based involvement of State scholars in solving problems:

"For too long," Gee argues, "the State's academics have hidden in ivory towers, often lending their considerable talents to Ohio's industry for profit but rarely working with government to find solutions to the problems of State and local government."

He is right. Gee's idea has never been tried in Ohio. Nothing about it suggests that it would be duplicative or that it would distract from the primary mission of the universities.

It seems to me that there has been a decade-long head start on that particular proposal and the work of the Levin School, and the seven or eight other urban universities in Ohio that have anticipated the work of the higher education reauthorization of this year really gives Ohio a head start, and joining in that effort is an important role for the urban universities of Ohio. I'm pleased to welcome Dr. Gee to that effort and take advantage of the chance to inform him of the work that you at Cleveland State and others have been doing for some time now.

Mr. SWEET. We believe you are in a unique position, given your former role in the legislature and as mayor of Akron and now in the Congress, to look at how we can more effectively link our Nation's urban universities to the issues confronted in their communities. We have done that for over a century in rural America through the land grant mechanism, and now we are pleased that the Congress is beginning to see the potential for similar kinds of mechanisms through title XI.

Mr. SAWYER. It is precisely the land grant model that provokes the work that we have been doing here this year and that Chairman Ford began in 1980 with the development of title XI in the first place. We think we have got demonstration grants begun this year and look forward to the work that will flower from that across the Nation.

Before we turn to questions and answers, why don't we add the second part of our panel.

Dr. McBay, you have been sitting there patiently. We look forward to your testimony and urge you to proceed as you will.

Ms. MCBAY. Thank you, Mr. Chairman. I appreciate the opportunity to participate in this series of hearings.

I have entered a longer statement in the record, but I would like to just make a few points from that document; in particular, I would like to comment on the implications of the demographic changes for educational attainment, the recruitment and retention of minority teachers, and some implications for educational policy.

In your hearing on May 26, you had testimony from William O'Hare at the University of Louisville, and he noted a couple of developments or changes between the 1980 and 1990 census that have specific implications for educational attainment, and I would like to remind you of those observations. In fact, you have already commented on one of them, and that is the increasing size of the minority population.

He noted that between 1980 and 1990 minorities accounted for 15 million of the 22 million increase in the population. In other words, 64 percent of that increase came from minority groups, and that 15 million increase represented a 32 percent increase in the overall minority population, and that is in comparison with only a 4 percent increase in the non-Hispanic white population. So we see the greater growth there.

The second point that he made related to the economic diversity within the minority population, and I think that is a very important point to underscore here. One of the points he makes is that nearly one out of every seven African American families can be considered affluent—that is, having income of $50,000 or more—and nearly one of every eight Hispanic families.

At the same time, he very carefully points out that 32 percent of African Americans are living in poverty and that is an increase from 29 percent in 1979. So clearly there is an increase in the poverty rate at the same time as some people are moving out of it and moving upward.

His comments also related to the spacial distribution of minorities, and there he was talking about the fact that African Americans, for example, in metropolitan areas are more segregated than any other minority group, that they are the least suburbanized. This is of special importance, this issue of living in the suburbs. Harold Hodgkinson of the Institute for Educational Leadership just released a report called "A Demographic Look at Tomorrow," and one of the observations he makes there is that America's best schools are located in the suburbs of our 40 largest metropolitan areas, and he also notes that our 40 worst schools are in the inner cities of those same metropolitan areas as well as some rural areas. So there is clearly a link between where you live and access to quality education.

There is also a lot of evidence from a number of studies about the clear correlation between socio-economic status and educational attainment, and let me just indicate some of the areas where there is evidence to support this link. One is in the outcome of ability grouping and tracking. We have an educational system that disproportionately places low income and minority children into lower track remedial classes, and that tracking begins sometimes as early as kindergarten. While their more affluent peers are moving forward, these children are left behind, and the gap increases to as large as 4 years during the K–12 years. It is very important that we pay attention to this practice of tracking because of its debilitating effects on low income and minority children.

One of the other areas where there is a clear correlation is in course placements—that is, whether or not you are in remedial or advanced general subjects. There is a recent study by the Department of Education that found that African Americans and Hispanics were almost twice as likely as whites to be enrolled in remedial mathematics, and if you take an income cut, low-income students were more than twice as likely as high income students to be enrolled in remedial mathematics.

If you look, on the other hand, at who is enrolled in higher level math courses, the study found that almost half of the students from high income families take algebra or advanced mathematics, and that was in contrast to only 15 percent of low income students taking those courses.

They also found a clear correlation between students' family income and their classroom achievements in science as well as in mathematics, with high-income students being provided opportunities for hands-on experience and opportunities that led to their having a greater understanding of what the scientific process is all about, a very critical experience.

There is also a relationship in terms of drop-out rates. For example, in 1990, 3.8 percent of white students in grades 10 through 12 dropped out, 5 percent of African American students, and 8 percent of Hispanic students.

There is also a relationship between socio-economic status and access to a rigorous academic program taught by well prepared, experienced, and certified teachers. The National Science Foundation funded a study that was conducted by Jeannie Oakes of the Rand Corp., and one of her findings was that secondary schools that had high proportions of economically disadvantaged and minority students tended to employ teachers who, on the average, were less frequently certified to teach science and mathematics. They were less likely to hold bachelor's or master's degrees in the very subjects that they were teaching.

There is also the relationship with school environment. You, I am sure, know of Jonathan Kozol's seminal report or book called "Savage Inequalities" which demonstrates very clearly the inequity in facilities and social support.

Historically, there has been a difference in standardized test score performance. For example, although blacks have made progress in recent years in terms of their average SAT scores, there is still essentially a 200 point difference if you look at the total combined scores, and there is also at the same time a clear correlation between socio-economic status and performance on standardized tests.

There is a relationship with high school graduation rates. While almost 70 percent of ninth graders graduated from high school in 4 years, only 59 percent of African Americans graduated in 4 years, and 52 percent of Hispanics did.

If you look at college going rates—and we were talking about higher education, or Mr. Sweet was a moment ago—if you look at the 1990 high school graduates, 65 percent of whites went on to college, only 46 percent of African Americans, and 57 percent of Hispanics. Once in college, you are not guaranteed graduation, and so if you take a look at how different groups are graduating from college, in 1990, 22 percent of whites who were 25 years and older had actually finished college, and that is in contrast to 11 percent for African Americans and 9 percent for Hispanics. So there is a difference then across racial and ethnic lines in terms of college completion rates.

Finally, in terms of preparation for success in college or direct entry into the workforce, all you have to do is read the reports that talk about the millions of dollars that are spent annually on remedial courses for freshmen and remedial training for new workers by businesses.

There is one promising finding, and I do want to note that, and that is an analysis of data from the High School and Beyond survey. A study by Pelavan and colleagues found that the best determinant of future college attendance was the enrollment in high school geometry. You probably heard about that.

Although minorities in general don't attend college at the same rate after 4 years of high school, among students who took geometry the difference disappeared: 80 percent of black students who took geometry, 82 percent of Hispanic students, and 83 percent of white students went on to attend college. So it is clearly a finding that we ought to take note of as we develop policy.

Just a note or two about the minority teachers and teachers of minority students. As you know, there is a very serious mismatch between the students who are in the classroom in terms of race and ethnicity and the teachers in front of the class.

A recent study by the National Education Association found little change in the racial and ethnic composition of the K–12 teacher workforce, with almost 87 percent of that workforce being white.

In terms of African Americans, African American students represent about 16 percent of the K–12 population, and African Americans represent only about 7 percent of the teacher workforce. As you know, that representation is predicted to decrease to about 5 percent by the turn of the century.

Now the underrepresentation of minorities in the teaching workforce is a serious cause for alarm, but, I tell you, equally as alarming is an observation by our own Department of Education. They have just issued a study which says that there is a disturbing nationwide pattern emerging that teachers who are less experienced and less well prepared to teach in their fields are the very teachers who are instructing children from the lowest academic and socioeconomic background. On the other hand, higher abilities children and those from advantaged backgrounds are more likely to have well trained, experienced teachers.

Now we have made that observation, and the question is: What is the action that is going to be taken on that observation?

Let me just note some areas in which I do think that policymakers ought to pay some attention. First, I feel very strongly and our organization feels very strongly that we ought to change the factory model education system that we have. This is the system that tracks students and that only produces an educated elite. We think that eliminating the practice of tracking is a major issue. In fact, the Department of Education's Office of Civil Rights has been making noises about filing a class action suit on behalf of low income and disadvantaged youth and minority youth because of this practice of tracking. I don't know if there is going to be follow-through on that, but there has been some discussion about that.

I think it is important to encourage the Department of Education, or the President, or whoever is going to be the education leader for the country, to lay out a clear vision of the kind of environment that we want to have so that all of our children can have a quality education. It seems to me that instead of focusing on strategies such as school choice and the GI Bill of Rights that will only lead to second-rate educational opportunities for the majority of low income and minority students, we ought to be talking about the characteristics that ought to be in place to ensure quality education for all students, and I'm thinking of a strong core curriculum, competent and motivated teachers, extensive parental involvement, the use of effective and innovative teaching strategies, access to state-of-the-art instructional technologies, and so forth. Of course, there should be a special emphasis on math and science—I don't want to leave that out.

Let me suggest that, given some of the comments that were made earlier and given the observations that I noted by Mr. Hodgkinson, we ought to consider targeting efforts in the areas that have the greatest needs—for example, if we know the worst schools are in the inner cities of 40 metropolitan areas, why not target efforts at those particular sites, meeting the educational needs of the low-income families who are in those metropolitan areas?

Within the metropolitan areas, why not concentrate in housing projects or in well defined low-income communities and try to meet the educational needs of the children there?

Let me suggest that we ought to consider creating a minority teacher leadership corps. I have in mind, and it has been suggested by others, an ROTC-like minority teacher leadership corps that would use scholarships as incentives obviously in exchange for joining the teaching force. I think this would be a way of attracting stronger students into the teaching profession.

Another area has to do with national teaching standards. The Congress has funded the National Board for Professional Teaching Standards, and it seems that you ought to then ask for and review the Board's progress and to determine what steps it has taken to ensure that those assessments don't represent yet another hurdle for minority teachers.

I have recently read of a study that causes some alarm in that regard. It is a study that was done by G. Pritchey Smith of the University of North Florida. He found that in 35 States almost 95,000 minority teachers had been tested out of teaching, and of that 95,000 minority teachers, 45,000 were African Americans, 35,000 were Hispanics, and the others were for other minority groups. So we cannot impose standards without doing something about the quality of the education that teachers receive as they are being prepared. Otherwise, we will simply have another hurdle, and you know what the results are going to be. What Mr. Smith has done is to document what the problems are.

The issue of parental choice: I have suggested earlier that the school choice proposal is a problem, whether it is school choice where you use vouchers for public or private schools or whether it is school choice within public schools. The point is, there aren't enough schools of choice, there aren't many vacancies in those that exist, and those schools, as you know, are able to decide which students they will accept. It is not clear to me that if you have students who have a significant college-going rate, high grade point average, and high SAT scores, why you would take students who are likely to change that outcome? Our goal ought to be to make sure that every school is a school of choice.

There are other areas that I talk about in the paper. Let me just mention them quickly. Special education (our concern is, a disproportionate number of Hispanic and black males are placed in special education classes; school finance; and equity in financing, as you know, is a major issue. Finally, a very serious problem, we think, that will continue to exacerbate the situation between students who are from more affluent backgrounds and those who are not, is the whole question of access to technology, and the use of advanced technologies in instruction.

Thank you very much for this opportunity.

[The prepared statement of Ms. McBay follows:]

PREPARED STATEMENT OF SHIRLEY M. MCBAY, PRESIDENT, QUALITY EDUCATION FOR MINORITIES NETWORK

Mr. Chairman, members of the Subcommittee on Census and Population, my name is Shirley McBay. I am President of the Quality Education for Minorities Network, a non-profit organization in Washington, D.C. established in July 1990 and dedicated to improving education for minorities throughout the nation. The Network is a focal point for the implementation of strategies to help realize the vision and goals set forth in the report: Education That Works: An Action Plan For The Education Of Minorities. The report was issued in January 1990 by the MIT-based Quality Education for Minorities Project, following more than two years of travel around the country, exploring effective programs and strategies to improve the education of minority children, youth, and adults.

I appreciate the opportunity to participate in your series of hearings on "America's Changing Profile" and to specifically comment on the implications of demographic changes for education policies and programs, educational attainment, and the recruitment and retention of minority teachers, particularly in mathematics and science.

BACKGROUND ON ISSUES/BARRIERS AFFECTING THE EDUCATIONAL ATTAINMENT OF LOW-INCOME AND MINORITY YOUTH

Poverty is a major deterrent to quality education and poverty among children in America is growing. In fact, "Children are the poorest age group in America. In 1990, one in five, or 12.7 million children, was poor, an increase of 2.7 million children from 1979." [1] Almost 44 percent of African Americans, more than 37 percent of Hispanics, and approximately 15 percent of whites under the age of 18 were living in poverty in 1990. For children under the age of six, in 1987, 48 percent, nearly one in two, of African American children were living in poverty, the highest percentage for any racial or ethnic group. Poor children are the least healthy and are at the greatest risk of school failure.

About a third of the more than 40 million students enrolled in our K–12 public education system today are minority students. Among these students, poor children are the most likely to be attending failing schools.[2] Despite proposals to use educa-

[1] "Kids Count Data Book 1992", Center for the Study of Social Policy, Washington, DC, page 12.

[2] *Ibid.* page 12.

tional vouchers to allow poor children to attend private schools or more successful public schools, without radical changes, the majority of children from low-income families will continue to attend weak public schools.

As in the past, low-income families will have to look to the public schools to equip their children with the knowledge and skills required for future success and security in the work place. The role of the public schools as equalizer and provider of equal educational opportunities is especially critical to the future well-being of low-income minority children and youth as workers, as family members, and as citizens. However, these schools will fail to serve this purpose for the majority of these children, unless policymakers take bold steps to improve our public schools.

Education is the historic gateway to a better life for all Americans, especially for minorities. However, across America, a grievous injustice persists: millions of African American, American Indian, and Hispanic children are behind most of their white peers before and after they enter kindergarten because they do not have access to educational programs and strategies that work (for example, in 1989 less than a third of African American children were enrolled in a prekindergarten program in contrast to 40 percent of white children).

By and large, low-income minority children are taught in an atmosphere of low expectations created in part by myths about minorities and about education, myths that are sustained by an obsolete, factory model educational system that disproportionately places minority children from low-income families into lower-track remedial classes, beginning for many as early as kindergarten.

Most low-income minority youth emerge from these classes (and from the academically thin, general and vocational track programs into which they are later counseled) without the ability to solve complex problems, to analyze abstract knowledge, to communicate with precision, or to deal with change and ambiguity. The system in place produces a small, educated elite that is disproportionately white and affluent.

While poverty clearly limits access to a quality education, it is not the only reason that minority students are disproportionately underprepared as they move from elementary to middle school to high school, and from high school graduation to college or the work force. Myths about minorities and about education continue to play a major role in shaping the attitudes of many Americans toward making quality instruction available to all students.

These myths include:

Myth #1: Learning is due to innate abilities and minorities are simply less capable of educational excellence than whites

Myth #2: The situation is hopeless; the problems minority youth face are so overwhelming that society is incapable of effectively responding

Myth #3: Quality education for everyone is a luxury since not all jobs presently require creativity and problem-solving skills

Myth #4: All we need are marginal changes

Myth #5: The problem will go away

Myth #6: Equity and excellence in education are in conflict

Myth #7: Educational success or failure is within the complete control of each individual, and in America anybody can make it

These myths are pervasive in society and in our educational system. As a result, we produce only an educated elite (estimated at 15% of all students) [3] that can meet "world class standards," a group too small to meet the demands of a "world class" economy.

Most of our graduates, but especially minority students from low-income families, do not have the high level skills they need to help position and secure America's leadership role in a global economy. This is occurring at a time when the percentage of minority students in our schools is significant and is steadily increasing (for example, 22 of the 25 largest school districts in the country are already predominantly minority; by 1995, minority students will represent at least 25 percent of the high school graduates in 19 states; and by 2010, Blacks and Hispanics will increase their percentage of the public school population to 34 percent, up from 25 percent in 1990).

Although the implications of these demographic trends for our work force and future security are clear, we continue to hold onto an educational system that disproportionately places low-income minority children into lower tracks where they are taught to memorize through drill and practice by the least experienced teachers,

---

[3] Hodgkinson, Harold, "A Demographic Look At Tomorrow," Institute for Educational Leadership, Inc./Center for Demographic Policy, June 1992, page 8.

with the fewest resources, and in a climate of low expectations. These students are treated as objects to be acted on rather than as active participants in their own learning. In short, we knowingly give these children less of everything they need to be successful. We marginalize their efforts and minimize their chances of becoming productive citizens and positive role models for their peers and families.

"Ability" testing, sometimes as early as pre-kindergarten, disproportionately places African American and Hispanic children into low-ability or special education classes from which it is almost impossible to escape. Such assignments essentially seal the fate of many of these children for a lifetime. As early as the third grade, a divergence in achievement appears, relative to their white peers, in reading, writing, mathematics, and science. The gap widens to as much as four years by the junior year in high school.

Policymakers ignore the evidence that when these children reach middle or junior high school, they disproportionately end up in remedial classes. For example, a June 1992 Department of Education study found that" tracking, low expectations and mind-numbing repetition account for much of American students' lackluster performance in mathematics and science." [4] The study also found that African Americans and Hispanics were almost twice as likely as whites to be enrolled in remedial mathematics, and that low-income students were more than twice as likely as high-Income students to be enrolled in remedial mathematics.

At the same time, almost half of the the students from high-income families took algebra or advanced mathematics in contrast to 15 percent of students from low-income families (see Table 1). In fact, 46 percent of eighth-graders took algebra or advanced mathematics, while the remainder took general or remedial mathematics. In addition, the study found a clear correlation between students' family income and their classroom achievements in science. Higher income students were provided more hands-on experience in science that led to greater understanding of the scientific process.[5] The evidence is irrefutable that our educational system is not working well for most students, but minority and low-income students are particularly underserved. For example, in 1988, 18.2 percent of Hispanic eighth graders were enrolled in algebra or advanced mathematics in comparison with 30.9 percent of white eighth graders. On the other hand, Hispanic eighth graders were twice as likely to be enrolled in remedial mathematics as white eighth graders that year (11.3 percent in contrast to 5.5 percent). The contrast is even more striking between students from low socio-economic status (SES) families and those from high SES families (15.5 percent versus 47.0 percent in algebra/advanced mathematics and 10.2 percent versus 3.7 percent in remedial mathematics).[6]

Table 1—Percentage of Public School Eighth-Graders in Different Types of Mathematics Classes

	Algebra/Advanced	Remedial
Socioeconomic Status:		
Low	15.2	10.2
Middle	28.3	6.4
High	47.0	3.7
Race/ethnicity:		
Asian	43.5	7.0
Hispanic	18.2	11.3
Black	24.6	10.0
White	30.9	5.5
American Indian	14.1	15.1

Source: Education Department, National Center for Education Statistics, "A Profile of American Eighth-Grade Mathematics and Science Instruction," June 1992.

Another major study found that the proportion of high-ability science and mathematics classes increased significantly as the proportion of white students increased.

[4] "Education Daily", Vol. 25, No. 138, July 20, 1992, page 1, commenting on: "A Profile of American Eighth-Grade Mathematics and Science Instruction," June 1992, National Center for Education Statistics, Department of Education.

[5] *Ibid.* page 3.

[6] *Ibid.* page 3, citing a table from: "A Profile of American Eighth-Grade Mathematics and Science Instruction," June 1992, National Center for Education Statistics, Department of Education.

On the other hand, classes having disproportionately large numbers of minority students were seven times more likely to be identified by teachers as low ability rather than high ability.[7] Low-income and minority students had less access than other students to the best qualified science and mathematics teachers.

Secondary schools with high proportions of economically disadvantaged and minority students employed teachers, on the average that were less frequently certified to teach science and mathematics, and were less likely to hold bachelor's or master's degrees in these subjects.[8] Policymakers have failed to act on other significant findings to the benefit of minority and low-income students. An analysis of data from the High School and Beyond survey found the best determinant of future college attendance to be enrollment in high school geometry.[9] While in general a much lower proportion of minorities than whites attended college within four years of high school, among students who took geometry, this difference disappeared: 80 percent of Black students, 82 percent of Hispanic students, and 83 percent of whites in this group attended college.

If low-income minority students continue in higher education, the majority will attend community colleges from which they will not likely transfer to a four-year institution. For example, approximately 42% of African American students in higher education are enrolled in community colleges, but their transfer rate to four-year colleges is only 18%, the lowest of all student groups. Of the minority students that do enter four-year colleges upon graduation from high school, only 40% will have earned a baccalaureate degree five years later.

In summary, demographic trends are such that minorities will represent an increasing percentage of the overall population while their poverty rates continue to increase disproportionately. These developments have clear implications for the educational attainment of this growing fraction of America's population because of considerable evidence of the correlation between socioeconomic status and educational attainment in several areas:

- In the outcome of "ability" grouping and tracking
- Course placements (remedial, general, or advanced)
- Dropout rates (e.g., in 1990 3.8% of whites, 5.1% of African Americans, and 8.0% of Hispanics dropped out of grades 10–12)
- Access to a rigorous academic program taught by well-prepared, experienced, and certified teachers School environment (level of expectations, quality of facilities, and social support available)
- Standardized test scores (e.g., a 200-point differential between African Americans and whites on average combined SAT scores)
- High school graduation rates (While almost 70% of ninth graders graduated from high school in 4 years, only 59% of African Americans and 52% of Hispanics did)
- College-going rates (among 1991 high school graduates: 65% of whites, 46% of African Americans, and 57% of Hispanics)
- College-graduation rates (in 1990, 22 percent for whites, 25 years and older, in contrast to 11 percent for African Americans and 9 percent for Hispanics)
- Preparedness for success in college-level work or direct entry into the work force (millions of dollars spent annually on remedial courses for freshmen and remedial training for new workers)

MINORITY TEACHERS AND TEACHERS OF MINORITY STUDENTS

The racial and ethnic makeup of our public school enrollment has grown more diverse over the past 20 years, and today almost one in three students is a member of a minority group. However, a recently released survey by the National Education Association found little change in the racial and ethnic composition of the K–12 teacher work force: almost 87 percent are white.[10] The following table illustrates the problem in the case of K–12 mathematics and science teachers.

---

[7] "Science and Engineering Indicators, "1991 Tenth Edition, National Science Board, page 29, commenting on Oakes J., 1990, "Multiplying Inequalities: The Effects of Race, Social Class, and Tracking on Opportunities to Learn Mathematics and Science," Santa Monica, CA, The RAND Corporation.

[8] *Ibid.* page 32.

[9] *Ibid.* page 28.

[10] "The Daily Report Card," July 7, 1992, commenting on "Status of the American Public School Teacher," a National Education Association Survey.

Table 2—Percentage of Minority Mathematics and Science Teachers in the Teacher Work Force, 1985–86, by Subject and Grade Range

Subject/Grade Range	Black	Hispanic	Indian
Mathematics:			
K–3	10	1	0
4–6	12	2	0
7–9	6	1	0
10–12	3	1	0
Science:			
K–3	9	4	0
4–6	8	4	0
7–9	6	1	0
10–12	5	1	1

Source: Professional Women and Minorities: A Manpower Data Resource Service, Commission on Professionals in Science and Technology, Ninth Edition, March 1991.

The underparticipation of minorities in the teaching profession is cause for alarm. However, far more serious is the following startling observation by the Department of Education: "A disturbing nationwide pattern is emerging: Teachers who are less experienced and less well prepared to teach in their field are instructing children from the lowest academic and socioeconomic backgrounds," while higher-ability children and those from advantaged backgrounds are more likely than low-ability or disadvantaged students to have well-trained, experienced teachers.[11]

This situation holds true in secondary school science and mathematics as well. For example, as Table 3 demonstrates and as the National Science Board recently reported, "secondary schools with high proportions of economically disadvantaged and minority students employ teachers who, on the average, were less frequently certified to teach science and mathematics and were less likely to hold bachelor's or master's degrees in these subjects." [12]

Table 3—Qualifications of Secondary School Teachers in High- and Low-ability Classes

[Percentage of teachers]

Teacher Qualifications	Low-ability Classes		High-ability Classes	
	Low SES, minority, urban	High SES, white, suburban	Low SES, minority, urban	High SES, white, suburban
Certified in science/math	39	82	73	84
Bacc. in science/math	38	68	46	78
Master's in science/math	8	32	10	48

Source: J. Oakes, "Multiplying Inequalities: The Effects of Race, Social Class, and Tracking on Opportunities to Learn Mathematics and Science," Santa Monica, CA, The RAND Corporation, 1990.

As is the case in more affluent schools, the following must also hold true for science and mathematics in schools attended by low-income and minority students:

• Teachers of mathematics and science must be specialists in their disciplines and be provided enhancement opportunities to further develop expertise in their areas.

• Teachers and students should have access to a computer network for instructional and/or research applications.

• The teaching of mathematics and science must include strategies and pedagogical techniques that accommodate the diverse ways in which students learn.

• Teachers must be prepared to expose students to laboratory activities, early research experiences. and mathematics and science competitions so that students can explore concepts and gain some experience with scientific discovery.

• Teachers and others who influence children and youth should be exposed in greater depth to the opportunities and requirements of various mathematics, science, and engineering careers.

---

[11] "Education Daily," *Op. cit.*, page 4.
[12] "Science & Engineering Indicators," *Op. cit.*, page 32.

MATHEMATICS AND SCIENCE TEACHER PREPARATION PROGRAMS

Policymakers must provide support for innovation and reform in the preparation and in-service enhancement of precollege teachers. Instructional programs for precollege teachers must prepare them to teach all students well, through content-based, hands-on experiences leading to mastery of key science and mathematics concepts, problem-solving skills, and necessary pedagogical skills.

Content preparation for secondary teachers must equal or exceed that generally required for baccalaureate degrees in the area of specialization. Teacher education programs must undertake the preparation of teachers as a partnership, a joint responsibility involving many departments at the college as well as the local school system and the community.[13]

Science and mathematics teacher candidates must experience scientific research firsthand and be well-trained in the use of technology. These are critical components if the nation is to have a teaching corps that is responsive to the community and society it serves, understands the dynamic nature of science and technology, and is able to use technology effectively as a teaching tool. All prospective teachers must be knowledgeable and understanding of the pluralistic nature of society and of their future classrooms. To be effective as teachers of students with a range of cultural backgrounds, their preparation must include a multicultural perspective, including an examination of the issue of historic exclusion of minorities and exclusion from the pursuit of careers in mathematics, science, and engineering.[14]

WHAT CAN BE DONE TO ATTRACT MORE MINORITY STUDENTS INTO MATHEMATICS AND SCIENCE TEACHING

To attract and nurture minority students at the pre-college level so that they will consider pursuing teaching careers, it is necessary to:

- promote the early identification and nurturing of students showing interest in mathematics and the sciences through Saturday academies, middle school and high school residential academies, and pre-college-to-college bridge programs;
- promote development of clubs and programs encouraging exploration of teaching careers, such as Future Science and Mathematics Teachers;
- encourage mathematics and science teachers and counselors to promote teaching as a career among students who have demonstrated interest and talent in mathematics and science; and
- promote more opportunities for students, particularly minority students, to serve as tutors to their peers or younger students or as laboratory assistants, thereby helping them to envision themselves in a teaching role.

If the children and youth of minority and low-income families are to be productive citizens in the 21st century, science and technology must be an integral part of their education and training. They must have access to quality mathematics and science instruction and to a rigorous academic curriculum. They must be taught and encouraged in a supportive climate by caring adults.

MAJOR EDUCATIONAL POLICY ISSUES AND COMMENTARY

If we are to provide a quality education for all children and youth, and to effectively address the myriad issues resulting from our changing demographics and historic neglect of the education of minorities, policymakers must address several major issues:

1. Our factory model education system.

Central to successfully meeting the educational needs of students historically underserved by America's educational system is the dismantling of the factory model educational system now in place. Our entire educational system must be restructured to eliminate the debilitating practice of tracking and to create an environment for success for all students.

Restructuring means making fundamental changes in the rules, roles, and relationships in schools. A restructured system would decentralize decisions about how to improve learning and would increase the involvement of teachers and principals in policy discussions. Policymakers would establish basic outcome objectives but would leave decisions about how to achieve those objectives to teachers, principals, parents, child development professionals, and other interested parties at the school

[13] "Together We Can Make It Work: A National Agenda to Provide Quality Education for Minorities in Mathematics, Science, and Engineering." The Quality Education for Minorities in Mathematics, Science, and Engineering Network, April 1992, page 18.

[14] *Ibid.*, page 19.

and community levels. In addition to outcomes prescribed by elected officials and policymakers, restructured schools would be guided by professional standards based on knowledge and skills developed through research and experience.

Such an environment would hold high expectations for all students and would respect and value the culture of every child in school. Such a system would create incentives that make the best teachers available for those who need them the most, would strengthen the bonds between schools and communities, would offer a rigorous academic curriculum, would provide access to social and cultural enrichment in and outside of school, and would help to revitalize the traditional faith within minority communities and families in the power of education to advance their children.

The major characteristics of this new environment would be the following:

- a strong core curriculum
- competent and motivated teachers
- extensive parental/community involvement in schools
- use of effective and innovative teaching strategies
- access to state of the art instructional technology
- year-round enrichment
- systematic assessment of student progress
- systematic exposure of students to career options
- a special emphasis on mathematics and science

2. Change at the local level where education takes place.

To produce the fundamental transformation of our educational system that is necessary, change must take place where education takes place; in schools and in communities across the country. While it is important to collect information on successful strategies and to influence policies and programs at the national level, it is also critical that demonstration projects supported by local alliances and partnerships be conducted. Such a focus would enable individuals at the local level to:

- help persuade people in local communities that change is possible if individuals and groups are motivated to act, and if they work together to meet common goals and objectives;
- help state and local policymakers, teachers, parents, professionals, students, and others develop a common vision of an educational system, upon which to base local goals and actions;
- help motivate people in local communities into individual and collective action to produce the local changes that are required; and
- help unite efforts in communities to produce change through a well thought out and systematic course of action that can draw on other resources throughout the country.

3. Special needs of low-income residential communities.

A comprehensive, sustained effort is needed to create a model approach for enhancing educational opportunities for socio-economically disadvantaged children and youth in housing developments and low-income residential areas, including rural sites. The purpose of such an initiative would be to create a supportive environment in which all children and youth in these communities would have access to the educational and social services, resources, and enrichment needed to succeed in school, to go on to college or the world of work, and to become productive citizens.

This could be achieved by focusing and coordinating resources and support services of a number of public and private educational and social services agencies, institutions, and organizations in specific low-income residential communities; attracting untapped resources in the larger community; involving the entire residential community in the educational process; and designing a model that would provide a range of educational and social services residents may require.

The proposed model is based upon the work of Clark Atlanta University and its efforts with two Atlanta housing projects adjacent to the University's campus. On August 28–30, 1992 the QEM Network is hosting a working conference to develop a national agenda for enhancing educational opportunities for children and youth in housing developments. The conference will bring together representatives from colleges and universities located near housing developments, tenants' associations, community-based organizations, human services agencies, and professional educational organizations.

4. National Goals for Education.

Much of the current national debate on education is tied to the national education goals adopted by the President and the Nation's Governors in 1989. The discussion around implementation of these goals is heavily weighted towards measuring student progress towards the goals. Very little is heard about ensuring that students from low-income families (who are disproportionately minority) are not overlooked in the rush to meet standards.

5. National Examination System.

There is the possibility that a national testing system of student achievement will be established. One such discussion concerns a multi-component examination (a written performance examination, student projects including group projects, and student portfolios). Thus far, the focus appears to be more on assessment models (and the ability to take the examination multiple times) than on the quality of instruction and strategies for ensuring that youngsters from disadvantaged backgrounds aren't simply sorted once again, but with a different battery of tests. Even administered on a voluntary basis, a national test may join the other major "voluntary" examinations (the SAT and ACT) which are voluntary, unless a student wants to go to college.

6. National Teaching Standards.

Legislation was approved by Congress to provide $5 million of federal funding for the National Board for Professional Teaching Standards. This board is developing "voluntary" assessments for elementary and secondary teachers. Although there is recognition of the critical need to increase the number of minority teachers in the classroom, it is important to ensure that National Board assessments do not represent yet another hurdle for minority teachers as many state-administered pre-professional teaching examinations do now, thereby undermining minority teacher recruitment efforts that are of critical importance to the education of students from low-income backgrounds.

7. Parental Choice.

Several issues are being considered by Congress in the area of elementary and secondary education. One is the Administration's school choice proposal. In the past, Congress has rejected proposals to adopt a voucher plan that would enable students to take government funds to a public or private school of their choosing. Now advocates of school choice are pointing to increasing support for such initiatives across the country as the basis for expecting that Congress will reconsider its position.

The school choice proposal raises a number of concerns, not the least of which will be the effect on low-income minority youngsters. It is clear that without adequate knowledge and understanding of options, and without low or no-cost transportation, minority parents are less likely to take advantage of choice, leaving their children in poorer quality schools. There are not many vacancies in "schools of choice" and schools are able to decide which students they will accept. Furthermore, we have experienced "Freedom of Choice" plans in the past. They led to court-ordered desegregation because they were being used to avoid school integration. Our goal should be to make every school a "school of choice." No child should receive an inferior education.

8. Special Education.

Another issue at the national level that is affected by demographic trends relates to efforts to expand the definition of students eligible for services under the Education for Individuals with Disabilities Act to include students with a condition known as "Attention Deficit Disorder." This condition is ascribed disproportionately to minority boys. Black and Hispanic male students are already disproportionately represented in special education classes, therefore, an expansion of the definition would represent yet one more way to enroll low-income and minority youngsters in special education.

9. School Finance.

Another area affected by the changing demographics is that of school finance. As predicted by some, a number of school-finance initiatives and experiments are being or will be undertaken, including privatization, where states will finance education through vouchers to parents (based on their choices of schools) rather than by directly financing schools. Because schools with large low-income and minority populations have traditionally suffered inequities in financial support, some of these possible "solutions" could actually exacerbate existing barriers to improvement of education for students from socio-economically disadvantaged backgrounds.

10. Other Issues affected by Demographic Trends.

Other factors affecting the availability of quality education to low-income and minority youth include the following:

- access to educational resources (computers and other technologies)

• educational decisions based on standardized testing results (since there is a known strong correlation between socio-economic status (SES) and student performance on these tests)

• teacher/administrator attitudes towards minority students

• distribution of financial resources to schools with high concentrations of low SES students

• home/community environment and parental/community involvement in schools

• the extent to which minority students participate in magnet and special theme schools that have been demonstrated to be effective in increasing student achievement

The outcomes of public policy and legislative discussions such as this one can clearly shape the nature and the quality of education available to students from low socioeconomic backgrounds.

Mr. Sawyer. Thank you very much, both of you, for your presence and for your contributions; and, Dave Sweet, again, thank you for your kind comments about the work that I have been doing with other colleagues here on behalf of urban education.

I am grateful for a number of the topics that you have both raised, particularly in terms of data use and how the large-scale findings of the census really can be augmented and developed through focused research and through continuous work throughout a decade, particularly during a period of such enormous change, to continue to monitor emerging trends so that we can respond to them more quickly than just every decade or decade and a half, which is the current situation that we find, particularly with regard to education funding on the Federal level.

Right now, title I dollars, for example, are being distributed according to formulas that are being driven by data that was based on 1979 realities, gathered in 1980, and the new data won't be available until some point next year at best. That is hardly real response in a time of intense change.

I am particularly pleased at the points that you raised, Dr. McBay. The example I always use is not geometry but, rather, algebra, that it may be the single most pivotal decision that a child and his or her parents make in the course of a lifetime. It may have more to do with the direction that that child takes, and it is for that reason that, in addition to the work that you heard described, that the Higher Ed Reauthorization included substantial work in terms of developing access to information and counseling systems at that middle school point where a child is making decisions about whether or not it is worthwhile to prepare, through course selection, even at that early age for the opportunity to go beyond.

The whole way in which we measure progress is pivotal not only for individuals but for our entire system. The National Council of Teachers of Mathematics has done an enormous amount of work over this past decade. If there is anything that it has found, in my view, that is important, it is that the whole business of choosing what it is that we are going to measure. It may have a great deal to do with the outcomes that we provoke, and in that sense it is far more important to decide early on what it is that we want children to learn and then, as you suggest, to develop the systems for the delivery of that learning and from that, the curriculum, the methods, and the materials. With that, you can finally develop the instruments by which to measure success instead of developing the instruments first and then rushing backwards in that developmental stream to get to the point where it is actually doing some good in schools and classrooms around the country.

Let me go back to the basic premises that each of you brought to this. I'm interested in the way in which one or more trends—when they come together at pivotal points, we find consequences that sometimes are instructive. If we look at the increase in single-parent and two-parent working families, does the literature tell us very much about the consequences of that rapidly growing phenomenon, in terms of academic achievement? Or, in fact, are our schools addressing that particular problem on either elementary and secondary or the higher education level?

I guess the question is, how have we been adapting institutionally to the two phenomena that each of you described in different ways: the changing demographics of the elementary and secondary school, and the quite rapid and profound change in the demography of the college campuses?

Ms. McBay. There are studies that show a relationship between the education of the mother and the success and achievement of her children in school. So clearly if you have a single female head of household who doesn't have a high school degree, then you would expect, based on the studies, that her children would not do as well.

Part of the problem is that many of the single heads of household that you speak of have been unsuccessful themselves in schools, and therefore they are hesitant, for a variety of reasons, including remembering their experiences, to actually participate in any significant way or to question in any significant way what is happening to their children. They don't have the information on which to help make the course selections that we were talking about before; in the case of selecting schools of choice, they don't have the information or the means of transportation.

So yes, I think there are some clear issues and problems.

Mr. Sawyer. But we don't know very much about the duration of the single parent status. We have some sense about the duration of two-working-parent status. Do you have any response to the notion that, because in single-parent families the parent tends to be younger—whether it is a question of the single status, the duration of that single status, or the age at which that child or young person becomes a parent in single status? Or is all of this so much a blend that we don't know very much about, and is hard to discuss?

Ms. McBay. I don't know about specific studies, I do know that there are programs. For example, in Albuquerque there is a New Futures Program where they take teenage mothers and provide them with educational opportunities to go back to school and, to have day care centers there for their children. That program has been extremely successful in terms of enabling the parent, or the mother, to then go on to get a job and to be supportive and a better first teacher of her children.

Mr. Sweet. In Ohio the State legislature passed a law recently requiring that AFDC recipients either obtain work or learning experience, and, in conjunction with the Cuyahoga County Department of Human Services, we established a college-entry pilot program AFDC recipients, largely women with children. We found that of the approximately 40,000 recipients, 13,000 had high school diplomas.

So the issue there was to see how we could develop a system—and, pragmatically, this is a system in which the State is paying for the work or training experience—that brings them into a university environment and gives them the support services, which include child care, so that they can progress toward a college degree.

This past year we had our first degree recipient from this program and it illustrates that such a program can have an impact and can give AFDC recipients who have high school diplomas the next set of skills so that they can compete in today's workforce.

I think there are many programs of that nature being developed by urban universities across the country.

Ms. McBay. In fact, LaGuardia Community College has a program that has been around for a number of years called the Middle College Program, in which students who have not finished high school and who have families are able to come to complete their work. They are more likely then to be successful because they are in a community of students who are nearer their age and have more responsibilities than they would if they were still in high school.

Mr. Sawyer. There is a widespread perception that programs aimed at students or others more broadly in society who are most in need have somehow failed. Do you share that perception?

Ms. McBay. Well, there was a recent article in the Post that talked about and celebrated the increase in graduation rates for African Americans over the last 20 years, and that is something of note. The problem is the quality of education that many of these students received, and many of them have gotten diplomas through the GED route.

You can see the inequity or the underpreparedness of many of these students when they go on to community colleges. About half—I guess 46 percent of African American students are in community colleges, and over 50 percent, 53 or 54 percent, of Hispanic students are there. You see what happens to them after that in terms of going from community colleges to 4-year institutions. The transfer rate is abysmal. For most students, it is about 28 percent; for African American studs, it is only 18 percent.

So there is a question here of preparedness. Clearly, financial assistance is an issue, but also many of these students leave community colleges without having completed a program or having some kind of a certificate that has some meaning.

Mr. Sweet. Similar to your example of the student reaching a crossroads at middle school level in terms of their math preparedness, a student entering a community college that doesn't think ahead in terms of preparing himself or herself for going forward into a 4-year curriculum is, I think, another challenge, and here is, a theme that you have struck on many occasions, an opportunity for building a partnership.

Universities and community colleges traditionally have not worked effectively together to address the needs of community college students. I think increasingly we are finding that the universities and community colleges are partnering up more effectively, but we have a long way to go to get the university faculty and the community college faculty pulling together for the benefit of those students.

Mr. SAWYER. Your responses raise a difficult dilemma. Where do we focus our efforts and our resources to make the most telling differences? Do we aim at those who are most in need? Do we aim at those who are most remedial? Are they the same? And, if they are different, do we have to choose?

Ms. MCBAY. Well, it is not in the best interests of the country to have anybody who is not able to contribute.

Mr. SAWYER. Clearly. We cannot afford to bear the burden. That was the whole point of my opening statement.

Ms. MCBAY. Right. I understand.

Mr. SAWYER. But we have to begin.

Ms. MCBAY. I would think that fully funding Head Start would be an important first step, and then following that with some kind of support at the K–5 grade levels. It seems to me those are very critical years. But it is very hard to pick out parts of the pipeline because each part is preparing the student for the next part, and when you have the advantages from having extra support, supplementary support, at one part, the next part has to be ready to build on that. Otherwise, you have lost—really, in a sense, you have wasted the resources that you put in the first part.

Mr. SWEET. And that is why it is so important to focus on the early childhood part of the pipeline, right at the beginning, and then move from there.

Mr. SAWYER. Let me ask you another question that deals with the dimensions of the phenomena. We know a great deal about the rapid change in the incidence of poverty. I'm not convinced that we have studied the duration of poverty to quite the same depth, and I'm not at all sure that we look at duration and concentration as well as incidence at the same time.

Can you talk at all about where the literature leads, where research is leading, what kinds of things we need to measure if we are going to get at the consequences of those phenomena? I mean they are the same phenomena, but they are different dimensions of the same question. Or am I not making any sense?

Ms. MCBAY. You are making sense. I just don't know the literature on this. I do know examples of programs where they have tied employment training opportunities for people who are on welfare. In Massachusetts in particular, the program was extremely successful there. So there is anecdotal evidence. It doesn't mean, of course, that studies don't exist that provide information on the concentration aspect of the problem.

Mr. SWEET. As you are well aware, the first thing to go in a grant proposal or in a foundation grant or Federal funding is the longitudinal tracking and the analysis of the policy that is being put in place, and your question illustrates the point that it would be great to establish a longitudinal tracking of the recipients of these degrees who were in the AFDC recipient category. However, the funding does not permit that.

As you are aware, we created a high school 10 years ago that is called the Law and Public Service Magnet High School of the Cleveland Public Schools, and we have tried our best to establish longitudinal data, tracking of those students and where they go, and how they then perform after exposure to this unique curriculum that has been developed. But there are very few funders out there that are willing to back university-related research on long-term longitudinal studies of this type.

Ms. McBay. I appreciate the importance of research, and, having been at MIT for 10 years, I could certainly attest to the importance of it. In fact, the focus, or a good bit of it, was on research. Many higher education institutions—I have to get this in—for a variety of reasons, spend more time on research and publishing papers and writing proposals and not enough attention to teaching and to the K–12 part of the pipeline.

But the point I want to make is that there is no secret about what it takes to successfully educate children. We have lots of examples of that. It is just that the less affluent students are not provided those opportunities.

So there is nothing, from my point of view, about the single-parent household that is that unique, it is just that the conditions are not there, the opportunities for supplementary education, for year-round schooling; enriching, reinforcing experiences are not there. This is true whether you are in a one-parent household or a two-parent household where the resources are not there. So there is no mystery here to me.

Mr. Sawyer. There are a number of phenomena that have yielded this maldistribution of resources. Let me just raise three of them that we have concentrated on, in this subcommittee, over the course of the conduct of the census, the generation of the data, and the discussion of the data as it has come from the census, all of which may have contributed in one way or the other to this maldistribution.

We have seen enormous regional population shifts over the course of this past decade—that is, across the continent, between regions. We have also seen this continued urbanization coupled with the exurbanization that Dr. Sweet talked about, and then we have seen, in addition, the enormous increase in immigration in a way that we haven't seen literally in a century.

Can you weigh those factors for me in terms of the consequences for maldistribution of resources?

Mr. Sweet. I would like to at least point to one issue that speaks primarily to the Midwestern cities, but I think it would be generalizable across most of our Nation's cities, and that is that historically we have seen the immigration, or the migration streams going into the central cities and then residents of the central cities aspiring to move to the suburbs, and so you have got a chain that has new immigrants arriving into our central cities and then people who have established themselves moving to the suburbs and then the people from the suburbs moving to the exurban areas and this continued shift.

What has happened in the cities like Cleveland and Akron and Cincinnati and Dayton and Toledo and some of the more mature, shall we say, economies is that the chain of outward movement continues. However, we have seen the inflow of new residents drop to a trickle, and that is because of the lack of job opportunities in the central cities. So what you see then is a decline.

Look across the Nation's major metropolitan areas, look at the central cities, and look at the loss of population in the central cities. It is not true that we have seen an increase in the outmigration, we have seen a decrease in the immigration, and, as a result, we see smaller populations, the gaps increasing, the socio-economic gaps that I have spoken to, and increasing challenges by those central city school districts and the central city governments in providing the necessary services for that more impoverished population.

So I think that one of the trends that is counter to the more traditional exploration of this topic is the lack of immigration into our central cities and the impact that that has had over the past decade or two.

Mr. SAWYER. I'm going to run out of time here before I have to go vote. I'm happy to come back to this panel. I want to make sure that we hear from our second panel as well, however. So I'm going to ask you one more question, and then let me ask you whether you would be willing to respond in writing to a series of other questions that we have.

I very much appreciate your contributions today. They really only begin to touch the veneer of the work both from the primary reading that we have done and the work that you have both been involved with. Other data indicate that we have an awful lot of work as policy-makers to do if we are going to understand the kind and character of change that we are undergoing.

But you both address a pivotal point. We talk about one kind of deficit after another around here, more than just the trade and the budget deficit, but the one that we don't talk about very much at all is the teacher deficit, the one that is coming upon us. It is not only a matter of urban and rural settlement patterns and the availability of convenience among teachers of a variety of different racial and ethnic backgrounds, but we have simply got an age problem in the teaching cohort in this country that I don't see us dealing with in any very real or focused way. It is as large a deficit as any that we are likely to face. It is going to produce out of the current teacher gap an absolute collapse of the floor on which current education is standing in the latter part of this decade.

The teacher gap in certain subject areas, those that you mentioned, Dr. McBay, is dire, and it affects both the work in understanding that problem in the kinds of institutional settings that led you to raise this. It is critical to the kind of work that is being done in the kind of institution, the urban institutions, Dr. Sweet, where you work.

Could the two of you discuss how we go about, in the very limited time that we have to address a problem that is inexorably descending on us?

Ms. MCBAY. I think there needs to be some opportunities, some funded opportunities for partnerships between some of the major urban universities and historically black colleges and other predominantly minority institutions that have teacher education programs. I think that partnership can help to ensure that the teachers who are prepared have the latest in terms of technology and an understanding how to use it. I think we also have to provide support for technology to be a part not only of the training but of the schools themselves.

Teachers have to have access to computers and to other forms of technology, and they have to know how to use them. So I think these partnerships could do that, coupled with the idea that I suggested earlier of having ROTC-like scholarships for students so as to attract students to teaching as early as high school—even before that, when they have, for example, experiences tutoring younger students.

Mr. SAWYER. When you say ROTC, are you talking not so much about the military style of the training as the commitment to serve?

Ms. McBAY. Yes, that you will get tuition assistance and other forms of assistance during your 4 years of study in college in exchange for an equal number of years teaching in an area where there is a great need. It seems to me this is one way to address the problem that I talked about earlier of having teachers in inner city schools that are not certified to teach the courses they are teaching. This is one avenue.

Also, there is this big move on to use retired military personnel or people who are leaving the military who have some math and science background. I think some major universities could actually develop a program, a 1-year or 2-year program, that would enable these people who have some knowledge of the subject, but who don't necessarily know anything about teaching, to become teachers. This could give us in a short time a ready pool of new teachers.

Mr. SWEET. I would like to pick up on that point, because I think one of the things that has to be attacked are certification and accreditation requirements. We in higher education are big on accreditation, and yet it oftentimes freezes us into an inability to change and address new opportunities such as not only the military retirees but other second-career people. There are so many people now that are confronting the need or the desire for moving from their current career into a second career. Many of those people are trained in math, science, and other kinds of disciplines that are very desperately needed in our school system, but they face a very difficult path in capturing that life experience and gaining credit for moving toward certification. We have to take a fresh look at certification and accreditation requirements as practiced by our universities.

Mr. SAWYER. One of the things I would like to ask you, not in this setting this afternoon, but to point us toward the literature that can best guide us as we try to strike a balance between a perhaps outmoded pathway to certification and the continuing need to maintain and refine and redefine the high quality skills necessary to address those populations that are most in need and most remediable. Clearly, current techniques may not be serving those needs well, but no technique may be even worse. Trying to strike a balance between those two will be very difficult.

I have to strike a balance between the work done in this subcommittee and the work that is done on the Floor.

Mr. SWEET. As a postscript, I might add, it is great to have a person who was formerly a teacher serving now in the Congress that understands the subtleties of these particular points.

Mr. SAWYER. Well, I don't know about formerly. I strongly suspect that in this kind of work as well as yours, once a teacher, always a teacher.

I will be back. Thank you. This hiatus may take a few minutes because there may be more than one vote, but it is my intention to return as quickly as possible.

[Recess.]

Mr. SAWYER. We are ready to resume.

The topic of our second panel is the transition from school to workplace. It is one of those topics that really expands on all of the concerns that we have been talking about this week, that we are going to be talking about next week, and so forth.

Our two panelists are Dr. Marta Tienda and Dr. Samuel Halperin. Dr. Tienda is the associate director of the population research center at the University of Chicago and a professor in the Department of Sociology at that institution. She has worked on the Census Advisory Committee on Population Statistics, and is a member of the Population Association of America and the American Sociological Association.

Dr. Halperin is the study director of the William T. Grant Foundation's Commission on Work, Family, and Citizenship. He directs the Foundation's Youth and America's Future Program, is the former president and director of the George Washington University Institute for Economic Leadership and former Deputy Assistant Secretary of HEW.

Welcome to you both. Dr. Tienda, if you would like to proceed, please.

STATEMENTS OF MARTA TIENDA, PROFESSOR OF SOCIOLOGY AND ASSOCIATE DIRECTOR, POPULATION RESEARCH CENTER, UNIVERSITY OF CHICAGO; AND SAMUEL HALPERIN, STUDY DIRECTOR, COMMISSION ON WORK, FAMILY, AND CITIZENSHIP, WILLIAM T. GRANT FOUNDATION

Ms. TIENDA. Thank you.

First, I would like to thank the Population Resource Center for organizing and assisting in compiling this hearing and to the subcommittee for allowing this opportunity to present some research findings and make some recommendations even though they will be bold.

For the past 15 years, I have investigated race and ethnic differences in labor market and educational outcomes. As I searched for explanations, it became very apparent to me that experiences of adolescents are pivotal for understanding the trends in social and economic inequality that I had been documenting among adults.

With support from Rockefeller and Russell Sage Foundation, Professor Joseph Hotz and I were able to launch a program of research to analyze race, ethnic, and gender differences in the transition from school to work. Dr. Hotz is the director of the population research center and professor of economics in the Harris School of Public Policy at the University of Chicago, and our work is truly interdisciplinary.

I'm here to share with you some preliminary findings from this research which illustrates the importance of race and ethnic differences in patterns of school departure and entry to the world of work among a cohort of young men and women. Our research program is timely in light of the increasing ethnic diversity of the U.S. population and the well documented projections that women and minorities will contribute disproportionately to the growth of the U.S. labor force into the next century.

As the workers of the future, youth must become the prime targets for dropout prevention programs and, for those who are not college bound, creative strategies that strengthen links between schools, vocational training programs, and employers. I will try to conclude then with recommendations for data collection and some of what I consider urgent research priorities.

Growing concern over the plight of America's youth has called attention to the rising numbers reared in poverty and in father-absent families, to high rates of school failure, particularly among minorities, and rising levels of youth unemployment. These problems are not confined to minority youth, but they certainly are more pervasive among them, and yet the weakened labor market position of minorities is puzzling when it is considered against narrower educational differentials between white and minority adults.

Although more black and Hispanic youth are graduating from high school than ever before, greater numbers of minority youth are confronting difficulties in the labor market whether or not they graduate from high school. This phenomenon requires a multi-focal vision of the school-to-work transition with a special emphasis of the experiences of youth who are not college bound and whose home and school experiences leave them equally ill prepared to enter the world of work.

Our approach to understanding ethnic variation in the school-to-work transition builds on several recent findings—namely that entry-level job opportunities for minorities shrank during the 1980's; that prolonged schooling is associated with higher levels of school joblessness at specific ages; and that economic payoffs to schooling have become more differentiated in recent years.

Prior research indicates that both the timing and the nature of the early labor market encounters as well as the linkages between the teen labor market experiences and early adult outcomes differ by race, but there is considerably less evidence about the Hispanic experience in this regard, and virtually nothing about the Asian experiences. Our work begins to fill a part of this gap by focusing on or including Hispanics in our research, and our recommendations will address needed extensions, including data collection that includes Asians.

Our empirical research is based on the National Longitudinal Survey of Youth, not census data. This survey is a representative sample of youth aged 13 to 20 years in 1978. The strengths of these data over prior surveys include the substantial oversample of Hispanics and blacks, very detailed longitudinal histories on schooling, labor force, and military experiences of the respondents, the availability of 12 years now of prospective data for the original respondents, and the availability of the measure of scholastic aptitude for all respondents that is based on the Armed Forces Qualifying Test, which I shall refer to as AFQT. I emphasize this because of the very important results when one analyzes this index.

We restricted our focus on individuals who were 13 to 16 in 1978, because we were interested in when school departures occur, the timing and the nature of first labor market encounters with respect to school enrollment data, and linkages between the very first labor market encounters and subsequent employment outcomes. These considerations are especially critical for minority workers.

Several features of our research program distinguish it from prior endeavors. First, we examined the employment experiences of minority and nonminority youth during the recent past rather than the distant past. Second, our broad comparative approach includes women and Hispanics, and, where possible, it distinguishes between white and nonwhite Hispanics. Third, we consider multiple definitions of school, job, and first school departure. This is very important because some results are sensitive to the operational definitions of first job. We distinguish first entry-level jobs, first steady jobs, and first full-time jobs.

In the short time I have available, I can only highlight some of the more significant results. In keeping with the subcommittee's interest on America's changing demographic profile, my testimony will emphasize, race, ethnic, and gender differences in patterns of school leaving and transitions to employment. Professor Hotz and I have prepared a fairly extensive background paper that contains greater detail about our findings which we have submitted to the staff.

On school departures, our results on patterns of school leaving reveal significant ethnic and racial differences in the timing and pace of school departure. Our inferences are based on life table estimates of cumulative proportions leaving school at specific ages according to the two criteria—that is, whether they remained out for 6 months or for a year or more—and these results are reported in tables A and B, which show that men tend to exit school more quickly than do women, but the differences in the rate of school leaving depend on race and ethnicity. White men and women prolong schooling more than their minority counterparts, while Hispanics exhibit the fastest pace of school withdrawal at very young ages. Over twice as many Hispanic women as compared to white or black women left school before the legal age to quit.

Our multi variate analyses reversed these results. That is, although the gross effects of race and ethnic origin on school departure are positive for both men and women, such that blacks and Hispanics exit school at a faster rate than their white counterparts, controlling for scholastic aptitude differences that are correlated with school retention reverses the rates of ethnic effects on school departure by our liberal criterion, and completely eliminates them for Hispanic men and women. That is quite notable in light of the well documented trends that Hispanics are not staying in school.

Ethnic differences in patterns of school withdrawal have profound implications for the long-term employability of young men and women. Although the premature school departure need not be definitive, there is mounting evidence that Hispanic youth are less likely to return to school or to receive general equivalency degrees. The patterns of school departure we have documented, thus, have profound implications for the workforce readiness of minority youth into the 21st century.

On labor force entry, our life table estimates of the timing of first jobs reported in figures 1(a) and (b), also reveal considerable diversity along race and ethnic lines. Although premature school departure renders Hispanics the most educationally disadvantaged group, it is black youth who encounter the greatest difficulties in the labor market. This generalization obtains for all definitions of first job.

That the labor market difficulties experienced by black youth carry into their early adult lives is clearly apparent in the timing of first full-time jobs. By age 20, 30 percent of white and Hispanic men have held full-time jobs compared to less than 20 percent of black men. Although lower shares of women than men worked full time by their 20th birthday, ethnic differences in entry to full-time employment paralleled the male pattern.

The slower rates at which blacks enter the labor market, which signal accumulating disadvantages in a life table framework, are clearly discernible in both sets of curves. The Hispanics-white disparities in the rate of labor market entry, while less pronounced in the black-white disparities, are statistically significant in all but one instance—namely, the Hispanic-white differences in the timing of first full-time employment for men.

Furthermore, the conclusion that black men experience the greatest difficulties entering the labor market is not altered by controlling for differences in scholastic aptitude or family background. However, this is not the case for Hispanic men. There were essentially no differences between Hispanic and white men in the rate of entry into either beginning or full-time jobs once differences in the AFQT scores and family background characteristics are standardized statistically.

Among women, an adjustment for differences in AFQT scores similarly did not eliminate the racial differences in the rate of attaining entry-level jobs. Black women, like their male counterparts, experience slower transitions into first jobs compared to white or Hispanic women of similar ability. However, no differences in the rate at which white and Hispanic women achieved entry-level jobs were evident among the respondents who were comparable in their AFQT scores and their family backgrounds.

Unlike men, racial differences in women's transition to full-time employment did not carry over into their full-time jobs. In other words, the rate of transition to full-time employment was no different among black, white, and Hispanic women with equivalent scores on the AFQT test and family backgrounds. Thus, for women, group differences in scholastic aptitude and family background account for the significant racial and ethnic differences in their rate of entry to the workforce.

Part of the delayed entry to the workforce experienced by black youth, particularly when compared to Hispanic youth, might stem from their slower rates of school departure, particularly before age 18, and in the figures we have plotted we compared the survival curves and the rate of entry into the workforce against one another. The extent of overlap between school and work, which is indicated by the area below the intersection between the two curves is much greater when the liberal definition of first job is used—that is, figures 2(a) and 2(b)—than when the restrictive definition is used—figures 3(a) and (b). Obviously, flexible employment, such as that captured by our liberal definition, is more compatible with school enrollment than is full-time work.

But despite the racial and ethnic differences in the timing of school departure and labor market entry, the results shown in figures 2 and 3 indicate substantial shares of youth do combine school and work during adolescence and during young adulthood. Short-term entry-level jobs are dominant at the younger ages, but steady jobs and full-time jobs that last for a year or more are not uncommon among 18- and 19-year-olds.

How work experiences while attending school influences later employment is not yet clear in the research, but we plan to scrutinize this further.

On wages, there is a presumption that there are advantages of early labor market entry because it supposedly builds work experience which is associated with higher earnings and occupations status at later ages. If the accumulation of experience occurs at the expense of lower educational attainment—that is, if employed youth withdraw from school at earlier ages—then the potential gains from early labor market experience may be totally offset during the early adult years, as earnings of the more highly skilled workers surpass those of less educated workers. In tables 5(a) and (b), which summarize wage and school outcomes for our three definitions of first job, we address this issue.

At the point of first contact with the labor market, race and ethnic differences indicate, quite surprisingly, that minority youth have a significant wage advantage in their first jobs. However, the minority advantage in wage rates is reduced when the analysis is restricted to first steady jobs, and among men ethnic differences in wages were statistically trivial in first steady jobs, but female wage gaps in steady jobs were significantly different by ethnicity, and were opposite to the ethnic differences in educational attainment.

All wage advantages of minority youth completely dissipate by the time they obtained their first full-time job. White men and women received the largest wage gains as they made the transition from entry-level to full-time jobs. Although blacks averaged half a year more schooling than Hispanics employed full time, they earned 50 cents an hour less on an hourly basis, and these are standardized for price index. Similarly, white women employed full time received $5.50 per hour compared to $5.01 and $4.84 for similarly employed Hispanic and black women.

These differences are all the more striking when mapped against the groups' average schooling levels at the time they attained their full-time jobs. There were no differences between black and white women, while Hispanic women completed one-half-year less of school. These results suggest that both color and credentials contribute to the profiles of labor market disadvantages of minority youth and that it is worth investing in resources to investigate the mechanisms responsible for the declining wage advantages of minority workers.

Several recommendations follow from our work to date. The first and foremost concerns the substantial race and ethnic differences in the rates at which young men and women leave school and enter the workforce. Among men, we observe pronounced race and ethnic differences in the probability of getting a job. In particular, it is black men who experience greatest difficulty entering the labor market. Unlike women, young men's wages are not differentiated by race and ethnic group membership.

I urge the subcommittee to support research directed to understanding the mechanisms and barriers that limit young black men's access to the labor market and the mechanisms that generate unequal wages for women of color. The research program I envision should be grounded in empirical analysis of secondary data, perhaps including the census, but should also include diverse methodologies to document whether and how discrimination may be responsible for the results we observe.

A second recommendation concerns data requirements to further research and knowledge about the school-to-work transition. Despite the great analytical potential of the NLSY for investigating various aspects of the school-to-work transition, I recommend that the subcommittee support appropriations for a new youth cohort. Respondents currently in the NLSY are now in their late 20's and early 30's, and those who were already in their late teens and early 20's were already too old when this cohort was begun to study the school-to-work transition. That means that cohort is currently beyond the transitional phase of their life course.

Given the dramatic changes in the racial and ethnic composition of the U.S. population during the 1980's that were driven by immigration and differential fertility, collection about today's youth seems a necessary adjunct for policy formulation about tomorrow's workers. Along this line, I recommend that the new youth cohort begin with younger children, kids in early adolescence rather than the large age spectrum used by NLSY.

Many scholars like ourselves have been forced to leave out the older ages when we do our analyses because of serious censoring problems. This is warranted to adequately portray the process of school departure. Legal restrictions on school departure notwithstanding, many youth, particularly minorities, leave school permanently before they are entitled to do so legally, and these are the kids most in need of attention of policymakers.

I also recommend that the new youth cohort include an oversample of Asian men and women. There was no mention of Asian population in the earlier panel. We know virtually nothing about the school-to-work transition of this rapidly growing and equally diverse minority population.

Third, I would urge the subcommittee to sponsor research on the significance of the Armed Forces Qualifying Test as a measure of scholastic aptitude and job readiness. The military interprets AFQT score as a measure of general trainability and uses the score to screen out individuals who are likely to have a low probability of success in completing military training.

Social scientists have used the AFQT as a general ability indicator, arguing that it performs like a scholastic aptitude test. But the typical employer does not have access to individuals' AFQT scores, nor are such standardized test scores available for typical job applicants.

Colleges and universities require some form of entrance exam for admission, and are there lessons to be learned from the military with respect to matching workers to job specialties based on this or a similar indicator of general trainability?

So, on this score I would like to thank the committee for inviting us to participate in this set of hearings and to address the subcommittee. Thank you.

[The prepared statement of Ms. Tienda follows:]

PREPARED STATEMENT OF MARIA TIENDA, PROFESSOR OF SOCIOLOGY AND ASSOCIATE DIRECTOR, POPULATION RESEARCH CENTER, UNIVERSITY OF CHICAGO

I. INTRODUCTION

I am Maria Tienda, Professor of Sociology at the University of Chicago and Associate Director of the Population Research Center of NORC and the University. For the past 1.5 years I have investigated race and ethnic differences in labor market and educational outcomes. However, in my search for explanations, it became all too apparent that experiences of adolescents are pivotal for understanding trends in social and economic inequality among adults. With support from the Rockefeller and the Russell Sage Foundations, Professor V. Joseph Hotz and I have begun a program of research to analyze race, ethnic and gender differences in the transition from school to work. Dr. Hotz is Director of the Population Research Center and Professor of economics in the Harris School of Public Policy at the University of Chicago.

I am here today to share with you some preliminary findings from this research which illustrates the importance of race and ethnic differences in patterns of school departure and entry to the world of work among a cohort of young men and women. Our research program is timely in light of increasing ethnic diversity of the U.S. population and projections that women and minorities will contribute disproportionately to the growth of the U.S. labor force into the next Century. As workers of the future, youth must be prime targets for drop-out prevention programs and, for those who are not college-bound, creative strategies that strengthen links between schools, vocational training programs, and employers. I will conclude with recommendations for data collection and about urgent research priorities.

II. BACKGROUND

Growing concern over the plight of America's youth has called attention to the rising numbers reared in poverty and in father-absent families; to high rates of school failure; and to rising levels youth unemployment. These problems, while not confined to minority youth, are more pervasive among them. Yet, the weakened labor market position of minorities is puzzling when considered against narrower educational differentials between white and minority adults. Although more black and Hispanic youth are graduating from high school than ever before, greater numbers minority youth are confronting difficulties in the labor market whether or not they graduate from high school. This phenomenon requires a multi-focal vision of the school to work transition, with special emphasis on the experiences of youth who are not college bound and whose home and school experiences leave them unequally prepared to enter the world of work.

Our approach to understanding ethnic variation in the school-to-work transition builds on several recent findings—namely, that entry-level job opportunities for minorities shrank during the 1980s; that prolonged schooling is associated with higher levels of youth joblessness at specific ages; and that economic payoffs to schooling have become more differentiated in recent years. Prior research indicates that both the timing and the nature of early labor market encounters, as well as the linkages between teen labor market experiences and early adult outcomes differ by race, but there is much less evidence about the Hispanic experience in this regard. Our work begins to fill this important gap in knowledge, and my recommendations address needed extensions in this line of research.

Our empirical research is based on the National Longitudinal Survey of Youth, which is a representative sample of youth aged 13 to 20 in 1978. The strengths of these data over prior surveys include: (1) the substantial oversamples of Hispanics and blacks; (2) the detailed histories on schooling, labor force and military experiences; (3) the availability of 12 years of prospective data for original respondents;

and (4) the availability of a measure of ability for all respondents based on the Armed Forces Qualifying Test.

We restricted our focus to respondents who were aged 13 to 16 in 1978 because of our interest in documenting when school departures occur; the timing and nature of the first labor market encounter with respect to school enrollment status; and linkages between first labor market encounters and subsequent employment outcomes. These considerations are especially crucial for minority workers. We were mindful not to repeat shortcomings of prior studies that have examined transitions to employment of high school graduates. Such approaches distort the school and employment difficulties experienced by the neediest youth.

In fact, several features of our program of work distinguish it from prior endeavors. First, we examine the employment experiences of minority and nonminority youth during the 1980s. Prior studies have suggested that youth entering the labor market during the 1980's have confronted different circumstances from youth cohorts who entered during the 1900s and 1970s.

Second, our broad comparative approach includes women and Hispanics, and where possible, distinguishes between white and nonwhite Hispanics. Most of the early studies on the school to work transition were limited to racial comparisons and to men. Employment policy for the 21st Century must be responsive to the growing diversity of the youth population, and the high rates of female labor force activity.

Third, we consider multiple definitions of first job and school departure. This is important because some results are sensitive to the operational definitions of first job. We distinguish between first entry level jobs, first steady jobs, and first full-time jobs. Furthermore, our operational definitions of first school departure distinguish between exits that lasted at least 6 months and those that lasted 12 consecutive months or more.

III. KEY FINDINGS

In the short time available, I can only highlight some of the more significant results. In keeping with the Subcommittee's interest on America's changing demographic profile, my testimony will emphasize race, ethnic, and gender differences in patterns of school leaving and transitions to employment. Professor Hotz and I have prepared a background paper that contains greater detail about our findings.

School Departures

Our results on patterns of school leaving revealed significant ethnic and racial differences in tile timing and pace of school departure. Our inferences arc based on life tables estimates of cumulative proportions leaving school at specific ages according to two criteria for departure, i.e., remaining out for 6 months or for one year or more. These results, reported in Tables 1a and 1b, show that men tend to exit school more quickly than women, but differences in the rate of school leaving depend on race and ethnicity. White men and women prolong schooling longer than their minority counterparts, while Hispanics exhibit the fastest pace of school withdrawal at younger ages. Over twice as many Hispanic women as compared to white or black women left school before the legal age to quit.

Our multivariate analysis reversed these results. That is, although gross effects of race and ethnic origin on school departure are positive for both men and women, such that blacks and Hispanics exit from school at a faster rate than their white counterparts (shown in Table 1 and Figures 2 and 3), controlling for ability differences that are correlated with school retention reverses the race and ethnic effects on school departure by our liberal criterion, and completely eliminates them for Hispanic men and women. A parallel story obtains for the restrictive definition of school departure after ability differences are taken into account, except that white Hispanic women exhibit a significantly slower pace of school departure compared to white women with similar AFQT scores. No comparable school retention effect emerges for Hispanic men whose AFQT scores are identical to those of whites.

Ethnic differences in patterns of school withdrawal have profound implications for the long term employability of young men and women. Although premature school departure need not be definitive, there is mounting evidence that Hispanic youth are less likely to return to school, or to receive a general equivalency degree. The patterns of school departure we have documented thus have profound implications for the workforce readiness of minority youth into the 21st Century.

Labor Force Entry

Life table estimates of the timing of first jobs reported in Figures 1a and 1b also reveal considerable diversity along race and ethnic lines. Although premature school departure renders Hispanics the most educationally disadvantaged group, it is black youth who encounter the greatest difficulties in the labor market. This generalization obtains for all definitions of first job. That the labor market difficulties experienced by black youth carry into their early adult lives is clearly apparent in the timing of first full-time jobs. By age 20, roughly 30 percent of white and Hispanic men had obtained a full-time job, compared to less than 20 percent of black men. Although lower shares of women than men had worked full time by their 20th birthday, ethnic differences in entry to full-time employment paralleled the male pattern. The slower rates at which blacks enter the labor market, which signal accumulating disadvantages, are clearly discernible in both sets of curves. Hispanic-white disparities in the rate of labor market entry, while less pronounced than the black-white disparities, are statistically significant in all but one instance, namely the Hispanic-white difference in the timing of full-time employment for men.

Furthermore, the conclusion that black men experience greatest difficulties entering the labor market is not altered by controlling for differences in ability or family background. However, this is not the case for Hispanic men. There were essentially no differences between Hispanic and white men in the rate of entry to either beginning or full-time jobs once differences in AFQT scores and family background characteristics arc standardized statistically.

Among women an adjustment for differences in AFQT scores similarly did not eliminate racial differences in the rate of attaining entry-level jobs: black women, like their male counterparts, experienced slower transitions into first jobs compared to white or Hispanic women of similar ability. However, no differences in the rate at which white and Hispanic women achieved entry-level jobs were evident among respondents who were comparable in their AFQT scores and family background. Unlike men, racial differences in women's transition to employment did not carry over into full-time jobs. In other words, the rate of transition to full-time employment was no different among black, white and Hispanic women with equivalent AFQT scores and family backgrounds. This means that groups differences in ability and family background account for the significant racial and ethnic disparities in entering the workforce based on the life table estimates.

Part of the delayed entry to the workforce experienced by black youth, particularly when compared to Hispanic youth, might stem from their slower rates of school departure, particularly before age 18 (see Table 1). Figures 2a and 2b, respectively, plot the cumulative proportions of men and women who departed school by specific ages (and remained out for at least 12 months) against the rates of transition to first entry level jobs. Figures 3a and 3b reproduce the same school departure plot, contrasting it with the rates of entry to full-time employment. The extent of overlap between school and work, indicated by the area below the intersection of the two curves, is much greater when the liberal definition of first job is used than when the restrictive definition is used. Obviously, flexible employment such as that captured by our liberal job criterion is more compatible with school enrollment than is full-time work.

These results show that whites were more likely than minority youth to have work experience of any type prior to school departure, although the ethnic and racial differences are more pronounced as the definition of jobs becomes more restrictive. For example, half of all white and Hispanic men who left school at age 16 had work experience according to our liberal criterion, compared to only 40 percent of black men who left school at this age. That black men's slower entry into employment is accompanied by less overlap with school (see especially Figure 3a), could aggravate their labor market disadvantages during early adulthood. Young women's tendency to combine school and work also showed greater racial and ethnic differences as the criteria used to define first jobs became more restrictive, but the pattern of differentials was not identical.

Despite racial and ethnic differences in the timing of school departure and labor market entry, results shown in Figures 2 and 3 indicate that substantial shares of youth do combine school and work during adolescence and young adulthood. Short-term, entry-level jobs arc dominant at younger ages, but steady jobs and full-time jobs that last for a year or more are not uncommon among 18 and 19 year-olds. How work experiences while attending school influence later employment outcomes is not yet clear, but we plan to scrutinize this issue further.

Wages

A presumed advantage of early labor market entry is that it builds work experience which is associated with higher earnings and occupational status at later ages. However, if accumulation of experience occurs at the expense of lower educational attainment—that is, if employed youth withdraw from school at earlier ages—then the potential gains from early labor market experience may be totally offset during the early adult years, as earnings of more highly skilled workers surpass those of less educated workers.

Tables 2a and 2b, which summarize wage and school outcomes for our three definitions of first job, addresses this issue. At the point of first contact with the labor market, race and ethnic differences in wages indicate, quite surprisingly, that minority youth have a significant wage advantage in their entry level jobs. However, the minority advantage in wage rates is reduced when analysis is restricted to first steady jobs. Among men, ethnic differences in wages were statistically trivial, but female wage gaps in steady jobs were significantly different by ethnicity, and were opposite ethnic differences in educational attainment.

All wage advantages of minority youth completely dissipated by the time they obtained their first full-time job. White men and women received the largest wage gains as they made transition from first entry level jobs to first full-time jobs. Although blacks averaged a half year more schooling than Hispanics employed full time, they earned $.50 less on an hourly basis. Similarly, white women employed full-time received $5.50 per hour compared to $5.01 and $4.84 for similarly employed Hispanic and black women. These differences are all the more striking when mapped against the groups' average schooling levels at the time of attaining full-time jobs: there were no differences between black and white women, while Hispanic women completed one half year less of school. These results suggest that both color and credentials contribute to the profiles of labor market disadvantages of minority youth, and that it is worth investing resources to investigate the mechanisms responsible for declining wage advantages of minority workers.

IV. RECOMMENDATIONS

Several recommendations follow from our work to date. The first and most important concerns the substantial race and ethnic differences in the rates at which young men and women leave school and enter the labor force. Among men, we observed pronounced race and ethnic differences in the probability of getting a job. In particular, it is black men who experience the greatest difficulty entering the labor market. Unlike women, young men's wages are not differentiated by race and ethnic group. I urge the Subcommittee to support research directed toward understanding the mechanisms and harriers that limit young black men's access to the labor market, and the mechanisms that generate unequal wages for women of color. The research program I envision should be grounded in empirical analyses of secondary data, but should also include diverse methodologies to document whether and how discrimination may be responsible for the results we observe.

A second recommendation concerns data requirements to further research and knowledge about the school-to-work transition. Despite the great analytical potential of the NLSY for investigating various aspects of the school-to-work transition, I recommend that the Subcommittee support appropriations for a new youth cohort. Respondents currently in the NLSY sample are now in late 20s to early 30s, and well beyond the transitional phase of their lifecourse. Given the dramatic changes in the racial and ethnic composition of the U.S. population during the 1980s that were driven by immigration and differential fertility, collection of data about today's youth seems a necessary adjunct for policy formulation about tomorrow's workers.

Along this line, I recommend that the new youth cohort begin with younger children—kids in early adolescence—rather than the large age spectrum used by the NLSY. This is warranted to adequately portray the process of school departure. Legal restrictions on school departure notwithstanding, many youth, particularly minorities, leave school permanently before they are entitled to do so legally. And, these are tile kids most in need of attention by policy makers. I also recommend that the new youth cohort include an oversample of Asian men and women. We know virtually nothing about the school-to-work transition of this rapidly growing and highly diverse minority population.

Third, I would urge the committee to sponsor research on the significance of the Armed Forces Qualifying Test as a measure of ability. The military interprets the AFQT score as a measure of general trainability, and uses the scores to screen out individuals who are likely to have a low probability of successfully completing military training. Social scientists have used the AFQT as a general ability indicator, arguing that it performs like a scholastic aptitude test. But, the typical employer does not have access to individuals' AFQT scores, nor are such standardized test scores available for typical job applicants. Colleges and Universities require some form of entrance exam for admission. Are there lessons to be learned from the military with respect to matching workers to job specialties based on this or a similar indicator of "general trainability?"

Our findings showing that race and ethnic variation in the transition to employment can be reversed or eliminated after adjusting for differences in AFQT scores and family background is both provocative and problematic. If the AFQT measure is truly an index of ability, then prior studies that failed to consider this influence on school departures and employment transitions may have misrepresented the significance of race. If, on the other hand, the AFQT index is capturing racial biases in the test itself, then our interpretation about its success in tapping ability differences among the groups is inappropriate. Until we can answer these questions satisfactorily, our findings about racial and ethnic differences must be regarded as tentative. However, our results underscore the urgency of scrutinizing the AFQT index and investigating how the use of this performance measure might be adapted to employment decisions in the civilian sector.

Thank you for the opportunity to address the Subcommittee.

Table 1a

Cumulative Percent Leaving School Using Two Definitions of First Departure: Young Men Aged 13 to 16 in 1978 by Ethnicity (Life Table Estimates)

	Liberal Definition[a]			Restrictive Definition[b]		
Age	Whites	Blacks	Hispanics	Whites	Blacks	Hispanics
≤ 13	-	0.3	0.7	0.1	0.3	0.7
14	1.3	1.4	2.6	1.0	1.2	2.0
15	4.8	3.9	6.6	3.9	3.1	5.3
16	12.2	9.2	15.9	10.3	7.5	13.4
17	26.0	23.3	33.0	23.1	20.0	28.6
18	49.7	50.5	57.1	44.9	45.0	50.3
19	71.0	75.7	77.3	64.6	69.2	70.1
20	80.1	87.6	86.8	73.4	81.7	81.5
21	85.0	92.6	91.6	78.7	87.9	88.0
22	90.9	96.0	94.5	84.9	91.6	91.7
23	96.2	98.6	96.8	90.4	94.9	94.5
24	98.6	99.9	98.6	93.1	97.0	96.7
25+	100.0	100.0	100.0	-	98.3	-
Age at First Departure						
$\bar{x}$	20.3	19.0	19.0	22.5	20.1	19.9
Median	18.6	18.4	18.3	18.7	18.6	18.4
[N][c]	[1265]	[797]	[511]	[1265]	[797]	[511]

Source: NLSY civilian sample

[a] Liberal Definition: Left school for 6 months or more.

[b] Restrictive Definition: Left school for 12 months or more.

[c] [N] is unweighted population in the risk set.

Table 1b

Cumulative Percent Leaving School Using Two Definitions of First Departure: Young Women Aged 13 to 16 in 1978 by Ethnicity (Life Table Estimates)

Age	Liberal Definition[a]			Restrictive Definition[b]		
	Whites	Blacks	Hispanics	Whites	Blacks	Hispanics
≤ 13	-	-	-	-	-	-
14	0.3	0.4	0.8	0.3	0.2	0.6
15	1.2	1.9	3.5	1.1	0.9	3.3
16	5.3	6.1	12.0	4.6	4.0	10.5
17	19.4	19.4	28.6	17.1	14.8	24.0
18	46.0	46.9	52.9	41.3	38.6	45.6
19	67.6	71.5	73.9	60.4	61.9	66.5
20	76.1	82.4	83.3	68.3	74.5	77.3
21	82.3	88.0	87.6	74.5	82.0	82.7
22	90.0	92.7	90.7	81.9	87.6	86.2
23	95.0	95.9	92.9	87.7	91.5	88.5
24	96.2	97.0	94.1	90.4	93.7	89.8
25+	-	-	94.6	-	-	-
Age at First Departure						
$\bar{x}$	20.3	20.0	20.3	22.4	21.3	21.9
Median	18.5	18.6	18.3	18.7	18.8	18.7
[N][c]	[1204]	[763]	[511]	[1204]	[763]	[511]

Source: NLSY civilian sample

[a] Liberal Definition: Left school for 6 months or more.

[b] Restrictive Definition: Left school for 12 months or more.

[c] [N] is unweighted population in the risk set.

Table 2a

Average Education, Hours, and Wages[a] at Time of First Job Using Three Definitions of First Job: Young Men Aged 13 to 16 in 1978 by Ethnicity (Standard Deviations)

Definition of First Job	Whites	Blacks	Hispanics
Liberal[b]			
Education	8.1 (1.2)	8.1 (1.3)	7.9 (1.3)
Hourly Wage, $	3.82 (1.55)	3.95 (1.93)	4.03 (1.86)
Weekly Hours	26.5 (14.5)	28.3 (13.7)	30.7 (14.7)
[N]	[1249]	[785]	[496]
Intermediate[c]			
Education	10.8 (2.0)	11.0 (1.8)	10.4 (1.9)
Hourly Wage, $	4.48 (2.25)	4.36 (2.01)	4.46 (2.02)
Weekly Hours	33.7 (12.5)	34.8 (11.8)	36.6 (11.8)
[N]	[1172]	[703]	[462]
Restrictive[d]			
Education	12.4 (2.3)	11.9 (1.9)	11.2 (2.1)
Hourly Wage, $	6.34 (2.72)	5.34 (2.16)	5.79 (2.51)
Weekly Hours	45.6 (8.8)	43.7 (7.9)	43.9 (7.5)
[N]	[916]	[475]	[363]

Source: NLSY civilian sample.
[a] Wages in 1982 dollars.
[b] Liberal Definition: any duration any hours.
[c] Intermediate Definition: 6 months duration and 15 hrs. or more per week.
[d] Restrictive Definition: 12 months duration and 35 hrs. or more per week.

Table 2b

Average Education, Hours, and Wages[a] at Time of First Job Using Three Definitions of First Job: Young Women Aged 13 to 16 in 1978 by Ethnicity (Standard Deviations)

Definition of First Job	Whites	Blacks	Hispanics
Liberal[b]			
Education	8.4 (1.2)	8.3 (1.3)	8.1 (1.3)
Hourly Wage, $	3.22 (1.61)	3.50 (2.08)	3.57 (3.02)
Weekly Hours	24.3 (13.5)	26.8 (12.2)	27.9 (13.9)
[N]	[1175]	[714]	[485]
Intermediate[c]			
Education	11.2 (2.0)	11.7 (1.8)	10.9 (1.9)
Hourly Wage, $	4.14 (2.63)	3.81 (1.57)	3.85 (1.69)
Weekly Hours	31.7 (11.0)	34.0 (11.0)	33.3 (10.2)
[N]	[1117]	[616]	[426]
Restrictive[d]			
Education	12.7 (2.1)	12.7 (1.8)	11.9 (2.0)
Hourly Wage, $	5.50 (2.51)	4.84 (2.28)	5.01 (2.05)
Weekly Hours	42.1 (6.3)	41.9 (6.5)	41.9 (6.5)
[N]	[820]	[396]	[281]

Source: NLSY civilian sample.
[a] Wages in 1982 dollars.
[b] Liberal Definition: any duration any hours.
[c] Intermediate Definition: 6 months duration and 15 hrs. or more per week.
[d] Restrictive Definition: 12 months duration and 35 hrs. or more per week.

Figure 1a

Timing of Labor Market Entry: Cumulative Proportions of Young Men Entering First Jobs Based on Liberal and Restrictive Definitions of Employment

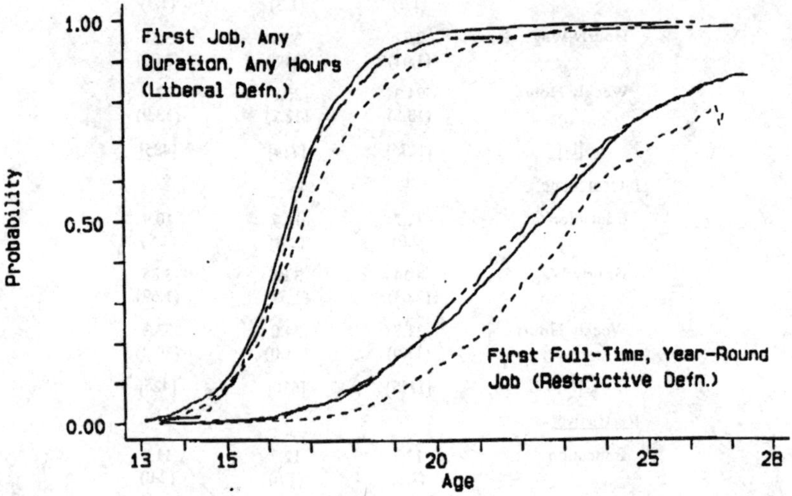

White ——
Black - - -
Hispanic — - —

Figure 1b

Timing of Labor Market Entry: Cumulative Proportions of Young Women Entering First Jobs Based on Liberal and Restrictive Definitions of Employment

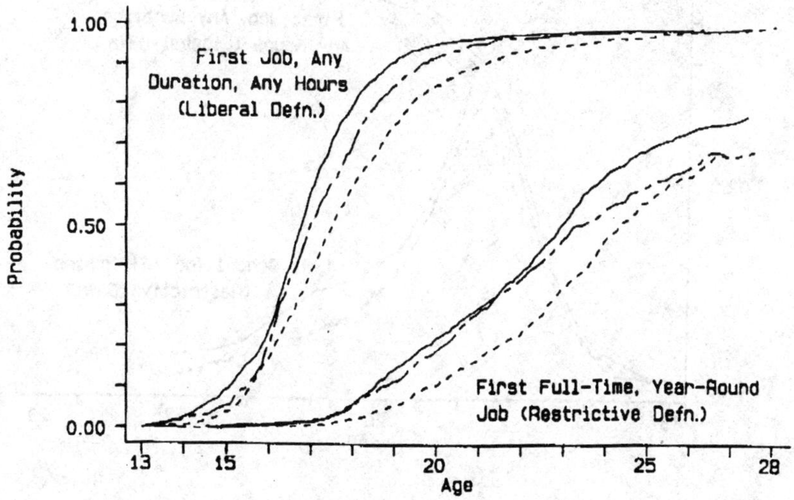

White ——
Black – – –
Hispanic –- - —

Figure 2a

Overlap of School and Work: Cumulative Proportions of Young Men Who Departed School and Began First Jobs of Any Duration or Time Commitment

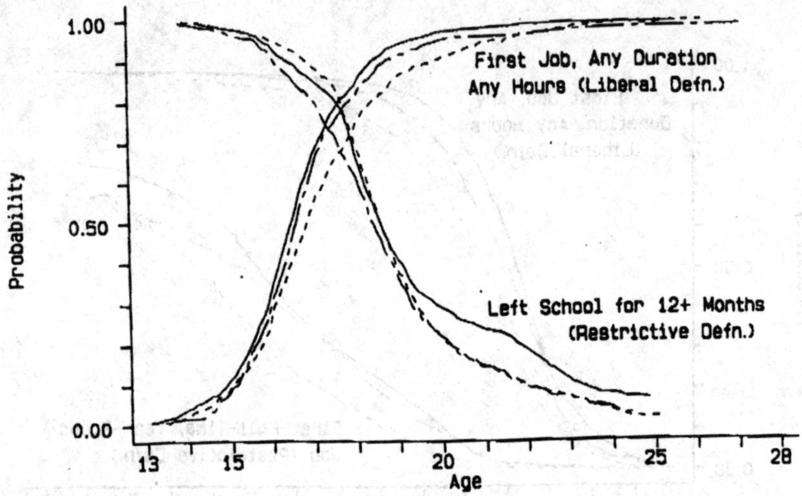

White ——
Black - - -
Hispanic — · —

Figure 2b

Overlap of School and Work: Cumulative Proportions of Young Women Who Departed School and Began First Jobs of Any Duration or Time Commitment

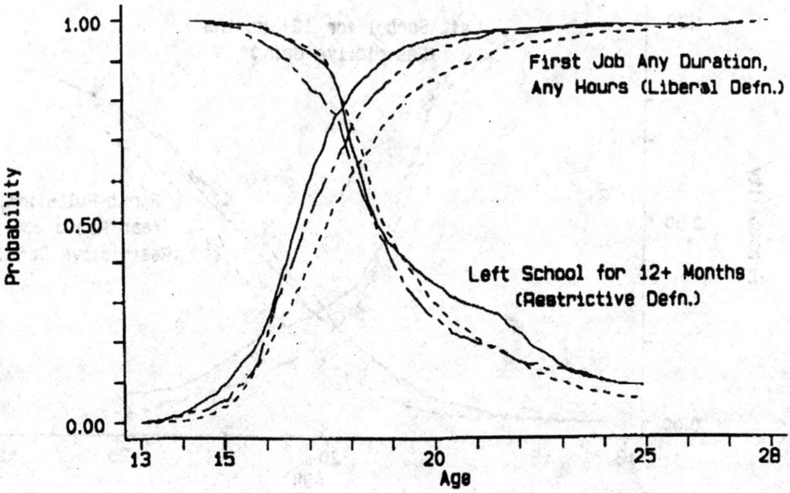

White ——
Black - - -
Hispanic —·—

Figure 3a

Overlap of School and Work:
Cumulative Proportions of Young Men Who Departed School and Began First Full Time Job

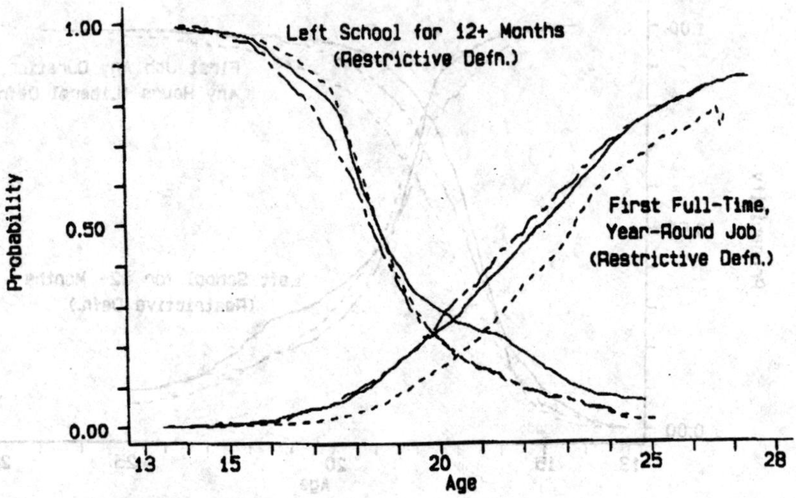

White ———
Black - - -
Hispanic —·—

Figure 3b

**Overlap of School and Work:
Cumulative Proportions of Young Women Who Departed School and Began First Full Time Job**

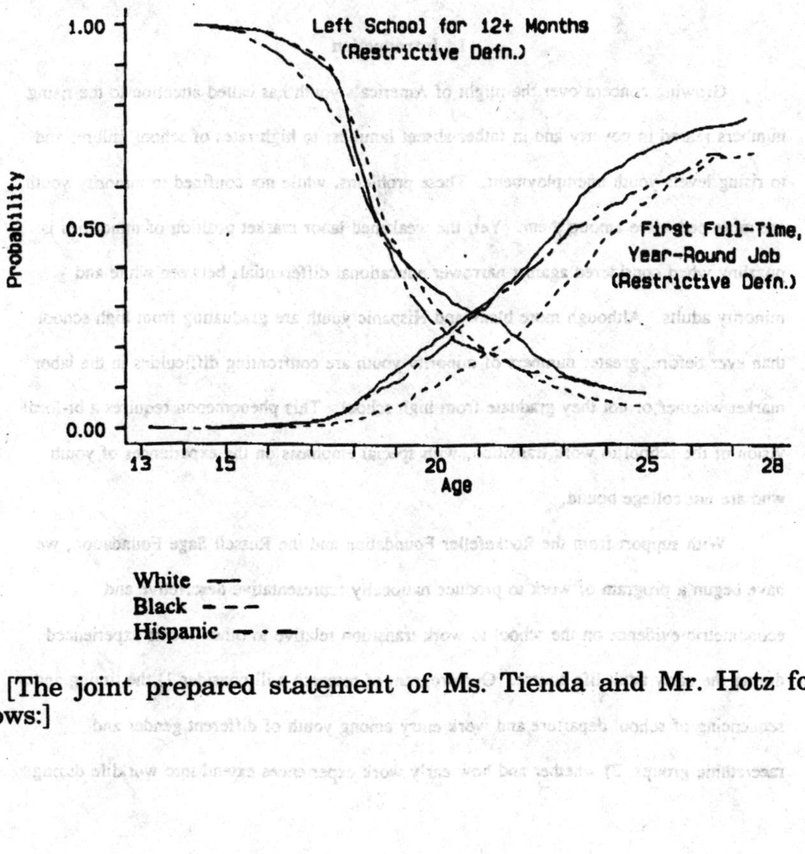

[The joint prepared statement of Ms. Tienda and Mr. Hotz follows:]

Gender and Ethnic Variation in the School-to-Work Transition

V. Joseph Hotz and Marta Tienda
University of Chicago

Background Paper for Testimony Delivered before the
Subcommittee on Census and Population
July 28, 1992

I. Introduction

Growing concern over the plight of America's youth has called attention to the rising numbers reared in poverty and in father-absent families; to high rates of school failure; and to rising levels youth unemployment. These problems, while not confined to minority youth, are more pervasive among them. Yet, the weakened labor market position of minorities is puzzling when considered against narrower educational differentials between white and minority adults. Although more black and Hispanic youth are graduating from high school than ever before, greater numbers of minority youth are confronting difficulties in the labor market whether or not they graduate from high school. This phenomenon requires a bi-focal vision of the school to work transition, with special emphasis on the experiences of youth who are not college bound.

With support from the Rockefeller Foundation and the Russell Sage Foundation, we have begun a program of work to produce nationally representative descriptive and econometric evidence on the school to work transition relative to other events experienced during the early adult life course. Our program of research will consider 1) the timing and sequencing of school departure and work entry among youth of different gender and race/ethnic groups; 2) whether and how early work experiences extend into worklife during young adulthood; and 3) the economic consequences of alternative pathways into the work force.

Our approach to understanding ethnic variation in the school-to-work transition builds on several recent findings--namely, that entry-level job opportunities for minorities shrank during the 1980s (Freeman and Holzer, 1986; Hirschman, 1988); that prolonged schooling is associated with higher levels of youth joblessness at specific ages (Mare and Winship, 1984; Mare, et al., 1984); and that economic payoffs to schooling have become more differentiated in recent years (Levy, 1987). Prior research indicates that both the timing and the nature of early labor market encounters, as well as the linkages between teen labor market experiences and early adult outcomes differ by race, but there is much less evidence about the Hispanic experience in this regard. Hispanic youth are at higher risk of failing to complete high school while black youth confront greater difficulties securing jobs. These outcomes could provide some leverage in determining how ethnicity influences the school-to-work transition of youth.

What follows is our initial foray to address these broad issues. We begin our presentation by describing the transition to work for a nationally representative cohort of young men and women aged 13 to 16 in 1978. Our general purpose is to document differentials in the timing of school departure and labor force entry among white, black and Hispanic men and women, and to provide tentative insights about the linkages between early work experience and employment status during young adulthood (i.e., circa age 25). Specific objectives include (1) charting ethnic differentials in the timing of school departures and first contact with the labor market using alternative definitions of "first job;" (2) characterizing ethnic differences in the nature of the early labor market encounters, and evaluating the rate of transition into employment using alternative definitions of first jobs; and (3) estimating labor supply functions to assess how early labor market experiences influence wages and worked in first full-time job.[1]

Following a brief and selective overview of the key findings and remaining gaps in the existing literature on youth employment (Section II), we describe the data used for the empirical analyses (Section III). Results that address our broad research goals are presented in Sections IV and V. The conclusion summarizes key results and outlines issues warranting further research.

II. Background

Although a substantial body of research has examined the transition from school-to-work (Mare and Winship, 1984; Hogan and Astone, 1986; Coleman, 1984; Rindfuss, et al., 1987), few studies have examined this critical transition for Hispanic youth (but see D'Amico and Maxwell, 1990). Even fewer studies have documented ethnic differentials in the **nature** of the first labor market encounter and its precise timing with respect to school departure. Guided by previous studies showing marked racial differences in the timing and sequencing of school departure and labor market entry (e.g., Coleman, 1984; Marini, 1984), we hypothesize that Hispanics may differ from whites and blacks in their early work experiences owing to earlier departures from school and lower educational attainment levels. Early labor market entry allows for the acquisition of valuable work

---

[1] We have prepared an extensive summary of the current theoretical and substantive research on the school-to-work transition, but opted to exclude it in this statistical portrait of the pathways from school to work of minority and nonminority youth.

experience, and may have lasting benefits for labor market careers. However, if work during adolescence prematurely curtails the acquisition of basic and job-related skills, the net benefits for young adults may be zero or negative over the long run.

Economic and sociological perspectives of the school-to-work transition, while differing in their emphases, have common grounds: (1) both acknowledge the value of skill acquisition early in the life cycle; (2) both suggest feedback effects from expectations and perceptions formed during initial work experiences and decisions about school completion as well as job selection among young adults; and (3) both recognize that labor market conditions determine the range of opportunities for acquiring early work experiences (Freeman and Holzer, 1986; Hirschman, 1988; Mare, et al., 1984). More generally, the theoretical considerations from economics and sociology suggest two general avenues through which early labor market experiences shape schooling decisions and subsequent labor market outcomes, namely individual behavioral responses (choices) and structurally circumscribed changes in opportunities.

Regarding the choice-based aspects of the school departure and potential impacts of youth employment experiences, it is widely recognized that many entry-level jobs may be "dead-end" jobs. However, experiences with such jobs may produce positive feed-back effects by encouraging students to prolong schooling by providing them first-hand evidence of the poor job opportunities available to persons with limited education. Thus, having worked in dead-end jobs may produce a positive long-term labor outcome by prolonging school departures and increasing skill levels among youth who enter full-time employment at later ages (see Meyer and Wise, 1982).[2] Alternatively, experiencing unemployment and fruitless job search or highly irregular employment at unrewarding jobs may reduce motivation to work and discourage school completion. This outcome may be especially likely among youth who can not appreciate the connections between basic competencies and the tasks performed in entry-level jobs. Such experiences may produce profiles of school failure and weakened labor market attachment as adults.

It is highly conceivable that minority youth are more likely than nonminority youth to experience negative feedback from entry into dead-end, low-pay jobs because: (a) they can not envision the stepping-stone function of entry-level jobs; (b) they recognize (quite realistically) the absence of employment opportunities that can ensure economic security and independence; and/or (c) the incentives to complete school are less compelling than those encouraging alternative pathways to adulthood. For example, minority youth are more likely than white youth to reside in families where higher levels of economic necessity may propel them into premature school withdrawal and full-time employment. However, the behavioral mechanisms that encourage some youth to remain in school while others exit prematurely in pursuit of labor market opportunities are not well understood. (See Cameron and Heckman, 1991, for results on the factors influencing schooling decisions of youth.)

In a widely-cited paper, Mare and Winship (1984) address this paradox of narrowing racial differentials in schooling outcomes as differentials in rates of joblessness between black

---

[2] Using the NLS-72, Meyer and Wise found that experiences of work during high school increases the probability of working in the future, and is associated with higher wages. However, their result was based on respondents who completed high school, which is a highly selective criterion to impose on minority youth.

and white men widened. They argued that the timing of school departure and military enlistment varied directly with employability, and that military enlistment provided non-college-bound youth an alternative to acquire more skills. In brief, the paradox of diverging racial differences in joblessness coupled with narrowing educational differences resulted because the least employable left school at earlier ages, thereby weakening their labor market prospects at older ages; at the same time, the more employable prolonged schooling either through military enlistment or college attendance. Mare and Winship's analysis ended in 1981, just prior to a deep recession, hence they were unable to document the role of cyclical downswings in limiting employment opportunities for youth who did versus those who did not prolong their schooling. Second, they restricted their focus to men, ignoring possible differences between the sexes, and they ignored Hispanic men. It is not obvious that their results for blacks and whites would fit the experiences of Hispanics, whose rates of military enrollment do not exceed their population shares, as do those of blacks. Although Hispanics have lower levels of schooling than whites, as a group, they tend to fare better than blacks on such outcomes as participation rates, unemployment rates, and wage rates (Bean and Tienda, 1987; Tienda and Stier, 1991). These facts, which have been replicated in a growing number of studies, suggest the provocative hypothesis that color (i.e., pigmentation) is directly related to employment outcomes independent of educational achievement and skills.

A second set of circumstances that influence youth employment experiences are more structural in nature in that they define the opportunities to secure employment. In many localities within the U.S., the late 1970s and early 1980s represented a period of slack labor demand (Cyert and Mowery, 1987; Kasarda, 1985; Wilson, 1987).[3] In fact, some scholars attribute the rising inequality among racial and ethnic groups to the reduction of unskilled and semi-skilled jobs during this period of massive industrial restructuring (Wilson, 1987; Kasarda, 1985). As a result of the tighter labor market and changes in the types of entry-level jobs available, many young adults entering the labor market during this period were more likely than prior entry cohorts to have negative employment experiences (D'Amico and Maxwell, 1990). Such experiences may not only have had immediate impacts in discouraging further job search, but may produce longer lasting "scarring" effects (Ellwood, 1982) not experienced by cohorts whose first exposure to the labor market occurred in less constrained eras. Thus, one hypothesis for increased race and ethnic inequality during the past 15 years or so is that as premiums on basic skill competencies rose, high school drop outs experienced higher penalties during the 1980s than did drop outs during the 1960s and early 1970s.

If such adverse outcomes were differentially felt by the minority youth, the changing labor market conditions of the last 10-15 years may have served to magnify the linkages between adolescent and adult labor market experiences relative to earlier periods of history. Thus, given changes in the structure of labor demand during the 1980s--the period we analyze--a working hypothesis differentiating our work from prior studies is that the linkages between early work experience and labor market standing during young adulthood have been weakened. This hypothesis is plausible if, as many studies have shown, the consequences of

---

[3] Lynch (1989) found significant effects of local demand conditions on re-employment probabilities for both men and women following the 1982 recession combined with strong race effects, but did not carry the analysis through the recovery.

premature withdrawal from school have increased (Levy, 1987), or, the likelihood of securing a good job has come to depend increasingly on prior school performance and perceived ability (Rosenbaum, 1989).

How incentives to prolong schooling and enter the labor market were experienced by youth during the 1980s, and whether there were differences along race and ethnic lines has profound implications for understanding the labor market standing of young adults in the 1990s. An important aspect of this question that has not been addressed in prior studies is whether tendencies to combine school and work as part of the transition to full-time employment have changed as a result of cyclical changes in the economy. There is conflicting evidence about whether and how employment during periods of school enrollment are of any significance for early adult employment. This is because most studies of the school-to-work transition have eschewed considering the nature of the first encounters with work on grounds that early work experiences (particularly those that occur during periods of enrollment) are highly complex and irregular (Lynch, 1989; D'Amico and Maxwell, 1990).[4]

While the above discussion suggests several interesting hypotheses about the nature and determinants of the school-to-work transition for youth, our initial foray into this arena is largely descriptive. Stated differently, our primary goal is to provide a comparative statistical portrait of the pathways to adulthood by examining the dynamic patterns of transition through

[4] For example, by restricting their analyses to individuals who graduated from high school, D'Amico and Maxwell bypass an important opportunity to examine the timing of school departure from school with respect to entry to the workforce. Similarly, in her analysis of re-employment probabilities of young workers, Lynch (1989) imposed severe sample restrictions that avoided a straightforward representation of the school to work transition. Such arbitrary decisions distort understanding of the school to work transition and build substantial selection biases into the results (see Cameron and Heckman, 1991).

a comprehensive set of labor force/schooling states over the early life course of white, black, and Hispanic youth. We use an event-history approach, focusing on patterns of transitions, their rates of occurrence and cumulative exposure to the labor market and education during the early stages of adulthood. Our multivariate analysis documents the process of school departure and labor market entry as well as the linkages between early work experiences and subsequent employment and wage outcomes.

III. Data, Variables and Methods

We use the National Longitudinal Survey of Youth (NLSY), a national probability sample of 11,406 individuals aged 14 to 21 as of January 1, 1979.[5] Several features of NLSY make it especially suited for the proposed objectives. First, blacks and Hispanics were oversampled, permitting race and ethnic comparisons of various aspects of the transition to adulthood. Second, the annual interviews solicited detailed information about respondents schooling, training and military experiences as well as detailed labor force histories. The latter is available on a weekly basis, and includes comprehensive information about jobs held from the time respondents first appeared in the sample. However, the NLSY provides more limited information about jobs held prior to 1978. That is, while the prospective employment information is quite complete, retrospective information about jobs and school activities is more limited. Finally, the NLSY exhibits a low attrition rate, just over 10 percent during the 12 year period we analyze.

[5] The NLSY gathered data on 1290 additional youth respondents who were in the military at the time of the 1979 interview. We restrict our focus to the civilian sample, excluding the over-samples of disadvantaged white youth, but including the over-samples of minority youth. This decision was based on extensive diagnostic analyses that revealed significant differences between the white random and nonrandom samples, but relatively minor differences between the Hispanic and black oversamples.

However, there are many ways the design of the NLSY limits the types of analyses we can perform. For example, many respondents aged 18 to 21 at the first interview (1979) have already completed or withdrawn from school and/or had multiple jobs. Although the NLSY obtains retrospective information about school and work behavior for the period prior to the first interview, this information is less complete than required by our focus on the *nature* of the first labor market encounter, the co-incidence of employment and school enrollment, and the linkages between first work encounters and subsequent full-time employment. After conducting considerable sensitivity tests, we determined that such left censoring could distort our understanding of the school to work transition. To minimize the difficulties introduced from left censoring, we restricted our analyses to individuals who were aged 13 to 16 as of 1978. For this age group we should, in principle, be able to observe the entire process of school departure and labor market entry. Our final sample of 2,889 young men includes 1,581 whites, 797 blacks, and 511 Hispanics, and our sample of 2,478 young women includes 1,204 whites, 763 blacks and 511 Hispanics.

Variable Definitions

Among the various definitions of first employment, the following are most common: first paid job; first full-time job; and first job after school completion. Each has its advantages and limitations, but in our judgement, the first--that is, the first job for pay--demarcates the point of entry to the labor market. Because the definition of first jobs is itself so varied in the existing treatments, we use three definitions of first job and two definitions of first school departure in the descriptive analysis. (In the interest of parsimony, our multivariate analyses use the most liberal and restrictive definitions of first job.) Specific operational definitions of school departure and first job are as follows:

1. **School Departure.** We examine first departure from school for at least 6 consecutive months (*liberal* definition) or at least 12 consecutive months (*restrictive* definition).[6]

2. **First Job.** We use three definitions of first job which are based on two criteria--weekly hours per work and duration of the job. For each job definition we know the industry sector, occupation, actual hours and wage rate. We have also coded the incumbents' education as of the beginning of the interval for each job.

(a) The *liberal* definition of first job includes any job of any duration or weekly hours. It comes closest to representing the first entry-level job.

(b) The *intermediate* definition of first job requires a duration of 6 months and at least 15 hours per week. It comes closest to the concept of steady work.

(c) The *restrictive* definition of first job requires a duration of at least a year on a full-time basis (i.e., 35 or more hours weekly), and represents first full-time job.

Our race and ethnic categories draw from subjective and objective items available in the NLSY. The race variable is based on a subjective assessment of respondents' race by the interviewer (at the time of the first interview). Interviewers were instructed to indicate whether respondents were black, white or some other race. Ethnicity reflects respondents'

---

[6] In this analysis we focus on first school departure, but subsequently intend to examine re-entry and exit behavior.

answer to the question, "What is your origin or descent?" based on 29 possible choices on a card listing.[7]

To identify Hispanics, we used the ethnicity codes from the screener interview rather than respondents' self report of Hispanic origin at the time of the first interview. Our decision was motivated by two factors. First, not only was the screener item the basis for generating the oversample of Hispanics, but more detailed questions about parents' origin were solicited at this time, thereby providing side information to verify the responses.[8] Hispanics can be of any race, but few studies have empirically examined directly the race of Hispanics. Because the race categories were obtained independently of ethnicity, we are able to distinguish between white and non-white Hispanics. Our multivariate analyses exploit this feature of the NLSY to ascertain whether and how color matters for Hispanics.

Other independent variables used in our multivariate analyses include respondent's age in 1978 (or age cohort), as a control for left-hand censoring of the school and work histories, race and ethnic group membership and several measures of family background (fathers' and mothers' education, family income as of 1979, and whether respondent lived with both parents at the first interview). A unique feature of NLSY is the availability of standardized test scores that tap ability differences among survey respondents. That is, the Armed Services Vocational Aptitude Battery (ASVAB), which is administered to individuals who

---

[7] Respondents were allowed to identify up to four groups, but were asked to indicate to which group they felt closest. We used this response to classify those individuals who reported more than one ethnic group.

[8] We differentiate four different groups based on the respondent's answer to the origin question: 1) Chicano, Mexican, or Mexican-American; 2) Puerto Rican; 3) Cuban, Other Hispanic, or Other Spanish; and 4) respondent does not identify with a Hispanic group in the "origin" question, but is identified as Hispanic by the screening interview. Unfortunately, sample sizes precluded more fine-grained analyses of Hispanic subgroups.

apply to any branches of the Armed Forces, also was administered to NLSY respondents regardless of military status in 1979. The Armed Forces Qualification Test, or AFQT, is the sum of the scores on four of the 10 subtests in the ASVAB: the Word Knowledge, Paragraph Comprehension, Arithmetic Reasoning and Mathematics Knowledge subtests. The military interprets the AFQT score as a measure of general trainability, and uses the scores to screen out individuals who are likely to have a low probability of successfully completing military training. Social scientists have used the AFQT as a general ability indicator, arguing that it performs like a scholastic aptitude test. (See Cameron and Heckman, 1991, for example.)

In addition to these covariates whose values are fixed over time, we include in our wage and hours regressions respondents' education and experience at the beginning of a job spell. To establish a link between early work experience and subsequent labor market status (timing, wages and hours of first full time job), we constructed a variable indicating whether respondents worked before their first school departure.

Methods

Our descriptive analysis of the process of school departure and labor market entry uses event history or life table methods to calculate the probability of exiting from school or entering the labor market (i.e., exiting joblessness). These techniques are well suited to handle problems of right censoring and attrition that characterize longitudinal data. Exit probabilities were derived from survival analyses computed separately for black, white and Hispanic youth using alternative definitions of first job and school withdrawal.

Subsequently we computed proportional hazard models using time to the first event (i.e., first school departure and first labor market entry). We also examine regression-based models of (log) wages on first jobs. In the statistical appendix we describe some preliminary procedures we implement to control for the possibility of selection bias in estimating the determinants of wages.

IV. Descriptive Results

School Departure

Tables 1a and 1b, respectively, summarize the pattern of school departure for young men and women by ethnicity. The entries for the liberal and restrictive definitions reflect the cumulative proportions who exited school and remained out for 6 and 12 months, respectively. Several generalizations are warranted from these results. First, there are significant ethnic differences in patterns of school departure for both men and women, although for women, racial differences are trivial under the restrictive definition.[9] Hispanic women's school departure pattern differs significantly from that of white and black women irrespective of the criteria used to define first exits. Second, men exit school at a faster pace than women, although gender differences in school departure depend on ethnicity. Third, the median age of first school departure for our youth cohort is relatively invariant across gender and race/ethnic groups--hovering around 18.5 years for both operational definitions. However, the mean age at first exit varies by ethnicity, reflecting significant differences in

[9] We computed a log-rank test to determine whether the race and ethnic differences in exit rates were statistically significant. Unless otherwise noted, only statistically significant differences are reported.

age-specific rates of high school noncompletion and distinct patterns of post-secondary enrollment (see Cameron and Heckman, 1991).

(Tables 1a and 1b About Here)

Ethnic differences in school departure rates are tiny for youth under 16 years of age, but they widen after the legal age for withdrawal from school. White men and women prolong schooling longer than their minority counterparts, while Hispanics exhibit the fastest pace of school withdrawal at younger ages. For example, over twice as many Hispanic women left school before the legal age to quit, as compared to black or white women. Premature school departure was more prevalent among men than among women, however. Approximately 10 percent of white men had left school (and remained out for at least a year) by age 16, compared to roughly 7 percent of black and 13 percent of Hispanic men. Women also prolong their schooling more than young men. Nearly 10 percent of white and Hispanic women remained in school beyond 24 years of age compared to 6 percent of black women. Whereas approximately three-fourths of minority women had left school and remained out for at least one year by their 20th birthday, only 68 percent of white women had done so.

Ethnic differences in patterns of school withdrawal have profound implications for the long term employability of young men and women. Although premature school departure need not be definitive, there is mounting evidence that Hispanic youth are less likely to return to school or to receive a general equivalency degree (Cameron and Heckman, 1991). On this basis, one might expect that Hispanic youth would encounter the greatest difficulties securing work, but as the following results show, this is not the case. Furthermore, the experience of nonminority youth clearly shows the importance of prolonging schooling as a necessary--albeit not sufficient--condition for enhancing labor market prospects during young adulthood.

Labor Force Entry

Life table estimates of the *timing* of first jobs (reported in Tables 2a and 2b for men and women, respectively) also reveal considerable diversity along race and ethnic lines. Premature school departure renders Hispanics the most educationally disadvantaged group, yet black youth encounter the greatest difficulties in successfully entering the labor market. This generalization obtains for all definitions of first job.[10] More specifically, nearly half of Hispanic and white men had held an entry-level job by their 16th birthday, compared to 40 percent of black men. By comparison, 40 percent of white women, 35 percent of Hispanic women, and 27 percent of black women had held an entry level job before reaching their 16th birthday.

(Tables 2a and 2b About Here)

The life cycle pattern of steady employment revealed similar ethnic differences. White and Hispanic men obtain steady jobs, indexed by our intermediate definition, at a median age of 18, but for black men, the median age at obtaining first steady job is about 1 to 1.5 years later. Stated as a cumulative probability, by age 18, nearly three-fifths of white and half of Hispanic men had held a 15-hour per week job that lasted at least 6 months, compared to only 40 percent of black youth. Gender differences in proportions who work

[10] Based on a log-rank test, one can reject the hypothesis that the age-specific proportions securing jobs was identical among race and ethnic groups for both men and women. Thus, race and ethnic differences are statistically significant. The only exception is the white-Hispanic difference in the timing of first full-time employment. However, for men, the black-white and black-Hispanic contrasts for full-time jobs were significantly different.

61-412 O - 94 - 9

appear to widen with age, particularly as the definition of first employment becomes more stringent. For women, the ethnic differences in the timing of first steady job were even more pronounced: 53 percent of white women, 40 percent of Hispanic women and 27 percent of black women had worked at least part time for 6 months or more by their 18th birthday.

That the labor market difficulties experienced by black youth carry into their early adult lives is clearly apparent in the timing of first full-time jobs. By age 20, roughly 30 percent of white and Hispanic men had obtained a full-time job which they kept for at least a year, compared to less than 20 percent of black men. Although lower shares of women than men had worked full time by their 20th birthday, ethnic differences in entry to full-time employment paralleled the male pattern. The black median age for full-time employment was about 1 year higher than for whites and Hispanics. By age 25, 10 percent fewer black men had held full-time, year-round jobs compared to their white and Hispanic age counterparts. Among women, approximately three-fifths of blacks and Hispanics had worked full-time before their 25th birthday, compared to over 70 percent of whites.

These racial differences in the rate of entry to first jobs are apparent in Figure 1 (1a and 1b for men and women, respectively), which displays the proportions of men and women making their first transitions into entry-level and first full-time jobs. Two noteworthy features of these plots are: (1) distinct differences in the steepness of the curves for entry versus full-time jobs and, (2) the consistently lower placement of the black curves relative to the white and Hispanic curves. With respect to shape, the entry-level job curves rise sharply until about age 18, and flatten out thereafter. The survival function for full-time employment rises less steeply and fails to reach the height of the entry-level function by age 25, the last age respondents were observed in this exercise. The *slower* rates at which blacks enter the labor market, which signal accumulating disadvantages, are clearly discernible in both sets of curves. Hispanic-white disparities in the rate of labor market entry, while less pronounced than the black-white disparities, are statistically significant in all but one instance, namely the Hispanic-white difference in the timing of full-time employment for men.

(Figures 1a and 1b About Here)

Work in School

As noted in Section II, an important issue in the analysis of the school-to-work transition is the extent to which youth gain work experience prior to leaving school, and its impact on the rate of successful transition to the labor force (see Meyer and Wise, 1982). Figures 2a and 2b, respectively, plot the cumulative proportions of men and women who departed school by specific ages (and remained out for at least 12 months) against the rates of transition to first entry level jobs. Figures 3a and 3b reproduce the same school departure plot, contrasting it with the rates of entry to full-time employment. The extent of overlap between school and work, indicated by the area below the intersection of the two curves, is much greater when the liberal definition of first job is used than when the restrictive definition is used. Obviously, flexible employment such as that captured by our liberal job criterion is more compatible with school enrollment than is full-time work.

(Figures 2a and 2b About Here)

(Figures 3a and 3b About Here)

Tables 3a and 3b provide detail on racial differences in the propensity to combine school and work depicted in Figures 2 and 3.[11] We first consider the evidence for young men presented in Table 3a. In general, whites were more likely than minority youth to have work experience of any type prior to school departure, although the ethnic and racial differences are more pronounced as the definition of jobs becomes more restrictive. For example, half of all white and Hispanic men who left school at age 16 had work experience according to our liberal criterion, compared to only 40 percent of black men who left school at this age. A similar pattern obtains using the intermediate definition of first job, except that the white male advantage vis-a-vis minority youth is even greater. Specifically, 35 percent of white men who left school at age 16 reported having held a steady job prior to leaving school, compared, respectively, to 23 and 14 percent of Hispanic and black men who first left school at the same age. About 9 percent of white youth who dropped out of school when they were 16 claimed they had held a full-time job for at least a year, but only 7 and 4 percent of black and Hispanic youth made this claim.[12] That black men's slower entry into employment is accompanied by less overlap with school (see especially Figure 3a) may be a key factor accounting for the disadvantages this group experiences during early adulthood.

(Table 3a About Here)

By age 19, the point at which half of all men had left school for six months or more, the vast majority (over 90 percent) reported some type of work experience. Approximately

---

[11] Percents reported in Table 3 refer to work experience prior to the beginning of the age interval at which school departures occurred.

[12] It is conceivable that employment during adolescence accelerates the rate of departure from school, but information available to us does not permit us to establish a clear causal ordering.

three-fifths of white and Hispanic men who left school at age 19 had held a steady job, while 20 and 15 percent, respectively, had already worked full-time. The work experience profile black men who left school at age 19 leaves them relatively disadvantaged vis-a-vis whites and Hispanics, as less than half reported having held a steady job, and less than 10 percent indicated they had worked full-time prior to leaving school.

Young women's tendency to combine school and work also showed greater racial and ethnic differences as the criteria used to define first jobs became more restrictive. For example, among Hispanic women who left school at age 16, nearly half had held an entry level job, compared to 42 percent of white women and 20 percent of black women. A different pattern obtains using the intermediate definition of first job in that the work experience advantage corresponds to white women: 16 percent of those who left school at age 16 had held steady jobs while enrolled in school compared to 13 and only 4 percent of Hispanic and black women, respectively, who left school at this age. By age 19, the point at which over half of all women had left school for at least 6 months, only three-fourths of black women compared to 86 and 92 percent of Hispanic and white women, respectively, had worked in an entry level job before leaving school at this age. Over half of white women and 44 percent of Hispanic women had held a steady job while enrolled in school among those who exited at age 19, while less than one-third of black women combined work and school prior to leaving school at age 19.

(Table 3b About Here)

Despite racial and ethnic differences in the timing of school departure and labor market entry, results shown in Figures 2 and 3, and Table 3 indicate that substantial shares of youth *do* combine school and work during adolescence and young adulthood. Short-term, entry-level jobs are dominant at younger ages, but steady jobs and full-time jobs that last for a year or more are not uncommon among 18 and 19 year-olds, particularly Hispanic and white youth. Moreover, full-time employment does not always follow school departure immediately.

Time from School Leaving to First Full-Time Job

Although full-time employment can accelerate the pace of school departure, it does not necessarily follow that having work experience while in school will result in full-time employment upon leaving school. Many youth experience a hiatus from the time between their first exit from school and the time they land a full-time job. This is clearly illustrated in Table 4 and Figure 4, which summarize rates of waiting times to full-time employment from the date of first school departure.

(Tables 4a and 4b About Here)

Whether we use a liberal (6 consecutive months of nonenrollment) or restrictive (12 consecutive months of nonenrollment) definition of school departure, black youth experience longest waiting times until their first full-time job. Among men, waiting times for blacks are approximately 6 months, compared to about 4.5 months for whites and Hispanics. Among women, waiting times average 6 to 7 months for blacks and Hispanics, compared to 5 months for whites. Essentially, women of color experience longer waiting times to first full-time job after leaving school than white women.[13] These results, depicted graphically in Figures 4a

[13] The difference between black and Hispanic women's waiting times was not statistically significant, while the minority-nonminority contrasts were significantly different. All comparisons for men are significantly different.

and 4b for men and women, respectively, reinforce the profile of disadvantage that characterizes black youth's transition school to work.

(Figures 4a and 4b About Here)

<u>Characteristics of First Jobs</u>

A presumed advantage of early labor market entry is that it builds work experience which is associated with higher earnings and occupational status at later ages. However, if accumulation of experience occurs at the expense of lower educational attainment--that is, if employed youth withdraw from school at earlier ages--then the potential gains from early labor market experience may be totally offset during the early adult years, as earnings of more highly skilled workers surpass those of less educated workers. Therefore, it is worthwhile to entertain the hypothesis that the advantages of early entry to the labor market may be lost if they come at the expense lower schooling. Tables 5a and 5b, which summarize wage and school outcomes for our three definitions of first job, provide insight into this question. At the point of first contact with the labor market, race and ethnic differences in educational attainment are tiny (mainly because school departures are restricted by law until age 16), but statistically significant nonetheless. Surprisingly, minority youth have a significant wage advantage in their entry level jobs. Specifically, Hispanic men received an hourly rate of $4.03 and averaged 31 hours of work per week, compared to an hourly rate of $3.82 received by white youth, who worked approximately 4 fewer hours per week. The first job hourly rate of black youth was $3.95, and they reported working an average of 28 hours per week.[14] Hispanic women averaged $3.57 in their first entry-level jobs, compared to $3.50 and $3.22 received by similarly employed black and white women.

(Tables 5a and 5b About Here)

The minority advantage in wage rates is smaller when one examines first steady jobs. Among men, ethnic differences in wages were statistically trivial, but female wage gaps in steady jobs were significantly different by ethnicity. By the time they were steadily employed, white women had completed 11 years of school and earned approximately $4.14 per hour. Black women averaged about half a year more education than white women when they held their first steady job, but their average hourly wage was lower--$3.81. Hispanic women completed almost one less year of graded schooling than black women by the time they were steadily employed, yet they earned the same average wage.

Finally, all wage advantages of minority youth completely dissipated by the time they obtained their first full-time job. White men and women received the largest wage gains as they made transition from first entry level jobs to first full-time jobs. White men averaged an hourly wage rate of $6.34 in their first full-time job compared to $5.79 and $5.34, respectively, for Hispanic and black men. Although blacks averaged a half year more schooling than Hispanics employed full time, they earned $.50 less on an hourly basis. Similarly, white women employed full-time received $5.50 per hour compared to $5.01 and $4.84 for similarly employed Hispanic and black women. These differences are all the more striking when mapped against the groups' average schooling levels at the time of attaining

---

[14] Ethnic differences in wage rates for men's entry level jobs are on the margin of statistical significance, p = .055. Unless otherwise noted, all other contrasts for both men and women are significantly different in a statistical sense.

full-time jobs: there were no differences between black and white women, while Hispanic women completed one half year less of school. These results suggest that both color and credentials contribute to the profiles of labor market disadvantages of minority youth.

Given the marked differences in race and ethnic wage differentials according to the three definitions of first job, we examined what share of each group entered the labor market through full-time employment, bypassing altogether the "exploratory" and "unstable" aspects of the youth labor market (Shore, 1972). We determined that minority men were more likely than whites to work full-time at their first labor market encounter. Specifically, 18 and 17 percent of Hispanic and black men worked full time in their first job compared to 14 percent of white men. These differences in the *first* labor market encounter may account for some of the wage advantage enjoyed by minority youth because employers often are willing to pay full-time employees more than those who work part-time (by presuming that the former have a greater commitment to work).[15]

However, other mechanisms operate to produce the observed cross-over in wages along race and ethnic lines (Mare and Winship, 1984). These include early disruption of school, which translates to flatter earnings profiles among older youth who truncated their school careers early; selection of the most able into prolonged schooling or military enlistment, and differential work experience trajectories produced by repeated difficulties in securing and maintaining jobs at specific ages. Thus, we turn to our multivariate analyses to examine the circumstances that produce distinct profiles of transition from school to work.

---

[15] An inspection of the industrial distribution of first jobs using the liberal and restrictive definitions did not reveal any obvious differences that could account for the wage differentials. That Hispanics were more likely to work in agricultural industries than either whites or blacks should produce opposite differentials because of the low pay associated with farm employment.

V. Multivariate Analyses: Cox and Wage Regressions

Our analysis proceeds as follows. First we estimate the timing of first school withdrawal and first job entry based on liberal and restrictive definitions of both events using cox regression techniques. Subsequently we evaluate the waiting time from first school departure to first full-time job. We conclude with a preliminary analysis of the determinants of (log) wage rates for first entry and first full-time job.

Tables 6a and 6b provide summary statistics for key background variables for men and women, respectively. The age distribution is quite similar among the three race and ethnic groups, but the youngest cohort is somewhat smaller than the other cohort groups. AFQT scores differ appreciably along race and ethnic lines, with black men scoring lowest at 48 points, whites the highest at 71 points, and Hispanic men between these extremes with 54 points. A similar ethnic pattern obtained for women, except that females scored slightly higher than their male ethnic counterparts. By construction, the AFQT index ranges from 0 to 105, and average scores for military populations range from 74 to 48 for whites and blacks, respectively. As a general ability measure, the AFQT varies positively with age, therefore only age-adjusted effects are meaningful. Inclusion of age cohort in the multivariate models also controls for differences in left censored employment and education histories.[16]

(Tables 6a and 6b About Here)

---

[16] There is no optimal solution for left censoring, particularly when the truncated history is selective. Although left censoring in employment and education histories is not great in these cohorts, it does exist. Controls for age cohort help monitor this problem, but they do not provide a completely satisfactory solution.

Black youth resided in families with the lowest family incomes in 1978, but Hispanics reported the lowest parental educational levels. Average white family incomes (from all sources) stood at approximately $22,000 in 1978, compared to roughly $11,000 and $13,000 for blacks and Hispanics, respectively. Hispanic parents attained approximately 8.5 years of graded schooling, while black parents averaged 10.5 to 11 years of schooling. Parents of white youth averaged 12 years of education.[17] Black youth were most likely and white youth least likely to have been reared in a parent-absent family. Just over half of young black men and women reported living with both parents when they were 14 years old compared to approximately three-fourths of Hispanic youth and 86 percent of white youth.

Waiting Times to School Departure

Tables 7a and 7b report the cox regression analysis of school departure for men and women, respectively. At first blush, the slower school exit rates of blacks relative to native whites are surprising in light of the life table estimates (Table 1) showing racial differences in exit rates that disfavored minorities, and they speak to our interest in racial and ethnic differences. Although these results are contrary to those produced by the life table analysis, they have a straightforward explanation. The *gross* effects of race and ethnic origin are positive for both men and women, such that blacks and Hispanics exit from school at a *faster* rate than their white counterparts. These are the basic results reported in Table 1 and Figures 2 and 3. However, controlling for ability differences that are correlated with school retention *reverses* the race and ethnic effects on school departure by our liberal criterion, and

[17] Because of nontrivial amounts of missing data on the parental education and family income variables, we included dummy variables for the missing cases. This was deemed preferable to losing observations and potentially introducing selection bias through nonresponse.

completely eliminates them for Hispanic men and women. A parallel story obtains for the restrictive definition of school departure after ability differences are taken into account, except that white Hispanic women exhibit a significantly slower pace of school departure compared to white women with similar AFQT scores. No comparable school retention effect emerges for Hispanic men whose AFQT scores are identical to those of whites.

(Tables 7a and 7b About Here)

Further adjustment for differences in family background among blacks, whites and Hispanics accentuates racial and ethnic variation in school departure patterns. This is particularly apparent when a restrictive criterion (i.e., nonenrollment for at least 12 months) is used to define school exits, as these results show that both Hispanic and black youth leave school at rates significantly below those of whites of similar family backgrounds and ability. Similarly, black and Hispanic women leave school for at least a year at a rate two-thirds as fast as white women with comparable ability and similar family backgrounds.

Substantively, the cox regression results indicate that once ability differences and family background are taken into account, white men exit school at rates 49 to 64 percent faster than black men, and about 24 percent faster than Hispanic men. Among women, adjustments for differences in ability and family background imply that white women's school exit rates are 36 to 50 percent higher than black women (using liberal and restrictive criteria for school departure), and 23 to 47 percent higher than those of white Hispanic women.

Higher AFQT scores prolong schooling by lowering exit rates between 1.5 and 2 percent for each raw score point. By any standard, this is a sizeable effect. Thus, it appears that racial and ethnic disparities in school leaving rates are largely mediated by differences in scholastic/job aptitudes as measured by AFQT scores. The AFQT result is robust, as it persists after introducing controls for family background (model 2) and irrespective of whether a liberal or restrictive definition of school departure is used. Of the family background variables, mother's education exerts little influence on men's departures from school, but father's education and higher family incomes lower men's exit rates in both the liberal and restrictive specifications. Results for women are generally similar except that mother's education also increases school retention for them. Interestingly, parent absence *per se* did not accelerate school departures once socioeconomic background is taken into account. However, living at home significantly increased school retention rates relative to living on one's own.

The significant age cohort effects for men in the restrictive specification indicate that left censoring may produce some distortion in the estimated effects, but given the consistency of results across the two specifications of the dependent variable, these distortions are not likely to be large.[18]

Age at First Job

Tables 8a and 8b summarizes the key results of the event history analysis of entry to employment. Our dependent variable is age at the occurrence of the first entry-level job (any duration and any weekly hours), or the first full-time job that lasted at least one year. Negative coefficients indicate a decreasing rate of entry to employment (that is, slower exits from the state of nonparticipation).

[18] We estimated a model that included year dummies to determine whether cohort effects might be due to period effects and discerned no significant pattern in the results. More importantly, the effects of age cohort were not washed out.

The life table analysis indicated that black men experience significantly slower transition rates to employment, compared to native whites, irrespective of the criteria used to define first job. This conclusion is not altered by controlling for differences in AFQT scores. Substantively, the implication is that black men who have AFQT scores comparable to those of whites make a significantly *slower* transition to entry-level and full-time employment. Stated differently, among black and white men who are statistically equivalent in terms of their AFQT scores and family background, black men's odds of securing entry-level or full-time employment are only .75 the odds of white men. However, there are essentially no differences between Hispanic and white men in the rate of entry to either beginning or full-time jobs once differences in AFQT scores and family background characteristics are standardized statistically.

(Table 8a About Here)

Among women an adjustment for differences in AFQT scores similarly did not eliminate racial differences in the rate of attaining their first job: black women, like their male counterparts, experienced slower transitions into first jobs compared to white or Hispanic women of similar ability. However, no differences in the rate at which white and Hispanic women achieved their first jobs were evident among respondents who were comparable in their AFQT scores and family background.

Racial differences in women's transition to employment did not carry over to entry into full-time jobs. The transition to full-time employment was identical among black, white and Hispanic women with equivalent AFQT scores and family backgrounds. This means that groups differences in ability and family background account for the significant racial and ethnic disparities in entering the workforce based on the life table estimates.

(Table 8b About Here)

The direct influence of family background and individual ability on the transition to work are substantively interesting not only because they circumscribe the effects of race, but also because they may hold a master key to understanding the mechanisms that maintain inequities along race and ethnic lines. Higher AFQT scores are associated with accelerated entry into beginning jobs for both men and women, and also women's transition to full-time employment. However AFQT scores slow men's rate of entry into full time employment--perhaps by prolonging school enrollment or encouraging military enlistment. The mechanisms producing this complex gender and race interaction in the effects of AFQT scores on entry to employment are not immediately apparent, but warrant much further investigation.

Family background is inconsequential for the rate at which young men secure entry-level employment, probably because most have some encounter with the labor market during adolescence, irrespective of their economic status. Apparently this is not so for young women. Maternal education accelerates the rate at which young women secure entry-level jobs. Furthermore, young women were 39 percent more likely to find an entry-level job if they lived at home in 1979 than their counterparts who lived on their own. The odds that young women would hold an entry-level job were higher for those reared in parent-absent families compared to those reared in two-parent families. This result appears to capture the work-inducing effect of economic need.

Results for the transition to full-time employment also revealed appreciable gender differences. Beyond the trivial effects of race and ethnic origin, only AFQT scores and two background variables accelerated young women's entry to full-time employment, namely living at home (versus on one's own) in 1979 and having acquired work experience before leaving school. Specifically, the odds of obtaining a full-time job were 28 percent higher for women who lived at home in 1979 versus those who lived on their own. Equally striking are the linkages between early work experience and the transition to full-time work for young women. The latter imply that the odds of full-time employment were 44 percent higher among women who reported having worked before leaving school compared to those who did not.

Although family background does not influence men's transition to an entry-level job, their effects were substantial for full-time employment. Specifically, father's education delayed young men's entry to first full-time job, while family income produced an offsetting positive effect. A much stronger influence on young men's transition to first full-time employment is that produced by the experience of having worked before leaving school, presumably in an entry level job, but possibly including steady employment. Substantively, this coefficient indicates that the odds of securing a full-time job were 32 percent higher for men who acquired labor market experience prior to leaving school relative to those who did not acquire such experience.

<u>Waiting Time from School Departure to First Job</u>

Table 9 provides further insight on the transition from school to work by estimating the rate at which young men achieve full-time employment subsequent to school departure.

Once again we find complex race and ethnic effects on the transition to full-time employment, but the patterns depend on gender and the criteria used to define school departure. For example, given that they exited school for at least six months, nonwhite Hispanic and black men entered full-time employment at a significantly slower rate than white men with similar AFQT scores. However, once family background is taken into account, only the negative effects for black men remain significant. Unlike men, adjusting for differences in AFQT scores eliminated racial differences in the rate of entry to full-time employment among women. Essentially this implies that among women who have left school, group differences in ability and family background mediate the race and ethnic disparities in the rate of entry to full-time employment.

(Tables 9a and 9b About Here)

Somewhat different results obtain for the restrictive definition of school departure. Although black and nonwhite Hispanic men experience a slower rate of entry to full-time employment vis-a-vis white men with equivalent AFQT scores, these apparent racial advantages disappear completely once differences in family background are standardized statistically. Among women with equivalent AFQT scores there are essentially no race and ethnic differences in the rate of entry to full-time employment. However, adjustments for differences in family background retard black women's transition to full-time employment subsequent to school leaving, and accelerate white Hispanic women's transition to full-time jobs relative to comparable white women.

Three more results from Table 9 deserve comment. One is the consistently strong and positive effects of AFQT scores on the rate of transition to full-time employment irrespective of the stringency of the school departure criteria used. Our estimates indicate that the elapsed time from school exit to job entry is shortened by approximately one percent for each unit increase in ability differences among men, and roughly two percent for young women. This finding suggests that AFQT is measuring more than just scholastic aptitude. We believe this index may also capture attributes associated with job readiness and/or skills.

Second, among the background characteristics, only family income influences men's rate of entry to full-time employment following school departure. For women, both family income and having lived at home at age 14 extend the time required to enter a full-time job. This most likely captures the school retention effects of living at home. However, the lack of uniform effects of family background on men's and women's transition to full-time employment subsequent to school departure suggests a complex gender interaction warranting further scrutiny in its own right.

Finally, experiences of work prior to school departure shortens the time required to acquire a full-time job after leaving school. This result is consistent with speculation about positive feedback links between adolescent and early adult work experiences, although the long term linkages are less clear. The ambiguous linkages between adolescent work experiences and subsequent adult employment outcomes is apparent in the wage analysis that follows.

Wage Analysis

In order to better understand and interpret the descriptive results showing a reversal in race differentials in wage rates during the school-to-work transition, we estimated wage functions for first entry-level and first full-time jobs using a semi-logarithmic specification.

Our first model estimates the main effects on (log) wage rates of race and ethnic origin, AFQT scores, and family background. To this baseline model we added respondents' education at the beginning of the job, and a cumulative measure of prior work experience (measured in weeks), and in the model predicting (log) wages of first full-time job, also the indicator of prior work experience prior to school departure.[19]

(Tables 10a and 10b About Here)

Key findings are as follows: First, race and ethnic effects on wages differ for men and women and according to the stringency of the criteria used to define first job. Among men, the only race effects on wages correspond to nonwhite Hispanics who are compensated 15 percent more per hour than statistically equivalent white men. However, there are no race and ethnic differences in wages received by men employed full time. By contrast, ethnic differences in wage rates persist for women whose family backgrounds are identical. That is, consistent with results reported in Table 5, entry-level wage rates received by nonwhite Hispanic and black women exceed those of whites by 20 and 10 percent, respectively. Women's wage gaps are patterned differently among those with full-time jobs. Although the wage premium for full-time workers corresponds to minority rather than majority women, it is blacks and white Hispanics (rather than nonwhite Hispanics), who out-earn their white counterparts by 7 and 14 percent, respectively. These seemingly counter-intuitive results partly reflect the tendency for Hispanic youth to enter full-time employment without part-time work experience.

---

[19] For first entry level jobs, prior work experience refers to episodes of uncompensated "employment." The average tenure prior to first paid job is 1.7 weeks for the sample as a whole.

Second, each year of formal schooling rendered men wage returns on the order of 3 percent for first entry-level jobs and nearly 4 percent for full-time jobs. For women, the wage returns to formal schooling where slightly higher, 6 percent for beginning and 5 percent for full-time jobs. Not surprisingly, experience effects are trivial for wages received in entry-level jobs, but substantial returns to prior work episodes are discernible for full-time employment. (Recall that experience is measured in weeks.) Finally, the anomalous result indicating negative wage returns for having acquired work experience before leaving school is unique to men. The negative wage returns to prior work experience require further investigation to determine whether they reflect selection effects, disruption effects, or unobserved heterogeneity.

VI. Conclusion

To recapitulate, the general questions motivating our empirical research focus on racial and ethnic differences in: (1) the timing of school departure and labor market entry; (2) the nature of the first labor market encounter; and (3) the consequences of adolescent labor market experience for employment outcomes during early adulthood. The event history analysis of school departure and labor market entry indicated considerable overlap between these two activity domains that are central in the lives of adolescents, but racial and ethnic differences were clearly indicated.

Although racial differences in the timing of labor market entry have been examined extensively, no prior study has examined racial differences in school to work transition among Hispanics. Our findings showing that race and ethnic variation in the transition to employment can be reversed or eliminated after adjusting for differences in AFQT scores and family background is both provocative and problematic. If the AFQT measure is truly an index of scholastic and/or job-related aptitudes, then prior studies that failed to consider this influence on school departures and employment transitions may have misrepresented the significance of race. If, on the other hand, the AFQT index is capturing racial biases in the test itself, then our interpretation about its success in tapping ability differences among the groups is inappropriate. Until we can answer these questions satisfactorily, our findings about racial and ethnic differences must be regarded as tentative. However, our results underscore the urgency of scrutinizing the AFQT index and investigating how the use of this performance measure might be adapted to employment decisions in the civilian sector.

There are other reasons for considering our findings tentative. The first is that we have not addressed possible biases stemming from unobserved heterogeneity. Second, our cox models do not consider covariates that vary over time. Rather, with the exception of educational attainment and job experience, we have restricted our independent variables to fixed characteristics obtained at the time of the interview. While instructive, this reduced form specification is warrants considerable elaboration. Third, the significance of race for Hispanics deserves further scrutiny. It is important, in particular, to determine whether our nonwhite effects basically serve as proxies for national origin distinctions, particularly between Puerto Ricans and other Hispanics. Fourth, we have not examined the role of military enrollment in mediating the school-to-work transition for minority men, and there is ample evidence indicating that this has made a difference for black men. Finally, documenting the selection process over the early life course transition from school to work in more substantive terms (i.e., how early school leavers differ from those who persist in school; how early labor market entrants differ from late entrants, etc.), should assist in the interpretation of the econometric solutions to "correct" for such biases.

Several recommendations follow from our work to date. The first and most important concerns the substantial race and ethnic differences in the rates at which young men and women leave school and enter the labor force. Among men, we observed pronounced race and ethnic differences in the probability of getting a job. In particular, it is black men who experience the greatest difficulty entering the labor market. Unlike women, young men's wages are not differentiated by race and ethnic group. These complex results emphasize the urgent need to support research directed toward understanding the mechanisms and barriers that limit young black men's access to the labor market, as well as the mechanisms that generate unequal wages for women of color. The research program we envision should be grounded in empirical analyses of secondary data, but should also include diverse methodologies to document whether and how discrimination may be responsible for the results we observe.

A second recommendation concerns data requirements to further research and knowledge about the school-to-work transition. Despite the great analytical potential of the NLSY for investigating various aspects of the school-to-work transition, our initial foray into this phenomenon also made us aware of numerous limitations of the NLSY. We recommend the need for a new youth cohort. Respondents currently in the NLSY sample are now in late 20s to early 30s, and well beyond the transitional phase of their lifecourse. Given the dramatic changes in the racial and ethnic composition of the U.S. population during the

1980s that were driven by immigration and differential fertility, collection of data about today's youth seems a necessary adjunct for policy formulation about tomorrow's workers.

Along this line, we recommend that the new youth cohort begin with younger children--kids in early adolescence--rather than the large age spectrum used by the NLSY. This is warranted to adequately portray the process of school departure. Legal restrictions on school departure notwithstanding, many youth, particularly minorities, leave school permanently before they are entitled to do so legally. And, these are the kids most in need of attention by policy makers. We also recommend that the new youth cohort include an oversample of Asian men and women. Virtually nothing is known about the school-to-work transition of this rapidly growing and highly diverse minority population.

Third, we recommend additional research on the significance and interpretation of the Armed Forces Qualifying Test as a measure of scholastic aptitude, labor market readiness, skills or other performance indicators. The military interprets the AFQT score as a measure of general trainability, and uses the scores to screen out individuals who are likely to have a low probability of successfully completing military training. Social scientists have used the AFQT as a general ability indicator, arguing that it performs like a scholastic aptitude test. But, the typical employer does not have access to individuals' AFQT scores, nor are such standardized test scores available for typical job applicants. Colleges and Universities require some form of entrance exam for admission. Are there lessons to be learned from the military with respect to matching workers to job specialties based on this or a similar indicator of "general trainability?" Our results suggest much can be learned about race and ethnic differences in school and civilian labor market outcomes from the experiences of the Armed Forces in recruiting, training and graduating minority youth and young adults.

Table 1a

Cumulative Percent Leaving School Using Two Definitions of First Departure: Young Men Aged 13 to 16 in 1978 by Ethnicity (Life Table Estimates)

	Liberal Definition[a]			Restrictive Definition[b]		
Age	Whites	Blacks	Hispanics	Whites	Blacks	Hispanics
≤ 13	-	0.3	0.7	0.1	0.3	0.7
14	1.3	1.4	2.6	1.0	1.2	2.0
15	4.8	3.9	6.6	3.9	3.1	5.3
16	12.2	9.2	15.9	10.3	7.5	13.4
17	26.0	23.3	33.0	23.1	20.0	28.6
18	49.7	50.5	57.1	44.9	45.0	50.3
19	71.0	75.7	77.3	64.6	69.2	70.1
20	80.1	87.6	86.8	73.4	81.7	81.5
21	85.0	92.6	91.6	78.7	87.9	88.0
22	90.9	96.0	94.5	84.9	91.6	91.7
23	96.2	98.6	96.8	90.4	94.9	94.5
24	98.6	99.9	98.6	93.1	97.0	96.7
25+	100.0	100.0	100.0	-	98.3	-
Age at First Departure						
$\bar{x}$	20.3	19.0	19.0	22.5	20.1	19.9
Median	18.6	18.4	18.3	18.7	18.6	18.4
[N][c]	[1265]	[797]	[511]	[1265]	[797]	[511]

Source: NLSY civilian sample

[a] Liberal Definition: Left school for 6 months or more.

[b] Restrictive Definition: Left school for 12 months or more.

[c] [N] is unweighted population in the risk set.

Table 1b

Cumulative Percent Leaving School Using Two Definitions of First Departure: Young Women Aged 13 to 16 in 1978 by Ethnicity (Life Table Estimates)

	Liberal Definition[a]			Restrictive Definition[b]		
Age	Whites	Blacks	Hispanics	Whites	Blacks	Hispanics
≤ 13	-	-	-	-	-	-
14	0.3	0.4	0.8	0.3	0.2	0.6
15	1.2	1.9	3.5	1.1	0.9	3.3
16	5.3	6.1	12.0	4.6	4.0	10.5
17	19.4	19.4	28.6	17.1	14.8	24.0
18	46.0	46.9	52.9	41.3	38.6	45.6
19	67.6	71.5	73.9	60.4	61.9	66.5
20	76.1	82.4	83.3	68.3	74.5	77.3
21	82.3	88.0	87.6	74.5	82.0	82.7
22	90.0	92.7	90.7	81.9	87.6	86.2
23	95.0	95.9	92.9	87.7	91.5	88.5
24	96.2	97.0	94.1	90.4	93.7	89.8
25+	-	-	94.6	-	-	-
Age at First Departure						
$\bar{x}$	20.3	20.0	20.3	22.4	21.3	21.9
Median	18.5	18.6	18.3	18.7	18.8	18.7
[N][c]	[1204]	[763]	[511]	[1204]	[763]	[511]

Source: NLSY civilian sample

[a] Liberal Definition: Left school for 6 months or more.

[b] Restrictive Definition: Left school for 12 months or more.

[c] [N] is unweighted population in the risk set.

Table 2a

Cumulative Percent with Work Experience Using Three Definitions of First Job: Young Men Aged 13 to 16 in 1978 by Ethnicity (Life Table Estimates)

Age	Liberal[a]			Intermediate[b]			Restrictive[c]		
	Whites	Blacks	Hispanics	Whites	Blacks	Hispanics	Whites	Blacks	Hispanics
≤13	2.3	1.4	1.1	0.7	0.8	0.6	0.2	-	0.4
14	7.6	5.5	5.1	2.1	1.7	1.4	0.6	0.2	0.7
15	21.5	16.9	18.7	7.2	4.8	5.4	1.2	0.7	1.4
16	49.6	39.7	46.3	22.9	13.0	17.0	3.4	1.3	3.4
17	75.4	63.5	72.6	42.3	25.8	34.8	6.6	2.4	6.9
18	89.3	79.6	86.6	57.3	39.7	51.6	12.0	5.7	12.3
19	95.6	88.4	93.3	68.6	52.5	63.4	19.8	11.4	20.5
20	97.7	92.7	95.8	77.1	62.8	71.6	28.9	18.3	30.4
21	98.6	95.5	96.5	78.8	72.3	78.8	39.0	27.9	41.8
22	99.2	97.4	97.2	85.2	80.0	85.2	49.8	39.4	53.3
23	99.4	98.6	97.9	90.6	87.1	90.6	61.2	53.4	64.2
24	99.6	99.3	98.3	94.3	92.8	94.3	72.4	64.5	73.3
25+	99.7	99.6	-	96.2	95.4	96.2	79.4	70.9	79.7
Median	16.5	16.9	16.6	17.9	19.4	18.3	22.5	23.3	22.2
[N][d]	[1265]	[797]	[511]	[1581]	[797]	[511]	[1265]	[797]	[511]

Source: NLSY civilian sample

[a] Liberal Definition: any duration and any hours.

[b] Intermediate Definition: 6 months duration and 15 hrs. or more per week.

[c] Restrictive Definition: 12 months duration and 35 hrs. or more per week.

[d] [N] is unweighted population in the risk set.

Table 2b

Cumulative Percent with Work Experience Using Three Definitions of First Job: Young Women Aged 13 to 16 in 1978 by Ethnicity (Life Table Estimates)

Age	Liberal[a]			Intermediate[b]			Restrictive[c]		
	Whites	Blacks	Hispanics	Whites	Blacks	Hispanics	Whites	Blacks	Hispanics
≤13	1.2	0.3	1.0	0.1	-	0.4	-	-	0.2
14	5.8	2.2	3.7	1.0	0.5	1.1	0.2	0.1	-
15	16.0	10.4	13.0	4.1	2.2	3.5	0.6	-	0.4
16	40.3	27.4	34.9	16.7	6.8	12.2	1.1	0.5	1.2
17	68.2	48.7	59.2	35.8	15.9	25.3	3.5	1.6	3.9
18	85.0	67.0	77.0	53.3	26.9	40.6	10.0	3.9	8.8
19	93.0	79.8	88.2	66.2	39.4	54.8	18.4	8.2	15.5
20	96.0	87.2	93.7	74.9	52.2	64.5	26.1	14.0	24.0
21	97.2	91.4	96.2	81.4	62.1	72.7	34.3	20.3	33.0
22	97.9	94.2	97.4	87.3	70.7	79.8	45.0	29.5	42.2
23	98.3	95.5	97.9	92.1	79.3	84.9	57.2	41.3	50.8
24	98.6	96.6	98.4	94.4	86.2	88.7	66.1	51.9	57.4
25+	98.8	97.7	98.7	95.4	90.3	91.2	71.4	59.6	62.6
Median	16.8	17.5	17.0	18.2	20.3	19.1	22.9	24.3	23.2
[N][d]	[1204]	[763]	[511]	[1204]	[763]	[511]	[1204]	[763]	[511]

Source: NLSY civilian sample
[a] Liberal Definition: any duration and any hours.
[b] Intermediate Definition: 6 months duration and 15 hrs. or more per week.
[c] Restrictive Definition: 12 months duration and 35 hrs. or more per week.
[d] [N] is unweighted population in the risk set.

Table [illegible]a

Percent With Work Experience by Age of First School Exit for at Least 6 months Using Three Definitions of First Job: Young Men Aged 13 to 16 in 1978 by Ethnicity

	Liberal[a]			Intermediate[b]			Restrictive[c]		
Age of School Exit[d]	Whites	Blacks	Hispanics	Whites	Blacks	Hispanics	Whites	Blacks	Hispanics
14	21.4	13.3	12.5	0.0	0.0	0.0	0.0	0.0	0.0
15	37.5	22.7	22.7	9.4	0.0	9.1	0.0	0.0	5.9
16	54.3	40.4	49.2	35.2	13.7	22.8	9.0	6.7	4.1
17	78.2	65.6	81.4	50.8	31.9	43.8	13.3	5.3	15.9
18	89.1	76.9	85.2	61.8	38.1	48.1	13.2	4.3	7.3
19	92.9	91.2	94.2	66.5	46.5	58.8	18.7	8.5	15.1
20	97.1	94.6	93.5	74.6	64.2	70.4	21.8	13.9	36.4
21	98.5	96.0	94.7	74.6	73.9	61.1	15.4	20.0	0.0
22	100.0	96.2	100.0	72.8	57.7	100.0	18.4	5.6	11.1
23	100.0	100.0	100.0	88.6	100.0	87.5	27.3	28.6	16.7
24	100.0	50.0	100.0	100.0	0.0	100.0	33.3	0.0	100.0

Source: NLSY civilian sample

[a] Liberal Definition: any duration and any hours.

[b] Intermediate Definition: 6 months duration and 15 hrs. or more per week.

[c] Restrictive Definition: 12 months duration and 35 hrs. or more per week.

[d] Age of first school exit at least 6 months; there were too few exits prior to age 13.

Table 3b

Percent With Work Experience by Age of First School Exit for at Least 6 months Using Three Definitions of First Job: Young Women Aged 13 to 16 in 1978 by Ethnicity

Age of School Exit[d]	Liberal[a]			Intermediate[b]			Restrictive[c]		
	Whites	Blacks	Hispanics	Whites	Blacks	Hispanics	Whites	Blacks	Hispanics
14	0.0	0.0	0.0	0.0	0.0	0.0	0.0	0.0	0.0
15	6.2	11.8	23.8	0.0	0.0	0.0	0.0	0.0	0.0
16	41.8	20.0	48.4	16.5	4.4	12.9	1.3	0.0	4.8
17	68.9	43.7	63.4	42.6	16.2	27.7	7.7	2.1	3.0
18	84.1	63.8	77.6	55.9	26.4	46.9	7.8	3.8	10.5
19	92.3	74.4	86.1	58.0	29.9	44.4	14.7	2.6	6.9
20	95.4	88.0	96.2	61.5	50.0	46.2	12.3	10.0	11.5
21	100.0	88.6	94.4	73.1	57.1	61.1	11.5	8.6	5.6
22	97.0	100.0	91.7	72.7	64.7	66.7	12.1	14.7	16.7
23	100.0	100.0	100.0	62.5	53.8	87.5	6.2	23.1	25.0
24	100.0	100.0	100.0	80.0	100.0	100.0	40.0	0.0	50.0

Source: NLSY civilian sample

[a] Liberal Definition: any duration and any hours.

[b] Intermediate Definition: 6 months duration and 15 hrs. or more per week.

[c] Restrictive Definition: 12 months duration and 35 hrs. or more per week.

[d] Age of first school exit at least 6 months; there were too few exits prior to age 13.

Table 4a

Waiting Times From First School Exit to First Full-time Job Using Two Definitions of School Departure: Young Men Aged 13 to 16 in 1978 by Ethnicity (in months)

Definition of School Exit	Whites	Blacks	Hispanics
Liberal[a]			
Mean	3.9	6.2	4.7
% censored	25.5	35.9	26.0
Median	2.9	4.7	3.6
[N]	[1265]	[797]	[511]
Restrictive[b]			
Mean	3.6	5.8	4.3
% censored	30.8	37.8	27.8
Median	2.7	4.3	3.3
[N]	[1265]	[797]	[511]

Source: NLSY civilian sample.

[a] Liberal Definition: Leaving school for 6 months or more.

[b] Restrictive Definition: Leaving school for 12 months or more.

Table 4b

Waiting Times From First School Exit to First Full-time Job Using Two Definitions of School Departure: Young Women Aged 13 to 16 in 1978 by Ethnicity (in months)

Definition of School Exit	Whites	Blacks	Hispanics
Liberal[a]			
Mean	4.9	7.6	6.8
% censored	33.2	48.0	46.4
Median	3.4	5.7	4.5
[N]	[1204]	[763]	[511]
Restrictive[b]			
Mean	4.6	6.8	6.3
% censored	37.6	49.5	48.7
Median	2.7	5.1	4.3
[N]	[1204]	[763]	[511]

Source: NLSY civilian sample.
[a] Liberal Definition: Leaving school for 6 months or more.
[b] Restrictive Definition: Leaving school for 12 months or more.

Table 5a

Average Education, Hours, and Wages[a] at Time of First Job Using Three Definitions of First Job: Young Men Aged 13 to 16 in 1978 by Ethnicity (Standard Deviations)

Definition of First Job	Whites	Blacks	Hispanics
Liberal[b]			
Education	8.1	8.1	7.9
	(1.2)	(1.3)	(1.3)
Hourly Wage, $	3.82	3.95	4.03
	(1.55)	(1.93)	(1.86)
Weekly Hours	26.5	28.3	30.7
	(14.5)	(13.7)	(14.7)
[N]	[1249]	[785]	[496]
Intermediate[c]			
Education	10.8	11.0	10.4
	(2.0)	(1.8)	(1.9)
Hourly Wage, $	4.48	4.36	4.46
	(2.25)	(2.01)	(2.02)
Weekly Hours	33.7	34.8	36.6
	(12.5)	(11.8)	(11.8)
[N]	[1172]	[703]	[462]
Restrictive[d]			
Education	12.4	11.9	11.2
	(2.3)	(1.9)	(2.1)
Hourly Wage, $	6.34	5.34	5.79
	(2.72)	(2.16)	(2.51)
Weekly Hours	45.6	43.7	43.9
	(8.8)	(7.9)	(7.5)
[N]	[916]	[475]	[363]

Source: NLSY civilian sample.
[a] Wages in 1982 dollars.
[b] Liberal Definition: any duration any hours.
[c] Intermediate Definition: 6 months duration and 15 hrs. or more per week.
[d] Restrictive Definition: 12 months duration and 35 hrs. or more per week.

Table 5b

Average Education, Hours, and Wages[a] at Time of First Job Using Three Definitions of First Job: Young Women Aged 13 to 16 in 1978 by Ethnicity (Standard Deviations)

Definition of First Job	Whites	Blacks	Hispanics
Liberal[b]			
Education	8.4 (1.2)	8.3 (1.3)	8.1 (1.3)
Hourly Wage, $	3.22 (1.61)	3.50 (2.08)	3.57 (3.02)
Weekly Hours	24.3 (13.5)	26.8 (12.2)	27.9 (13.9)
[N]	[1175]	[714]	[485]
Intermediate[c]			
Education	11.2 (2.0)	11.7 (1.8)	10.9 (1.9)
Hourly Wage, $	4.14 (2.63)	3.81 (1.57)	3.85 (1.69)
Weekly Hours	31.7 (11.0)	34.0 (11.0)	33.3 (10.2)
[N]	[1117]	[616]	[426]
Restrictive[d]			
Education	12.7 (2.1)	12.7 (1.8)	11.9 (2.0)
Hourly Wage, $	5.50 (2.51)	4.84 (2.28)	5.01 (2.05)
Weekly Hours	42.1 (6.3)	41.9 (6.5)	41.9 (6.5)
[N]	[820]	[396]	[281]

Source: NLSY civilian sample.
[a] Wages in 1982 dollars.
[b] Liberal Definition: any duration any hours.
[c] Intermediate Definition: 6 months duration and 15 hrs. or more per week.
[d] Restrictive Definition: 12 months duration and 35 hrs. or more per week.

Table 6a

Background Characteristics of Respondents by Ethnicity and Race: Young Men Aged 13 to 16 in 1978 (Means or Percents)

	Whites	Blacks	Hispanics
Cohort			
13	20.9	18.4	20.0
14	26.1	26.7	28.8
15	28.5	26.6	23.5
16	24.4	28.2	27.8
AFQT	70.9	47.6	54.5
(s.d.)	(20.0)	(18.5)	(20.4)
[N]	[1211]	[772]	[481]
Father's Education	12.4	10.4	8.5
(s.d.)	(3.3)	(3.3)	(4.7)
[N]	[1177]	[584]	[403]
Mother's Education	11.9	10.9	8.1
(s.d.)	(2.4)	(2.5)	(4.3)
[N]	[1208]	[722]	[463]
Live w̄ Both Parents at 14	86.8	55.7	71.2
[N]	[1262]	[796]	[510]
Family Income, 1978	22,004	10,974	12,964
(s.d.)	(13,599)	(8,084)	(9,893)
[N]	[1042]	[645]	[424]

Source: NLSY civilian sample.

Table 6b

Background Characteristics of Respondents by Ethnicity and Race: Young Women Aged 13 to 16 in 1978 (Means or Percents)

	Whites	Blacks	Hispanics
Cohort			
13	18.4	18.7	17.8
14	25.5	26.6	29.2
15	27.6	27.5	28.6
16	28.5	27.1	24.5
AFQT	73.1	50.1	55.7
(s.d.)	(17.0)	(16.7)	(18.4)
[N]	[1149]	[745]	[488]
Father's Education	12.2	10.2	8.6
(s.d.)	(3.2)	(3.5)	(4.5)
[N]	[1114]	[560]	[430]
Mother's Education	11.9	10.7	8.0
(s.d.)	(2.4)	(2.6)	(3.9)
[N]	[1156]	[710]	[484]
Live w̄ Both Parents at 14	86.5	52.0	76.0
[N]	[1203]	[759]	[509]
Family Income, 1978	22,523	11,453	13,305
(s.d.)	(12,839)	(10,131)	(9,282)
[N]	[959]	[654]	[431]

Source: NLSY civilian sample.

Table 7a
Determinants of School Departure Rates Using
Two Definitions of Exit: Young Men Aged 13 to 16 in 1978
(Asymptotic Standard Errors)

	Liberal[a]		Restrictive[b]	
	(1)	(2)	(1)	(2)
Cohort				
14	-.003 (.061)	-.013 (.062)	.102 (.064)	.097 (.065)
15	.108 (.061)	.093 (.062)	.244 (.064)	.232 (.064)
16	.036 (.063)	.014 (.063)	.214 (.065)	.197 (.065)
Ethnicity/Race				
Hispanic-White	-.073 (.068)	-.217 (.073)	-.076 (.070)	-.274 (.076)
Hispanic-Non-White	-.077 (.095)	-.078 (.099)	.003 (.097)	-.200 (.100)
Black	-.305 (.055)	-.401 (.059)	-.367 (.056)	-.487 (.060)
If Foreign Born	-.213 (.096)	-.254 (.097)	-.257 (.098)	-.303 (.099)
AFQT	-.022 (.001)	-.019 (.001)	-.026 (.001)	-.022 (.001)
Mother's Ed.[c]		-.013 (.009)		-.012 (.009)
Father's Ed.[c]		-.021 (.007)		-.035 (.008)
Family Income[c]		-.007 (.002)		-.009 (.002)
If Live at Home, 1979		-.159 (.094)		-.115 (.096)
If Live in Female-Headed Household at 14		.090 (.060)		.071 (.060)
Log Likelihood	-16152.6	-16089.6	-15403.3	-15332.1
[N]	[2464]	[2459]	[2464]	[2459]

Source: NLSY Civilian Sample
[a] Liberal Definition: Left school for 6 months or more.
[b] Restrictive Definition: Left school for 12 months or more.
[c] We have included dummy variables for observations with missing responses on these items.

Table 7b
Determinants of School Departure Rates Using Two Definitions of Exit: Young Women Aged 13 to 16 in 1978
(Asymptotic Standard Errors)

	Liberal[a]		Restrictive[b]	
	(1)	(2)	(1)	(2)
Cohort				
14	.056 (.064)	.039 (.065)	.039 (.067)	.017 (.068)
15	.028 (.063)	.026 (.064)	.068 (.066)	.057 (.067)
16	-.214 (.065)	-.194 (.065)	-.077 (.067)	-.064 (.068)
Ethnicity/Race				
Hispanic-White	-.085 (.068)	-.264 (.073)	-.177 (.071)	-.385 (.077)
Hispanic-Non-White	.098 (.102)	-.003 (.104)	.045 (.103)	-.070 (.106)
Black	-.208 (.056)	-.305 (.059)	-.315 (.057)	-.408 (.061)
If Foreign Born	-.434 (.096)	-.473 (.097)	-.452 (.099)	-.494 (.100)
AFQT	-.013 (.001)	-.011 (.001)	-.017 (.001)	-.015 (.001)
Mother's Ed.[c]		-.019 (.009)		-.024 (.009)
Father's Ed.[c]		-.020 (.008)		-.022 (.008)
Family Income[c]		-.008 (.002)		-.006 (.002)
If Live at Home, 1979		-.420 (.092)		.378 (.093)
If Live in, Female-Headed Household at 14		.008 (.059)		-.046 (.060)
Log Likelihood	-15522.8	-15427.3	-14814.4	-14720.3
[N]	[2375]	[2368]	[2375]	[2368]

Source: NLSY Civilian Sample
[a] Liberal Definition: Left school for 6 months or more.
[b] Restrictive Definition: Left school for 12 months or more.
[c] We have included dummy variables for observations with missing responses on these items.

Table 8a
Determinants of Transitions to Employment Using Two Definitions of First Job: Young Men Aged 13 to 16 in 1978
(Asymptotic Standard Errors)

	Liberal[a]		Restrictive[b]		
	(1)	(2)	(1)	(2)	(3)
Cohort					
14	-.029	.032	-.063	-.064	-.068
	(.060)	(.060)	(.072)	(.072)	(.072)
15	-.248	-.247	-.121	-.123	-.107
	(.060)	(.060)	(.072)	(.072)	(.072)
16	-.517	-.515	-.130	-.135	-.113
	(.061)	(.061)	(.073)	(.073)	(.073)
Ethnicity/Race					
Hispanic-White	-.068	-.029	.054	.017	.000
	(.067)	(.070)	(.076)	(.081)	(.081)
Hispanic-Non-White	-.162	-.129	-.199	-.235	-.183
	(.096)	(.100)	(.113)	(.118)	(.117)
Black	-.270	-.286	-.317	-.288	-.308
	(.052)	(.055)	(.062)	(.066)	(.066)
If Foreign Born	-.063	-.038	.154	.129	.096
	(.094)	(.094)	(.108)	(.109)	(.109)
AFQT	.004	.002	-.001	-.001	-.002
	(.001)	(.001)	(.001)	(.001)	(.001)
Mother's Ed.[c]		.012		-.008	-.010
		(.009)		(.010)	(.010)
Father's Ed.[c]		.006		-.019	-.021
		(.007)		(.009)	(.009)
Family Income[c]		.001		.005	.004
		(.002)		(.002)	(.002)
If Live at Home, 1979		-.063		.131	.113
		(.094)		(.115)	(.115)
If Live in Female-Headed Household at 14		.056		-.007	.007
		(.057)		(.068)	(.068)
If Work before School Departure	--[d]	--[d]			.275
					(.070)
Log Likelihood	-16553.5	-16510.3	-12818.6	-12778.9	-12757.5
[N]	[2464]	[2459]	[2464]	[2459]	[2027]

Source: NLSY Civilian Sample
[a] Liberal Definition: Any duration, any hours.
[b] Restrictive Definition: 12 months or more duration and 35 or more hrs per week.
[c] We have included dummy variables for observations with missing responses on these items.
[d] Endogenous to liberal model; not included.

[illegible]

Determinants of Transitions to Employment Using Two Definitions of First Job: Young Women Aged 13 to 16 in 1978 (Asymptotic Standard Errors)

	Liberal[a]		Restrictive[b]		
	(1)	(2)	(1)	(2)	(3)
Cohort					
14	-.195 (.063)	-.188 (.064)	-.017 (.083)	-.015 (.084)	-.010 (.084)
15	-.249 (.063)	-.220 (.063)	-.054 (.082)	-.059 (.083)	-.061 (.083)
16	-.485 (.063)	-.443 (.064)	-.027 (.081)	-.051 (.081)	-.058 (.082)
Ethnicity/Race					
Hispanic-White	-.122 (.067)	-.066 (.070)	.051 (.083)	.047 (.089)	.023 (.089)
Hispanic-Non-White	-.041 (.098)	-.100 (.100)	-.239 (.135)	-.203 (.138)	-.231 (.139)
Black	-.274 (.056)	-.299 (.059)	-.133 (.070)	-.117 (.074)	-.116 (.074)
If Foreign Born	-.021 (.092)	-.021 (.093)	.034 (.114)	.038 (.115)	.019 (.115)
AFQT	.009 (.001)	.008 (.001)	.011 (.001)	.010 (.002)	.008 (.002)
Mother's Ed.[c]		.030 (.009)		-.003 (.012)	-.001 (.012)
Father's Ed.[c]		-.011 (.008)		-.002 (.010)	-.004 (.010)
Family Income[c]		.003 (.002)		.003 (.003)	.003 (.003)
If Live at Home, 1979		.332 (.085)		.261 (.113)	.246 (.113)
If Live in Female-Headed Household at 14		.139 (.058)		-.074 (.075)	.087 (.075)
If Work before school Departure	--[d]	--[d]			.364 (.075)
Log Likelihood	-15573.9	-15501.3	10616.3	10580.9	10568.3
[N]	[2375]	[2368]	[2375]	[2368]	[2368]

Source: NLSY Civilian Sample

[a] Liberal Definition: Any duration, any hours.

[b] Restrictive Definition: 12 months or more duration and 35 or more hrs per week.

[c] We have included dummy variables for observations with missing responses on these items.

[d] Endogenous to liberal model; not included.

Table 9a
Determinants of Transitions From Two Definitions of First School Leaving to First Full-time Job: Young Men Aged 13 to 16 in 1978
(Asymptotic Standard Errors)

	Liberal[a]		Restrictive[b]		
	(1)	(2)	(1)	(2)	(3)
Cohort					
14	-.006 (.073)	-.004 (.074)	-.069 (.077)	-.090 (.077)	-.105 (.077)
15	-.070 (.073)	-.078 (.073)	-.122 (.076)	-.134 (.076)	-.120 (.076)
16	-.025 (.073)	-.037 (.074)	-.078 (.076)	-.092 (.076)	-.060 (.076)
Ethnicity/Race					
Hispanic-White	.091 (.076)	.136 (.080)	.116 (.078)	.188 (.082)	.152 (.082)
Hispanic-Non-White	-.264 (.114)	-.203 (.118)	-.240 (.115)	-.146 (.119)	-.105 (.119)
Black	-.220 (.062)	-.145 (.065)	-.185 (.063)	-.103 (.067)	-.121 (.067)
If Foreign Born	.195 (.109)	.174 (.110)	.213 (.111)	.191 (.112)	.198 (.112)
AFQT	.009 (.001)	.008 (.001)	.011 (.001)	.009 (.001)	.007 (.001)
Mother's Ed.[c]		.001 (.011)		.003 (.011)	.000 (.011)
Father's Ed.[c]		-.007 (.009)		-.001 (.009)	-.005 (.009)
Family Income[c]		.011 (.002)		.015 (.003)	.013 (.003)
If Live at Home, 1979		.170 (.114)		.172 (.117)	.162 (.117)
If Live in Female-Headed Household at 14		-.051 (.067)		.019 (.068)	-.009 (.069)
If Work before School Departure	--	--[d]			.583 (.070)
Log Likelihood	-12422.2	-12374.1	-11678.5	-11633.6	-11584.0
[N]	[2369]	[2364]	[2236]	[2232]	[2203]

Source: NLSY Civilian Sample
[a] Liberal Definition: Left school for 6 months or more.
[b] Restrictive Definition: Left school for 12 months or more.
[c] We have included dummy variables for observations with missing responses on these items.
[d] Endogenous to model; not included.

Determinants of Transitions From Two Definitions of First School Leaving to First Full-time Job: Young Women Aged 13 to 16 in 1978 (Asymptotic Standard Errors)

	Liberal[a]		Restrictive[b]		
	(1)	(2)	(1)	(2)	(3)
Cohort					
14	-.044 (.085)	-.024 (.086)	-.022 (.090)	-.001 (.090)	-.003 (.090)
15	-.060 (.084)	-.048 (.085)	-.013 (.087)	-.005 (.088)	-.018 (.088)
16	-.073 (.083)	.106 (.084)	-.090 (.086)	-.127 (.087)	.129 (.087)
Ethnicity/Race					
Hispanic-White	.074 (.084)	.160 (.090)	.114 (.086)	.220 (.091)	.194 (.091)
Hispanic-Non-White	-.287 (.140)	-.145 (.143)	-.219 (.140)	-.065 (.143)	-.104 (.144)
Black	-.014 (.072)	-.090 (.075)	-.122 (.073)	-.186 (.078)	-.202 (.078)
If Foreign Born	.154 (.118)	.167 (.119)	.257 (.119)	.271 (.119)	.255 (.119)
AFQT	.020 (.002)	.017 (.002)	.023 (.002)	.020 (.002)	.017 (.002)
Mother's Ed.[c]		.011 (.012)		.019 (.013)	.015 (.013)
Father's Ed.[c]		-.012 (.010)		-.016 (.010)	-.012 (.011)
Family Income[c]		.009 (.003)		.007 (.003)	.007 (.003)
If Live at Home, 1979		.317 (.122)		.369 (.125)	.306 (.125)
If Live in, Female-Headed Household at 14		-.113 (.077)		-.097 (.079)	-.124 (.079)
If Work before school Departure	--	--[d]			.617 (.075)
Log Likelihood	-10097.2	-10050.3	-9471.6	-9424.4	-9386.7
[N]	[2254]	[2247]	[2127]	[2120]	[2120]

Source: NLSY Civilian Sample
[a] Liberal Definition: Left school for 6 months or more.
[b] Restrictive Definition: Left school for 12 months or more.
[c] We have included dummy variables for observations with missing responses on these items.
[d] Endogenous to model; not included.

Table 10a
(log) Wage Regressions for Two Definitions
of First Job: Young Men Age 13 to 16 in 1978
(standard errors)

	Liberal[a]		Restrictive[b]	
	(1)	(2)	(1)	(2)
Cohort				
14	.115 (.029)	.091 (.031)	.017 (.031)	.037 (.031)
15	.118 (.030)	.063 (.040)	.032 (.031)	.061 (.031)
16	.137 (.030)	.053 (.051)	.016 (.031)	.046 (.031)
<u>Ethnicity/Race</u>				
Hispanic/White	.029 (.049)	.030 (.049)	.076 (.050)	.071 (.049)
Hispanic/Non White	.150 (.075)	.150 (.075)	.071 (.079)	.071 (.079)
Black	.037 (.033)	.033 (.033)	.043 (.035)	.003 (.036)
If Foreign Born	.085 (.060)	.091 (.060)	.001 (.061)	.024 (.060)
AFQT	.001 (.001)	.000 (.001)	.005 (.001)	.003 (.001)
Mother's Ed[c]	-.001 (.005)	-.001 (.005)	-.001 (.005)	-.003 (.005)
Father's Ed[c]	.002 (.004)	.002 (.004)	.014 (.004)	.010 (.004)
Family Income[c] ('000, $)	.000 (.001)	.000 (.001)	.003 (.001)	.003 (.001)
If Lived at Home, '79	-.077 (.053)	-.075 (.053)	-.055 (.055)	
If Lived in Female Headed Household at Age 14	.033 (.033)	.031 (.033)	.038 (.034)	
Ed. at Job Start		.031 (.016)		.043 (.006)
Exper at Job Start[d]		.003 (.002)		.003 (.000)
If Work before school Departure	—[e]	—[e]		-.102 (.034)
Constant	1.15 (.077)	.972 (.120)	1.17 (.079)	.871 (.088)
R^2 (x100)	1.89	2.20	11.5	17.9
[N]	[2300]	[2299]	[1778]	[1688]

Source: NLSY Civilian Sample
Note: All Models net of foreign birth status
[a] Liberal Definition: any duration, any hours.
[b] Restrictive Definition: 12 months or more and 35 hours or more per week.
[c] We have included dummy variables for observations with missing responses on these items.
[d] Recorded in Weeks: Refers to work experience in unpaid jobs for liberal definition.
[e] Endogenous to outcome; not included in models.

Table 10b
(log) Wage Regressions for Two Definitions of First Job: Young Women Age 13 to 16 in 1978
(standard errors)

	Liberal[a]		Restrictive[b]	
	(1)	(2)	(1)	(2)
Cohort				
14	.096	.050	-.039	-.038
	(.032)	(.035)	(.034)	(.033)
15	.158	.049	-.015	-.018
	(.032)	(.046)	(.034)	(.033)
16	.231	.065	-.022	-.023
	(.033)	(.060)	(.033)	(.032)
<u>Ethnicity/Race</u>				
Hispanic/White	.095	.099	.209	.136
	(.057)	(.056)	(.059)	(.057)
Hispanic/Non White	.173	.196	.099	.050
	(.085)	(.085)	(.098)	(.094)
Black	.106	.097	.147	.075
	(.037)	(.037)	(.039)	(.039)
If Foreign Born	.018	.026	-.009	.011
	(.059)	(.059)	(.063)	(.062)
AFQT	.001	.000	.010	.006
	(.001)	(.001)	(.001)	(.001)
Mother's Ed[c]	-.008	.007	-.017	.007
	(.006)	(.006)	(.006)	(.006)
Father's Ed[c]	-.006	-.006	.001	-.005
	(.004)	(.004)	(.004)	(.004)
Family Income[c] ('000, $)	.001	-.001	.004	.003
	(.001)	(.001)	(.001)	(.001)
If Live at Home, 1979	.008	.009	.035	-.010
	(.052)	(.052)	(.056)	(.054)
If Live in, Female-Headed Household at 14	.038	.039	.054	.054
	(.035)	(.035)	(.036)	(.035)
Ed. at Job Start		.061		.052
		(.018)		(.007)
Exper at Job Start[d]		.0002		.001
		(.0003)		(.000)
If Work before school Departure	—[e]	—[e]		.005
				(.034)
Constant	.863	.492	.556	.267
	(.084)	(.138)	(.092)	(.094)
R^2 (adj)	3.30	3.87	17.03	24.51
[N]	[2190]	[2186]	[1468]	[1389]

Source: NLSY Civilian Sample
Note: All Models net of foreign birth status
[a] Liberal Definition: any duration, any hours.
[b] Restrictive Definition: 12 months or more and 35 hours or more per week.
[c] We have included dummy variables for observations with missing responses on these items.
[d] Recorded in Weeks: Refers to work experience in unpaid jobs for liberal definition.
[e] Endogenous to outcome; not included in models.

Figure 1a

**Timing of Labor Market Entry:
Cumulative Proportions of Young Men Entering First Jobs
Based on Liberal and Restrictive Definitions of Employment**

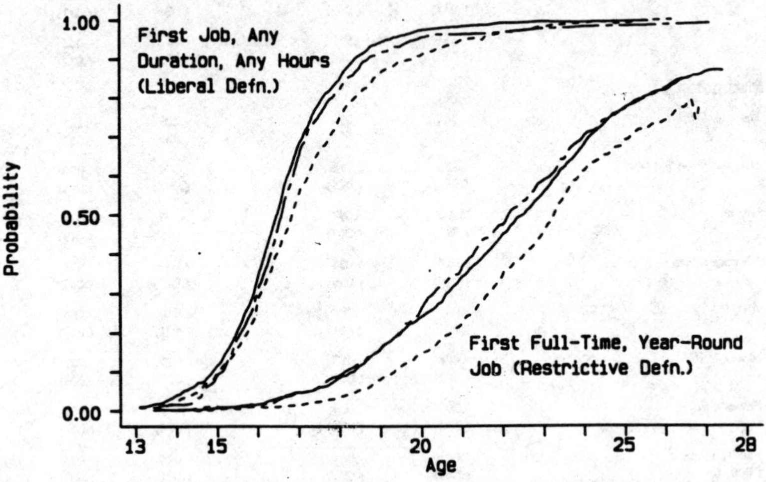

White ——
Black - - -
Hispanic —·—

Figure 1b

Timing of Labor Market Entry:
Cumulative Proportions of Young Women Entering First Jobs Based on Liberal and Restrictive Definitions of Employment

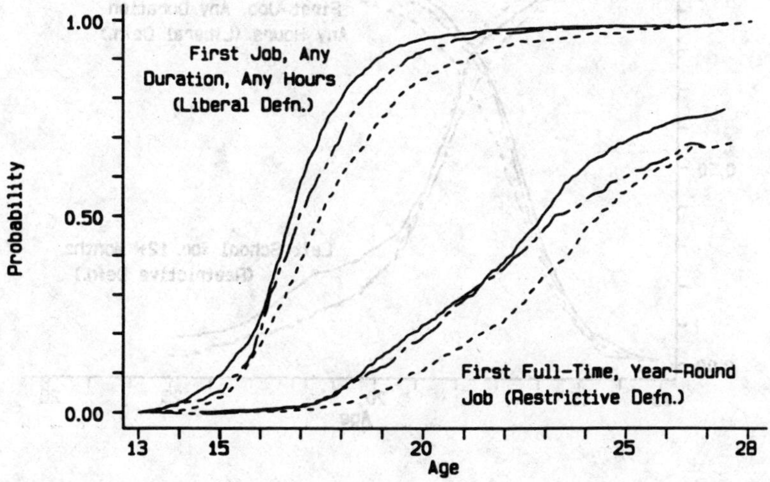

White ——
Black - - -
Hispanic —·—

Figure 2a

Overlap of School and Work:
Cumulative Proportions of Young Men Who Departed School and Began First Jobs of Any Duration or Time Commitment

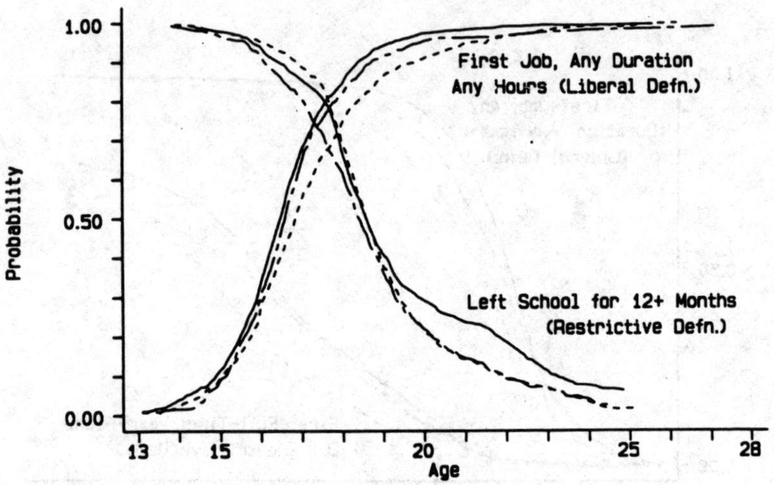

White ——
Black - - -
Hispanic —·—

Figure 2b

**Overlap of School and Work:
Cumulative Proportions of Young Women Who Departed School and
Began First Jobs of Any Duration or Time Commitment**

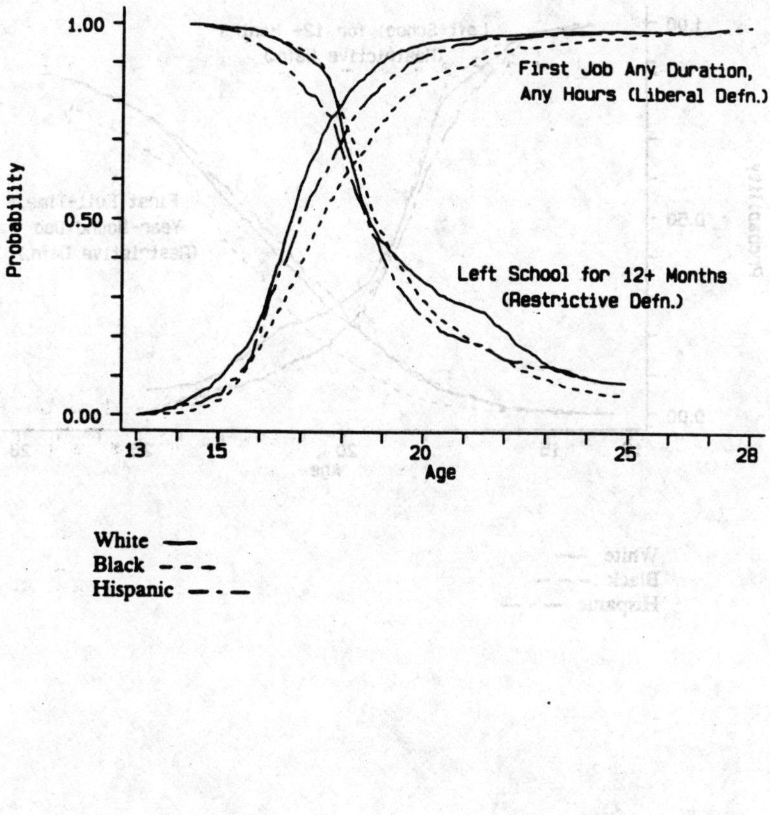

Figure 3a

Overlap of School and Work:
Cumulative Proportions of Young Men Who Departed School and Began First Full Time Job

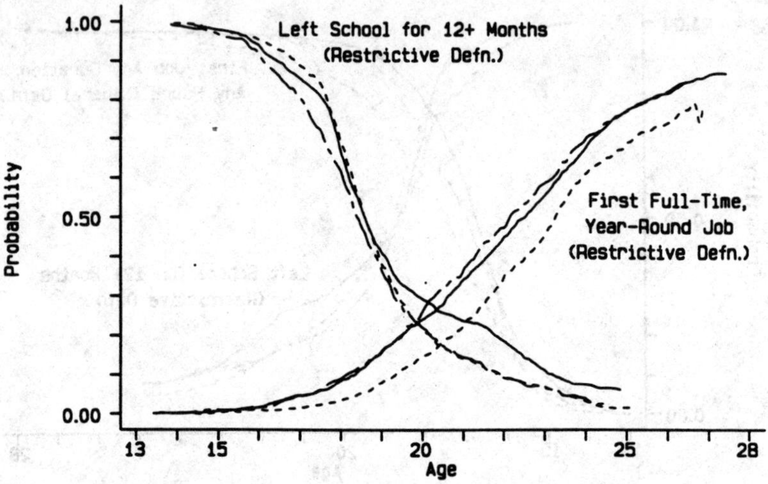

White ——
Black - - -
Hispanic —·—

Figure 3b

Overlap of School and Work:
Cumulative Proportions of Young Women Who Departed School and Began First Full Time Job

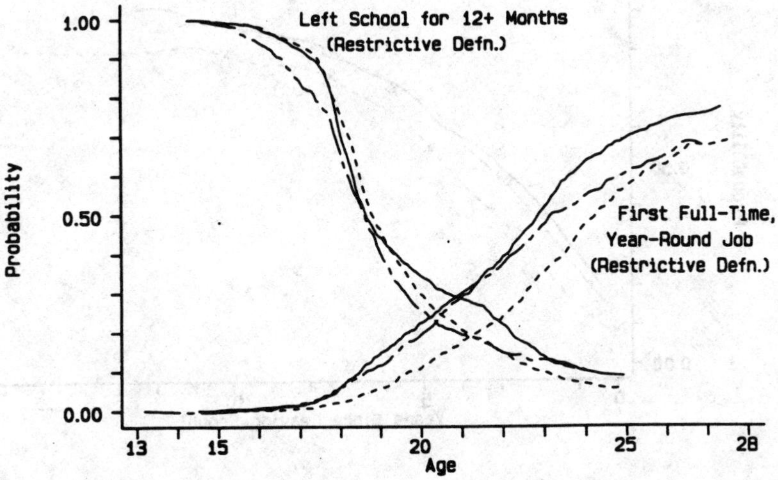

White ——
Black – – –
Hispanic — · —

Figure 4a

Waiting Times from First School Exit (for at least 12 Months) to First Full-Time Job: Young Men

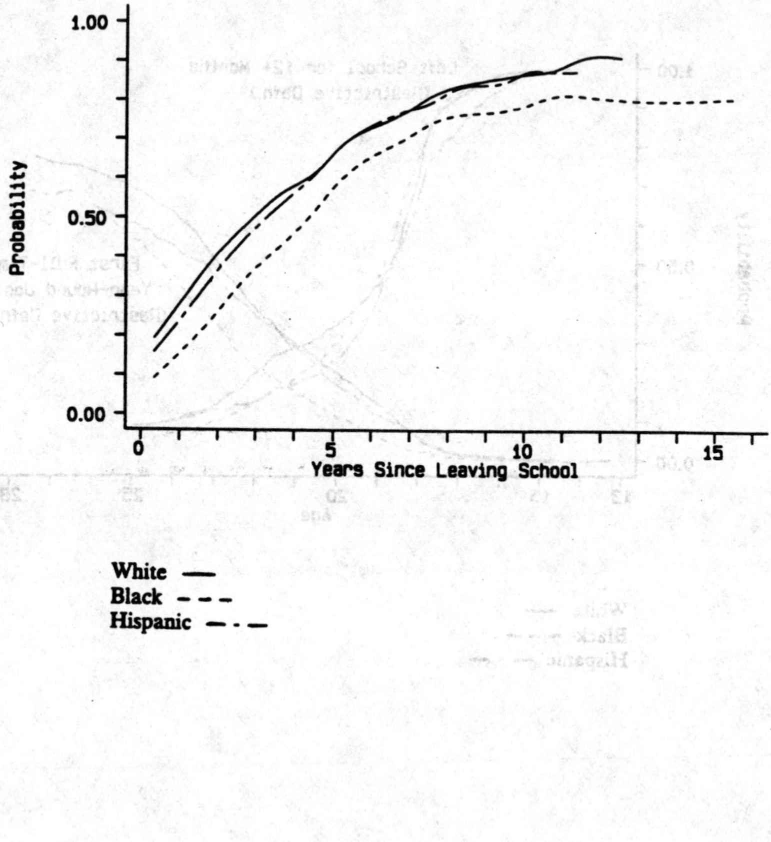

Figure 4b

Waiting Times from First School Exit (for at least 12 Months) to First Full-Time Job: Young Women

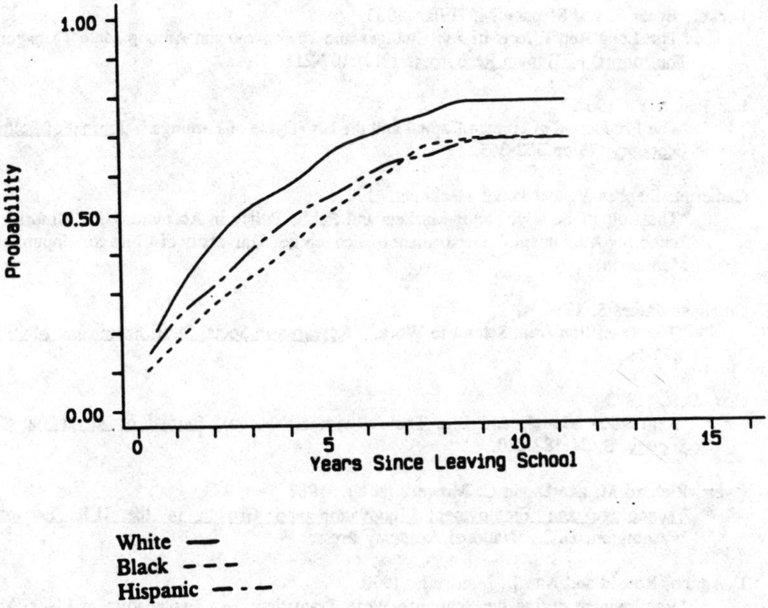

References

Bean, Frank D. and Marta Tienda. 1980.
The Hispanic Experience in the United States. New York. Russell Sage Foundation.

Becker, Brian E. and Stephen M. Hills. 1980.
"Teenage Unemployment: Some Evidence of the Long-Run Effects on Wages." The Journal of Human Resources, 15(3):354-372.

Becker, Brian E. and Stephen M. Hills. 1983.
"The Long Run Effects of Job Changes and Unemployment Among Male Teenagers." The Journal of Human Resources, 17(2):197-211.

Ben-Porath Y. 1967.
"The Production of Human Capital and the Life Cycle of Earnings." Journal of Political Economy, 75 pp.352-365.

Cameron, Stephen V. and James Heckman. 1991.
"The Role of Family, Labor Markets and Public Policy in Accounting for Minority Schooling Attainment." Department of Economics, University of Chicago: Unpublished Manuscript.

Coleman, James S. 1984.
"The Transition from School to Work." Research in Social Stratification and Mobility, 3:27-59.

Cox, D.R. 1972.
"Regression Models and Life Tables (with discussion), Journal of Royal Statistical Society, B, 34:187-220.

Cyert, Richard M. and David C. Mowery (eds.). 1987.
Technology and Employment: Innovation and Growth in the U.S. Economy. Washington, D.C.: National Academy Press.

D'Amico, Ronald and Nan L. Maxwell. 1990.
"Employment during the School-to-Work Transition: An Explanation of Black-White Wage Differentials and Bifurcation of Black Income." Paper presented at 1990 PAA Meeting in Hayward,CA.

Ellwood, David. 1982.
"Teenage Unemployment: Permanent Scars or Temporary Blemishes." In Freeman, Richard B. and David A. Wise (eds.), The Youth Labor Market Problem: Its Nature, Causes and Consequences. Chicago: University of Chicago Press. Freeman, B. Richard and Harry Holzer.

Lynch, Lisa M. 1989.
"The Youth Labor Market in the Eighties: Determinants of Re-employment Probabilities for Young Men and Women." Review of Economics and Statistics, (February):37-45.

Mare, Robert and Christopher Winship. 1984.
The Paradox of Lessening Racial Inequality and Joblessness Among Black Youth:Enrollment, Enlistment, and Employment, 1964-1981." American Sociological Review, 49:39-55.

Mare, Robert, Christopher Winship and Warren Kubitschek. 1984.
"The Transition from Youth to Adult: Understanding the Age Pattern of Employment." American Journal of Sociology, 90(2):326-351.

Marini, Margaret Mooney. 1984.
"The Order of Events in the Transition to Adulthood." Sociology of Education, 57(April):63-84.

Meyer, Robert H. and David A. Wise. 1968.
"High School Preparation and Early Labor Force Experience". In Freeman, Richard B. and David A. Wise (eds.) The Youth Labor Market Problem: Its Nature, Causes and Consequences. Chicago: University of Chicago Press.

Mincer, J. 1962.
"On-the-Job Training: Costs, Returns and Some Implications," Journal of Political Economy, 70, pp. 50-79.

Rindfuss, Ronald R., C. Gray Swicegood and Rachel A. Rosenfeld. 1987.
"Disorder in the Life Course: How Common and Does It Matter?" American Sociological Review, 52(December):785-801.

Rosebaum, James E. 1989.
"What if Good Jobs Depended on Good Grades?" American Educator (Winter):10-15, 40-43.

Shore, Milton F. 1972.
"Youth and Jobs: Educational, Vocational, and Mental Health Aspects." Journal of Youth and Adolescents, 1(4):315-323.

Tienda, Marta and Haya Stier. 1991.
"Joblessness and Shiftlessness: Labor Force Activity in Chicago's Inner City." To appear in volume edited by Christopher Jencks and Paul Peterson.

Wilson, William J. 1987.
The Truly Disadvantaged. Chicago: University of Chicago Press.

Mr. SAWYER. Thank you very much.

Dr. Halperin.

Mr. HALPERIN. Mr. Chairman, my expertise is in tracking the prospects of the approximately 20 million 16- to 24-year-olds who are unlikely to attend post-secondary education at any time during their working years. They are what our Commission on Youth and America's Future has termed "the forgotten half."

Who are the forgotten half? In nonstatistical terms, they are the young people who build our homes, drive our buses, repair our automobiles, fix our televisions, maintain and serve our offices, schools, and hospitals, and keep the production lines of our mills and factories moving.

To a great extent, the forgotten half determine how well the American family, economy, and democracy function. They are also the thousands of young men and women who aspire to work productively but never quite make it to that kind of employment. For these members of the forgotten half, their lives as adults start in the economic limbo of unemployment, part-time jobs, and poverty wages, and, of course, many of them never break free.

In 1988 when our first Forgotten Half report appeared, most Americans mistakenly believed that economic times in this country were good and that the future was very bright. We pointed out then, however, that most young workers had been in an economic depression dating back to at least 1973. Today, of course, all Americans know that our economy is in deep trouble and that our future as a nation is in doubt.

We called then for a variety of actions, both public and private, to reverse this long-term earnings decline. We argued that investment in people, our present and our future workforce, was the only sure path to economic prosperity and social harmony. Invest in workers, we said, and grow the economic pie for all Americans.

Today, however, and unfortunately, we can update the statistics that we used in 1988 to show the falling incomes and the rising poverty rates. If you look at the numbers in the middle of page 2 of the statement, we are talking here about heads of families aged 25 or less. You will notice that the inflation-adjusted income for high school dropouts, for high school graduates, and for those who have one to 3 years of college is substantially less in 1990 than it was in 1973. Indeed, for high school dropouts, in inflation-adjusted dollars, we are talking about purchasing power that is just slightly over half of what it was in 1973.

Only college graduates had a slight increase in purchasing power. If you look at poverty rates among high school dropouts, the increase from 1973 to 1990 was almost 57 percent, for high school graduates the poverty increase was 28 percent, and even college graduates had an increase in poverty rates, but of course much, much smaller; less than 6 percent, compared to the other groupings.

Mr. Chairman, in the question period of the previous panel, you asked where our priority ought to go. That, of course, is not a research question but one of political will, political feasibility, but I do think that the numbers at the bottom of page 2 give you at least one person's response to your question, which is that our young have been getting poorer.

Our older Americans over the age of 65, while there are still many in poverty, many in hard straits, have invariably been doing better. I think that calls for some questioning about priorities and who should pay and who should invest in America's future. I think the numbers there are self-explanatory.

On May 11 of this year, the Census Bureau reported that the percentage of workers unable to support a family of four at the poverty line had sky-rocketed over the past 11 years. In 1979 about 12 percent of all full-time, year-round workers earned below poverty-level wages, but in 1990 that figure had jumped by two-thirds to 18 percent. In other words, almost one worker in five, 14.4 million workers, were earning below the poverty level.

Now the group that we studied, the forgotten half, the non-college-bound, workers under age 25, were especially hard hit. In 1979, about 23 percent of them earned below the poverty line, but by 1990 that percentage had almost doubled to over 43 percent. These were the lowest wages for the largest number of workers in any year since the records were begun in 1964. So the long-term trend starting in 1973 continues and is, of course, quite depressing.

One-fourth of black workers and nearly one-third of Hispanic workers were paid below poverty level wages in 1990, but it is very important to counter some of the prevailing myths and images. Seventy percent of all the low-wage workers were not minority, they were white, nor were the low earners mostly high school dropouts; on the contrary, 77 percent of these low-wage earners had completed high school. Indeed, the proportion of low-earning young workers with a high school diploma rose from 13 percent in 1979 to 21.5 percent in 1990, a jump of two-thirds.

In 1991, the jobless rate for high school graduates not going on to post-secondary education was 25 percent—again, the highest rate since 1983. For 1990/91 dropouts, the official unemployment rate was 40 percent. However, those youth under age 25 who had gone to college enjoyed the lowest unemployment rate, 8.3 percent.

With your permission, Mr. Chairman, I would like to have entered into the record an excellent and up-to-date analysis of the youth unemployment situation in this country prepared by my colleague Alan Zuckerman, who is the executive director of the National Youth Employment Coalition.

There are undoubtedly several reasons for the sharp declines in earnings and for these shocking increases in poverty. However, it is clear to most Americans who think about it that education, training, economic development, international competitiveness, national prosperity—the future of our country, in short—are now interdependent as never before in our history.

Schooling and training pay off. They pay off in higher productivity, higher wages, higher tax yields, and, above all, they pay off in the avoidance of costly social pathologies and costly anti-social behaviors. So, as a people, what do we do? Well, at a very minimum, we have to put a much higher priority in this country on education and training. We need to serve far more than the 1 to 5 percent of the eligible youth who are today served in such programs as the Jobs Corps; as the Job Training Partnership Act; in apprenticeships; in youth service and conservation corps; in career academies; in tech-prep; in cooperative education and the like.

Since even 1 or 2 years of post-secondary education pay off for both the individual and for the society, I think we have to encourage many more young people, perhaps as many as 70 percent of our young people, to continue their academic and their technical skill development after high school. For too long we have been saying to young people, "Graduate from high school, and you'll be on easy street." Well, nothing could be further from the truth. Some post-secondary education for most of our young people is absolutely essential.

Now we don't have in this country national policies. What we have are lots of programs. Last year, in a study we commissioned and published called States And Communities On The Move: Policy Initiatives To Create A World-Class Work Force, we documented 60 different State and local policies, not Federal policies but State and local policies, that governmental leaders and industry leaders and others believe are going to help our young workers become world-class producers. There isn't one answer, there isn't one program. There is a whole series of things that people are trying, and unfortunately, we do not know at this point which are the most effective in cost and benefit terms.

But, as we indicate in the various chapters of States And Communities On The Move, there is major attention being given to the development of a national apprenticeship system with young people, substantially younger than those who are now enrolled in apprenticeship—the average age today is around 29—we are talking now about programs for high school youth, connecting them with community colleges and other institutions.

Tech-prep or so-called 2-plus-2 which endeavors to integrate academic and vocational education and to articulate secondary schools with community colleges and other institutions is spreading with the help of the Carl Perkins Act which the Congress has authorized and funded.

There is also a plan afoot to significantly expand the Job Corps over the next 5 years to increase the number of slots, the number of centers. That is, by most expert opinion, a very cost-effective investment. There is a major study being conducted on how to use the facilities, the personnel, the expertise of the armed forces and the National Guard and their network of people, facilities, and equipment to assist in the training of America's young.

The adolescent female is a particularly important target under the Family Support Act, under the Jobs Program. And then, of course, there are all kinds of local alliances, community alliances, between employers, schools, parents, and young people.

But I want to come to this point. Overall, there is a very unfortunate, perhaps typically American way of doing business, which is that you create lots of programs, lots of categories, and overall there is no system, and there are some very basic questions about what kind of a system do we want to have in this country that have not been satisfactorily answered by anyone.

For example, I list four questions on page 5:

What is the public responsibility to assure that all young people have the opportunity to access needed labor market services, including counseling and training when they first enter the labor market?

What agency or institution, or combination thereof, should have the lead responsibility for providing the specific school-to-employment transition services?

What role should the private sector play in the process, including their role in determining education and training curricula and in financing the system?

Who should be responsible for providing the architectural framework that fits together the pieces of a comprehensive school-to-employment transition system?

These are very large and thorny questions, but I'm confident that we can answer them effectively if we have the will to do so, and that is why I am greatly encouraged by the commitments made by Governor Clinton, by the Democratic Party Platform, on July 14. I just want to quote one section. It said: "A competitive American economy requires the global market's best educated, best trained, most flexible workforce. An expanding entrepreneurial economy of high-skill, high-wage jobs is the most important family policy, the most important urban policy, the most important labor policy, the most important minority policy, and the most important foreign policy that America can have."

We on the Commission, which is a bipartisan commission, certainly hope that the Republican Party convening next month will make similar commitments to investing in our Nation's vital human resources, particularly our youth who are, or will soon be, our country's front line workers.

Thank you, Mr. Chairman.

[The prepared statement of Mr. Halperin follows:]

PREPARED STATEMENT OF SAMUEL HALPERIN, STUDY DIRECTOR, WILLIAM T. GRANT FOUNDATION'S COMMISSION ON WORK, FAMILY, AND CITIZENSHIP

Mr. Chairman: In accepting your invitation to appear here today, I have made it clear that I am neither a demographer nor a statistician. My expertise is in tracking the prospects of the 20 million 16–24 year-olds who are unlikely to attend post-secondary education in their working lifetime. They are what our Commission has termed (in two 1988 reports [1]) "The Forgotten Half." As we wrote:

> Who are the Forgotten Half? In non-statistical terms, they are the young people who build our homes, drive our buses, repair our automobiles, fix our televisions, maintain and serve our offices, schools, and hospitals, and keep the production lines of our mills and factories moving. To a great extent, they determine how well the American family, economy, and democracy function. They are also the thousands of young men and women who aspire to work productively but never quite "make it" to that kind of employment. For these members of the Forgotten Half, their lives as adults start in the economic limbo of unemployment, part-time jobs, and poverty wages. Many of them never break free.
>
> Our study . . . has convinced us that, as young Americans navigate the passage from youth to adulthood, far too many flounder and ultimately fail in their efforts. Although rich in material resources, our society seems unable to ensure that all our youth will mature into young men and women able to face their futures with a sense of confidence and security. This is especially true of the 20 million non-college bound young people we have termed the Forgotten Half.

In 1988, at a time when most Americans mistakenly believed that economic times were good and the future bright, we pointed out that most young workers had been in an economic depression dating back to at least 1973. Now, all Americans know that our economy is in deep trouble and our future as a nation in doubt. We called for a variety of actions—public and private—to reverse this long-term earnings decline. We argued that investment in people—our present and future workforce—was

[1] The Forgotten Half: Non-College Youth in America and The Forgotten Half: Pathways to Success for America's Youth and Young Families.

the only sure path to economic prosperity and social harmony. Invest in our workers, and grow the economic pie for all Americans.

Today, we can update the statistics we used four years ago on falling incomes and rising poverty rates: (The following figures were prepared by Professor Andrew Sum of Northeastern University, Boston.)

Median Incomes (Inflation-adjusted) and Poverty Rates for Young Families with Children, 1973–1990

[By educational attainment of family head]

	Median Income		Poverty Rate Percentage	
	1973	1990	1973	1990
High School Dropout	$18,842	$10,213	32.2	56.6
High School Graduate	28,410	20,000	11.1	28.0
1–3 Years of College	31,710	27,000	8.1	18.2
College Graduate	37,757	38,700	2.1	15.8

Young Get Poorer, Elderly Get Richer, Middle Class Shrinks

[In percent]

	Under 18		Over 65	
	1969	1989	1969	1989
Under Poverty Line	19.4	29.1	42.0	31.5
Middle Income	74.6	62.5	51.3	59.1
High Income	6.0	9.4	6.7	9.4

On May 11, 1992, the Census Bureau reported that the percentage of workers unable to support a family of four at the poverty line had skyrocketed over the past 11 years. In 1979, 12.1 percent of full-time year-round workers earned below poverty-level wages, while in 1990 that percentage had risen to 18—almost one worker in five or 14.4 million workers.

Workers under age 25 were especially hard hit: In 1979, 22.9 percent of them earned below the poverty line, while in 1990 that percentage had almost doubled to 43.4 percent. These were the lowest wages for the largest numbers of workers in any year since records were commenced in 1964.

One-fourth of black workers and nearly one-third of Hispanic workers were paid low wages in 1990. However, 70 percent of all low-wage workers were not minority, but white. Nor were the low earners mostly high school dropouts; 77 percent of them had completed high school. Indeed, the proportion of low-earning young workers with a high school diploma (but no college) rose from 13 percent in 1979 to 21.6 percent in 1990—a jump of two-thirds.

In 1991, the jobless rate for high school graduates not going on to postsecondary education was 25.3 percent, the highest rate since 1983. For 1990–1991 dropouts, the official unemployment rate was over 40 percent. However, those youth under age 25 who had gone to college enjoyed the lowest unemployment rate: 8.3 percent.

With your permission, Mr. Chairman, I would like to have entered into the record an excellent and up-to-date analysis of youth unemployment, Against All Odds, by my colleague Alan Zuckerman, Executive Director, of the National Youth Employment Coalition. I have attached his statement to my own prepared text.

* * * *

There are, undoubtedly, several reasons for these sharp declines in earnings and shocking increases in poverty. However, it is clear that education, training, economic development, international competitiveness and national prosperity are now interdependent as never before.

Schooling and training pay off in higher productivity, higher wages, higher tax yields, and in avoidance of costly social pathologies and anti-social behaviors. So, as a people, we must put a higher priority on education and training. We need to serve far more than 1–5 percent of the eligible youth currently enrolled in programs like Job Corps, JTPA, apprenticeships, youth service and conservation corps, career academies, Tech Prep, cooperative education, and the like.

Since even one or two years of postsecondary education pay off for both the individual and the society, we must also encourage and make it possible for at least 70 percent of our young people to continue their academic and technical skill development after high school.

As we pointed out in our 1991 study, States and Communities on the Move: Policy Initiatives to Create a World-Class Workforce, there are other actions that should be supported at all levels of government and society in order to help our young workers become world-class producers:

• major attention is being given nationwide to developing a youth or student apprenticeship system to meet the needs of persons younger than are now typically enrolled in apprenticeship.

• 2 + 2 Technical Preparation (Tech Prep), which endeavors to integrate academic and vocational education and define a clearer articulation between secondary schools and postsecondary technical training institutions, is spreading with new funding under the Carl Perkins Vocational and Technical Education Act

• a significant expansion of the Job Corps, a youth employment and training program that most experts consider a cost-effective investment, is being advanced in Congress, through the appropriations process, over a five-year period

• major study is being conducted to determine how the Armed Forces and the National Guard, with their network of people, facilities and equipment, can be mobilized in the post-Cold War era to assist in training America's young

• adolescent females are an important target population for the JOBS program under the Family Support Act of 1988

• community alliances involving the business community in facilitating access by youth to the labor market, often modeled after the Boston Compact, continue to develop in various metropolitan areas while a wide variety of school/business partnerships are emerging and becoming more sophisticated and demanding

Overall, there is developing a series of discreet, and sometimes competing, categorical programs. However, basic questions about the character of a school-to-work transition system have not yet been satisfactorily answered. Specifically, there is not yet any agreement on four key questions relative to the school-to-employment transition:

> 1) What is the public responsibility to assure that all young people have the opportunity to access needed labor market services, including counseling and training, when they first enter the labor market?
>
> 2) What agency or institution, or combination thereof, should have lead responsibility for providing specific school-to-employment transition services for young people?
>
> 3) What role should the private sector play in the process, including their role in determining education and training curricula and financing the system?
>
> 4) Who should be responsible for providing the architectural framework that fits together the pieces of a comprehensive school-to-employment transition system?

These are large and thorny questions, but I am confident that we can answer them effectively—if we have the will to do so. And that is why I am greatly encouraged by the commitments made by Governor Clinton and by the Democratic Party Platform adopted on July 14:

> A competitive American economy requires the global market's best educated, best trained, most flexible workforce. . . . An expanding, entrepreneurial economy of high-skill, high-wage jobs is the most important family policy, urban policy, labor policy, minority policy and foreign policy America can have."

We can also hope that the Republican Party, convening next month, will make similar commitments to investing in our nation's vital human resources, particularly our youth who are, or will soon be, our country's front-line workers.

[The analysis prepared by Alan Zuckerman, Executive Director, National Youth Employment Coalition follows:]

UNEMPLOYMENT RATES

• The odds of urban youth having a job are slim. Youth unemployment is double the rate for adults.

• Minority youth unemployment remains double the rate for all youth.

• By official counts, one out of five teenagers (16–19) who is actively looking for work can't find it.

• Nearly three million 16–24 year-olds are actively looking, but can't find a job.

REAL JOBLESSNESS

• The "real jobless rate" for youth is worse. Nearly one out of three teenagers (16–19) is unemployed, has given up looking for a job out of frustration, or has had to settle for a part-time job even though full-time work is needed.

• The "real jobless rate" for teenagers in 1991 was 31.2%

STATE AND CITY TEEN JOBLESSNESS

• Official youth jobless rates are in double digits for all but two states (Nebraska and South Dakota).

• Major cities with the highest teenage jobless rates are: Baltimore, Riverside-San Bernadino (CA), Detroit, New York City, and Phoenix.

WORKING YOUTH

• Only 42% of all teens are working compared to an employment-to-population ratio of 62% for all Americans.

• For urban teens, the situation is most dire. During the first three months of 1992, in New York City, for example, only one out of eight teens were employed.

INTRODUCTION

Youth unemployment has consistently been double the rate for adults and minority youth unemployment has remained double the rate for all youth. Unemployment is not spread evenly across the country and the odds of getting a job are much lower for youth living in major cities than for youth living outside major urban areas.

SMALL PERCENTAGE OF TEENAGERS WITH JOBS

If that's not bad enough, the Bureau of Labor Statistics (BLS) Employment to Population ratio, paints a far more severe, and disturbing, picture of the employment prospects for young people in our major cities getting jobs and entering the mainstream. BLS's Current Population Survey documents the percent of all youth, rich or poor, Black or White, Anglo or Hispanic, who have jobs. Nationally, at the time of the BLS survey, 42.1% of all 16–19 year-olds were employed, as compared with 62.1% of the total civilian population. However, in 1991, only 16.9% of all 16–19 years-olds in New York City were employed. That means that only one in six New York City teenagers had a job. And it's getting worse. For the first three months of 1992, the employment/population ratio for 16–19 year-olds dropped to 12.6%. (See The New York Times, June 2, 1992). In other words, only one of every eight teenagers in New York City is working. While New York is the toughest place for teens, a teen's prospects are only slightly better in Chicago (22.5%) or Los Angeles (29.5%).

The sample is too small to identify the ratio of teenage workers to all teens in poor, inner city neighborhoods like Bedford-Stuyvesant, Anacostia, North Philadelphia, Watts, or Roxbury. But we do know that minority unemployment has run double the rate for all youth. If we assume that ratio applies to the employment/population ratio and use the 1991 figure of only one in six New York City teenagers with a job, a reasonable estimate would be that one in twelve youth in poor, minority urban communities are employed. How do young people, especially poor young people, learn the basic rules about a job, if they have only a one in twelve chance of having a job?

UNEMPLOYMENT RATES

In May 1992, the official national unemployment rate rose to 7.5%. 9,500,000 people who were looking for employment could not find a job. The news for young people was even more discouraging with official youth unemployment at 14.5% in May. This rise in unemployment is occurring at a time when the civilian labor force grew by more than 330,000 jobs in May, with an average growth of more than 300,000 jobs since November, 1991.

Millions of 16–24 year-olds are graduating from high school and college and their unemployment rate is 14.5%, which means that 2,960,000 16–24 year-olds can't find a job. For 16–19 year-olds the unemployment rate is even higher: 20% in May. These figures tell a story of dashed hopes and uncertainty for millions of young people.

There is a broad gulf between society's message of opportunity and hope, "stay in school, work hard, learn a skill," which is as American as apple pie, and the harsh reality of 14.5% official unemployment rates. If you are age 16–19, one out of every five of your peers who is looking for a job can't find one. High unemployment rates and low wages create a skepticism among many young people, especially the "forgotten half," those who are unlikely to enroll in postsecondary education.

According to the William T. Grant Foundation Commission on Work, Family and Citizenship, "The basic truth faced by too many youth is that regardless of how well schools do their job and regardless of how well high school graduates learn basic skills, most large, established employers typically wait until these same youth—with no greater educational skills and no advanced work skills—reach age 20–22, even 25, before hiring them." (The Forgotten Half, 1988) Unfortunately, young workers are not prized, nurtured and developed by the American economy.

STATE AND CITY JOBLESS RATES

The current recession continues to take a heavy toll on all areas. Real joblessness has increased by 19% since the recession began in June 1990. In America's largest metropolitan areas, real joblessness is up by 29%.

The official unemployment rate for teenagers in 1991 was in the double digit range in all but two states (Nebraska and South Dakota). When the numbers of teenagers who have given up the job search out of frustration and those who have had to settle for part-time jobs even though they want full-time work are taken into account, the "real jobless rate" for youth was 31.2% in 1991. In America's largest cities, the real jobless rate for teenagers was 34.5%. Major cities with the highest teenage jobless rates in 1991 were Baltimore (46.1% real youth jobless rate); Riverside-San Bernadino (CA) (45.7% real youth jobless rate); Detroit (44.8% real youth jobless rate); New York City (41.9% real youth jobless rate); and Phoenix (40% real youth jobless rate).

ROADBLOCKS TO EMPLOYMENT

Perhaps the geography and economy of inner cities is wrong for young people. The jobs in the central core demand high skills while the new shopping malls and expanding service economy are more often located in the suburbs. Urban youth live in proximity to jobs for which they lack qualifications while the jobs in the suburbs are beyond their reach for lack of adequate transportation.

Even recent high school graduates and college graduates face a tight job market. Young people who have stayed in high school and graduated find themselves competing with dropouts for low-paying service jobs which require minimal education. Even college graduates are finding the transition to work difficult and entry-level management positions few and far between. The hopes of young job applicants are being dashed by the harsh reality of today's job market.

The current economy is placing roadblocks in the way of young people of all incomes, education, ethnicity and geography as they seek summer jobs. While the dropout might have the toughest chance of getting a job, anecdotal evidence and stories on television and in the press support the impression that high school and college graduates are having a difficult time getting a job this summer. As one employer told me recently, "How can I hire youth this summer, when I have laid off people who have worked with me for years?"

THE COSTS

My greatest fear is that when the odds of succeeding and getting a job which can support a family are this low, many young people reach the conclusion that they don't have chance. Despair and hopelessness lead to destructive behavior. When these perceptions are based on reality, it is difficult for the teacher in elementary school or high school or the vocational instructor or counselor in a "second chance" program to convince young people that there is a payoff for doing well in school. There is no way to measure this change in attitude, but we shouldn't underestimate its effect.

Lost productivity is impossible to measure, but idle labor is as wasteful as idle capital. If we could harness the energy of almost three million unemployed 16–24 year-olds, we could produce more goods and services and increase demand as young workers purchase food, clothing and services. When youth are employed and learn a skill, it leads to self-sufficiency.

The social costs of crime, welfare, and vandalism are apparent. Los Angeles reminded us that wholesale destruction is still a possibility. But these visible symptoms are small compared to the losses when youth don't believe they have a future.

For example, University of Chicago sociologist William Julius Wilson suggests one measure of social costs is a Marriageability Index. His thesis is that it is rational for many young women not to want to marry the father of their child because the chances of his getting a job are slim. Many young women choose to be single parents rather than accept responsibility for dependent children and a dependent father.

INVESTING IN YOUTH—THEY ARE OUR FUTURE

To paraphrase H.L. Mencken: For every complex problem, there is a solution which is obvious, simple to implement, inexpensive—and wrong. There is no quick, easy and cheap solution to the dilemma of joblessness among young workers. We need to improve the skills and capacity of youth; that's the supply side. And we need to create more jobs; that's the demand side. Finally, we have to make a special effort in large cities, where unemployment is most severe.

The National Youth Employment Coalition's members work with youth and with organizations that help youth make this difficult transition to work and self-sufficiency. Preparation for work must begin in elementary school. Employment competencies must be built into child and youth development. Finally, we must maintain and build a first-rate "second chance" system for youth who need an extra boost. However, all of this human development will be wasted unless we create more demand for young workers, especially in our cities. The demand side is difficult, but it must include apprenticeship, youth service and conservation corps, and other service and job creation efforts. We must also help employers to recruit, train and hire young workers. A growing economy and a society committed to genuine full employment is essential to the future of our nation.

Mr. SAWYER. Thank you both.

Just on that last note, while I appreciate the citation of at least one, I note that both parties have been arguing that they are somehow agents of change going on right now. The truth of the matter is that change is going on and what they need to do is to compete to help move this Nation in a way that makes those currents productive instead of beating against the current and destroying that very fragile ship that is our Nation in the process. Change is happening, and it is happening at a pace that we need to be able to understand and measure, and I appreciate your comments with regard to that.

The supplementary documents that you both offer, both Dr. Tienda and Dr. Hotz's paper as well as Alan Zuckerman's paper, will be included as part of the record of this hearing.

Let me ask you a question about several dimensions of the same problem. I talked to the previous panel about some of that. You both have referred to the kind of education and post-secondary training that yield income advantages, and you have talked about those that yield a measure of employment stability. Looking at some of the different segments of our population, which is more important, or are they simply different dimensions of the same phenomenon?

Ms. TIENDA. I don't think it is an either/or issue. This is a country that is founded on inequality, and the real question is: What are the tolerable limits of inequality that we are willing to sustain?

In my judgment, we have learned to tolerate levels of inequality that are virtually incompatible with our democratic philosophy and our ideology of equality of opportunity. There is no equality of opportunity in this country for some people, and what we need to do is make sure that we do at least provide that chance. One cannot look at the results for young black men and say that they have opportunity.

So if we have the political will to reduce inequality in this country, then we will not have the rising poverty rates that we have. If we have rising poverty rates for everybody, then we have to ask:

Why is it that some people have much higher rates of rising poverty than others? Those are the issues that we have to address.

If the country is in a recession, of course there is going to be rising poverty and there is going to be rising unemployment. That begs the question as to why some groups are more vulnerable to that rising inequality. If it is a matter of education, that is something where one can intervene and try to design a responsible policy for. If it is a matter of your color, your birthplace, and your gender, then I think the problem is much more difficult but, nonetheless, equally important to deal with head on.

Mr. HALPERIN. I think it is important that we not put all the burden for change on the education and training system. Those are major social institutions, and they have a heavy load to bear. But in our study of "the forgotten half," we pointed out the things that could be done to strengthen the family, to strengthen the community, to use the workplace as an educational institution, to use young people themselves as a resource to solve many of the problems of our society, and, of course, to strengthen and improve the education and training system.

I would point out, as Dr. Tienda did, that these things are not neatly separable. We know that educational attainment—that is to say, more years of schooling—correlates with greater physical health, greater family stability, two-parent families, greater participation in civic activity, in voting, all of these things are important to the flourishing of our society. So we can't think solely in terms of income.

I titled my paper "Education, Training, Competitiveness, And Economic Development." It could have been, "How do you save American democracy?"

Mr. SAWYER. I think you are right. I think it really is at the very pivot point of what we are talking about in these hearings.

I asked the question in that way, though, because you just touched on it when you talked about the role of the workplace itself in terms of training. The truth of the matter is that, however informal it may have been, the workplace has been the locus of continuous training for the American workforce as equipment, techniques, materials changed over time, never more rapidly than in the last quarter of a century. The American worker who has been in the workplace has benefited from that and elevated to the degree that he has been able to remain in the workplace.

We have a very great tension that is rapidly evolving, however, where we are seeing increasing rates of unemployment among particular categories of teens and young adults who do not have that purchase on that first entry point for durable work opportunities. At the same time, we are seeing the potential for rapidly exploding shortages in specific categories of work opportunities as that population bulge moves beyond its primary years and out of entry-level positions and finally into retirement.

There is a real tension there. If stability and entry, regardless of wage, is not there, then we do not have the locus of the best opportunity, the best traditional opportunity, that we have had for continued education and training. In fact, if we think in terms of the amount of capital plant that is allocated to education in this country, we are barely keeping pace, given the movement of population, with the ability to educate young people whose populations are as mobile as they have become. It is just very difficult for school systems, just to reduce it to its lowest common denominator, to plan for the long-term demographic consequences of the hills and valleys that they have been experiencing over the last 20 years and are likely to continue to experience, regardless of birth rate, just given the mobility of the Nation.

Mr. HALPERIN. I have stressed the importance of thinking systematically because, for example, the youth unemployment and underemployment problem has been with us for well over a generation. This is not a recent phenomenon. In general, the unemployment rate for young people is double what it is for adults. This won't be solved by thinking of a stopgap program with a few million or even a few billion dollars. We have to think about the whole transition from adolescence into adulthood and responsible participation not merely as workers but also as parents and as citizens.

Again, I refer to States and Communities on the Move because it shows that there is a lot of creative thought going on around the country, but we don't have any overall plan. We haven't figured out yet whose responsibility it is to pay for this, what is the proper role of business. Our leading employers know that they must invest in their workforces, otherwise they will not be competitive. Unfortunately, something like only one-half of 1 percent of our 19 million employers invest in the upgrading of their workforce.

So we need a national policy that goes beyond schools and goes beyond youth but encourages employers.

Mr. SAWYER. It would give investment tax credits, for example, for the kind of investment in human skills levels that are the concomitant of elevated production techniques. As equipment becomes obsolete, workers become obsolete with them. If we could invest in, or, as we once did, if we were to resume the kind of investment in new capital equipment necessary to keep the Nation productive, it would be of little use without comparable investment in the skills to keep it functional.

Ms. TIENDA. There are very good projections available from the Department of Labor, the Bureau of Labor Statistics, on what occupations, what industries, at a very detailed level, are expected to grow and how much they are expected to grow. Those projections are not off the map in the sense that they are not for the year 2050 but for the year 2000 and the year 2010. Those are the years that we are talking about moving the kids who are now in school into the workforce.

So, in a sense, there could be a goal that one could strive for if we began to to try to match the demand side of the equation, which we can produce kind of as independent tabulations, and the supply side, which we produce demographically in terms of differential rates of growth, with some surprises because of immigration and booms and busts in certain age groups, but, in the main, we do have the parameters of that matching. What we haven't done is put in place the programs to try to make the match happen.

Along those lines, what we have done has been—I believe our policy failure is precisely the point that Dr. Halperin was emphasizing, that we don't have the follow-through. We try for a lot of quick fixes. We do a program—for example, millions of dollars to spend on the STEP program. It is a well conceived program, but you cannot get kids from the inner city who are disadvantaged, give them two summers of training, a quasi-program of school enrichment while everybody else is catching up to them, so they slide behind, and do it again another summer.

The main effect is getting them a job, and then after, when they really need it, when they enter high school, when they are most at risk to dropping out is when we stop the program. That doesn't make any sense.

I mean one can look at it rationally and say, "Why did we spend so much money on a program and then want to replicate it in every possible JTPA site we could find?" You know, I have to scratch my head and say this doesn't make any sense, but it seemed like we had a good thing going and we were pretending to do something for disadvantaged youth. Pretending doesn't help.

Mr. SAWYER. I hope we were doing more than pretending. I hope we were learning something about what works and what doesn't. But clearly, as a question of scale, it hasn't been sufficient. It hasn't been a failure of programs, it has been an unavailability of programs on any scale that might have made a difference.

We are looking at a population bulge that is going to have real consequences. We have looked to the consequences for programs like Social Security and have begun to make the decisions now necessary to accommodate the inevitable consequences of that into the future.

But it comes to the question of a productive population rapidly moving, in a very short period of time, into a dependent population, followed on by a less well trained workforce in terms of the needs of the workplace, and smaller population in size. It seems to me that one of the things we are likely to see is a retention of trained workers who have had that purchase on the workplace for a long period of time and the training and education that goes with being in an active job being retained in that workplace for a longer period. The consequences in terms of entry-level opportunities for that following generation are critical, just as are the opportunities for promotion, so that what was once an entry-level job with a ladder in front of it, or increasingly, a series of trapezes, simply becomes a step-stool on to which you step and stand for an extended period of time. We have got to come to grips with that.

Does any of the work that you have done give us any hint as to the direction we might follow as we deal with what I see as a likely consequence between this intergenerational competition?

Ms. TIENDA. I think the policies are more than just focusing on the workers and their employability. That is only half of the equation. The other half is exactly as you suggested on the changing character of the job opportunities.

There has been a considerable amount of work by economists, predominantly those in the Northeast, NBER and affiliated institutions, that document the trend in wage growth and what are the forces driving the flatness and the slower wage growth. So that doesn't affect only young and minority workers, it affects all the workers, which is why the poverty rates and the differences in income have been flattened out during this period.

61-412 O - 94 - 11

So the question is, why did we let the minimum wage stay as low as it has for so long and allow that amount of purchasing power for the very poor to take place? Why have we seen the deterioration of unions that have made possible for semi-skilled workers a family wage, that was possible in the seventies, and that is what is basically driving—two of the forces that are driving the wage inequities at all levels.

So it is not just a credentials/schooling phenomenon, because if we had suddenly a society where everybody had a high school education, we would still have substantial inequality, and we have to come to grips with that because the quick fix from a policy standpoint is, get these kids out of school. Well, they are graduating, and the most telling case is the experience of young blacks, because they have the highest graduation rates of the minority population.

And look at young girls. Even those who are teen mothers have higher high school continuation rates given that they have had a birth. So does that guarantee them a pathway to a successful family life or longer-term trajectory? and the answer to that is a very mixed one; some of them get out, and some of them don't.

So it is not a guarantee, and once we come to terms with that and say, well, what is necessary for people to have family wage, for workers to have a family wage so that they don't have poverty wages, and we are willing to deal with that, then we can ameliorate the problems that we are discussing, and that will provide incentives for young kids who have all the competing opportunities on the streets. We are competing minimum wages that we know are inadequate with many lucrative opportunities on the streets. It is a hard act to follow in some cases where all they see are hope and despair.

Mr. SAWYER. Dr. Halperin.

Mr. HALPERIN. We have some status problems that have to be confronted. The fact of the matter is, the American people seem to have bought into the notion that to be a success you have got to be a college graduate—"dumb people" don't go on after high school, they go into the workforce; the smart people go to college—and, in fact, the Census Bureau makes it very clear, the rewards for going on to college are very pronounced. But we have got to break that. We have got to show parents and students that there are important occupations that lead to high wages, that lead to the ability to get married, to have children, to have a home, to buy an automobile, and to educate your own children.

The problem there is that many people don't know about those new occupations and what is required to be able to succeed in them. Our counselors don't know, our teachers don't know; many of these jobs were not here 20 years ago.

Employers take on a large part of this role in various industries, but we need more employer participation, because it is not only a question of their immediate workforce needs, it is also a question of whether these young people will be able to buy the products and the services that employers have to offer. In other words, we really all prosper or we all suffer.

That is a long-range view, and, of course, in many parts of American life we have been characterized by very short-range thinking.

That has got to be broken, and we have to think systematically and think about the different contributions that have to be made.

The necessity for much larger investments in post-secondary education is now upon us; I think we have to recognize this.

Relating back to your question to the previous panel about minority teachers, I think we need bold thinking. We have a number of programs to encourage young people to think about teaching as a career. We have Teach For America; we have the Teacher Corps Reborn; we have specialized programs for engineering and for science and mathematics. But why not a more universal program such as has been proposed, again by one of the candidates, to let someone study anything that he or she wants to study, get all the money necessary to buy that training, and then pay it back, pay it back with either community service in teaching or in law enforcement or in social work, etc., or through a surcharge upon your income tax? I don't think that is a partisan proposal, I think that is a question of how do you build from models and demonstrations and puny programs to something universal that opens up opportunity to everyone.

Mr. SAWYER. In fairness, there are supporters of similar proposals on both sides of the aisle in this Congress, but it will almost certainly require that kind of presidential leadership to make it happen on a scale necessary to have the kind of consequence that you are talking about.

Mr. HALPERIN. I would like to make it clear, I know that President Bush has sent up legislation with regard to youth apprenticeship, with regard to systemization of the Job Training Partnership Act, and all of these things are to the good. None of them, however, on either side of the aisle, address the magnitude of the problem and the opportunity that lies before us.

Mr. SAWYER. We are in agreement on that.

Let me shift. You both suggested earlier, in one way or another, our lack of information, particularly about some immigrant populations. Let me ask you a series of questions about that. What do we know about the consequences that the age of immigrants, at the point at which they arrive in the United States, has on their participation in the workforce? What do we know about educational backgrounds of immigrants?

I have done a good deal of work in literacy questions, and one of the real abrasion points is that there are enormous numbers of people who are illiterate in English and perfectly literate in their first language.

What do we know about variation in the point when immigrant children enter the school system, and how does that affect their performance in school?

Finally, I guess, what kinds of training do immigrant populations, as diverse as they are, bring with them that have proven most helpful in making the kind of transition to the workplace successfully that we need to learn from? And, I guess as a part of that, what kinds of additional training do we need to look toward? The whole range of questions is about a portion of our population that has never been as significant as it is today.

Ms. TIENDA. I think that is a very large area about which we are just beginning to gain some understanding, and it is important, I think, to make a distinction between immigrants and refugees, because the kind of support, the social contract, if you will, between the Federal Government and immigrants versus refugees is very different. So that is a starting point.

Mr. SAWYER. Both phenomena had a very high level by comparison to the recent years.

Ms. TIENDA. Absolutely. But for the immigrant population, it is more indirect. It is through the schools, and it is not in any kind of direct assistance, as is provided for refugees, because there are many cash assistance programs and health assistance programs that are available to refugee populations that are not available to immigrants, and, in fact, there is a moratorium. I have gone through all the legislation recently on immigration where the Congress specifically prevents legal immigrants from having any access to means-tested income programs for a period of 3 years. For the legalized population, that was extended to 5 years.

But the broader questions that you ask, I think, don't admit of any easy answers, because you find, for example, if you just focus on the Asian population, there is a big myth that has to be debunked, and it can only be done if we begin to ask questions and document what this population is all about, the myth of the model minority. The Asians are becoming very, very frustrated with that mythology because they are extremely diverse, and one of the very striking statistics that I saw for the San Diego School District compared the native populations, immigrants, the Hispanics, blacks, and various Asian groups. The Hmong had extremely high test scores, and they come from a background of extreme disadvantage. It is not the case, apparently, in Minnesota.

Some of the research that has been done at ISR into this population shows that there are some very interesting patterns that make that possible, and that has to do with the sib ship structure, where the older siblings sit down with the younger siblings and help them through their homework because they cannot go to their parents who don't speak the language, and any of us who have taught at all and tutored realize that you learn the material when you tutor. That is how I learned statistics. I was tutoring other people, but I got paid for it, so I had to learn it. I had an incentive. But I learned statistics that way.

So that sort of solves that little mystery, but there are many Asian groups who have an enormous amount of pressure to go in what their parents consider to be safe occupations: "No, we don't want you in humanities, we don't want you into drama, we want you in a safe occupation, engineering and science," and they get a lot of pressure from the other side. Even if they get to institutions like the University of Chicago, it is enormous pressure that they experience when getting a B-plus for them is seen as something terrible, and they want to know why they got a B-plus.

The amount of pressure that you feel, and you have that kind of experience with Hispanic students, who are also at the University of Chicago. Some of them, as I was telling the dean, can hardly write a paragraph. How did they get through the system, and how did we admit them, and are they going to go through another revolving door?

So we have a range of outcomes, and I don't think to place all the blame on the school system is a problem, but I think there have been some ill-fated programs like bilingual education that, in idea, and theory, and conception, was very illuminated but in actual implementation and execution has turned into many, many disastrous consequences where it has served to accentuate inequality rather than prevent it and minimize it.

So the immigrant experience does pose very large challenges to our school system. We did not find any effects of immigrant status, however, on the school-to-work transition. The immigrant status never emerged as a significant predictor once you standardized for family backgrounds and AFQT scores.

The problem is, in reality, we can't standardize people the way we can do it statistically. So all of that is kind of a big spoof for what the world might be if we could social engineer at every level, and that does raise again questions of what it is that are the ability or aptitude or experience differences that manifest themselves as differences by immigrant status and by national origin.

Mr. HALPERIN. One of your colleagues on the other side of the Hill likes to say that we need not merely simplifiers but complexifiers, and indeed we need a great deal more research about what works for different ethnic and racial groupings.

But my understanding of this general field is that the worst thing we can do is try to tailor programs to different racial or ethnic minorities. We have many successful programs. The Rockefeller Foundation has funded, with substantial numbers of millions of dollars, training programs which have very high success rates among folks who happen to be predominantly Hispanic, for example, in San Jose, CA, and elsewhere, but they didn't set out to create a program that would work for Hispanics, they tried to incorporate some of the principles of best practice that Dr. McBay referred to earlier in the last panel.

Mr. SAWYER. And it is that about which I am asking rather than the specific programs for specific populations. Rather, what are we learning from a variety of populations about what works best generally?

Mr. HALPERIN. Well, again, you have a listing in her testimony of some of those principles, but my understanding is that, first of all, the programs need to be intensive rather than the kind of drop in/drop out kind of programs. They have to be intensive and extensive over a period of time.

The average JTPA program, for example, invests about $1,800 to $2,300 for a young person, or older worker, over maybe 16 weeks. That is not enough to make up for a lifetime of problems and disadvantage. There has to be extensive investment in the same way that, as a nation, we invest something like $5,000 per year per higher education student over 4 years or more. So there is $20,000 versus an $1,800 to $2,300 investment.

It has to be interprofessional. Anyone who thinks that educators have the answers or that trainers have the answers or that the health profession has the answers or that social workers have the answers is foolish. We need collaboration on a scale that we have never enjoyed before to cross these professional lines.

Those are some of the principles, and there is a very simple one, and that is, the more time you spend on tasks, the more you learn, and we don't work hard enough. Our expectations, our standards, for what we demand of our students of all ages are not high enough. So it isn't just a Government program, people have to invest more of themselves in success. But it is not one or another of these principles of success; we need them all involved in our program design.

Ms. TIENDA. For immigrant children, we cannot compromise on the importance of English and acquiring English skills early on. And I'm not against maintaining second languages—both of my children are fluent in Spanish—but it is absolutely essential that adequate proficiency in English be acquired very quickly in the schooling career, and that is where I think we are making a mistake in trying to be too accommodating where the total immersion programs or the transitional programs are going a little too far. We should insist that the acquisition of English skills is not compromised in any way, shape, or form, because that is essential to work in the United States, enclaves notwithstanding.

So I think the research is very clear on the importance of English ability. It does limit options, and it is an accumulating disadvantage that plays itself out in all sorts of ways in the workforce.

Mr. SAWYER. It is a debate that has gone on for a long time in this country and one that is likely to intensify again as a product of increased need, but I cannot disagree with you about the critical importance of language acquisition. It is fundamental.

What does it tell us when we see the dramatic increase in poverty rates—if poverty rates are one measure of success or lack of it—among those with one to 3 years of college? Does it tell us about the kinds of jobs that people are looking for or that are accessible to that level of education? What does it tell us about that kind of outlook at the same time that we advocate that that level of training and education is an absolute necessity, a growing necessity, in the course of the coming decade?

Dr. Halperin, can you help me?

Mr. HALPERIN. I think it tells us more and more and more. That is to say, while there has been a dramatic increase in the poverty rate among those who have had one to 3 years of college, that increase has been substantially less than among those who have less than one to 3 years of college. That is to say, we have got to make it possible for people to act on their own observation of the real world.

People know that you have to have skills to sell in the marketplace, and that is why, in Dr. Sweet's testimony you will recall, he pointed out that the so-called nontraditional student is no longer nontraditional; that is the majority now. People who are 27 years old—that is the median age now in our colleges and universities—30 years old, 40 years old, 50 years old need more education and training. We have these cliches about life-long learning, but it is real. People are going to have to be trained and retrained many times in their working lives.

Mr. SAWYER. The cliche—if I could interrupt for just a second—I think goes back to the myth that we have been living with for the last 20 years that people somehow are going to take a hiatus and retrain in large-scale ways two or three times in the course of a working lifetime. That is just not going to happen with any large number of people. The real hope is to find an opportunity for training and learning in the course of that working lifetime as a part of work.

I'm sorry to interrupt.

Mr. HALPERIN. I think we need to look at other countries' experience in solving these same problems. Other countries have known for a long time that unless they export they will die. So they have constructed systems—again, systems—so that at any age a person in Sweden, for example, can go back to a training center and get new skills in a new profession or upgraded skills in his existing profession. We don't do that in the United States. We make people run through all kinds of hoops, swear poverty, swear incompetence or something, before we will give them very minimal training. That, I think, is one of our big needs for reshaping our own thinking.

We have to provide the wherewithal for people who want that training to be able to afford it. You have a mortgage to pay, you need transportation to get to that training program, you may need medicine for your kids or for yourself. This is not charity, this is not philanthropy, this is an investment, because when that worker gets the new skills he or she will be able to pay it back to the Treasury in the form of higher tax payments for State, local, and Federal Government.

Economists have long urged us to make a distinction between investment and spending. They are not the same. When we pay off the savings and loan crisis, there isn't anything that comes back to us in the way of productive investments. When we invest in our workforce, we are going to get something back.

Ms. TIENDA. May I suggest that part of the reason that these are higher over time, one way you could produce these numbers, especially among the college graduates, is that the waiting time from school departure to actually landing a job has increased. It could be either search costs have been increasing, and I think there is substantial evidence of a lot of unemployed college graduates. Eventually many of them are going to get a job, but sometimes it takes them longer. If they are a mechanical engineer, they may get a job in some nonmechanical-engineering firm, but they will get some wages. In the meantime, if you use a cross-sectional measure to capture poverty rates you are losing a lot of the dynamics, and I think the Survey of Income and Program Participation is better geared to help us disentangle that hiatus.

For youth, the various groups that we looked at in NLSY, we show an average from school departure to full-time job of 3.6 months. That is a long time, and if you amortize that over a year it can put you into poverty if you are only going to get a low-wage job. So one has to calibrate this with respect to some time references. The poverty rates are based on annualized measures, and then we have a snapshot, and that seems to be a very important circumstance.

Mr. SAWYER. I keep mentioning that I'm going to ask all of you to respond to questions in writing. One of those questions in writing I want to ask you about is specifically the kind of data we need.

But, just as important, we need to look, I think, with great care at how we go about the business of capturing that data. For too long we have over-relied on a very unwieldy long-term structure of a decennial census, and we haven't really built data. At least my fear is that the structure of the census may not dovetail effectively with the kind of specific research work that flows out of universities and that might make use of better structured long-term data and data that can be collected more frequently than every 10 years.

You talked about making opportunity accessible, and we have looked at the way in which manufacturing jobs and other kinds of decent opportunities, accessible entry-level opportunities, have moved away from inner cities, the very place where the need is perhaps measurably the greatest.

As we look at the way in which we try to address that particular problem, do we know enough about whether people with lower levels of education are sufficiently mobile to follow jobs, not just within the metropolitan area as it spreads more broadly but as job opportunities move regionally?

Then it comes down, I think, to me, to a question about whether or not we ought to be preparing young people, particularly at entry level, for jobs likely to be within their communities, or do we prepare young people to take advantage of jobs wherever they may be found in an increasingly mobile society?

Mr. HALPERIN. I think we need to be able to prepare young people for careers and not for jobs. My understanding of labor market predictions is that they are very unreliable. Technologies spring up, and they destroy industries, they build industries, they create situations that you could not predict two, or three, or 4 years before. But you can give people basic skills, particularly the so-called higher order learning skills, so that people are flexible, so they can change, so they can learn on the job, so that they can take stress, so they can solve problems.

Now that is a tall order, and not too many of us, if any, know how to do this, but we have to aim for that direction. I don't think it is really feasible on a national scale to, say, train the people of Akron for the jobs that are going to be in Akron very far out; maybe a couple of years but not very far out. What you have to make sure is that folks in Akron have the ability to roll with the punches, and to come back, and to find their role, their career.

Again, status is very important here. If we tell people that you are going to be on easy street with a 4-year liberal arts education, we have to make sure that that is an honest promise. I don't think it is. I think people have to have skills to sell in the marketplace. We need generalists as well as technical people, but we have to make certain that people are not frittering away their time in 4 years of study.

A lot of people go to college, as we all know, because that is another way to put off the decision about, "What am I going to do when I grow up?" If you ask a high school class, "What are you going to do when you graduate from high school?" almost 100 percent of them will say, "I'm going to college." We know that isn't true; only about 56 percent of the high school graduates do go on to any college, and only about 24 percent of the total population are college graduates. But we have got to give people some realistic understanding of what the world is like out there.

We need to rebuild our employment services. We don't have a labor market information system the way most European countries do so that they can tell you about where the jobs are. It is not only the disadvantaged person who has trouble with mobility, moving from Pennsylvania or Ohio to where the jobs are somewhere else; it is very educated people too. The information about what is happening right now is not readily available. And, of course, counseling, guidance—a very big problem in this country; we don't have enough of it. The average German worker or French worker has a whole array of people behind him to help him make more rational decisions.

Ms. TIENDA. Well, I guess I don't think that it is so perfect in Germany or France or many of the European countries. In Spain they had very, very high unemployment rates for a long time and very high rates of dependency of 25-year-olds, 30-year-olds still living with their parents because they couldn't find employment.

Mr. SAWYER. Let me just say in response to that, I just finished doing a presentation before a representative body of members of the European Parliament who represent both the north and south of Europe, and the phenomenon which I described to them, which was in somewhat greater detail but essentially the same phenomenon that I talked about applying to the United States, began to get heads nodding in that room more intensively than it does among American counterparts. They recognized themselves in the kinds of descriptions that I offered of the United States.

The phenomena that we are talking about I'm convinced are global clearly, and they are happening throughout the advanced industrialized world, and it is not something that the United States is going to have to face alone, but in terms of national competitiveness we need to be on the cutting edge of change.

Ms. TIENDA. That is exactly my understanding of the industrialized countries' trajectories with respect to unemployment and wages and globalization, etc.

I have done a considerable amount of work on migration and employment to the extent that one can with the U.S. Census. The decennial census is so ill suited to address questions of migration and employment precisely because you know residence 5 years ago with respect to the date of the census, and for college students there is a lot of moving between, and it doesn't give you a way of following a cohort longitudinally, and that becomes very important because the decisions for moving are not only made on the basis of jobs. If they are, they also imply social costs, and you have to ask yourself, how is it, if we have such terrible information networks, that undocumented immigrants get jobs that they do in this country, and the reason is, they have access to information that is very well orchestrated and they have the social supports in places and communities. It is not a random draw across this country. So that is a very important story.

But we also have to ask ourselves about the general migration and employment relationship and the national versus the local labor markets. For lower skill levels, we really are talking about local labor markets, and the kind of range of opportunities that individuals with high school educations or non-college educations are willing to consider are very different from the range of locations and destinations that college-educated youth are willing to consider.

So that in order to look at these questions more successfully we need to have longitudinal data. Census data simply will not do the trick.

One of the classic cases is the case of the Puerto Rican population where it is the case that they are moving out of New York that has had declining opportunities for them and where they have experienced a very poor fate. On the other hand, those that are left behind are precisely those that are least able to take advantage of those opportunities, and it makes for a very substantial bifurcation and concentration of poverty. But the census data cannot deal with that.

The census of Puerto Rico has a bit more fine-tuned migration data by annualized years, but, again, you can't match it very clearly with the U.S. census to see what the flow is between Puerto Rico and the mainland, so we are always left in a quandary trying to use econometric methods to suggest what the dynamics are and come very close to finding the real answers.

Mr. SAWYER. In this body we have discovered something about that. We have found that the Congressman from the Bronx was born in Puerto Rico, while the Delegate from Puerto Rico was born in the Bronx.

Dr. Halperin.

Mr. HALPERIN. I didn't want to imply that we have to copy other countries' systems. I do think we need to be aware of them and see what we can learn from them.

Less than a month ago I was visiting working retraining programs in Holland and in Germany, and there I saw multi-million-dollar equipment, the latest that money could buy, and workers coming from various firms, not just from one firm, and they were learning how to advance to the highest levels in the printing industry, for example, printing and graphics. They were using multi-million-dollar computer-driven lathes, which we do have in some of our vocational schools and community colleges, but not many.

We need to pay attention. That is in our self interest, to pay attention. We don't have a policy again for worker retraining that will enable people to use that new equipment which technology is thrusting upon us at an incredible rate.

Mr. SAWYER. You guys are making my job very difficult. I have outlined a series of questions here, and I'm just crossing them off one by one as you answer previous questions. We are covering my ground awfully well.

I had hoped to conclude with a question about the broad-based characteristics of apprenticeship programs in other places that we can learn best from. You started to talk about that. Can you expand on that and develop it, because it really goes at those populations that in many ways define that forgotten half.

They are also the populations that have the greatest difficulty obtaining purchase on entry and duration in the workforce and are the populations that will define the difference between whether we succeed into the next century the way we succeeded in the last, or whether we become more like those great European powers that went through the better part of a century in trying to figure out how to emulate the lessons we learned at the end of the last.

Mr. HALPERIN. Let me put your question in a somewhat broader context. I think apprenticeship is one way to go, but it is only one way. There is cooperative education, there is work-study, there are internships, there is shadowing, there are various kinds of ways to bridge the gap between formal, abstract, conceptual learning in the classroom and the world of work. What do they have in common?

I think the successful programs that the American people will build, first of all, don't foreclose opportunities for higher education. We can't afford a class-stratified system. People always have to know that they haven't finished their education but there is a way to go beyond at some point in their life when they are ready for it.

There has to be hands-on work. Many people are simply not learning, the way you and I are conversing today, through the ears. A lot of people have to work with their hands. They have to understand how things work before they get into the theory, and so many of the advances in educational research and learning theory tell us that we have to find the different ways that learners succeed.

Again, all of the things that I have mentioned have this hands-on, contextual learning, experiential base, and we need to do more of that. Vocational education has been doing it for a long time. We have got to do more of it.

We need to integrate academic education and workplace skills. We need to figure out how to provide a system of incentives for people to have success. People are not going to go through lengthy training programs unless they have heard, they have seen, some relative, some friend, who has had a payoff from that. So there has to be, if not a job guarantee, at least a very good prospect from the labor market system that doesn't yet exist that there will be a reward for that effort.

These are some of the principles. We have to figure out if there are wage increments while you go through this, and you are working for an employer. While you are simultaneously in an apprenticeship type program, does the employer give you somewhat higher wages when you learn on the job, when you are more productive, when you take on assignments ahead of what is normally expected? There have to be incentives, and we haven't figured out what those incentives are.

Mr. SAWYER. Is it an incentive to the worker, or is it an incentive to the employer to give it to the worker, or is it both?

Ms. TIENDA. I think it is both.

Mr. HALPERIN. I think in a well constructed system it is both. Again, the ultimate beneficiary is the American people because we are going to be more productive, our wages are going to be higher, we are going to be more competitive in the world, we are going to have a higher standard of living.

But in the microcosm, it is the student as worker who needs some incentives. We have to get our teachers out of the isolation of the classroom and let them see what goes on in the workplace, and the workplace, by the way, isn't just in manufacturing or in the building trades, which is where our traditional apprenticeships have been. There can be apprenticeships, as there are now in the United States, in hospitals, in universities, in local governments, in retailing, in wholesaling, in transportation and communications. We have to think much more imaginatively about all of the ways that young people can learn careers and, again, not just jobs.

Mr. SAWYER. Credentialing and accrediting doesn't have to take place only in institutions of formal learning.

Ms. TIENDA. But I have an excellent example.

Mr. SAWYER. Go ahead.

Ms. TIENDA. On this paper that we working on, Professor Hotz and I, we had the pleasure of having a young man, a Puerto Rican, who is participating in the Summer Research Opportunity Program. He was about to leave the university after his BA, but not knowing what he wanted to do. He is in the Economics Department, and he doesn't feel he has a good take on what an economist does. But by having him on our project for the summer—he is paid by this program—he has gotten a sense for what research is all about. He generated many of the tables, he has been reading documents, and he said for the first time yesterday as we were having our meeting, "I've decided I'm going to stay in economics; I'm going to go on to graduate school." In this example, what we have is a mentoring program, a connection that gives the vision, the translation from the academics, those pages in the exams, to the actual execution of some of the functions that take place within this role we call professorships.

The same can be said for many other kinds of experiences. Science education—when I think of how I was taught science in grade school out of a book with this person in a white coat called a scientist, I thought, "Oh, wow, what it would be to be a scientist." It was so far away from my world, versus how my son is receiving science training at the University of Chicago Lab School, where he has hands-on experiments already in the third grade, that he can begin to see what science is all about. He thinks science is what he wants to do, not read books. he wants to do science, he wants to do computers, because that is part of his world, and there is no substitute in any field with creativity of trying to translate along the lines that Dr. Halperin was suggesting to make all the difference.

Mr. SAWYER. Just the fact that you say you learned science and your son is doing science is all the difference in the world.

Ms. TIENDA. And that is exactly what these various programs under the rubric of apprenticeship, I think, are all about.

Mr. HALPERIN. Of course, the Congress for a long time has recognized the truth of this kind of learning. You have had thousands of interns throughout the year as well as in the summer who are shadowing, who are learning. We hope they are learning the right things, but the point is, they are learning about what actually happens, and that is the kind of lesson that we need to translate into every facet of the American economy.

Mr. SAWYER. If we could only bring adult supervision to the process, we would be in good shape.

Ms. TIENDA. We all have our role then.

Mr. SAWYER. Yes.

Thank you both very, very much.

I spend a great deal of time talking with my staff about the importance of looking for points of cross-connection between disciplines. Those places are where we can look for opportunities for innovative solutions. I don't think that I have been involved in the last 6 years in a hearing that has focused that quite as clearly as the commentary and suggestions that have flowed from the four witnesses that we have heard this afternoon, and I just want to thank you very much for your contributions today; they have been very important.

Ms. TIENDA. You are welcome.

Mr. SAWYER. We stand adjourned.

[Whereupon, at 4:13 p.m., the subcommittee was adjourned.]

AMERICA'S CHANGING PROFILE: "WHERE WE'RE GOING: EDUCATION AND WORKFORCE TRENDS"

WEDNESDAY, JULY 29, 1992

House of Representatives,
Subcommittee on Census and Population,
Committee on Post Office and Civil Service,
Washington, DC.

The subcommittee met, pursuant to call, at 10:08 a.m., in room 311, Cannon House Office Building, Hon. Thomas C. Sawyer (chairman of the subcommittee) presiding.

Mr. Sawyer. Good morning.

We are in the second day of our third set of hearings to look at demographic trends as they flow from the kinds of changes that we have seen in the last decade or so measured on at least scale by the 1990 census and in much greater detail in the kind of scholarly work and research that has been exemplified by some of the witnesses that we have had before us in the last several weeks, and we are looking at the policy implications that may flow from those kinds of examinations of trend lines. We will look at the changing workforce and whether the emerging American workplace is prepared to respond to the needs of that labor force and, perhaps even more importantly, vice versa.

Yesterday we looked at how demographic trends are driving the need to reconsider the role of educational institutions and the direction of educational programs. We looked at how young people are making the transition from school to the workforce. Views differ widely, but the lessons of 1990 and the findings of that work and the continuing research that comes from it are really inescapable.

Among the kinds of things that we have heard about prior to today are that minority children comprise a growing share of the school population. A lot of those minority children have tended to be poor. They are more likely to drop out before completing high school. They are less likely to achieve thorough and adequate training in math and science, just to name two disciplines of high value. And they are less likely to pursue an education beyond high school.

Younger minorities, particularly African American males, find it more difficult to secure full-time employment, the kind of employment that results in both steady wages and a decent standard of living.

More than ever, these kinds of trends, these and others, demand our attention. These kinds of trends and others we will hear about today will, in some ways, define our choices because they describe an emerging workforce. Less than 15 years from now, that emerging workforce will start to replace the single largest population bulge in our history, the so-called baby boom generation. The question that continues to recur is whether or not newer, younger entrants to the workforce will have the necessary skills to secure steady employment and realize income advantages.

The answer, I suspect, is far from academic. It will determine whether or not Americans in the next century can meet the burdens of supporting two generations, one on either side. One will be younger, less white, more mobile, increasingly foreign born, the other older, more indigenous, more place bound, and certainly numerically large. These are two generations whose needs and expectations will be great and often divergent. They are two generations that may well be in competition for the same limited resources, the resources that that emerging workforce will have to produce and sustain with far fewer people than they will be expected to support in comparison to the recent past.

The question that we have posed today, not just on behalf of this subcommittee but in terms of the way in which other entities in this Congress make use of that kind of flow of information, is how we can best prepare for that future. Will that workforce add to the competition for resources, or will it be strong enough to ease the tensions that are the inevitable product of demographic change?

Our witnesses today have studied the labor force and the workplace in great depth. Their conclusions may not be the same, but they are all important. I look forward to hearing their findings and conclusions today.

I am particularly pleased to be joined today by Connie Morella, the gentlelady from Maryland whose work on the Post Office and Civil Service Committee and previous work in earlier Congresses on the Subcommittee on Census and Population has been exemplary. Her current work, particularly with regard to the Federal workforce, is charting new ground.

It is a pleasure to have you here. Would you like to make an opening statement?

Mrs. MORELLA. I'd love it. Thank you.

Thanks, Mr. Chairman, and I certainly want to thank you for your invitation to attend this series of hearings on demographic trends. You and your staff have done a terrific job of establishing these meetings regarding the census figures, and I appreciate the fact that you are trying to keep Members of Congress apprised of the progress. I want to acknowledge your hard work and your diligence.

I did have an opportunity to look at some of the testimony that will be presented to us today. During the past year we have seen parts of the statistics, but to see it compiled with explanations and possible outcomes is certainly very revealing, interesting, and I hope we can do something more with it.

At one point in your testimony, Mr. Chairman, you said that America's children are more culturally diverse and economically disadvantaged than their parents and grandparents. That is certainly a very sad point for us to digest. Certainly as a parent and as a grandparent also—and I believe I am expressing the feelings of all parents and grandparents—we have lived and worked so that our offspring can enjoy a better life than we, and I hope that by looking at the issues now we can help to change the gloomy possibility.

As Roz Kleeman has artfully expressed in her testimony, the traditional family has now become a "historic artifact." It has become so because of necessity. Single-parent families, live-in parents, grandparents, sheer economic necessity, the whole range is before us, and we must preplan for this reality and eventuality.

The data that Census '90 has rendered is eye opening and challenging. We must make aggressive strides to counteract the negative implications, and by planning in advance that is a definite possibility.

Adequate health provisions, including pre- and post-natal provisions, effective education geared to workforce projections, family-friendly policies are just the foundation toward building a strong, competitive, motivated workforce.

We know that the workforce of the next decade will include a larger percentage of women, minorities, and older workers. As a matter of fact, we know that two out of three of the new entrants into the workforce by year 2000 will be women and minorities.

I would also like to add, particularly with implementation of the Americans With Disabilities Act, we are going to have more disabled persons in our workforce, and so I hope that studies and statistics have been conducted which include all of those projections. I am looking forward to hearing the detailed testimony. I want to welcome the witnesses.

I also want to point out that in my jurisdiction of Montgomery County, MD, I did have a forum on family-friendly workplace policies, and we included on our panel those corporations that had won awards for demonstrating that you can enhance productivity and elevate morale if you can make accommodation for the changing family structure.

We did have a representative of OPM who was there also, and, as the GAO report will demonstrate, we do have a task before us in terms of remediation with regard to family-friendly workplace policies for the Federal sector. I'm committed also to working toward that, and, again, I thank you for the invitation to be here and look forward to hearing the witnesses.

Mr. SAWYER. Thank you very much for being here and for those thoughtful comments.

Our first panel this morning is made up of three witnesses: Sar Levitan, who is the director of the Center for Social Policy Studies; he is a research professor of economics at George Washington University and chaired the National Commission on Employment and Unemployment Statistics. He enjoys a wide range of consultancies across both governmental and private entities.

Arnold Packer is a senior fellow at the Institute for Policy Studies at Johns Hopkins University. He is the former Executive Director of SCANS, the Secretary's Commission on Achieving Necessary Skills. He was the deputy director and co-author of the Hudson Institute's Workforce 2000 study, and Assistant Secretary for Policy Evaluation and Research at the U.S. Department of Labor in the late seventies.

Our final witness on the first panel is Lawrence Mishel, who is the research director at the Economic Policy Institute, the author of a number of EPI publications, and specializes in fields of productivity, competitiveness, income distribution, labor markets, industrial relations, and training and human resource policies.

With that brief introduction, let me say welcome and turn to Dr. Levitan to begin.

STATEMENTS OF SAR A. LEVITAN, DIRECTOR, CENTER FOR SOCIAL POLICY STUDIES, GEORGE WASHINGTON UNIVERSITY; ARNOLD H. PACKER, SENIOR FELLOW, INSTITUTE FOR POLICY STUDIES, JOHNS HOPKINS UNIVERSITY; AND LAWRENCE MISHEL, RESEARCH DIRECTOR, ECONOMIC POLICY INSTITUTE

Mr. LEVITAN. Thank you, Mr. Chairman.

As you and Congresswoman Morella just stated, our labor market is going to be facing a lot of challenges. I understand that you have heard already a great deal of gloom and doom, and you might hear some more from my learned colleagues on this and the next panel.

I therefore decided to depart from gloom and doom for a change and tell you about some things that you folks don't have to worry about. I singled out three issues that the media and that many analysts who should know better keep on scaring us with and which I think are greatly overstated. The three issues are: Our workforce is ill prepared to master the rapidly changing technology; the second trendy idea is that declining birth rates during the 1970's and during the 1980's will create labor shortages; the third trendy idea, which is very much publicized these days by the Government, is that Government regulation is responsible for declining productivity growth. Let me take up each one of these.

There is no question that the workplace is being transformed, but at a much slower rate than is generally recognized. If you take the latest Bureau of Labor Statistics projections, which is the subject for this hearing, during the next 13 years, we find that the Bureau of Labor Statistics estimated that by the year 2005 for every computer programmer added to the workforce there will be five sales persons and cashiers, three office clerks and receptionists, three food servers, and two janitors. Quite clearly, a great deal of our workforce is not going to require much training or particular change in their occupation.

As a matter of fact, the most numerous occupation in the American labor market is that of secretary. There are 4½ million secretaries in the labor force now, according again to the BLS, but the skills of a secretary have changed very little since the typewriter was introduced in 1870. Whether the secretaries operate a manual or electric typewriter or computer, the secretary's skills have remained essentially the same: an ability to operate a machine and, more significantly, spell correctly. I might add that the spelling is not so much necessary now because there is some kind of a gremlin inside a computer which I can never understand but which tells the secretary how to spell things.

The same thing if you looked at cashiers——

Mr. SAWYER. I wish they could do as well for punctuation.

Mr. LEVITAN. Well, that will be the next invention.

The computer may automatically record the transactions of the cashier, but the goods that the stores sell are not free. Even with optical scanners, that so impressed President Bush lately, someone besides the customer must manage the cash register whether the payments are made with plastic cards or old-fashioned cash.

There is another factor that should be considered that would prevent rapid change in technology. The lack of capital will impede the rapid expansion of new technology. Virtually all capital-intensive industries have massive investment in existing facilities, and they cannot afford to squander these resources to change for the new technology.

The evidence seems to me overwhelming that the economy is not generating an extraordinary demand for new skills—my colleagues may disagree with that, but we will hear from them—and that new technology is not radically skill requirements.

The second issue that we hear very frequently is that we are going to face labor shortages. Even today with 10 million unemployed, there is still talk that labor shortages will develop some time when the economy resumes growth. The assumption that slow growth of the labor supply will be a cause of labor shortages ignores empirical evidence. The demand for labor continues to rise, but at least two or three important sources would prevent sustained labor shortages.

First, employers and workers will not be able to afford, as they did in the last two decades or so, early retirement. Cost of pensions and cost of health care is going to rise. Therefore I don't think that early retirement will prevail as it did in the past. We will therefore have some extra supply of labor force, and, of course, as you in Congress have already indicated 9 years ago in the Social Security amendments, the normal age of eligibility will increase early next century from 65 to 67. So, again, we are going to have an additional supply of labor.

Second, if there are sustained labor shortages, what we can do is open the gates to immigrants more than we did 2 years ago. Millions of skilled and unskilled workers are knocking at our doors. In the case of sustained labor shortages, of course we can invite these potential workers who are knocking at the doors to come in.

Finally, labor shortages could be diminished by increasing the hours of work. That may scare some, but it wouldn't be too great a problem to increase their hours by 1 hour. That would be the equivalent of increasing the labor force by some three million workers.

Labor shortages should be viewed as a challenge and a blessing rather than a problem. Full employment has been a goal whose achievement should be welcomed rather than viewed with concern.

The third issue that I want to touch on is that Government regulations have reduced the growth of productivity during recent years. I want to make that on an entirely nonpartisan basis. Deregulations of American industry started under Carter, continued under Reagan and under Bush. Vice President Quayle is, of course, a great proponent of deregulation, so it is a nonpartisan issue, but, at the same time, productivity has not responded to the decline in Government regulation.

During the past 3 years, productivity per worker hour in the private sector has risen at a fraction of 1 percent compared with 2.3 percent during the 3 years before the deregulation became Federal policy. We must conclude that Government intervention in the free market, whatever the merits or fault, has hardly been a culprit for the declining growth in productivity during recent years.

Finally, I want to add a point which does not deal with projections of the labor force but which is in the direct jurisdiction of your subcommittee. In recent years the Bureau of the Census has stopped collecting a lot of data or making unpublished data available to consumers. It is no conspiracy, just that the resources have been cut, which led to reducing the supply of available data.

An illustration of this phenomenon surfaced a couple of months ago when there was a great hullabaloo about the overworked American labor force. The theme has been, they are working longer. I think that the evidence was very inconclusive. BLS or the Census Bureau have not been very helpful in supplying relevant data because in 1987 they stopped collecting data on weeks of work during the year, and therefore we don't know how much working time has increased, but, again, this is something that is worth the consideration of this committee. I don't want to let you off completely without any worries.

Thank you, Mr. Chairman. My 7 minutes are up.

[The prepared statement of Mr. Levitan follows:]

PREPARED STATEMENT OF SAR A. LEVITAN, DIRECTOR, CENTER FOR SOCIAL POLICY STUDIES, GEORGE WASHINGTON UNIVERSITY

Given the broad agenda for this hearing, I singled out several topics for my presentation, focusing on the education/labor market connection. I also suggest that concerns about the impact of immigration, new technology, labor shortages, and government regulations have been overemphasized. Finally, I recommend some needed labor market reforms addressing the needs of the working poor.

A. THE EDUCATION/WORK CONNECTION

Education constitutes the principal investment of time and money in preparation for work. Measured by length of schooling, Americans have been one of the most educated people in the world for a century or more. Today 85 percent of 25 to 29 year-olds have completed at least four years of high school, and nearly a quarter have finished four years of college. The educational attainment of the 25 to 64 year-old working age population now approximates that of incoming cohorts, and consequently the attainment level of the work force is not likely to increase in the 1990s.

Unlike several of our major economic competitors, the American system of preparation for work stresses educational attainment or "aptitude" tests rather than qualitative standards or occupationally-specific assessments of knowledge or skills. The emphasis on longer education has unquestionably produced a more qualified work force, but it also encourages educational inflation and enables some individuals to obtain credentials by accumulating "seat time" rather than skills. From the employers' perspective, the lack of educational standards means that credentials present an uncertain value, which in turn promotes educational inflation because employers try to minimize their hiring risk by stressing longer attainment. Governmental policy has greatly influenced rising educational attainment, through an extensive network of public postsecondary schools, grants and loans, tax subsidies, and the educational benefits provided through military service.

Educational Background, 1940–89

[in percent]

	Proportion completing 4 years of high school		Proportion completing 4 or more years of college	
	25–29 year-olds	25–64 year-olds	25–29 year-olds	25–64 year-olds
1940	38.1	25.7	5.9	4.8
1950	52.8	36.0	7.7	6.5
1960	60.7	45.3	11.0	8.4
1970	75.4	61.1	16.4	12.1
1980	85.4	75.0	22.5	18.9
1989	85.5	82.0	23.4	23.4

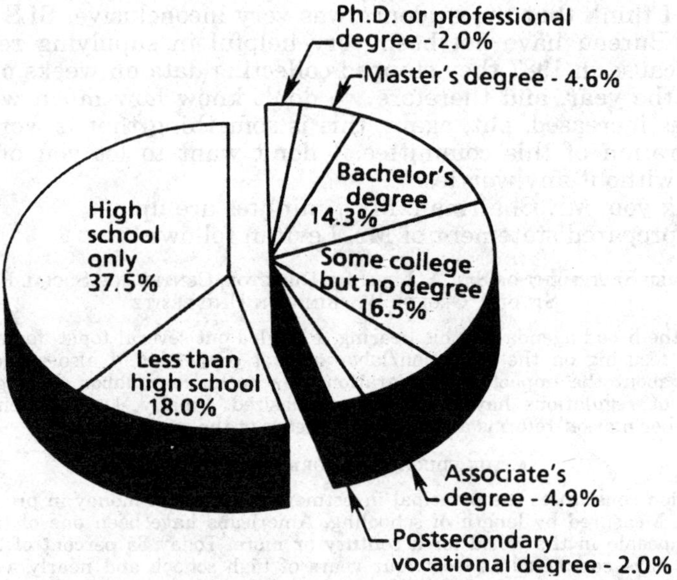

Source: U.S. Bureau of the Census, *What's It Worth? Educational Background and Economic Status: Spring 1987* (Washington: U.S. Government Printing Office, October 1990), Current Population Report, Series P–70, No. 21, p. 7.

From an individual's perspective the economic value of education is bountiful, although much of this return is apparently attributable to credentials rather than capability. In 1987 workers with bachelor's degrees earned twice as much per month as those who did not continue beyond high school, and four times more than those who did not complete high school. This educational "bonus" decreased during the 1970s, but rose during the next decade to levels above those of the early 1970s.

Earnings account for about two-thirds of aggregate income. However, since almost all men ages 25 to 54 have worked in the postwar period, and because income data are much more extensive, they are used here as a proxy for earnings. Granting the lack of statistical rigor, the data provide insights into the economic rewards of education by tracking the income of five age cohorts (table). The income of 25 to 34 year-old college graduates equalled or exceeded that of 45 to 54 year-old men with only a high school diploma despite two decades more work experience.

Table 1, A college education has become not only more lucrative, but almost necessary to avoid stagnant or declining career earnings

Men's Income by Educational Attainment

[1990 dollars]

	Elementary school	1–3 years High School	High School Only	1–3 Years College	College Graduate
25–34 years old					
1949	$10,269	$13,832	$15,593	$15,780	$17,864
1958 *	12,562	17,794	19,513	20,908	24,850
1969	17,615	22,202	26,565	28,373	33,929
1979	14,144	19,398	25,222	26,892	30,635
1989	11,004	14,728	21,081	24,243	31,410
33–44 years old					
1949		16,037	17,778	19,994	25,948
1958 *	14,548	19,638	22,207	26,232	32,180
1969	20,026	26,104	30,340	36,211	46,578
1979	17,984	21,940	31,439	35,190	45,494
1989	12,659	16,609	26,351	31,840	43,084
145–54 years old					
1949		16,194	18,606	20,685	28,002
1958 *	14,269	18,822	22,614	26,498	38,378
1969	20,192	25,895	30,383	36,015	48,432
1979	18,997	26,227	32,679	35,630	49,452
1989	15,073	21,231	29,621	36,130	50,594

* 1959 income data not available.
Source: U.S. Census Bureau, 1950 Census of Population and Current Population Reports, Series P–60, various years.

The income differential based on educational attainment rose during the past decade. Recent college graduates are now quickly reaping an increased income level above their less-educated contemporaries that previous generations of college graduates took decades to attain. At the other end of the educational spectrum, workers are increasingly facing the prospect of minor income gains or even declines as their careers progress. In contrast, young men with no more than a high school education in 1949 nearly doubled their real average income by the time they reached middle age.

National standards

Potentially promising is the development of voluntary national test standards. In the absence of standards, workers and the economy suffer a shortfall in competence because the yardstick for credentials is largely time spent in school, rather than mastery of knowledge or skills. Americans recognize the importance of education for occupational success, but many students seem to act as if their educational achievement and schoolwork have little relevance to their future careers. The immediate rewards of educational achievement are often slim because many employers are unwilling to hire youth fresh out of school for career-track positions, and discrimination, although illegal, remains a fact of life. Consequently many youngsters, who tend to have limited horizons, view educational effort—and sometimes graduation itself—as marginal to their careers, and instead pursue paid work or leisure activities that are frequently dysfunctional. The fact that employers tend to ignore grades and test scores, and many postsecondary schools admit high school graduates regardless of achievement, actively discourages educational effort.

National standards are necessary for practical, legal, and equity considerations. Employers have little reason to rely upon educational credentials which are not based on reasonable standards, and may represent radically different achievements from one school to the next. Rigor and consistency are also necessary to address equal opportunity challenges, which many job tests have failed to meet. Nonuniform standards penalize students who attend "tougher" schools or enroll in more difficult courses, and may encourage many to seek frivolous courses in order to boost "paper performance.

About 80 percent of adults favor standardized national tests, and 70 percent favor a national curriculum. Students themselves support the idea of high school graduation tests, including half of students who had failed such tests. A higher proportion of minority than white students endorsed graduation tests. Adoption of standardized tests raises problems and necessitates additional investments. There is a need first to determine what the tests will measure. If the standards are set at adequate levels, many students now automatically promoted will likely fail, which may in turn raise dropout rates. In the absence of extra help, students at risk may become victims of the tests.

Youngsters from poor or single parent homes can benefit from special assistance, but the most effective approach would be to ameliorate these conditions in the first place, a task which of course must be addressed outside the school system. Programs that expand employment opportunities, raise earnings, prevent out-of-wedlock births, provide child support and child care, and secure minimally decent health care and affordable housing are desirable in their own right. They are also critical tools for achieving educational improvement and better preparation for work.

Existing federal programs directed at the poor who are most in need of educational assistance require added funding if the programs are to serve all those seeking aid. Congress has boosted appropriations for preschoolers served by the Head Start program.

However, the "Chapter 1" program, targeted to assist elementary and secondary students who perform poorly in school, has concentrated its limited funds on elementary pupils. As a result, aid to youngsters who require continuing help in secondary schools is normally unavailable.

B. THE WORKING POOR

The American economic and political system has produced vigorous economic progress, facilitating upward mobility. Millions moved out of poverty into the middle and upper classes, and the number of poor workers continued to decline until the 1970s. Individuals who fail to apply themselves are likely to be impoverished, and poverty, conversely, can breed dysfunctional behavior. Greater commitment to work and skill training can rightly be expected among many of the able-bodied poor. But blind faith in the free market system and a blanket indictment of the poor are unwarranted. The difficult living conditions of poor workers and the complex factors that account for their existence should not be ignored. Government intervention is essential to improve their lives and prospects.

The working poor remain America's glaring contradiction. The concurrence of work and poverty is contrary to the American ethos that a willingness to work leads to material advancement, and it negates the prevalent view that the cause of poverty among adults capable of work is deviant behavior, particularly a lack of commitment to work.

The increased incidence of poverty among workers, combined with population growth, significantly augmented the overall number of poor workers. From 1979 to 1989—both final years of long economic recoveries and therefore comparable periods in the business cycle—the number of full-time, year-round poor workers rose by 38 percent, from 1,365,000 to 1,887,000, and rose to 2,038,000 in 1990 as a result of a recession which began in mid-year. The number of partially working poor rose 26 percent from 1979 to 1989, and by 30 percent from 1979 to 1990. Although 1991 data are not yet available, the recession has undoubtedly further exacerbated the problems of the working poor.

Troubling earnings trends

Earnings inequality has grown since the 1970s, with the bottom fifth of earners bearing the brunt of the burden. The U.S. Census Bureau tracked low earnings trends for the past quarter century by examining inflation-adjusted earnings of less than $11,570 in 1989 dollars, roughly equivalent to the poverty threshold for the average-sized poor working family of 3.8 individuals. In the last two decades, the share of low earners in the work force remained relatively constant, but only because of increased paid work time among women. The share of the work force that labored full-time, year-round rose from 56 to 61 percent in the decade after 1979. Inflation-adjusted hourly earnings have dropped. The proportion of full-time, year-round workers with low earnings grew since 1979 even before the recession's onset, and reached nearly one in five in 1990. Due to earnings growth and smaller households, the poverty rate among low earners dropped by nearly half between 1964 and 1979, before climbing during the next decade. However, poverty rates have continued to fall among full-time, year-round low earners.

Growing earnings inequity is attributable to a variety of factors, including greater employer demand for college-educated workers, the fall in the value of the minimum wage, international trade, the decline of labor unions, the shift in the work force from manufacturing to the service sector, and immigration. The relative importance of these factors varies greatly for different types of workers. It is difficult to single out the most important influence, because wage inequality has risen within each group of workers with similar educational, occupational, and industrial characteristics. Even less clear are the reasons why these factors have contributed to earnings inequality.

Employer preference for more educated workers is no doubt an important contributor to the increasingly skewed earnings distribution,. but its influence has been exaggerated. The fact that overall inequality has grown while educational attainment differentials have narrowed indicates that other factors are relevant. Moreover, the historical trends are not consistent. In the two decades following Work War II low earners experienced greater wage increases than high earners—a development little influenced by rising educational attainments. Similarly, low earners in a wide variety of industries have lost ground in the past decade, which diminishes the importance that some have attached to industrial restructuring and international trade.

C. NOT TO WORRY

It might be useful to comment on some trendy notions that presumably adversely affect labor markets. I will single out four such notions: immigration, technology, labor shortages, and government regulation.

Undocumented immigrants

Federal law attempts to limit the number of immigrants, but is often overwhelmed by foreigners seeking a better life and employers desiring cheap labor. Consequently many undocumented aliens reside in the United States illegally. A large proportion of undocumented immigrants are poor, although they are often not counted in the published statistics. Many were poor upon entering the United States, they may lack schooling or facility in English, and their illegal status often bars them from taking advantage of assistance that could help them escape poverty.

To stem inflow of illegal immigrants, the 1986 Immigration Reform and Control Act instituted sanctions on employers who hire them. Employers face civil fines of up to $10,000 and a criminal penalty of up to $3,000 for each illegal alien hired, as well as a maximum six months' imprisonment. Ineffective enforcement, combined with questionable voluntary compliance by employers and reportedly widespread use of forged documents, has frustrated efforts to reduce illegal immigration. Although admittedly a crude measure, border apprehensions are the only available gauge of illegal immigration. After dropping to 891,000 in 1989 following the amnesty law, apprehensions rose to 1,113,000 by 1991 despite a recession, which normally dampens the inflow.

The 1986 immigration law also included a major humanitarian component by offering amnesty to immigrants who entered the country illegally. Three million illegal residents applied for amnesty under two separate provisions. Nearly 1.8 million applied under a program that granted amnesty to individuals who have lived in the United States continuously since 1982. Another 1.3 million applied for amnesty under a special agricultural worker program, which qualified farm workers employed for at least 90 days between May 1985 and April 1986. As of February 1992, the U.S. Immigration and Naturalization Service (INS) has granted temporary residence status to 2.7 million applicants, 90 percent of the total. The INS estimated that roughly an additional 2 to 3.5 million illegal immigrants resided in the United States in 1990.

The vast majority of amnesty applicants were young, single Mexican men. Over half of the total lived in California. At the time of application, nearly two of every three aliens performed unskilled work as operators, fabricators, and laborers, or were employed in service jobs.

Amnesty applicants who reported their hourly wage earned 39 percent less than the median for all wage and salary workers in 1988: $5.00 verses $8.26 hourly. However, workers who had the longest tenure either in the United States or with one employer earned the highest wages among illegal immigrants, possibly indicating upward job mobility.

Data are scarce on the effect of immigration, legal or illegal, on the wages of American citizens. Immigrant competition probably depresses the earnings of low wage native workers, although to date researchers have not found strong or consistent effects. Immigration policies must strike a balance between the nation's traditional open door to the "tired, poor, huddled masses" with their impact on wages of native American workers.

High technology skills

The work place has been changing at an accelerated pace and there is every indication that this transformation will continue. It is, however, easy to overstate the impact of these changes. Computer technology is going to generate a wide variety of service jobs. These include both the most sophisticated and demanding and the most mundane and boring work. The Bureau of Labor Statistics estimated that by the year 2005, for every computer programmer added to the work force during the next 13 years, there will be five sales persons and cashiers, three office clerks and receptionists, three food servers, and two janitors.

It follows that the work place a baker's dozen years hence is not going to be much different than it is today. Even if more robots perform some of the more repetitive labor that is now being done by humans, the robots will replace only a tiny fraction of the 147 million workers who will be in the labor force by 2005.

Lack of capital will also impede the rapid expansion of new technology. Virtually all capital-intensive industries have a massive investment in existing plant facilities, and they cannot afford to squander these resources through the wholesale replacement of working machinery. More importantly, the financial constraints on capital formation necessarily limit the rate at which new technologies are introduced.

The most numerous occupation in the American economy is that of secretary. Today there are some 4.5 million of them performing diverse chores in the work place. Despite radical improvements in office equipment, the skills of a secretary have changed very little since the typewriter was introduced in the 1870s. Whether secretaries operate a manual or electric typewriter or a computer, the necessary skills have remained essentially the same—an ability to operate the machine and, more significantly, to spell correctly. Indeed, the importance of the latter skill has diminished because computers include dictionaries.

Technology may result in a similar pseudo-transformation of the jobs performed by the nation's 2.5 million cashiers. The computer may automatically record transactions, but the goods that the stores sell are not free. Even with the optical scanners which so impressed President Bush, someone besides the customer must manage the cash register whether payments are made with plastic cards or old-fashioned cash, which is unlikely to become obsolete.

The evidence seems to be overwhelming that the economy is not generating any extraordinary demand for new skills and that new technology is not radically changing skill requirements.

Labor shortages

Even as 10 million remain unemployed, today's conventional wisdom is that slower population growth will inevitably produce labor shortages. Official sanction of this view was supplied by former Labor Secretary Elizabeth Dole, who said, "Because the number of new workers will continue to fall, businesses will be scrambling for talent throughout the 1990s."

The assumption that slow growth of the labor supply will be the cause of labor shortages ignores empirical evidence. The historical record indicates that economic factors are much more important than population growth in determining labor shortages. Moreover, if demand for labor continues to rise, at least two important sources could prevent sustained labor shortfalls.

First, companies have been downsizing their labor force by encouraging early retirement, but at considerable costs if the companies provide pensions and health insurance which employers may not be able to afford in the future. National policy will soon also discourage early retirement. The 1983 Social Security amendments, which will gradually raise the normal age of eligibility from 65 to 67 after the. turn of the century, are a harbinger of this development.

Second, opening the gate for immigrants is another historical means of increasing labor supply. Millions of skilled and unskilled workers are knocking at our doors. In case of sustained labor shortages, Congress could amend present law and allow for increased immigration.

Finally, labor shortages could be diminished by increasing the hours of work. Increasing the work week by one hour would be equivalent to a rise of nearly three million additional workers.

Labor shortages should be viewed as a challenge and a blessing rather than a problem. Full employment has been a goal whose achievement should be welcomed rather than viewed with concern.

Government regulations and productivity

One fashionable idea receiving wide currency in recent years is that government regulation has stymied productivity growth. Presumably, if government ceased to interfere with free markets, productivity would return to the levels the economy enjoyed in the 1950s and the early 1960s.

There is no question that government regulations have reduced measured productivity growth. Achieving clean air, clear water, and safety in the workplace has its cost. However, even ignoring the benefits to society, the best available estimates about the impact of regulations upon productivity suggest little relationship between measured productivity and governmental regulations.

The Carter, Reagan, and Bush administrations have reduced governmental intervention in the workplace, but productivity has not responded to these changes. Indeed, during the past three years productivity per work hour in the private sector has risen at a fraction of one percent compared with an annual increase of 2.3 percent during the three years before deregulation became federal policy. We must conclude that governmental intervention in the free market, whatever its merits or faults, has hardly been the culprit for the declining growth in productivity during recent years.

D. NEEDED REFORMS

When parents are unable to provide basic necessities for their children, further government assistance is necessary. Helping parents earn an adequate living is the first line of defense. The reintroduction of a public jobs program, abolished in 1981, would provide employment to individuals otherwise unable to find work. However, work alone is insufficient, as nearly nine million Americans remain impoverished despite their work efforts. A livable wage is especially important to young adults starting families, but since 1973 the earnings of 20- to 24-year-old men not in school full-time have declined after adjusting for inflation. More young women are working, and although the gender gap has narrowed, women's average wages are still significantly below men's. In the 1960s and most of the 1970s, the minimum wage yielded full-time, year-round workers who were single parents with two dependents an annual income that raised them above the poverty threshold, but in 1992 the minimum wage provided for less than 80 percent of that standard. In addition to raising the minimum wage, the current earned income tax credit should be amended to consider family size in providing support for low earners.

Lack of affordable child care is a serious impediment to employment for many mothers, particularly single women. Finding affordable care is becoming increasingly difficult because grandmothers and aunts are likely to be either working or living too far away to watch their kin's children. Despite increased governmental help, low income parents need further child care assistance to secure employment.

Beyond employment and income assistance, renewed federal efforts to meet the basic health needs of American families are necessary. Some 35 million Americans have no health insurance coverage and their numbers are rising. Congress has devoted considerable attention and resources to the medical problems of the elderly, but little to the working poor or near-poor without children. A new federally subsidized health insurance system or an extension of medicaid could fill this gap.

The nation faces a considerable challenge in molding its work force to meet present and future needs. But the obstacles should not be overestimated, nor should we waste time or resources addressing trendy "crises" scarcely likely to materialize. The private sector will shoulder most of the burden of maintaining our competitiveness in an increasingly internationalized economy. Education is one area where government is preeminent. Ensuring a quality education for all Americans, despite its lack of novelty, trendiness and sex appeal, remains the most important contribution that government can make to meeting the challenges ahead.

E. DATA ADEQUACY

Finally, a comment on a matter which directly concerns the jurisdiction of this subcommittee. To meet the economic, social, and demographic challenges ahead, we must first of course understand them. The information provided by the U.S. Census Bureau and the Bureau of Labor Statistics, which this subcommittee oversees, is the most important analytical tool we possess. I submit for the record a Joint Economic Committee report that my colleague, Frank Gallo, and I prepared on the quality of work force-related statistics and the reforms needed to better understand the changes that confront the nation. I would like to emphasize the importance of better utilizing the information already at hand. Computer advances enable the agencies to much more fully mine existing survey data, but for budgetary reasons most of this potential remains unrealized. [Editor's note: The report has been retained in the subcommittee's files.]

The Bureau also pays insufficient attention to statistics critical to understanding the changes which are the subject of today's hearing. For example, earlier this year a well-publicized debate emerged whether Americans were overworked. But Census statistics could shed little light on this important issue, because after 1987 the agency stopped publishing data on how many weeks Americans worked per year.

Mr. SAWYER. Thank you very much, Dr. Levitan.

Let me just emphasize—I should have said it beforehand—while we have set a 7-minute testimony limitation, it is the full intent of the chair to be as flexible as the witnesses need.

Mr. LEVITAN. I wish, Mr. Chairman, you told me that 10 minutes ago.

[Laughter.]

Mr. SAWYER. Well, the fact that it was 10 minutes ago when I should have said it is evidence of the flexibility, I suppose, and I hope that you will take advantage of the question period to expand in any direction that you think would be useful to us.

I particularly appreciate your comments about support for the Census Bureau, the expansion and perhaps even modification of the direction of data gathering and its frequency. We are in the midst of a time, whether we agree about its consequences, of substantial change, and it is important that we know about it.

Rather than go on further at this point though, let me turn to our second witness and ask you, Dr. Packer, to proceed if you will.

Mr. PACKER. Thank you, Mr. Chairman. It is a pleasure to be here even if I have to follow Sar Levitan, who is a tough act to follow.

It seems to me that the Congress and next administration will have to face three questions: First, is the world transforming rapidly? Is all this talk about globalization and new technology and demographics meaningful or just something that magazine writers use to fill their publications? The second question is: Is the United States adjusting to that transformation? And then the third question is what to do about it if the adjustment is not going well.

Contrary to my distinguished colleague, I do believe that the world is transforming, and I do believe the data indicate very clearly that the transformation is not going very well for many Americans.

Of all the data that we have, one particular set characterizes the problem best for me. They appear in the Learning A Living report that the SCANS Commission presented when it terminated a couple of months ago, and, with your permission, Mr. Chairman, I would like to submit that report for the record.

[The above-mentioned report has been retained in the subcommittee's files.]

Mr. PACKER. In 1969, a large majority of American males who had managed to acquire a high school diploma could support a family, and today that is no longer so. The share of African American males with 12 years of education unable to support a family of four above poverty rose from 20 percent in 1969 to 43 percent in 1989.

What that essentially says is that in 1969 an African American male who had managed to get a high school diploma had a four-in-five chance of being able to raise his family above the poverty level if it was a family of four. By 1989, that probability had come close to one in two. For white males, the figures had risen from 8 percent to 23 percent, a trebling.

I think what that clearly brings us to is the choice that an influential recent report stated in its title: "America's Choice: High Skills or Low Wages." The idea that one need not acquire high skills because there will be good-paying secretarial jobs that do not require high skills is a very dangerous idea. It does not serve either the country or the young people who are going to school very well. If you don't have good skills, you are very unlikely to be able to earn a decent living in the 21st century. If your State does that, your State will be in bad shape. And, it is true for the Nation as a whole. The choice, high skills or low wages, is the critical issue.

We stated that choice somewhat differently in Workforce 2000, there we said if the country wants to grow by 3 percent a year then it will have a skills shortage.

The real question is how to improve the skills of today's and tomorrow's workers. The Secretary's Commission on Achieving Necessary Skills (SCANS) identified a set of competencies that are closely associated with higher performance jobs and higher wages. This is not a projection, this is not guess work. When we looked out into the field and inventoried those skills and compared skills with wages we found that higher levels of those skills meant a difference of $11,000 a year. Workers were brought substantially above the poverty level if they had higher levels of these skills.

What are these skills? They are things such as planning time and developing and following schedules, working in a team, negotiating, explaining to others what has to be done. People with these skills are comfortable with technology and can interpret instructions. They can use that little gremlin in the computer and even come out with the correct spelling of "potato," I would imagine.

They know how to find information. They understand that they work in a system of people and procedures that define the way things are done. They can read and write and have the personal qualities that make for a good worker. And when I say "read and write," reading scores by themselves do not tell you anything unless you know what is to be read and what is to be done with the information. So reading as a prescription is not specific enough.

I would like to move next to the question of demographics. Mr. Chairman, you pointed out the changing age distribution of our workforce, and I think that is the most important demographic shift. By 2005, the median age of the labor force will be 40.6 years. That is about what it was in 1962 but 4 years older than the median in 1990. Until 2005, the number of nonworkers, primarily children and older workers, dependent on each working American will decline. In 1990 there was an equal number of workers and nonworkers in the United States, but by 2005 there will only be 9 nonworkers per 10 workers. By 2010, as you point out, Mr. Chairman, the tide will turn as the oldest baby boomers start to retire. Then the burden of support on those of working age will grow.

Now if it is acceptable to the country to require all of us to work until we are 70 and go back to a 50-hour week, I guess that is OK. But if people think earlier retirement is still desirable and that a shorter work week, given family responsibilities is desirable, we will have to raise productivity. Then we must begin to get back to the productivity growth rate of the fifties and sixties.

In Workforce 2000, we pointed out that productivity in the service sector grew by 1.4 percent annually between 1955 and 1970 but actually fell between 1970 and 1985. So we are going to have to change the productivity in the service sector, and we believe that that is going to require higher skills.

The other demographic shift is the change to a more female and less white workforce. According to the latest projections from the Bureau of Labor Statistics, the labor force will grow by about 26 million persons between 1990 and 2005 as 56 million persons not in the labor force enter it and 30 million others leave the labor force.

While 18 million white men will enter, 14 million white men will leave, so that white men will only make up 15 percent of the net—and let me emphasize the word "net"—addition to the labor force, and their share of the total 2005 labor force will shrink to 38.2 percent.

Women of all races will be almost half of the entrants but only 43 percent of the leavers, so that females will constitute half of the net additions. Minorities of both sexes are projected to be 35 percent of the entrants and 54 percent of the net additions to the labor force.

These demographic changes, as important as they are, should not be a cause of alarm. Indeed, the shift to minorities and women can be a great opportunity for the United States. According to some studies that I did while still at the Hudson Institute, the requirement for new skills can be divided between demographic shifts and new job requirements; only 10 percent of the upgrading is required because of demographic shifts, 56 percent is due to the changing job requirements if—let me emphasize if—if the economy grows. If you stay with a slow-growing economy and a 7.8-percent unemployment rate, obviously there will be no skills shortage. All those highly skilled unemployed or underemployed workers will surely demonstrate that there is no skills shortage today. There is no capital shortage either, for those firms that have idle equipment. We hope these are short-term considerations that will end when an economic recovery begins.

Shortages of skills and capital have to do with the strength and duration of the recovery. We are a functioning economy. We will not have empty shelves because people can't do the work or we have no equipment. We do not face a crisis. A shortage will appear as a continuing stagnation in wages, productivity, and competitiveness. A shortage does not halt production but limits potential economic growth. A shortage is a dream killer, it does not kill the economy.

With enough capital and skill we could grow faster, there would be more good jobs. With a 3 percent growth rate, disposable income can grow by 1.7 percent a year, we found in Workforce 2000. With fewer skilled workers, we would still grow, but disposable income would grow only .6 percent per year, and I think Larry Mishel will tell us that, for most people, that will mean diminishing income.

The debate is not over whether there is or is not a skill shortage, that is a semantic argument. Everyone that I know agrees that we have a choice between a high skill or a low wage economy, and everyone agrees that we should take the high skill path. The issue is how to take the path. How do we convince firms——

Mr. SAWYER. Let me ask you to suspend for just a moment here. We have got a vote that is coming up, and I'm trying to pick a good point at which to break so that we might go and complete our vote in the next 10 minutes. Inasmuch as I question whether you are going to get through the rest of your testimony in the next 3 minutes, I think we would be better off suspending here and let you come back and talk about the direction that we ought to take and your conclusions rather than try to rush it at this point.

So we will stand suspended here for a moment while we go vote, and we will be back. Thank you.

Mr. PACKER. Thank you.

[Recess.]

Mr. SAWYER. Thank you very much for your patience.

We think we actually have a reasonable window of time here, so, without any greater pause, you just go right on ahead, Dr. Packer.

Mr. PACKER. Thank you.

So the question is, if the high skill, high wage path is the one to be taken, how do you do that? How do you convince firms to become high performance employers that seek high skills and are willing to pay high wages for those skills, and what do you do about education and training? Then you must think about how demographic change alters the human resource strategy.

Let me begin with the last question. I think what demographics ought to make people alert to is that students are different. Irrespective of race and gender, humans vary and have different strengths and different learning styles. The old assembly line, "everybody has to learn the same thing in the same way" technique has most likely passed its usefulness.

The SCANS report proposes that schools provide students with a resume of their achievements, and that resume emphasizes strengths rather than punishing weaknesses. As one commissioner said, "our approach is more like competing in the decathlon than entering in one track and field event. In the decathlon, I made up for my weakness in the shot put by doing better in the hurdles," he said.

Instead of concentrating on minimum competency, schools should seek maximum development of student talents. That may mean customizing instruction instead of mass production. We think, in the SCANS Commission, that "school to work transition" is the wrong term, what you really require is "school and work integration" around a common language.

John Bishop at Cornell traces the lack of effort among American high school students to employers' lack of interest in the high school transcript. If you want that interest, you need a transcript that speaks to what employers want. That is why we recommend the resume.

Also, Congress should see to it that the National Assessment of Educational Progress and the Dictionary of Occupational Titles speak in one tongue. Earlier this month, the Departments of Education and Labor entered into a contract with the American College Testing Organization and the Council of Chief State School Officers to develop a way to assess the SCANS skills of the population at large. The Dictionary of Occupational Titles is also being changed. If they talked in the same language—and, of course, I would suggest the SCANS language—then you could make a decent estimate as to whether there will be a skills shortage or not.

But as important as that is for Congress, it is more important for individual youngsters. They have to be aware of their own personal skills gap, to acknowledge the difference between what they know and what the job of their dreams requires. Knowing what one needs to know and being able to get those skills need not wait until the student is finished with high school.

As my young research assistant said, "I feel that I'm paying to learn in college much that I could have learned in high school, and I have this foreboding that my real learning will not begin until I start work." Changing that foreboding requires a common language between business employers and schools. That is the contribution of the SCANS Commission. But languages die unless they are used in conversation by educators, employers, and the Government in this case.

In summary, a high performance economy requires a high performance human resource system. The major challenge for education and training does not arise because of changing demographics but, rather, from changing requirements for skills. The first step toward reducing the gap is an ongoing conversation, in a common language, between employers and educators.

Thank you, Mr. Chairman, and I'll be pleased to answer any questions you may have later.

[The prepared statement of Mr. Packer follows:]

PREPARED STATEMENT OF ARNOLD H. PACKER, SENIOR FELLOW, INSTITUTE FOR POLICY STUDIES, JOHNS HOPKINS UNIVERSITY

Good Morning, Mr. Chairman. It is a pleasure to be here today and to speak to you about the implications of demographic trends for the workforce. My name is Arnold Packer. At present, I am a Senior Fellow at the Johns Hopkins Institute for Policy Studies where I direct a newly formed SCANS/2000 Program.

Up until May of this year I was Executive Director of the Secretary of Labor's Commission on Achieving Necessary Skills or SCANS. The SCANS Commission of 31 leaders from business, labor, education, and government worked from May of 1990 to April of this year and produced a number of reports, including *Learning a Living: A Blueprint for High Performance.* (With your permission, Mr. Chairman, I would like to enter that report into the record.) Some of the 31 SCANS Commissioners are advisors to me at the SCANS/2000 Program.

Prior to that assignment I was Deputy Director of the Work Force 2000 project at the Hudson Institute and co-author of the *Work Force 2000* report. William Brock who chaired SCANS and launched the Work Force 2000 project when he was Secretary of Labor, is also an Advisor to the SCANS/2000 Program.

The goal of the SCANS/2000 Program at Johns Hopkins is to expand on the work of SCANS and Work Force 2000. Our vision is American workers doing high-performance work at good wages. Our challenge is to contribute to the development of human resource policies that will help bring about this vision during a period of rapid change.

CHANGING REQUIREMENTS

Corporations, governments, non-profit institutions, and the world of work are being transformed as economies globalize, technologies advance, and demographics shift. The United States is not adjusting well to the transformation. Earnings have fallen for most workers over the last twenty years and family incomes have been maintained only by sending more family members to work.

In 1969, unskilled or semi-skilled workers in the U.S. could earn 20 to 40 times as much as workers in many countries of the developing world. Since then, technology and globalization increased wages in nations such as Korea and Taiwan while wages in the U.S. fell. In 1969, a large majority of American males who had managed to acquire a high school diploma could support a family. Today, American males with only a high-school education find it much harder to earn even a poverty-level wage. The share of African-American males with 12 years of education unable to support a family of four above poverty rose from 20% in 1969 to 43% in 1989; among whites the comparable figure rose from 8% to 23%.

The choice before us is whether we will continue to allow the earnings of American workers to stagnate or, instead, take steps to increase their skills, productivity, and wages. The title of an influential recent report stated the alternatives clearly: *America's Choice: High Skills or Low Wages. Work Force 2000* expressed the choice a little differently, stating that the skills of American workers must increase substantially or the nation will not be able to grow rapidly enough to improve the American standard of living.

These findings are now generally well accepted, most agree that the nation needs to restructure, reform, improve and invest in education and training. Today's real debate revolves around how to improve the skills of today's and tomorrow's workers—those already in the workforce and those still in school. The relevant questions are:

• What, how, and who to teach, and

• How to achieve a high-performance economy that will seek and reward a skilled workforce.

These new questions were addressed by the Secretary of Labor's Commission on Achieving Necessary Skills (SCANS). SCANS identified a set of competencies that are closely associated with higher-performance jobs and higher wages. The SCANS research found that workers exhibiting higher levels of these skills earned an additional $11,000 annually.

SCANS research found that workers earning a decent living are competent at a handful of things. For example, they can plan their time and develop and follow schedules. They can work in a team, negotiate, and explain what has to be done. They are comfortable with technology and can interpret instructions. They know how to find information and use a computer. Most importantly, they understand that they work in a "system" of people and procedures that define the way things are done. Also they can read and write and have the personal qualities that make for a good worker. The Commission believes that these skills are essential to a successful adjustment to the new economic, technological, and demographic conditions.

CHANGING DEMOGRAPHICS: AGE, RACE, AND GENDER

I want to emphasize the relatively modest role that the growing number of women and minorities in the workforce is playing in the adjustment process. The changing age of Americans will be much more important. The youngest of those born in the baby boom of 1946–62 have past their 30th birthday and the older ones are campaigning to be President and Vice-President.

By 2005 the median age of the labor force will be 40.6 years, about what it was in 1962, but four years older than the median was in 1990. Until 2005, the number of non-workers—primarily children and older persons—dependent on each working American will decline. In 1990, there was an equal number of workers and non-workers in the United States, but by 2005 there will only be 9 non-workers per 10 workers. By 2010, however, the tide will turn as the oldest baby boomers start to retire. Then the burden of support on those of working age will grow.

In other words, the next twenty years offer a window in which to correct the problems that were not addressed in the last twenty. Productivity must begin to grow at rates like those of the 1950's and 60's and much faster than it has in recent years. *In Work Force 2000* we pointed out that productivity in the service sector grew by 1.4% annually between 1955 and 1970 but actually fell between 1970 and 1985.

Mr. Chairman, your letter of invitation asked about the impact of demographics on the challenges facing us. Yes, the workforce is becoming more female and less white. According to the latest projections from the Bureau of Labor Statistics, the labor force will grow by about 26 million persons between 1990 and 2005 as 56 million persons begin to look for work and 30 million leave the workforce. While 18 million white men will enter, 14 million white men will leave; so that white men will only make up 15% of the 26 million net additions and their share of the 2005 labor force will shrink to 38.2%. Women of all races will be almost half of the entrants but only 43% of the leavers, so that females will constitute 50% of the net additions. Minorities of both sexes are projected to be 35% of the entrants to the labor force and 54% of the net additions to the labor force over the 15 years from 1990 to 2005.

These demographic changes, as important as they are, should not be a cause for alarm. According to an analysis that I made of the need for upgrading the U.S. labor force, the demographic shift accounted for only 10% of the challenge. Much more important was the changing nature of the job requirements. I estimated that the changing mix of jobs will generate 56% of the training requirement.

SKILLS SHORTAGES

Let me spend a moment to define a "skills shortage" as I use the term. As many highly skilled, but unemployed or underemployed workers will attest, there is surely no generalized skills shortage today. And many firms with idle equipment will claim that there is no shortage of capital either. These are, we hope, short-term considerations that will end when an economic recovery begins in earnest.

Shortages of skills and capital have to do with the strength and duration of the recovery. Even in this long-term sense we should recognize that ours is a functioning economy and employers will adjust to the availability of capital and skill. When the recession ends, shortages will not empty the shelves of supermarkets nor will factories be idled because of a lack of skills or equipment as, for example, is often the case in Russia. In that sense, the U.S. does not face a crisis of capital or skills. The shortage will appear as a continuing stagnation in wages, productivity, and competitiveness.

Thus, the shortage shows itself not as halting production but rather as limiting potential economic growth. This shortage kills our dreams. With enough capital and skill we could grow faster. There would be more "good" jobs. In *Work Force 2000* we found that the current level of skills was inadequate to support growth of 3% annually between 1985 and 2000. An economic growth rate of 3% requires a higher skilled workforce. A growth rate of 3% would allow for higher wages and for disposable income to grow by 1.7% annually while eliminating the budget deficit. *Work Force 2000* also contained a lower economic growth path. This low-wage path requires fewer skilled workers, but disposable income grows by only 0.6% annually.

The debate over whether there is or is not a skill shortage is a semantic argument. Almost everyone agrees that there is a choice and advocates taking the high-skill, high-wage path. While it is easy to write articles and make speeches about what a "shortage" means, it is a waste of Congress's time and energy to debate whether there is a shortage when everyone agrees that skills need to be improved.

ELEMENTS OF A HUMAN RESOURCE STRATEGY

The issue that is worth time and much Congressional energy, is: How does the nation take the high path? How do we convince firms to become high-performance employers that seek high skills and are willing to pay high wages? What do we do about education and training so that firms who choose high performance will know that they will be able to find capable workers? And, does demographic change alter the human resource strategy we should adopt?

Let me begin with the last question. Demographic change should alert us to an obvious fact that educators have recognized for a long time but which has not yet significantly changed education. The NY Times recently reported on research findings explaining the male reluctance to ask directions when lost. The researchers report this phenomenon to be a result of the differences in the way men and women locate themselves spatially. There is also some evidence from Holland that females do better in mathematics if it is taught in a non-traditional fashion.

There is no need to argue about whether mathematics should be taught differently to men and women. The point is that humans, irrespective of race and gender, vary and have different strengths, weaknesses and—the point of this discussion—learning styles.

The best-known researcher on this subject is Howard Gardner of Harvard whose has developed a Theory of Multiple Intelligences. He posits seven such intelligences: linguistic (poets and speech writers), musical, logical/mathematics (academic and IQ tests), spatial, kinesthetic, and intra-personal and inter-personal intelligence. Education should foster all of these, not only the intelligence that can be measured by multiple choice exams.

The recent SCANS report proposed that schools provide students with a resume of their achievements. The resume accommodates Gardner's idea of different intelligences. The Commission recognized that work rewards one for doing well while school tends to punish weaknesses. As one athletic Commissioner said: "Our approach is more like competing in the decathlon than entering in one track and field event. In the decathlon, I made up for my weakness in the shotput by doing better in the hurdles." Instead of concentrating on minimum competency, schools should seek maximum development of the student's talents. This means customizing instruction instead of mass producing a uniform product.

A COMMON LANGUAGE

The next century will emphasize school-and-work integration rather than school-to-work transition. Life-long learning means that the transition is never complete.

Integration of school and work requires a common language that will be shared by school and work. With a common language, one can focus on the gap between what is known and what is required to be known. John Bishop at Cornell traces the lack of effort in American high school students to employers' lack of interest in the high school transcript. Establishing interest requires a transcript that speaks to what employers want. But if every employer states his or her wants in their own terms there is no way that schools can produce a uniform transcript. That is why SCANS recommended a resume that educators, employers, and youngsters all understand.

Similarly, if the Congress wants to develop human resource policy, then it has to know something about the gap between the capacity of today's workforce and the requirements of tomorrow's workplace. Capacity estimates are now provided by the National Assessment of Educational Progress (NAEP) and job requirements by forecasts of the future economy coupled with data compiled for the Dictionary of Occupational Titles (DoT). But NAEP and DoT use different terms. A crosswalk between the two data sets was developed for *Work Force 2000* so that we could estimate the skills gap. The effort was arduous and, in many ways, unsatisfactory.

Congress should see to it that NAEP and DoT speak in one tongue. Earlier this month NAEP and the Department of Labor entered into a contract with American College Testing and the Council of Chief State Officers to begin to develop a NAEP exam for the SCANS skills. The Dictionary of Occupational Titles is also being revamped. If that revamping ended with a way to describe jobs in SCANS terms then Congress will have a way to estimate the nation's potential skill shortage.

As important as it is for Congress to be aware of the nation's skills gap, youngsters (and those who advise them) need to be aware of their own personal skills gap. They need to acknowledge the difference between what they know and what the job of their dreams requires. Note this awareness requires a leap to an imagined occupational future. If all you want to be is a "hamburger flipper" there is no gap. Wanting to own a chain of restaurants, however, requires more and different skills. Similarly, if the nation will accept a low-wage future then there is no skills shortage.

Choosing high wages requires investing in human resources. Among the first steps should be getting educators and employers to share a common language. It is hard for a student to choose between a year of chemistry and a year of geometry when the employer says "I need a problem solver," especially if the employer has not specified the types of problems to be solved.

The Department of Labor, through its Commission on Work-based Learning, and the Department of Education are supporting the development of industry skills standards. Presumably, these standards will define the "problems" that workers in that industry must solve. If all industries would describe the standards using a common language then the schools could respond.

Moreover, the response need not wait until the student is finished with high school. As my young research assistant said the other day: "I feel that I am paying to learn in college much that I could have learned in high school and I have this foreboding that my 'real' learning will not begin until I start work." Changing all of that requires a common language between business and schools.

A common language is the contribution of the SCANS Commission. But languages die unless they are used in conversation—by educators, employers, and the government in this case. There are many things the Congress could do to foster that sort of conversation, and most would require little if any new funds. I have already mentioned the need to align the DoT with the NAEP surveys. Current efforts of the Departments of Labor and Education could be strengthened. More could be done in assessment. Demonstration projects could be valuable. The first step, however, is to decide to take action to make the choice of high skills and high wages more reality than rhetoric.

In summary, a high-performance economy requires a high-performance human resource system. The major challenge for education and training does not arise because of changing demographics, but rather from changing requirements for skills. The first step for reducing the gap between the current level of skills and what is needed for a high performance economy is an on-going conversation, in a common language, between employers and educators. SCANS may have defined that language but it will not live unless the two parties use it to communicate.

I would be pleased to answer any questions you might have.

Mr. SAWYER. Thank you very much, Dr. Packer.

Dr. Mishel.

Mr. MISHEL. Thank you.

I am here to provide doom and gloom, and it is not so much that I enjoy that, it is the only thing that appears through my eyeglasses, and although I do think that there are ways out of our problems, I am sure that pursuing the same path we are on now won't get us the solutions we need and the type of basically income growth and standard of living that we potentially could have.

I want to address the future by first discussing the recent past, because some analyses of the future ring more true than others in the context of what we already know of what is happening and the clearest evidence we have of the future is, in fact, what we know has happened.

I see in the last 12 or 15 years that we have encountered two layers of problems. The early layer was the one that came in full in the early 1980's. It is the problem of the dramatic fall in wages of the noncollege-educated workforce, the fact that 80 percent of the workers in this country had lower wages by the end of the 1980's than in the early 1980's, a situation that was particularly severe for men, for blue-collar workers, for those with less than a college degree.

The wages of male high school graduates fell 16 percent from 1979 to 1991, and I think for me the statistic that symbolizes the problem the most is, what are the wages that a young male high school graduate can earn? This is not a dropout, this is someone who did schooling, and the young male high school graduate in 1991 earned 26 percent less than one in 1979 and around 30 percent less than a young male high school graduate in 1973. This is a dramatic erosion of the earnings opportunities of a broad segment of the workforce.

And I say "broad" because many times people have an overestimate of how many people have completed college in our workforce. In fact, it is less than 25 percent of even people in their thirties that have a college degree. There are a fair number of people who have gone to some college—1, 2, or 3 years—but, in fact, the wages of people who have some college education are basically very similar to those people with a high school degree and move just like those with a high school degree.

So for all intents and purposes, we have a workforce, even the young workforce, those people, let's say, between 25 and 34 who have completed their schooling—we have a workforce of which 75 percent are not college graduates. So when we talk about the falling wages of high school graduates, we are really talking about what has happened to the vast majority.

This has not only been a problem for men, the wages of young women high school graduates have fallen 16 percent over the last 12 years. All these statistics and more than you ever want to know are in the document I submitted as my testimony.

That is the first layer of problem, and that is the one that is now more familiar. I want to talk about a new layer of problem, and this can be characterized by: The bright spots of the 1980's have now dimmed. That is, there were groups that still enjoyed wage growth in the early and mid 1980's, that by the late 1980's and early 1990's it was no longer the case.

For instance, one of the success stories over the 1980's was that the wages of women were rising in real terms, and that was the case, for instance, of the median woman worker; their wage rose 5 or 6 percent between 1979 and 1989. However, the wages of women have been falling rapidly over the last 2 or 3 years, and that decline has wiped out just about the entire gains of the 1980's.

Over the 1980's, the wages of college graduates grew, although modestly. Starting in 1987, the wages of college graduates and of people just coming into the workforce with college degrees has been declining. A male college graduate's wage in 1991 was 5 percent lower than in 1987.

The reason for the emergence of basically depressed wages and earnings opportunities for white-collar workers and college-educated workers is not because we have been producing so many college graduates that we have a surplus of them driving down their wage, which was the case in the 1970's.

The worrisome part of this is that there has been a very slow growth in demand for white-college and college-educated workers as we have seen the collapse of Wall Street, and the finance sector, and insurance, and real estate, and banking, and we have seen that the "lean and mean" philosophy in manufacturing has now gone beyond the blue-collar sector to the white-collar sector and there is restructuring in retail trade and other industries which are severely reducing their white-collar employment.

A confirmation of these trends is the nature of the current recession. I have become a convert of late to the notion that this is a heavily white-collar recession, something that I didn't think was the case a year ago. I have been convinced because of the following two types of efforts.

One is, if you just look at the increase in the number of people unemployed, you will see that the rise of white-collar unemployed comprises more than 50 percent of the rise in unemployment. This is not to say that blue-collar workers haven't been intensively hurt by the recession. Blue-collar workers have much higher unemployment rates than white-collar workers; white-collar workers now have unemployment rates which are still less than what blue-collar workers had before we went into the recession, but the fact is that white-collar workers have been far more affected in this recession than in any recession we have had in the post-war period.

The other trend that suggests problems to me is not just the rise of white-collar unemployment but the fact that white-collar employment has grown extraordinarily slowly, as pointed out by the Bureau of Labor Statistics in an article a few months ago, so that basically the job opportunities for white-collar workers is still growing but much slower than it was, for instance, in the 1980's.

So I think we have come to the end of the white-collar boom that we experienced, and I think, in fact, a lot of the reason that there is so much political turmoil, that there is such a low level of consumer confidence can be traced to the problems of the white-collar and college-educated workforce, that what we have is not only those folks who have been somewhat immune from the economic problems of the 1980's now face not only a higher risk of unemployment but that their wages and incomes are now falling, which I think is the bigger item, and I think that that is one major element for the lack of confidence.

The other is that I think that people understand, after all the dramatic problems we have had, that this is not a short-term, cyclical phenomenon, that we have long-term problems, and that our incomes are not going to be growing quickly in the near future, once we get out of the recession, that we face fundamental structural problems of generating income growth for the American population.

One dramatic way to illustrate this is the fact that I believe that it is true that the younger families today will probably not obtain the incomes that earlier generations had. We already have people in my cohort earning less than the people who were 10 years ahead of me. The people 10 years behind me have started out much lower than what I did in my cohort and are unlikely to achieve what has been achieved in my sort of 10-year cohort, and this is essentially the way I view our problems of slow income growth.

Slow income growth does not mean that no one has more income in 1 year than the next or over 10 years. The problem of income growth, the way it has been carried out, the mechanism is that young people start out with lower incomes and they progress more slowly as they age, and when they reach middle age—and we will take a broad interpretation of what that is—they will achieve not as much as what an earlier generation had when they were in their high earning years, and I think that is a problem.

Let me now turn to the future, and the question is, as my colleagues have been talking about: What are the trends with regard to the skills required on the job? What are the skills of the available workforce? How is it that we get to a high wage growth path for the U.S. workforce?

My belief is that we are firmly on a low wage economic growth path and that we have been on that growth path for some 15 years or more. So it is not actually just a choice between whether we go higher or low. No one from any Government office has announced that we are now going to pursue a low wage path to growth, but one should be able to read the information about how people have been doing and understand that, in fact, there has been an implicit strategy about how we are to integrate ourselves in the global economy that is based on the fact that we intend to have slow wage growth or declining wages as one of our major weapons, and there won't be a press release announcing it.

So the question is whether we are going to shift paths or continue down the same path. You may know, in fact, that the U.S. workforce is the only one of the advanced countries that had lower wages over the last 10 years. Other countries were having real wage growth while our workers were seeing wages rise slower than inflation, and a slow inflation rate to boot.

What is the evidence about what the jobs of the future are going to be and the skills required for them? One set of evidence involves looking at BLS employment projections, and I have done that, and I think the way one should address projections of the future is to ask, what do the future trends look like relative to past trends? I think it would be very misleading when we just talk about the future without any yardstick for knowing is that change large or small.

For instance, when we talk about the composition of the workforce, a lot of what we see in the future has already been happening in the past. With regard to, for instance, minorities, there was actually a faster integration of minorities into the workforce over the last 12 years than is expected over the next 15, especially for African Americans. That is not the case for Hispanics.

So I think we need to hold up a yardstick to the projections, and when you do that, you see that the expected growth in the skill requirements for jobs, the types of skills that workers need, the education required of them, will need to be higher in the future than now. In other words, employers will be requiring workers to have more skills and education.

However, the rate at which that is increasing would be expected to be much slower if the projections were true in the 1990's than it was in the 1980's, which it wasn't in the 1970's, than it was in the 1960's. That is, we don't have an explosion of skill requirements facing us, we actually have an economy which is very slowly producing the need for higher skills.

Another set of evidence about what the future holds is normally considered that the wages of college-educated workers have grown faster than those for less educated or high school graduates, so that the wage gap between college workers and high school workers has grown, and economists pursuing this type of research have shown that this represents a bidding up of the premium for education, or the premium for skill, and I think that that is true in part. What people don't appreciate is that the reason there has been a growing gap between the college wage and the high school wage is primarily the deterioration of a high school wage. The wage of a college graduate in 1989 was just marginally above that of 1979, but what happened was a dramatic erosion for everybody else.

Nor does a ratio of college to high school wages tell you much about what is happening on average because remember, I said that the college workforce is just 25 percent, and the people in the denominator of the high school workforce are 75 percent. So a ratio of 25 percent to 75 percent doesn't tell you what is happening to the person at the 50th percentile in any way or what is happening on average.

I think most convincing to me that the wage data do not suggest that we are going to have a rapid explosion of jobs requiring college degrees is what I have already said has happened, which is that since 1987 the wages of white-collar and college-educated workers has begun to fall.

Now, guaranteed, it has not fallen as fast as that of high school graduates, so that for any individual graduating high school it is still economically rational to go to college because you will be better off than if you don't. However, the situation we are now in is, if you compare the wages in every education group in 1989, they were far lower than they were in 1973. Let me explain that. In 1973 the wages of college graduates fell dramatically. That was because we had a surplus of college graduates, because we had a big baby boom, because there was a draft and a lot of the baby boom went to college—baby boomers of the male variety—and it drove down the wages.

If you realize that the college wage grew just modestly in the 1980's, then you realize that the losses from the seventies were never recouped and that the college wage was 12 percent lower in 1989 than 1973, and there was a dramatic erosion of the wages of high school graduates, there was an erosion of the wages of people with one to 3 years of college.

The only reason why, on average, our wages haven't fallen more is that we have been shifting. There are proportionately fewer high school dropouts and more high school graduates. There are proportionately fewer high school graduates and more college graduates. If we had not been upscaling our workforce educationally, our wages would have dropped some 10 to 14 percent on average from 1973 to 1989. In fact, it was a much lower 3 or 4 percent percent. So I don't find as convincing that there is going to be a white-collar boom, a big boom for technical, managerial, executive, white-collar professional workers in the 1990's.

Another area of evidence that people use to talk about the future skills, and it is the one we know the least about, which is not what kind of occupations we are going to be in, not what kind of industries we are going to be in, but what happened to the particular types of jobs.

For instance, Dr. Levitan talked about how the job of a secretary has changed over time. I rather think it has been more dramatically upgraded in skill level than he does, but the biggest force that is going to change what skills the workers of the future need is not so much what occupations they are in but whether a bank teller's job, a blue-collar operative's job, a telephone operator's job is going to require a lot more skills now in the future than in the past and not so much whether we have more service workers than manufacturing workers or more white-collar workers than blue-collar workers.

All the evidence suggests—as slight as it is—that there has been no giant leap forward in the skills required for particular jobs. It has grown; it has grown dramatically in a small minority of firms that are considered leaders in the field, that are cutting edge, high performance firms, and there is a lot of misleading information on the street, so to speak, about the dramatic changes in jobs.

I will just give an example of a report by the National Association of Manufacturers with Towers Perrin, a consulting group, which I consider is just trying to profit from trying to publicize the idea of labor shortages. They do a survey of NAM members and get a response of 10 percent, so they claim they have some kind of valid survey, which in an academic journal wouldn't even be considered.

So you start with totally weak data, and then you claim there is a labor shortage. Well, the labor shortage they say there is among small manufacturers, the occupation that they say is most in shortage, is common laborer. Among all manufacturers the skills that are short are operatives, regular blue-collar operatives, and skilled blue-collar workers. The ones where there is no shortage are basically the white-collar technical workers in manufacturing. But the headlines to this are, "Great Skill Shortages."

This is not to say that there aren't any skills shortages, particularly in manufacturing, but just that there is misleading information, and I don't believe that any skills shortage in the manufacturing sector has been a constraint on particularly our large manufacturers to upgrade their technology to implement new work systems.

When we are talking about manufacturing, we are talking about the highest wage sectors that have the cream of the crop. It seems very clear to me that they have not been constrained by a lack of available skills.

I want to say a word about the demographics of the future and close with some implications for policy. The demographic trends are important. As my Congresswoman said, some two-thirds of the workforce is going to be minority and female in the entrants, and I think it is important to think about both of those categories separately. One major reason is that all the major evidence that I have seen has convinced me that women are smarter and better educated than men, and there is no reason to believe that a large share of the future workforce being female——

Mr. SAWYER. That is a very safe thing to say with your back to a largely Federal workforce.

Mr. MISHEL. Well, it is Federal evidence.

So I don't see, at least in terms of skills, that there is much of a problem with regard to having women being a larger share. I think the issue has to do with work-family connections and other issues. It is not a skills question. The problem that women face in a labor market is not the skills they bring in, it is what happens to them once they are in, and all the evidence is that the educational upgrading that is going on is happening much more among women than men, college completion rates, et cetera, so that in the future there will be a fair distance between the average education levels of women than men.

With regard to minorities, I think it is important to note that the big growth is really basically Hispanics, partly due to future immigration but partly due to past immigration, that the composition of the workforce is not becoming very much increasingly more African American, for instance.

But it is also important to note, as the Census Bureau just did in one of its reports, that there has been a dramatic improvement in the education levels of African Americans. It is not a very well known fact. It is not only that more African Americans have completed high school, it is also, if you look at other data, that their test scores have risen dramatically, and there has been a substantial closing of the gap between whites and blacks.

It is not that blacks still are not scoring less, and it is not that we don't need to do more both for whites and for blacks in schooling, but the degree to which one might imagine the disadvantage of having a more increasingly black workforce is substantially lessened over the last 20 years.

Last, for some policy implications, my basic point is that we have a major problem with the types of jobs that are available to people and the wages that are paid to them. That is the major problem confronting us: Are we going to do something that is going to provide a decent and rising standard of living for the vast majority, something we have not done?

How do we do that? Well, it is clear to me that we can't do it alone by raising the skills of the workforce. This is not to say that education isn't important, does not have economic benefits, does not have benefits for producing better citizens. It is that to be honest with the American people we must say, to have a high wage growth path, we must not only invest in our people, we must make sure that there are high skill, high wage jobs available to them, which leads to another very uncomfortable truth: If you want to go on a high wage path, one must block the way to the low wage path. I don't think there is any real way to do it.

It is not going to be by exhortation by the President or the Secretary of Labor that gets companies to change the way that they use their workforces, that upgrade technology to put in lean production systems, to have labor-management cooperation. Every company makes decisions and will be increasingly making decisions, are they going to produce in the United States, or are they going to produce in Mexico or some other lower wage country. They are going to make a decision about whether they are going to try to bust their union or they are going to work with their union. They are going to decide, are we going to try to have a workforce filled with part-timers without benefits or temporary workers without permanent status?

Companies are going both ways, and some companies at the same time. You know, part of them are doing a high wage path, and part are doing a low wage path, and it seems to me that the role of policy is going to have to be to inhibit the pursuit of the low wage path, and I think to be honest with the American people we have to discuss that.

Last, some comments about the Census Bureau, as my college, Dr. Levitan, did so. On the one hand, I want to contrast the Census Bureau with the other agency that deals with labor market trends, BLS, and I think the Census Bureau is to be praised for dealing with issues of income and wages forthrightly in reports and addressing the issue over the last several years, something I fought BLS for not doing. There has been very little attention in BLS publications to any problems dealing with wages.

While praising Census relative to BLS on that score, it fails on another score, and that is, I'm shocked by the increased politicization of the press releases accompanying reports. This has not had to do with any one single report, it is a trend I have noticed over the years, especially anything to do with incomes and wages that are hot political topics, and I guess I rely on, and reporters rely on, these press releases to be an accurate portrayal of what is in the information. But what you get these days is, if there is any good news, it is in the first paragraph; any bad news, you might get it later; and I think that is not an appropriate way for a statistical agency which is supposed to be above the political fray to present its evidence.

This is not to say there is a bias in particular with regard to the studies themselves, but we have allowed the politicization of the selling, the marketing, of the reports, and I find that extraordinarily disturbing.

Thank you.

Mr. SAWYER. Thank you, gentlemen.

Dr. Levitan, I have no choice but to turn back to you and see whether there was anything that you wanted to add to your comments.

Mr. LEVITAN. Thank you, Mr. Chairman. Yes, I would like to comment on what we have just heard.

Since I am the only one who stuck to the 7 minutes, I appreciate the extra time.

Mr. SAWYER. That is exactly why I'm turning back to you.

Mr. LEVITAN. The reason I did not talk about reduced wages—in my prepared statement I do have a few paragraphs on that—the point is that the assignment here was to talk about the labor force, and I thought I should stick to the job description.

However, I think that obviously we are facing very, very real problems, except that my good friend Dr. Packer has touched on the wrong points. First of all, to rely upon SCANS, the Secretary's Commission on Achieving Necessary Skills is a misplaced trust. SCANS is a series of platitudes covered by a very nice glossy cover, very beautifully printed, but it is just a bunch of platitudes.

Dr. Packer says that we need to talk in a common language. I thought we should, yes. English, I think, is the language, and I don't think that Dr. Packer has discovered something else. I'm not raising a debate about bilingualism, I think we still should stick to a common language. I agree that we do need some standards for achievements, but that is a different issue.

If we are going to have standards of achievements, then we should also be concerned about those who will fall behind, and those who will fall behind will be mostly minorities, and therefore we have to invest much more in them to keep them in school rather than just say we are going to pass standards of achievement and not worry about the consequences.

If we look at the data, it is quite clear that we have more and more people going to college, more and more people have the skills. The question is not whether they have the skills needed in the labor market. The big problems, of course, are minority students—I don't mean by minority just racial, but the minorities are those who complete 10 or even 12 years of schooling and cannot read and write. That is where we have to make the investments.

But the point is that the reason wages are declining is that we are not putting in enough investment. We are not saving enough, and therefore we don't have enough investment. Our national debt is increasing. I don't know why we didn't point it out before, but I'm sure that my two learned colleagues will agree with me.

But the real problem, I think, is that the problem is not in the schools, the problem is not in the labor market, the problem that we are facing today is in the family. The breakdown or the erosion of the family, particularly the black family, is the source of most of our major problems, the source of the poverty, and, of course, attached to that is the misguided public policies that we have experienced in the last 12 years. But, as I said before, I don't want to make this a partisan discussion, God forbid. But the fact is, that is what we have to worry about, the erosion of the family.

I'm only an economist, and some would say a poor economist, and I am not a preacher, but I know if two-thirds of black kids are born out of wedlock, then the chances that those kids are going to live in poverty are six times greater than kids born in a two-parent family. So that is the problem that we have to address.

There is one more point which I am surprised that Dr. Packer, a former Assistant Secretary for Policy in the Labor Department, did not mention, or to bemoan the fact that once upon a time a full-time wage earner working year-round could support a family of four without dropping in poverty. A major reason for that was that the minimum wage required employers to pay those wages. Now, the minimum wage falls short by about 20 percent to even get a woman with two children out of poverty.

I think that Dr. Packer has moved away too long from what he was telling me when he was in the Labor Department as far as minimum wage is concerned. We need policies that would provide incentives for the people who are now at the bottom of the economic ladder, for the people who are not working, for the people whose wages have been declining, as was pointed out by Dr. Packer and Dr. Mishel. Right now incentives open to them to overcome the obstacles they face in the labor market are grossly inadequate.

We have to create incentives for them that would convince them that if they behave with rectitude, they are going to follow old-fashioned precepts, then they are going to be able to succeed. If that sounds very conservative, I want to add that I am one of the very few who still admit to being a card-carrying liberal.

Thank you, Mr. Chairman.

Mr. SAWYER. Thank you for your comments.

First of all, everyone should understand, this is a conversation that didn't begin here today and isn't going to end here today, but I thought that perhaps Dr. Packer might like to reply before we go into questions.

Mr. PACKER. Well, Dr. Levitan has kept me on the right track for, I guess, 20 years now. But I would like to respond to his comments——

Mr. LEVITAN. Some things you haven't learned.

[Laughter.]

Mr. PACKER. And I still haven't learned. Life-long learning for me is life-long listening to Sar Levitan explain the right way.

But I would like to talk a bit about the SCANS report and what is meant by a common language. Obviously, we are all going to be speaking English, but if anybody has tried to talk to a Government agency these days, you realize that English alone will not carry you past the front door.

Schools talk in terms of 11th-grade English. Job applications usually talk in different terms. So the youngster says, frequently with justification, "Why do I have to learn this? It will not be used."

I met just Monday with representatives of business and the College Board, talking about 12th-grade mathematics. There really is an issue as to whether the geometry curriculum, which was generated in the 14th century, still is pertinent in the 21st century, and the obvious answer is, it is not.

The need to understand what a rhombus is or what a co-tangent is now less important than understanding what a mean and standard deviation are, but high schools today will teach you the former and not teach you the latter.

In English, again, this same College Board group will examine what 12th-grade English should teach. In school work, you are given a minimum number of pages to write. You learn to pad your material. If you go to college and fill two blue books, that is typically a good idea. When one comes to the business world or even the Government world, cutting it down to one or two pages is frequently the challenge, not seeing how many words you can put in. So school and work are very different worlds with very different languages.

I would suggest that part of the reason for the numbers that Larry Mishel rightly points to is that we are teaching the old skills and the world requires new skills. It seems just common sense to suggest that if you just keep teaching people how to make buggy whips they will not earn the kind of living in the 21st century that all of us want, and I'm sure all the members of the committee want.

Mr. SAWYER. Thank you, all three, very much for a series of provocative statements.

Let me at this point insert into the record the opening statement of Congressman Ridge who had to go back to the floor to participate in the debate on the rule and turn initially for questions to Mrs. Morella in recognition of her patience.

[The prepared statement of Hon. Thomas J. Ridge follows:]

PREPARED STATEMENT OF HON. THOMAS J. RIDGE, A REPRESENTATIVE IN CONGRESS FROM THE STATE OF PENNSYLVANIA

Mr. Chairman, I would like to commend you for scheduling this series of hearings. As the Subcommittee that has jurisdiction over the Bureau of Census, it would be pointless for us to have invested all the time that we have over the past 4 years in overseeing the 1990 Decennial Census, if once the data is released we do not conduct hearings such as these to evaluate what that data tells us about the characteristics of the American people.

Examining America's changing profile has never been as important as it is today. All you have to do is read a current newspaper or magazine to know that we, as policymakers, need a better understanding of the identity of the American people. The media has been saturated with stories on both the decline of the American cities and the decline of family values.

Once the Los Angeles riots themselves subsided, the question all public officials were faced with was what the riots were telling us about the ineffectiveness of our existing social programs. Today we will hear from witnesses about urban change and ghetto revitalization. It is my hope that the distinguished witnesses will be able to give us some insight into why programs will or will not work, given the current structure of our cities.

Lawmakers cannot live in a vacuum when developing programs and it would be foolish for us to implement policies without knowing who it is that would be effected by those policies. Before we create what possibly could be bad solutions to the problems facing this country, we need to have a better understanding of the people that reside in this country and what their specific needs are. If we do not, then it would be like a coach developing a game plan without first knowing who the players are and what talent they posses.

I welcome our distinguished witnesses and look forward to hearing their testimony.

Mrs. MORELLA. Thank you, Mr. Chairman.

I found it very stimulating and, again, as the chairman said, all of the comments that were made have been very provocative, some in agreement, some not. Certainly there is initiative for us to move ahead. Dr. Levitan talked about the fact that the family is deteriorating, disintegrating, and, of course, in so doing it is changing:

there is no longer the two-parent family we can look to. There are all of the variations in single heads of household.

So tying in with what you also have given as your three points: first, of all you say that technology is not radically changing; second, you say that there is a labor shortage, but, that is great; and then, of course, Government regulations which you say place too much emphasis is on regulations resulting in an impediment.

If there is the difficulty with the family and if we do have a labor shortage, then it seems to me one of the things we are saying is that child care, attention to the variation in families, is critically important. When it comes to labor shortages, we should look to compressed time, flex-time, job sharing, the kinds of things that accommodate the family changes that can enhance the productivity in the situation. We should look to some of the things that Congress is now doing, some innovations in our welfare reform, including—I won't say "workfare" because that is an overused term, but giving some waivers to some of these States, like our State of Maryland, to try some different things—the carrot particularly, rather than the stick approaches.

I would just like your comment on what I'm saying. Is that correct? Would you agree with me on those statements?

Mr. LEVITAN. Yes, I certainly would say amen to everything you said. The only thing is, I wish you had added one more point. would you agree that we need to focus on the two-thirds of black kids and the 20 percent of white kids who are going to be born out of wedlock?

We start, of course, with prenatal care. Head Start should be provided on a full basis. Schools, instead of starting at 9 and closing at 3, should be open to coincide with the working hours of parents. I don't know how many billions that will cost, we have to face up to it. Otherwise, if we don't, as a matter of public policy, try to help the family to cope under current conditions, then I think by the time they get to school it is too late. By the time they get to school, the school has to worry about discipline and devote less time to teaching. Whether they teach trigonometry one way or another, that is a very interesting point for great scholars like Dr. Packer—I'm picking on you today.

Mr. PACKER. I know.

Mr. LEVITAN. But I haven't had a chance now for quite some time.

What we do need is to assure that schools be able to teach. Right now in many areas of the country, or many communities, that is not so, and that is not going to be accomplished easily. To change conditions requires billions of dollars of investment. And, to increase productivity, you also have to have a more active Government role in order to encourage investment. To blame it on the school and bashing the NEA or the AFT, that is not going to do any good. We have to realize that we have to change our policies as we did in the thirties. We realized that the public policy was not meeting the needs of families, and we enacted all sorts of legislation. We did it during the New Deal; we have to do it in the nineties.

But the point is to put the emphasis in the right place, not to publish another glossy SCANS.

Mrs. MORELLA. I tend to agree with you, and I think the public policy has let the children down when you look to the future.

I would agree with you that Head Start is a program which is going to cost a great deal more money for all of the eligible children to be able to receive the benefit of the program. For every dollar that we put into it—and it has been in existence long enough for us to know this—we gain six dollars in benefits.

As a country, I think we have to learn to be less short-range visioned and look more long range. We seem to have the, "I want what I want when I want it, and if I don't get it I'll tear the place down," attitude.

Even in the Head Start program we passed a component called Even Start, which will help to bring parents, whether it is a single parent or two parents, up to par so that they can move along with their children. So I tend to agree with you on that.

Dr. Packer, you have taken this all very good-naturedly, and you know Dr. Levitan, looking to you as a colleague—this gives him kind of the springboard. But I wanted to also comment on the fact that you did seem to stress high skill versus low wage, and that has been torn down by your two colleagues here on the panel who seem to think it isn't quite as simplistic as that, there is not really the equation. I wonder if you want to comment on that as a solution, or do you see it actually as a solution?

Also, the other point I raised to you when I personally greeted you is, when you give the statistics with regard to the African American males with 12 years of education unable to support a family of four above poverty rose from 20 percent in 1969 to 43 percent in 1989 compared to the comparable white figure which was 8 percent in 1969 and 23 percent in 1989, and I did ask you, what about the females? and I think you said there are no statistics. Why?

Mr. PACKER. The data are harder to interpret for women in the 1969 to 1989 period where there was such a rapid increase in the female participation in the labor force. But I gather Larry Mishel, in his new work, is going to bring new data to bear on that issue.

Mrs. MORELLA. Because if you want to see the deterioration of the family, I think particularly the African American female who is a mother, or a grandmother, is bearing a tremendous burden in that particular regard.

Mr. PACKER. Part of that family problem arises because it's hard to raise a family without a decent job. Whether the female or the male is heading the family, a decent job is what is necessary.

I think with regard to the evidence on skills, it is true, as Larry Mishel says, what you earn with a college degree did not rise very much in the eighties and has fallen since. Still, as Larry says, the economically wise decision is to get that college degree because the premium, the difference, in having that degree is at historic highs and very much higher than it was in 1973. Data in the glossy-covered SCANS report does indicate that the SCANS skills make a difference of $11,000 a year.

So I think while it is important to worry about how the labor market will utilize that set of skills, it is extremely important for family purposes and others to make sure that the skills are there. I think a lot of the problem in the poverty household is not a lack of morality, it is a lack of hope, and that lack of hope comes from not having an opportunity to get a decent job and having the sinking feeling that, because I dropped out of high school, I don't have the skills for that job. The way to keep kids in school is to teach them stuff that they find interesting and relevant to their roles out of school. I don't think that is a modest issue.

In my judgment, education is not the only thing, but it sure beats whatever comes second as a way out of the problem. And you are quite right about Head Start; that should be fully funded. You are quite right about changing the labor market, but a lot of the things you suggest require better skills. That is, if you are going to have compressed time and flex-time, that means you have to have workers that are self-motivated and can figure out for themselves what needs to be done. The old-fashioned method didn't require many skills: "Come in at 8 o'clock, you punch a time clock, you do what I tell you when I tell you and how I tell you, and you go home at 4 o'clock, or 5 o'clock." That doesn't fit in a two-worker family or a one-parent, one-worker family. What does fit is, "Look, I'll tell you in general what needs to be done. Do it flexibly. I trust you have the skills and the motivation to do the job right." That is a different way of educating people.

Mrs. MORELLA. You are talking about a general educational background rather than the high technology skills that are imperative.

I want to turn now to Dr. Mishel, who is a really brilliant constituent of mine, Mr. Chairman. He recognizes the value of women in the workforce and what they can offer.

Mr. SAWYER. You would never pander to a constituent, would you, not in an election year?

Mrs. MORELLA. No.

Mr. SAWYER. No.

Mrs. MORELLA. Actually, it is interesting, because, picking up on what you said, Dr. Packer, he talks about the gap between the high school and college wage and the slowly increasing need for higher skills.

I was reminded of a hearing that I recently had on two of my pieces of legislation which dealt with sexual harassment. Really, the bills weren't sexual harassment bills, but it ended up being like that. It had to do with promoting apprenticeships in nontraditional roles for women and then science and engineering roles for women, and what they had in common was that those of the white-collar profession were hitting a glass ceiling and those in the blue-collar were hitting a brick wall.

We had a woman garbage truck driver. She had just barely a high school education—maybe a GED that she actually got—and she was a single head of a household, and she was asked, "Why did you pick that job if you got such harassment?" She had to pick up her work orders in the men's room. I mean that ended up being harassment. She said, "Because it pays better." Well, that pay was better than being a kindergarten teacher, and that is saying something else about skills and values and why some people will go into some of those particular professions.

I just wonder if we can equate that.

Mr. PACKER. If you take the look at the ratio of, say, engineers' salaries to teachers' salaries in the United States compared to those in Japan or Germany, it is clear that we in this country do not respect education as much as those other countries do.

Mrs. MORELLA. And it may mean that all of this emphasis on higher education is not as important as just teaching basic literacy, open-mindedness, in terms of the jobs for the future. Is that also something that is happening?

Mr. PACKER. Well, working with cultural diversity is indeed one of the skills that we located as being crucial to being able to succeed in the 21st century. Yes, you do need to have that openness. A broad education usually leads to that.

Mrs. MORELLA. Yes.

Dr. Mishel, I wondered if you wanted to add anything. You certainly did offer some fascinating trends and developments in your comments on the Census Bureau versus the Bureau of Labor Statistics. I was trying to figure out how should they do it. Should they not issue press releases or just do a news story?

Mr. MISHEL. Just a straightforward press release would do. I mean I'm saying BLS needs to do the studies and Census needs to release them in a better way.

I want to comment on this family business, because I think it is vastly exaggerated, what we are talking about here. I think we are mistaking female-headed families for kids born out of wedlock; they are not the same thing. The vast majority of women who are heads of families are divorced, separated, widowed, and never married. Female-headed families is not a permanent state of being, it is something that families go into and come out of. The actual major growth of female-headed families occurred in the 1970's, not the 1980's. It has been going on for much longer. It is going on around the world in the advanced countries.

The major reason why we have a growth in poverty is not the rise of female-headed families; there has been a rise in poverty among married-couple families. What has happened is that we have had what you would call adverse demographic trends. I mean the more female-headed families, the more poverty you are likely to have, and that has been going on.

What has changed in the last 10 years is that economic growth used to diminish poverty, and the character of our economic growth didn't do that in the eighties, it actually exacerbated poverty, so that you have an economic situation that is not ameliorating sort of an adverse demographic trend, you have it exacerbating it.

I think we should recognize that some 80 percent of families are married couples, that the vast majority of children live in married-couple families. This is not to say that there aren't great issues to be concerned about with regard to female-headed families, and I think what you are trying to identify I value greatly, which is—I'll put it very strongly—Why is it that a woman separated from the paycheck of a man is almost necessarily poor?

In other words, it is not a natural state of being that a woman needs a man's paycheck to not be poor, and I think that is one way to look at the female-headed issue. It is not necessarily misbehavior, although, you know, clearly there is a lot of adverse—things that people are doing that don't make sense but make sense within the life they face, but that in the overall benefit of the country and their own benefit don't make sense.

I'm not saying that people don't contribute to their own problems and that we don't have things to solve that are not economic in nature, but I think it is vastly exaggerated especially because it reduces the problem of poverty to an image in people's minds which is black, female-headed, out of wedlock kids, ghettos, which is a small part of the overall rise in poverty, although something that we should be concerned about.

Lastly, I would just say I'm glad I'm not sitting between my two colleagues.

[Laughter.]

Mrs. MORELLA. I have no other questions, but I thought to myself as you had each spoken that I have really not asked you all the questions I had thought of; I also thought, I wonder if the three of you could ever sit down and come out with one paper with the three names in terms of a census.

Mr. MISHEL. The answer is yes.

Mrs. MORELLA. Maybe you could.

Mr. MISHEL. I think so, actually.

I would say that the differences between Dr. Packer and me are not that we don't need more skills, but it is the degree to which it is worthwhile to talk about upgrading skills without talking about the fundamentals of what jobs are out there, and I don't think he disagrees with me that the evolution of the job structure is not what we want. I think we would both agree that it is sub-par in terms of the jobs being offered in the future and what has been offered in the past. The question is, you know, couching a program for human investment and whether we consider that is the constraint on future growth or whether it is not—you know, how much we have to do sort of both things at once, get better jobs and better skills.

Mr. PACKER. I don't think we disagree that we have to do both things at once. You have to get better jobs, and you have to get better skills, and you have to work on both problem areas.

Mr. LEVITAN. I am not as optimistic as my two colleagues. I think if we would write one paper there would be a lot of footnotes with dissents, and as to what we should emphasize, how much we emphasize the family, how much new skills, and so on, it would be a very, very confusing paper. I think we should write separately.

Mr. SAWYER. I'm not sure you could write a paper. I suspect you could write a book between you.

Mrs. MORELLA. That is absolutely right—exactly.

I want to thank the panel and thank you, Mr. Chairman.

Mr. SAWYER. Thank you very much.

I have got dozens of questions here.

Mr. MISHEL. Mr. Chairman, could I interrupt for a moment? I just want to say that I'm a single parent this week and I have to pick my kids up at one o'clock. They are preschool kids. So I need to leave here shortly.

Mr. SAWYER. I appreciate that, and I am not going to ask many questions. Let me try to consolidate them into categorical questions, if I could.

One of the things we haven't talked an awful lot about is the age structure of the workforce. We have touched on it, but we haven't talked an awful lot about it. Clearly, if there is a place in the American workforce where the majority of workers traditionally have acquired the skills they needed for each succeeding year of employment, it has been in the workplace itself, and as we see a very large population bulge spread across that workforce up and down the ladder, there are fewer open rungs on that ladder for a succeeding generation.

It is a phenomenon that I'm not sure we have confronted in quite this way in the modern history of this country, where the avenue toward the skills that are needed most is precluded by the occupancy of a previous generation to quite the degree that we are likely to face as a result of the age structure of the current population.

Do we know very much about the longevity of jobs themselves? Is it important? Is it important to understand where the opportunities will make themselves not only for entry but for promotion within a workforce for a successor generation? And this gets to the second question, whose burden in supporting that larger dependent population at some point, perhaps a later point than currently, but at some point in the foreseeable future. Do we know enough about duration of jobs or the way in which we ought to be going about substituting for training on the job for a successor generation?

Mr. LEVITAN. Well, if you assume that occupational requirements have not changed very radically, as I tried to argue before, then I think that opportunities are going to continue to exist as they did by and large in the past. If, again, people retire at a later age, there would be fewer opportunities for younger people to step in. But by and large I don't see major changes in the next 10 or 20 years, although I will hasten to admit that I still have difficulty in finding out what is happening in 1992, and I certainly don't know what is going to happen in the year 2002 or 2012.

But the fact is that we have always been talking about changes in the labor force, and these changes are slow, and the labor force adjusts to it, employers adjust to it, the educational system will adjust to it, except that lately we have not done the right things as far as public policy is concerned, and we have fallen behind.

Mr. SAWYER. I'm asking questions that really do impose on public policy at a time when, for example, the military is seeing a substantial down-sizing and an increase in the forced departure of some folks who had thought of themselves as career participants in the military. It nonetheless continues to recruit and make space. It is an "up or out" policy. That does not exist in large measure in our workforce.

There are large numbers of people who value stability over movement and advancement. If, in fact, job skills are not changing at a very rapid pace, then we see very little incentive to upgrade or move if stability and security become the highest value in individual decision-making for an entire generation.

Is there anything that we need to worry about in those terms? Question one. And, question two: if we are seeing happen to incomes what you have described, will the income or productive capacity of that smaller generation in successorship be sufficient to support the economic demands of a larger dependent elderly population?

Mr. LEVITAN. I think advancement comes with seniority, and certainly you in Congress know that seniority is a very important institution, and it applies also to a large extent also in the private sector. In my own business, you get older, you teach less, and you get paid more, and that is the way I think we are going to continue.

So, again, I am not in a mood today to worry too much about the year 2002. I think we ought to change what we are doing today as far as public policy is concerned. But I don't see that there would be any radical changes in opportunities for people as they enter the labor force in the years ahead.

Mr. SAWYER. Any other perspective?

Mr. PACKER. Well, I think Sar has proven again that he is right. We could not write a joint paper.

I think your point is very well taken, Mr. Chairman. After the baby boom starts to retire, living standards will decline for most Americans, or will continue to decline for most Americans, unless we can boost the productivity of the labor force.

Skill requirements are not changing rapidly enough. Unless we can require more skills and pay for those skills too, then the problems that you point to will come about.

Now there has been an extraordinary shift in the thinking, if not yet the practice, of American corporations. American corporations need to move to flat organizations away form the hierarchy with all the brains at the top and all the heavy lifting at the bottom. That is not a system that will be competitive. Competitiveness requires total quality production or total customer satisfactory or Dr. Deming's method, or whatever you wish to call it. We are going to have to have success throughout the organization and that we no longer can preserve the idea that all the wisdom is at the top of the organization, along with the very high salaries, that has characterized the 1980's.

Mr. SAWYER. Dr. Mishel.

Mr. MISHEL. On the first question about basically job mobility, job tenure, the answer is, we don't know as much as need to know. What we have some idea of is the tenure of people in particular employers. We have very little information, or very few studies survey employers and the jobs that they have. We have a lot of information about the supply side of the market, the workforce, and very little about the demand side, the jobs of employers and whether—my bias is to believe that jobs are not getting longer, that you are not there longer, as I thought you might be suggesting, but shorter, although I will tell you that all the evidence on that is weak and there is the frequently expressed notion that people have to change jobs so many times over their lifetime. I have never been able to find out how that has been substantiated or where that comes from, unless anyone else knows. I mean you commonly hear that, that in the future people are going to have to change much more often in the past.

Mr. SAWYER. If they are going to stop and retrain and go back to new careers, I haven't seen it happening except in the rare instances that are so extraordinary, they make news when they do.

Mr. MISHEL. Yes.

Mr. SAWYER. It has just not happened.

Mr. MISHEL. I would agree with you. In my view, the biggest gap in our training, our post-secondary system, is the lack of skill development on the job. We are one of the few countries that has no policy whatsoever in that area, or a very weak policy, and that is a great area of concern of mine that we have to move forward in.

I will refrain from saying anything about the training of the future workforce to carry the load of the dependents in the year 2020 or 2050 because I haven't examined that question.

Mr. SAWYER. Thank you.

One of the kinds of questions that keep recurring is—and I want to go back, as Dr. Levitan suggests, to the jurisdiction of the committee—is that we seem to know a great deal about the incidence of phenomena but we know very little about intensity or quality or duration of phenomena.

You talk about singularity among parents. We really don't know very much about how long it lasts, the age at which it starts, the consequences that are age dependent, or the duration. I suspect that all of those, although I don't have any data to back it up, have profound effects on the performance of any given family and, consequently, of specific family structure.

Mr. MISHEL. I praised the Census Bureau in this regard. I just want to praise the SIPP Program, the Survey on Income and Program Participation. It is a panel of households, people. I mean it is of short duration. At some level, you want to follow people over decades, not over a two-and-a-half-year period or whatever it is. But it is very much a step in the right direction, and I know it is a mammoth undertaking.

Mr. SAWYER. One of the other arenas that this particular subcommittee is working on is trying to plan for 2000 and beyond and to come to grips not only with the way in which we conduct the decennial census, but the kind of information that we try to gather. Perhaps we should move some of that information and expand that information base into more frequent, less intensive measurements of a broad sample of a population, rather than trying to use this enormous and unwieldy, every-10-year technique to gather all the information from which other data can flow.

In any event, let me go back to the subject of immigration. We talked about that. What do we know about immigrants today and the consequences that has for either the benefit or burden on a workforce? What do we know about age of entry or level of education, skills level, economic stability, English language skills, and so forth, and what are the consequences? What should we know?

Mr. LEVITAN. We do know something about it, and that is the immigrant, as long as he or she lives, their wages keep on increasing. But the problem of immigrants is that they may have an impact on the lower level jobs. How much this is a factor we really don't know, but the fact is that a lot of the work done by immigrants today, particularly those who are undocumented, they do the work at lower wages and therefore—and sometimes maybe even below the minimum wage—and, to that extent, like in anything else, there are some gainers and some losers, and the people at the bottom of the economic ladder may be victims of immigrants who work at the low wages.

In other words, if we decrease the supply of people working at lower wages, we might have more chances for those at the bottom. But we really don't know or have enough data on it.

Mr. SAWYER. I'm trying to see what I have not asked or has not been addressed in one way or another.

Mr. LEVITAN. While you are thinking of the next question, we do have longitudinal data, the National Longitudinal Survey, in your State, by the way, in Columbus. They did collect data, starting in 1968, for various age groups. The trouble is that it is expensive, and people dropped out of the survey, and the support for that survey has declined very radically.

There is another survey in the neighboring State of Michigan, PSID.

What does that stand for?

Mr. MISHEL. Panel Study on Income Dynamics.

Mr. LEVITAN. Yes, and that one has also traced families for more than 20 years. So we do have some longitudinal data on what is happening to the labor force over the years.

Mr. MISHEL. It is very dated, and it takes a long time to get current information from any of those sources.

Mr. PACKER. But it is crucial. I mean the idea of changing welfare to make it a temporary situation requires understanding how people change over the years. The census has always been a snapshot kind of situation, and people don't have very good memories about the past. So you need the data that can only be found by expensive longitudinal studies. But I'm sure you know the old story about the drunk who was looking for his key under the light even though he had dropped it in the dark.

Mr. SAWYER. You look where the light is.

Mr. PACKER. He went where the light was, right, and going where the data is cheap is not always——

Mr. MISHEL. That was an economist, not a drunk.

[Laughter.]

Mr. SAWYER. You have some distance in order to meet your family obligations, don't you?

Mr. MISHEL. Yes. I'm sorry.

Mr. SAWYER. I appreciate very much the contributions that you have all made this morning. Frankly, we have covered most of the territory that I had wanted to. I would appreciate the opportunity to submit questions in writing, not exhaustive, but, nonetheless, if you would be prepared to respond, I would appreciate it.

Mr. PACKER. Yes.

Mr. SAWYER. The materials that you have submitted will be inserted as part of the record. I thank you very much for your time here this morning.

Mr. PACKER. Thank you.

Mr. MISHEL. Thank you.

Mr. LEVITAN. Thank you.

Mr. SAWYER. Our second panel this morning is comprised of Rosslyn Kleeman, the Director of the Federal Workforce Future Issues, General Government Division of GAO. Like our previous witnesses, her credentials are exhaustive and impressive. Our second witness is Maureen Steinbruner, the executive vice president of the Center for National Policy, who has similar kinds of credentials.

If you would both identify your colleagues who are with you for our record, we can proceed with Rosslyn Kleeman.

STATEMENTS OF ROSSLYN S. KLEEMAN, DIRECTOR, FEDERAL WORKFORCE FUTURE ISSUES, GENERAL GOVERNMENT DIVISION, U.S. GENERAL ACCOUNTING OFFICE, ACCOMPANIED BY CURTIS COPELAND, PROJECT MANAGER; AND MAUREEN S. STEINBRUNER, EXECUTIVE VICE PRESIDENT, CENTER FOR NATIONAL POLICY, ACCOMPANIED BY IRA FORMAN, FELLOW IN AMERICAN POLITICS AND THE ECONOMY

Ms. KLEEMAN. Thank you very much, Mr. Chairman.

I have with me Curtis Copeland, one of our evaluators, who has worked on the reports that you have from the General Accounting Office. I would like to submit my full statement for the record and give you a shortened version.

Mr. SAWYER. Without objection.

Ms. KLEEMAN. Workforce 2000, a report that has become a reference tool for the personnel management community, predicted that several demographic facts would shape the economy and the workforce of the future. Two of these predictions—that there would be generalized labor shortages and skills mismatches—have been discussed here today and debated by labor economics and other experts.

Given the questions that have been raised about these predictions, we decided to concentrate our efforts on the other elements of the Workforce 2000 report—that is, on the demographic changes in the workforce that have occurred and are expected to occur.

The most dramatic of these changes in recent decades has been the wholesale entry of women into the labor force. As figure 1 in my testimony shows, in 1950 only about one-third of all women were in the civilian labor force. By 1990, women's labor force participation rate had increased to nearly 60 percent. During that same period of time, men's labor force participation rates fell by about 10 percentage points to about 76 percent in 1990.

I might add, since our work is primarily about Federal employees, in that same period of time from 1976 to 1990, the number of men in the Federal workforce decreased by about 100,000, and the number of women increased by about 200,000. This is particularly dramatic when you think that about 100,000 clerical jobs have disappeared during that time and women are usually identified with clerical jobs.

The most dramatic change in women's labor force participation rates has been among married women with children. As figure 2 in my testimony shows, less than 19 percent of married women with children under age 6 were in the labor force in 1960, but by 1990 nearly 60 percent of such women were in the labor force. Labor force participation rates for married women with children ages 6 to 17 increased from 39 percent in 1960 to nearly 75 percent in 1990.

Relatedly, there has been a dramatic increase in the proportion of families in which both husbands and wives are in the labor force. In 1960 less than 32 percent of working husbands' wives were in the labor force. By 1990 that percentage had more than doubled to nearly 70 percent.

These statistics clearly indicate that the traditional family in which the wife stays home while the husband works is now a thing of the past. As fewer and fewer households have care givers in the home during working hours, more and more employees face the challenge of trying to manage personal responsibilities from the office or from the work site.

A number of employers have changed their human resource policies to help employees balance their work and family responsibilities. There are a lot of new programs on flexible work schedules, flexi-place, job sharing, flexible benefits—that kind of thing. The key word and the key element in work-family programs is "flexibility." I might add that the private sector employers that we have talked to tell us that they don't put these programs into place just to be nice; they have really paid off in increased recruiting and retention of the better workers and in increased productivity.

The second demographic trend we examined in our study was the increasing percentage of racial or ethnic minorities in the civilian labor force. In 1980 minorities represented about 17 percent of the workforce. By 1990 this had increased to nearly 21 percent, and BLS officials predict a continuation in this trend into the next century, with minorities expected to represent about 27 percent of the labor force by the year 2005.

Figure 3 shows that while the number of whites in the labor force is expected to increase by about 17 percent between 1990 and 2005, the number of blacks is expected to increase by over 30 percent, and Asians and Hispanics are expected to increase by 75 percent during this period.

In response to or in anticipation of these changes, many employers have initiated programs to recognize the increasing cultural diversity of their workforce. Particularly, they have instituted training programs to discuss cultural diversity.

A third demographic trend we have discussed in our report was the aging of the workforce. In a sense, this phenomenon is nothing new. As figure 4 shows, while the median age of the civilian workforce has been rising since 1980, the median age is still not as high as it was in 1962 and is not expected to reach that level again until the year 2005.

In some ways, the changes in the age composition of the labor force will be different from what we have experienced to date. Figure 5 shows that between 1975 and 1990 there was a middle-aging of the workforce. From 1990 to 2005 the greatest increase in the labor force is expected to be in the 55-and-older group.

The aging of the labor force is, to date, believed to have had a number of positive economic effects. However, the long-term consequences may be of more concern. By the second or third decade of the 21st century, a significant portion of the labor force will be eligible to retire, and perhaps a larger portion than at any time in American history. If the large number of baby boom generation workers retire and the relatively smaller post-baby boom generation is insufficient to take its place, officials that we interviewed said that there may be generalized tight labor markets.

Some employers we talked to are devising incentives to encourage the use of older workers. Some private sector employers are allowing elder employees to transition to part-time schedules and are hiring retired workers for occasional or temporary jobs. If there is widespread use of such programs, the labor shortage scenario could change.

Because the work of my group is particularly concerned with the Federal civil service, I should mention that all the demographic changes that I have discussed—the feminization of the labor force, the increasing presence of minority and older workers—are also occurring in the Federal workforce, and we believe that the Federal Government must devise strategies to deal with these demographic shifts. However, because the demographic composition of the Federal workforce differs by agency and by region, a single strategy or set of strategies probably won't be appropriate in all circumstances.

I might add that the demographic changes in the general workforce are similarly varied. We should be looking at regional differences and occupational differences there as well as in the Federal labor force, and use different approaches for them also.

The inescapable conclusion one draws after looking at the issues of demographic changes is that today's labor force is dramatically different from that of the past, and it is no great stretch of the imagination to predict that the labor force of the next generation will be different than today's.

For the changes that have occurred already, the relevant question is: Have employers adapted to the changed conditions? Have they recognized that employees need help in balancing work and family life? Have they recognized and used the strengths of a diverse workforce? And for the changes that are still to come, the relevant question is: What should we do to prepare for the labor force of the future?

Some employers, as I mentioned, have recognized the changing dimensions of the workforce and are changing their human resource policies to respond to or to anticipate those changes. We strongly believe that these policies will pay dividends in improved recruitment, retention, and productivity, and that those employers who adopt such changes appear to be better positioned to prosper and grow in the 21st century.

That concludes my prepared statement, Mr. Chairman. I would be glad to answer any questions you have.

[The prepared statement of Ms. Kleeman follows:]

PREPARED STATEMENT OF ROSSLYN S. KLEEMAN, DIRECTOR, FEDERAL WORKFORCE FUTURE ISSUES, GENERAL ACCOUNTING OFFICE

The civilian labor force has changed dramatically in recent decades and is expected to change even more in the decades to come. In response to or in anticipation of those trends, a number of employers are modifying their human resources policies to better enable them to attract, develop, and retain a productive workforce.

The most dramatic of recent demographic changes has been the wholesale entry of women into the workforce, particularly married women with children. The "traditional family," in which the wife stays home while the husband works, and the ability of workers to separate their work and family lives have become historical artifacts. in recognition of this new environment, more and more employers are offering child and elder care assistance, flexible work schedules, flexible benefits, parental leave, and other human resources programs to help their employees balance work and family responsibilities.

Another demographic trend is the increasing representation of racial or ethnic minorities in the labor force. By the year 2005, minorities are expected to represent 27 percent of the labor force, with the highest percentage increases between 1990 and 2005 occurring among Hispanic and Asian/other groups. Some employers have initiated training programs to recognize the increasing cultural diversity of their workforces.

A third trend is the aging of the labor force, driven largely by the aging of the baby-boom generation. Although the effects of this change to date are believed to have been positive, tight labor markets may occur in the second or third decades of the 21st century if large numbers of baby-boom generation workers leave the labor force. Some employers have developed strategies to allow phased retirement and/or to utilize the skills of retirees.

All of these demographic changes are also occurring in the federal workforce. The percentage of the federal workforce that was women rose faster between 1976 and 1990 than in the nonfederal sector. The federal workforce is also more minority based and older than the nonfederal sector.

Some employers have responded to recent demographic changes in the workforce and are anticipating those changes that are expected to occur. These employers appear better positioned to prosper in the 21st century.

Mr. Chairman and Members of the Subcommittee: I am pleased to be here this morning to discuss our recent reports describing the changing workforce and the programs some employers have developed to respond to those changes.

In 1987 the Hudson Institute Published *Workforce 2000*—a report that has become an essential reference book for the personnel management community.[1] Among the demographic "facts" that the report said would shape the economy and the workforce of the future were: (1) tighter labor markets due to slower workforce growth and a smaller reservoir of well-qualified talent; (2) a continued "feminization" of the workforce (i.e., a growing percentage of the workforce that is female); (3) the increasing representation of Blacks, Hispanics, Asians, and other minorities in the workforce; and (4) the aging of the workforce. Our report on *Demograghic Issues Facing the Federal Government* examined each of these changes in some detail.[2] A second report on the *Comparison of Federal and Nonfederal Work/Family Programs and Approaches* described what some employers are doing to respond to the feminization of the workforce.[3] Today I will discuss these changes in the labor force and describe what some employers are doing to respond to them.

TIGHT LABOR MARKETS/SKILLS MISMATCHES

One of the more controversial predictions in Workforce 2000 was that slow labor force growth, caused by declining birth rates in the post-baby boom generation (those born after 1964), would result in tighter labor markets by the year 2000. The report's prediction that a skills mismatch would emerge between the abilities of new workers and the increasing skill requirements of new jobs has also been controversial.

Several labor economists and other experts have questioned whether these conditions will occur by the turn of the century. For example, officials at the Bureau of Labor Statistics (BLS) told us that labor shortages are usually limited to certain occupations, industries, and geographic areas or for short-term periods. They also pointed out that while the supply of labor has been slowing, the demand for labor has decreased as well. With both supply and demand decreasing, widespread labor shortages are, they believe, unlikely to occur. Studies by the Economic Policy institute, the Congressional Research Service, and the Commission on the Skills of the American Workforce, also question the labor shortage/skills mismatch scenario.

Given the questions that have been raised regarding labor shortages and skills mismatches predicted in Workforce 2000, we believe that it is more prudent for employers attempting to prepare for the future to focus on those elements of the report on which there is widespread agreement—the demographic changes in the workforce that have occurred and are expected to occur.

---

[1] William B. Johnston, *Workforce 2000: Work and Workers for the 21st Century,* (Indianapolis: Hudson Institute, June 1987).

[2] *The Changing Workforce: Demographic Issues Facing the Federal Government* (GAO/GGD–92–38, March 24, 1992).

[3] *The Changing Workforce: Comparison of Federal and Nonfederal Work/Family Programs and Approaches* (GAO/GGD–92–84, April 23, 1992).

THE FEMINIZATION OF THE WORKFORCE

The most dramatic of these demographic changes in recent decades has been the wholesale entry of women into the labor force. Between 1950 and 1990, the female civilian labor force increased by nearly a million workers each year. By 1990, nearly 57 million women were working or looking for work—more than a 200-percent increase since 1950. in comparison, during this 40-year period the number of men in the labor force increased by only about 55 percent.

Another way to see this change is by looking at labor force participation rates—that is, the percentage of the population that is working or looking for work. As figure 1 shows, in 1950 only about one-third of all women were in the civilian labor force; by 1990, women's labor force participation rates had increased to nearly 60 percent. During this same period men's labor force participation rates fell by about 10 percentage points to about 76 percent in 1990. BLS has predicted that women's participation rates will continue to increase through the year 2005 while men's participation rates will continue to decline.

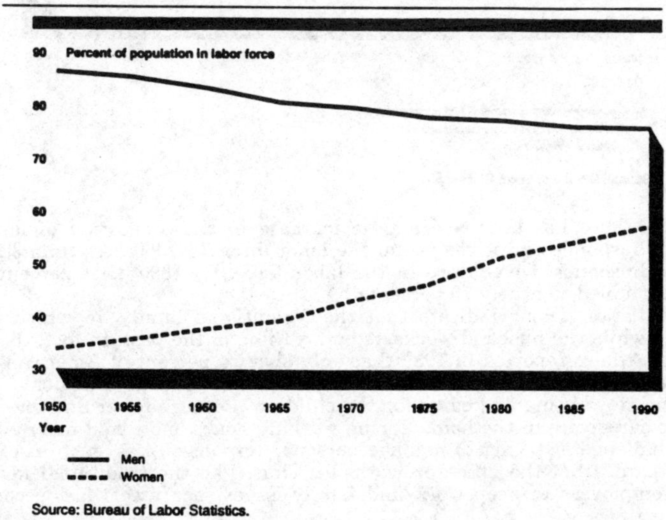

Source: Bureau of Labor Statistics.

The most dramatic change in women's labor force participation rates in recent decades has been among married women with children. As figure 2 shows, less than 19 percent of married women with children under age 6 were in the labor force in 1960. By 1990, nearly 60 percent of such women were in the labor force. Labor force participation rates for married women with children ages 6 to 17 increased from 39 percent in 1960 to nearly 75 percent in 1990.

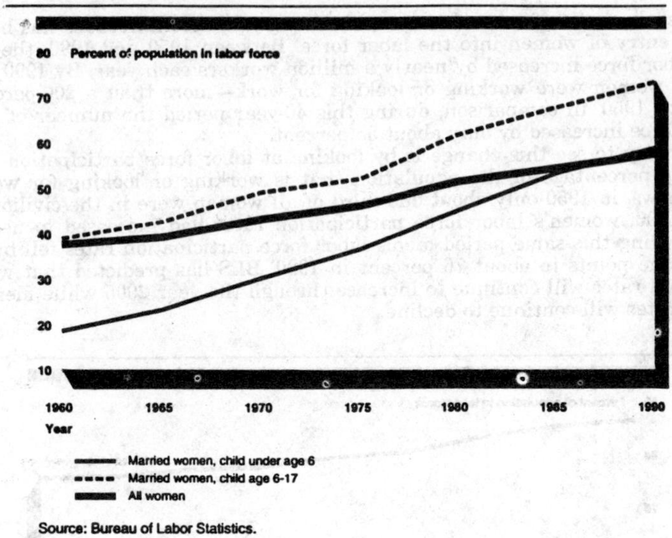

Source: Bureau of Labor Statistics.

Relatedly, there has been a dramatic increase in the proportion of families in which both husbands and wives are in the labor force. In 1960, less than 32 percent of working husbands' wives were in the labor force. By 1990, that percentage had more than doubled to nearly 70 percent.

These statistics clearly indicate that the "traditional family, in which the wife stays home while the husband works, is now a thing of the past. In fact, the Bureau of National Affairs reported in 1989 that only about 4 percent of American families fit the stereotypical image of the father who works outside the home and the mother who stays home and cares for the children. Because fewer and fewer households have caregivers in the home during working hours, more and more employees face the challenge of trying to manage personal responsibilities, such as child care and elder care, from the office or worksite. Thus, like the traditional family, the ability of employees to keep work and family issues separate is fast becoming an historical artifact.

Employees and employers increasingly realize that traditional human resources policies, such as rigid work schedules and leave programs, are not conducive to achieving a work/family balance. This imbalance has also been shown to cause increased turnover and absenteeism and lower productivity. Therefore, a number of employers have changed their human resources policies to help employees balance their work and family responsibilities, adopting such programs as flexible work schedules, increased use of part-time employment and job sharing, flexible benefits and dependent care spending accounts, flexible work place arrangements, use of sick leave to care for family members, child care centers and referral programs, elder care assistance, and counseling and training programs. The key element in these employers' work/family programs is reportedly increased flexibility to accommodate workers' needs.

Our report on *The Changing Workforce: Comparison of Federal and Nonfederal Work/Family Programs and Approaches* discusses the development of work/family programs by 16 leading nonfederal employers, including IBM, AT&T, American Express, Levi Strauss, and the States of New York and California. These employers often believed the programs helped them reduce turnover, improve productivity, and become more competitive employers, and several had done studies that demonstrated those effects.

The number of employers adopting these policies and programs has increased rapidly in recent years. For example, BLS reported that the percentage of employees in medium and large private sector firms offering child care assistance was five times greater in 1989 than in 1985. The percentage of state and local government employees eligible to receive child care assistance more than quadrupled between 1987 and 1990. Still, only a small percentage of all employers currently offer such programs. They are most common among relatively large firms. A 1991 study by Hewitt Associates found that 66 percent of the more than 1,000 major U.S. employers they surveyed provided some form of child care assistance.

Some companies have undergone a complete metamorphosis in their human resources policies. For example, in 1950 IBM did not hire married women and the company's female employees had to quit when they got married. It was assumed their husbands would support them. Now, IBM's Policies are designed to attract and retain women (as well as men). The company offers a range of programs built upon a recognition that the spheres of work and family are inextricably linked. In 1991, IBM was named by the Families and Work Institute as one of four U.S. companies having the most developed set of work and family programs.

In summary, then, a number of employers are adopting programs and

Policies to accommodate the "new workforce" brought about by the entry of women into the workforce. However, it should be emphasized that these programs and policies are not solely for women. Both women and men need human resource policies designed to help them balance work and family responsibilities.

INCREASING PERCENTAGE OF LABOR FORCE WHICH ARE MINORITIES

The second demographic trend we examined in our study was the increasing Percentage of racial or ethnic minorities in the civilian labor force. Minority representation in the employed labor force increased slowly until about 1970, but since then this representation has accelerated. By 1980 minorities represented about 17 percent of the workforce; by 1990 this had increased to nearly 21 percent. BLS officials predicted a continuation of this trend into the next century, with minorities representing 27 percent of the labor force by the year 2005.

As figure 3 shows, the representation of certain racial or ethnic groups in the labor force is expected to increase faster than others in the coming years. BLS predicted that while the number of Whites in the labor force is expected to increase by about 17 Percent between 1990 and 2005, the number of Blacks is expected to increase by over 30 percent, and the number of Hispanics and Asian/other minorities is expected to increase by about 75 percent during this period.

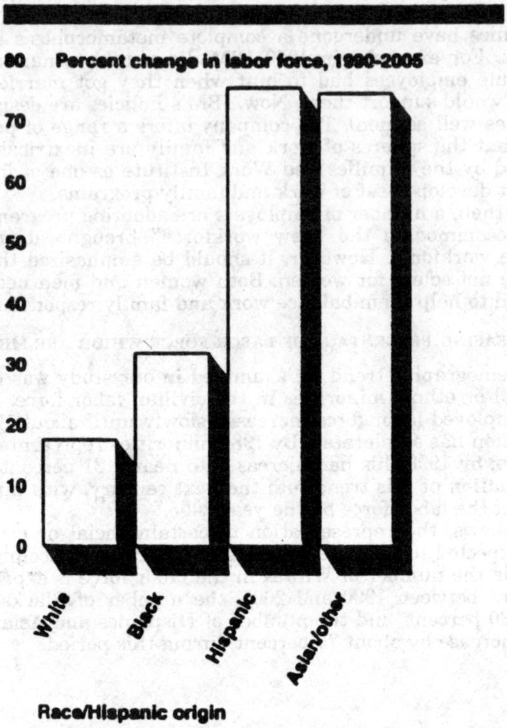

Source: Bureau of Labor Statistics.

In response to or in anticipation of these changes, some employers have initiated programs to recognize the increasing cultural diversity of their workforces. For example, Digital Equipment Corporation began a training program that helps employees understand the behavioral and business implications of a diverse workforce. The program stresses that differences are beneficial to the corporation because the workforce and customer base of the organization are changing. Similarly, several AT&T business units have established diversity training programs, workshops, and publications for their employees. AT&T has also established a cross-business unit diversity team to discuss other diversity initiatives.

AGING OF THE WORKFORCE

A third demographic trend we discussed in our report was the aging of the workforce. In a sense, this phenomenon is nothing new. As figure 4 shows, while the median age of the civilian labor force has been rising since 1980, the median age is still not as high as it was in 1962 and is not expected to reach that level again until the year 2005.

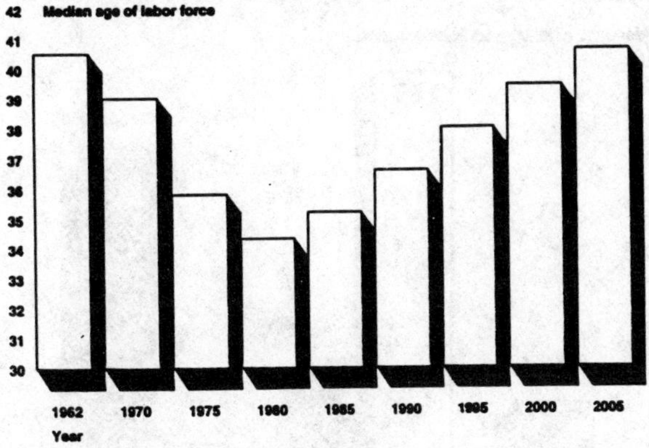

Source: Bureau of Labor Statistics.

In some ways, though, the changes to come in the age composition of the labor force will be different from what we have experienced to date. As figure 5 shows, between 1975 and 1990 the 25-to-54 age group grew more rapidly than any other age group in the labor force. Thus, what we have seen to date has been the "middle-aging" of the labor force. From 1990 to 2005, though, the greatest increase in the labor force is expected to be in the 55-and-older group. These changes reflect the movement of the 76 million person "baby-boom generation" (those born between 1946 and 1964) through the labor force age categories. The first baby boomers will turn 55 in the year 2001, with the last of that generation reaching 55 in 2019.

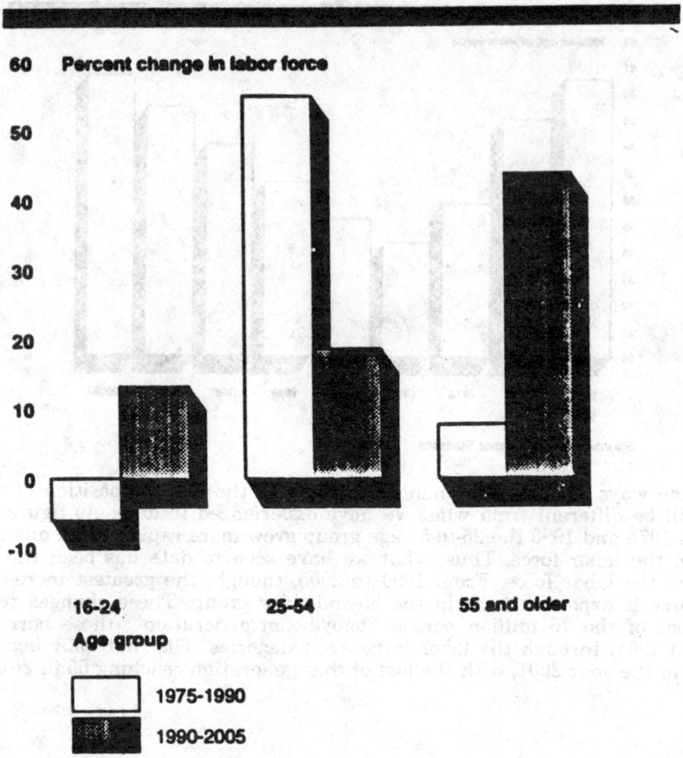

Source: Bureau of Labor Statistics.

The aging of the labor force has, to date, been believed to have had a number of positive economic effects, with the more experienced "middle-aged" workers being more productive and having a higher national saving rate. However, the longer term consequences may be of more concern. By the second or third decades of the 21st century a significant portion of the labor force will be eligible to retire—perhaps a larger portion than at any time in American history. Retirement trends indicate that workers increasingly leave the labor force as soon as they are able to do so. If large numbers of baby-boom-generation workers retire and the relatively smaller post-baby boom generation is insufficient to take its place, officials we interviewed said there may be generalized tight labor markets during the second or third decades of the 21st century. However, they said that predicting changes that far into the future is extremely risky. For example, if employers devise incentives to encourage older workers to delay their retirement plans or to utilize the skills of older workers, these tight labor markets may never exist.

Some employers are doing just that. For example, the Travelers Corporation established a job bank for its headquarters retirees in 1981, and it has since expanded the program to include non-Travelers retirees. The retirees fill positions ranging from unskilled production through data entry to professional. A study by the Commonwealth Fund found the program saved the company money, provided staffing flexibility, and offered other advantages, such as improved employee morale and an expanded temporary employment pool. G Corporation has also established a retiree job bank. The company asks retiring employees if they are interested in returning to work on a short-term basis. Those interested are called back as the need arises, and they are rehired through a contract agency so that their pensions are not affected. The company also has a phased retirement program that allows pension-eligible employees who are at least 60 years old to go on a part-time schedule but still be treated as full-time workers for pension accrual and insurance purposes. The program was initiated to allow a more gradual transfer of technology than traditional retirements allow.

IMPLICATIONS FOR THE FEDERAL EMPLOYER

All of the demographic changes I have discussed—the "feminization" of the labor force and the increasing presence of minority and older workers—are also occurring in the federal workforce. Between 1976 and 1990, the percentage of the federal workforce that was women rose faster than in the nonfederal sector. The number of federal Professional and administrative jobs held by women in the federal government rose by 162 percent during this period—10 times faster than the rate for men. The federal workforce also has a higher percentage of minorities than the nonfederal sector and is about 5 years older than its nonfederal counterpart. Therefore, the federal government must also devise strategies to deal with these demographic shifts. However, because the demographic composition of the federal workforce differs by agency and region, a single strategy or set of strategies will Probably not be appropriate in all circumstances. Demographic differences by region are also apparent in the nonfederal labor force.

CONCLUSION

The inescapable conclusion one draws after looking at the issue of demographic change is that today's labor force is dramatically different from the labor force of 20 and certainly 40 years ago. Likewise, it is no great stretch of the imagination to predict that the labor force of the next generation will be different from today's. For the changes that have occurred already, the relevant question is "have employers adapted to the changed conditions?" Have they recognized that employees need help in balancing work and family life? Rave they recognized and utilized the strengths of a diverse workforce? For the changes that are still to come, the relevant question is "what should we do to prepare for the labor force of the future?"

Some employers have recognized the changing dimensions of the workforce and have changed their human resources policies to respond to or anticipate those changes. They have also found that these policies can pay dividends in terms of improved recruitment, retention, and productivity. These employers appear better positioned to prosper and grow as we head toward the 21st century.

This concludes my prepared statement. I would be happy to try to answer any questions you might have.

Mr. SAWYER. The GAO is always within the prescribed time limit.

Ms. KLEEMAN. Thank you very much. We try.

Mr. SAWYER. I am operating under a prescribed time limit as well. Let me ask just one question before I go. I'm not quite sure how long it is going to be. I hope we can all hang in here for a few minutes, because I'm not sure how many votes there are going to be.

You suggest that the middle-aging of the workforce will yield a higher savings rate. My question is, when past generations of workers got to a particular age, their demands on income became less, the house began to get paid off, the kids were off to school, and that was generally taken care of. Much of that has been deferred for a large portion of this emerging middle-aged generation, and it is hardly a generation that has shown a propensity to save by comparison to its predecessors.

Is your conclusion about this middle-aged workforce based on past performance of age cohorts at this particular stage of life, or is there something that leads us to believe that this whole group of people is going to change the generational pattern of behavior?

Ms. KLEEMAN. We haven't done any economic studies of that age group, but I would predict that because we have better retirement, better pension plans, and many of the people are choosing to retire earlier, that that may make a difference.

Another thing has been the increase in two-worker families that will cause this middle-age group to have slightly better wages per family. Not being an economist, I'm afraid I can't give you a very detailed answer to that.

I do think there is another problem with this mid-aged group that is very serious. There is a bulge of middle managers right now. We are restructuring our whole workforce. One report that I read said that by the year 2000 we will have over 81 million managers in the 35-to-55-age group, and, at the same time, they will only have 61 million workers in the 20-to-35-age group to manage. So I think that we are going to have to look to a lot of issues related to that middle-age group that you are talking about.

Mr. SAWYER. We will all be managing each other.

I will be back shortly.

Ms. KLEEMAN. All right.

[Recess.]

Mr. SAWYER. You are all very patient, and I appreciate that very much.

Let me turn to Maureen Steinbruner.

If you would introduce your colleague for the record, we can keep track of him.

Ms. STEINBRUNER. Thank you, Mr. Chairman.

My colleague, whom you know, is Ira Forman, who has worked with me on the research that we are reporting on in today's testimony, and he is a native of the great State of Ohio—a proud native of the great State of Ohio.

Let me say first of all, I think you flagged an interesting issue this morning that there was some perhaps significant disagreement. I would like to weigh in on the side of those who say we have a problem. I think we do have a problem. I think the problem that your committee is looking at today is one that Alan Greenspan should be looking at every day in every way.

The workforce issues being considered by this subcommittee will be central, I believe, in determining how much the overall U.S. economy is able to grow in the United States in the 1990's. Midline Government economic growth projections, the official Government projections, now indicate that if trends continue, the U.S. standard of living will grow by about 13 percent over the decade of the 1990's, the decade we are in.

If this proves to be the case—and it looks like it is going to be on the high side at this point—it will be the smallest increase in per capita income in decade over decade terms of the entire century except for the decade 1910 to 1920 when per capita income did not grow and the 1930's, a decade in which it first fell sharply and then increased for a net of 12 percent. So we are talking 1930's here, if I could be colloquial.

By contrast, our standard of living grew in both the 1970's and 1980's by 18 to 19 percent. This means that in each of the past two decades, neither one of which is now considered by the public to have been particularly praiseworthy in economic terms, we had a much better per capita growth record than is currently expected for this decade. Why? Because of the nature of what has been happening to our workforce and because of how growth in the workforce growth has built our economy.

Per capita or per person output, or standard of living, which is very important to all of us, is the basis of our personal income. It, of course, also dictates how much the Nation as a whole can afford in terms of health services and education, medical research, clean air, and roads, the whole ball of wax.

Growth in our standard of living depends on two factors very simply. One factor is how productive the working part of the population is, and the other is what proportion of the population is working. Output per worker, or, more precisely, output per hour and workers, or the number of hours per population, multiplied, gives you output per person; that is, productivity times labor force participation equals standard of living.

How efficient we are, how many of us work, and how much absolutely dictate the prosperity we are able to achieve as individuals, as families, as communities, and as a nation.

As many analysts have observed and as some of your panelists mentioned this morning, growth in one of the two factors in the standard of living equation, productivity or output per worker, has been slowing for some time. Because of the facts of our current demographics, however, this slowdown now presents us with a problem, or challenge, unlike any we have seen in the postwar period.

I would like to go back and put a little historic context on what we are looking at. In the 1950's, U.S. output per hour, productivity, was increasing at a very rapid clip, so much so that we were able to reduce the portion of the population in the workforce and yet still have higher incomes. The baby boom was expanding the dependent part of the population at the low end, and at the high end, in the older age groups, earlier retirement of male workers, as has just been referred to, was more than offsetting increases in women's labor force participation. More goods and services with less effort was the story of the 1950's U.S. economy, producing a standard of living growth for the decade of a little under 17 percent. That is why it felt so good.

In the 1960's, productivity was increasing at a rate comparable to that of the 1950's. Population and work effort continued to decline over the first part of the decade, but by about the middle of those years the first baby boom cohorts began to enter the workforce. The result was that the proportion of the population in the workforce was about the same at the end of the decade as it was at the beginning.

The 1960's saw, in effect, a steady amount of population work effort along with rapid increases in output per worker. The increase in standard of living that this produced was enormous, almost 30 percent for the decade.

By the beginning of the 1970's, we were entering a period in which labor force participation would increase a great deal. The trend toward greater labor market representation for women in all relevant age ranges combined with growth in the younger worker cohort. The result was a great upward surge of paid work and paid work seeking. This combination posed great difficulty in terms of unemployment toward the end of the seventies, as you will recall. We were not able to find enough slots in the workforce for all those new workers, at least not in highly productive or well paid jobs, and that began the trends that we heard about from the earlier panel.

We did expand the service sector and the retail trade sector to take advantage of the additional pairs of hands, but we added those jobs at low wages. With a large supply of new labor, the relative price of labor declined.

Real hourly productivity increased over the 1970's at about half the rate of the 1960's. We partly made up the difference with the increase in workers but were not able to match the per capita growth performance of the 1960's.

The 1970's saw an increase in population work effort which, together with slower productivity growth, gave us a total increase in output per person for the decade of a little under 19 percent, which means that the 1950's, the 1970's, and, as we will see, the 1980's were similar in standard of living growth—not as good as the 1960's—but what was going on underneath in terms of how we were producing that standard of living was very different when you look at the different decades.

When we look at the growth record of the 1980's, which has been much discussed and debated but which I believe is still not well understood in demographic terms, what we see is that during this past decade hourly productivity grew more slowly than in any other postwar decade. We are definitely on a downhill track here. People have observed that, and it is a problem. However, we again increased our labor force participation.

During the 1980's, the U.S. standard of living increased slightly less than the 1970's, about 18 percent overall, very comparable. But the population work effort increases were a much larger part of the 1980's equation, a very different story. An increase in the work contribution of the population is not, I would submit, what we traditionally think of as prosperity. The record of the postwar period in this regard is summarized in figure 1.

The direction of these trends is the reason why the current workforce picture merits close attention as we look toward the future and why emphasis on both the quality and the opportunities of today's workforce is so essential. We are unlikely to be able to repeat the work increases of the 1980's except by increasing hours. The labor force slack is just not there.

To look at the labor force side for a moment, going into this decade approximately 192 million Americans were aged 16 and over. That is your labor force pool in absolute terms, as you know. Of that number, some 45.5 million were in what might be described as a pool where they were not candidates for full participation. A little over 10 million were high school age. They are supposed to be in school.

Fifty and a half million were between the ages of 18 and 22. Now, as we heard from Larry Mishel, there are about a quarter of those people who are in college, who complete college education. At a minimum, that is 3.8 million people still in school—it is probably larger than that—and then a very large number, almost 32 million, are people 65 and over. You might want to talk about that, the implications of that, at the end.

That leaves a primary labor force pool of about 146 million, a number that includes many individuals who might be thought of as unlikely labor force participants—for example, some mothers of very young children, some people who are too severely ill or disabled to work—the new legislation will help with that, but it won't completely change the equation there—people in prisons, people whose skills or training are so poor that there are few, if any, jobs for which they are qualified.

However, even without taking these unlikely workers out of the primary pool, we are nonetheless already at an effective labor force participation rate of about 85 percent, because there were about 125 million workers in 1990. Factoring in the unlikely workers means we are really pushing the limits in terms of additional workers per population.

This is a little bit of a different way of thinking about the so-called labor force shortage: it is the proportion of the population in the labor force overall.

Reflecting the impact of these trends, which were already under way at the end of the past decade, for the first time in at least a generation American workers were apparently starting to put in more hours on average as we entered the 1990's. Professor Levitan referred to the evidence. The evidence is not great, as you know, and I would encourage you to look at the statistical validity of what we have and also some ways to gather better data.

Our numbers do indicate, however, that there may be a bend in that trend, and in some regards people may think that is a good thing, but I think in other regards we have to agree that increasing work again is not what we consider prosperity. The total increase we see now is not very large, but it does look as if it might be a real change in trend.

Social Security Administration analysts have been assuming a slight decrease in hours in their midline estimates, which I referred to before, and this is certainly reasonable in relation to longer-term historic trends. The bottom line is, though, if hours do not increase and the proportion of the population in the workforce by and large cannot increase much because of demographics, then we simply have to do a better job of increasing productivity, as reflected in both overall output and in real wages. This is the case if we want to improve our standard of living only by the amount it improved in the 1980's and no more. It is a large and important task. This subcommittee is to be commended for helping raise this issue as a priority.

Just to finish up, I would like to offer an amendment to what I think Larry Mishel described as the options between a low wage/high growth strategy. I think we are really, unfortunately, on the path of a low wage/low growth strategy, and that is not going to make any of us feel very good.

Thank you.

[The prepared statement of Ms. Steinbruner follows:]

Prepared Statement of Maureen S. Steinbruner, Executive Vice President, Center for National Policy

The workforce issues being considered by this Subcommittee will be central in determining how much the overall U.S. economy Is able to grow in the United States during the 1990s. The labor force increases of the past couple of decades cannot be repeated in this decade. This fact contains very serious implications for the economy, implications that we need to address as a nation.

In order to appreciate why this is so, we need to step back and look at where the U.S. economy has been and where it is going in terms of the nature of its aggregate performance.

Mid-line government economic growth projections indicate that if recent demographic and economic trends continue, the U.S. standard of living will grow about 13% over the 19905.

If this proves to be the case, it will be the smallest increase in per capita income, in decade-over-decade terms, of the entire century, except for the decade 1910 to 1920, when U.S. per capita income did not grow, and the 1930s, in which we had first a sharp fall and then an increase, for net growth of about 12%.

By contrast, our standard of living grew in both the 1970s and 1980s by 18 to 19 percent. This means that in each of the past two decades—neither one of which is now considered by the public to have been highly praiseworthy in economic terms—we had a much better per capita growth record than is currently expected for the 1990s.

Why? Because of the nature of what has been happening to our workforce.

HOW STANDARD OF LIVING GROWS

Per capita or person output, or "standard of living," is the basis of personal income. In addition, of course, it also dictates how much the nation can afford in terms of health services and education, medical research, clean air and roads, regional theater and children's museums, pop music and avant garde art, theme parks and National Parks, aerospace technology and telecommunications infrastructure.

Growth in our standard of living depends on two factors. One factor is how productive the working part of the population is and the other is the proportion of the population in the work force.

Output per worker (or, more precisely, output per hour) and workers (or, number of hours) per population, multiplied, are equivalent to output per person. Productivity times labor force participation equals standard of living. How efficient we are, how many of us work, and how much dictate the prosperity we are able to achieve as individuals, as families, as communities, and as a nation.

As many analysts have observed, growth in one of the two factors in the standard of living equation—productivity, or output per worker—has been slowing for some time. Because of the facts of our current demographics, however, this slowdown now presents us with a problem, or challenge, unlike any we have seen in the postwar period.

THE HISTORIC CONTEXT

In the 1950s, U.S. output per hour, or productivity, was increasing at a very rapid clip, so much so that we were able to reduce the proportion of the population in the workforce and still have higher incomes. The baby boom was expanding the dependent part of the population at the low end, and at the high end, in the older age groups, earlier retirement of male workers was more than offsetting increases in women's labor force participation rates.

More goods and services, with less effort, was the story of the 1950s U.S. economy, producing standard of living growth of a little under 17 percent.

In the 1960s, productivity was increasing at a rate comparable to that of the 1950s. Population work effort continued to decline over the first part of the decade, but by about the middle of those years, the first baby boom cohorts began to enter the workforce. The result was that the proportion of the population in the workforce was about the same at the end of the decade as it was at the beginning.

The 1960s saw, in effect, a steady amount of population work effort along with rapid increases in output per worker. The increase in standard of living that this produced was enormous, almost 30 percent for the decade.

By the beginning of the 1970s, we were entering a period in which labor force participation would increase a great deal. The trend toward greater labor market representation for women in all relevant age ranges combined with growth in the younger worker cohort. The result was a great upward surge of paid work and paid work-seeking.

This combination posed great difficulty in terms of unemployment toward the end of the 1970s. We were not able to find enough slots in the workforce for all of those new workers—at least, not in highly productive or well-paid jobs. We did expand the service sector and the retail trade sector to take advantage of the additional pairs of hands, but we added those jobs at low wages. With a large supply of new labor, the relative price of labor declined.

Real hourly productivity increased over the 1970s at about half the rate of the 1960s. We partly made up the difference with the increase in workers, but were not able to match the per capita output growth performance of the 1960s. The 1970s saw an increase in population work effort, which together with slower productivity growth, gave us a total increase in output per person of a little under 19 percent.

That brings us to the growth record of the 1980s, which has been much discussed and debated, but which is still not well understood in demographic terms.

During this past decade, hourly productivity grew more slowly than in any other postwar decade. We again increased our labor force participation. During the 1980s, standard of living increased slightly less than in the 1970s, about 18 percent. But population work effort increases were a larger part of the 1980s equation.

An increase in the work contribution of the population is not what we traditionally think of as "prosperity." The record of the postwar period in this regard is summarized in Figure 1.

The direction of these trends is the reason why the current workforce picture merits close attention as we look toward the future, and why emphasis on both the quality and the opportunities of today's workforce is so essential.

We are unlikely to be able to repeat the work increases of the 1980s except by increasing worker hours. The labor force slack is just not there.

WHY LABOR PARTICIPATION CAN'T GROW MUCH

Going into this decade, approximately 192 million Americans were age 16 and over. Of that number, some 45 and a half million were not candidates for full participation in the workforce:

- A little over 10 million people were high-school age, 16 to 18.
- 15 and a half million were between the ages of 18 and 22. Of this age group, about a quarter now complete four years of post-secondary education. That's an additional 3.8 million people in school.
- 31.5 million were people 65 and over.

That leaves a primary labor force "pool" of some 146.3 million, a number that includes many individuals who might be

thought of as "unlikely" labor force participants. These are, for example, some mothers of very young children; people who are too severely ill or disabled to work; people in prisons; and people whose skills or training are so poor that there are few, if any, jobs for which they are qualified. Even without taking these "unlikely" workers out of the primary pool, we are nonetheless already at an effective labor force participation rate of about 85 percent, because there were about 125 million workers in 1990. Factoring in the "unlikely" workers means we are really pushing the limits in terms of additional workers per population.

Reflecting the impact of these trends, which were already underway at the end of the past decade, for the first time in at least a generation American workers were apparently starting to put in more hours, on average, as we entered the 1990s. Using Bureau of Labor Statistics data on workers working (an unpublished series), and published data on hours worked, we have calculated that the annual hours worked by Americans increased each year but one after 1982. [see Figure 2].

The total increase was not very large, but it does look as if we may be experiencing a real break in the postwar trend to shorter hours. Social Security Administration analysts have been assuming a slight decrease in hours in their mid-line estimates. This is reasonable in relation to longer-term historic trends, but if hours do not increase, and the proportion of the population in the workforce by and large cannot increase much, then we have to do a better job of increasing productivity, as reflected in both overall output and in real wages.

This is the case if we want to improve our standard of living only by the amount it improved in the 1980s, and no more.

It's a large and important task. This Sub-committee is to be commended for helping raise this issue as a priority for all of us.

FIGURE 1: COMPONENTS OF NET CHANGE IN U.S. GNP PER CAPITA (per cent)

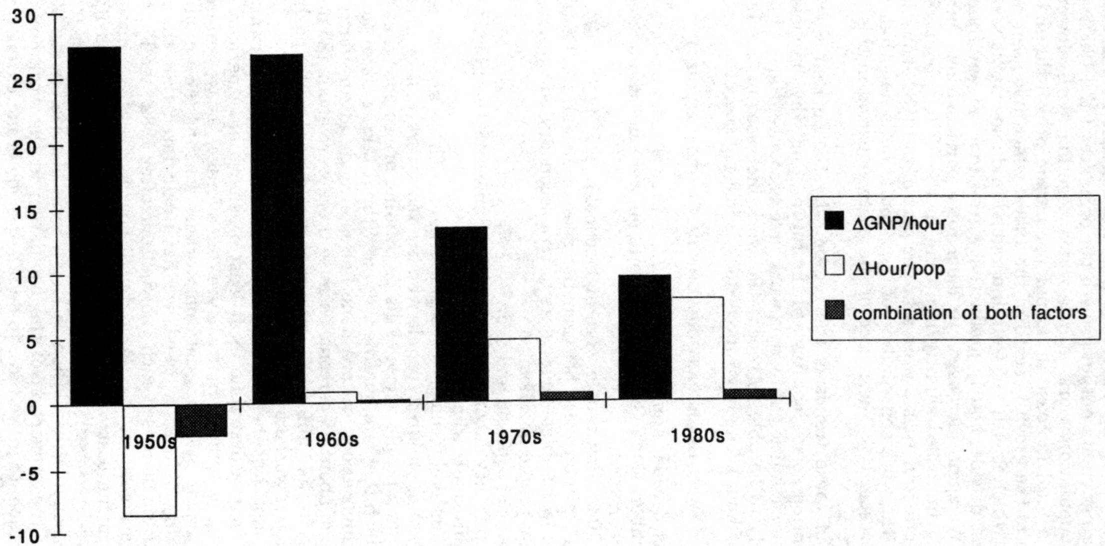

FIGURE 2: ANNUAL U.S. HOURS PER WORKERR

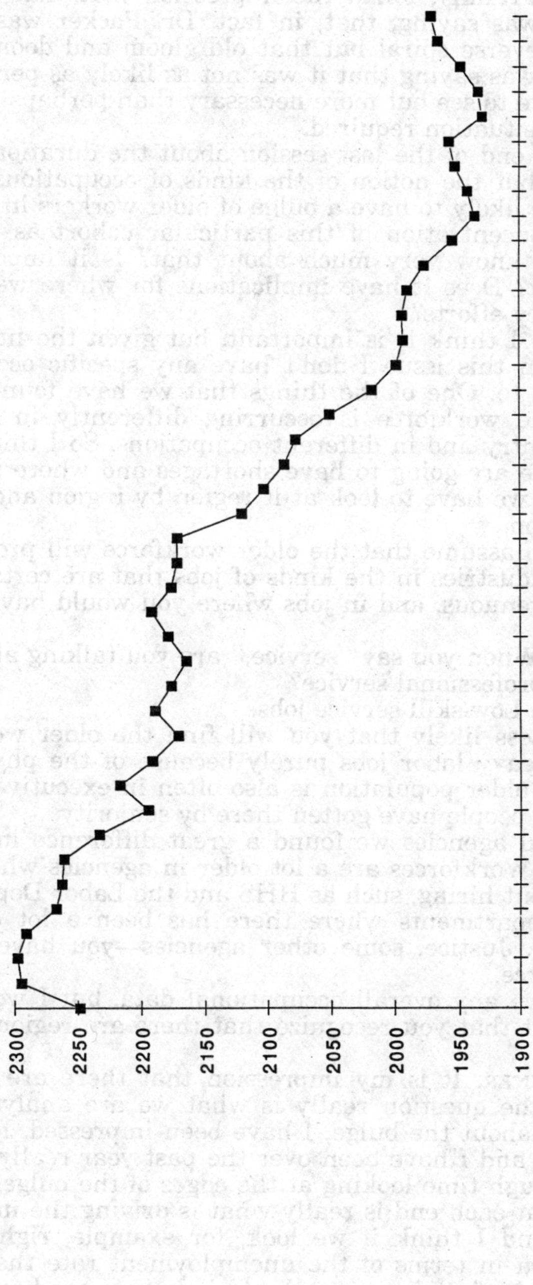

Mr. SAWYER. Frankly, I had the impression that that was precisely what he was saying, that, in fact, Dr. Packer was talking hopefully of a reverse spiral but that old gloom and doom on the end down there was saying that it was not as likely as perhaps Dr. Packer might like to see but more necessary than perhaps Dr. Levitan thought the situation required.

I asked at the end of the last session about the duration of jobs. Let me add to that the notion of the kinds of occupations and industries that are likely to have a bulge of older workers in the next 15 years, the concentration of this particular cohort as it moves through. Do we know very much about that? Is it important to know about that? Does it have implications for where we concentrate public policy efforts?

Ms. KLEEMAN. I think it is important, but given the little work we have done on this issue I don't have any specific occupations that I can point to. One of the things that we have found is that the aging of the workforce is occurring differently in different parts of the country and in different occupations. So I think as we look at where we are going to have shortages and where the older workers will be, we have to look at it region by region and occupation by occupation.

I think we can assume that the older workforce will probably be in the service industries in the kinds of jobs that are certainly not as physically strenuous, and in jobs where you would have a flexible schedule.

Mr. SAWYER. When you say "service," are you talking about low-skill service or professional service?

Ms. KLEEMAN. Low-skill service jobs.

I think it is less likely that you will find the older workers in production or heavy labor jobs purely because of the physical demands. But the older population is also often in executive and top level jobs where people have gotten there by seniority.

Across Federal agencies we found a great difference in average workforce ages. Workforces are a lot older in agencies where there hasn't been recent hiring, such as HHS and the Labor Department. In the other departments where there has been a lot of recent hiring—Defense, Justice, some other agencies—you have a much younger workforce.

So I don't have any overall occupational data, but I would urge as you look at it that you recognize that there are regional differences.

Ms. STEINBRUNER. It is my impression that there are data out there. I think the question really is what we are analyzing, and when we think about the bulge, I have been impressed, looking at the data, as Ira and I have been over the past year really, that we don't spend enough time looking at the edges of the bulge, that the rate of change at each end is really what is driving the impacts on the economy, and I think if we look, for example, right now at what is going on in terms of the unemployment rate that part of what we should be focusing on is the fact that we are beginning to see a bit of an uptick due to those baby boom kids, children of the baby boom generation, arriving at the very early edges of labor force participation age, and anything that this committee could do to encourage the Government as a whole to pay more attention to those larger cycle demographic effects and their edges I think would be very, very constructive.

Mr. SAWYER. Let me ask the same kind of question with regard to the consequences of the composition of the workforce, the characteristic changes, the racial composition, the ethnic composition, the condition of personal economic status, and the consequences that those will have, the increasing numbers in categories of those kinds of measures, the trend lines with regard to past capacity to participate in a fully productive way.

Have we looked at the way in which those fairly rapid changes in composition will change our capacity to increase productivity of the workforce?

Ms. STEINBRUNER. Again, your panelists this morning reflected the fact that there has been a fair amount of attention to that in the Workforce 2000 kinds of issues.

I guess I may be in a slightly different position from many people on this. I think what I see in the data is the possibility that we have absorbed a lot of the change already that we are going to see and that we have a workforce composition that will change at the margin, but, you know, women in a given cohort who are going to come into the labor force, they are basically there, and those changes——

Mr. SAWYER. I'm not talking about those who are not participating who will be coming in, I'm talking about the substantial changes and projectable changes in the makeup of the population itself.

Ms. STEINBRUNER. And I guess I'm arguing perhaps that, in a contrarian fashion, in some sense we have already—we are well on the way to experiencing the impact of that, it is out there right now, and the fact is, we should have started taking account of this about 10 years ago.

We don't give enough attention to the individual workers we have in the labor force. We wait for more; we throw away the ones we have. You know, it is the psychology of, "Well, just keep moving," that is very American and very healthy in a lot of ways, but it also means that you don't look at people as something you are making an investment in, you look at them kind of like a consumption item, and I think we really have to change that and that in the end will be driven by compositional changes that are already having an impact.

Mr. SAWYER. Let me ask if, in fact, that sense of an older, more feminized, more traditional minority workforce is a set of phenomena that is well upon us in the population at large. If, in fact, the Federal workforce is well ahead of that curve generally in the population, what kinds of things have we learned in that Federal workforce? What are we doing in the Federal workforce that we ought to replicate? What are we doing that we ought to avoid? What kind of lessons are we learning as a product of this ability to look beyond the horizon through a Federal workforce?

Ms. KLEEMAN. I'm not sure that we have learned any of these lessons in the Federal Government. We are much older. Our average age in the Federal Government right now is about 42, and that is the age that they expect the civilian labor force in the year 2005. Also, our education level is much higher; about 34 percent of the

Federal workforce has at least a college degree, and I think it is around 22 percent in the general workforce.

But I don't believe we have learned any lessons that we can pass along.

Mr. COPELAND. Clearly, the Federal Government is experiencing all the phenomena that the non-Federal sector has experienced. About 70 percent of Federal employees are married and living with their spouse and 75 percent of those spouses are also working. So we have really a workforce of dual-career couples.

However, surveys which we did, indicated that even though about 40 percent of the Federal workforce is on flexible work schedules, most of the people that aren't on flexible work schedules say that they would like to but their agencies or their supervisors won't let them.

So we found that there has been sort of a spotty record on responding to demographic changes, with certain agencies doing a lot and other agencies not doing very well. We recommended that the Office of Personnel Management establish an office of work/family programs to try and coordinate what the different agencies are doing and to act as a technical advisor. In June they established that office, and hopefully that development will spur greater interest on the part of Federal agencies to respond to these changing conditions.

Ms. KLEEMAN. I know we are very behind in the Federal Government in skills training, which is something that everyone is predicting will be very important. We are just now looking at skills training for some of the entry-level Federal employees where there are problems, but many of the private sector companies have recognized this for some time.

I know the Federal Reserve Bank of Boston has had skills training for their entry-level people for quite some time, and they pay them while they are taking skills training. They are finding that their entry-level people are at about the 8th-grade level in reading and writing, so they find that skills training is very valuable. Some private sector companies, such as Motorola, also give basic skill training. It saves them money in the long run. They figure it saves about $33 on every dollar they invest in skills training.

So this is an area where I'm afraid the Federal Government is just catching up. We are going to have to recognize that skills training will be important because of these future demographic changes.

Mr. SAWYER. Each of you has been putting together, synthesizing, an enormous amount of data in order to come to the presentations that you have brought us here today. What kinds of information did you find most lacking? What sorts of things should we be looking at as we try to reform the data gathering process broadly through the decennial census in the course of the next few months in order to get ready for 2000? What kind of data ought to be moved into other kinds of data collection systems, not in the decennial census at all but rolling mechanisms throughout a decade, and what kind of data simply don't exist that ought to be developed?

Ms. KLEEMAN. We are able to get pretty much all of the data that we need on Federal employees from the Central Personnel Data File. Although there are a few gaps, OPM is working on those. Some of the gaps have been on employees' educational level and keeping track if additional education as they stay in the workforce.

We have done quite well in getting information from the Bureau of Labor Statistics. There are some problems right now in developing wage data that is needed for introducing locality pay for Federal employees. That has been kind of slow, due in part to a period when the Bureau of Labor Statistics funds were in danger of being cut back. But, for the most part, we haven't found lack of data to be too great a problem.

Sometimes when I come into my office and I see the computer printouts stacked so high all over, I wonder if we aren't getting too much. But I think that is not a problem right now.

You certainly ask many more questions with computerized data than you did before, and I don't think—have you found anything?

Mr. COPELAND. We really didn't try and determine all the lackings of the data. We were pretty much overwhelmed by how much was there.

The data that exists is usually sufficient to determine the general dimensions of workforce change. What is often lacking though, is information regarding the questions you have asked—the "why" questions. Why are things happening the way that they are? Oftentimes, no amount of data will answer that question.

Ms. STEINBRUNER. Yes, I think that there is, obviously, a lot of data out there, and we are doing better in general, simply having it available in a form that people can use. Ira reminds me that in terms of looking at how many hours people are actually putting in on the job, the information is not as useful as it could be.

The other thing I would say is, your reference to what goes on between the census years, I think that is very important. Waiting for this great big tranche of data every 10 years, then it is 2 or 3 or 4 years after that before it's available—if we could do something smaller-scale in between that was more update oriented but also question driven, it would keep.

You know, your questions about the data change, because you are looking at the phenomena out there, and the questions you are asking, for example, about the impact of the composition of the workforce, well, we will want some updates on that kind of question, and it may very well be that it would be useful to consider somewhat different methodologies from the ones that we have very locked in now, just as you are considering different methodologies for the census itself, and I would just encourage you to think about that a little bit.

Mr. SAWYER. I think you have hit it right on the button. We have only recently begun to look with the seriousness that we do today at the rolling and regional character of economies and the way it affects different parts of the country very, very differently at exactly the same time.

We don't know very much about how economic effects resound back and forth among regions or whether or not there is a cause and effect there involved at all.

Ms. STEINBRUNER. It is very important—very, very important.

Mr. SAWYER. Yes. And it seems to me that as long as we are looking at snapshots that are that far removed from one another—snapshots, if they are close together, you can——

Ms. STEINBRUNER. You can make a movie out of.

Mr. SAWYER. Yes. But when they are a decade apart it is hard to tell what is going on in between, and it seems to me that that is an arena in which we can do substantially better in answering many of the kinds of dimensional questions that we don't have answers to today.

Between all of those things that we have heard from others this morning and the things that you have offered today, I guess the one question that I have that remains, other than those that may occur to us as we are in the business of putting this together and may ask you to share, is where there are things that you have heard in the course of today's hearing that you would like to respond to, or react to, or comment upon.

Ms. KLEEMAN. No, I can't think of anything. We have recognized the disagreements that you heard a little bit of here today on skills mismatches and labor shortages. We will certainly be watching these issues, particularly regarding the Federal workforce.

Mr. SAWYER. Are you in the process of identifying potential skills mismatches?

Ms. KLEEMAN. We are looking at a good number of workforce future issues. Right now we are concentrating in two areas, the first of which is what to do about the changing demographics. We are getting more and more into some of the work/family and other issues. The second thing that we are into right now is looking at who is coming into the workforce, particularly the Federal workforce.

We are quite alarmed to know that the average entry-level age in the Federal workforce is over 31 years of age right now, and this is for entry-level jobs. Those entering the Government aren't your young kids out of college, although we did hear that the age of those attending colleges has gone up. But we are very concerned about that.

Mr. SAWYER. That is very close to the average age of the college campus today. I mean it really doesn't come as a surprise, seeing what is happening all across the country.

Ms. KLEEMAN. I think we still hear that the average graduation age is about 27. But we are watching who is coming into the Federal workforce and doing a lot of work in that area.

If you have specific areas on occupations or things of that sort that you would like us to look into, we would be glad to.

Mr. SAWYER. Thank you.

Ms. STEINBRUNER. I have great respect for Sar Levitan, but I think I would like to just go on the record in disagreement with something that he said. The idea that a secretary today doesn't have to have different skills—I have been a secretary at various times in my life, and I still sit down and pop into the job from time to time, and, believe me, working a manual typewriter and working a word processor, having to maybe use data bases as well as word processing software, that is not the same job, it is just not the same job. That is one side of the equation.

The other side of the equation is the people coming into the job. You can be recruiting a receptionist today who possibly has very, very inadequate language skills but is still trying to take phone messages and write down the things that he or she needs to write down. We had a workplace 50 years ago in which people who did not have great grammar, spelling, whatever, could still do—you could go and work on an assembly line, for example, and get paid a fairly decent wage, and the fact that you could not put together a standard English language sentence would not be a problem. Now you might be in that job trying to operate a robotics machine or something.

There has been a lot of change in the nature of the jobs that are out there, and, in fact, if we want to continue to keep up with our international competitors, I think we have to have more change in that direction rather than less.

Ms. KLEEMAN. One of the things that Maureen just said reminded me that I read recently that one-third of the banks in this country now give English language training. That is a tremendous difference in workforce training.

Mr. SAWYER. It may say something about the number of banks that are headquartered in California.

Ms. STEINBRUNER. For now.

Ms. KLEEMAN. The article didn't say where the banks were.

Mr. SAWYER. Thank you all very much. I appreciate your being here. I very much appreciate the contribution to the record that we have today.

Ms. STEINBRUNER. Thank you very much.

Ms. KLEEMAN. Thank you.

Mr. SAWYER. If there is no further business to come before us, we stand adjourned.

[Whereupon, at 1:20 p.m., the subcommittee was adjourned.]

[Additional material submitted for the record follows:]

PREPARED STATEMENT OF MICHAEL R. LOSEY, PRESIDENT AND CEO, SOCIETY FOR HUMAN RESOURCE MANAGEMENT

Mr. Chairman and Members of the Subcommittee:

The Society for Human Resource Management (SHRM) welcomes this opportunity to submit this statement on changing demographics and the workplace. SHRM is the leading voice of the human resource profession, representing the interests of more than 50,000 professional and student members from around the world. Formerly the American Society for Personnel Administration, SHRM provides its membership with education and information services, conferences and seminars, government and media representation, and publications that equip human resource professionals to become leaders and decision makers within their organizations. We would like to share with you some of the findings of SHRM's issues management program relative to the impact of changing household structure on the American workplace.

Changes in U.S. family structure which began over 30 years ago have affected the workplace in ways both small and profound. Thirty years ago, the typical American family consisted of a married couple with children and a single (male) wage earner. Not surprisingly, workplace policies reflected this view of the family.

Today, this diversity of household arrangements in the U.S., make it difficult to determine if there is a "typical" American family any longer. Certainly, a one-size-fits-all approach is no longer adequate. Consequently, workplace policies designed for the family of 1960 have been and continue to be reformulated to meet the needs of today's workforce.

Whereas one-income families were the norm in 1960, for example, two-income households became the norm during the 1980's. Employers responded with policies ranging from "cafeteria" benefits and flexible working hours to child care assistance and spousal relocation. Continued changes in the two-income family, including rising birth rates among women in their 30's, are expected to foster demands for even greater workplace flexibility over the next decade.

Single-parent families, including single-father families (which according to recently released Census data were the fastest growing family group in the U.S. over the last decade), have posed their own challenges for employers, and now the rise of the no-parent family also looms.

In 1980, according to Census data, 4% of all American children lived in institutions, foster care or a household headed by a relative other than a parent. By 1990, this figure was up to one in ten, according to a study by the Annie E. Casey Foundation. Consequently, as grandparents and other relatives assume caregiving roles without necessarily having legal custody, employers have had to grapple with a new kind of family that may not rely on the legal definition of dependent.

Similarly, domestic partnerships (two adults living together and sharing expenses in a committed relationship) have also become more common in the last decade and also challenge the traditional definition of "family" in terms of workplace policies and benefits.

Finally, while employers have typically focused on the immediate needs of their current workforces, more are beginning to turn their attention to the workforces of the future: today's children. The effect of household instability on children has long been debated, but evidence is mounting that children who grow up in a household in which one or both parents are physically, financially or emotionally absent have long-term difficulties in the school system and, later, in the workplace.

Increasingly, employers are coming to the realization that they cannot build strong companies on fragmented families. These employers are working to craft policies that support rather than ignore the American family and its changing needs.

Successful integration of work and family is a complex problem, and companies across the United States are engaged in a variety of exciting, progressive experiments in meeting the needs of their work forces. Ironically, the proposed mandated family leave legislation may well stifle some of the creative work-family projects companies are undertaking while at the same time doing nothing for the small business owners who are not yet able to provide family-friendly benefits. For this reason, SHRM continues to oppose mandated family leave.

In 1988, SHRM conducted a benchmark survey of corporate work-family policies and last month released "Work & Family," a follow-up to that original report. We believe the findings of this survey will be useful to this Committee as you deliberate the issue, and an executive summary is attached for your use. The survey documents a groundswell of employer activity in the area of family-support benefits. Through our publications and educational programs, SHRM continues to encourage our members to develop family-friendly policies in their own organizations, and we applaud those employers across the country that have already done so.

Thank you for allowing us to submit this statement for the record.

AMERICA'S CHANGING PROFILE: "HOW WE COMPARE: THE GLOBAL PICTURE"

TUESDAY, SEPTEMBER 22, 1992

HOUSE OF REPRESENTATIVES,
SUBCOMMITTEE ON CENSUS AND POPULATION,
COMMITTEE ON POST OFFICE AND CIVIL SERVICE,
Washington, DC.

The subcommittee met, pursuant to call, at 1:05 p.m., in room 311, Cannon House Office Building, Hon. Thomas C. Sawyer (chairman of the subcommittee) presiding.

Member present: Representative Sawyer.

Mr. SAWYER. Good afternoon. I am pleased to welcome everybody to what is the last in a series of hearings that has spread across this spring and summer and fall to talk about demographic trends and their policy implications.

In our earlier hearings, we discussed an awful lot of changes in the composition and distribution of our population that reflect the way in which we are really redefining who we are, where we are going, and how we live. We learned that our Nation's future is increasingly being defined by two generations: one, numerically large and older, indigenous, more place bound; the other younger, more racially diverse, less affluent, more mobile.

We found that a quarter of us are people of color who are, as traditionally defined, minority populations, the fastest growing populations in the United States. This growth is being driven by higher rates of natural increase and record levels of immigration.

We found that 8 percent of our population is foreign born, the largest number of foreign-born people in our Nation's modern history. Immigrants are more likely to be young and to settle in cities. Their children are contributing both to the cultural wealth and diversity of our schools, and to the challenges that those institutions and others like them face. So it is no surprise that urbanization continues in the United States.

A century ago, for the first time, half of us lived in urban areas. Today, that new threshold that we have crossed has some three-quarters of us in metropolitan areas. Cities, however, are no longer the centers of manufacturing that they were becoming a century ago. Outmigration of jobs from urban centers has and is creating an entrenched economic underclass whose problems are only compounded by their concentration.

And so we find that poverty, as well, is concentrated in urban areas, and children are increasingly its victims. One in every five

American children is poor. The consequences of that growing number are alarming for our future.

At the same time, the Nation is aging. By 2030, the number of elderly will have doubled. The needs of the elderly population will be greater by virtue of their sheer numbers alone.

These and other demographic forces are leading to a collision of needs among different segments of the population. The challenge that all of us face is to define, understand, to balance and address those increasingly distinct, sometimes disparate and often competing interests.

But the United States isn't changing in isolation. The same kinds of demographic forces that affect our Nation can be seen on a larger scale around the world.

International migration is becoming a tidal wave of human movement. It is being spurred by fragile economies and political change—in some cases, political upheaval. There are nearly 18.5 million refugees in the world, more than at any time since the Second World War. Millions more are continuing to migrate in search of economic opportunity or to reunite with family members, or for any of the other traditional forces behind global migration.

Immigration compounds the pressures of internal migration; that is to say, the movement already taking place within national boundaries. Like us and other developed nations, the world is becoming more city-based. That threshold that we crossed a century ago, the world just recently crossed, where almost half of all humanity now lives in urban areas.

Cities in industrialized nations are increasingly ill-prepared to absorb the flood of people searching for jobs. In developing nations, rapid urban growth has outpaced the ability of governments to provide basic human services. And so it is no surprise to those of us here, who have seen those same patterns, that urban poverty is pervasive in developing nations.

But in some cases rural poverty is often even more severe. It affects absolutely everybody, regardless of age.

Which brings us to the fact that the world, like us, is aging, but not evenly. In industrialized nations, including the United States, about one out of four people will be 65 years or older by the first third of the 21st century. In developing countries, more people are young; only about one out of eight are 60 or older. This marked contrast in age structure complicates the already uneven distribution of the world's population between developed and developing nations.

Rapid and profound demographic change drives and is driven by economic and technological development. This sea change is influencing the relationship between nations and the ability of governments to address the needs of their own increasingly diverse populations, and the competitions between and among them.

Today we are going to look at global population characteristics and migration patterns. We are witnessing demographic change that I think is no overstatement to describe as global in scope and titanic in effect. The real problem for those of us who are trying to come to grips with it is not only making policy based on it; but simply measuring the pace of global change is, in many ways, nearly as great a challenge as responding to the consequences of that change.

So I am particularly grateful for the witnesses that we have here today. I have looked at your testimony, and I am just enormously impressed. It is accurate to describe you as leading experts in your fields. I look forward to your review and discussion.

And just in closure, before I turn to our witnesses, let me thank Jennifer Williams of CRS for her invaluable assistance to staff in preparing for these hearings; and to Jane DeLung and Shelley Kossack of the Population Resource Center for their support and guidance.

Our first panel today is composed of Barbara Boyle Torrey, who is the president of Population Reference Bureau. She is the Chief for the Center for International Research, up until recently, at the U.S. Bureau of the Census; recently nominated to the board of directors of the Population Association of America, and a member of the National Academy of Sciences Committee on Population.

Dr. Charles Westoff is the Maurice P. During professor of demographic studies and sociology and faculty associate, the Office of Population Research, at Princeton. From 1975 through this year, he was the director of the Office of Population Research at Princeton, a member of the board of directors of the Population Resource Center, and the Population Reference Bureau. He recently participated in the African Development Bank Conference, and comes here from there, I understand.

It is a pleasure to welcome both of you.

STATEMENTS OF BARBARA BOYLE TORREY, PRESIDENT, POPULATION REFERENCE BUREAU; AND CHARLES F. WESTOFF, MAURICE P. DURING PROFESSOR OF DEMOGRAPHIC STUDIES AND SOCIOLOGY AND FACULTY ASSOCIATE, OFFICE OF POPULATION RESEARCH, PRINCETON UNIVERSITY

Mr. SAWYER. Let me turn first to Barbara Torrey.

Ms. TORREY. Thank you. I think what I will do, instead of reading my testimony, is I will——

Mr. SAWYER. I want you to feel free to take as much time as you want. I really enjoyed your testimony, and would welcome you—would urge you to either use it, expand upon it; but whatever you do, don't truncate it for my sake.

Ms. TORREY. I think what I will do is use the figures as a way of talking and making my points on the figures themselves, which are in the back of my testimony. I actually thought you were giving my talk. Let me give you a few of my numbers.

Mr. SAWYER. Actually, mine was prepared before we received yours, and I didn't know whether we were talking back and forth between staffs or what.

Ms. TORREY. Not that I know of, but I am impressed.

Let me describe initially, what most people think of when they think of world population is, they think of this enormous growth rate. And we have three different groups of population projections. The Census Board, World Bank, and the United Nations are all within a range of each other, so that there are not significant differences. And we all show that the world's population is likely to increase 50 percent by 2020, and it is almost certainly going to double by 2040.

And you can make different kinds of assumptions, but most people are looking at those kinds of numbers.

On figure 2, you can actually see how much of that increase is coming in the developing world. It is, almost 90 percent of all of the increase is in the developing world today; and less and less will come from the developed world itself.

But on figure 3 is what I really focus on. I tend to be optimistic and think that the world could probably handle 11 billion people, but the thing that is of concern to me is how fast those people are joining us. And you can see on figure 3 that we went from 1 billion population to 2 billion, and it took us 124 years. The next billion was added, from the second to the third billion, in 34 years; and that was in our lifetime, or some of our lifetimes. And that was—it took us a long time.

We are now adding a billion people to the world's population every decade. And this is very rapid for the next five decades, much more rapid than has ever happened in the past.

When people talk about things speeding up, you can take a look at this figure and realize what they are talking about. This is despite the fact that, on figure 4, you can see how countries are actually reducing their fertility rates. And we keep forgetting, even though the population of the world is increasing, this is despite the fact that the total fertility rates have been coming down quite dramatically in many countries.

The United States, in 1842, had a total fertility rate of 6 children per woman. That is about where many of the African countries are today. It took us 58 years to drop to 3.5 births. It took Colombia and South Korea 12 years to do the same thing. These are phenomenal drops, and we are not recognizing—when people focus only on population growth, they are not recognizing these huge changes in half a generation happening in many of the countries in the world.

Despite these kinds of decreases in total fertility rates, however, you can see on figure 5 the doubling time of many of these countries; and this is what they call population momentum, that even when the fertility rates are coming down, they have so many women in their childbearing ages, that you have some of these countries doubling in a single generation. That is a huge increase. That is faster than has happened almost any other place in history; and as you can see, most of these countries are the ones that don't have the infrastructure, don't have the education and human capital yet which they would need to make this a much easier adjustment.

You can see the doubling time for the United States, given current fertility rates, is 83 years; Japan is 191 years, and my guess is they may never double again, given that.

One of the questions we looked at in terms of how to think about where people might want to focus is to look at population density. In figure 6, actually we said, OK, what are the 10 most dense countries in the world? And it was a surprise. Three of them are three of the wealthiest countries in the world—the Netherlands, Belgium, and Japan; and three of them are some of the poorest countries in the world. So population density is not by itself telling us a lot about the economic conditions, or whatever, in the countries themselves.

But what does—and what we try to do then is say, OK, let's take countries that are very dense that are also growing very fast; and when we did that, figure 7 shows you that of those eight countries, these are countries that are already very dense and are going to double in the next 30 years, and six out of the eight countries are in Africa.

And if I were to worry—I mean the older I get, I am more careful about what I worry about. But if I were to worry, I would worry about countries that are already very dense and also growing very rapidly, and that this is the list.

Now, let me pick up on one of the things, Congressman Sawyer, that you were saying, which is what I think is one of the really significant trends—which is the urbanization of the world. While the world population is doubling, actually the urban population is tripling. And you can see that on figure 8. The world is about 50 percent urban now; but it is going to 61 percent by 2020. This is very rapid, and most of it, again, is taking place in the developing world itself.

When you talk about urbanization, most people think of Mexico City, and in fact, most of the growth in urban populations is not coming in the megacities, it is coming in the cities that are below 2 million, fortunately.

I think this is an optimistic trend. Most people are very concerned about it and see it as a problem, but people—urban populations behave differently than rural populations. Their fertility rates decline, their life expectancy increases, their education increases, they have more opportunities.

But they also consume differently, urban consumers all over the world. There is an urban culture that crosses national boundaries, and that, it seems to me, is to the benefit of the urban countries that are exporting, such as the United States. Most of our exports are implicitly for urban areas; and with the huge growth around the world like this, it seems to me that we should be able to take advantage of that.

At the same time that you have drops in fertility rates, what that really does is help make the world middle-aged; and this is also an optimistic trend, I think. And figure 10 shows you actually how the world is becoming middle-aged very rapidly. And you can see that although the developing world is considerably older than—the developed world is older than the developing world, in fact, the developing world itself is aging.

What happens is, you also have an aging labor force, which means you have got increased productivity. Aging people consume different kinds of things, they are more settled, they get married, they have children. There is a lot less crime. And when people have asked me, why is the crime rate in almost every country so highly correlated with age, you know, my sense is that we need to sleep more, and you have less people who are tired and not running around.

Anyway, on figure 11 you can see actually what the United States looks like in this, and we are today about 9 years older than the world in general. But even Kenya, which is one of the youngest countries in the world today, is aging very rapidly there. And this aging is going to produce a lot of changes; and it will be partly economic change, partly demographic change, itself.

Figure 12 actually goes to the extension of that, which is the world becoming aged. And we are so used to, in the United States, seeing the aged as a problem; and in fact, of course, in world history it is a triumph. The luxury of being able to worry about the problems of the aged, people forget about. And as I get older, I realize how happy I am to be living in this century. But even the aging is happening very, very rapidly.

Mr. Sawyer. We assume you will be even happier to be living in the next century.

Ms. Torrey. Right. I am counting on it.

When you look at how fast countries have aged—France was really one of the first countries to get to 14 percent aged; it took France 115 years. That is very slow; the society can adjust to that. It is taking the United States about 66 years to do that. It is happening much faster both in—Japan and the Soviet Union are aging very, very quickly. Japan is the fastest aging country in the world today. It is going to take them 26 years.

One of the interesting things is, Japan has had a demographic advantage over the United States for many years. They were younger than we were. They are now passing us very, very quickly. And they will be much older than we will be for the rest of this century.

Let me finally get a little bit closer to home, which is one of my favorite topics, which is North America, and figure 13 really shows what North America demographically looks like. All of the trends we have been talking about are actually in a microcosm in North America, because we have a developing country as a neighbor. And you can see that by the year 2000, these three countries will be 400 million people. That is going to be considerably larger than the European Community. Even if the European Community hangs together, they are going to be 330 million.

We are going to be 400 million consumers. And it seems to me that these three countries form a very potent potential market, larger than any other market in the world, when you take into account the economic resources that are available to this market and the human capital itself.

I am going to stop there and let Charlie Westoff continue and focus in more on some of these issues.

Mr. Sawyer. Well, thank you very much.

[The prepared statement of Ms. Torrey follows:]

Prepared Statement of Barbara Boyle Torrey

Mr. Chairman and Members of the Subcommittee:

To understand how the United States will change, we have to understand the global context of population trends. The world now is changing so fast that there are no historical precedents for the changes. It no longer is enough to understand only the present; we also need to anticipate the future. Anticipating the future requires understanding past trends and making relative comparisons to provide the context for current analysis.

Projections about the future decrease in reliability the longer the time horizon. Some kinds of data are more reliable than others. And some of the most reliable data come from population projections. Most of the population of 2010 already are born, and their characteristics are already known. That is even more true in the

United States, where fertility rates are relatively lower, than in developing countries, where fertility is higher. Therefore, there is a level of predictability with short-term population projections that does not exist with other projections, such as economic ones.

The three major producers of global population projections—the United Nations, the World Bank, and the U.S. Bureau of the Census—all agree that the world's population is likely to double in the next 50 years. While estimates for specific countries may differ, the order of magnitude of the middle projections for the world are similar. These middle projections assume that fertility in every country with rates above replacement will fall to replacement levels, and that fertility in countries with rates already below replacement will generally stay where they are or return to replacement levels. The projections also assume that mortality improvements will continue, but in the developed countries such improvements will not occur as fast as they have in the recent past.

The United States today is the third largest country in the world, having moved up to third place when the Soviet Union dissolved. But by 2030, we are likely to drop to fifth place, being surpassed by the rapidly growing populations of Indonesia and Pakistan. And by 2050, projections indicate that the United States will drop to sixth place when it is surpassed by the population of Nigeria.

Almost all of future world population growth will occur in the developing countries (figure 1). In the next 30 years, almost 3 billion people will be added to the developing world at the same time that 140 million are added to the developed world. In 2020, about 95 million will be added in a single year in the developing world, compared with only 2 million in the developed world (figure 2). Behind these broad population trends are three considerations that are likely to change the context of the United States' place in the world: the rapidity of future population changes; the rapid pace of urbanization; and the "middle aging" of the world's population.

THE RAPID CHANGING OF THE WORLD

Global population changes in the next 50 years will come faster than in any period in human history. Because the changes are happening so quickly, the public and private sectors in the United States will have to become increasingly flexible to adapt to the changes and take advantage of them. A few examples of how fast countries and the world are changing are:

- It took 124 years for the world population to increase from one billion to two billion people (1801–1925). It will take only 11 years to add the sixth billion (figure 3).
- It took 58 years for the U.S. total fertility rate to drop from 6 children per women to 3.5 children per woman; in South Korea, it took only 12 years (1961 to 1973) (figure 4).
- Household sizes are changing as rapidly as the fertility rate. In the United States, the average household size was 3.3 persons in 1960; it is 2.6 today. In many developing countries, the size is much larger, but dropping fast. The social support structure that the extended family provides in traditional cultures often collapses with rapid changes from extended to nuclear families.
- At 1990–91 growth rates, it will take the United States about 83 years to double its population; it will take Nigeria just 22 years (figure 5). Today Nigeria is the eleventh largest country in the world; by 2050 it will probably be the fourth largest.

The most rapid growth is occurring in countries with the least amount of infrastructure. Growth itself will induce some needed changes. But induced changes may not be able to keep up with very rapid growth. Therefore, the speed of change is likely to be important in determining how populations adjust to their growing numbers.

Rapid population growth also means rapid increase in population density:

- Population density in the United States in 1991 is an estimated 71 persons per square mile. In the former Soviet Union, it is 34; and in West Germany, it is 588. The most densely populated country in Europe is the Netherlands, with 1,146 persons per square mile. But the most densely populated country in the world is Bangladesh, with 2,255 persons per square mile (figure 6).
- The population density of the developed countries is going to change very slowly over the next several generations. In the United States, our population density is estimated to increase from 71 persons per square mile in 1991 to 83 persons per square mile in 2020.
- Eight developing countries already have population density that is 150 percent or more of the world average and will at least double by 2020 (figure 7). All but

Syria and Pakistan are in Sub-Saharan Africa. This kind of growth creates enormous pressures on land use and the broader environment.

These rapid population changes in the next 50 years mean that the United States will have to become increasingly flexible, first to accommodate to the changes, then to realize the new opportunities, and finally to take advantage of them.

URBANIZATION OF THE WORLD'S POPULATION

While the world's total population is projected to double over the next 50 years, the urban population is likely to double in just 30 years, increasing between 1990 and 2020 from 2.6 billion to 5.0 billion (figure 8). A world urban culture is developing through the mass media. Urban people soon may share more of their culture with people in other urban areas around the world than with people in their own country's rural areas. The urbanization of the world will foster the evolution of a global culture.

- In 1991, nearly 50 percent of the world's population was urban; by 2020, 61 percent of the population will be living in urban areas.
- Today there are about 94 cities with a population of 2 million or more; by 2000, there are likely to be 128 cities that size.
- However, most urban growth will occur in cities that have under 2 million inhabitants today (figure 9).

Urban populations in developing countries have lower fertility and mortality rates than their counterparts in rural areas. They have more education and higher income. They also have different expectations than rural populations; they consume more and different kinds of products, in part because of their higher income.

The United States has one of the most sophisticated urban cultures in the world. And much of our foreign trade is for urban markets. The urbanization of the world is likely to be to the advantage of countries that export urban goods and services.

THE AGING OF THE WORLD'S POPULATION

At the same time as the world's population is doubling and its urban population is tripling, it also is becoming middle aged. Fifty percent of the world's population is under 24 years of age today (figure 10). In developing countries overall, the median age is about 22 years, and in Kenya it is only 15 years. By 2020, the median age of the world population will be 30 years and in developing countries, 28 years. Median age is increasing in every region of the world (figure 11).

In the United States, the median age was 19 years in 1860, 28 years in 1970, and 33 years in 1991. That makes it about 9 years older than the median age of the world's population today.

Developing countries with low life expectancies and high fertility rates have young populations, with most adults within one generation of each other. In developed countries today, adults typically span three generations, each with very different levels of education. In developing countries, elementary school enrollment increased between 1965 and 1986 from half to more than three-fourths of the corresponding school-age population. And the differences among the generations in educational attainment produce very different expectations, and different options for fulfilling those expectations. Educational diversity among the generations is increasing in most countries of the world.

The middle aging of the world's population creates a number of opportunities because it represents an increase in the educational attainment and experience of the labor force. Middle-aged populations also consume more, produce more, and have more income than younger populations. Middle-aged populations have lower dependency ratios (number of old and young dependents per working-age population) than younger populations. This means they can save and invest more if they can gain discretionary income.

The longevity of the world's population is one of the triumphs of human history. And it is happening at an unprecedentedly rapid rate. It took France 115 years for its population age 65 years and over to increase from 7 percent to 14 percent of its total population; it will take the United States 66 years, and it is taking Japan 26 years to make the same transition (figure 12). This will dramatically increase Japan's aged dependency burden. It is, however, the kind of problem that most people in human history would have liked to share.

RECENT DEVELOPMENTS

Two developments on the international scene have consequences for future population trends. The first development is the creation of the Newly Independent States out of what was the Soviet Union. The second is a growing recognition of the increasing interdependence among the three countries of North America—Canada, Mexico, and the United States. Let me discuss each development in turn.

The Newly Independent States (NIS)

The Newly Independent States (that is, the former Soviet Union) together represented the third largest country in the world in 1990. And their 1990 labor force was 29 million larger than the U.S. labor force. But the average annual growth rate of the NIS labor force in 1990 was half the growth rate of the United States labor force (0.7 percent versus 1.5 percent, respectively). The success of the current economic transition and the role of the NIS as a future market for U.S. goods will depend partly on the increase in labor force productivity which, in turn, will depend partly on the human capital of the current and future labor force. Some comparisons:

• 78 percent of U.S. adults over age 25 years have finished high school, compared with 52 percent in the Newly Independent States.

• But, in the NIS today, a higher estimated percentage of 25 to 29 year olds have finished the equivalent of high school (92 percent) than in the United States (85 percent).

• The United States has a higher percentage of college graduates among 25 to 29 year olds (23 percent) than in the NIS (15 percent).

• From 1990 to 1993, the size of the annual increments to the NIS joint labor forces will be smaller than the annual increments in the next 20 years. Therefore, these years offer the best opportunity in two decades to minimize the effects of unemployment in a restructuring of the centrally-planned economies of the NIS.

The United States and the European Newly Independent States are demographically mature societies that are now facing the inexorable aging of their populations and slowing of their labor force growth. The combination of their demographic realities and their economic expectations for real growth is likely to result in labor constraints and dislocations in the last decade of the 20th century. But when the Newly Independent States get their economies growing in real terms again, they will represent one of the largest groups of consumers in the world, with considerably more income than the first and second largest consumer markets (China and India, respectively). That is why it is so important to work with the emerging statistical systems in each one of the Newly Independent States to ensure that, when their economies begin to grow in real terms, the consumer and producer markets in these countries will be well described to U.S. businesses. U.S. businesses need new data to take advantage of these large markets that have had repressed consumption for so many years.

The North American Community

The evolving economies of Canada, Mexico, and the United States are making these countries increasingly interdependent. By population size, these countries represent the third largest consumer market in the world, after China and India. By 2000, China and India will each have over 1 billion, and Canada, Mexico, and the United States combined will have about 400 million consumers (figure 13). By that year, the European Community will have over 330 million, and the Newly Independent States will have about 312 million.

Within the North American community, we are already increasingly living and visiting with each other. Today, Mexicans are the largest group of foreign-born population in the United States, and Canadians are the second largest. The United States is expecting a 21 percent decrease in new entrants into the labor force (ages 20–24 years) between now and the year 2000. Mexico is expecting a 35 percent increase in this age group. Within the three countries of North America, then, there is the potential for a virtually steady flow of new labor force entrants over the next 10 years.

Because of the increasing importance to the United States of the North American labor force and consumer markets, it will be crucial to see that the statistical offices of the three countries coordinate their statistical descriptions of these markets. Carefully designed and coordinated regional statistics are needed for businesses, as national boundaries tend to become less meaningful in the international economy. The three countries of North America are fortunate to have enormous natural and human resources. And we are diverse enough to make use of comparative advantage and efficient divisions of labor if we have the data and analysis to show where these divisions and advantages lie.

CONCLUSION

The challenges in a rapidly changing world are to quantify the changes and to make information about these trends accessible to policymakers and private businesses alike. The United States needs a long-term perspective on current issues. Many of the future changes represent opportunities; in order to take advantage of the opportunities, we have to be able to understand and then to leverage them. Future population increases will occur so rapidly that we need to anticipate them so we can manage them. Increases in education and the middle aging of world population should help the process of adjustments. But they cannot be taken for granted when the population increases are happening so rapidly in the countries that can least afford it.

SOURCES

International data are from the International Data Base, U.S. Bureau of the Census, including *World Population Profile reports for 1987, 1989, and 1991,* U.S. Government Printing Office, Washington, D.C.

U.S. data not in the various issues of the *World Population Profile* are from U.S. Bureau of the Census, *Statistical Abstract of the United States 1991,* 111th Edition, U.S. Government Printing Office, Washington, D.C., 1991; and *Current Population Survey* for March 1991.

Data on the Newly Independent States are from Barbara Boyle Torrey and W. Ward Kingkade, "Population Dynamics of the United States and the Soviet Union," *Science,* 30 March 1990, Vol. 247, pp. 1548–1552.

Figure 1.
World Population by Development Category: 1950 to 2020

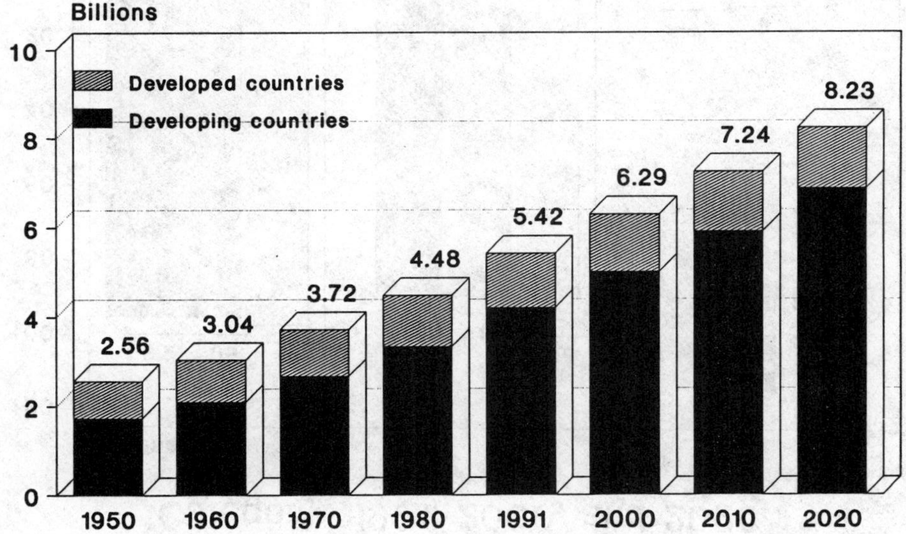

Source: Center for International Research, U.S. Bureau of the Census.

Figure 2. Millions of Persons Added Each Year to World Population, by Development Category: 1991, 2000, and 2020

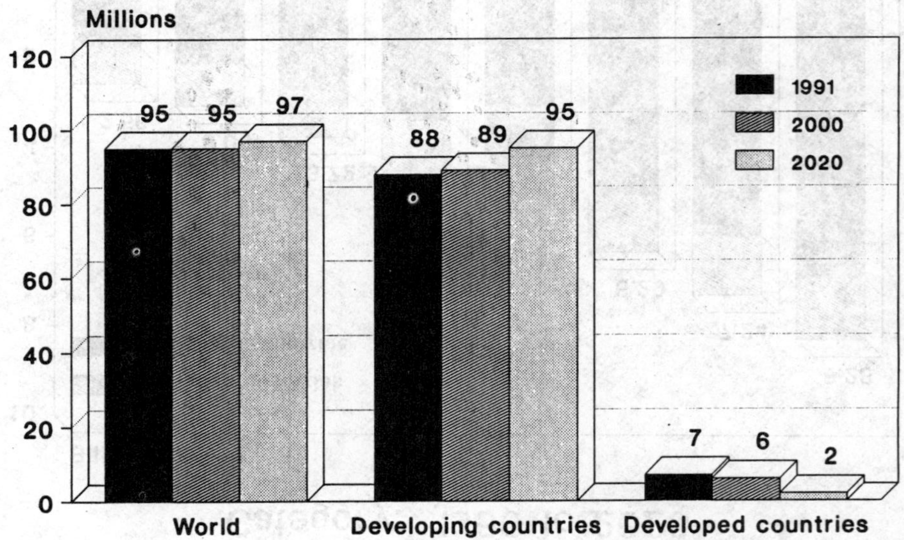

Source: Center for International Research, U.S. Bureau of the Census.

Figure 3.
Number of Years Between Each Billion Persons Added to World Population

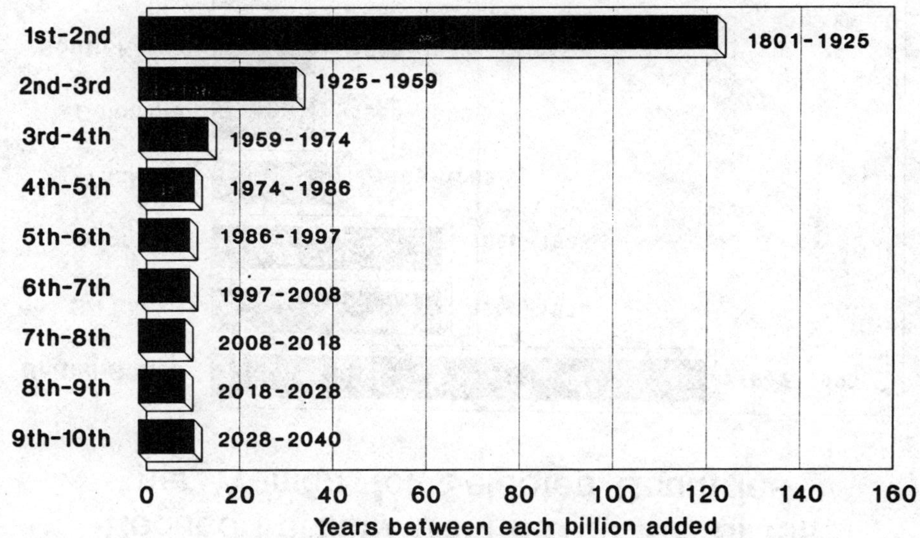

Source: Center for International Research, U.S. Bureau of the Census.

Figure 4. Number of Years Taken to Reduce Fertility from 6.0 to 3.5 Births per Woman, for Selected Countries

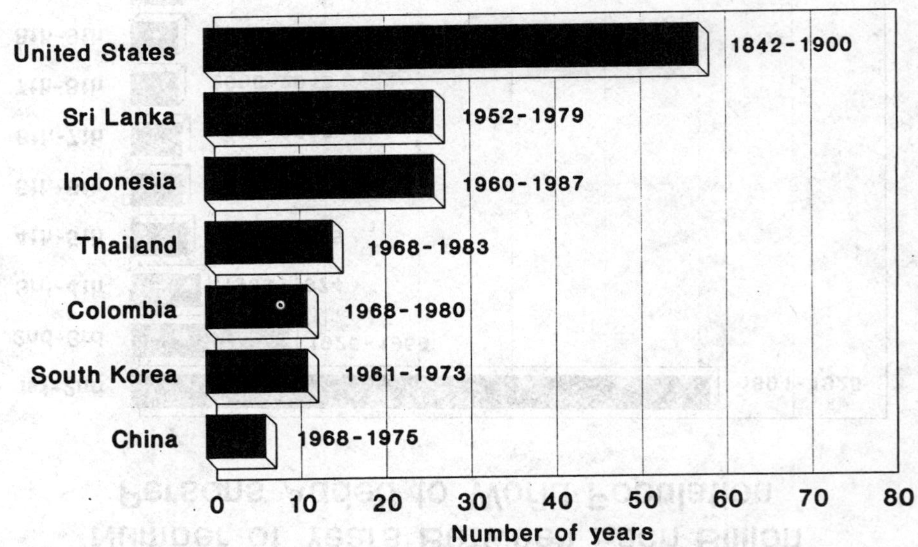

Source: Center for International Research, U.S. Bureau of the Census.

Figure 5. Number of Years It Would Take to Double the Population at 1990-91 Growth Rate, for 10 Largest Countries

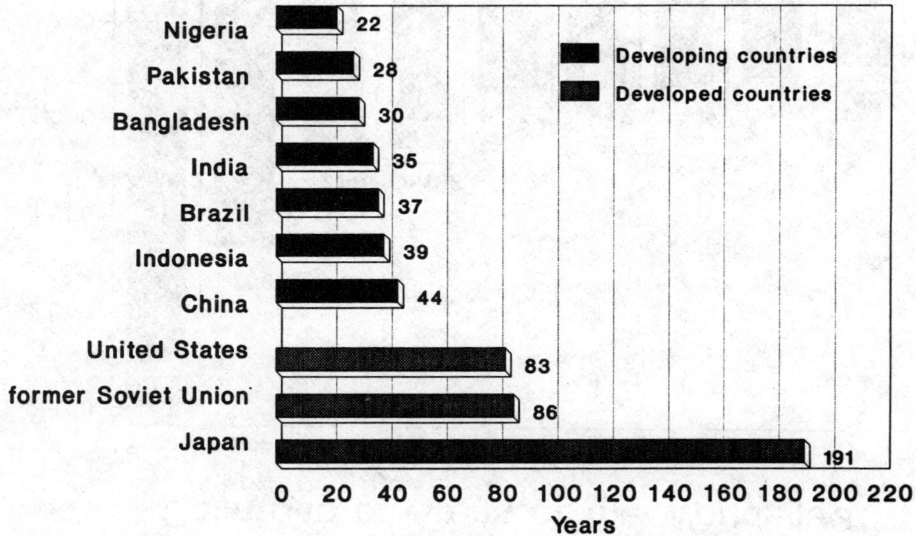

Source: Center for International Research, U.S. Bureau of the Census.

Figure 6. The Most Densely Populated Countries or Areas of the World: 1991

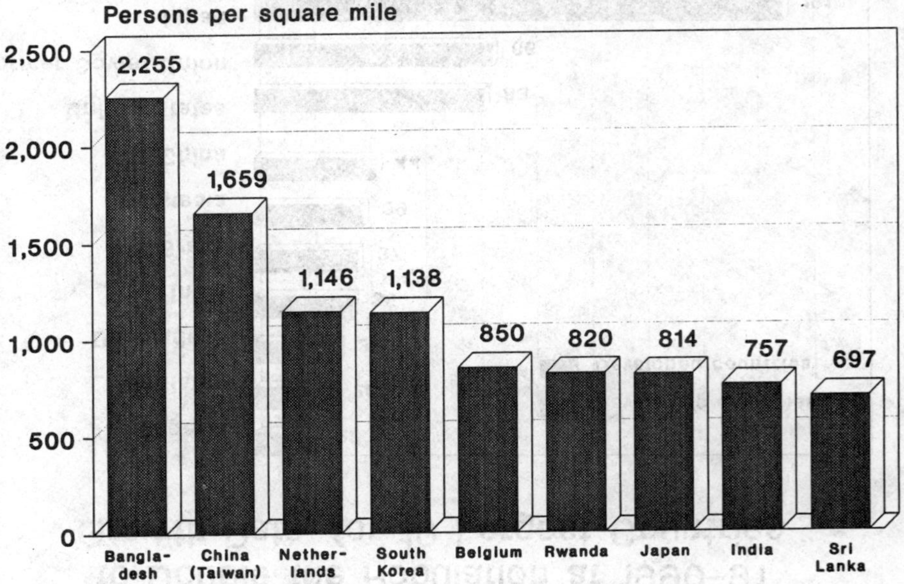

Source: Center for International Research, U.S. Bureau of the Census.

Figure 7. Countries Whose 1991 Density Is 150 Percent or More of World Average and Will at Least Double by 2020

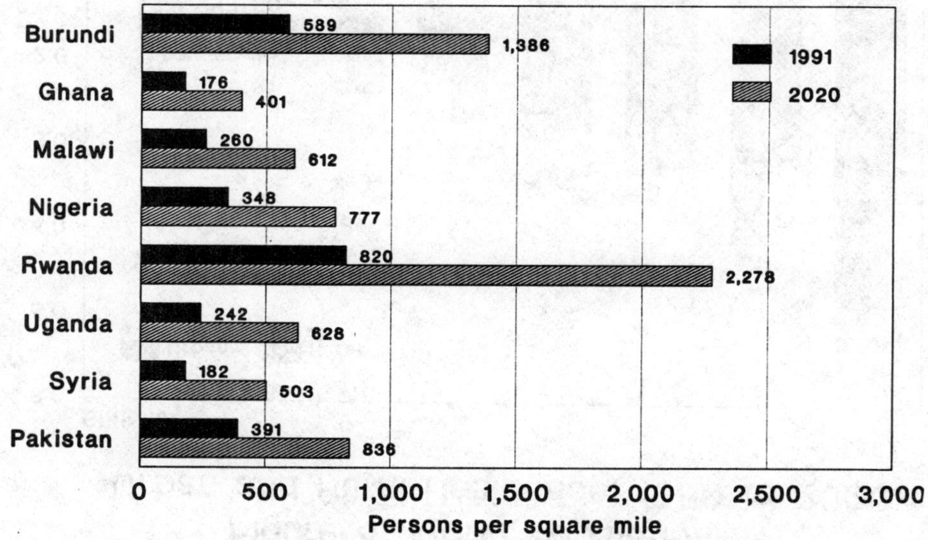

Source: Center for International Research, U.S. Bureau of the Census.

Figure 8. World Population by Urban and Rural Residence: 1950 to 2020

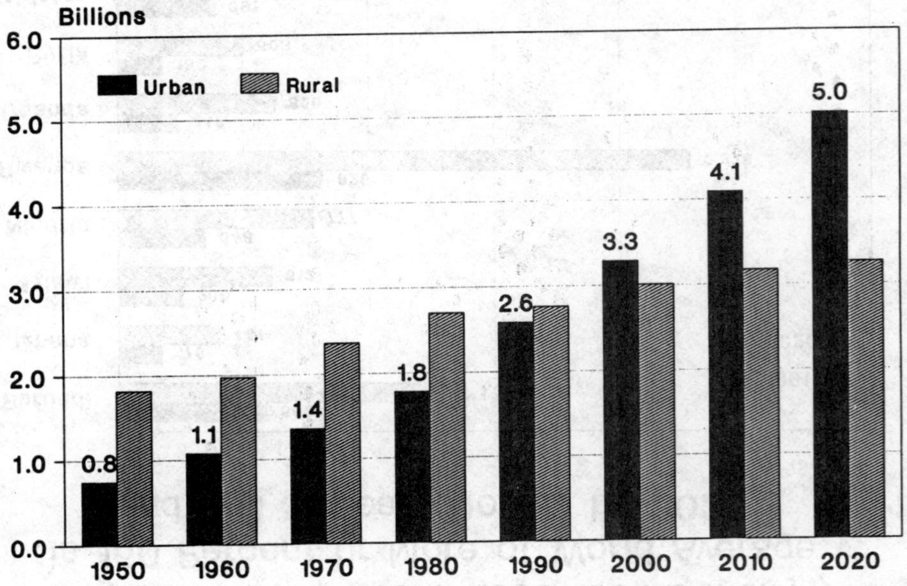

Source: Center for International Research, U.S. Bureau of the Census.

Figure 9. Percent of World Population by Residence Category: 1991 and 2000

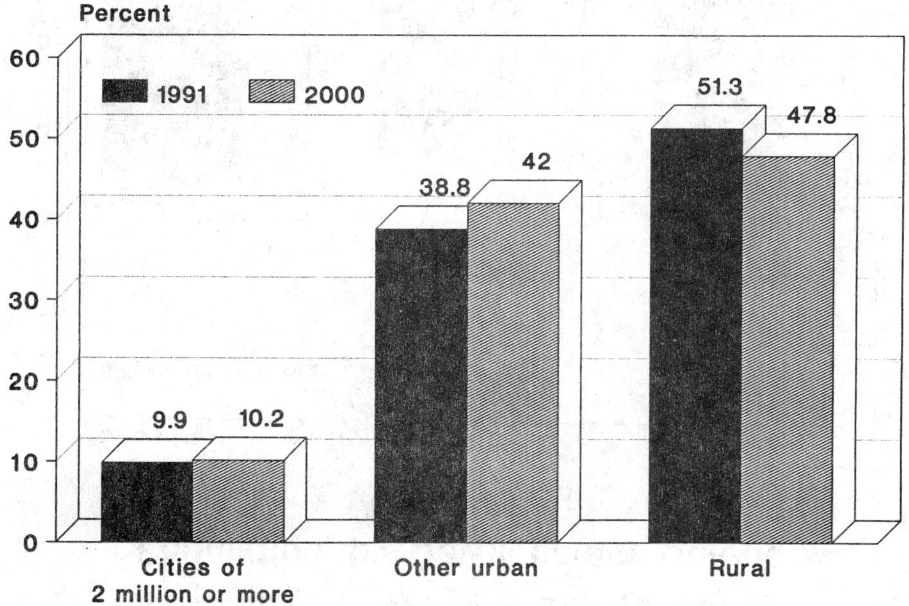

Source: Center for International Research, U.S. Bureau of the Census.

Figure 10. Median Age of World Population, by Development Category: 1991 to 2020

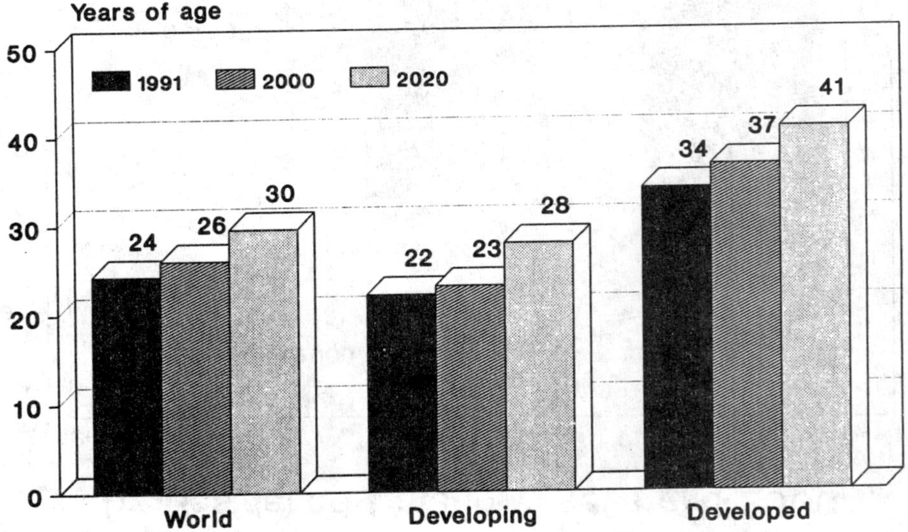

Source: Center for International Research, U.S. Bureau of the Census.

Figure 11. Median Age of the Population in Selected Large Countries: 1991 to 2020

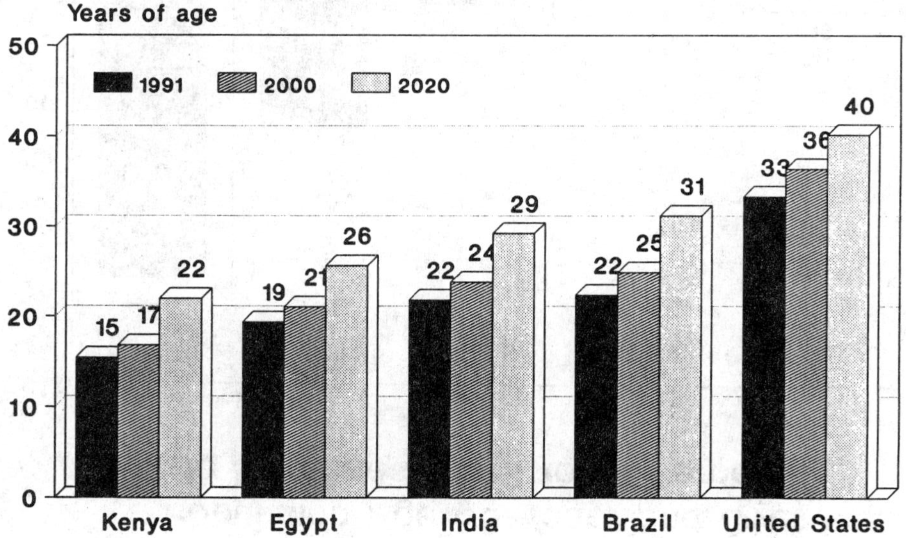

Source: Center for International Research, U.S. Bureau of the Census.

Figure 12. Number of Years Required for Population Age 65 Years and Over to Increase from 7 to 14 Percent

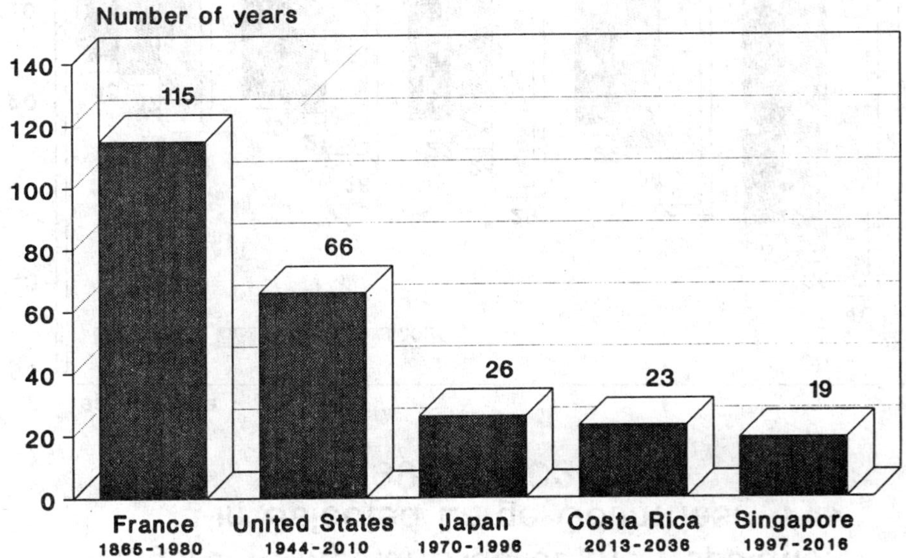

Source: Center for International Research, U.S. Bureau of the Census.

Figure 13. Population of Canada, Mexico, and the United States: 1991, 2000, and 2020

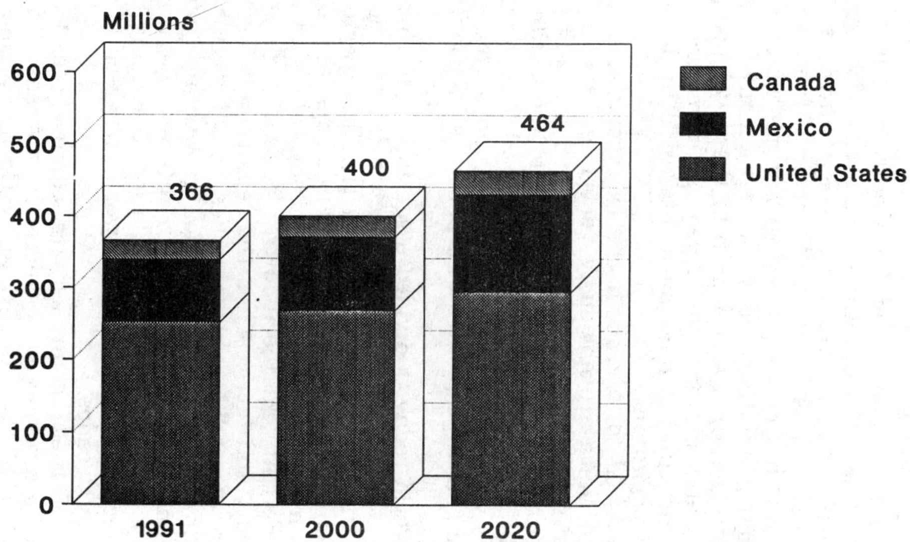

Source: Center for International Research, U.S. Bureau of the Census.

Mr. SAWYER. Dr. Westoff, if you would like to proceed, and then we will turn to questions.

Mr. WESTOFF. Thank you. Mr. Chairman, about half of my professional life has been devoted to the study of American fertility and population change. Twenty years ago, during the Nixon administration, I served as Executive Director of the Commission on Population Growth and the American Future, which tried to formulate a national population policy. Since then my interests have moved to the international scene, both in the developed and in the developing countries; in the past 2 years, I have concentrated on Africa, and in particular, I have been interested in assessing the demand for family planning.

I was asked to talk about the U.S. population in global perspective, and there are obviously very many points of possible entry into that subject one could focus on: contrasts in fertility and population growth; in labor force or employment differences; urbanization, which has already been discussed; age structure differences, which have already been discussed and so on. I have elected to focus on the large picture of differences in population growth and fertility.

The world today is divided essentially into three categories that differ in the stage they have reached in what demographers have labeled the "fertility transition." The first group to complete this transition to low fertility, which includes the United States, are those countries in the West and in several Asian countries, notably Japan. Fertility has been low or declining for several decades in this group, and has reached the replacement level; that is, a total fertility rate of 2.1, which implies an ultimate stationary population or lower. Rates of population growth are correspondingly low. The demographic momentum for future growth in this category of nations is limited, and the populations are aging rapidly. These are the developed countries of the world in which birth rates declined over many decades.

Some of these countries are currently experiencing negative rates of natural increase, where the number of deaths exceeds the number of births, for example, Germany and Hungary. Many others are close to zero rates of natural increase. Fertility rates are extremely low in some of these countries: 1.5 in Japan, 1.2 in Hong Kong, 1.3 in Italy and in Spain, 1.6 in Europe as a whole.

By comparison, in our country, the total fertility rate is 2.0, and the annual rate of natural increase is eight-tenths of 1 percent, a rate higher than in Europe, where it is two-tenths of 1 percent. It should be noted that these are rates of natural increase. They do not include net migration, which is a significant component of population growth in the United States, some 30 or 40 percent of its annual growth.

The future of fertility in this group of developed nations is a matter of speculation. There have been radical social changes affecting marriage, the family, and the status and roles of women in these societies over the past 30 years or so that do not suggest a return to early marriage or to larger families. Indeed, one can make a persuasive case for the advantages of low population growth, despite the usual misgivings about the aging of population and the concerns about who will pay the pension bills.

The second category of countries are those in the developing world that have experienced rapid or significant recent declines in fertility. Much of Latin America falls in this category. For example, the total fertility rate in Brazil is now probably below three births per woman. Nonetheless, because of the demographic momentum for further growth that its youthful age structure implies, the rate of natural increase in Brazil is close to 2 percent, and even under the most optimistic assumption about the future course of low fertility, the population of the Latin American region will increase by more than 80 percent before it stops growing, adding at least another 300 million persons in 50 years.

China is another member of this second category. Its population, which is now close to 1.2 billion, is expected to grow by another 200 million before stabilizing. As everyone knows, the enormous reduction of Chinese fertility to a level near replacement has been the result of direct government policy.

India is the other giant in this group. Its population is now approaching 900 million. Although its fertility has evidently declined significantly to a level possibly now below 4.0, the momentum for future population growth is enormous. Again, under the most optimistic assumptions about future growth, India will add another 400 to 500 million persons in the next 25 to 30 years.

The third and last category consists of those countries that have yet to enter the fertility transition or that are just beginning to show signs of some change. Most of sub-Saharan Africa, much of the Middle East, and some major countries in Asia, such as Pakistan and Iran, fall in this category. The African population picture is dramatic indeed. Although the total population of this vast continent is currently only 650 million, 45 percent of whom are under 15 years of age, the rate of growth is 3 percent as a consequence of an extremely high fertility rate in excess of six births per woman and a death rate that has declined rapidly. From one point of view—and this is important to remember—the fact that the African population has grown rapidly in the last few decades can be regarded as a triumph over the forces of mortality. On the other hand, unless fertility comes down rapidly, mortality is likely to rise in the classical Malthusian sense.

Consider the demographic implications of maintaining constant fertility in Africa with continuing improvements in life expectancy, which may be inconsistent, as I have just noted. The United Nations projection with this assumption leads to the absurd result that by the year 2050, within the lifetime of many of today's children, the population of Africa would exceed the total population of the world today. Now, such a projection cannot, of course, be taken literally, but it does underscore dramatically the need to reduce fertility.

Such a projection makes another important point, namely, that controversies about the implications of population growth for economic development or for the environment become quite academic. Such numbers are simply unsustainable. Even assuming a very rapid decline in fertility, the population of Africa would grow to 1.7 billion by the year 2050.

Now let me say a few words about the implications of all of this for the United States. What does the rapid population growth of the Third World mean for the United States? Its implications for the countries involved are serious indeed, whether one focuses on questions of income growth, environmental impacts, or political stability. But aside from humanitarian concerns, what is the American stake in all of this?

The answer depends upon our beliefs in the increasing globalization of the economy, in the implications for world order and for national security, and in the fragility of the world ecosystem.

The economic aspects seem clear enough. The economy is sensitive to international market conditions in terms of markets for U.S. exports, which requires not only competitive strength in the American economy, but also income growth abroad; that is, the ability to afford U.S. exports. Whether the hundreds of millions of residents of the less-developed countries are a potential economic opportunity for the U.S. economy or an ever-increasing dependency burden is not independent of future population growth in these countries.

The implications for national security relate to how rapid population growth contributes to political instability, to migration and refugee pressures, to increasing population pressures on urban infrastructures, to the problems of vast uneducated, youthful populations and the frustrations of the more educated unemployed, to the enormous problems of providing employment to ever-increasing numbers of potential workers, and so forth.

On the ecological side, we have been repeatedly warned in recent years of the global nature of environmental threats related to climate changes, ozone depletion, pressures on water resources, soil erosion, deforestation, waste disposal problems, biodiversity and so on; the list sometimes seems endless. Although it is clearly the United States and the other economically developed nations of the world that are disproportionately contributing to the variety of environmental problems because of their high levels of consumption and use of certain technologies, many Third World countries are also developing, and their rapid population growth will simply exacerbate the environmental impact.

Demography may not be destiny, but it is hardly irrelevant.

Let me close on a note about data needs, which I understand is the main purview of your committee. Most of the countries of the Third World do not have regular censuses or vital registration systems. As a result, much of our knowledge about fertility and child mortality derives from national sample surveys. In this connection, I would like to mention an invaluable resource, which is the Demographic and Health Surveys Project that has been conducted under the Agency for International Development contracts since 1984. These population surveys not only chart trends in fertility and child mortality, but also collect an enormous amount of useful information about child health, immunization, AIDS, nutrition, contraceptive knowledge and practice, the demand for family planning, and so on. It is important that this source of information be maintained and regularized, and that its geographic coverage be expanded.

Thank you.

Mr. Sawyer. Thank you very much.

[The prepared statement of Mr. Westoff follows:]

Prepared Statement of Charles F. Westoff, Maurice P. During Professor of Demographic Studies and Sociology and Faculty Associate, Office of Population Research, Princeton University

Mr. Chairman and Members of the Subcommittee:

I am a professor of demographic studies and sociology at Princeton University's Office of Population Research. About half of my professional life has been devoted to the study of American fertility and population change. Twenty years ago, during the Nixon administration, I served as executive director of the Commission on Population Growth and the American Future, which tried to formulate a national population policy. Since then my interests have moved to the international scene both in the developed and in the developing countries; in the past two years I have concentrated on Africa and, in particular, I have been interested in assessing the demand for family planning.

The world today is divided essentially into three categories that differ in the stage they have reached in what demographers call the "fertility transition". The first group to complete the transition to low fertility, which includes the United States, are those countries in the West and in several Asian countries, notably Japan. Fertility has been low or declining for several decades in this group and has reached the replacement level (a total fertility rate of 2.1, which implies ultimately a stationary population) or lower. Rates of population growth are correspondingly low, the demographic momentum for future growth is limited, and the populations are aging rapidly. These are the developed countries of the world in which birthrates declined over decades. Some of these countries are currently experiencing negative rates of natural increase, where the number of deaths exceeds the number of births (e.g. Germany and Hungary); many others are close to zero rates of natural increase. Fertility rates are extremely low in some of these countries: 1.5 in Japan, 1.2 in Hong Kong, 1.3 in Italy and in Spain—1.6 in Europe as a whole. By comparison, in our country, the total fertility rate is 2.0 and the annual rate of natural increase is 0.8 percent, a rate higher than in Europe, where it is 0.2 percent. It should be noted that these are rates of natural increase only; they do not include net migration, which is a significant component of population growth in the United States.

The future of fertility in this group of developed nations is a matter of some speculation. There have clearly been radical social changes affecting marriage, the family, and the status and roles of women in these societies over the past 30 years or so that do not suggest a return to early marriage or to larger families. Indeed, one can make a persuasive case for the advantages of low population growth rates despite the usual misgivings about the aging of the population and the concerns about who will pay the pension bills.

The second category of countries are those in the developing world that have experienced rapid or significant recent declines in fertility. Much of Latin America falls in this category. For example, the total fertility rate in Brazil is now probably below 3 births per woman. Nonetheless, because of the demographic momentum for further growth that its youthful age structure implies, the rate of natural increase in Brazil is close to 2.0 percent, and even under the most optimistic assumption about future low fertility, the population of the Latin American region will increase by more than 80 percent before it stops growing, adding another 322 million persons in 50 years.

China is another member of this second group. Its population, which is now close to 1.2 billion, is expected to grow by another 200 million before stabilizing. As everyone knows, the enormous reduction of Chinese fertility to a level near replacement has been the result of government policy.

India is the other giant in this group. Its population is now approaching 900 million. Although its fertility has evidently declined significantly to a level possibly below 4.0, the momentum for future population growth is enormous. Again, under the most optimistic assumptions about future growth, India will add another four to five hundred million persons in the next 25–30 years.

The third and last category consists of those countries that have yet to enter the fertility transition or that are just beginning to show some change. Most of sub-Saharan Africa, much of the Middle East, and some major countries in Asia such as Pakistan and Iran fall in this category. The African population picture is dramatic indeed. Although the total population of this vast continent is currently only 650 million—45 percent of whom are under 15 years of age—the rate of growth is 3.0 percent as a consequence of an extremely high fertility rate in excess of 6.0 births per woman and a death rate that has declined rapidly. From one point of view, the fact that the African population has grown rapidly in the last few decades can be regarded as a triumph over the forces of mortality. On the other hand, unless fertility comes down rapidly, mortality is likely to rise. Consider the demographic implications of maintaining constant fertility with continuing improvements in life expectancy: The United Nations projection with this assumption leads to the absurd result that by the year 2050 (within the lifetime of many of today's children), the population of Africa would exceed the total population of the world today! Such a projection cannot, of course, be taken literally, but it does underscore dramatically the need to reduce fertility. Such a projection makes another important point, viz., that controversies about the implications of population growth for economic development or for the environment become quite academic; such numbers are simply unsustainable. Even assuming a very rapid decline in fertility, the population of Africa would grow to 1.7 billion by 2050.

IMPLICATIONS FOR THE UNITED STATES

What does the rapid population growth of the third world mean for the United States? Its implications for the countries involved are serious indeed, whether one focuses on questions of income growth, environmental impacts, or political stability. But aside from humanitarian concerns, what is the American stake in all of this? The answer depends upon our beliefs in the increasing globalization of the economy, in the implications for world order and national security, and in the fragility of the world ecosystem.

The economic aspects seem clear enough. The economy is sensitive to international market conditions in terms of markets for U.S. exports, which requires not only competitive strength in the American economy but also income growth abroad, i.e., the ability to afford U.S. exports. Whether the hundreds of millions of residents of the less developed countries are a potential economic opportunity for the U.S. economy or an ever-increasing dependency burden is not independent of future population growth in these countries.

The implications for national security relate to how rapid population growth contributes to political instability, to migration and refugee pressures, to increasing population pressures on urban infrastructures, to the problems of vast uneducated youthful populations and the frustrations of the more educated unemployed, to the enormous problems of providing employment to ever-increasing numbers of potential workers, etc.

On the ecological side, we have been repeatedly warned in recent years of the global nature of environmental threats related to climate changes, ozone depletion, pressures on water resources, soil erosion, deforestation, waste disposal problems, biodiversity, and so on—the list is endless. Although it is clearly the United States and the other economically developed nations of the world that are disproportionately contributing to the variety of environmental problems because of their high levels of consumption and use of certain technologies, many third world countries are also developing, and their rapid population growth will simply exacerbate the environmental impact.

Demography may not be destiny, but it is hardly irrelevant.

DATA NEEDS

Let me close on a note about data needs, which is the concern of this Subcommittee. Most of the countries of the third world do not have regular censuses or vital registration systems. As a result, much of our knowledge about fertility and child mortality derives from national sample surveys. In this connection, I would like to mention an invaluable resource, which is the Demographic and Health Surveys project that has been conducted under AID contracts since 1984. These population surveys not only chart trends in fertility and child mortality, but also collect an enormous amount of useful information about child health, immunization, AIDs, nutrition, contraceptive knowledge and practice, the demand for family planning, and so on. It is important that this source of information be maintained and regularized and that its geographic coverage be expanded.

Mr. SAWYER. Those bells mean that I have to excuse myself. I will go and do my duty and return.

[Recess.]

Mr. SAWYER. Thank you very much for your patience. I have a whole series of questions I would like to ask you about in broad terms. Let me turn to some of the more direct ones first.

Dr. Westoff, you began by mentioning some of the statistical concerns, the measurements that are of real importance to you. Ms.

Torrey, you eliminated from your testimony some of the things that you said about measurements.

Let me begin by asking you where you see the current deficiencies in global demographic characteristics, how those measures might be improved, and particularly how we might go about the business of reconciling the differences among the various measurement systems around the globe, particularly at a time when, if we take seriously all the discussion about globalization, we don't even speak the same language in terms of measurements with the other side of the world.

Mr. WESTOFF. Well, as I noted in the conclusion, most of our information about fertility, mortality and related subjects for the developing countries of a current nature, come from these demographic health surveys; and they are terribly important. And they have been sponsored by AID; and presumably they are about to give another 5-year contract for continuation of this project, although who knows what happens to AID? I mean, there are all kinds of rumors about that, as well, and foreign aid bills in general.

But one defect of this is that it relates only to those countries which are part of the AID family, and it leaves out some significant parts of the world. The alternative, I suppose—which was the case when the World Fertility Survey, its predecessor, was in business during the 1970's—the United Nations picked up that part of the coverage where AID didn't operate; but the United Nations has its own financial problems now.

But the irony of this is that—one irony which relates to what you were asking is that the kinds of information that are being collected as part of this project are highly standardized, highly uniform. The questions are the same; and as a matter of fact, I designed the questionnaire that is being used all over the world. And so it enhances enormously international comparability. That is not the case in Europe.

So where countries do their own thing, you know, you have all kinds of—there really is an irony here, because more developed countries have in a certain sense a weaker statistical system which feeds very well their own needs, perhaps, but does not lend itself as neatly to international comparisons as in the developing countries.

Ms. TORREY. Let me talk about the one area that I am concerned about—well, the two areas. One is the newly independent states of the ex-Soviet Union. When we were working with them from the Census Bureau, they had been so closed for so many years that they did not even know how to do good sample surveys. And they are really desperate to figure out how to do this. They cannot take censuses to find out information about themselves like they used to in the past. And it seems to me the United States has a vested interest in working on this to help them collect statistics in a way that we can understand and use ourselves.

The other one, of course, is North America—what I have always been interested in is the role of the Eurostat, which is always a passive role in Europe, but they do combine data from other European countries. And we don't have anything quite equivalent to that for the North American area; and it is very useful to have countries coordinating their statistics so that we can understand them.

Mr. SAWYER. We talk repeatedly, particularly in those two arenas that you mentioned, about both tracking the effectiveness of AID on the one hand, and describing an environment appropriate for investment on the other—perhaps the larger way to develop the kinds of markets that you are talking about, Dr. Westoff. Yet we don't have a very good way to do either one. It is particularly frustrating when we talk about trying to assemble the economic resources of a continent in a way that reconciles the assets with one another, and we don't even have a very good way to describe it.

Can you talk about the specifics of either of those circumstances? I guess North America is particularly timely today. But it is one that is not going to go away, even if short-term accommodations between Mexico and the United States can be arrived at for the sake of a treaty.

Ms. TORREY. I think it is so much in our self-interest, I must say, that we need to know what is going on. A very nice thing about statisticians is that they really feel they are a profession unto themselves, and they really do want to work together. And it is probably not a lot of technical assistance needed in these two areas of the world, except at the beginning.

I think in developing countries it is a much bigger issue, obviously, trying to set those systems up.

Mr. SAWYER. We talk a lot about urbanization and the way that the world is becoming much more urban, much more metropolitan, and doing so very rapidly, and doing so in a more dispersed way than perhaps in the past. Have we learned any lessons from the last hundred years among the developed nations that would be of benefit as we try to address this phenomenon at an even greater pace among currently developing nations?

Mr. WESTOFF. I am not sure whether we have or not. As you noted in your introduction, I was at a conference a couple of weeks ago in the Ivory Coast that the African Development Bank was sponsoring, their first foot in the water on the population subject. And they came up with—at this conference, many came up with all kinds of recommendations, one of which was to try to slow the rates of urbanization in Africa, as though you could wave some magic wand and do this. And it seemed to me to be utterly silly.

Mr. SAWYER. I am not asking anybody if we have learned how to alter the tides of the waves, just whether we have learned to be better surfers or navigators.

Mr. WESTOFF. I don't think so.

Ms. TORREY. Well, since World War II, certainly, there has been a lot of urban planning in the Western world, and there are—I know that AID has a whole area that looks at urban problems and urban issues themselves, and they certainly are transferring some of that knowledge. The problem is, a lot of it is very expensive, so that you have people growing up now without any planning at all.

Mr. SAWYER. Certainly, urban areas have been places of growing wealth, of cultural richness, of opportunity. They have also been, in many places, just cesspools of real deprivation, need, and squalor.

Mr. WESTOFF. I might just note, one of these surveys that has just been completed in Zambia, which is the most urban of the African countries, is the first one to indicate that the downward trend of infant and child mortality has been significantly reversed; and this—within the last 5 years or so. It may be because of the spread of AIDS in that population, but because it has been going on for a dozen years, it is more likely to be the collapse of its economy and the health system.

Mr. SAWYER. Just intuitively, it would seem that any time you have populations gathered in concentrations that the hunt for finding focused solutions to problems is great. At the same time the whole critical-mass syndrome would lead you to believe that those very same problems might be compounded in their intensity.

Do we know very much about those two phenomena?

Mr. WESTOFF. Well, we may. I don't. By the same logic, it is also, if you look at the history of cities in Europe, you know, back in the Middle Ages, evidently, these were the places where infections spread and epidemics took off. I mean, density has both rewards and costs associated with it.

Mr. SAWYER. I guess the question is, is population density a problem in and of itself; or really is it only a problem when combined with other phenomena—poverty, lack of health care, lack of housing, growth?

Mr. WESTOFF. I think clearly the latter. You can look at parts of Manhattan in the middle of the day, some of the most affluent sections of the city, and it is pretty densely populated. So it obviously depends upon what is associated with it in terms of socioeconomic characteristics.

I don't think you can really infer anything from density alone.

Mr. SAWYER. What do we know about why fertility rates tend to decline when affluence increases; or does affluence increase when fertility rates decline? What does that mean in terms of policy?

Mr. WESTOFF. Well, the conventional wisdom on this subject for many decades now has been that fertility rates in the West historically—it doesn't go back more than a hundred years—and in the developing nations today will come down as economic development proceeds; and that the—sort of the extreme version of that proposition is that unless you have rapid rises in per capita income growth, you are not going to realize declines in fertility.

But there is enough contrary evidence now to indicate that, for one reason or another—one of the reasons perhaps being that there is a latent demand even in some African countries for the reduction of fertility, or at least for the control of the spacing of births, that family planning programs have had an enormous impact. I think it is hard to prove this, but certainly I think the evidence is pretty overwhelming in places, in parts of the world where economic development has not exactly been overwhelming. So that both of these things tend to operate and tend to reinforce each other and interact.

So if you are going to wait for economic development to reduce the fertility of countries in Africa, there is just not enough time for that.

Mr. SAWYER. Do we, in fact, need to begin to tame the waves and manage the tides? Is that what you are suggesting, rather than simply to navigate them?

Mr. WESTOFF. Well, I think we need to provide the technical assistance, for which there is some demand. I think that—I just finished some research which indicates that the mass media can have an enormous effect on attitudes toward this in a couple of African countries, three African countries, that I have looked at. So that these large families which are built into the agrarian economies and into the traditions of these societies are not immutable.

Mr. SAWYER. What can we say about age competition in the global setting? Do we have—I mean, it has become a commonplace political dialogue in this country. Do we have a sense of comparability globally?

Ms. TORREY. You mean competition among different——

Mr. SAWYER. Among different age cohorts.

Ms. TORREY. Yes. Also, it depends in part on what the human capital is attached to each one of these cohorts, and that does vary a lot. So that even if you have much larger cohorts in one country than another, they can compete. Education is the key to finding out what their comparative advantages are. So we can't look at just the population by itself.

Mr. SAWYER. Tell me what you mean by that. You are going to have to expand on that, develop it a little bit.

Ms. TORREY. This is actually something that I am going to be interested in doing some more research on, is that I think people have looked at this and are talking about it in relatively simplistic terms. And they talk about large populations and developing countries competing with the labor forces in developed countries; and I think it is more complicated than that.

I think we need to look at what the education is of these different groups and the new entrants into the labor force. Because that is—the education is probably going to be as important as the numbers themselves, and will probably be the key to understanding how these are going to shift over the next 10, 15, and 20 years.

Mr. SAWYER. Was it your testimony that highlighted the difference in high school graduation rates in the newly independent states?

Ms. TORREY. Yes.

Mr. SAWYER. And on the one hand, where their high school graduation rates were significantly higher than those of the United States?

Ms. TORREY. Yes.

Mr. SAWYER. Where our college and postgraduate rates, among those who did graduate, were significantly higher than theirs. I mean that seems to indicate a strengthening of the middle in the newly independent states and a widening of the gap that we have perceived between the best and the worst educated in the United States.

Ms. TORREY. It is very interesting. We looked at how the median age in the newly independent states was changing; and it was changing very rapidly—not the median age, the median educational attainment—and it is within 1 year of the United States now. And in fact, in my mind, that is probably very hopeful, because——

Mr. SAWYER. Except that it is within 1 year of the United States, concentrated at the median, whereas ours are concentrated at the poles.

Ms. TORREY. That is exactly right. That is exactly right.

Mr. SAWYER. What are the implications? What will it mean for markets and other kinds of things developing over the next 20 years?

Ms. TORREY. Well, let me do my research on this, and I will come back. But surely what we have is an increasingly bimodal distribution in terms of human capital, and if not, increasing relative to some of these other countries that do a better job of keeping all of their kids in high school. Our dropout rate is high relative to a lot of other countries, and certainly high relative to the newly independent states. And that is going to be an important criterion of how that cohort competes.

We also have the best education in the world in the United States. So those cohorts who stay in school are going to do fine competing, and I think we are going to have to work out how we—how this is going to be distributed.

Mr. SAWYER. Dr. Westoff, let me ask you one last question. I have a number of other questions. I would hope that we might submit to you for response or however you choose to treat them.

But the last implication that you talked about in your testimony was with regard to environmental effects of population. You enumerated all of those elements, including ozone depletion, pressures on water resources, soil erosion, deforestation, waste disposal problems, biodiversity. Is it fair to say that every one of these is compounded by rapid population growth and unfocused development?

Mr. WESTOFF. Yes. I think the short answer is yes.

It has been several decades now that people in social and biological sciences at work on these issues have been trying to get the right handle on the relationship between population growth and environmental impacts, and I think we had—as a matter of fact, the appropriate way to think about it, in my opinion, is the same way, the same logic, that we built into our report in 1972 on Population and The American Future that the Rockefeller Commission, that I was involved with, that population growth tends to exacerbate and intensify these problems. And there are a whole series of problems—including environmental ones—which make the solution more difficult because it shortens the time for sensible solutions.

So I think that that is the way to think about it. It has a multiplier effect as well.

Mr. SAWYER. So that the opportunity to solve problems in concentrated settings is overwhelmed by the numbers. That was the question I was getting at earlier. Have we learned very many lessons from all of that?

Mr. WESTOFF. We mustn't forget the other side of it. Because, if you look at what the United States and Europe is doing to its environment, we are making, as I say in this paper here, more than a—a very disproportionate contribution to it, a negative contribution to it, because of the technology and per capita income and consumption.

Mr. SAWYER. Thank you both very much for your presence here today. I enjoyed the testimony from both of you. And, Dr. Westoff, thank you very much for the extra effort to put yours together. And, Ms. Torrey, I appreciated having yours as well.

Our second panel today is comprised of Doris Meissner, who is the senior associate and director of the Immigration Policy Project, Carnegie Endowment for International Peace. She is the former Acting Commissioner of the Immigration and Naturalization Service, former executive director of the National Women's Political Caucus, a member of the board of trustees of the Refugee Policy Group.

Michael Teitelbaum is a program officer for the Alfred P. Sloan Foundation. He served with the U.S. Commission for the Study of International Migration and Cooperative Economic Development, has taught through the Office of Population Research at Princeton University and Nuffield College in Oxford, England, and is a former staff director of the House Select Committee on Population. Welcome.

STATEMENTS OF DORIS M. MEISSNER, SENIOR ASSOCIATE AND DIRECTOR, IMMIGRATION POLICY PROJECT, CARNEGIE ENDOWMENT FOR INTERNATIONAL PEACE; AND MICHAEL S. TEITELBAUM, PROGRAM OFFICER, ALFRED P. SLOAN FOUNDATION

Mr. TEITELBAUM. I am coming home, Mr. Chairman.

Mr. SAWYER. Mrs. Meissner? You may proceed when you are ready.

Mrs. MEISSNER. Thank you very much, and thanks for the invitation to join you for this hearing.

When we move from the information that was presented in the earlier panel to the question of global—or international—migration, we are obviously moving to one of the implications of demography as we see it around the world. In talking about international migration, I think it is very important always to remember that the vast majority of people who move—who are migrants—actually move within their own countries and are basically part of the urbanization phenomenon that you talked about in your opening statement.

A much smaller number move within particular geographical regions in the less developed world. The smallest number cross international borders and go to other regions of the world. So it is important to keep the scale in perspective.

On the other hand, it is also the case that the numbers who are crossing international borders and moving or trying to move—to the industrialized world are growing significantly. And it poses a series of questions that are going to be very much with us in this post-Cold War era and will represent one of the major issues that we confront in a post-Cold War world.

I would like to spend this time talking about what I see as some of the primary reasons international migration because they, of course, are the basis for policy responses.

First of all, we cannot forget that the world that we live in is a world that has been, in the last two decades, marked by wars in many areas of the globe. And those wars have been wars that have disproportionately affected civilians. About 90 percent of the victims of those wars have been civilians. So huge numbers of displaced persons and refugees have been created. And those wars are not ending. As we have seen in ex-Yugoslavia and possibly other areas on the rim of the Soviet Union, there is every reason to believe that war will continue to be with us.

Depending on what kind of a foreign policy we have had toward the parts of the world that have been in war, we have called the victims refugees in some cases and treated them that way. In some cases we viewed them as asylum seekers. In other cases we have viewed them as illegal immigrants. By and large, those distinctions have been conditioned by policy rather than by an fair-minded view of the circumstances that the people have found themselves in.

But the reality that we face today is that there are about 18 to 20 million people in the world that are in a refugee-like status. They are under the care of the international humanitarian system, and there are probably an equal number that are displaced within their own countries that are beyond the reach by and large of the international assistance organizations. Those are very, very large numbers of people.

The second major trend has to do with economic development and the lack of progress that we have seen in the 1980's. The 1960's and 1970's, as a matter of fact, were good decades as far as development was concerned. There were important gains in important parts of the world.

But, by and large, those gains were reversed in the 1980's as a result of recession, debt, conflict. And that happened just at the time that major numbers of new workers were coming into labor markets as a result of high birth rates in the 1950's and 1960's. In the 1980's—and continuing today—there has been a conjunction of seriously decreased growth and significantly increased numbers of new workers. That has significantly increased pressure for international migration.

Third, international connections are required in order for people actually to migrate. When one talks about migration, it is very easy to feel besieged, as if everybody is moving at every moment.

In fact, migration occurs very selectively. Flows are not random. They track well-established connections between countries. The connections come about through history, and they tend to be a function of colonial patterns in the past, such as the connection, for instance, between France and Algeria. They are a result of wars that have been fought between countries—the U.S. relationship with South Korea, for instance. They are a result of long-standing labor recruitment policies—the phenomenon of Turks in Germany, for instance.

But such international connections are increasing rather than decreasing. They are increasing as a function of global economic interdependence. Not only are they increasing, but they are supported or facilitated by speedy communication and by cheap travel which enable people to move in ways that never were the case before.

Finally, there is a receptivity to migration that exists in many industrialized nations. In the United States and in many other western nations, we have social and moral beliefs that support migration. The most fundamental one is that we believe in the unity of families. We believe in people who come being allowed to have family members with them. That is an important ingredient in social stability in a nation like ours, but it also supports migration. Likewise, our humanitarian tradition of generosity to refugees is a philosophical element of our character that fosters migration.

In addition, our economy and the economy of most advanced industrialized nations are good for migration. We have experienced significant growth in our low-wage and service sectors. The jobs that we have created by and large in the last decade are attractive to migrants, and the disincentives for illegal immigration are rather timid and largely ineffective.

What I conclude from all of this is that the dilemma of international migration pressures will not recede. It is a dilemma that will not solve itself, because opportunities in the west to migrate will remain modest in comparison with the numbers of people that are likely to want to move.

The important thing is that we recognize that international migration pressures are a structural characteristic of broad, fundamental political economic and social realities of the world that we live in. To address those realities effectively, we must have policies that go beyond the conventional control, admissions and humanitarian measures that we have relied on to date. Managing migration pressures must become part of the central objectives of our foreign policies for the future.

In my statement I have given you some ideas on how policy might address those realities. I will stop at this point in terms of my remarks, however if you would like to discuss policy responses in the question and answer session, I would be, of course, happy to do so.

Mr. SAWYER. Thank you very much.

[The prepared statement of Mrs. Meissner follows:]

PREPARED STATEMENT OF DORIS MEISSNER, SENIOR ASSOCIATE, CARNEGIE ENDOWMENT FOR INTERNATIONAL PEACE

Thank you for the invitation to appear as an expert witness and to contribute to the subcommittee's deliberations on global migration. issues. I do so in my capacity as an independent scholar with the Carnegie Endowment for International Peace, where I direct its immigration policy program.

In your examination of the 1990 U.S. census and the policy implications arising from contemporary demographic trends, you are wisely addressing global issues as a crucial area for inquiry in your set of hearings on America's Changing Profile. U.S. demographic trends are indeed a manifestation of conditions and dynamics that are worldwide in their origins and significance.

As the committee's review has surely shown, immigration now accounts for the largest share of growth in the U.S. population. Moreover, 85% of today's immigrants come from Latin America and Asia, a dramatic shift from the historical pattern of American immigration in which Europeans came here to populate a young, developing land. Although immigration accounted for a greater percentage of the U.S. population in the early 19005 than it does today, the immigration of more than 9 million new residents in the 1980s ranks it as the decade of the largest number of immigrants in our history. And those levels of immigration will continue and may increase in the 19905.

Today's immigration is in one sense a continuation of our historical tradition as a nation of immigrants. In another sense, our current immigration experience is a reflection of global economic, political and demographic forces that are newly upon us and that will require substantially new attitudes and policies, if we are to cope successfully. In sketching the issues and suggesting responses, my testimony draws upon "Managing Migrations," an article I wrote for the Spring, 1992 issue of Foreign Policy, and work I have been doing with the Trilateral Commission, an organization of American, Western European and Japanese leaders from diverse sectors of their societies, that is examining emerging foreign policy problems.

Through the ages, migration has functioned as a primary source of human progress that has been a positive force for individuals and civilizations alike. However, because today's migrations are increasingly generated by wars, human rights deprivations and poverty, large numbers on the move can be the source of political instability and dangerous upheavals.

The vast majority of migrants move within their own countries, the next-largest share move across national boundaries within the less-developed world, and a relatively small share cross borders to the West. Although proportionately small, the numbers coming to the West are sizeable and growing. Broadly speaking, they fall into five categories: legally admitted immigrants and temporary residents; contract labor migrants; illegal migrants; asylum-seekers; and refugees.

There are many significant issues associated with the first two groups. However, it is the latter three categories—illegal immigrants, asylum-seekers and refugees—around which the migration debate in the industrialized world is revolving today. Although the three groups are distinct in law and policy, related conditions, singly and in combination, have generated them.

The large and growing numbers on the move can be attributed to these conditions:

Wars and civil strife

The 1970s and 80s have been marked by protracted war and civil strife in many countries and regions of the world. Many of the conflicts, such as those in Southeast Asia, southern Africa and Central America, were fueled and sustained by U.S.-Soviet antagonisms. Ninety percent of the casualties in these proxy wars have been to civilians.

The peril to non-combatants, duration and devastation of both the proxy wars and other civil strife situations have caused massive population displacements. Depending on the international politics of the situation, the victims became refugees (Cambodia, Vietnam, Afghanistan), asylum-seekers (Ethiopia, Nicaragua, Sri Lanka) or illegal immigrants (El Salvador, Somalia, Haiti).

Nor are such wars behind us. The carnage in ex-Yugoslavia is an ominous warning of the humanitarian dilemmas ushered in by the end of the Cold War. What makes ethnic cleansing so alarming from a global migration standpoint is that creating refugees is the objective, not simply the byproduct, of the conflict.

Economic development patterns

Many of the development gains of the 1960s and 70s slowed or were reversed in the 1980s, due to war, recession and debt. Thus, job creation and improvements in living standards lagged seriously at a time when high 1950s and 60s birth rates poured unprecedented numbers of new workers into labor markets. Where cross-national linkages existed, either through longstanding labor market relationships such as Mexico and the U.S. or historic ties such as northern Africa and Europe, South-North migration accelerated.

In addition, export-led development strategies that have prevailed in many countries, particularly in Asia, together with overpopulation, poverty, or unemployment, seem to induce emigration. Even Japan is no longer impervious to migration pressures. Contingents of illegal residents come from Taiwan, South Korea, Bangladesh, the Philippines, Thailand, and Pakistan. The explanation is Japan's international role as a leading source of investment capital. The same can be said for the U.S. and other nations. Major capital flows and investment seemingly bring with them migration in a reverse flow.

International connections

International migration flows are not random. They track close connections that have been established, often decades ago, between and among nations. These connections are rooted in colonialism, war and military occupation, labor recruitment, and economic penetration. Thus, Indians move to England and Canada, their commonwealth partners. Korean war brides led the way for today's sizeable Korea-U.S. flow. Turkish guestworkers in Germany sent for family members instead of returning to them at home. Cuban elites, who identified with capitalism and whose wealth derived from American investment, fled to Miami after the 1959 revolution.

Once migration footholds are established, family members join successful migrants, remittances link communities across great distances, and established immigrant groups help the newly arrived find work and negotiate seemingly alien ways and places. Migration itself then becomes a new connection between nations, evolving into a social process that is increasingly sustained by factors that are largely beyond the realm of government action or the economic impulses that originally generated it.

Colonialism and military occupation may be outdated forms, but new, analogous transnational linkages are being created as economic interdependence deepens. These linkages give rise to continuingly new forms and sources of migration.

Receptivity to migrants in advanced industrial nations

A complex set of supply/demand interactions must exist for migration pressures to become actual flows. Migration to industrialized societies occurs in response to humanitarian and social beliefs that are the basis for admitting refugees and family members of earlier immigrants.

Moreover, the economies of developed nations fuel migration movements. International trade and markets have restructured developed country economies in ways that expand the supply of low-wage jobs, especially in major cities. Traditional manufacturing jobs have diminished, often replaced with lower paid, less skilled production jobs, and service sectors have grown very rapidly, creating substantial numbers of new, low-wage jobs. Immigrants are often more likely than indigenous workers to take these jobs, a trend that seems unlikely to change soon.

Although certain levels of immigration can make important contributions to the economic health of developed countries, migration is not the answer for overpopulation vis-a-vis jobs in less-developed countries. Under any realistic scenario, immigration opportunities in the West will remain modest when viewed against the employment needs of the rest of the world.

Thus, the dilemma posed by international migration pressures will not solve itself; it requires concerted efforts and new priorities by individual nations and the international community. International migration is a structural characteristic of broad social, economic and political themes in today's world. What is required is a wide-ranging mix of policies at national, regional and international levels.

The broad objective should be to manage migration pressures in ways that (a) eliminate involuntary migration due to life-threatening circumstances, both political and economic; (b) prevent sudden mass movements and humanitarian emergencies; and (c) establish mechanisms to control, regulate and channel flows that are, to some extent, inevitable.

To those ends, I would like to sketch some ways to think about the migration policy challenge in both national and international policy arenas.

National policies

Clearly defined, publicly debated migration policies need to be established by many more than just the traditional immigration nations. Although nations need new policies to address new migration pressures, the controversy swirling around the issues in Western Europe illustrates how difficult and volatile the subject can be.

Public political discourse in France by mainline politicians now includes references to the "noise" and "smells" created by immigrants. In Germany, vicious attacks on foreigners by youth groups have electrified an already tense legislative debate on proposed changes to the constitution to tighten political asylum procedures. Political elites fear that the immigration issue will again cast Germany into the role of antiforeigner in international eyes.

Western European nations have begun to arrest smugglers, standardize border controls, deploy mobile forces in remote border spots, and penalize airlines and other carriers for failing to check documents. These are all reasonable steps which are routine, acceptable elements of immigration regulation in traditional immigration nations. In addition, migration policies should embody effective labor market controls, legal protections for non-citizens, access to citizenship, and timely adjudication of political asylum claims.

But it is also essential to develop systems that admit specified levels of new immigrants. The most objectionable policy in the court of public opinion is one where the nation appears unable to control a basic element of sovereignty, choosing who resides in the country. This abdication of choice is what exists today in the form of burgeoning asylum caseloads in many developed countries. Long-staying asylum populations symbolize national vulnerability.

This is not the case when a nation determines that it has reasons—humanitarian, economic self-interest, whatever—to invite some foreigners to join the society, and decides whom and how many. Those reasons exist for most developed nations today; presenting them and developing policy accordingly will contribute importantly to the cause of migration regulation and control.

Finally, a crucial aspect of national policy debates involves questions about the integration of newcomers. Whether by choice or happenstance, many developed nations, including Japan, have become immigrant nations to varying extents.

Regardless of what steps nations take to respond to future migration pressures, substantial populations of immigrants now reside in industrialized nations and are likely to remain. Postponing the cost and commitment required for successful integration is, under these circumstances, dangerous social policy. The challenge is one of successfully integrating newcomers and, most importantly, their children. It is a challenge that faces the U.S. anew, as well as many other nations.

International policies

Migration policy measures that utilize law enforcement, visa and admission criteria, and timely political asylum procedures are necessary but not nearly enough. Migration pressures must be addressed with policies of far greater scope and ambition than those encompassed by the framework of traditional humanitarian and immigration control policies. Sadako Ogata, the United Nations High Commissioner for Refugees, has urged that the issues be treated not only "as a matter for humanitarian agencies of the UN but also as a political problem which must be placed in the mainstream of the international agenda as a potential threat to international peace and security."

Heeding this warning will require fundamental shifts in foreign policy. For more than 40 years, and especially since the Helsinki Accords were adopted in 197S, freedom of movement as a fundamental principle of international human rights was central to the Cold War struggle. Against the backdrop of stringent exit controls, freedom of movement increasingly took the form of promoting the right to leave.

Defining freedom of movement in a new day requires recasting the fervor and effort the West devoted to promoting the right to leave to underscore its corollary, the right to stay. Most international migration today is an act of desperation, not choice. The vast majority of individuals prefer home and will stay there, if conditions are even barely tolerable. It is that impulse that policy must build on; freedom of movement should reflect options and choice, not the sole avenue for survival.

An international ethos anchored in the right to stay would require:

• **Sustained development, balanced growth and population stabilization in the countries which now house the majority of the world's population.** A crucial question for the future is how a rich world of stable population size can interact with a less developed world of dramatic population growth? The enormity of the task is illustrated by these numbers. By 2010, about 730 million new workers will have entered the labor force in the developing world. During the period of the most robust job growth in the U.S. in the 1980s, to provide a comparison, the economy produced 2 million new jobs annually. The need to generate jobs is unprecedented.

Another illustration of the scale of what is required comes from information about migrant remittances. Foreign exchange generated by remittances is estimated to be $66 billion, a number second only to oil sales, whereas official development assistance stands at about $51 billion. Officially tallied remittances come largely through contract labor programs. The actual figure, because of sizeable informal flows that have not been measured, is far higher. Thus, international migration is a key element sustaining many nations' economies.

Development policies that provide some measure of economic hope for individuals and nations without stimulating substantial new migrant flows are a threshold challenge for the international community.

• **Foreign policies and international priorities that emphasize broad-based improvements in human rights conditions.** Vast numbers of people do not enjoy the most fundamental protections. Combined with extreme poverty and information, through mass communications, about conditions elsewhere, widespread human rights deficiencies are a major reason for today's migrations.

Past policies have tended to concentrate on individual, extreme cases of dissidents and groups that have been individually persecuted by enemy governments. Future policies must focus far more broadly on overall human rights conditions, regardless of whether particular governments are friend or foe, with the objective of changing conditions that deprive large numbers of people of basic rights and freedoms.

With tensions emanating from ethnic clashes and separatist movements on the rise, human rights imperatives may require redrawing borders in some cases and addressing aspirations for minority or group rights and protections, guaranteed by regional or international bodies, in others. In addition, international humanitarian agencies and activities must command more resources, coordinate more effectively, and develop comprehensive emergency response capabilities that today reside only with military services.

In that connection, the aftermath of the Cold War has brought with it political solutions, however tenuous, for countries like Nicaragua and Cambodia. Effective repatriation of refugees that have been in neighboring countries is considerably more expensive and complex than providing care in camps. If repatriation and reintegration of these populations fail, they could become new sources of international migration, for people once moved are likely to move again.

• **Effective conflict resolution mechanisms and interventions.** The Kurdish exodus from Iraq after the Gulf war prompted the international community to take the unprecedented action of declaring this humanitarian emergency a threat to regional peace and stability, opening the way for intervention, for humanitarian purposes, within a sovereign state. The circumstances were unique, yet the UN action signalled the changing parameters of sovereignty and the role international bodies and consensus may play in redefining it.

Preventing ruinous migrations must be among a set of priority, shared international political and collective security objectives. The task is to address emerging crises that could lead to protracted refugee or other artificial migration situations before they take firm hold and become irreversible. Tests of this proposition have been the Organization of American States (OAS) effort to dislodge the coup in Haiti and the UN effort to avert further bloodshed in Yugoslavia. Unfortunately, the outcomes have been disappointing and largely ineffective, at least to date, in each case.

• **Dramatic reductions in arms sales, production and military spending.** Not only have war and armed struggles victimized defenseless populations, the percentage of national budgets devoted to military spending has taken limited resources away from needed social spending in many countries in both the developed and developing world. However, the military/non-military balance has been particularly distorted in many high emigration countries. The International Monetary Fund (IMF) states that a 1% reduction in defense spending internationally would free up $140 billion. This would more than compensate for shortages in capital to devote to development and human resources investments.

• **Decisions on trade that expand access to the markets of advanced nations.** Today's consensus models for economic development stress market-based structures and international trade as the routes to growth and prosperity in less developed countries. Yet the very products most likely to be competitively produced by less developed countries are often those which advanced countries continue to protect. Migration pressures are centrally affected by this standoff. The Caribbean Basin Initiative, for example, had as an explicit purpose to reduce migration pressures through trade and development. It has had only marginal, if any, success in that realm because the very products—sugar, apparel, leather—most likely to create jobs are barred from the U.S. market.

The nexus between trade policy and migration is poorly understood and represents an area of policymaking that is key. The emergence of three major trading blocs, for example, could lead to growth in world output and increased trade without mitigating migration pressures, if large areas of Africa and Latin America and parts of Asia are unable to make progress in the world economy. At the same time, we have only the most rudimentary understanding of how migration pressures are affected by economic integration initiatives such as the North American Free Trade Agreement (NAFTA).

Europe's experience in this regard has been a positive one. Formal economic integration has been underway for more than 30 years. From the outset, it acknowledged a place for labor mobility. When labor mobility provisions became effective in 1968, Italian emigration north had diminished because Italy's economic growth, largely stimulated by other EC measures, had begun providing enough jobs to employ new workers. For Spain, the experience has been similar, and both countries, longstanding migrant-source states, now attract, rather than export, workers.

The change occurred not only in response to newly-available markets, but also because of Europe's political commitment to a common future and the accompanying substantial resource flows from northern to southern Europe for social purposes. The shift suggests that the circumstances compelling people to emigrate can change over the course of 10 to 20 years, given investment, expanded market access, and other benefits attendant to economic integration.

Paradoxically, migration concerns are a serious deterrent to broader economic integration. With wage differentials of 10 to 1, the U.S. and Mexico, for example, have taken great pains to establish that NAFTA will not encompass labor migration issues.

Although free trade is likely to produce growth, it does not follow that migration pressures will necessarily diminish. This is because growth is not synonymous with economic development. The economy must improve in specific ways to diminish migration pressures. Mexican wages do not need to increase to the point that they equal those in the U.S., but the gap must narrow and improvements in economic and social well-being must be broadly experienced throughout Mexican society to overcome longstanding migration pressures and illegal immigration connections.

This requires targeted private investment and aggressive public investment in social programs and national infrastructure. Such investment is unlikely if the private sector and marketplace incentives alone constitute the engines of growth. The goal should be for Mexico to become the Italy of the Western Hemisphere, not a permanent low-wage mecca.

NAFTA does not seem to envision such a future at all, although it may serve as a first step in that direction. If so, the agreement is a positive development from a migration standpoint. If not, we will have missed a historic opportunity to address migration pressures that affect Americans in critical ways. Just as we are learning that development must become "user-friendly" where environmental issues are concerned, the migration implications of particular development, investment and trade strategies must also be treated as issues of crucial importance.

* * * * *

To the extent that nations have migration policies at all, most, including the U.S., handle them as narrow, particularistic functions. However, the causes of contemporary migrations are deeply embedded in the social, economic and political conditions of our times. To be effective, policy must go beyond conventional control and humanitarian measures, so that managing migration pressures becomes part of nations' central economic, political and security objectives.

Thank you.

Mr. SAWYER. Mr. Teitelbaum?

Mr. TEITELBAUM. Thank you, Mr. Chairman.

It is a pleasure to be back in the House of Representatives. I wouldn't have thought I would say that when I was here. It wasn't entirely an orderly place in which to work, but it is nice to be back.

Mr. SAWYER. There are some who say it hasn't gotten any better.

Mr. TEITELBAUM. I have been asked to provide some commentary on recent and perspective trends in global migration insofar as they relate to economic trends and social progress in industrialized and developing nations. Now, Mrs. Meissner and I did not—I did not actually know she was going to be on the program, and we did not speak, but, as you will see if you have looked at our testimony, there is a good deal of commonality in the things we say.

Mr. SAWYER. There are times you even quote the same sources.

Mr. TEITELBAUM. Oh, do we? Oh, good.

Mrs. MEISSNER. Probably each other.

Mr. TEITELBAUM. So I will associate myself with almost everything that she said and take my time to draw your attention to some central points that I think that anybody who is fair-minded, and is not pushing a particular line on this subject, would have to agree are central points about recent experience with international migration.

First, the absolute numbers of recent international migration are of large magnitude, and are generally thought by observers—though there is a good deal of murkiness in these data—to be accelerating over the past 5 to 10 years, and especially directed toward industrialized countries of Europe and North America.

Now there is a good deal of murkiness about the numbers, and I can go into that if you want. There are attempts to get harder numbers on international migration, but it is actually quite difficult to do. Even the very definition of what is a person who is migrating internationally varies from country to country. And so it is awfully difficult to put together comparable data.

But as an order of magnitude, at least, if one tries to guess—estimate—the numbers of people who are currently resident outside their nations of birth, it would be in the range, I think, of 95 to 110 million people.

Now, that does not include a number unknown to me, but described to me as in the 25 million range, of persons who live in the same place, but happen to now be located in countries other than that of their nationality because of the breakup of the Soviet Union. And there will presumably be more of those over time, if the Czech and Slovak Federal Republic does indeed break up. Then there will be Czechs living in Slovakia and vice versa. The numbers there are not very large, I don't think.

In the former Soviet Union the numbers are quite large, but I am not including them, because I don't know how to deal with them. They are not really international migrants.

The OECD recently published its annual appraisal of global migration trends, and I quoted from it in my written testimony as saying that "in most OECD countries the upward trend in international migratory movements that had become quite marked by the mid-1980's was stronger and gaining ground by 1990 and 1991." It then goes on—without the quote now—to report further that the juxtaposition of large and rising immigration flows with another characteristic that you heard from the previous panel—historically low levels of domestic fertility has resulted—the two opposing trends has resulted in a rapid increase in the demographic impacts of immigration in all OECD countries. That is point one.

Point two: these flows of international migrants have become increasingly volatile and quite unpredictable. I list in my testimony a few examples of those which will immediately be familiar. What happened in Germany and Eastern Europe, which seems like a century ago, but say 3 years ago, something like that, when several millions of people suddenly moved. The sudden departure of hundreds of thousands of Soviet Jews, mostly for Israel, a number that—as I recall a paper I read on this topic—is equal to the total number of Soviet Jews who had left the Soviet Union in all preceding years. But it took place in a year or two.

Then let us not forget the 4 to 5 million persons who fled the Iraqi invasion of Kuwait and the Gulf War that followed, and the newspaper estimates of 2 million people displaced from the republics of the former Yugoslavia.

The other thing to remember about these kinds of phenomena is that if one goes to Europe one finds a great deal of anguish and worry about much larger potential flows of this unpredictable volatile type, with all kinds of numbers thrown around. Most demographers don't believe them to be real, and yet one sees them in the newspaper every day—20 million former Soviets heading west, that kind of number.

So whatever the reality of that, the fear is there, the anxiety is there, and that point should not be forgotten.

Third, the current numbers of international migrants who are resident outside their own countries are heavily concentrated in certain world regions. They are not evenly distributed around the globe. In sub-Sahara and Africa, which previous witnesses have referred to in a different context, is the region or subcontinent par excellence of international migration, with 35 million estimated people resident outside their country of nationality.

And then one takes Asia, which is a much bigger place demographically than sub-Saharan Africa, at 15 to 20 million; the Middle East again, a much smaller place, about 15 to 20 million; 15 to 20 million in west Europe; and 25 to 30 million in the United States and Canada, i.e. North America.

And then, finally, one should remember that within these regions to which most migrants move internationally—in which most of them can be found—there is a heavy internal concentration of those migrants. So that in the United States, only five States, perhaps six States, and within them only a few metropolitan areas, account for the bulk of international migrants resident in the United States. And that means that from the point of view of a Member of Congress, it can be a different world depending on whether the Congressman comes from where I came from, Missouri, say, or even Ohio, or whether one comes from south Florida or southern California or New York. They are just different places in terms of what we are talking about here.

Mr. SAWYER. There are other differences between southern Ohio and southern California, but they are probably not worth going into.

Mr. TEITELBAUM. Would you like to comment on them?

Mr. SAWYER. No, no, no.

Mr. TEITELBAUM. Probably a few earthquakes, although there have been some in Ohio.

The fourth point: this really seconds Doris Meissner's point, that whatever the size of these flows and however they may be accelerating, they really represent only a small minority of any country's population. Most people just don't move, and most people certainly don't move internationally across borders, or at least that has been the way—that is, all we can speak about is what we know to have happened so far.

Even if you take the most extreme cases, such as Cuba, or probably the most extreme would be Afghanistan, one might have thought everybody left. In fact, it is hard to get over 25 percent of the population leaving, even under terrible circumstances like Afghanistan. Cuba is 10 percent, and one thinks of it as a major out-migration country. Haiti is comparable.

So it is important to remember that, as she said, that while there are large flows and they are accelerating, it is not a situation in which everyone is on the move and there are—to go back to your metaphor of tidal waves—these are not uncontrollable tidal waves. In fact, there is a very substantial level of national control over entry. However ineffective as Doris Meissner said may be some of those controls, there is much less migration as a result of those controls than there might well have been expected to be.

Fifth point: that the impacts of this international migration on economic trends and social programs are actually remarkably difficult to assess, and suffer from a very unsavory combination—they are not only difficult to assess, but they are subject to strong ideological biases of various kinds. It depends on one's political orientations, or even one's disciplinary orientations, how one views the impacts.

I will give a few examples here, but I won't belabor them. Obviously, it goes without saying in the House of Representatives that issues of ethnicity, race, religion, nationality are important differences of opinion on this subject.

I do want to talk about the perspective of international migration as a "factor movement," that is simply the movement of a factor of production—labor—comparable to the flow of capital or commodities or manufacturers. This is a common point of view. One hears it frequently from some economists, but not all economists, I should say. And it ignores a rather obvious fact, a rather objective reality: that while many immigrants are indeed workers (although many are not workers), they are not merely workers. They are human beings. Unlike Toyotas. These may be very good motor cars, but they are not human, I don't think, the last I looked.

Immigrants are flesh and blood human beings. They have all the attributes of human beings, and the impacts they have upon the societies into which they move, and the impacts those societies have upon them, embrace all the noneconomic elements of human relationships. In the real world, these impacts are perceived by the public and by their representatives, whether or not they are perceived by analysts looking at the situation through a set of prisms or blinders, one might say.

The best summary I can find of the importance of this human dimension comes from the late Swiss writer and architect, Max Fritsch, who summed up the European experience with gastorbeiter programs, the guestworker programs in which millions were recruited actively by many European countries for work in the post-war period. He said—and we can't really interpret what the emotive quality he intended by this—he simply said it, and I think it is remarkably spare and elegant. He said, "we asked for workers, and people came." I think that sums it up. That is the difference in perspective.

The time scale is also important. The impacts of immigration may be invisible for long periods of time and then suddenly can break out in vicious physical assaults, mayhem, riot, bombings, fire bombings, and xenophobic right-wing neo-Nazi revivals. All of a sudden, almost out of nowhere from the point of view of people unaware of the perceptions of the population or what has been going on. It happens typically when the economy sours, or perhaps when some political extremist or extremist group decides to mobilize a latent kind of animus toward foreigners.

I just saw in today's Wall Street Journal, on the plane coming down, that the estimate now is that in Germany this year the neo-Nazi assaults on asylum hostels and foreigners on the street—it is not limited to hostels—there are in excess of 1,000 incidents, violent incidents, attacks on foreigners now recorded this year, resulting in 10 deaths and 700 injuries.

I don't know how good those data are. It is a newspaper report. But there is no doubt to anyone who follows what is going on in Germany that this is a major set of events that is emerging here and is causing all kinds of perception problems for the German state from the point of view of its neighbors. There is a history here, after all—which most of us would like to forget—about Germany, but some people are reminded of it by these kinds of terrible episodes.

Time scale also matters with respect to refugees. Refugees are typically highly dependent residents, highly dependent upon public welfare and income transfer programs in the short-term. But over the longer term they may become (they also may not become), productive citizens and no longer a dependent population. So the general point is the time scale in which one assesses effects matters a lot.

Finally, the cost-benefit kind of approach to the impacts of large-scale immigration. I have tried to read most of the studies that have been done estimating costs and benefits of international migration, and as you know if you've looked at them, they come up with wildly differing results, I mean ranging from large positive to large negative net costs.

The problem is it is very hard to measure the cost, very hard to measure the benefits. The benefits are typically concentrated among the immigrants, and let's say their employers and some others. The costs are typically widely dispersed, if there are costs, among others who may not even be aware that they are incurring any costs. Some of the benefits may be immediate. Some of the costs may be deferred.

How does one measure the cost of certain things? What does one say about the cost to Germany and what has happened in the last year that I just described? How do you put a Deutschemark figure on the cost of that kind of political situation?

There is also no consensus——

Mr. SAWYER. Even harder to put a pound figure on it.

Mr. TEITELBAUM. Yes. Well, it is going down now.

There is also no consensus as to whether costs should be figured at marginal cost or average cost. How should one factor in the cost of infrastructure? If it is there already, shouldn't one take a percentage of it for each additional immigrant? Or should one say, well, it is a sunk cost. It is cost free to add the additional person on the highway system or the water system or whatever.

All of these decisions have to be made by the analysts in this cost-benefit analysis accounting system. And since the analysts are often of one view or another as to how they would like it to come out, it is not too surprising that the results are wildly differing.

Which leads me to the biases of those making these kinds of assessments, because this project has attracted some of the most ideological of protagonists, especially in Europe, but also in the United States.

In Europe I will just give a quick litany of the exaggerated emotional groups that have taken a lead in this: The National Front in France, which started out and was laughed at by the political class, and is now a threat. In Germany, the Republican party and the People's Union, two parties that are showing increasing returns to their exaggerated policies on this subject.

And, of course, then the neo-Nazi groups. I can't really tell you how they are organized or where they come from, but they are obviously there.

In Austria, there is the Freedom Party. In Switzerland, there is a party with the unlikely name of the Auto Party, which as I understand it initially started—it organized on a platform of eliminating the speed limit on the autobahns in Switzerland, and found that anti-immigrant rhetoric got more votes than eliminating the speed limits. And there is another party as well.

In the United States, anyway, on these kinds of ideological debates, it is the usual suspects. The Wall Street Journal's editorial pages which are well-known, the Heritage Foundation, the Cato Institute, the Mexican-American Legal Defense and Education Fund, the American Civil Liberties Union, white supremacist groups of various ilks, not to mention the more moderate but nonetheless advocacy groups that are pushing particular economic lines or ethnic agendas or political agendas.

Unfortunately, one has a complicated subject that is very hard to assess, and a lot of advocacy with a lot of exaggeration. That is not a good combination.

So what is in prospect? Well, I try to outline in my testimony—and I won't go through it in any detail—three predictable things that I think are pretty sure to happen and three things that are quite unpredictable. Let me just summarize them quickly.

The first two predictables are rapid demographic growth—you have already heard about that—and its son or daughter, rapid labor force growth, with a lag of 15 to 20 years. These are near certain, as you have already heard. To put some numbers on the labor force side of this, for the next 20 years, the ILO—the International Labor Office—projections show that over the next 20 years, in the less-developed world, the economically active population is projected to increase some 732 million people in 20 years.

Now, since in my experience on Capitol Hill, large numbers have a rather numbing impact on discussions, let me use two comparisons to put that 732 million into perspective. Compare it first to the past two decades of labor force growth in the less-developed world, vis-a-vis the projected next 20 years. The past 20 years growth was 650 million. So you will get a flavor that there is more coming, not a great deal more, but more coming in the context that Doris Meissner mentioned of less satisfactory rates of economic growth over the immediate past decade than had preceded.

Then compare the labor force growth projected over the next two decades in the less-developed world with the total labor force of the entire industrialized world—which is the number of jobs, if you will, that have been accumulated over their histories collectively. And that number comes to 585 million, as the total labor force of the industrialized world to be compared against 732 million estimated or projected increase over the next two decades in the less-industrialized world.

A third predictable Doris Meissner has already mentioned, so I won't be saying anything about it: that the option of international migration is likely to continue to increase and to spread more widely, even to now remote parts of the Third World.

Now, the unpredictables are whether future economic growth in less-developed countries will be of a character and of a pace that will be sufficient to accommodate the kind of labor force growth that I have just alluded to. They will have to be remarkably successful in economic development over the next 20 years to succeed at that. That is number one.

No. 2, the scale of increase in labor force is so large that, even at the highest levels one could credibly anticipate, international migration is unlikely to be of a large enough magnitude to be significant in providing jobs for that kind of labor force growth.

The second unpredictable is what will happen in the former Warsaw Pact states. If anyone can tell me what will happen there, then I will try to spell out the migration implications of that. But since I don't think we know what is going to happen there, it is very, very unpredictable.

And the third is what kinds of wars can we expect to see? Doris Meissner has already alluded to the product of such wars, and I don't think we expected the Iraqi invasion of Kuwait or the Gulf War to occur. So, under those circumstances, it makes it rather difficult to predict where the next one will be, but that makes for a very unpredictable situation.

I would say in that regard that, while it is very unpredictable, there is a very high likelihood that such wars will take place somewhere. And given migration implications that can arise and we have seen arise, and given the desperate human suffering that results and the dangerous political forces unleashed by such human suffering—I hope that the State Department and the intelligence agencies are paying a lot of attention to this, recognizing they can't predict, but at least they should be managing a watching brief.

I think I will stop there, Mr. Chairman.

[The prepared statement of Mr. Teitelbaum follows:]

PREPARED STATEMENT OF MICHAEL S. TEITELBAUM, PROGRAM OFFICER, ALFRED P. SLOAN FOUNDATION

Mr. Chairman, members of the subcommittee:

I am Michael S. Teitelbaum. I am a demographer by specialization, formerly on the faculties of Princeton and Oxford Universities, and currently at the Alfred P. Sloan Foundation in New York. So that you will know something about me, let me say quickly that between 1978 and 1980 I served as Staff Director of the House Select Committee on Population (during which time I had cordial professional relationships with your predecessors as Members and Staff of this Subcommittee). From 1987 to 1990 I served as a Commissioner on the U.S. Commission for the Study of International Migration and Cooperative Economic Development. More recently I was elected First Vice President of the Population Association of America, and appointed one of nine members of the Commission on Legal Immigration Reform, established by the 1990 Immigration Act. I appear here at your request, and in my personal professional capacity.

I have been asked to provide commentary on recent and prospective trends in global migration insofar as they relate to economic trends and social progress in both industrialized and developing nations.

Since my comments must be very brief here, let me draw your attention to five central points that jump out immediately from any fairminded look at recent experience with international migration:

First, the absolute numbers of recent international migrants—though the estimates are quite soft at the margins—are clearly of very substantial magnitude. Moreover, there is general agreement that the international flows of people have been accelerating considerably in recent years, especially in the experience of the industrialized countries of Europe and North America.

Some 95–110 million persons are currently resident outside their nations of birth.

The most authoritative appraisal of global migration trends, published by the OECD last month, reports that in "most OECD countries, the upward trend in international migratory movements that had become quite marked by the mid-1980s, was stronger and gaining ground by 1990 and 1991." It reports further that the juxtaposition of large and rising immigration flows with historically low levels of domestic fertility has led to a rapid increase in the demographic impacts of immigration in all OECD countries.

[OECD, Trends in International Migration: Continuous Reporting System on Migration (SOPEMI) 1992, Ch 1.]

Second, international migration flows have become increasingly volatile and unpredictable.

In recent years there have been substantial, and wholly unpredicted, pulses of international migration in various world regions:

• several millions who moved from Eastern Europe to (former) West Germany, Austria, and elsewhere in Western Europe;

• the hundreds of thousands of Jews from the former Soviet Union who have moved to Israel;

• the 4–5 million persons who fled Iraq's invasion of Kuwait and the subsequent Gulf War.

• the estimated 2 million displaced from the republics of the disintegrating Yugoslavia.

Moreover, there have been widespread speculations about much larger impending pressures for outmigration from the former Soviet Union, former Yugoslavia, Poland, Romania, and elsewhere in Eastern and Central Europe.

Third, the current numbers of international migrants resident outside their own countries ("stocks") are heavily concentrated:

• 35 million are in sub-Saharan Africa alone
• 15–20 million in Asia and the Middle East
• 15–20 million in West Europe
• 25–30 million in U.S./Canada
• 4–5 million in Australia

Within these regions, international migrants are also heavily concentrated. In the United States, most live within only 5 or 6 states, and in a few areas. Hence the perception of immigration can vary dramatically, depending upon whether one is in southern California or Missouri, south Florida or South Carolina.

Fourth, only a small minority of a country's population ever emigrates, and their reasons for doing so are highly diverse.

Even in extreme cases (Afghanistan, El Salvador, Cuba), the percentage who leave the country is in the range of 10–25 percent.

The fact that the absolute numbers of international migrants are now very large should not convey a false impression of footloose masses roaming uncontrollably across international borders.

Moreover, people move international for a wide variety of reasons, often overlapping, including: the economic demands of migrants, employers, and politicians; ethnic and family ties; political persecutions; mass expulsions; wars both international and civil; famines; natural disasters; environmental crises or degradations; etc.

Fifth, the impacts of international migration upon economic trends and social programs are extraordinarily difficult to assess, and are subject to strong biases—depending upon the commentator's ideological and/or disciplinary orientations.

A few examples should suffice:

1. It is obvious that the virtues/drawbacks of particular immigration streams are viewed quite differently by different groups, often along dimensions of ethnicity, nationality, race, religion, etc.

2. Those who describe immigration as a "factor movement" of labor (comparable to the flow of capital, manufactures, or commodities) ignore a rather obvious reality: many (not all) immigrants are indeed workers, but they are not merely workers.

They are human beings—flesh and blood—with hopes, fears, loves, hates, politics, religions, languages, values, cultures. The impacts they have upon the human societies into which they move are not merely on its labor force, but upon all these noneconomic elements of the receiving human society, and in the real world these impacts are perceived by the public.

The late Swiss writer Max Fritsch, speaking of the European experience with the immigration of millions of "guestworkers" during the postwar period, put it best: "We asked for workers," he said, "and people came."

3. The time scale over which the impacts of immigration are assessed is critical. Even very large movements may be absorbed without apparent impact for many years, as in Germany, France, and Italy—only to suddenly break out in vicious riots and assaults, or neo-Nazi revivals, when the economy sours or extremists mobilize. Refugees may be highly dependent upon public welfare in the short term, but may become productive citizens over the longer term. The general point is that timescale matters—a lot.

4. "Cost-benefit" analyses of the impacts of largescale immigration produce wildly differing results. Both the benefits (typically concentrated among immigrants and

their employers) and the costs (typically widely dispersed) turn out to be extremely difficult to measure. There is no consensus as to whether costs should be figured at "marginal" or "average" levels; how the accounting should be done for infrastructure costs (roads, water supply, school buildings); nor how to measure the fiscal impacts upon oversubscribed services with rapid cost inflation such as health care.

Unfortunately, assessment of the impacts of immigration is not only highly vulnerable to the biases of the assessor, but has attracted some of the most ideological of protagonists—especially in Europe, but also on the American scene.

In Europe, one need only mention the emotional claims of the National Front of Jean-Marie Le Pen in France; in Germany, the "Republican Party" and "People's Union", not to mention the neo-Nazi groups; in Austria, the "Freedom Party"; in Switzerland, the "Auto Party" and the "Swiss Democratic Party".

In the U.S., the subject has been heavily lobbied by the Wall Street Journal's editorial pages, the Heritage Foundation, the Cato Institute, the Mexican-American Legal Defense and Education Fund, the American Civil Liberties Union, various white-supremacist groups, not to mention numerous economic, ethnic and political interest groups.

WHAT IS IN PROSPECT?

One illuminating way to visualize international migration is as a point of deepening intersection between Western industrialized countries and the third world.

Demographic and economic differentials between these groups of countries, already large and in many cases still increasing, are producing rising "potentials" for international migration. Such potentials may be realized, or not, depending upon a complex mix of policy, history and communication.

Somewhere between these two polar extremes lie the rapidly-changing countries of the former Warsaw Pact, in which economic differentials vis-a-vis the West are currently very large, but demographic rates are rather similar.

From this demographic-economic perspective, we can see at least six elements that will underlie future international migration trends, of which three are relatively predictable, and the other three almost wholly unpredictable.

THE PREDICTABLES:

Predictables #1 and #2: The first two predictable elements emerge from the powerful forces of demographic change in the countries of origin.

Demographic projections provide useful future insights for perhaps 20 years. Labor force projections (demographic projections with additional assumptions as to future labor force participation rates by age and sex) are useful for perhaps a decade or so.

Both have weaknesses, but they still are better guides to the likely future than are economic or political projections.

The high demographic growth rates of the postwar third world are well known, and need not be reviewed here. Because of the powerful in-built "momentum" of this population growth, further demographic increases of very large magnitude are near-certain.

The latest UN projections indicate that the population of the less developed countries can be expected to increase by some 1.5 to 2 billion people between 1990 and 2010.[1]

With a wholly predictable lag of about two decades, this powerful acceleration resurfaces as very rapid labor force growth.

Rapid labor force growth is almost certain to continue well beyond the end of the century, due to high fertility of the past two decades, even though fertility rates in many (though by no means all) third world countries have begun to decline.

The ILO projections for the next twenty years show a further increase of some 732 millions in the economically active population of the less developed world.

Since big numbers have a tendency to become rather numbing in government, let me use two comparisons to put this number into perspective. First, compare this 732 million increase over the coming two decades with the the increase in the same regions over the past two decades: 650 million.

Second, compare the 732 million increase, over the next two decades, with the total size of the industrialized countries' current labor forces, a labor force size accumulated over the whole of their histories: 585 million

---

[1] Calculated from United Nations, World Population Prospects 1988 (New York: 1989), Table 1.

Predictable #3: Access to the option of international migration is likely to continue to increase, and to spread more widely, even to now-remote parts of the world.

The technological improvements in transportation and communication that have transformed all of our lives are now penetrating into previously-isolated populations in Asia, Africa and Latin America. Hundreds of millions of people who, only a couple of decades ago, would have lived out their lives within a few kilometers of their birthplaces now have the real option of seeking to migrate internationally.

Long distance migrations from one continent to another, previously high-risk and costly enterprises, have become quick and inexpensive. Films, television, and VCRs have brought to the attention of remote millions the economic attractions of life in other areas. International telephone and fax communications have allowed migrants to maintain close ties with family and friends that previously would have had to be sacrificed.

THE UNPREDICTABLES:

Unpredictable #1: Will future economic growth in less developed countries be of a character and pace sufficient to accommodate such magnitudes of growth in those seeking employment?

The decade of the 1980s has been an unhappy one in this regard. But those who attempt to forecast should be honest, and above all humble. In reality, we lack the tools needed to make plausible forecasts as to the coming decades (economic growth is a remarkably complex phenomenon, subject to the viscissitudes of nature, politics, and (perhaps) even culture.)

Two things are reasonably certain:

1. the coming two decades will have to be remarkably successful ones in economic terms if the third world is to be able to create sufficient employment to keep its already high rates of underemployment from rising still higher.

2. the scale of projected third world labor force growth (730+ million in 20 years) is so large that, even at the highest credible levels, international migration cannot be large enough to be a significant factor in providing the jobs needed.

Unpredictable #2: The nations of the former Warsaw Pact provide a more complicated picture in some respects.

They have long had somewhat higher fertility and mortality rates than Western nations, but their fertility was still quite low, so we should not expect to see the very rapid increases in economically-active population that can be rather clearly foreseen for the third world. (Before the collapse of Communism, these countries used to complain of "labor shortages", though in reality these were reflections of the inefficiencies of the command economy.)

With economic transformation will come at least transitional increases in unemployment and under-employment. Also, the depressed exchange rates of their currencies are already producing very large (e.g. 10-fold) differentials in earning power vis-a-vis comparable Western employment.

The combination of rising unemployment and enormous earning differentials provides powerful economic incentives for migration movements, and these are already in process. Unlike the third world, however, these large differentials in employment prospects and earnings potential may be relatively short-term, e.g. a decade in duration.

No one can really know: the future course of political and economic change in these countries is one of the most unpredictable forces of the near-term future.

Unpredictable #3: The Gulf War of 1990–91 and the current slow-motion disintegration of Yugoslavia forces us to recognize a final area of exceptional uncertainty: where violent conflicts might occur from which large populations might be forced to flee.

The Iraqi invasion of Kuwait and subsequent events provoked the hasty movement of some 4–5 million persons, with very considerable economic loss and human suffering involved. Many were not even nationals of the combatant countries, because by 1990 the Persian Gulf had become a region of heavy immigration, largely of workers from the Middle East and Asia. Others fell victim to internal ethnic fissures within Iraq that led to the suppression and flight of large numbers of Kurdish Iraqi nationals.

The migration impacts of the Yugoslav civil war cannot yet be assessed, though millions are already in flight from the violence and from the ghostly reappearance of the "ethnic cleansing" seen during World War II.

While it is very likely that there will continue to be such conflicts—both international and internal—the locations and magnitudes cannot be clearly predicted. At the same time, the high likelihood of such powerful migration pulses, and the desperate human suffering and dangerous political forces they unleash, warrant a serious "watching brief" of potential trouble spots by the State Department and intelligence sectors.

In summary, Mr. Chairman:

International migration is a subject characterized by truly exceptional difficulties for objective analysis, and by large degrees of uncertainty—all surrounded by an envelope of excessive enthusiasm for unrealistic models by otherwise objective analysts, or by flagrant excesses on the part of ideological and interest-group advocates. (In the perceptive words of an old Chinese proverb, "Strong and bitter words indicate . . . a weak cause.")

The combination of complexity, uncertainty and rhetorical excess makes a heady brew, unlikely to produce much in the way of clarity or consensus. Congressional deliberations about immigration reform during 1990 presented a particularly chaotic episode, dominated by advocates and last-minute horsetrades rather than careful deliberation. The subject is an increasingly important one, in humanitarian and economic terms alike, and it deserves the kind of orderly, balanced and informed consideration that I hope this Subcommittee can encourage.

Thank you for your kind attention.

Mr. SAWYER. Thank you both very much.

Just a couple of brief observations. You probably can't predict earthquakes any better than we ever could, but we know that they will occur. And so we seek to be as prepared as we can for those dislocations, even though we still can't pinpoint them with any real success.

Just let me offer a couple of other observations.

As you suggested, the absolute size of migrations may not be great in and of themselves, but the real pain that they produce and the real pain that provokes them and the further perceived dislocation are significant, particularly in their growth in relative size in today's world.

You are right certainly about time scale being critical to that perception, slow and fast. There are grave differences, even though the absolute size may not be enormous.

When you were talking about Germany and the consequences of that older indigenous, wealthier, more stable population and the consequences of perceived rapid movement—or the threat of rapid movement—of younger, more mobile, less affluent, more needy population, I couldn't help but think that what you were describing was a formula for Los Angeles. The events that we saw there this spring certainly took place in an environment that we are coming to perceive in those terms.

And while they haven't provoked the rise of political extremism to the same degree that you described in various parts of Europe, that it may well be that, like earthquakes, it would be difficult to pinpoint whether that would occur in Los Angeles or Washington or Atlanta or New York or any of the other places where those phenomena emerged. It is still possible to predict a likelihood of their emergence one place or another.

In that sense, I very much appreciate what you have to say. I am grateful, I guess I should say.

Mrs. Meissner, you asked us to return to the policy implications of all of this. Maybe this is the best time simply to say, why don't you go back? And if you are looking for a place to start, I am interested in the way in which the commitment of the international community to the ideal of the right to leave has in many ways driven many of the pressures that yielded the effects of the last 4 years. That entails one set of problems, but the right to stay imposes a whole different set of demands and expectations that the international community places in settings where they might be most called for. Would you expand on that?

Mrs. MEISSNER. Well, the idea of leaving your country to escape persecution is obviously an idea that is extraordinarily important. But in a Cold War setting we were able to be really very high-minded in the way that we celebrated it. There is no question that we used the idea of people leaving Communist countries as a propaganda point every bit as much as we facilitated departure to protect people that were suffering, having been political prisoners or the like.

Where we found ourselves at the end of the Cold War was with an international attitude toward Communist countries, at least, that said that if you can leave, you are a hero. And that worked very effectively when Communist countries, in fact, stood at the gate and controlled very, very arduously the opportunity for people to leave.

But now we are in a situation where we won. And by saying we won, I mean that the principle of freedom of movement which we had fought very hard for in our international relations, when the principle of freedom of movement became possible from Communist countries, it becomes the problem of answered prayers. You need to be very careful of what you wish for because the wish might be granted.

As Michael said, the numbers of people that were predicted to leave the east and the Soviet Union were exaggerated. The experience is that not nearly those numbers are leaving. Nonetheless, over time, there are very large numbers of people from that part of the world that wanted to leave, and our devotion to the notion of the right to leave applied, of course, not just to communist countries. It was taken up by others around the world.

I would argue that we now have to find a way—if we are going to be serious about migration pressures around the world we have to find a way to reverse that psychology. Now, by reverse the psychology I don't mean keeping people penned up in their own countries. I certainly don't mean returning to a situation where movement and exit are restricted. What we do need to do is concentrate seriously on people's ability to live where they currently live in a way that allows them to survive economically and to be safe politically.

Mr. SAWYER. Measuring whether or not the door is open, the right to leave, whether the gate is open is relatively easy. It becomes extremely difficult to define and impose what we mean by the kinds of conditions that make it not only a right, but possible for people to stay—if that is what you are talking about—the conditions in which people live.

Mrs. MEISSNER. Exactly.

Mr. SAWYER. I mean, it seems to me that the international community has a great deal to say to one another who think of themselves as friends and collaborators, and the whole notion of Helsinki. But it runs the risk of taking on the attitude of, "You mind your own business, these are our people, we will take care of them the way we want to," if we start talking about the rights and terms and conditions in which people can stay.

Mrs. MEISSNER. What you want to have, of course, is a situation where people migrate as a matter of free choice, not as a matter of economic survival or of staying alive in terms of personal danger. And what we need to do is to be focusing much more heavily on economic development issues around the world, and we need to be focusing much more heavily on what the real ingredients of democracy are, apart from simply having elections and saying that that meets the test. I mean, the real test of democracy is if people enjoy some measure of human rights that allows them to survive in their own societies and resolve conflicts peacefully.

Mr. SAWYER. Do you include in that rights of repatriation, rights of restitution of property, those kinds of tangible measures of one's——

Mrs. MEISSNER. Those certainly come into play.

Repatriation is a wonderful example right now of a task that the international community is facing in a number of refugee situations where conflict is at least receding, although it may not be entirely over. And what we are finding with repatriation, of course, is that it is an enormously expensive proposition.

The international community is spending large sums of money in Cambodia, for instance, not only on repatriation but on trying to restore a situation where people can survive in the ways that I have argued, economically and politically. One has to wonder in how many places we can muster those kinds of resources.

In terms of our own nation and where we experience migration pressures, Haiti probably represents an example in this hemisphere where the Cambodia approach ultimately is the only approach that will create any kind of a future for that country. Will that happen? Is there—is there the money for it in the first place? And, beyond that, is there any real commitment to it?

But until we begin to think of countries like that in terms of substantial resources and political commitment we won't really be seriously addressing long-term migration pressures.

Mr. SAWYER. Mr. Teitelbaum, you suggested that no one would have predicted Kuwait, and that is probably true. But almost everybody predicted Yugoslavia, almost everybody. And we found ourselves impotent as a world community to do anything about it. Europe appeared paralyzed and the rest of us unwilling to take that step that was taken in Kuwait. Is it a question of mustering sufficient will?

Mr. TEITELBAUM. Well, yes, I think it is will, but it is also the scale of what happened in Yugoslavia. The nature of that civil war I am not sure was predicted, certainly not by me. I think people thought that the federation might not hold together in some form, but for it to disintegrate in the way it has, and for the reappearance in the world's vocabulary of "ethnic cleansing," which goes right back to the 1930's, I think that has surprised a lot of people. The viciousness of the assaults of various kinds, and the passions of the——

Mr. SAWYER. Except that everybody who talked about the motive for what was likely to happen—I mean, we even have a word for it that is 75 years old, Balkanization—spoke to those very forces that were likely to be the explosive ingredient in the whole mix.

Mr. TEITELBAUM. Well, I think you are right there. I don't think we were ready collectively, and it is hard to get ready collectively for what has happened in Yugoslavia. The European Community has had other agendas to deal with.

Mr. SAWYER. Sure.

Mr. TEITELBAUM. The unification of Germany has been something of a distraction for German government over the past several years. And, on that score, I want to make one point that I think is important to keep in mind: This subject that we are dealing with here today of refugees, immigration, used to be a "low politics" question. I don't mean to demean it. I just mean that it wasn't on the agendas, on a daily basis, of the Chancellor of the Federal Republic or the Premier or the President of France or the Prime Minister of Britain.

Mr. SAWYER. Or the President of the United States.

Mr. TEITELBAUM. Or the President of the United States. It was just not on that agenda. It was at lower levels of government. It was in the Ministry—as the French call it—the Ministry of National Solidarity or the Ministry of Employment or the Home Office that dealt with these kinds of questions.

It is now a "high politics" issue. Much to the surprise, I think, and probably much to the chagrin of the Presidents and the Premiers and the Prime Ministers who would rather not deal, I think, with these kinds of emotional, destructive issues. It is now one of the issues, among several, but not a lot, that present serious complications for the future of European integration.

The turmoil in the currency markets that we saw last week in Europe, how does that relate to what we are talking about here? But it does. If you read the standard accounts of what happened, you will find, I think, a conventional description and not controversial—that German unification was achieved by the German Government—the West German Government—on terms that were unduly favorable to the East, partly to restrain the migration of East Germans to West Germany, but partly just to keep things together.

That resulted in the Bundesbank jacking up interest rates to unrealistically high levels in order to restrain resulting inflationary pressures. The European monetary system amplified that through the European Community, and led to all kinds of unexpected consequences from a decision about what the conversion rate should be between the Deutschemark and the East German mark upon unification.

But that is what I mean by "high politics" questions. These issues are now integral to the future of European integration.

The second point is that—to go back to Doris Meissner's comment about creating the opportunities for people to live productively in their countries of origin—foreign assistance is not a big enough flow to make much of a difference in that regard. The biggest flow is trade, and trade policy is driven by all sorts of issues other than this issue that we are talking about. The main forces that drive trade policy are domestic politics in France, in the United States, in Germany and Japan, and many of those trade policies have very perverse outcomes with respect to providing employment in these countries of origin of prospective migrants.

We end up doing one thing with our foreign assistance program—enhancing foreign assistance to the Philippines because of serious problems in the Philippines' economy—and, with the other hand, devastating the Philippines' economy because of the sugar program in the United States, which wiped out three-quarters of their export potential for sugar. So there is an example of how domestic interest group politics on totally unrelated issues end up being the determining factors in this issue.

Mr. SAWYER. Well, clearly, it is different in different places. If there was a single issue that binds together the difference in your response to the Gulf and Yugoslavia, it is a difference in the willingness to intervene in what is an otherwise perceived as a sovereign situation. We don't have very many instrumentalities of international policy to deal with that sort of thing. But we know that these things are predictable.

In September, right after the coup when Russia was putting together the infrastructure of an international state, their Foreign Minister, Kozyrev, was talking about CSE as a potential instrumentality of avoiding the kinds of ethnic and population conflicts that he knew were about to emerge inside what was coming to be seen as a very soon-to-evolve former Soviet Union.

We have not taken those steps. And yet the failure to have such an instrument, whether it is CSE or some other instrument, clearly has brought about terrible consequences in a place where it was just as predictable. I mean, we sit here today with proposals calling upon others for voluntary restraints in terms of international arms sales and yet we have great difficulty in exercising that same restraint ourselves.

I just would agree that when you say that it is complex, that, in fact, it is.

I have gotten completely off the direction of the kinds of questions I was going to ask you, and I have a ton of them. I would ask that you, if you would, be willing to respond, however briefly or whatever length you might be willing to, to written questions.

I guess, in the end, though, what this really comes back to is, as we try to measure what is going on among ourselves, we have never had, at least not in a century, the difficulty that we have had in the course of this year in measuring ourselves. What is happening within the United States, certainly an environment we know far better than most of the rest of the world, the techniques we have used have posed a real challenge to us in knowing the kinds of answers to the questions of where we are going, why we are going there, and how we are living and what the implications are.

That is difficult in the environment in which this subcommittee has primarily been responsible. If what we are trying to do is reconcile those measurements, as they change, to meet the needs of the United States, and seeing the broader needs of the rest of the world, are there measurements that you see as particularly vulnerable, that are particularly needed in terms of international cooperation and effort by this country?

Mr. TEITELBAUM. Measurement, did you say?

Mrs. MEISSNER. Measurements?

Mr. SAWYER. Measurements of demographic movement around the world.

Let me give you an example. Tomorrow I have a resolution before the Foreign Affairs Committee asking that one of the real gaps in the kinds of sanctions that were passed earlier this year with regard to Bosnia be addressed, and that is that we really don't have a very good way to measure, to inventory, to itemize the movement of people as a result of the refugee problem that has occurred in Yugoslavia.

I don't think that there is a single thing that we can do that is within our immediate grasp that offers us better hope of saving substantial numbers of lives with people in the current circumstances than to take names and promise to count later. I mean, that has an implication in terms that go right back to the precedent that you cited when you talked about cleansing, and it goes right back to 47 years ago in Germany.

If we have names, we have a better chance of holding people accountable. It is one of the ways to save lives. That is a very crude and certainly fragile circumstance, but are there measures that we need to undertake?

I was asked a question the other day about Africa; what we know, what is going on, what we are doing, how we are addressing the problem that has emerged in headlines in recent weeks and months, but whose implications just go very, very deep, particularly when you think about the amount of volatility in that part of the world and the accumulation of weapons on one side and their absence on another.

What should we, as a community of nations, be moving together to measure when we are trying to understand the movement of people around the world between frontiers?

Mrs. MEISSNER. I would just, if I understand what—if I understand the use of the word "measure," I would say that these are not measurement issues in terms of the international community. I think we know a good deal, at least we know enough about what is happening demographically around the world to reach some judgments.

My sense of——

Mr. SAWYER. I would have to disagree, since both of you suggested, to begin with, that we have difficulty even defining what we mean by the various categories of movement. If we can't define that, I don't know how we can measure.

Mrs. MEISSNER. My own view is we know enough about the categories of movement to begin to think differently about how we respond. And if we give a much higher priority to movement-related issues as a critical element of reformulating policies, then the impetus to refine our understanding of the actual scale of the numbers of people and so forth will flow from that.

My own sense is that we don't know enough—that there are measurement questions that have to do with linkages. Michael has mentioned about trade. It is absolutely true that trade is by far the most important element of economic growth that is available, and, yet, we really know very, very little about how trade, how actions in the trade field interact with and mitigate migration pressures.

I mean there is a great deal to know of, what I would say, a cross-disciplinary nature, and we have not asked the questions, and we don't know how to come up with the information and the data that we need because they have not been important policy areas to probe. Because migration and international movement have not been among the things that have motivated policy thinking, research and discussion and an awareness, leaders around the world simply haven't focused on the issues.

There is enough data available to suggest urgency. If the issue becomes a more important one in the minds of decision-makers, the rest of the measurement needs, it seems to me, will flow from that.

In that regard, I think Yugoslavia, while it is a very, very sad situation, can also be a test from which we learn. When all is said and done, the Berlin Wall only came down, what, 2 or 3 years ago? It will be 3 years this fall. So if you want to date the end of the Cold War from there, it is really a very short period within which to be asking of the international community, you know, a total rethinking of its role and its capabilities. But, Yugoslavia should produce that. If it doesn't, the war really will be a double tragedy.

Mr. TEITELBAUM. I would say, Mr. Chairman, that there are a couple of things on the data side, or the definition side, that you might want to think about. First, it would be awfully nice if there could be some negotiations internationally toward some common definitions of what an international migrant is. It is fairly simple. But if you want to compare fertility, as you heard the previous panel talk about, there is an internationally agreed definition of what a live birth is.

Mr. SAWYER. Sure.

Mr. TEITELBAUM. And that did require some States to change their own definitions a bit to comply with the WHO convention, the conventional definition of a live birth. There is some fuzziness around the margins, but basically there is an international standard there. This is not true when it comes to international migration. It would be nice to start discussions along those lines.

On that score, though, I have to say that governments may not wish to have data widely known about what is happening. They may find it convenient to be very slow to publish data, for example, or to put categories on things that make them less politically threatening in some way or other to them. And that is a reality. Since governments collect the data, they also publish them and classify them, and that makes it more difficult.

There is one international effort that has been in place for quite a while that probably could be enhanced. It has always been starved for funds. It is a monitoring system, an international monitoring system on international migration, operated by the OECD in Paris, and it is the only place you can go to get some sort of commonality of data from a reasonably wide variety of countries, with some analysis on an annual basis.

My understanding, that has been run on a shoestring for many years and is now being enhanced a bit, but it is only because of the high politics issue that it has gotten more attention.

There is also a slow-fast part to this, or a speed question. These national data systems are very lumbering beasts. They take a long time to collect data, then they have to digest them, and then they have to publish them, make them available, then they have to be mailed. So there is a very long lag built into those kinds of systems.

For the kinds of things you are talking about, Mr. Chairman, it might be worth considering whether some competent statistically oriented people, such as the Census Bureau, or U.N. Population Division, might be empowered and funded to be available at short notice to do counts—short-term, immediate, emergency counts—of what is happening on a more than erratic random basis, which is the way we tend to get these estimates of two million Yugoslavs in flight. Who knows where those numbers come from.

But it might be worth considering that there would be value, from a humanitarian perspective and other perspectives, in having some attention paid to emergency data gathering when emergencies occur.

Last point, on the United States: We don't have very good data on immigration. The Immigration Service is quite aware of that failing and has done a lot, actually, in the last 5 years or so to improve the quality of its data collection and tabulation, but it still has a good way to go. And there are almost no funds available from government sources to support analysis of those data because the subject falls between the stools of government agencies and is on nobody's stool squarely. As a result, you have very little governmentally funded research on international migration.

I would report to you on a workshop I attended last week at the National Academy of Sciences, in which there was an anguished discussion about the apparent collapse of an effort to add a series—I think it was three questions—to the control card of the Current Population Survey that would allow the Current Population Survey data to be analyzed with respect to whether the person is native-born or foreign-born. The cost mentioned was $100,000 to $150,000 dollars a year to do this, and it collapsed for want of money.

Well, that is an oddity, it seems to me. That should be rectified because those are valuable data that ought to be tabulatable by nationality, nativity—where the person was born, and allow one to look at the economic experience of immigrants in the United States, for example.

Mr. SAWYER. Thank you. I thank you both.

I guess I agree completely that matters of high policy elevate and focus technical need for measurement, for definition, clarifying the understanding of what motivates it.

I also have come to believe that often those measurements themselves can be an important ingredient in elevating the urgency of high policy. We are all better off when we understand with clarity the phenomena that are going on around the world, and it is to that end that we have conducted these hearings.

I don't think that there is a single phenomenon that is going on in the world today that more draws together the understanding of what is going on in our country and our relationship with the rest of the world, at a time when that is more important than it has been—well, certainly since the end of the Second World War. We are defining who we are going to be as a nation, and we are defining it in terms, at least in significant part, what we have been talking about here and for the last few months.

I am particularly grateful for your willingness to take part in this hearing today and hope that some of the more detailed questions that we might offer to you, you would find time to respond to.

We hope to produce a public record of these proceedings, perhaps in a way that would be more widely accessible than committee prints are sometimes, and so the work that goes on in the remaining months of this year, I hope, can be important to sharing a wide range of issues of the kind that you have elevated here today, and that your colleagues have over the recent months.

Thank you very much for being with us.

If there is no further business before us today, we stand adjourned.

[Whereupon, at 3:25 p.m., the subcommittee was adjourned.]

○

61-412 O - 94 (460)

ISBN 0-16-043596-X
90000
9 780160 435966